The Mellen Biblical Commentary

Intertextual

New Testament Series

in Twenty-Two Volumes

General Editor

George Wesley Buchanan

The Mellen Biblical Commentary

Intertextual

New Testament Series

in Twenty-Two Volumes

Volume 1
Book 2

The Gospel of Matthew

George Wesley Buchanan

Wipf & Stock
PUBLISHERS
Eugene, Oregon

Wipf and Stock Publishers
199 W 8th Ave, Suite 3
Eugene, OR 97401

The Gospel of Matthew, Volume 2
By Buchanan, George Wesley

ISBN: 1-59752-8676
Publication date 8/10/2006
Previously published by Edwin Mellen Press, 1996

PREFACE TO VOLUME TWO

Those who use volume two of this commentary series without having first read volume one may find concepts, traditions, customs, terms, and abbreviations with which they are not familiar. If that occurs they may turn to volume one and find the information needed either in the preface or the introduction.

TABLE OF CONTENTS

CHAPTER THIRTEEN

MATTHEAN PARALLELS TO THE HEXATEUCH

Matthew	First Testament
Jesus told a parable about the future Kingdom of God, its greatness and its coming (Matt 12:1-52).	Balaam blessed and described a glowing future for Israel (Num 23-24).

And it happened when Jesus finished these parables, he went away from there (Matt 13:53).

The division in Matthew that corresponds to Numbers in the Pentateuch is the same division that Bacon noted as a separate unit.[1] Like the "Leviticus" section, it has two divisions, the first comprised two chapters and the second consisted of one. Further agreement in organization is that like chapters 8 and 9, chapters 11 and 12 described activity of Jesus, whereas chapters 10 and 13 were teaching sections or discourses of Jesus. Just as Numbers began with an extensive treatise on the Levites, so the "Numbers" section of Matthew devoted attention at the beginning to the Levites whom John came to cleanse and whose ministry was succeeded by the superior ministry. The rebellious Levites of Numbers were replaced in Matthew by the rebellious scribes and Pharisees. The blessed land and people prophesied in Numbers was countered by the parables about the Kingdom of God. The "Numbers" section is coherent with the "Leviticus" section; it begins after the familiar transition passage and continues until the end of the section where there is another similar transitional sentence. "Numbers" differs from "Leviticus" in that it follows Numbers in proper sequence.

[1]B. C. Bacon, Studies in Matthew (New York: H. Holt & Co., c1950), pp. 288-296.

TEXT

13:1In that day Jesus, after he had gone out of the house, sat down alongside the sea, 2and many crowds were brought to him so that he went down into a boat to be seated, and all the crowd was standing on the shore.

TECHNICAL DETAILS

The beginning and final parables in this chapter were introductory and conclusive. They are not among the six parables whose subject is the Kingdom of Heaven. The first and the eighth tell about the character, methodology, and purpose of telling parables. Jewish and Christian parables are very similar to Greek fables, but not completely. Whereas Greek fables, such as, "The Dog in the Manger" or "The Fox and the Grapes," are general stories that can be used over and over again in many situations, Jewish and Christian parables were composed and used as illustrations to answer one particular question.

In addition to its midrashic coherence, Matt 13 is structurally organized so that the six medial parables form an inclusion. The first and sixth of these parables are about good and bad things--the weeds and the wheat, the good fish and the bad fish. In between these two parables are two pairs of matching parables. All six are parables of the kingdom. One of the ways early Jewish and Christian scholars emphasized a point was to bring together several illustrations of one subject. For example, instead of one beatitude, the author of Matt 5 brought in eight beatitudes which teach basically the same point--the Kingdom will come to those who are passively righteous. Rabbis often gathered together for emphasis several scripture verses that are very closely related (e.g., Mek Shirata 4.1-12).

The six parables between the introduction and conclusion in Matt 13 are all about the Kingdom of Heaven. This is a central chapter of the gospel and it contains the central point. This group of six parables, in turn is sandwiched in between two other parables, one as an introduction and the other as the conclusion. Furthermore the first half of the chapter is addressed to the crowd, and the second half is addressed to the disciples. As Wenham has observed, this chapter is too well organized to presume it was dependent upon Mark.[2] Gerhardsson concluded, after studying all three synoptic forms of the parable of the sower,

> We have here another example of a block of traditions being found in the purest condition in Matthew.[3]

---

[2]D. Wenham, "The Structure of Matthew XIII," NTS 25 (1979):516-22.

[3]B. Gerhardsson, "The Parable of the Sower and its Interpretation," NTS 14 (1968):191.

COMMENTARY

After Jesus had gone out from the house. There is no indication before this verse that Jesus had been in a house, but the house from which Jesus left was evidently the one in which he lived at Capernaum, alongside the Sea of Galilee (Matt 13:1). This was either his original home, or more likely the monastery where he lived.

The crowds were gathered to him. The crowds at this point were not yet hostile. They were positively interested. This is an editorial comment, very much like the setting given at the beginning of the Sermon on the Mount (Matt 5:1-2) where the crowds and the disciples were present, and Jesus sat down to teach (Matt 13:2). Being seated was the normal position for a teacher in antiquity.[4] In the Near East, still today, listeners crowd so close to a speaker that he or she needs some barrier to enable the speaker to move and speak. Jesus got into a boat and moved far enough out into the sea to provide the necessary barrier. Contrary to Patte, who thought the parables were directed to the disciples,[5] the main parables were for the crowds. They were delivered in code so that the Romans could not get the message. The disciples did not need to learn the message of the parables, because they already knew the mysteries of the Kingdom of Heaven. Only the interpretive parables--the sower and its interpretation (Matt 13:13-23)--were for the disciples.

TEXT

Matthew	First Testament
[3]Then he spoke to them many things in parables, saying:	For just as rain comes down and snow from heaven and does not return there unless it water the land and make it produce and sprout.
Look! **A sower** went out to **sow** [grain], [4]and while he was sowing, some [seed] fell on the path, and the birds, after they came, consumed it. [5]Other [seed] fell among the rocks where it did not have much soil, and at once it dried up, because it did not have depth of soil, [6]and after the sun arose it was scorched, and because it	Then it gives **seed to the sower** and bread to the eater, thus will be my word which goes out from my mouth. It will not return to me empty (Isa 55:10-11). He will be like a tree planted alongside streams of water, which produces fruit in its season. Its

[4]So also B. M. Newman, "To Teach or Not to Teach (A Comment on Matthew 13.1-3)," BT 34 (1983):139-43.

[5]D. Patte, The Gospel according to Matthew (Philadelphia: Fortress Press, c1946), p. 183.

had no root, it **was dried up**. [7]Other [seed], however,	leaves **do not dry up**, and all that it does succeeds (Ps 1:3).
fell among **the thorns**, and the thorns grew up and choked it,[8]but [still]	Do not **sow** among **the thorns** (Jer 4:3).
other [seed] fell on good soil and continued to produce grain--some, a **hundred** [measures], some sixty, and some thirty. [9]He who has ear let him hear.	Then Isaac sowed in that land, and he harvested in the same year a **hundred** measures (may-ah she-ahr-eem, מאה שערים). Yahowah blessed him, and the man became rich (Gen 26:12-13).

TECHNICAL DETAILS

This parable is not a variant form of the parable of the seed growing secretly in Mark 4:26-29, as many have thought. They are both complete parables, but they were formed on separate bases and have different messages.

COMMENTARY

Many things in parables. Lowe and Flusser interpret this text by saying that Jesus taught the disciples everything, but that he compensated the crowds by telling them parables.[6] Gundry thought he taught so that he might confuse the false disciples, who lacked understanding. These lacked understanding because they refused to understand. The parables were a means of obscuring the truth to them.[7] All of these missed the whole point of the parables. This was not alternate information; it was not intended to obscure the truth from stubborn disciples; it was the same information told in code. Those who knew the code could understand the same data the disciples knew. It was the Romans from whom the message of the parables was obscured. They did not refuse to understand; they wanted to find out the message, but they did not know the code.

Via held that for Matthew the parables were told to be understood by the disciples only, but he did not offer any reason why this should be done. He thought Mark had to allegorize them because Mark thought the parables in themselves were useless.[8] If that were true it would be so only because Mark did not know the code. Via noticed that Mark explained Matthaean parables, but he

---

[6]M. J. Lowe and D. Flusser, "Evidence for Corroborating a Modified Proto-Matthaean Synoptic Theory," NTS 29 (1983):38.

[7]R. H. Gundry, Matthew (Grand Rapids: Eerdmans, 2d c1994), pp. 250, 256.

[8]D. O. Via, Jr., "Matthew on the Understandability of the Parables," JBL 84 (1965):430-32.

still thought Mark was the source for Matthew rather than vice versa. Evans suggested that the sower parable was a midrash on Isa 55:10-11 and Deut 6:6-13.[9]

Crossan claimed the parables were valid teachings on the basis of dissimilarity. This means that there are no such forms as parables in the scripture or early Jewish literature, and there are none in later Judaism or Christianity. Parables are unique to Jesus, according to Crossan. He said that without the principle of dissimilarity there is no "critical possibility of ascertaining Jesus' own teaching."[10] He is wrong on three points: 1) The assumption that there are no parables in the FT, intertestamental literature, or Rabbinic literature;[11] 2) that dissimilarity is a valid criterion for determining the teachings of Jesus. This presumes that Jesus taught only unique things and that no one could add a unique teaching to the words attributed to Jesus; and 3) dissimilarity is the only way to ascertain the teachings of Jesus.[12] His definition of the parables of Jesus is also in error. He said parables are

> essentially moral stories inculcating universal ethical truths, and ontologico-poetic-articulation of the kingdom's in-breaking upon himself![13]

Wow! Is that clear? Jesus was not just an innocuous teacher of ancient wisdom as Crossan held.

This entire unit is an introduction to the parables that follow. It was intended to give the reader a clue to the fact that parables are not intended to be ordinary narrative to be understood as a simple message. They were used as code to communicate messages to some people but to communicate no secrets to others who might be eavesdropping. Even the parable included in this unit was designed to explain why parables were used at all. This explanation was reinforced with a proof text from Isaiah. Those who had eyes to see and ears to hear were the apostles, but there were also others who were familiar with Jewish tradition and scripture who would understand certain parts of certain parables. This pro-apostolic affirmation is contrary to the anti-apostolic view of the author of Mark, who

---

[9]C. A. Evans, "On the Isaianic Background of the Sower Parable," CBQ 47 (1985):464-68.

[10]J. D. Crossan, "The Seed Parables of Jesus," JBL 92 (1973):262.

[11]M. D. Goulder, Midrash and Lection in Matthew (London: SPCK, 1974), pp. 47-69, has shown how similar rabbinic parables are to the Matthean parables. He has identified 100 rabbinic parables and five parables in the FT. There are at least 300 rabbinic parables.

[12]For other criteria and illustrations see Buchanan, Jesus: The King and his Kingdom (Macon: Mercer U., c1984).

[13]Crossan, "Seed Parables," p. 264.

used very few parables in his gospel. Like farmers who sowed grain expecting a harvest, most of the time they were not disappointed, even though they did not always reap as large a crop as they wanted.

There are many parables in the FT and intertestamental literature. Parables are still being used in the Near East in the twentieth century as a means of communication in a resistance movement under careful enemy observation. Fisk told of some conversations he held with Lebanese after the Israelis had overwhelmed their nation. He quoted a resistance leader, named Khalil Jerardi:

> "The brutal practices of the [Israeli] occupation army are in the interests of the resistance," he said. "The arrests the Israelis make are of ordinary people. When this happens, the people become more united. The resistance needs this badly." Who is the resistance? Jerardi's voice did not change. "The resistance is national, but its ideas are those of Islam. And it is based on the principle that God opposes tyranny. This is the truth of the resistance. Some statements issued in Beirut in our name are untrue. Yassir Arafat says untrue things. The resistance is not led by commanders--by a Mr. X or a Mr. Y, as the media say--it is directed by the ideas of Islam."
>
> He spoke more literally that I realized. Only later would a village sheikh tell me the reality behind this "direction" of the resistance. The village Imams, he said were asked to mention certain words in their sermons. The requests came from Beirut, often from the Hezbullah; sometimes, not always, the code-words were devised by Iranians. These words--"great books", "olive groves", "sweet fruits", there was no limit to the combinations--would mean nothing to the village sheikhs. Nor to most of their worshippers. But a few, perhaps only one man, in the mosque would understand their import. They would be a message. That is how the suicide bombers of Lebanon used to receive their orders.[14]

Jews in the time of Jesus held the same position in Palestine that Moslems and Christians hold in that same land today. Two thousand years ago, the land Jews claimed as their country was occupied by Romans who treated Jews very much the same way Israelis today treat Palestinians. Jews 2,000 years ago had secret resistance forces just as Palestinians do today, and they used similar ways to communicat with one another under the watchful eyes of the occupying forces. There were certain code words that had special meanings to those who had ears to hear, but only those could understand. Those who could understand were the ones to whom it was given to know the "mysteries of the Kingdom of Heaven."

---

[14]R. Fisk, Pity the Nation: The Abduction of Lebanon (New York:MacMillan, 1990), p. 578.

Explaining the relationship between being learned and not being learned, Rabbi Haninah bar Papa said,

> The holy One blessed be He does not measure according to the human measure. Human beings fill the empty vessel, but do not fill the full [vessel], but [the method of] the holy One blessed be He is not thus. He fills the full [vessel], but he does not fill the empty [vessel], as it is said, and he said, **If you really hear** (11:13) (literally, "If hearing you will hear"). [This means] if you are hearing [now], you will hear [in the future], but if not, you will not hear [in the future] (bBer 40a).

This is partially similar to the statement, "He that has ears to hear, let him hear," but it does not require the fifth-column situation that is inherent in the invitation to hear, if you have the proper ears or insights for it.

Without an appreciation of the problems of communication during a fifth-columnist movement it is impossible to understand the significance of the parables of Jesus. These parables were not innocent stories to be told to children for entertainment. Underground resistance movements have traditionally used similar methods of conducting their resistance against the occupation troops. Via missed all of this when he held that "the parables in themselves are useless." The parables were very useful. They provided an important means of communication to an underground movement under the watchful eye of the government in power.[15]

In rocky places . . . among thorns. The Greek word (paráh, παρά) that is rendered here "on" would normally be translated "beside" or "alongside," but it probably reflects the Hebrew ahl (על) which can mean both "on" and "beside." The birds would more quickly find seed on a path than beside it. The path, rocky places, and thorns are not places where farmers normally sow grain, neither in the United States nor in the Near East. Farmers normally sow their seed only on good ground where there is a chance that it will grow. Jeremias tried to justify the text by saying that in the Near East farmers sowed their seed first and plowed afterward.[16] This position has been refuted by several scholars, one of which was Payne.[17] Payne examined several references to sowing, cultivating, and reaping and found nearly all put sowing before plowing, but there were some instances where plowing followed sowing. Essame also called attention to Jub 11.1,

---

[15]Via, "Matthew," pp. 430-32.

[16]J. Jeremias, The Parables of Jesus tr. S. H. Hooke (New York: Scribner, 1972), p. 12.

[17]P. B. Payne, "The Order of Sowing and Ploughing in the Parable of the Sower," NTS 25 (1978):123-29.

which reported that birds ate seed that had been sown but had not yet been plowed under.[18]

The problem here is the American understanding of the word translated "plowing." No farmer who expected wheat to grow, would have "plowed" wheat under, using an ordinary plow that plowed deep enough to turn up hidden rocks and cover wheat with six inches of soil. Farmers in all countries know better than that. American farmers would not call the kind of action required to cover wheat "plowing," but "harrowing." It covers wheat by about one inch of soil, but it does not turn up huge rocks upon which wheat should not have been planted. Gundry tried to make excuses for the farmer's stupidity in planting the grain where he did.[19]

All explanations and attempts to justify a farmer sowing wheat on roadways, rocks, and among weeds, however, are beside the point. The parable was never designed with the thought that the hearers would believe farmers sowed their fields in that way. There really is no story here of a farmer who sowed grain on roadways, rocks, and among weeds. This is the nonsense portion of the parable. The only message of the parable has to do with communication through code in the presence of eavesdropping Romans.

The nonsense element of this parable was given to alert Jesus' audience to the fact that Jesus was not really talking about farming but about something else--something people could understand only if they had ears to hear (Matt 13:9). Those who had ears to hear realized that Jesus was speaking in code so that listening Romans could not understand the message he wanted to communicate. In this context about parables, the mysterious message was apparently an explanation for his use of parables in open teaching (Matt 13:4-7).[20] Gerhardsson said the disciples were the ones who had ears to hear; the crowds did not.[21] If there was no one in the crowd who might understand the hidden meaning of the parables, it would have been a waste of time to have included them in the discussion. Jesus could have limited his audience to his disciples, if he had chosen to do so. He spoke to the crowds so that those in the group who knew enough about scripture and Jewish tradition might learn the secret message. It is also not true that the only message Jesus wanted to give to the crowds was the Sheh-máh (שמע). That message could have been told directly without a parable.[22]

---

[18]W. G. Essame, "Sowing and Ploughing," ExpTim 72 (1960):54.

[19]Gundry, Matthew, p. 251-54.

[20]Contra G. Kennedy, "Nothing Without a Parable," H. K. McArthur (ed.) New Testament Sidelights (Hartford: Hartford Seminary Foundation, 1960), 10-26, who held that parables were always applicable to everyone. He said they were lucid and not dark mysteries.

[21]Gerhardsson, "Parable," p. 174.

[22]Gerhardsson, "Parable," pp. 176-79.

Other seed fell on good soil. This means that some people understood the message of the parables. On the one hand, there were in his audience disciples who were trained in "the mysteries of the Kingdom of Heaven" (Matt 13:11). These knew the secret doctrines of the sect, so they did not need to have it told to them in code, although they also knew the code. All Christians and Jews had secret catechisms, peculiar to their sect or group. A sect's catechism was sometimes called gnóh-sis (γνῶσις) or special knowledge. Sometimes it was called the "mysteries of the Kingdom of Heaven" (tah mys-táy-ree-ah tays bah-sil-áy-as tohn oo-rah-nóhn , τὰ μυστήρια τῆς βασιλείας τῶν οὐρανῶν) the "knowledge" (dah-áht, דעת), or the "oral torah" (toh-ráh sheh-beh-ahl péh, תורה שבעל פה. On the other hand, however, there were Jews not trained in these secrets, other Jews who had been trained in other sects, and eavesdropping Romans. Any leader who wanted a large popular support had to communicate openly to these uncatechized or differently catechized Jews, but this was dangerous. By speaking publicly an underground leader might disclose to the eavesdropping Romans the real purpose of his message. If that happened, Romans would quickly remove him from the political scene, just as they already had removed John the Baptist.

Although apostles might be persecuted and even killed by Romans if they happened to say something that gave away these secrets, Jesus assured them that God would not blame them for this. God would put into their mouths that which they should say. They were legal agents, speaking only in behalf of God who was their principal. As God's agents the apostles were only means through which God could speak. Therefore God was responsible for the consequences of his apostles (Matt 10:19-20).

Some a hundred. Matthew, like many other good rhetoricians, often organized things into threes: 1) 100, 2) 60, and 3) 30. It is not certain what this 100 meant so far as a harvest is concerned. It was probably based on the bumper crop Isaac raised when he began farming among the Philistines. Isaac is reported to have raised 100 measures (Gen 26:12-13), but that does not say how much land it required to raise a hundred measures. It was enough to make Isaac rich, so it was not considered an ordinary crop. It was a very successful harvest. When Jesus told the parable, comparing the success of his teaching to the success of Isaac's farming, he intended to say that some people understood 100% of what he wanted them to know when he told parables.

TEXT

Matthew	First Testament
10When the disciples had come to him, they said, "Why in parables do you speak to them?" 11In reply, he said,	

"To you it has been given **to know the mysteries** of the Kingdom of Heaven, / but to those it has not been given. / [12]Whoever has it shall be given to him, / and he will be increased, / but to the one who does not have, / even that which he has shall be taken from him.

The one who reveals **mysteries makes known to you** what will be [in the future] (Dan 2:29).

There is a God in heaven who reveals **mysteries and makes known** to King Nebuchadnezzar what will happen at the end of the days [of this evil era] (Dan 2:28).

[13]Because of this **I speak to them in parables**, because even though **they see, they do not see**, and while they **are hearing,** they do not **hear nor understand."**

I will open my mouth in parable; I will disclose riddles from antiquity,
which we **have heard, and understood**, and our fathers have told us (Ps 78:2-3).

[14]Also the prophecy of Isaiah is fulfilled in them which says:

You will surely hear but not understand;
You will certainly see but not perceive.
[15]The mind of this people has become fat;
they heard with heavy ears,
and they covered their eyes,
lest they see with their eyes,
hear with their ears,
and understand with their minds,
and turn, and I will heal them (Isa 6:9-10).

COMMENTARY

Why in parables do you speak to them? In answer to this question, Matthew employed "because" (hó-tee, ὅτι), whereas Mark used "in order that" (hín-ah, ἵνα). Supposing that Matthew used Mark, Via held that Matthew "softened" the expression. According to Mark Jesus did not want the crowds to understand, whereas in Matthew Jesus dealt with a situation in which most of the crowds were not able to understand.[23] The situation is more complex than Via thought. The "them" in this sentence refers to the crowds, who are clearly distinguished from the disciples in this pericope. The crowds were hard of hearing. No one had taught them the code necessary for understanding. There was no opportunity whereby Jesus could teach them openly the needed code. He had to take them as they were and hope that some of them might grasp certain parts of his message through

[23]D. O. Via, "Matthew on the Understandability of the Parables," JBL 84 (1965):430-32.

parables. Those in the crowds who would not understand at all were the Romans. God had covered their eyes and blocked their ears so that they could not understand the message that was being communicated to the chosen people. Cerfaux compared the three synoptic versions and concluded that the earliest form is found in Matthew.[24]

To you it has been given. I.e., "God has given you." The passive voice was used to avoid the use of the divine name, but each sect believed that God was its founder, and God was the one who gave them their catechism. They were the elect of God and had been privileged by this special knowledge (Matt 13:11) just as the message was given to King Nebuchadnezzar in a dream (Dan 2:28). The king, however, and all of his gentile counsellors were unable to decipher the mysteries. Daniel, the Jew, was the one who understood these mysteries, and he was able to tell Nebuchadnezzar what was going to happen in the future (Dan 2:28-45). Like Daniel of old Jesus' followers had this special knowledge the gentiles could not understand. That which they understood was that Jesus was the Messiah, and they anticipated the events that would happen in the near future. As the Messiah, Jesus was God's legal agent and spoke God's words. The messages Jesus taught the disciples were messages from God. The disciples were privileged to know the mysteries Jesus tried to communicate to others. "Those" who were not as privileged as the disciples were the crowds--all others who heard the parables.

The mysteries of the Kingdom of Heaven. The mysteries that Daniel understood were the events related to the image of the king's dream. This image was the gentile king, and, like the gentile empire that had ruled Palestine since 586 B.I.A., it was destined to be destroyed. That which would follow would be the Hasmonean kingdom. The Hasmonean kingdom was the kingdom which **the God of heaven will set up**, and **it will never be destroyed nor will its sovereignty be left to another people** (Dan 2:44). The mysteries of the king's dream were the mysteries of the Kingdom of heaven, which was the liberated Davidic kingdom, and it would not be ruled by another people. In NT times, this kingdom was ruled by another people--the Romans. Those who had ears to hear knew about the Book of Daniel and the Hasmonean victory. They were expecting the Kingdom of heaven to be returned. That was the mystery the Romans could not decipher.

The mysteries included the knowledge that unlocked the code for messages they wanted to communicate. Those who did not know the special code could at least recognize FT allusions and typologies. They could also recognize Jewish traditions which the Romans would not know. By alluding to these in parables Jesus was able to tell them what he wanted them to hear. The better they knew

---

[24]L. Cerfaux, "La Connaisancedes Secrets du Royaume d'apres Matt. XIII.11 et Paralleles," NTS 2 (1955/56):238-49.

their traditions and scripture, the more they could understand. Some understood very much (a hundred fold), some less--"60" or "30." Any was better than nothing, and this seemed the only method by which Jesus could make his message popular to Jews but not to Romans (Matt 13:11). The only ones Jesus wanted to understand nothing were the Romans.

Whoever has it shall be given to him. This means the one who had a good knowledge of tradition and scripture would learn still more about Jesus' message (Matt 13:13). As other scholars have thought, this may once have been a pithy proverb that dealt with wealth and poverty: the ones who had money could earn interest and become richer, but those who were poor would have to borrow money, giving up hours of labor to repay the interest on the money they borrowed. In this way the poor became poorer.[25] Here, however, the wealth and poverty apply to knowledge and ignorance. Jesus was not limited in his communication to the preaching he, himself, did. He trained his apostles, taught them chreias and parables, and sent them out to communicate his message. They were his recruiters, messengers, and fishers of men--and they were trained to speak in code.

Hear and you will not understand (Isa 6:9-10). Isa 6:9-10 was a very important text for the early church that often had to speak in code (John 12:40; Acts 28:26-27; Rom 11:8). Some scholars think Matt 13:14-15 is an intrusion, added by the later church, but Cope argued that it is essential to the chapter. He has shown that this is one of the texts upon which Matthew constructed the entire unit, Matt 13:1-52.[26] By relating the parables to FT texts, Cope has shown that the passage involved was composed by one editor at one time. This means these parables should be studied together to find a unified meaning that is coherent. They were not pieced together from hypothetical sources like "Q," and the Gospel of Mark. Wenham, Lowe, and Flusser have all concurred in that judgment. Lowe and Flusser have noticed that the entire eight parables have an evident Hebrew basis, but the interpretations, both of the sower and of the weeds and wheat, are all non-Hebraic Greek.[27] This implies that the interpretations are midrashim composed by the later church.

Those who would hear and not understand were the Romans who would be eavesdropping. Hagner was correct in holding that this doctrine of election is a two-edged sword. Some are predestined to be elected and some are destined to be excluded. Grace was not extended to all. These mysteries were not intended

---

[25]So Allison: W. D. Davies and D. C. Allison, Jr., Critical and Exegetical Commentary on the Gospel according to Saint Matthew (Edinburgh: T. & T. Clark, c1991), p. 391.

[26]O. L. Cope, Matthew: A Scribe Trained for the Kingdom of Heaven (Washington, D.C.: CBS Press, 1976).

[27]D. Wenham, "The Interpretation of the Parable of the Sower," NTS 20 (1974):299-319; Lowe and Flusser, "Proto-Matthaean," p. 36.

to be known by the non-elect.[28] This was not a de-segregationistic doctrine. Neither the author of Daniel nor of Matthew had any thoughts of co-existence as equals among all believers. The ones who wrote the literature and the people to which they belonged believed they, themselves, were among the elect who knew the mysteries of the Kingdom of Heaven. They had no feelings of sadness for those who were excluded.

The prophecy of Isaiah. This verse contains a chiasm. First there is "ears" and then "eyes." In the next line there is "eyes" and then "ears."

TEXT

Matthew

16**Blessed**, however, **are** your eyes, because they **see**,/ and your ears, because they hear./
17I tell you under oath,/
"Many prophets and just men / have longed **to see** what you see,/
but they did not **see**, /
and hear what you hear,/
but they did not hear."

Psalms of Solomon

18.6God will cleanse the Israelites for the day of mercy and blessing, for the day of election when he leads up his Messiah. 7**Blessed are** those who exist in those days, **to see** the good things of the Lord which he will do in the coming generation.

COMMENTARY

Pious Jews then found and today still find occasions every day to give blessings. This is part of their faith. When Mary went to her Aunt Elizabeth to tell her of her pregnancy, Elizabeth at once said, "Blessed are you among women, and blessed is the fruit of your womb" (Luke 1:42). When John was born, Zecharias said, "Blessed be the Lord God of Israel, because he has visited and performed redemption for his people" (Luke 1:68). An unknown woman from a crowd called out to Jesus, "Blessed be the womb that bore you and the breasts that nursed you" (Luke 11:27). An unknown poet of NT times said those who existed in the days of the Messiah would be blessed, because they would see the good fortune of Israel when God gathered the tribes together in Palestine (PssSol 17.50). Those Israelites would be blessed who would live to see the day of mercy and blessing when the Lord brought to Israel his Messiah who would do many good things for Israel (PssSol 18.6-7).

[28]D. A. Hagner, Word Biblical Commentary: Matthew 1-13 (Dallas: Word Books, c1933), p. 375.

The eyes of the apostles were blessed, because they knew the mysteries and understood the hidden meanings of the parables that followed in Matthew 13. It was through these mysteries that the good news was proclaimed. The mysteries were that the Kingdom was soon to be restored to the Jews on the promised land. In the judgment of Jews of NT times, all prophets prophesied only for the days of the Messiah, but the days of the Messiah were for them far in the future. The disciples, however, were alive in the days of the Messiah. They would see the kingdom come about which the mysteries were designed. The just men were those like Abraham (Gen 15) and Phineas (Num 25; Ps 106:30-31), whose work and faith were reckoned to them as righteousness. They were the ones who had performed works of supererogation. They had laid up virtues in the treasury of merits in heaven so that the Kingdom of Heaven could come, but they did not live to see the kingdom come. Therefore, the disciples were about to gain benefits that the prophets and just men of the past only longed to see and hear, but were unsuccessful. God had given the disciples the privilege of knowing the mysteries of the Kingdom of Heaven. This was a blessing greater than any received by the great saints of the past.

TEXT

18You, then, hear the parable of the **sower**: 19From everyone who hears the word of the Kingdom and does not understand [it], the evil one comes and seizes that which was sown in his mind. This man is [the one who functions as] **the [seed] which was sown along the way.** 20Now **the [seed] which was sown among the rocks** is [the parabolic equivalent of] the one who hears the word, at once receives it with joy, 21but has no **root** in himself, but is ephemeral. When tribulation and persecution come on account of the word, at once he is caused to stumble. 22The [seed], however, **that was sown among the thorns**--This man is the one who hears the word, but the anxieties of the age and the vanity of wealth **choke** "the word," and he becomes unfruitful. 23But **the [seed] which was sown on good ground**--This is the one who hears the word and understands, who bears fruit and **produces--some a hundredfold, some sixty, and some thirty**.

TECHNICAL DETAILS

This unit is clearly a midrashic interpretation of the parable of the sower. The commentator picked out words and phrases from the parable and interpreted them the way he understood them, weaving the words of the parable intertextually into his homily. Gerhardsson said,

> The parable and the interpretation fit each other as hand fits glove. If the parable--in the only form we know it--is from Jesus, so is

the interpretation. If the interpretation is secondary, then the parable, in the form we know it, is too.[29]

It is true that these two units are closely related, perhaps even as hand and glove, but the hand is not the glove, and the text is not the interpretation. The text must always precede the midrash, and the interpretation is almost always composed by someone who did not write the text but who considers the text valid. In this case the message of the interpretation is different from that of the text.

The parable of the sower probably was composed by Jesus, but the interpretation was not, although it contains some of the words of Jesus. It is a sermonette that was added by the later church. It was either composed by Matthew or by someone who wrote before Matthew organized this chapter. The parable itself (Matt 13:4-8) probably referred to the percentages of the messages that the hearers were able to grasp through the code. Some could understand more than others.

The expositor who interpreted the parable for the church, however, thought it referred to the faithfulness of the ones who heard. All heard, but not all were faithful. In this later interpretation the preacher had a different audience. He thought that it was desirable for all the crowd to understand. He did not have the problem of the eavesdropping Romans. If anyone did not understand at all it was not because God stopped up his or her ears and covered the eyes, but because the evil one came and snatched away the person's understanding. Some members of the Christian crowd were enthusiastic, but ephemeral; others heard the message and understood it but were afraid to act on the basis of its message. The good seed, however, heard, understood, and had the faith and courage to live the faith they accepted. This midrashic sermonizer was not the last person to misunderstand and misinterpret the words of Jesus. Words that are spoken or written in code specifically so that some people will misunderstand them are often misunderstood by others, as well.

COMMENTARY

Hear the parable of the sower. Matt 13:4-8 is the parable of the sower. That which follows (Matt 13:19-23) is an interpretation of that parable. Cave correctly follows Jeremias in thinking that this interpretation of the parable is not a genuine parable of Jesus. Rather it is an interpretation of the parable by the later church.[30]

---

[29]Gerhardsson, "Parable," p. 192.

[30]C. H. Cave, "The Parables and the Scriptures," NTS 11 (1964/65):382.

Everyone who hears the word of the Kingdom. All who hear the parable told or read hear the way the word of the kingdom will be communicated, because that is the message of the parable. Parables that follow will tell the word of the kingdom, but not all will realize that it is the word of the Kingdom or know what specific information the parables were designed to tell.

Has no root in himself. There are variants for this verse. Luke 8:13 does not have the pronoun "himself." Mark has "themselves." Some Syriac versions have "it" or "him" (ἀυτῷ=בו) instead of "himself" or "itself (ἑαυτῷ)." This makes good sense, because it has "word" for its antecedent.[31] This would mean the person involved would have no root in the word and therefore would perish.

Although there were undoubtedly people in the early church who responded to the good news in all of these ways, this interpretation is probably not the one intended by the parable. Out of 52 verses, these first 23 are all introductory. It evidently seemed important to Matthew that the people who read these parables realize that they would not be understood correctly unless the reader had some of the knowledge of which Jesus spoke.

At once he is caused to stumble. The medieval Hebrew text has a variant: "Satan makes [them] forget it from their mind." Pseudo-Cementine apparently used this text "A wicked demon steals the words of salvation and snatches them from memory" (Recog 1.26, 1-2).[32] This version is coherent with verse 19 which shows the evil one taking away that which is sown in the mind.

TEXT

24 Another parable he provided them, saying,
"The Kingdom of Heaven is like a man sowing good seed in his field.
25 While men slept, his enemy came and sowed weeds in the midst of the wheat
and went away. 26 When, however, the stalk grew and produced fruit, then also
the weeds became evident. 27 The servants of the manager said to him, 'Sir, did
you not sow good seed in your field? From where, then, does it have weeds?'
28 He said to them, 'An enemy has done this.' The servants said to him, 'Do you
want us, then, to go out and uproot them?' He replied, 29 'No! lest while you are
gathering the weeds you uproot also the wheat. 30 Let them both grow together until the harvest. Then, in the time of the harvest, I will say to the harvesters.
"Gather first the weeds, and tie them into bundles to burn, but the wheat gather
into my granary."'"

---

[31] J. Joosten, "The Text of Matthew 13.21a and Parallels in the Syriac Tradition," NTS 37 (1991):153-59.

[32] So G. Howard, "The Pseudo-Clementine Writings and Shem-Tob's Hebrew Matthew," NTS 40 (1994):624.

TECHNICAL DETAILS

Kingsbury holds that only Matt 13:24-26 of this unit can be attributed to Jesus. The rest has all been added by later editors and commentators.[33] That does not seem necessary, since the whole passage is unified and makes sense the way it has been finally canonized.

COMMENTARY

Another parable he provided them. The parable was designed for the crowds, but it may have been one of those that Jesus provided for his apostles to use in their preaching to the crowds. This is another parable about sowing. It was placed in the same chapter as the first parable in this series so as to keep all the material about the same topic organized together.

Good seed in his field. This is a typical introduction to a parable. The rabbinic formula was lah-máh ha-dah-váhr dóh-may (למה הדבר דומה) (What is the thing like?) is usually followed by a statement such as this. Jesus did not mean that the Kingdom of Heaven was like a man who did as the parable said, but the situation related to the coming of the Kingdom of Heaven was like the situation given in the parable.

Most rabbinic parables begin in response to a question asked by students of some rabbi. The rabbi then would tell a parable to illustrate the answer he wanted the students to understand. One example was illustrated by Rabbi Shimon ben Yohai. His students asked why manna from heaven came down to the Israelites every day rather than once a year. He told them that this could be compared to a king of flesh and blood (a gentile king), who had only one son. He first provided for his son's maintenance by giving him an allowance once a year. This meant that the son would visit his father only once a year. Then the king changed his policy and paid his son's allowance every day, so he would get to see his son every day. The same would be true with the Israelites. Since they received only enough manna for one day they had to worry that there would be enough for the following day. This required them to turn to their Father in heaven every day (bYoma 76a).

The rabbi knew how often the manna fell from heaven. He did not know much about the way kings handled their family economic problems. It is not likely that a prince would come to see his father only when he needed money, but the rabbi needed an illustration that taught about the manna from heaven. The rabbi made up a royal situation that suited his needs. It was not intended to give an accurate factual account of royal household economy. To understand the purpose of the parable it was necessary to know the question asked of the rabbi which

---

[33] J. D. Kingsbury, The Parables of Jesus in Matthew 13 (St. Louis: Clayton, 1977), p. 65.

prompted the parable.[34] There are many rabbinic parables dealing with a king and his son. These never have anything to do with Royalty. They are always stories in which the king is God and the son is Israel, and the message is about Israel and God. A parable functions as a crucible that contains something else. The listener has to recognize the substance the crucible contains rather than the crucible.

In Matthew the parables of Jesus do not always give the question that prompted the composition of the parables. By the time Matthew composed his gospel, these parables had probably already been collected and formed into literary units that the apostles might use for their preaching and discussions with Palestinian leaders.

Parables of Jesus are some of the most likely teachings of Jesus to be valid, not because they are dissimilar to anything anyone else ever taught, but because they are coherent among themselves, are coherent with the chreias, and because none of them presumes a geographical area different from Palestine or of a time different from the period during which Jesus lived.[35]

Sowing good seed in a field is a normal task for a farmer. There is nothing peculiar about that. The question is: "How is this related to the Kingdom of God?"

Weeds. (zizania, ζιζάνια) were well-known weeds in Palestine. They were probably the same weeds that are called darnel today, but no one is certain. Darnel is a bearded plant that initially looks like wheat.

Manager. The Greek word, oi-koh-des-pó-too (οἰκοδεσπότου), literally, means, "the ruler of the house." In this context, it was the man who owned the farm. He was evidently a gentleman farmer who had employees that actually performed the manual labor.

An enemy has done this. Crossan and Gundry followed Jeremias in explaining how this suspicion might be raised by arguing that there were many more weeds than would normally be expected, but there is nothing in the parable to indicate that this was the case. Like others Crossan, Gundry, and Jeremias tried to justify a surprising deduction.[36] Both have become captivated by the "crucible" and have missed the content. Like many other parables, without knowing the question it was intended to answer, the event is not completely rational. Even if there are many weeds in a wheat field, a farmer does not normally assume that some enemy of his has deliberately planted them there while the farmer was not

---

[34]Buchanan, Jesus, p. 207.

[35]See further Buchanan, Jesus, chapter 2.

[36]Jeremias, Parables, p. 225; Gundry, Matthew (Grand Rapids: Eerdmans, 2nd c1994), p. 264.

watching.[37] Weeds normally appear in seeded fields even without the interference of an enemy. Their presence is nothing that causes alarm and throws suspicion on anyone.[38] This probably means that the parable was intended to illustrate a situation in which the damage was caused by an enemy. Since the parable is no longer in its original context, we can only conjecture the dramatis personae involved and the situation that prompted the parable.

Since there are other chreias and parables that picture Jesus in conflict with the Pharisees in defense of the tax collectors, this seems like the place to begin. This parable is one in which the whole situation is compared to something related to the Kingdom of Heaven. In the promised land, there were "weeds" popping up everywhere, and, from the point of view of the Pharisees, these were the tax collectors. They did not come up voluntarily, however, the way weeds spring up in a field of wheat. These had been appointed by the enemy, Rome. Initially, these tax collectors seemed to be neighboring Jews, no different from those around them, until suddenly they began to collect taxes for Rome. Then they were recognized as enemies. It was the enemy, Rome, that was responsible for these.

Let them both grow until harvest. There were Zealots and Sicarii among the Jews who took every chance they could find to kill the tax collectors, which they called "weeds." Their answer, in the language of the parable, was to pull them up wherever they were found so that the good wheat, the loyal nationalists, could grow unimpeded. The counsel of the parable was that there might be some damage done that way to the nationalists themselves (wheat). Until the wheat had completely headed and was ready for harvest, some of these "plants" that had seemed to be "weeds" might turn out to be "wheat." This was the case with some, if not all, of Jesus' disciples. Although they had been wealthy businessmen and tax collectors, they gave all they had to Jesus' movement, together with their dedication and leadership skills. It would have been unfortunate if these had all been killed before their conversion to become followers of Jesus.[39] There was no intention, however, for those who remained Roman collaborators to go unpunished when

---

[37]W. G. Doty, "An Interpretation: Parable of the Weeds and Wheat," Int 25 (1971):189, who thought of a parable as a miniature comedy or tragedy, missed the whole point of the enemy in pre-70 I.A. Palestine. He commented, "They do not react to the enemy, but ask what they should do with the weeds. The enemy has no further function or role than sowing weed seeds among the good seed (wheat). He is then dismissed from the story."

[38]Crossan, "Seed Parables," p. 260, said, ". . . the owner recognizes that inemical activity alone can explain the presence of (so many?) tares." But there is no indication in the text that this was an unusually large number of weeds.

[39]See further Buchanan, "Jesus and the Upper Class," NovT 7 (1964):195-209 and Jesus: The King and his Kingdom (Macon: Mercer U., 1984):171-90.

the kingdom actually came. They would surely get their just treatment. At the final time, they would be burned.

When dealing with real weeds and real wheat, there is no way that waiting would change the outcome.[40] Weeds keep on being weeds and wheat keeps on being wheat. They just have different destinies. With tax collectors, however, there was a possibility for change. The tax collectors were Jews by birth. They had been appointed tax collectors by an enemy. It was possible for them to repent and become loyal parts of the Kingdom of Heaven.

Since Jesus was addressing himself to a serious recruitment program directed to, and later also by, these very tax collectors that the Pharisees wanted uprooted, it seems proper and necessary for him to compose parables such as this one to defend his actions. He had probably had enough success among these wealthy Jews employed by the enemy Rome to realize that there was some real talent there. There was also some latent loyalty to the Kingdom of Heaven when the need was properly presented to them. One of these tax collectors had repented and become one of Jesus' apostles. Another, Zacchaeus, was not only a tax collector, but a chief tax collector. When he received Jesus' message, he volunteered to take half of his possessions to repay former injustices so that he could have a clear conscience and no debits in the treasury of merits and demerits. The rest he would give to the poor, which probably means he would join Jesus' monastic movement, contributing all of the remaining possessions to the community called "the poor" (Luke 19:19). Success stories like this convinced Jesus of the wisdom of calling these "sinners," "harlots," and "weeds" to repentance before the "harvest."[41]

Smith observed a close relationship among the words involved in this parable and the Markan parable of a plant growing mysteriously. He presumed that Matthew had used Mark and altered the parable to suit his needs.[42] Since both parables dealt with plants growing there was naturally some similarity of words. It is possible that both gospel writers depended upon a third document, but no dependence at all is necessary. The Matthaean parable has as its main point the question of those included and those excluded in judgment. The Markan parable (Mark 4:26-29) called attention to the vicious battle that would be fought in the Kidron Valley, following the prophecy of Joel 4:13.[43]

---

[40]B. Charette, The Theme of Recompense in Matthew's Gospel (Sheffield: JSOT Press, c1992), p. 145, said, "Before harvest there is always time for weeds to be changed into wheat." Really? Has anyone ever seen it done?

[41]Buchanan, Jesus, pp. 141-43.

[42]C. W. F. Smith, "The Mixed State of the Church in Matthew's Gospel," JBL 82 (1963):150-52.

[43]Buchanan, Jesus, pp. 208-11.

At the time of the harvest. The harvest referred to here is the final battle held in the Kidron Valley when all the gentiles would be gathered there to join battle with the Jews at Jerusalem. There the enemy would be cut down in war and destroyed (Joel 3[M4]:3-21). This is the way the "weeds" would be "burned." The harvest is clearly an idiom here used metaphorically, but it does not refer to the end of the world, as Gooding thought.[44] It refers to the successful battle against all Jewish enemies. After the war, the Jews would live in peace on their land.

Tie them into bundles to burn. At harvest time, farmers in the Near East do not bundle up their weeds and burn them. They cut the grain near the heads. Then they burn off the straw together with the weeds.[45] That which was expected to be gathered at "harvest" time would be all of the children of Israel from the various countries to which they have been exiled. Then there would be a final judgment, and the "weeds" would be burned (Isa 40:11; Ezek 34:11-25). The gathering of the weeds was one of the nonsense parts of the parable included to alert the reader or hearer that the subject of the parable was not weeds and wheat but saints and sinners at the judgment.

There was no disagreement on this point. Like the Pharisees, Jesus understood that the Kingdom of Heaven would have only righteous people as citizens. Finally, the sinners would be destroyed; the bad fish would be thrown out; the weeds would burn. The only question was one of time. Jesus said Jews should be patient so that no righteous people would be destroyed or thrown out by mistake.

TEXT

Matthew	First Testament
[31]He offered them another parable, saying, "The Kingdom of Heaven is like a grain of mustard seed, which a man took and sowed in his field. [32]On the one hand, it is the smallest of all the seeds, but on the other hand, after it **has grown up**, it became greater than all the vegetables, and it became **a tree**, so that	The **tree grew** and became strong, and its top reached heaven, and it could be seen to the end of all the earth. Its leaves were beautiful, and its fruit was plentiful. In it was food for everyone. The beasts of the field

[44]D. W. Gooding, "Structure Littéraire de Matthieu, XIII, 53 a XVIIII, 35," RB 85 (1978):231.

[45]W. Corswant, "Agriculture," Dictionary of Life in Bible Times (New York: Oxford, 1960), p. 24.

the birds of heaven even came and pitched their tents (kah-tahs-kay-noón, *κατασκηνοῦν*) **in its branches.**"

had shade under it. **The birds of heaven lived** (yeh-dur-óhn, ידרון; eh-nós-soo-ahn, *ἐνόσσευον*) **in its branches**, and all flesh was fed from it (Dan 4:9).

All **the birds of the heaven made their nests** (kin-ne-noó, קננו; LXX eh-nós-soo-sahn, *ἐνόσσευσαν*) **in its branches** (Ezek 31:6).

Over them **the birds of the heaven** dwell; they sing from among **the branches** (Ps 104:12).

TECHNICAL DETAILS

In the triple tradition, Matthew and Luke agree on the following words which are not included in the Markan parallel: **The Kingdom of Heaven is like, which a man takes** (Matt 13:31; Luke 13:18); **after it has grown up, a tree,** and **in its branches** (Matt 13:32; Luke 13:19). Contrary to the Markan priorists, the agreements between Matthew and Luke against Mark are not "minor."

COMMENTARY

Mustard seed. A small seed that looks very much like a turnip seed. It is smaller than wheat, barley, millet, and other grains grown in Palestine. It was frequently used as an illustration of something small (mTohar 8.8; mNid 5.2). Mustard plants and seeds are known all over the Near East, Europe, and America. The plant has yellow flowers and grows taller than most wheat, but it does not become a tree.

Becomes a tree. Crossan asked, "Why begin with a mustard seed if one intends to end with a tree (*δένδρον* in Q) rather than a bush (*λάχανον* in Mark 4:32)?" His only solution was to assume that the biblical allusions were later additions.[46] This is a normal question. It never happens to mustard seed in any country. Mustard seeds grow up and become mustard plants.[47] Patte called it

[46]Crossan, "Seed Parables," p. 255.

[47]Crossan, "Seed Parables," p. 260. Mark 4:31-32, not realizing the significance of that Daniel quotation, modified the parable so that the mustard seed grew up to become "the largest of all garden herbs." This made it rationally acceptable for those, like Mark, who did not understand the code to these riddles. Scholars like G. E. Post, "Mustard," Hastings Dictionary of the Bible

"a shrub or tree with branches big enough for birds to make their nests in them (13:32)."[48] Plummer said, "'tree' (δένδρον) does not necessarily mean a timber-tree. We speak of a rose-tree and a gooseberry-tree."[49] This is straining, and Plummer said that in an effort to make sense of a statement that was not intended to make sense. Not many people call a gooseberry bush or a rose bush "a tree." It is only in poetry, such as the song, "On the Street Where You Live," in My Fair Lady, where there are "lilac trees in the heart of town."

Lilac bushes were not called lilac trees because that was the normal name for lilacs but because a one syllable word was needed for the poetry. There was also a special reason why the mustard seed in the parable Jesus told grew up to become a tree. The reference to the tree was put into the parable to direct the listeners, "who had ears to hear," to the quotation from Daniel 4 and alert them to the fact that there was a hidden message in this parable for those who knew their scripture and Jewish tradition. The message of the parable had nothing to do with mustard seeds and trees. It was about the Kingdom of God in a land ruled by outsiders. The mustard seeds and trees were only "crucibles" designed to contain the disguised message. Mark failed to get the point of the parable, so he "corrected" it so that it would make sense without the code. Instead of "tree" he put "greater than all of the [other] vegetables" (Mark 4:32). This shows the secondary character of Mark's version of the parable.

Pitched their tents. Crossan asked, "Why use a mustard plant if one intends to have birds nesting in its branches?"[50] Gundry called attention to the extent of the hyperbole. He correctly said that the birds build their nests in the Spring before the mustard plant could have grown large enough for any of the birds to build nests in its branches.[51]

The problem becomes greater if one were to translate the Greek correctly. These birds do not nest; they pitch their tents. This is a military expression designed to alert the reader to the fact that there is another message to be communicated here--one that involves military tents. Birds dwell in branches, as the

---

3, p. 463; H. A. W. Meyer, A Critical and Exegetical Handbook on the Gospel of Matthew (New York: Funk & Wagnalls, 1884), p. 258; and A. Plummer, An Exegetical Commentary on the Gospel according to S. Matthew (London: Stock, c1920), p. 194, have also tried to justify the parable by holding that the mustard plants sometimes grow large in the Near East--ten to twelve feet tall, and Arabs sometimes call herbs, "trees." This still is not a tree that "reaches heaven." Those who understand "the mystery of the Kingdom of Heaven" or parabolic code would not have this problem.

[48]Patte, Matthew, p. 195.

[49]Plummer, Matthew, p. 194.

[50]Crossan, "Seed Parables," p. 255.

[51]Gundry, Matthew, p. 267.

Aramaic and Theodotian's Greek of Dan 4:9 both say. They also build nests and hatch their young in branches of trees, as the LXX says, **hatched their young in its branches**. Ezek 31:6 described a great tree where birds made their nests (LXX **hatched their young**). Birds make nests, hatch their young, and dwell among branches of trees, but birds do not build or pitch tents. This was a clue to the listeners that Jesus was not talking about birds at all, but about troops. See the commentary on Matt 8:20.

McArthur[52] was convinced that the best reading of the text shows that the tree is original, but he objected

> . . . contrast is a legitimate part for a parable but not incongruity. The contrast between the small mustard seed and the large plant makes a point in the contrast of Jesus' ministry, but a mustard seed that turned into a tree would be a monstrosity not characteristic of the parables correctly attributed to Jesus.

McArthur and Crossan[53] missed the point at which this resembles other parables. Like many other parables of Jesus, this riddle was not intended to provide a lesson on agronomy. Most Near Eastern farmers would have known that mustard seeds do not grow up to become trees. They grow up and become mustard plants, but it is precisely this distortion which would have given the one who had ears to hear the clue to the intended message of the parable.

There were probably four messages for those who had ears to hear:

1) All they had to do was remember the content of Dan 4 or Ezek 31 or go back and look them up to learn that the Daniel tree was part of a dream that represented a kingdom that reached heaven and its dominion extended to the end of the earth (Dan 4:22). Ezekiel compared Pharaoh of Egypt and his kingdom to a huge cedar tree in Lebanon. The Kingdom of Heaven was to be like one of those nations. These were both political kingdoms, one was Babylon and the other was Egypt. The Kingdom of Heaven would become a great kingdom like one of those.

2) The second message was that the Most High rules the kingdom of men and gives to whomever he chooses (Dan 4:17, 25, 32), and he would force even gentile kings to acknowledge him (Dan 4:37).

3) This kingdom, represented by a tree, was ruled at one time by Nebuchadnezzar, but after it had passed through the hands of three other beasts,

---

[52]H. K. McArthur, "The Parable of the Mustard Seed," CBQ 33 (1971):198-210, quote from p. 210. R. W. Funk, "The Looking-glass Tree is for the Birds," Int 27 (1973):3-9, argued that Jesus deliberately picked a small mustard bush in contrast to the cedar of Lebanon because of the humble size. Even though he studied this passage in relationship to Ezekiel and Daniel, Funk did not see the reason for these references.

[53]Crossan, "Seed Parables," p. 253-59, concluded that the original parable did not have any reference to a tree or birds' nests, so he dismissed the quotation from Daniel.

it was finally given to the Jews under the leadership of the Son of man (Dan 7:13) at exactly the time when Judas overpowered the Syrians sufficiently to cleanse the temple. This knowledge enabled Jews to understand the third message which was that the Kingdom of God was like the Hasmonean kingdom that had been ruled by the foreign nations until the Son of man was vindicated in the heavenly court.

4) The fourth message was that the "birds" that found shelter in the branches of the great "tree," in Jesus' time, were to live in tents and follow Jesus. The Romans missed all of these messages.[54] So have many twentieth century scholars.

TEXT

[33]He spoke to them another parable: "The Kingdom of Heaven is like leaven which a woman took and hid in three measures of flour until the whole [container of flour] was leavened."

COMMENTARY

The Kingdom of Heaven is like leaven. The importance of the leaven metaphor is that leaven is very infectious. It is not necessary to add yeast to flour to make it leavened. It has only to be moistened to be considered leavened. For Passover, it is important to have flour that has not been leavened. Therefore care had to be taken that no moisture reached the wheat from the time it headed out until the flour was moistened just before the bread was put into the oven. There must elapse only 18 minutes between the time the flour is moistened until the unleavened bread is taken out of the oven.

Today most Jewish bakers can manage this operation within 11 minutes. If any flour is accidently moistened or becomes moldy, it must be discarded. Vessels that can hold moisture must be broken. If a small bit of leavened flour falls into a pot of dough, 60 times as large as the leavened flour, the whole is considered leavened. The dough must be discarded and the pot must be broken.[55] Because leaven is considered infectious, it was used metaphorically to describe a political or religious movement. That is what Jesus meant when he warned his disciples to watch out for the leaven of the Pharisees, Sadducees, and Herod (Matt 16:6; Mk 8:24-15; Lk 12:1). He meant that these groups were busy

---

[54]Buchanan, Jesus, pp. 212-13. The secretive way in which messiahs communicated is evident when Sabbatai Zevi carried a fish around in a baby basket to let Jews know that under the zodiacal sign of Pisces Israel would be redeemed from pagan rule. See J. Kastein, The Messiah of Ismir, tr. H. Peterson (New York: Viking, 1931), p. 73.

[55]R. I. Rabinowitz, "Mazzah," Encyclopaedia Judaica 11, pp. 1155-58.

propagating their doctrines everywhere. Like leaven, they were corrupting the nation. Rabbis complained to the Lord:

> Master of the ages, it is revealed and known to you that we want to do your will. Who is hindering? The leaven that is in the dough and subjection to the gentiles. May it be your will that we may escape from their hands (bBer 17a).

This was also true of leaven that must permeate into loaves. Aune correctly said,

> While modern critics speak of the 'messianic secret' of Mark, the evangelist himself was concerned with the 'secret of the kingdom of God' (Mk. iv.12). This secret is clarified by the parables of Matthew xiii.[56]

Hid in three measures of flour. Three measures of flour is about 1 1/2 pecks or roughly a third of a bushel (40 liters). It normally takes about three cups of flour to make a loaf of ordinary white or whole wheat bread. A third of a bushel of flour would make much more bread than the average family could eat. This exaggerated amount of flour was probably given to clue in the listeners to the fact that Jesus was talking about something other than a house wife baking bread.

When leavened bread is desired, there is no need to hide the leaven that is used.[57] It can just be added since there is no secrecy involved, but Jesus was using code language to talk about something that was secret. At the time he was speaking, the Kingdom of Heaven was in hiding. The Romans did not know it existed. This was an underground movement that was quietly, infectiously, working its way through the land. With the rapidity of leaven in a loaf, this undercover movement would take control of the whole situation, and soon everyone would find out what had been happening.[58] This parable is consistent with the parable of seed growing secretly or the mustard seed that grew up and became a tree. At the right time, the grain would be ready for harvest and the leavened loaf would be ready for the oven. These were different metaphors for the same event. It

---

[56]D. Aune, "The Problem of the Messianic Secret," NovT 11 (1969):25.

[57]There is also no reason to think the number three refers to the deity, as Funk thinks (R. W. Funk, "Beyond Criticism in the Quest of Literacy: The Parable of Leaven," Int 25 [1971]: 149-70, esp. p. 167). Funk said "leaven" is the loss of the received world; "hide" means mystery; and "three measures of meal" equals the presence of God (p. 167). Three measures would make a fantastically large number of loaves, but that was intended to alert the Jewish listener that Jesus was not really talking about bread at all. Funk has used the scripture as an ink blot test by which to infuse his own theology.

[58]With Constantine's conquest, Eusebius said all those Christian disciples, who had been consecrated to the Word and yet were secretly concealed, appeared openly (HE 10.iv.60).

meant that the Kingdom of Heaven was about to come into existence in the land of Palestine.

In his customary way the author of GosThom 96 elaborated on Matthew's text by noting that the resulting loaves would be large.

TEXT

[34]All these things Jesus spoke in parables to the crowds, and without a parable he spoke nothing to them, [35]so that which was spoken through the prophet might be fulfilled, saying,

Matthew	First Testament
I will open my mouth with parables; I will produce hidden things from the foundation of the world.	**I will open my mouth with a parable; I will produce riddles from** ancient times which we have heard and learned, which our fathers have told us, [which] we will not hide from their children, narrating to the next generation the praises of Yahowah and his strength (Ps 78:2-4).

TECHNICAL DETAILS

In his parallel to Matt 13, Mark included first the parable of the sower and its interpretation. He followed these with the parable of the seed growing secretly, which is not included in Matthew, and finally, the parable of the mustard seed. Mark introduced these parables with the statement, "He taught them many things in parables" (Mark 4:2) and concluded with, "And with many such parables as these he spoke the law to them" (Mark 4:33). For Mark, this was not just a summary of the first half of the list of parables. It was a final summary. These were all the parables he included, but he noted that there were many more--at least the three or four that Matthew had in his collection. There are several summary statements in Mark which summarize that which is included in the Matthaean parallel. For example, at the end of the Sermon on the Mount, Matthew has, "When Jesus finished these words, the crowds were surprised at his teaching, for he taught them as one having authority and not as their scribes" (Matt 7:28). "These words" consist of the Sermon on the Mount (Matt 5:1-7:29).

Mark did not record the Sermon on the Mount; he only summarized it: "They were surprised at his teaching, for he was teaching them as one having authority, and not as their scribes" (Mark 4:22). Mark reported only that teaching had taken place; he did not tell what it was. It is clear from these summarizing statements in Mark that Mark had access to materials that he was summarizing but omitting. He may have been using Matthew as his source, but Matthew was not the only source. He also included the parable of the seed growing secretly (Mark 4:26-29), which Matthew omitted. His sources did not include the hypothetical "Q," because "Q," by definition, is that material found both in Matthew and Luke, but not in Mark.

COMMENTARY

Jesus spoke in parables. This is a summary statement, but not a conclusion. Each parable was introduced as "another parable," but this was the half-way mark. Matthew had already told the parable of the sower and given its interpretation. Then he included the first triad of parables. He still had three more parables plus the concluding parable to report in Matt 13. At this mid-way he summarized that which had been reported.

The crowds. This editorial comment is coherent with Matt 13:2-3, "Many crowds were gathered to him . . . and he spoke many parables to them." The editor structured this setting for the parables, just as he placed the Sermon on the Mount to be an antitype to Moses on the mountain with the crowds of people at the base of the mountain. Moses came down and addressed the crowds.

Spoken through the prophet. This refers to the word of God which was spoken through the legal agency of the prophet. This so-called "prophet" was a Psalmist, but rabbis frequently referred to any text of the FT which they needed as if it were prophecy that was destined to be fulfilled in the days of the Messiah.

I will open my mouth with parables. This is the second text used in this unit to justify the use of parables and to explain the way they were used. These proof texts show that the Messiah was supposed to speak in parables. It was thus prophesied in the word of God. The first text (Isa 6:9-10) was used to provide a textual basis for justifying Jesus' use of parables and to introduce an interpretation of the parable of the sower. This was followed by three additional parables. The second text (Ps 78:2) follows another parable about sowing and introduces another interpretation of the parable followed by another three parables. This text is placed in the middle of the unit on kingdom parables and is part of a well-organized structure.

I will produce hidden things. That is what these parables were. They were riddles, code messages, hidden messages which only those who knew their scripture and Jewish tradition could understand. These were messages the Jewish nationalists did not want Rome to understand. To them they were hidden, because Romans did not have ears to hear.

From the foundation of the world. This is the reading of some major texts, including Sinaiticus (א,CDθW). Other texts omit kós-moo (κόσμου) "of the world," reading only kah-tah-boh-láys (καταβολῆς) "foundation." This is a translation of the Hebrew, kah-dáhm (קדם), "ancient times," "antiquity," etc. (Ps 78:1). LXX 77:2 has ap archáys (ἀπ' αρχῆς) "from the beginning." This is a better translation of the Hebrew than Matthew has. The ancient teachings were hidden away in scripture, Jewish history, and tradition. They had been there from the foundation of the world.

TEXT

[36]Then, after he had left the crowds, he went into the house, and his disciples came to him, saying, "Interpret for us the parable of the weeds of the field."

COMMENTARY

He went into the house. This is a transitional sentence, moving from the FT text to the interpretation of the parable of the weeds and seeds. The geographical situation continues to be coherent. Jesus moved from the crowds beside the sea to his home near the sea, probably at Capernaum. His home near the sea may have been a monastery which was also the home of the disciples, because when he entered his house, the disciples went with him. The transition in teaching was made also. He shifted from the crowds to the disciples.

Interpret for us the parable. In the first half of chapter 13, Matthew included first the parable of the sower, then its interpretation. This second half begins with a parable of the weeds, followed by its interpretation. Matthew's organization is consistent.

Matthew pictured Jesus spending time training his disciples by answering their questions and providing them parables for their preaching. The parable of the sower was probably the teaching of Jesus, but the interpretation which follows is the addition of the later church. The same is true with this parable. Wenham wondered why the parable was so nearly like that in Mark whereas there were variances between Matthew and Mark in the interpretation.[59] This is nothing new. The parable constituted the words of Jesus, and later editors were reluctant to change these. The interpretation, however, is the work of the later church, and editors felt free to change later additions at will. Testing the possibility that Matthew used Mark and changed it somewhat, Wenham concluded that that hypothesis made no sense. He held that Matthew and Mark had both used an earlier source which Matthew followed faithfully and Mark changed. This is the solution

---

[59]Wenham, "Parable of the Sower," p. 301.

proposed earlier by Parker and supported later by Lowe and Flusser.[60] Another possibility is that Mark used Matthew.

TEXT

The Commentary on the Parable

[37]The one who **sowed the good seed** is the Son of man, [38]and **the field** is the world. The **good seed** are the sons of the kingdom, but the **weeds** are the sons of the evil one. [39]**The enemy** who **sowed** them is the devil. **The harvest** is the end of the age, and **the harvesters** are angels. [40] Therefore, just as **the weeds are gathered and burned** in fire, thus it will be at the end of the age. [41]The Son of man will send his angels, and they will **gather from** his kingdom all the stumbling blocks and those who commit lawlessness (Ps 37:1), [42]and they will throw them into the oven of fire (Dan 3:6). In that place there will be wailing and gnashing of teeth. [43]Then the righteous will shine like the sun in the Kingdom of their Father. He who has ears, let him hear.

The Commentary on the FT

Matthew	First Testament
[37]The one who sowed the good seed is **the Son of man,** [38]and the field is the world. The good seeds are the sons of the kingdom, but the weeds are the sons of the evil one. [39]The enemy who sowed them is the devil.	Look! With the clouds of heaven one like a **Son of man** is coming up to the ancient of days (Dan 7:13).
The harvest is the end of the age,	Put in the sickle, for **the harvest** is ripe (Joel 4:13).
and the harvesters are **angels.** [40]Therefore, just as the weeds are gathered and burned in fire, thus it	Then Yahowah my God will come. All his **angels** will be with him (Zech 14:5).
will be **at the end of the age.** [41]The	You will rest and will stand in your allotted place **at the end of days** (Dan 12:13).

[60]P. Parker, "A Second Look at the Gospel before Mark," JBL 100 (1981):389-413; and The Gospel before Mark (Chicago: U. of Chicago, c1953); Lowe and Flusser, "Proto-Matthaean Synoptic," pp. 25-47.

Son of man will send his angels,	The appearance of the fourth is like the **Son of God** (Dan 3:25).
and they will **gather from** his kingdom **all the stumbling blocks and**	"I will surely **gather from** the face of the ground (האדמה, hah-ahd-ah-máh)" says the Lord, "**all . . . the stumbling blocks [and] the wicked ones** (Zeph 1:2-3).
those who commit lawlessness,	Do not be jealous of **those who commit** wickedness (Ps 37:1).
42**and they will throw them into the oven of fire**.	**They will throw them into the oven of fire** (Dan 3:6).
	You brought them out of Egypt, out of the **oven of** iron (1 Kings 8:51; cf. Deut 4:20; Jer 11:4).
In that place there will be wailing and **grinding of teeth**.	The wicked will see and become angry. He will **grind his teeth** and tremble (Ps 112:10).
43Then **the righteous will shine like the** sun in the Kingdom of their Father. He who has ears, let him hear.	Many of those who sleep in the ground will wake up--some to life of the age and others to disgrace and rejection of the age. Those who make [others] wise **will shine like the** brightness of the firmament, and those who make the many **righteous**, **like the** stars for the age and until [the next age] (Dan 12:2-3).

TECHNICAL DETAILS

This is a masterful midrash. The author, first of all, commented on the parable of the wheat and the weeds, selecting words from the parable which he thought were important. These he quoted and defined. While defining them, he also wove into his midrash several strategic passages from the FT. The fact that he treated the parable of the Sower the same way he treated the FT intertextually means that in his judgment the teachings of Jesus had scriptural authority already by the time he wrote.

COMMENTARY

The one who sowed the good seed. "The one who sowed good seed" is the one mentioned in Matt 13:24. In the parable (Matt 13:24-29), this was probably God, but since the Son of man was believed to be God's legal agent, the interpretation is legitimate. This is the beginning of an interpretation of an earlier parable (Matt 13:24-29). The Son of man was the new Judas the Maccabee, and the end of the age was the end of the new Syrian Greek age, which came to an end with the success of the Hasmonean rebellion.

The field is the world. "The field" is the one mentioned in Matt 13:24. There seems to have been a Hebrew origin, both to the parable (Matt 13:24-29) and also the interpretation (Matt 13:37-43). The word for "world" is kós-mos (κόσμος), which is one of the words that would normally render the Hebrew ah-deh-máh (אדמה). Ah-deh-máh can also mean "land," namely the promised land. In the parable, the field was probably meant to be the promised land. The later church either misinterpreted the Hebrew by mistake or it intentionally changed its original meaning to expand the territory. If the field is the world then the world is not the same as the Kingdom of Heaven, as Patte held.[61]

The sons of the kingdom. This is the same as the parable intended--the good Jews and/or Christians on the promised land.

The sons of the evil one. Functionally, these were the tax collectors and other Jews who mingled with the Romans.

The enemy who sowed them. More specifically, the enemy was Rome who lured Palestinian Jews to become rich by collecting taxes. For Jews and early Christians terms like Satan, the devil, the evil one, etc. were not just abstractions. They were identified with local and current enemies.

The harvest is the end of the age. The expression "the end of the age" is a typical Matthaean expression (Matt 13:30, 39, 40, 49; 24:3; 28:20). The only use of the verb sun-teh-láys-thai (συντελεῖσθαι) in the Gospel of Mark occurs in parallel with this expression of Matthew's (Mark 13:4). The end of the age meant the end of the common era that was ruled by gentile idolators while the Jews and/or Christians were subjects to this foreign power on the promised land. Whenever this common age would come to an end, the holy Jewish or Christian age would begin. The "end of the age" in Matthew and the "end of days" in Daniel are terms describing the same portion of the cycle. The end of days in Daniel refers to the end of the era ruled by Antiochus Epiphanes. It came to an end after the Hasmoneans overpowered the Greeks and gained control of the Davidic kingdom

---

[61]Patte, Mattthew, p. 197.

again. This was a type for which the anticipated antitype would have been the downfall of the Roman empire and the establishment of the Kingdom of God with its capital city at Jerusalem, and its king, a Jewish messiah.

The term "harvest" sometimes referred to cutting down the enemy in battle, just as harvesters cut grain. Joel described the battle at the end of the common age as a harvest scene that would take place when all the gentiles would gather and be defeated in the Kidron Valley east of the temple in Jerusalem. At this military "harvest" the Lord would use his sickle to mow the gentiles down like grain, while Jews would reign victorious (Joel 3:9-21). Jeremiah compared Babylon to a threshing floor. At harvest time it would be trampled (Jer 51:33).

The commentator correctly related the destruction of the wicked to gathering weeds in the parable. He also correctly related this end of the age to the end expected in Daniel and the gathering expected in Zephaniah and Joel. When Jews and Christians spoke of the "end of the age," it was almost always in joyous expectation, because the age they wanted to end was the age of gentile rule over the promised land. There is one exception. Hai Gaon was speaking about "the age to come," after the Messiah had been revealed, the dead had been raised, and the temple was reestablished in Jerusalem. Then Jews would "dwell in their kingdom until the end of the age." This was the Jewish age about which he was speaking. When would the holy, Jewish age come to an end? Hai Gaon said,

> There are some who say until the completion of 7,000 years from the days of creation (3240 I.A.).[62]

His logic was that since 1,000 years in the sight of the Lord was as a day, there should be six common days (millennia) from the creation of the world. The sixth of these would be from 1240 to 2240 I.A. Then the sabbath rest of one holy "day" (1,000 years) would allow Jews to rule the world for their age of a millennium, from 2240-3240 I.A. This deduction, however, is unique. Most ancient Jews and Christians spoke of the end of the common gentile age when they spoke of the end of the age. That is the case with all of the references to the end of the age in the Gospel of Matthew (Matt 13:39, 40, 49; 24:3; 28:20).

The harvesters are angels. Jewish holy war theology depended heavily on angels to come to the aid of Jewish troops in battle. When the Israelite troops fled from the Egyptians, the angel of the Lord went before the Israelites and followed after them to provide protection (Exod 14:19). It also went before the Israelites to blot out the tribes of Canaan, who were enemies of the Israelites, to be overcome so that the Israelites could possess the land (Exod 23:23; 32:34). Zechariah promised that at the end of the age, the gentiles would be gathered in the Kidron Valley for

---

[62]See Buchanan, Revelation and Redemption: Jewish Documents of Deliverance from the Fall of Jerusalem to the Death of Nahmanides (Dillsboro, c1978; sold by Mercer U. Press), p. 129.

war. At that time, God would come, and all his angels with him, and they would fight against those enemy nations (Zech 14:3-5).

During the Maccabean rebellion divine beings were reported to have appeared in heaven on horseback with golden armor overpowering the Syrian Greeks in behalf of the Jewish troops (2 Macc 3:25). Jesus expected that when the Son of man came into his glory and sat on his glorious throne in Jerusalem, he would not come alone. All of his angels would come with him (Matt 25:31), just as Zechariah prophesied. As the Lord's legal agent Jesus thought he had authority to expect God to send him more than 12 legions of angels, if Jesus chose to ask him (Matt 26:53). When these angels came with the Son of man, they would destroy all of the enemies that threatened the chosen people.

He will gather from his kingdom. Matthew rendered the Hebrew of Zephaniah differently from the RSV. Most scholars take ah-sáhf (אסף) to mean "sweep away," probably derived from shah-fáh (שפה), a word whose basic meaning is "to rub off." The word ahsh-páh (אשפה), however, means "quiver," a container where arrows are gathered (Ps 127:5). LXX rendering of Zeph 1:2 is "omit" or "abandon" (ek-láyp-say ek-lip-é-toh (*ἐκλείψει ἐκλιπέτω*). Matthew evidently understood ah-sáhf to mean "gather," the most normal meaning for the word, because he rendered it by soo-lég-eh-tai (*συλλέγεται*) (Matt 13:40) and su-léx-oo-sin (*συλλέξουσιν*)--to gather or collect (Matt 13:41). According to Matthew, Zephaniah thought God promised to gather everything from the face of the ground[63]--human beings, beasts, birds, the stumbling blocks, and the wicked ones (Zeph 1:2-3). Matthew was not concerned about the birds, beasts, and the human beings in general. He was only interested in the stumbling blocks and the wicked ones, and God's purpose for gathering them was only that he might destroy them by burning (Matt 13:40-42).

"His kingdom" was not the church as some commentators hold. As McIver said,

> This kingdom cannot be conceived in terms of reign but only in terms of territory that one can enter and from which one can be excluded . . . Nor is this the only language associated with the kingdom that is best understood in terms of territory. Take, for example, the frequently occurring image of entering the kingdom found in 5:20; 7:21; 18:3; 19:23-24; 21:31.[64]

---

[63]The word Zephaniah used was אדמה, which can mean "land," "ground," "earth," "soil," or "country." Zephaniah probably used the word to mean ground or land. Matthew seems to have taken it to mean the promised land.

[64]R. K. McIver, "The Parable of the Weeds among the Wheat (Matt 13:24-30, 36-43) and the Relationship between the Kingdom and the Church as Portrayed in the Gospel of Matthew," JBL 114 (1995):655.

Harrisville said further,

> What happens most to the Kingdom of God is that it is 'entered.' Next in order is the kingdom as 'preached.' . . . The kingdom as 'inherited' assumes third place . . . The kingdom as sought or awaited, as given or received, is in next to last place; and the kingdom as seized, shut up, promised, prepared, assigned or shared is in last place.[65]

These are things that do not happen much to a reign. The kingdom mentioned in Matt 13:43 was not a reign, and it was not the world as other scholars think. His kingdom was the land of Palestine, the kingdom of the Son of man. There was a strong belief among Jews and early Christians that the land of Palestine would not be restored to the chosen people until all sin and sinners were removed from the land. Finally, the sinners would be destroyed; the bad fish would be thrown out; the weeds would burn.

Throw them into the oven of fire. This alludes to the oven of fire into which Shadrach, Meshach, and Abednego were thrown by the king and from which they all escaped unharmed. The gentiles, however, who wanted them killed were later thrown in and were burned instantly. As antitypes of the situation in Daniel, the angels were the equivalents of Shadrach, Meshach, and Abednego, and the antitype of the Son of God who was seen with them in the oven of fire (Dan 3:25) was the Son of man. The sons of the evil one were the antitypes of the Babylonian counsellors of the king.

The righteous will shine. This is a summary drawn from Dan 12:2-3, which is a poetic couplet.

> Those who make [others] wise **will shine like**
> **the** brightness of the firmament,
> and those who make the many **righteous**,
> **like the** stars for the age and until [the next age].

"The many" are the members of the congregation of Israel. In Daniel, they were the Jews who survived the Maccabean Rebellion. They were the same people as the "saints of the Most High" (Dan 7:18). They were citizens of the Davidic kingdom after the Hasmonean victory. Those who made them righteous were the ones who redeemed them by paying off their indebtedness in the heavenly treasury. They were the soldiers who fought the war and pious Jews who died for refusing to abandon their faith in the time of persecution. In the heavenly court (Dan 7) these courageous and faithful Jews were the ones who brought

[65] R. A. Harrisville, "In Search of the Meaning of 'The Reign of God,'" Int 47 (1993):143-45.

about the verdict of "righteous," "innocent," "not guilty," or "sinless" for all the surviving Jews of the kingdom. The righteous ones would be the sinless citizens of the new Davidic kingdom (the wheat) after the Romans had been driven out and the wicked people (the weeds) were all destroyed.[66] The Kingdom of their Father was the same as the Kingdom to be ruled by the Son of man, when he would come into his glory and sit on his glorious throne, and the saints would inherit the kingdom prepared for them (Matt 25:31-34).

He who has ears. Plummer missed the coded method of communication by parables. He said,

> All have ears; and therefore all are responsible for refusing to listen. A man cannot plead that he was unable to hear.[67]

Jews were very careful to see that not all could hear. These messages were designed for the Jews who knew the code. Those Jews who knew their scripture would not have needed Jesus to interpret it for them--least of all the disciples who knew the mysteries of the Kingdom of Heaven. Matthew introduced this interpretation scene to clarify the point for readers who might not otherwise understand all of this and to remind readers that these parables were all told as code for the nationalists to understand, but not the Romans. Even Matthew's explanation would make no sense to the Romans, just as it has not made sense to many Christians for hundreds of years.

TEXT

44The Kingdom of Heaven is like a treasure hidden, which, after a man found, he hid, and from his joy went out and sold all that he had and bought that field.

COMMENTARY

A treasure hidden. Most texts add "in the field," but Sinaiticus and the medieval Hebrew text omit these words. The explanation given by most scholars of this parable does not make sense.[68] One of the ideas is that a common day laborer

---

[66]On this see further Buchanan, New Testament Eschatology: Historical and Cultural Background (Lewiston: Mellen, c1993), pp. 120-60.

[67]Plummer, Matthew, p. 196.

[68]J. Schniewind, Das Evangelium nach Matthaeus (Göttingen: Vandenhoeck & Ruprecht, 1950), p. 173, for example, tried to compare "God's rule" to a field with a treasure in it. Also Kingsbury, Parables, p. 116. This makes no sense. Jesus compared a kingdom, which is a geographical territory, to a field, which is also a geographical territory, but to compare an action to an object is difficult.

found a hidden treasure while digging in his employer's field. Derrett argued that the finder was entitled to do the things he did in order to obtain the treasure. This was legally appropriate,[69] but that does not answer the problem of the day worker having enough possessions to buy the field. Those who understood parables realized that Jesus was not really talking about a field or a chest full of hidden gold and jewels.

This was not just any ordinary field. It was the field, the very special field. It was not really a farmer's field at all. It was the promised land, the main purpose of all of these kingdom parables. Jews realized, more than others, that this was the land of milk and honey. It was an important land bridge between great countries, like Egypt and the Orient. It was able to tax other countries heavily for crossing this territory. As a buffer state, it could strike deals with opposing countries for the privilege of cooperating with Palestinian Jews in matters of trade and warfare. In ways like this Palestine was able to live rather prosperously without taxing its own citizens much.

Sold all he had. Scholars have also been embarrassed by the ethics of the worker who cheated his employer out of the treasure that was rightfully his.[70] Crossan, for example, thought that Jesus' parable would have instigated a moral shock in a Jewish audience.[71] Plummer recognized the obvious morality question, but justified it: "But even if he was guilty of sharp practice, that ought to afford no difficulty."[72]

The mystery of this parable, however, removes both the problem of ethics of the employee and the problem of his ability to buy the field. For those who considered this land their promised right, there has never been an ethical problem about taking it whenever possible. They have felt no "moral shock" about driving out the inhabitants of that land and then sitting under the vine and fig tree after they had killed the person who built the house and planted the trees. Israelites took it from the Canaanites by warfare, and did not feel the least bit guilty about it. The Hasmoneans took it from the Greeks through warfare and negotiations with the Romans. There is no account of Jews being guilt ridden because of their unfairness to the Greeks. There is no record of reparation payments offered to the Greeks. The same was true of the Christian conquest and expansion during the time of Constantine. Eusebius reports only joy over the victory of Christians

---

[69]J. D. M. Derrett, "Law in the New Testament: The Treasure in the Field (Mt. XIII.44)," ZNW 54 (1963):31-42.

[70]J. D. M. Derrett, Law in the New Testament (London: Darton, Longman & Todd, c1970), pp. 4-14, said the act "is hardly loving one's neighbor as oneself." Jeremias, Parables, p. 139.

[71]J. D. Crossan, Finding is the First Act: Trove Folktales and Jesus' Treasure Parable (Philadelphia: Fortress, 1979), p. 90-91.

[72]Plummer, Matthew, p. 197.

which he interpreted as God's new intervention, providing Christians with a new Exodus.

Individual Jews and Christians may feel guilty about taking someone's field unjustly, but nations of Christians and Jews, justifying themselves by manifest destiny beliefs seem able to keep themselves from being overcome with guilt over their unjust conquests. The parable was told to people who felt divinely appointed to "find" a treasure in the promised land. In order to make this discovery fruitful, they were encouraged to join a monastery, which involved selling all that they owned and contributing the proceeds to a group that called itself "the poor," so that it could finance the endeavor of obtaining the promised land. Jesus and his apostles had made precisely the kind of sacrifice this parable advocates, and they encouraged others to do the same.

TEXT

45Again the Kingdom of Heaven is like a merchant looking for choice pearls,
46and after he had found one very precious pearl, he went away and sold all that he had and bought it.

TECHNICAL DETAILS

This has often been recognized as a "twin" to the parable of the treasure in a field. Glombitza observed that these parables are separated in the Gospel of Thomas, but, following Bultmann, Glombitza concluded that Matthew has them together the way they were originally.[73] It is not certain whether Matthew has them correctly organized or not. They may have been told at the same situation, but at different times. Matthew organized his materials very well according to a well-planned structure,[74] putting teachings together, miracles together, redemption midrash together, etc. Therefore, he may have obtained them from separate sources and put them together because of the similarity of form and message. Nonetheless, wherever or whenever Jesus told the parable of the pearl merchant, the message is the same as the parable of the treasure in the field.

---

[73]O. Glombitza, "Der Perlenkaufmann (Eine exegetische Studie zu Matth xxiii.45-6," NTS 7 (1961):153-61, also followed Bultmann in thinking that the parable of the fish net belonged with both of these. Glombitza's interpretation of all three of these as offering salvation to all overlooks the social and political situation in which they were told. J. Wellhausen, Das Evangelium Matthei (Berlin: G. Reimer, 1904), p. 70, also considered the forms in Matthew to be primary to those in the Gospel of Thomas.

[74]See Cope, Matthew, pp. 13-31, for an explanation of the way Matthew organized chapter 13. See also Buchanan, Jesus, pp. 105-106.

COMMENTARY

Looking for choice pearls. The Kingdom of heaven was not like a merchant; it was like a situation in which a merchant did as the parable described. The merchant was assumed to be an astute judge of pearls. That was his business.

He sold all that he had. The merchant recognized the great value of that one particular pearl. Like the treasure in the field the pearl was priceless. The Kingdom of Heaven was compared to the precious pearl in that it was the very best way anyone might invest his or her money. The pearl could only increase in value, and the land of Palestine, once under unrestricted control of Jews and their messiah, would be an immeasurable source of wealth.

Both parables indicate that there is no price too high to pay. The person who recognizes that it is the Kingdom of Heaven that can be acquired should give up everything he or she has to obtain it. This is the very message Jesus expressed in the chreias when he told people to leave families, jobs, and everything to which they were devoted and become his disciples. In this chapter, at least, there is no obvious incoherence in these teachings. The only difference is the trouble caused to twentieth century scholars. The pearl merchant was expected to have sources for obtaining money, whereas the employee who found the treasure in the field was not. The employee seemed to be cheating the employer, whereas the pearl merchant was expected to drive the hardest bargain that he could. Most scholars have felt no moral shock at the idea of a merchant negotiating for a purchase. That is a normal part of business.[75]

TEXT

47Again the Kingdom of Heaven is like a fish net, thrown into the sea. It gathers from every kind [of sea creatures]. 48When it has been filled, they draw it up onto the shore. Then they sit down and gather the good ones into a container, and they throw out the worthless ones. 49This is the way it will be at the end of the age. The angels will come out and separate the evil ones from the midst of the righteous, 50and they [the angels] will throw them [the evil ones] into the furnace of fire. In that place there will be wailing and gnashing of teeth.

COMMENTARY

Like a fish net. This parable seems to have the same point as the parable of the weeds in the field except that the element of the enemy and the destiny of the righteous is not included, so the parable follows more clearly. The parable seems to teach patience in judgment. Fishermen could not be selective about the fish

---

[75]Glombitza, "Perlenkaufmann," NTS 7 (1961):153-61, conjectured that this was an allegory in which God was the pearl merchant and Jesus was the pearl. No such allegory is necessary.

they wanted to catch into their nets, but they could sort them after they were brought into the boat. In the same way the angels would sort out the evil ones and discard them in the fiery furnace.

Every kind [of sea creatures]. Jews, of course, were forbidden to eat fish that did not have scales and fins; therefore, these were considered "worthless." It was not just because Jews did not like eels, catfish, shell fish, frogs, and turtles that these creatures were considered worthless. They were worthless to Jews, because they were forbidden by law. The fact that Jews were not permitted to eat them did not mean these sea beings would never live in Palestinian waters. The person who refused to touch "worthless" fish would never become a fisherman, because these lived side-by-side with the fish that had scales and fins. A fisherman had to accept them all at the beginning.

Gather the good ones into a container. There was a time when these would have to be segregated, but that could not happen before the "worthless" ones had been touched. All the fish were drawn into the boat or up on land, and then they were divided. Only the good fish were kept. The "worthless" ones were thrown out. That is the way it would be in the Kingdom of Heaven. There existed, in Jesus' time, both faithful Jews and also those who had compromised with the Romans. These wealthy, liberal Jews were the ones the Pharisees wanted destroyed at once, but Jesus encouraged patience--the patience of a farmer or a fisherman.

At the end of the age. The end of the age was the end of the common, pagan era in which Jews and Christians then lived. It would continue until the Romans were overthrown, and the Jews would be established as rulers of the promised land. When the last battle of the war would be over, a court trial was expected, and the Jews who were faithful at that time would be judged kah-sháyr (כשר), but the unfaithful Jews would be excluded from the kingdom. Matthew even went so far as to indicate the final torture they would suffer. This was a typical Matthaean interpretative addition to the parable. The parable stopped with the assurance that the unrighteous Jews would not be included in the Kingdom. They would be separated from the righteous just as the weeds would be singled out from the wheat and as the unapproved fish would be separated from those that had scales and fins.

It was assumed that all sin and iniquity would be destroyed or removed before the Kingdom could be reestablished on the promised land. Jeremiah said that when the Lord restored the fortunes to Judah and Israel and rebuilt them as at first that he would cleanse them from all guilt and rebellion (Jer 33:7-8). Zechariah imagined an angel putting all of the iniquity of the land into a basket, putting a lid on it with a heavy weight to keep it down, and having it removed from the land and taken into Babylon (Zech 5:5-11). The motivation of this vision was to transfer all of the Palestinian guilt to the Babylonian gentiles, so that the gentiles would be punished for the crimes Jews had committed. An early Jewish poet looked forward to the time when God would restore a new king, the Messiah of the Lord, to the throne of Jerusalem. At that time there would be no unrighteousness in the land. The place would be free from sin (PssSol 17.36). Coherent with this belief was the message of the parable of the fish net and the weeds in the field. At the end of the age the weeds would be burned, and the fish that were not kah-sháyr would be thrown out. In the new "field" of Palestine there would be no sinners (weeds or bad fish) to attract the Lord's punishment. With no sins deserving punishment, the chosen people would receive only blessings from the Lord's hand.

From the midst of the righteous. These are the same harvesting angels who were delegated by the Son of man to gather up all of the stumbling blocks and doers of evil (Matt 13:41).

TEXT

51"Do you grasp all of these things?" They said to him, "Yes." 52Then he said to them, "Because of this every scribe instructed in the Kingdom of Heaven is like a man who is the ruler of a house, who takes out from his treasury old [things] and new."

COMMENTARY

Do you grasp? Literally, "Can you bring together?" The idea Jesus was asking was could the disciples "put two and two together and make four." This required a knowledge of the code in which Jesus spoke, the mysteries of the Kingdom of Heaven. This question was not limited to the parable about sorting out fish. The question was applied to the entire chapter, the whole collection of parables. He meant, "Do you follow the significance of these coded messages?"

Because of this. "This" includes the entire message of the parables that were collected into this chapter.

Every scribe. Scribes belonged to an honorable profession. They associated with famous people. Ben Sira contrasted them to the craftsmen who made pots and other objects with their hands. The scribes were the lawyers and judges. They studied history, prophecy, and the law of the Most High. They understood the hidden meanings of the proverbs and the puzzles of the parables (Sir 38:31-39:3).

Instructed in the Kingdom of Heaven. The Greek word for "instruct" is the same as "becoming a disciple" or "being disciplined." This may refer to those who have become disciples of Jesus, or it may simply refer to those who have become trained in the mysteries of the Kingdom of Heaven, whether they had become disciples or not. It was their task to understand the hidden codes of the mysteries.

In some way they had become adequately trained in scripture and Jewish tradition to be able to understand the code Jesus was using and so understand all of these parables.

Old and new. The analogy is to a man who owns many possessions that have been collected in the family for many years. He could bring out antiques and modern furniture and equipment. The scribe that was well-trained also had a large collection of parables, scripture, Jewish traditions, and other knowledge that would enable him or her to deduce hidden means that were spoken in code through parables. A good example of that is the scribe who wrote the interpretation of the wheat and the weeds (Matt 13:37-43. See above). He first developed a midrash on the basis of Jesus' new parable (Matt 13:24-33). This was his use of the new, but he also worked into this midrash some relevant passages of scripture (Dan 7:13; 12:2-3, 13; Joel 4:13; Zech 14:5). That demonstrated his use of the old.

This was the final time in this dissertation on the Kingdom of Heaven that Matthew interrupted the sequence of the parables to remind the reader that special knowledge was required for understanding these parables correctly. They were spoken in code. This was necessary to communicate to some people without disclosing the message to others who would be listening. The twentieth century reader should take these admonitions seriously and not try to understand the parables as clear meaningful narratives that make sense for everyone just the way they are.

As Cope has shown, Matt 13:1-52 forms a complete unit which is held together by two FT texts. The parables employed in this sermon were judiciously chosen. There were three twin parables, one set of which was divided for organization purposes. The six parables included in this small narrative were all about the Kingdom of Heaven and were coherent with 12 other parables contained in the Gospel of Matthew. Of the 18 parables Matthew recorded, 17 of them were parables about the Kingdom of Heaven or of judgment. Matthew evidently used only parables that suited his editorial structure and his point of view. Luke has some parables that were not designed to teach the Kingdom of Heaven as directly as Matthew did.[76]

TEXT

[53]Now it happened when Jesus had finished these parables, he left there.

COMMENTARY

This is Matthew's editorial sentence to alert the reader that he or she has come to the end of one section and the beginning of the next. The word "finished" is regular, and the reference to his leaving that geographical spot is also

[76]Cope, Matthew, pp. 13-29.

included in the summary in Matt 11:1 and 19:1, as well as here. This is the end of the "Numbers" section, which began with Matt 11:2. That which is to begin with the next sentence is the Deuteronomy section. The following parallel passages will show the relationship of Deuteronomy to Matthew 13.

MATTHEAN PARALLELS TO DEUTERONOMY

Matthew	Deuteronomy
Jesus entered into his own father land. He taught the people, but they doubted the wisdom of his teaching.	Moses told the Israelites to enter the land promised to them.
They were scandalized because of him. He could not do mighty deeds there because of their lack of faith (13:54-58).	People doubted Moses' wisdom and sent spies. They brought back a bad report. Later they failed to enter the land, because of their lack of faith (1:19-46).

TEXT

54Now after he had come to his home town, he taught them **in their synagogue**,
so that they were **surprised and** said, "From where does this man get this wisdom and these miracles? [**55Is not** this **the son of the carpenter**? Is not his mother called Mary, and are not his brothers James, Joseph, Simon, and Judas? 56Are
not his sisters all with us? Then, from where does he get all these things?]"
57And they were offended by him. **But** Jesus **said to them, "A prophet is not
without honor** except **in his own home** town and in **his** house."

58He did not do many miracles there because of their unbelief.

TECHNICAL DETAILS

The bold faced type in the unit above are the identical words that are used in the parallel Lukan passage. In that sermon, that is given below, the same words will also be shown in bold faced type. Matt 13:54, 57 constitutes a chreia. The necessary four points of a responsive chreia are here: 1) The speaker is identified. Although the word "Jesus" is not used, the context shows that the subject is Jesus. 2) The situation that prompted the speaker to speak is given. 3) The response is quoted, and 4) the entire unit is very brief. Verses 55 and 56 are editorial expansions. The passage makes sense without them. The Markan parallel (Mark 6:1-6) includes the expansion, and there is no way from these verses alone to tell whether Matthew used Mark, Mark used Matthew, or both used an earlier source. Luke's version developed the unit into a sermonette (Luke 4:16-29). The Lukan homily used not only the chreia but also the editorial expansion.

COMMENTARY

His home town. The Greek pah-treé-dee (πατρίδι) could mean his home country, but, so far as the record shows, Jesus never left his home country. Therefore the distinguishing factor of his "father land" must be the municipal location within Palestine. Matthew did not say what this town was. The place where Jesus went, as if it were his home, was Capernaum. This, of course, may have been his monastic home as distinguished from his birth place.

The son of the carpenter. This is a Near Eastern way, of saying "carpenter." If his father had been a carpenter, it was assumed that the son would be a carpenter, and vice versa.

Over the centuries there have been many imaginary expansions of this brief narrative. Barklay, for example said,

> In those days a carpenter did not buy his wood from the saw-mill or from the wholesaler. He went out to the hill-side, chose his young tree, swung his axe, cut it down and carried it home on his shoulder. Certainly Jesus was no weak and anemic person; so he must have been bronzed and weather-beaten, in the perfection of physical manhood.[77]

The Greek word for carpenter is téhk-tohn (τέκτων). From this we get such English words as architect and technology. The word, téhk-tohn (τέκτων), had a wide possibility of usages. It could apply to a common laborer who whittled, made lumber, or did the manual labor required to construct furniture or houses. It could also refer to the general contractor who designed the houses and supervised the laborers. For example, Homer described one carpenter, Harmon, as the one who built the entire Trojan navy (Iliad 2.5, 59-64) and the carpenters who built Paris' entire palace and court yard (Iliad 6.313-16).

There is not much evidence in Jesus' teaching of his familiarity with carpentry nor of his association with the poor.[78] One parable, the story of the man who built a house on rock rather than sand (Matt 21:42), and another reference to a man who first sat down and counted the cost of constructing a tower before he began to build (Luke 15:18-30), are the only indications that Jesus knew anything about construction. These, of course, were questions the owner, architect,

---

[77]W. Barclay, The Mind of Jesus (London: SCM, c1960, 1961), p. 10. For similarly bold and unsupported claims see H. Branscomb, The Teachings of Jesus (Nashville: Cokesbury, c1931), pp. 213-14, and J. W. Bowman, Jesus' Teaching in its Environment (Richmond: John Knox, c1963), p. 27.

[78]See Buchanan, "Upper Class," p. 195-209; and Jesus: The King and his Kingdom (Macon: Mercer, c1984), pp. 171-90, for further evidence of Jesus' association with the wealthy.

or contractor would consider--not the common laborer.[79] This reference to carpentry (Matt 13:55) is found only in the expansion to the chreia, rather than in the chreia itself.

This wisdom. This does not suggest, as many commentators hold, that Jesus was unschooled and unlearned. The number of his teachings in chreias and parables show that he was very intelligent, and he was pictured as outwitting all of the lawyers the Pharisees brought against him. He was probably trained by John the Baptist in the Nazoraion sect of Judaism. His home community was probably not surprised at his intelligence and training, but at the direction of his scholarship. Instead of exhibiting his learning about construction, he was devoted to religion and politics. This was a surprise. Religion and politics are seldom safe subjects of conversation, and his particular brand disturbed the people in his home community.

His brothers . . . and . . . sisters. This is contained only in the expansion to the chreia, but there seems no reason for it to have been added if it had not been true. Jesus evidently belonged to a family, originally, and later joined a monastery, fulfilling all the demands of that vocation. His mother was evidently called Mary, and she was not a perpetual virgin.

They were offended by him. Not only did Jesus not gain new recruits from his home community, but instead he found rejection.

A prophet is not without honor. This is a litotes expression. A litotes is an expression where two negatives are used to say something positive. To say a prophet is not without honor means a prophet has honor.

TEXT AND MIDRASH

Luke's Homily	Matthew
4:16**He came to** Nazareth, where he had been brought up, and, according to his custom on the Sabbath day, he entered **into the synagogue**, and stood up to read [the scripture]. 17There was given to him the scroll of the prophet Isaiah, and, after he had opened the scroll, he found the place where it was written: 18"The Spirit of the Lord is upon me, be-	13:54**After he came to** his home town, he taught them **in their synagogue**, so that

[79]On this see further, Buchanan, "Monasticism and the Economic Classes," Jesus, pp. 171-90.

cause he anointed me to announce
good news to the poor. He has sent
me to proclaim release to the
captives, and the opening of the eyes
of the blind, to provide release to the
prisoners, [19]to proclaim the year of
the Lord's favor" (Isa 61:1-2).
[20]Then he closed the scroll,
gave it back to the attendant, and sat
down. The eyes of all those in the
synagogue were directed to him,
[21]and he began to say to them, "Today this scripture is fulfilled in your
ears." [22]Then all bore witness to him
and **were surprised** at the gracious
words which went out from his
mouth, **and they began to say,**

"Is not this the son of
Joseph?"

[23]Then **he said to them**, "You will
surely tell me this parable, 'Physi-
cian, heal yourself! The things that
we heard had happened in Capernaum, do also here in your home
town.'" [24]Then he continued, "I tell
you under oath, **'A prophet is**
not accepted
in his home town.'
[25]Truly I tell you, there were
many widows in Israel during the
days of Elijah, when the heaven was
closed for three years and six
months, and there was a great famine upon all the land, [26]but to none
of them was Elijah sent except **to**
Serepta of Sidon . . . a widow

they **were surprised**

and **said**, "From where does this
man get this wisdom and these
miracles?
[[55]**Is not this the son of**
the carpenter? Is not his mother
called Mary, and are not his brothers
James, Joseph, Simon, and Judas?
[56]Are not his sisters all with us?
Then, from where does he get all
these things?]" [57]And they were
offended by him.
But Jesus **said to them,**

"A prophet is
not without honor except
in his own home town and in **his**
house."

woman (1 Kings 17:9). [27]There
were also many lepers in Israel in
the days of Elisha, the prophet, but
none of them was healed except
Naaman, the Syrian."
[28]Then, after they had heard
these things, they all were filled with
anger, [29]and they arose and threw
him out of the city, and they led him
to the edge of the cliff upon which
the city was built in order to throw
him down, [30]but he passed through
their midst and left.

TECHNICAL DETAILS

This is a good illustration of the way texts are used and midrash is developed. Whether the author of the midrash is a lawyer pleading a case or a preacher composing a sermon, the place to start is with the text. The preacher, lawyer, or teacher started with a text that was considered valid. For the Christian or Jewish midrash, this usually meant a FT text. The fact that Luke's text was from a teaching of Jesus, encased in a chreia, meant that the teachings of Jesus were treated like the FT. Jesus was a true prophet and apostle of God, and this was a true teaching of his. The first to embellish this chreia was one who had this chreia as part of a collection of the teachings of Jesus. He added vss. 55 and 56 to clarify the situation. Luke found this expanded chreia in some collection, possibly in the Gospel of Matthew itself or the Gospel of Mark. There is only one small clue to suggest that Luke used Matthew or his source rather than Mark or his source: Both Luke and Matthew use the expression "the son of . . . " For Matthew this is, "Is not this **the son of** the carpenter?" Luke has, "Is not this **the son of** Joseph?" Mark has, "Is not this the carpenter?" Apart from this expression, Luke did not comment on any expression that is unique either to Matthew or Mark.

Luke took the text from his source and filled in many of the uncertainties. Matthew's text did not say what Jesus' home town was; Luke identified this, perhaps inaccurately, as Nazareth. Luke distinguished this from the other possibility of Capernaum, where Jesus had apparently performed miracles. From his text, Luke learned that Jesus taught in the synagogue, meaning that he taught them many times. That was his custom on the Sabbath day. Luke altered this to concentrate on one special event when Jesus gave his opening sermon. Luke further understood the text's statement, "He taught them," to mean that he first read a text from Isaiah which itself was a commentary on the Leviticus text on Jubilee release (Lev 25:10). Then, returning to his text, Luke gave the response of the congregation with some expansion. Apparently acquainted with the methods the rhetoricians taught for developing a homily from a chreia, Luke supplied Jesus with a proverb (which he called a parable) and two illustrations from the FT to support his argument, after which he gave further response on the part of the congregation, accentuating the extent of Jesus' rejection.

Luke had a text that showed Jesus was not accepted in his own home town. His homily expanded that rejection to show that the Jews rejected him, but like Elijah and Elisha, Jesus was accepted by the gentiles, like the widow of Sidon and Naaman, the Syrian. Luke's attitude reflects a conflict between Jews and gentiles toward Jesus that Matthew did not show. Matthew's point of view was pro-Jewish, whereas Luke's attitude was anti-Jewish or pro-gentile.

The homiletic nature of the Lukan passage shows that the sermon Jesus was reported to have preached in the synagogue was a Lukan addition. The chreia, already expanded by Matthew and/or Mark, was developed into a sermon by Luke. This means that the Lukan sermon is not the ippsissima verba Iesou as many have claimed. The only saying of Jesus preserved in the chreia is, "A prophet is not without honor except in his own home town and in his house" (Matt 13:57). Luke paraphrased that, as was the custom of preachers, to read, "No prophet is accepted in his home town" (Luke 4:24). This is not a primary report of a historical event. It is a text report in the form of a sermon built on a secondary text. The primary text is the chreia that holds the saying of Jesus.

The author of this midrash thought the Matthaean (or possibly Markan) unit was God's word, so he treated it as scripture. He formed his midrash on the new chreia he had at his disposal and also scripture passages from the old Hebrew scripture.[80]

---

[80]Not noticing the relationship of Luke's homily to the text on which it was based, M. Burrows, "The Origin of the Term, 'Gospel,'" JBL 44 (1925):31, was followed by E. F. Scott in saying, "[this Lukan homily] is one of the most historical incidents in the Gospel narrative."

CHAPTER FOURTEEN

MATTHEAN PARALLELS TO THE HEXATEUCH

Matthew	Deuteronomy
After the death of John, the people followed Jesus to the wilderness (14:1-14).	After the defeat by the Amorites, Moses led the Israelites to the wilderness (1:41-2:1).
People could not buy food in the wilderness. Jesus multiplied the loaves and fishes so that there was more than enough (14:15-21).	Could not buy food from Sihon, so they conquered the land and took cattle and booty (2:26-35).
Jesus performed many great deeds, stilling the storm, walking on the water, and healing diseases. Peter asked to be able to walk on water but he could not, because he lacked faith (14:22-36).	The Lord showed the people his greatness by conquering nations for them. Moses asked to see more but was not allowed because of the sin of Moses and the people earlier (3:1-29).

TEXT

14:1 At that time, Herod the tetrarch heard the report of Jesus, 2 and he said to his
servants, "This is John the Baptist. He has been raised from the dead, and because of this the miracles have taken place through him"; 3 for Herod had seized
John, bound him, and put him in prison because of Herodia, the wife of his
brother, Phillip. 4 John used to say to him, "It is not lawful for you to have her,"
5 so [Herod] wanted to kill him, but he feared the crowd, because they held him
as a prophet.

TECHNICAL DETAILS

There are three small agreements of Matthew and Luke against Mark in this passage. Matthew and Luke both call Herod **the tetrarch** (Matt 14:1; Luke 9:7), whereas Mark called him, "the king" (Mark 6:14). Matthew and Luke both also used the same term to say that Jesus was John the Baptist, **raised from the dead** (Matt 14:2; Luke 7), whereas Mark 6:14 used a different form of the verb.

Matt 14:1-2 seems to be a responsive chreia: 1) The speaker (Herod) is identified; 2) the situation which prompted Herod to speak is given (Matt 14:1); the speaker's response is given; and 4) the entire unit is very brief--only two verses in length. Matt 14:3 begins with a rhetorical interpretation. The interpretation of any chreia, of course, normally was composed by a different and later author from the one who composed the chreia.

COMMENTARY

Herod the tetrarch. This was Herod Antipas, son of Herod the Great. He ruled Galilee and Peraea after the death of Herod the Great. He was never king, as Mark held. The only Herods who were kings were Herod the Great and Herod Agrippa I.

This is John the Baptist. Herod was probably speaking typologically rather than historically. He probably did not believe that John had been raised from the dead physically. He was speaking picturesquely to relate the activities of Jesus to those of John the Baptist. It was like saying, "He is a Benedict Arnold," "She is a real Jezebel," or "This is another Francis Assisi." There is little to question the report that Jesus and John were closely allied. Reportedly John was the one who baptized Jesus; he may also have anointed him. John expected Jesus to use his skills and organization to get him released from prison. Jesus paid high tribute to John as the greatest of the prophets, as the Elijah who was to come. When asked by what authority he did the things he did Jesus responded in effect that his authority was from the same source as John's. Even the effort of the Fourth Gospel to picture John as only a "voice," claiming that he was not as important as a servant who loosens his master's sandals, is an obvious over-kill in an effort to play down the importance that John apparently provided in the early period of Christianity. It is not necessary to fight anything that does not exist.

Herod had seized John. Cope failed to recognize the literary form, chreia, on which Matt 14:3-12 commented, but he nevertheless, has correctly analyzed this entire unit, grammatically and historically, observing that Matthew had not yet reported the event of John's death, so he interrupted his narrative, told of John's death, and then continued in verse 13 to tell of Jesus' reaction to Herod's observation.[1] The intrusion began with the word "for" (gar, γάρ). Josephus described in greater detail the death of John. He said Herod placed John in prison at Machaerus before he had him killed, because John had too much influence among the people and might lead a sedition (Ant 18.116-19). When Herod became worried also about Jesus it was because of "the powers which were working in him" (Matt 14:2). These powers were evidently very much like those which John had been doing before he was killed. They were not healing miracles. They were forces that were threatening to Herod. Luke said the Pharisees warned Jesus that Herod was looking for him so that he could have him killed, as he had arranged for John to be killed (Luke 13:31-33). According to Matthew, when Jesus heard of Herod's intentions, he left the area and went into hiding (Matt 14:13).

It is not lawful. This is not something that John had said only once. The imperfect tense of the verb means that he frequently said this. It was his custom to do so. He evidently made a good deal of noise about the topic--enough to have irritated Herod.

Lev 20:21 prohibits a man from taking his brother's wife. This is impurity. Slavonic Josephus concurred that John was in conflict with Herod over the matter of Herod's having taken his brother Phillip's wife. According to this text John warned Herod that because of his action Herod would be cut off by a heavenly sickle (Wars, Loeb, Appendix 11; see also Joel 3). Slavonic Josephus, however, is a late text and may have been influenced by the Matthaean account. John apparently played the same role with Herod and Herodias that Elijah had played in his relationship with Ahab and Jezebel (1 Kings 21).

TEXT

Matthew	First Testament
[6]When the birthday celebration of Herod was taking place, Herodias' daughter danced in the midst and pleased Herod. [7]Because of this he took a vow that **he would give to her whatever she might ask.** [8]Having been prompted earlier by her mother, she said,	What is your request Queen Esther? **Whatever your request it will be given to you**, up to half the kingdom, and it shall be done (Est 7:2).

"Give me here on a platter the head of John the Baptist." [10]The king, having been disturbed, on account of the vows [he took] and those who were reclining

[1]O. L. Cope, "The Death of John the Baptist in the Gospel of Matthew; or, the Case of the Confusing Conjunction," CBQ 38 (1976):515-19.

together, commanded that it be provided, [11]and after he had sent [a messenger], he beheaded John in prison, and his head was brought on a platter and given to the girl, and she took it to her mother. [12]Then his disciples came, took the corpse, buried it, and after they left they reported to Jesus.

COMMENTARY

The birthday celebration of Herod. Royal birthday parties were celebrated by pagan kings, and the Herods followed the gentile practice. Jews objected to it. This entire story of John's death is told in Matthew in 12 verses (Matt 14:1-12). Mark told the same story in 16 verses (Mark 6:14-30). This does not prove that Matthew abbreviated Mark as Meier claimed.[2] The opposite is at least as possible, holding that Mark added some words to clarify the narrative. This is one of the things people used to do with midrash. The evidence points both ways, and the interpretation a scholar gives is usually determined by a prejudice one way or the other. There is nothing in this passage to rule out either the Griesbach hypothesis or the two-source hypothesis. The following parallels will show the problem involved.

Matthew	Mark
14:3:"Herodia, the wife of his brother."	6:17: "Herodia, the wife of **Phillip**, his brother."
14:4: "For John said to him, 'It is not lawful for you to have her.'"	6:18: "For John said to **Herod**, 'It is not lawful for you to have **the wife of your brother**.'"
14:5: "And wanting to kill him,	6:19: But Herodias held a grudge against him and she wanted to kill him, **but she was not able**, because
he was afraid of the crowd, because they held him to be a prophet."	Herod was afraid of John, knowing that he was a righteous and holy man, and he kept him secure and listened to him gladly.
14:7: He took a vow that he would give her whatever she might ask.	6:23: He swore to her, "Whatever you ask I will give you--**up to half of my kingdom.**"

Herodias's daughter danced. This seems like a fictional account patterned after the story of Esther. It does not seem reasonable for a tetrarch's wife to want her own daughter to appear as a public dancing girl at a drinking party.

---

[2]J. P. Meier, "John the Baptist in Matthew's Gospel," JBL 99 (1980):399.

The head of John the Baptist. This is a dramatic story intended to show how much Herod's wife resented John the Baptist because he criticized Herod and Herodia, and the story blames this incident for John's death, claiming that Herod was disturbed and did not really want to do it, but there are some problems with this report.

The king. Herod Antipas was really never a king. He was a tetrarch, one who ruled 1/4 of the country. The only Herods who were kings were Herod the Great and Herod Agrippa I.

He beheaded John in prison. The messenger probably did the murderous work, but the act was attributed to Herod, because he was the principal responsible for the act, whereas the messenger was only the legal agent through whom Herod acted.

His head was brought on a platter. The implication of this story is that Herod sent at once, while the birthday party was going on, and had John beheaded and his head returned, but according to Josephus, the distance involved would have made this impossible. According to Josephus' account, John was killed in Machaerus, a long journey from Tiberias, for a different reason altogether. The report was given by Josephus in relationship to a major battle Herod lost with the Arabian king, Aretas:

> Some Jews thought the destruction of Herod's army was a much deserved vengeance by God for having killed John, who was called the Baptist. Herod had him put to death [even though he was] a good man who had commanded the Jews to live virtuous lives and to practice justice toward one another and piety toward God while engaging in a baptism. Baptism appeared to him to be acceptable to God, not as a request [for pardon] of certain bodily sins, but for the consecration of the body, the soul having already been cleansed through righteousness. When others joined the multitude of those who had repented, for they had been aroused by hearing [his] words, Herod became frightened. Such ability to persuade people might lead to some type of revolution, because they thought it was right to do everything according to his counsel. It seemed much better [to Herod], before something surprising took place, to get rid of him than to regret it after the fact. John was sent by Herod, bound, to Machaerus, the previously mentioned fortress, and there killed (Ant 18.116-19)

According to Matthew, Herod's birthday party was going on in Galilee, where Herod was tetrarch, probably at Tiberias. According to Josephus, John had been put in prison at Machaerus, about 100 miles away. When the most rapid means of travel would have been horse-back or donkey-back, it would have been impossible to have made that round-trip journey on the same day, let alone the same night. Slavonic Josephus' report also tells about John's accusation of Herod, but does not tell of the birthday party or of John's death. It seems more likely that John was imprisoned and killed, because Herod thought he was a political threat, but kings in those days often killed people for almost any reason at all, so the story given in Matthew would have been accepted as reasonable, if not studied critically, although it is probably not an accurate account.

From the days of Herod the Great until after the Bar Cochba defeat Jews and Christians had to express their nationalistic feelings in code. The death of John the Baptist was a real tragedy, but any Jew or Christian who objected openly about the murder of John was a in danger. Jews and later Christians learned coded ways to lament. The only way Jews and Christians could preserve their nationalistic views in their literature was to hide them in code. The narrative of John's death was told in such a way as to allow believers to lament without arousing the suspicions of the Romans. This story gives the impression that John the Baptist was in no way related to an insurrection but instead was killed because he had criticized Herod Antipas and his wife, Herodias.

It is undoubtedly true that Herod Antipas had Herod killed, but the Matthean and Markan accounts about the way it happened is probably a fictionalized account based on the Purim festival. The Purim festival is an annual event at which Jews dramatize their hostilities toward the gentiles. At this feast Jews read the entire Book of Esther, which is a novel, supposedly taking place in Susa, the capital of Persia when Ahasuerus was king. At one banquet, the king's wife embarrassed the king before his nobles. He had her displaced and advertised for another queen. The Jewess Esther won the contest.

The king's most trusted friend was Haman who was honored by everyone except Mordecai, the Jew, who sat outside the gate but refused to honor Haman as he came by. Haman planned to have Mordecai killed, but Mordecai acted first and prompted his niece, Esther, to prevent this act, together with the persecution of other Jews in the kingdom. Queen Esther went to the king and obtained his favor. The king offered her anything she wanted--even half of his kingdom. Queen Esther asked that Haman be invited to attend a banquet she would prepare. Before the banquet was held the king learned of a time Mordecai saved the king's life, so he honored Mordecai by putting royal robes on Mordecai and his horse and having Haman lead the horse through the city announcing that Mordecai was honored by the king.

When the king asked at the banquet what Queen Esther's request was, she asked that Haman be hanged and the Jewish people be saved from persecution. With the Persian king's permission, Jews then killed all of their enemies in the kingdom, and Mordecai became the most honored person in the kingdom next to the king himself. He became the new Joseph or Daniel.

Like the story of Esther, the setting for the narrative about the death of John was at a royal banquet. The queen became involved through her daughter and was promised anything she wanted, even as much as half his kingdom, according to Mark 6:23, even though Herod was not a king and had no authority to give away any of his tetrarchy which he ruled only under the dominance of Rome. Like Esther this queen wanted the death of a prominent man. In the story of John the Baptist, Herodias played the role of Esther. She succeeded in getting the one killed she wanted, and this all took place at a banquet where Herod's wife was promised to receive any request she might make. John the Baptist was the new Mordecai who failed to honor the royalty of the kingdom. The tragedy was that Herodias was not a true antitype of the faithful Esther. Instead she was the villainess. Instead of risking her life to save John the Baptist, the new Mordecai, she was the one who had him killed. Instead of the new Haman being killed to please the new Esther, it was the new Mordecai who was killed. Instead of the Jews having the privilege of killing all of their enemies, they continued under subjection of the Romans under the agency of Herod.

This is only a deduction based on the story of John's death that does not make sense but resembles the Purim Festival and the story of Esther. Mark's addition of "up to half my kingdom" (Mark 6:23; Esther 5:6; 7:2) makes Matthew's subtle, coded allusions more obvious. In favor of this explanation is the fact that Jews through the centuries have related their feasts to local, current events. The story of John's death may once have been dramatized at a Purim festival to express the mourning Jews and early Christians felt about John's death. The tragedy was cleverly lamented at Purim, contrasting this Purim to the Purim reported in the Book of Esther, just as Ps 74 contrasted the destruction of the temple at Jerusalem with the Lord's deliverance of his people from Egypt at the sea (Exod 15).[3]

Since it was not safe for Jews and early Christians to report history that threatened Rome, this drama may have been included in the gospels as a coded account that reflected Jewish and early Christians' feelings without stirring up more hostility from the Romans. Since no one has made sense out of the Matthean and Markan account this additional solution might be considered as a possibility. Every reader may judge whether or not it makes sense.

TEXT

[13]When Jesus heard [about John's death], he went away from there in a boat to a wilderness place alone. When the crowds heard [that Jesus had left], they followed him on foot away from the villages. [14]When he came out [Jesus] saw a great crowd, and he had compassion on them and healed their afflictions.

[3]See further Buchanan, "The Fall of Jerusalem and the Reconsideration of Some Dates," RevQ 53 (1989):31-48.

Matthew	First Testament
[15]When it was evening the disciples came to him, saying,	You shall remember all **the way** which Yahowah your God has led you these forty years
"It is a **wilderness place**, and the hour has already gone. Dismiss the crowds so that they may go away into the villages and buy food for themselves." [16]Jesus said to them, "They have no need to leave.	**in the wilderness** (Deut 8:2). A man came from Baalshalishah, and he **brought** to the man of God **loaves** of the first fruit, twenty **barley loaves** and a sack of fresh
You give them [something] **to eat**." [17]They said to him, "We do not have [anything] here except five	grain. [Elisha] said, "**Give** [it] **to the people** and **let them eat**." His servant said, "How can I set this before
loaves and two fish." [18]Then he said, "**Bring** them here to me." [19]After he had commanded the crowds to recline on the grass, he took the five **loaves** and the two fish. Then he looked up to heaven, blessed **the loaves of bread**, broke [them] and **gave** [them] **to the** disciples, and the disciples [gave them] **to the crowds**.	a hundred men?" [Elisha] said, "**Give [it]** **to the people and let them eat**, for thus said Yahowah, '**Eat and have some left**.'" He set [it] before them. **They ate and there was** some **left over**, according to the word of Yahowah (2 Kings 4:42-44).
[20]**All ate and were satiated**, and	You **will eat** meat, **and** in the morning **you will be satiated** with bread, and you will know that I am Yahowah, your God (Exod 16:12).
there were 12 baskets full of **pieces [of bread]**	Moses said to them, "It is **bread** which Yahowah **has given you to eat** . . . The one who had much had
left over.[21] There were about 5,000 men eating, besides women and children.	nothing **left over**; the one who had little had no shortage (Exod 16:15-18).

TECHNICAL DETAILS

This unit occurs in the triple tradition, and the following words occur in Matthew and Luke against Mark: **He separated, the crowds followed him** (Matt 14:13; Luke 9:10-11); **He healed their afflictions** (Matt 14:14; Luke 9:11); **and,**

the crowd[s] food (Matt 14:15; Luke 9:12, 13); **but they, not . . . except** (Matt 14:16; Luke 9:13); **to the crowd[s]** (Matt 14:19; Luke 9:16); and **the pieces [of bread] left over** (Matt 14:20; Luke 9:17).

In addition there were the following passages found in Mark that Matthew and Luke do not have. **Then he said to them, "You come by yourselves to a desert place to rest a while," for there were many who were coming and going, so that they did not have free time even to eat** (Mark 6:31); **because they were like sheep that did not have a shepherd** (Mark 6:34); **200 denarius worth of bread, and give it to them to eat; but he said to them, "How many [loaves] of bread do you have? Go and see." When they found out they said** (Mark 6:37-38); **And the two fish he divided among all** (Mark 6:41), and **And of the fish** (Mark 6:43). The Markan texts that do not occur in Matthew or Luke seem like homiletical expansions. These are some of the agreements, both in omission and in addition, of Matthew and Luke against Mark that Streeter has called "minor."

This homily was placed in this position for at least two purposes:

1) In parallel with Deuteronomy 2:26-35 it was needed to provide an antitypal situation. When the children of Israel needed food in the wilderness and could not buy any, they conquered the land and took cattle and booty. Their need was met. In a similar situation, a new crowd of Israelites needed food, and the food was provided.

2) This homily was based primarily on the Elisha provision, supplementing it with words like "satiated," "bread," "left over," and "eat" from the story of the manna. When there was a small amount of loaves and grain and a large number of people to feed, Elisha, the man of God, ordered his servant to set it before them and assured them that there would be enough and some left over. He was confident of this because he had it on the authority of the word of Yahowah. In the new provision, Jesus, the man of God, also made a similar order, and there was enough and some left over. These two scriptural proofs were enough to satisfy Matthew. He found one text from the Torah and one from the prophets. Since it takes two witnesses in court to prove a case, Matthew considered this case proved. From a legal point of view "it happened." Sceptical Christians may still wonder if it really happened.[4]

COMMENTARY

He went away from there. This is the fifth withdrawal scene Good noticed, but it has only two parts: 1) The threatening situation was the death of John, and 2)

[4]For a closer parallel to the same narrative in the Fourth Gospel see Buchanan, "The Samaritan Origin of the Gospel of John," Religions in Antiquity, ed. J. Neusner (Leiden: E. J. Brill, 1968), pp. 169-70.

the withdrawal was of Jesus leaving whatever place he then was.[5] As Cope has shown, this is a continuation of the story that ends in Matt 14:2: "He [John] has been raised from the dead, and because of this, the miracles have taken place through him."

Matthew did not tell from what place Jesus left nor to what place he went. Jesus reportedly crossed the lake and went into some wilderness area. Since he left after he heard that Herod beheaded John, it suggests that he had been in Galilee, Herod Antipas' tetrarchy, and crossed the Sea of Galilee to be in Herod Phillip's tetrarchy, assuming that if John was a threat to Herod Antipas that Jesus would be too. This adds to the possibility that Herod killed John for some reason other than his criticism of his personal behavior, since it is not likely that Jesus was also involved in that event. In the Johannine account, however, Jesus multiplied the loaves in the area of Tiberias (John 6:23).

According to Matthew Jesus and John were very close, and John's death was a real blow to Jesus. It gave him cause for mourning and and also fear for the safety of his own life. Allison has astutely shown how closely Matthew has paralleled the lives of Jesus and John:[6]

John	Jesus
Herod the tetrarch was responsible for John's death	Pilate the governor was responsible for Jesus' death
John was seized (κρατέω, 14.3)	Jesus was seized (κρατέω, 21.46, etc.)
John was bound (δέω, 14.3)	Jesus was bound (δέω, 27.2)
Herod feared the crowds because they held John to be a prophet (14.5)	The chief priests and Pharisees feared the crowds because they held Jesus to be a prophet (21.46)
Herod was asked by another to execute John and grieved so to do (14.6-11).	Pilate was asked by others to execute Jesus and was reluctant so to do (27.11-26)
John was buried by his disciples (14.12).	Jesus was buried by a disciple (27.57-61).

The crowds followed him on foot. The role of the crowds in this pericope is that of following Jesus--not just academically, but also on foot--and Jesus' attitude to them was one of compassion. If he crossed from the area of Tiberias, the crowds that followed him probably walked around the north end of the Sea. The Greek word translated "villages" is normally rendered "cities," but there are no cities

---

[5]The first scene was Matt 2:12-15.

[6]W. D. Davies and D. C. Allison, Jr., A Critical and Exegetical Commentary on the Gospel according to Saint Matthew (Edinburgh: T. & T. Clark, c1991) II, p. 476.

in that region, so the author must have intended the small towns and villages by the designation.

This is a desert place. The importance of being in a desert place is that Moses also led the crowd of Hebrews into the wilderness after they had fled from Egypt. Moses also had the problem of providing food for such a large crowd at that.

You give them [something] to eat. This narrative was placed in the Gospel by the editor in this particular place to make it an antitype of Moses' experience in providing food for the Israelites in the wilderness.

No one knows how this multiplication of loaves was to be understood. Earlier scholars have suggested that the people really had enough food in their bags with them, but they did not want to share it. When Jesus began the sharing process, the miracle that took place is that the crowds began to share theirs, so that no one went hungry. Others have imagined that Jesus was near a cave where he had a huge storage of food from which the disciples brought out supplies.[7] The most likely explanation is discovered when the homily is noticed. The author of this homily composed his small sermon primarily on the Elisha text, but also using the narrative of the manna, following the legal and rhetorical rules of the day. This was a prophetic passage; all prophecy was believed to be fulfilled in the days of the Messiah; these were days of the Messiah; everything that was in the world was in the scripture; this was in the scripture; therefore Jesus, the new man of God, must have performed something like this. All the homiletician had to do was fill in the details.[8]

He . . . blessed the loaves. The appropriate blessing here is probably the same one used at the Last Supper, which is also an ancient blessing over bread at almost every Jewish meal (mBer 6.1): "Blessed are you, Lord our God, king of the age [to come], who brings forth bread from the [promised] land" (bah-roókh ah-táh a-doh-nái el-oh-háy-noo, meh-lehk hah-oh-láhm, hah-móht-see lékh-ehm min hah-áhr-etz, ברוך אתה יי אלוהינו מלך העולם המוציא לחם מן הארץ).

There were 12 baskets full of pieces [of bread] left over. In addition to being the antitype of the miracle of Moses providing food for the Hebrews in the wilderness, this story is also an antitype of Elisha. One of the Jewish eschatologists said

[7]This theory was first suggested by K. F. Bahrdt, Briefe über die Bibel in Volkston von einem Prediger auf dem Lande (Halle: J. Fr. Dost, 1782). It was later summarized by A. Schweitzer, The Quest of the Historical Jesus tr. W. Montgomery (New York: MacMillan, c1966), p. 39. Bahrdt said, "It is more reasonable here to think of a thousand ways by which Jesus might have had sufficient supplies of bread at hand, and by the distribution of it have shamed the disciples lack of courage, than to believe in a miracle" (p. 41).

[8]Allison, Matthew, p. 485, also thought the Matthean narrative was much influenced by 2 Kings 4:42-44.

that in the days of the Messiah the treasure of manna would descend from on high and provide the people manna to eat (2 Bar 29.1-8).

According to the word of the Lord. Where did Elisha get his text to know that this was the word of Yahowah? Probably from the story of the provision of manna in the wilderness (Exod 16:12-18). If so, either Elisha had a variant text or else he distorted the text a little, ignoring the negative before "left over." Like modern lawyers, some ancient legalists sometimes argued a case on the basis of part of a sentence, omitting the words that change the meaning. Elisha found the following words in the Exodus text: "bread," "eat," "be satisfied," and "be left over." This was all from the word of Yahowah. He took this as a promise that the people could "eat and have some left over." The Matthean midrash is evidently a midrash on a midrash. Matthew had more than one precedent for his homily. He used texts from both Exodus and Second Kings. The Second Kings passage had earlier used the Exodus text.

TEXT

Matthew	First Testament
22 Then [Jesus] brought the disciples to get into the boat and proceed to the other side [while he remained] until he dismissed the crowds. 23 After he had dismissed the crowds he went up into the mountain **alone** to pray. When it was evening he was there **alone**,	Who **alone** spread out the heaven (Job 9:8a).
24 and the boat [with the disciples] was already many stadia away from the land, being battered by the waves, for [the boat] was facing the wind. 25 **At the** fourth **watch** of the night, [Jesus] **came** to them,	The Egyptians **came** after them . . . in the midst of the sea. It happened **at the** morning **watch** (Exod 14:23-24).
walking on the sea. 26 When the	He **walks on** the waves of **the sea** (Job 9:8b).
disciples saw him **walking on the sea**, they said, "It is a ghost!" and	The Israelites **walked on** dry land in the midst of **the sea**, and the **water** was for them a wall on their right and on their left (Exod 14:29).
	The Israelites **were very much**

they cried out from fear. 27At once	**afraid**, and **they cried out** to the Lord (Exod 14:10).
Jesus **spoke to** them **saying,** "Courage! I am. **Do not be afraid.**" 28In reply, Peter said to him, "Lord, if you are [the one speaking], command me **to come** to you **on the water.**" 29He said, "Come," and after he had come down from the boat, Peter **walked on** **the water** and came to Jesus, 30	Moses **said to** the people, **"Do not be afraid"** (Exod 14:13). The Israelites **walked on** dry land in the midst of the sea, and **the water** was for them a wall on their right and on their left (Exod 14:29).
but seeing the **wind**	The Lord made the sea **walk** with a strong east **wind** (Exod 14:21).
he **was afraid, and** as he began to sink, **he cried out,**	Israelites **were very much afraid, and they cried out** to the Lord (Exod 14:10).
"**Lord, save** me." 31At	The **Lord saved** Israel on that day (Exod 14:29-30).
once Jesus **extended his hand** and took hold of him. Then he **said to** him, "Man of little faith! Why did you doubt?" 32As they went up into the boat, the wind stopped. 33Those in the boat worshiped him, saying, "Truly you are the Son of God."	Moses **extended his hand** over the sea, and the Lord drove the sea back with a strong east wind (Exod 14:21). Moses **extended his hand** over the sea, and the sea returned (Exod 14:27). Send out **your hand** from on high. Rescue me and **deliver me** from much water (Ps 144:7).

TECHNICAL DETAILS

Studying the difference between this Matthean text and its Markan parallel, Carlisle noticed that the Markan version was expanded, although he presumed at the outset that Matthew was secondary and therefore had made the omissions. The midrashic nature of this unit in Matthew is so obvious that it is unlikely that

Matthew would have formed it by copying Mark and editing out a few expressions. Matthew's midrash is ten verses long, and it is all developed from Exodus 14. Four verses of this midrash (Matt 14:24-28) are parallel with Mark, and the Markan verses also have the same parallels that Matthew has for those four verses. To presume that Matthew used Mark it would be necessary for one to imagine that Matthew copied four verses from Mark, then suddenly recognized that this was a midrash on Exod 14, supported by Job 9:8, which was also a midrash on Exod 14. He then would have turned to those passages, and composed a continuation of Mark's midrash, producing a coherent unified midrash. It is far more reasonable to think that Matthew composed his entire midrash as one composition and that Mark copied four verses of this narrative, omitting the rest of the homily. The only other reasonable solution is to presume that both gospels had access to some unknown source which Matthew copied entirely, and Mark used only the first part. Even if that were true, it is clear that the Matthean text as it now exists is a primary text, and the Markan parallel is secondary. This is further confirmed by the unity of the Matthean midrash. This is evident from the chiasm that holds two parts of the midrash together:[9]

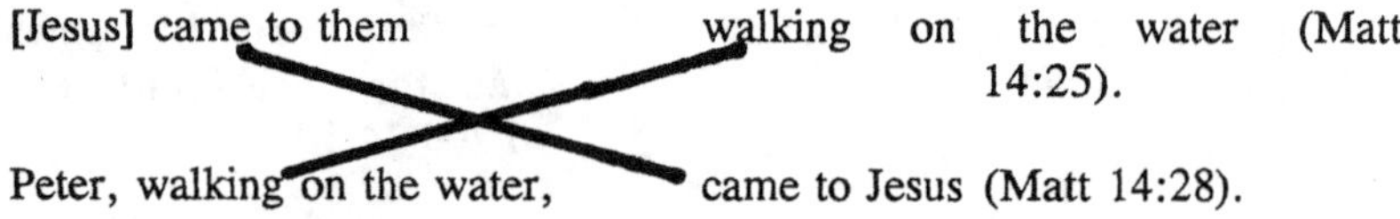

Carlisle further noticed, correctly, that Matthew presented Jesus with a much closer attachment to his disciples than Mark had, and Matthew had a greater interest in the church than Mark.[10] This suggests that Matthew was earlier and closer to Palestine than Mark. According to Mark Jesus' attitudes toward the 12 was always negative. A possible reason for this is that Mark was written later than Matthew, after the fall of Jerusalem, somewhere in Pauline territory where he picked up Paul's negative attitude toward Jesus' disciples. It is not likely that Jesus had actually been as hostile toward those apostles who had left all their wealth, businesses, and social positions to follow him as Mark depicts.

From the words in bold faced type both in Matthew and in Exodus 14 and Job 9:8, it is clear that this narrative was intentionally constructed as a midrash on Exodus 14 and Job 9:8. Jesus was pictured as an antitype of Moses. Like Moses, he confronted people who were his followers who were crying out in fear of being killed. He calmed them by showing the control he had over the forces of nature. Like Moses, he extended his hand to save. Like Moses he told the people not to be afraid but only to trust. Jesus both walked on the water and enabled

---

[9]Allison, Matthew II, p. 508.

[10]C. R. Carlisle, "Jesus' Walking on the Water: A Note on Matthew 14:22-23," NTS 31 (1985):151-55.

Peter to walk on the water as well. Moses not only walked through the sea but he led the Israelites to walk through the water on dry land. Both Jesus and Moses saved the people involved even though they lacked faith.

Since this is a midrash about Jesus, it was not composed by Jesus. The question arises, "How did the author get the data he needed to compose the narrative?" The answer is, "From the scripture and some understood doctrines of logic." The scripture was Exod 14 and possibly Job 9:8. The rules of logic involved are: 1) There is nothing that is in the world that is not in the scripture. 2) There is no before and after in scripture, and 3) all prophecy is prophesied only for the days of the Messiah.

Once a person was convinced that Jesus was the Messiah, the new Moses, he or she had only to look in the scripture to find the unknown history of Jesus. Since Jesus was the new Moses, and these were the days of the Messiah, he must have done all the things Moses did. Since Moses performed a saving miracle with the water, Jesus must have done that, too. It was only a matter of deducing from the scripture the historical event that must have happened. Once such an event can be deduced, there is no question about its veracity. It has been attested by scripture. According to rabbinic logic this narrative has been legally "proved," but that does not mean it happened.

Many things can be legally true or philosophically proved that are false. It is unfair, however, to blame a legalist for proving a case by accepted rules of logic and rhetoric. Twentieth century logicians might question the validity of the rules and become convinced that this reported event did not happen, but that does not mean the author was a malicious fiction writer or fraud. The author was following contemporary homiletical doctrines. The teachings of Jesus are to be found in the chreias and parables of Jesus. Homiletical compositions are additions of the later church.

There are only three occurrences of the expression "Son of God" in the NT that have the dependent genitive before the governing noun (the-óo whee-ós, *θεοῦ υἱός*). These are Matt 14:33; 27:43; and 27:54. Mowery concluded correctly that this phenomenon can be explained either of two ways: 1) emphasis or 2) Matthew's use of a source. All other usages of the expression are written whee-ós too the-óo (*υἱός τοῦ θεοῦ*).[11]

COMMENTARY

Went up into the mountain to pray. This does not tell where Jesus was, geographically. On three sides of the Sea of Galilee there are hills or mountains. At the northeast corner is old Mount Hermon (modern Golan Heights).

[11]R. L. Mowery, "Subtle Differences: The Matthean 'Son of God' References," NovT 32 (1990):193-200.

Battered by the waves. Literally this means that the boat was being tortured by the waves.

At the fourth watch of the night. Between 3:00 and 6:00 o'clock in the morning. This was the Matthean parallel to the Exodus "morning watch" (Exod 14:24). Since the event reported about Moses took place on the morning watch, the narrative composed about Jesus must also have occurred on the morning watch.

Courage! I am. Do not be afraid. Since Moses told the Israelites not to be afraid (Exod 14:13), Jesus must have told the disciples not to be afraid. This all comes from the scripture. Several times in the gospels, Jesus is reported as having said, **I am**. This is not "I am the Messiah," "I am here," "I am he," but just **I am**. This is probably an allusion to Exod 3:14, **I am what I am**, or **I will be what I will be** (eh-heyéh asháyr eh-heyéh, אהיה אשר אהיה). The LXX translation for that is eh-góh ay-mee hah óhn (ἐγώ εἰμι ὁ ὢν), **I am the existent One**. This may have been a way of claiming legal identity with Yahowah. The Messiah was understood to have been Yahowah's legal agent, and as such was legally God. The admonition not to be afraid frequently occurs in the Bible. This was the message of the angels to Daniel, Mary, the shepherds, as well as the message of Jesus to the disciples.

To come to you on the water. Matthew used the word "water" here instead of "sea" to avoid repetition. In the Moses story, it was not only Moses, but all the Israelites who were able to walk on dry land in the midst of the water, with water walled up on the right and the left (Exod 14:29). Since all prophecy was prophesied only for the days of the Messiah, the Messiah must not only have walked on the water himself, but also have enabled other Jews to walk through the water safely. All the homiletician had to do was think of a way this could take place in the area of the Sea of Galilee rather than the sea at the eastern border of Egypt.

Jesus had said, **I am**. Peter said, "If you are." Jesus had not said simply, "I am Jesus." He said, **I am**, which identified him legally with God who spoke to Moses in the bush. Peter knew he was Jesus, but he was testing Jesus' divine authority. He was asking Jesus to prove it. As God's legal agent Jesus seemed able to control the forces of nature, the way Moses, Joshua, Elijah, and Elisha had done, but Jesus had appointed Peter as his apostle or legal agent. If Jesus really had the authority to transfer his ability to his apostles then they would know both that he was God's legal agent and that they had the same authority as he had, just as was affirmed in Matt 10 when Jesus commissioned them.

The wind stopped. This further affirmed Jesus' divine authority. He not only controlled the waters of nature, but he controlled the wind. This was proof enough to the disciples. They finally gave the answer to the question, "Who or what is he?" He said, **I am**, and the apostles responded, "You are the Son of God," which is another way of saying he was the Messiah or the king of Israel. The title "Son of God" is one frequently applied to kings. Pharaoh was called the son of Re, and Alexander the Great was called the son of Zeus. This was another way of saying they were the legal agents of the deity on earth.

Jesus extended his hand Moses extended his hand over the sea, and in this way he saved the Israelites (Exod 14:21, 27). The homiletician reasoned that the Messiah, too, must have performed a saving act by extending his hand, so he simply filled in the details.

Truly you are the Son of God. Only God can control the sea, the wind, and the storms. Only his legal agents have the authority to instigate action to overpower the forces of nature. It was Moses who extended his hand to make the sea open up and later close; it was Jesus who could walk on the water and enable Peter also to walk on the water. This power proved to his disciples that he was the Messiah, the Son of God.

TEXT

34After they had crossed over they came to the land of Gennesaret. 35When the men of that place recognized him, they sent into that whole surrounding region, and they brought to him all those having illnesses, 36and they begged him that they might only touch the hem of his robe, and whoever touched [it] were healed.

COMMENTARY

The land of Gennesaret. This territory was on the west side of the Sea of Galilee. Therefore, if anyone follows the crossings of the sea, it seems that Jesus started the movement of chapter 14 on the west side of the sea. When Jesus heard of John's death he crossed the sea to arrive on the eastern shore, in the territory of Herod Phillip. It was from there that he multiplied the loaves.

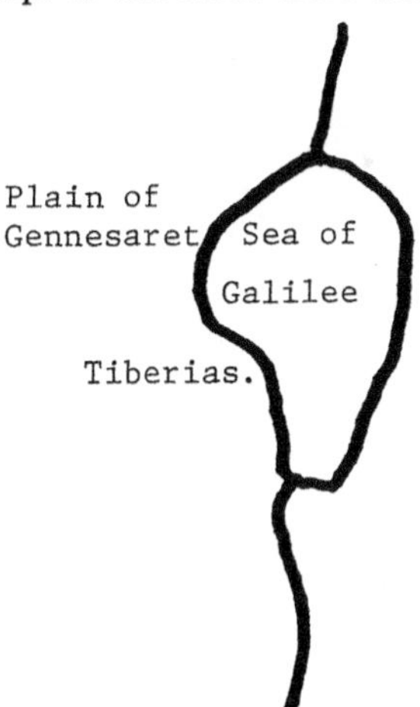

Then after he and his disciples crossed the sea again, they came to Gennesaret, which was on the west side, the place from which he started. He had returned to the territory of Herod Antipas, his most threatening opposition.

This has very little historical value, because Matthew organized this material to suit his literary structure. He structured the antitypes of the exodus across the sea at the border of Egypt, the provision of manna in the wilderness, and the revelation at the burning bush in the area around the Sea of Galilee where there was both sea and wilderness.

The hem of his robe. Ancients believed that there was magic in the touch. If they could not touch a person, if they could just touch his clothing, or even a scarf, or some handkerchief that he had touched, they might be healed. If that was not possible they planned to have his shadow fall on some sick person to be healed. Matthew reported another instance whereby a woman touched the hem of his garment and was healed from her hemorrhage (Matt 9:20-22). Hutter found two cases in Akkadian literature where someone seized the hem of a king's robe as a way of asking for mercy. Hutter compared this to Saul when he took the hem of Samuel's robe (1 Sam 15:17-28) and the woman who touched the hem of Jesus' robe.[12]

[12]M. Hutter, "Ein altorientalischer Bittgestus in Mt 9 20-22, " ZNW 75 (1984):133-35.

CHAPTER FIFTEEN

MATTHEAN PARALLELS TO THE HEXATEUCH

Matthew	First Testament
Conflict with Pharisees over the commandments. Pharisees had broken them and would be uprooted (15:1-14).	Commandments and admonitions to keep them. Rewards and punishments for keeping and breaking commandments. Moses foresaw that the Israelites would break commandments and be scattered (Deut 4:44-6:25).
Jesus healed demon possessed, dumb, blind, maimed, and lame people so that the multitudes glorified the God of Israel (15:21-31).	Those who keep commandments will become prosperous and all sickness will be healed by the Lord (Deut 7:12-16).
Jesus fed the hungry multitude multiplying the loaves and fish (15:31-39).	Lord let Israelites be hungry and fed them manna that they might know that people do not live by bread alone (Deut 8:1-10).

TEXT

Matthew	Mark
15:1Then **Pharisees and scribes from Jerusalem** came **to** Jesus, saying	7:1The **Pharisees and** some of the **scribes**, having come **from Jerusalem**, gathered **to** him. 2When they saw some of his disciples that with common hands, that is unwashed, they ate bread--3for the

2"**Why do your disciples** transgress **the traditions of the elders**, for they do not wash their **hands** when **they eat bread?**" 3In reply, **he said to them,**

"Why do **you** transgress **the commandment of God** on account of **your tradition?**"

Pharisees and all the Jews if they do not wash their hands they do not eat, holding to the tradition of the elders, 4and many other things there are which they received by tradition to observe, immersions of cups, pots, and pans--5and the Pharisees and the scribes asked him, "**Why do your disciples** not walk according to **the traditions of the elders**, but with common **hands they eat bread?**" 6**He said to them**, "Well has Isaiah prophesied concerning you hypocrites, as it is written, 'This people honors me with their lips, but their heart is far removed from me. 7In vain they worship me, teaching doctrines that are human commandments' (LXX Isa 29:1). 8Having abandoned the commandment of God, you keep the human traditions 9Then he said to them, "**You** have annulled well **the commandment of God** in order that you might keep **your traditions.**"

TECHNICAL DETAILS

Matthew has here a responsive chreia: 1) The speaker is identified; 2) the situation is given which prompted him to speak; 3) the speaker's answer is given; and 4) the entire unit is succinct. Neither Bultmann nor Dibelius discussed the literary structure of this unit. Dausch, Lohmeyer, M'Neile, and Meyer[1] all studied these three verses as if they were an integral part of the entire discussion, Matt 15:1-20, not noticing this chreia on which the rest of the discussion is based. The chreia is the text for the commentary, Matt 15:4-20, and the text was composed before the commentary. It also has its own meaning apart from the commentary that was added later. There was probably an extensive discussion between the

[1]P. Dausch, Die Drei älteren Evangelien (Bonn: T. Hansstein, 1952), pp. 228-31; E. Lohmeyer, Das Evangelium des Matthäus (Göttingen: Vandenhoeck & Ruprecht, 1926), pp. 243-51; A. H. M'Neile, The Gospel according to Matthew (London: MacMillan, 1915), pp. 221-29; H. A. W. Meyer, Critical and Exegetical Hand-Book to the Gospel of Matthew, tr. P. Christie (New York: Funk & Wagnalls 1884), p. 279.

Pharisees and Jesus on the topic of transgressing traditions. Jesus evidently did not justify his actions according to any law or custom. He simply replied ad hominem, "You transgress even the sacred scriptures!" This has all been capsuled into a chreia.[2] It would have been Jesus' disciples who composed the chreia on the basis of the event and the response of Jesus. Chreias are the units that can be judged most reasonably to contain the sayings of Jesus.

TEXT

Matthew	First Testament and other Jewish Literature
15:1 Then Pharisees and scribes from Jerusalem came to Jesus, saying	They [Aaron and his sons] shall **wash their hands** and their feet lest they die (Exod 30:21).
2 "Why do your disciples transgress the traditions of the elders, for they do not **wash their hands** when they eat bread?" 3 In reply, he said to them,	All the elders of the city nearest to the slain man shall **wash their hands** over the heifer whose neck was broken in the valley (Deut 21:6).
	Then the Spirit of god clothed Zechariah, son of Jehoida, the priest, and he stood over the people and said, "Thus said God,
"**Why do you transgress the commandment of God** on account of your tradition?"	'**Why have you transgressed the commandment of Yahowah**? You have not prospered, because you have abandoned Yahowah, and he

[2] K. J. Thomas, "Torah Citations in the Synoptics," NTS 24 (1977):90, held that the question between Jesus and the Pharisees was resolved in Jesus' favor by the end of the first century. His basis for this was Rabbi Eliezer's judgment, "The scholars concurred with Rabbi Eliezer that in a matter between a son and his father and mother they might open (break a vow) for him for the honor of his father and mother" (mNed 9.1). It is true that Rabbi Eliezer made this judgment, but there is little basis for assuming that he was a Pharisee or that the Pharisees accepted his judgment. There are only five places in the entire Mishnah and Tosephta where the Pharisees are mentioned (tBer 3.25; mSab 1.15; mHag 3.25; mSot 15.11; mYad 2.20; mSot 3.4; mYad 4.6-8). The famous rabbi Johanan ben Zakkai referred to the Pharisees as if he were not a Pharisee himself. Furthermore there are many anti-Pharisaic statements in the Talmud, a condition one would not expect of literature composed entirely by Pharisees. See further A. Guttmann, "Pharisaism in Transition," Essays in Honor of Solomon B. Freehof (Pittsburg: Rodef Shalom, 1964), pp. 202-19; and Buchanan, The Consequences of the Covenant (Leiden: E. J. Brill, c1970), pp. 259-67.

has abandoned you'" (2 Chron 24:20).

I know that you will become thoroughly disobedient; you will become thoroughly irreligious, **not observing the commandments of God**, but the commandments of human beings (TAsher 7.5).

COMMENTARY

Then Pharisees and scribes. Here was a delegation sent from the nation's capital city to investigate Jesus' activities. The text does not say whether they came of their own volition or whether they were sent in some official capacity. The Pharisees were members of a popular Jewish sect; the scribes were lawyers.

Mark's edition of this is a paraphrase. He said "the" Pharisees and "some of the" scribes "having come" from Jerusalem "gathered to him." Mark then took a few verses to explain to his reading public that which Matthew's readers already knew--the traditions of the elders. After that explanation, Mark's readers were also prepared to understand the second point of the chreia.

The traditions of the elders? The traditions of the elders were legal precedents, the contemporary rules by which the interpretation of the scripture was governed. These rules were accepted by the local courts. The offense is plain. The disciples did not wash their hands before they ate. This was not an offense against good sanitation and hygiene. It was a ritualistic taboo. It was a standard liturgy which was known by all Palestinian Jews. Because of this Matthew had no need to explain what it was. Mark's later or foreign audience, however, needed an explanation, so Mark developed a small commentary on this chreia (Mark 7:1-9).

Transgress the commandment of God. Matthew did not report in this unit what it was that the Pharisees did to transgress the scriptures. This chreia seemed to the people who composed it clear enough to remember the details of the incident. The best clue, then, is from the punch line for the chreia which is also a quote from scripture (2 Chron 24:20)--an astute way to conclude an argument. Those who understood the message of the chreia recognized the quotation from the scripture. The context of that quotation followed the death of the priest Jehoida. At that time the leaders of the nation abandoned the temple and the God of their fathers and worshiped asherim and idols. Then the nation failed to prosper, so the prophet Zechariah told them the reason for their problems. They had transgressed the commandment of God. In this chreia Jesus probably intended to picture the

Pharisees, who had come from Jerusalem, as the current equivalent of the leaders in Jerusalem during the time of Zechariah who had abandoned the religion of their fathers. The tradition of the elders that the Pharisees accused Jesus of having transgressed was the current antitype of the practices of the leaders of Jerusalem after the death of Jehoida.

Respect for quotations is shown in the fact that the Matthean editor did not change the chreia but instead interpreted it by making an addition. This is what rhetoricians would have done. The later church also expanded the chreia for use in Mark's gospel so that a different group of readers could understand it. It would not make sense to assume that Matthew used Mark's nine-verse sermonette and abbreviated it in such a way that it emerged with a perfect chreia. Rabbis said that the words of the scribes are more demanding (choh-mayr . . . may, . חמר מ . .) than the words of the Torah (mSan 11.3). The scholars said that "they do not judge the words of the Torah from the words of the scribes nor the words of the scribes from the words of the Torah" (mYad 3.2). This chreia, like the Sermon on the Mount, shows that Jesus had not abandoned the Torah. He claimed its authority.

TEXT

Matthew	First Testament
[4]For God said, **Honor your father and your mother**	**Honor your father and your mother**, just as Yahowah your God has commanded you, so that your days may be extended and so that he may prosper you on the land which Yahowah your God gives to you (Deut 5:16; cf. Exod 20:12).
and he **who curses his father** or **his mother** let him **be put to death**.	Every man **who curses his father** and **his mother** shall **be put to death**; he has cursed his father and his mother. His blood be upon him (Lev 20:9; cf. Exod 21:17).

COMMENTARY

For God said. This is the beginning of the church's interpretation of the chreia. Mark has "Moses said" (Mark 7:10; cf. also Matt 22:31//Mark 12:32//Luke 20:37). These both have the same meaning. Since Moses was considered God's legal agent, that which Moses said God said. It is regularly Matthew who calls the scripture that which God said. This means it is found in the FT, but the chreia did not say what God said or where it was found in the scriptures. In some way the Pharisees broke the commandments found in the scripture, even though they upheld their own tradition. Matthew provided the texts he presumed the chreia omitted. In a true Matthaean fashion, two texts are supplied to prove that God said this. Matthew regularly supplied two, because it requires two witnesses in court to prove a case.[3] These are both texts dealing with the responsibilities of children to parents. The tradition Matthew thought the Pharisees broke was in taking an oath not to provide for their parents. He considered this to be cursing. Rabbis also used Lev 10:9 to interpret the commandment to honor parents (Exod 20:12; Mek Bahod 8.1-5).

Honor your father and your mother. This means providing for them in their old age. Children who do this for their parents enable their parents to live long. They also set the precedent for their children to treat them the same way, so that they may live long on the land. Rabbis said honoring one's parents provided them with food and drink and clean garments (Mek Bahod 8.1-3).

TEXT

Matthew	First Testament
[5]But you say, "Whoever **says to his father or mother**, '[By the] gift [on the altar], [may all these unmentioned curses come upon me], if you benefit from me,' [6]he will not **honor** his **father or** his **mother**. So you overrule the word of God on account of your tradition."	The one who robs **his father and his mother and says**, "It is no transgression," is a colleague of a destroyer (Prov 28:24). **Honor** your **father and** your **mother** that your days may be extended on the land which Yahowah your God gives you (Exod 20:12).

COMMENTARY

Curses his father or his mother. Although this offense required the death penalty, rabbis held that a person was not guilty of this offense unless he cursed them using the Tetragrammaton. If he used some substitute name while taking an oath against them he was not guilty (mSan 7.8). Curses were normal parts of oaths.

[3]For example: Parading Virtue (6:2-5); Praying and Fasting (6:16-18); Birds and Flowers (6:26-29); Dogs and Hogs (7:6); Bread and Fish (7:9-11); Volunteers (2 chreias: 8:19-22); Mingling and Fasting (9:10-15); Patches and Wineskins (9:16-17); Jesus and John (10:16-18). There are double proof texts in the following verses: 15:4; 19:5; 19:18-19; 21:13; 21:42; 22:37-39; 27:9-10. The following verses are "second endings" to chreias: 9:13; 12:50; 18:4.

Oaths usually had these parts:

1) a sacred being or object by whom or what the oath was taken (here the gift on the altar);

2) a list of curses the oath-taker was willing to accept (here understood but omitted);

3) if he did not do as he said or if that which he said was not true (here if he provided for his parents in their old age). Many times the oaths were minced, omitting the curses, but allowing them to be understood as was done here.

Will not honor his father or his mother.[4] When oaths like this were made, the Pharisees upheld the oath, and the parents were neglected. The commandment to honor your father and your mother meant you should provide them food, shelter, and clean garments in their old age (Mek Bahod 8.1-4). Monks broke this commandment when they vowed that they would give all that they had to the monastic order. This meant that they would take oaths not to honor their father and their mother by providing for them in their old age. This was a responsibility most Jews took very seriously, and monks had to justify breaking it on the basis of Torah expediency. It was better to break one law so that the kingdom could come when all laws could be kept than to continue in bondage unable to keep the law.

When the prospective follower of Jesus asked permission first to bury his father he meant that he would follow Jesus as soon as he had fulfilled the commandment to care for one's parents until they had died and were honorably buried (Matt 8:22). Ben Sirach said one who honored his mother was laying up treasures [in heaven]. The one who honored his father would have the joy of his children and would obtain the attention of God when he prayed. He should help his father in his old age and never irritate him as long as the father lived. Such honor would cancel iniquities (Sir 3:1-16). It would also set an example to his children, so that they would take care of him in the same way when he became old. The one who abandoned his family to join a monastery, however, depended on the other monks to take care of him in his old age.

Matthew had been nurtured in the belief that caring for one's parents was a major religious duty, so he failed to appreciate the monastic vows Pharisees upheld. Matthew thought those who became monks were breaking the two commandments he listed. This seems very unlikely to have been the original meaning Jesus intended in the commandment the Pharisees broke, because Jesus also required his followers to take monastic vows that let the dead bury their own dead. Matthew represented the later church; he used the text in the way that was useful to his day and supportive of his own legalism. Even though Matthew was a legalist, which Jesus was not, and even though he interpreted the chreia to suit his own needs, he also preserved unchanged chreias that were exactly contradictory

[4] See Buchanan, "Some Oath and Vow Formulas in the New Testament," HTR 58 (1965):319-26.

to the message he defended. This is consistent with normal scribal integrity. Matthew treated the chreia constructed around a saying of Jesus in precisely the same way the English jurist, Maine, said was typical of ancients in dealing with law. They were very careful to uphold the ancient law, but they interpreted it in such a way as to change or even nullify it. Then they observed the new interpretation and ignored the original law which remained on the books. In fact the law was changed, but in fiction it remained the same.[5]

TEXT

7Hypocrites! Well did Isaiah prophesy about you, saying,

Matthew	First Testament
8"**This people**	The Lord said, "Therefore **this people** draws near with its mouth and
honors me with its lips, **but their mind is far from me.** 9In vain they **worship me**, teaching teachings [that are] the **commandments of human beings."**	**with its lips** [people] **honor me,** **but its mind is far from me.** Uselessly you **fear me.** [Its] doctrine will be **commandments of human beings** (Isa 29:13).
10Then, calling to the crowd, he said to them,	
	Go, say to this people,
"**Hear** and **understand:**	"**Hear and hear,** but do not **understand**" (Isa 6:9).

11That which	enters the mouth	does not make the person common, but
that which	comes out of the mouth--	this makes the person common."

TECHNICAL DETAILS

Verses 10 and 11 constitute a chreia, and the punch line is a poetic couplet. This is the basis for an interpretation that follows in Matt 15:15-18.

5H. S. Maine, Ancient Law (U. S. A.: Dorset Press, c1986), pp. 22, 26-28.

COMMENTARY

Honors me with its lips. This is still addressed to the Pharisees whom Jesus had already accused of breaking God's commandment, according to Matthew. Then he was pictured as applying a text from Isaiah to show their superficiality.

Commandments of human beings. All commandments have been instituted by human beings, but not all have the same authority. Part of the dogma of Judaism and Christianity was that Moses was an apostle or legal agent of God. Therefore the commandments of the Torah which have been ascribed to him are considered the word of God, because Moses wrote them under the Lord's authority. This is also true of writings attributed to David or Solomon. Since they were both kings they were also recognized as legal agents of the Lord. Jesus was an apostle of the Lord for the same reason. Words written either by Jesus or his apostles were also considered words of the Lord, who acted as principal in the composition. Prophets whose prophecies were later proved correct were also accepted as the Lord's apostles, and their words were the word of the Lord, legally. Commandments of human beings were those commandments that were made by someone who did not have God's authority for their action.

Hear and understand. This means the people to whom Jesus was speaking should not be like the Jews to whom Isaiah spoke. Isaiah's audience heard but did not understand. Jesus wanted his audience both to hear and to understand.

Makes the person common. This passage is usually translated "defiles the person." The Greek word koi-noí (κοινοῖ) means "become common," but most scholars think the context here requires that the meaning be extended to mean more than make common, but even to defile. The words "common" and "defilement" have different meanings, even though the two are associated. Peter is reported to have held that he never ate anything that was either common or unclean (Acts 10:14). This means that food could be either common or unclean. He avoided both possibilities. When David came to the priest, Ahimelech, asking for bread, Ahimelech said he had no common bread (léh-khem chohl, לחם חל) but only holy bread (léh-khem kóh-desh לחם קדש) that was permitted to be eaten only by priests in a condition of holiness. Ahimelech extended this rule to include others who had kept away from women and so were holy (1 Sam 21:4).

The things that are common (chóhl, חול) are not holy (kódesh, קודש) (Lev 10:10; Ezek 22:26). Holy things are God, Sabbaths, feast days, the chosen people, Jerusalem, the promised land. Common things are the six working days of the week, gentiles, pagans, idolaters, and foreign lands. Although these are all bad from a Jewish or early Christian point of view, they do not defile. Paul said he was convinced by Jesus that nothing was common in itself; if someone thought it was common, to that person it was common (Rom 14:14). Paul may have learned this rule from the teaching in Matt 15:11. The same notion would apply to something that was holy. If Ahimelech, for example, considered the bread in his possession was in a condition of holiness, then to him it was holy, and he was obligated to treat it as something holy.

There have always been some Jews and some Christians who have eaten things that are considered by the pious to be common, and they continue to be members of the faith, but most people do not ordinarily eat things that Jews considered defiling. A Jew who eats pork or shell fish does not have to go through the liturgical cleansing process as he or she would if he or she were defiled. Foods that are not approved by dietary laws are common and illegal, from a biblical point of view, but they do not defile. Things that defile are corpses, lepers, excrement, menstrual blood, semen, drainage from boils or other skin diseases. Most of these go out of people. They are not usually eaten by human beings. A dog, however, might eat the meat of a corpse. If it should, the dog would be unclean for three days until all of the meat is decreed to have been digested. If a dog that had eaten corpse's flesh within three days should enter a house, coming under a roof, it would defile the house. If, however, it only lay across the threshold, without entering the house completely, the question was debatable. Rabbi Jose said it would only defile the house if it lay with its mouth outward and its rear end inward. Although the corpse's flesh entered the dog's mouth, it would not normally be vomited out; it would come out from the other end of the alimentary canal. Excrement defiled (mOhol 11.7).

A person who is defiled is not common but unclean, and he or she has to perform required rituals and sometimes receive a pronouncement by a priest before being called "clean" again. Matthew knew about uncleanliness (ah-kah-thar-seé-ah ἀκαθαρσία). It was associated with bones of corpses (Matt 23:27). He only twice mentioned unclean spirits, and that was to report that Jesus gave the apostles authority over them (Matt 10:1) and to tell what happened when an unclean spirit left a man (Matt 12:43). Mark, on the other hand, mentioned unclean spirits 11 times, and Luke, six times. When Matthew used the verb koin-ó-oh (κοινόω), he evidently meant something was made common; when he meant something was unclean he used the term akatharsía. He apparently knew the difference.

Since Matthew had just finished reporting on the evils of taking oaths and vows of celibacy he was speaking of words that come out of people's mouths. Words would not defile, but they might make common. Through speech a person might remove himself or herself from the holy community and become a pagan, gentile, and an idolater. In the chreia Jesus accused the Pharisees of having transgressed the commandment of God. This meant they, like the Jerusalem leaders in Zechariah's time, had become common. Through words people could blaspheme, deny their faith, take oaths to idols, or uphold a pagan religion.

This suggestion is further supported by the interpretation given in verses 15-20. The point of the saying, then, might be that a Jew was permitted to eat food that was not sold at a store that was kah-sháyr (כשר) without being excommunicated, but he might not blaspheme, take oaths or vows by a pagan deity, or deny his or her faith and still belong to the holy congregation. A priest, however, who wanted to remain worthy of his office, would not make his clean, pious alimentary canal common by means of filthy food (4 Macc 7.6), such as that sold by gentile stores and not approved by dietary laws.

TEXT

Matthew	Fisrt Testament
[12]Then when the disciples had come to him, they said to him, "You know that the Pharisees, when they heard the word, were offended." [13]He, however, said in reply, "Every **plant** which my heavenly Father has not **planted**	Your people will be righteous--all of them. For the age they will inherit the land, **the shoot of my planting**, the work of my hands (Isa 60:21).
will be uprooted. [14]Let them go.	Look! I have appointed you today over the gentiles and over the kingdoms, **to uproot** and to break down . . . to build and **to plant** (Jer 1:10).
[They are blind leaders of the blind. If the blind leads the blind, both **will fall into** a ditch]."	The one who digs a pit **will fall into** it (Prov 26:27). He makes a pit, digging it out, and he **will fall into** the pit he has made (Ps 7:15).

TECHNICAL DETAILS

This is a responsive chreia from a literary point of view. 1) the speaker is identified; 2) the situation is given to which Jesus responded; 3) his response is quoted; and 4) the unit is very brief. It is also one of the teachings that grew out of a council meeting held after the apostles had returned from one of their missions. They were giving Jesus an account of the events that occurred while they were "fishing for men." It was in sessions like these that much of the information was communicated that was recorded in chreia form. The disciples evidently took notes of Jesus' advice, put them in chreia form so that they could easily remember them, and have them on hand the next time the situation occurred. This chreia is also coherent with other teachings in parables and chreias. Here, Jesus is shown in conflict with the Pharisees, as is evident in many other chreias. He also used metaphors related to farming or gardening which are similar to those used in the parable of the weeds and the wheat. The final scene of that parable pictured the weeds being thrown into the fire with the wheat safely stored in the granary. When the "harvest" comes, only the grain that has been planted will be reaped. That might not include the Pharisees. Like Jeremiah, Jesus was the one who was appointed to do the planting and the uprooting.

Matthew put two chreias (Matt 15:1-3 and 15:12-13) together in the same chapter, because they both dealt with conflicts Jesus had with the Pharisees. Appropriately, he put the chreia first that showed Jesus insulting the Pharisees by implying that they were idol worshipers and that their tradition was an act of transgressing. Of course, that would have provided an occasion for the Pharisees to have been offended. The Pharisees evidently heard something Jesus said, and they fully understood. That was why they were offended. Initially, however, these two chreias may have taken place at very different times and occasions.

COMMENTARY

Heard the word, were offended. The term "word" here reflects the Hebrew dahváhr (דבר), which has a wider meaning than simply a word in a sentence. It means a thing or a matter. It means that when the Pharisees heard the things that Jesus had been doing and saying, they were offended. When the disciples were concerned about the Pharisees being offended and not following Jesus' movement, Jesus responded that this indicated their position in God's original plan. Jesus did not consider the politically astute thing to do and work out a compromise with them. In other parables, Jesus was shown in direct conflict with the Pharisees, some more that others. This conflict evidently became worse as time went on. There may have been a time when Jesus and the Pharisees worked together, because the disciples seemed alarmed that Jesus had fallen out of their favor. It is only a conjecture that the reason for their fall-out was Jesus' association with the tax collectors. That is the issue about which he seemed to be in greatest disagreement with them, but no record is given of Jesus before he began to associate with tax collectors and sinners.

Let them go.[6] This is the basic quotation of the chreia. The clause, "Let them go," may have been added later, or it may be integral to the saying. Jesus seemed willing here to accept the break with the Pharisees and not try to make amends so as to regain their favor. He concluded that they were not part of God's plan or they would support his program. God was frequently pictured as the farmer, with Israel as the plant (Isa 5:1-7; 60:21; Jer 45:4; Ezek 17). Like Jeremiah,

---

[6]H. A. W. Meyer, Handbook, p. 282, argued mistakenly that the plants to be burned were not the Pharisees but their teachings. Just as "weeds" represented sinners in the parable of "Wheat and Weeds," so the "plant" here represents rejected members of the community (Matt 3:10; Isa 5:7; Sir 3:28). So also T. Zahn, Das Evangelium des Matthäus (Leipzig: A. Deichert'sche Verlag, 1910), p. 525, and M'Neile, Matthew, p. 227.

however, Jesus was appointed as God's agent. He would be the one who uprooted and destroyed, planted and rebuilt. If the Pharisees gave Jesus too much trouble, when the kingdom came, he might root them out. Nevertheless, his idea about the way to treat weeds was to wait until harvest time to separate them from the wheat. The same was true of tax collectors and other sinners.

Blind leaders of the blind. This is probably not an original part of the quotation of Jesus. Matthew made many second endings to chreias in his effort to have at least two witnesses to support a case. The chreia is complete without verse 14. Paul said, "You are persuaded that you are a guide of the blind, a light for those in darkness, an instructer of fools, a teacher of children" (Rom 2:19-20). This insulting statement is not a part of the chreia which contains a summary of Jesus' response. These insults, whereby people were called "hypocrites," "snakes," and "vipers," are all editorial additions that were probably added by Matthew himself.

TEXT

15Peter, replying, said to him, "Interpret for us the parable." 16Then he said, "Are you also still **ignorant?** 17**Do you not understand** that everything **that enters the mouth goes into** the stomach and is discarded **into** the toilet? 18**The things that go out of the mouth** go out from the mind, and they are **the things that make the person common,** 19for from the mind go out conflicts, evils, murders, adulteries, fornications, stealings, false witnessings, blasphemies. 20These are **the things that make the person common**. The act of **eating with unwashed hands** does not **make the person common.**"

TECHNICAL DETAILS

The bold face words in this unit are those that were also used in one of the previous chreias (Matt 15:10-11), showing that this is a midrash on those verses. If Matthew composed Matt 15:15-20, then someone else composed Matt 15:10-11, and Matthew had access to it before he wrote Matt 15:15-20. Although Jesus is pictured as giving both the initial statement (Matt 15:10-11) and the interpretation, at Peter's request, these are only literary forms. Matt 15:10-11 is a chreia, which is a literary form designed to preserve the basic points of a teacher's teaching. Chreias were usually composed by a teacher's disciples to preserve succinctly the basic teachings of their teacher. The odds are that this chreia contains an accurate saying of Jesus. This is the kind of literary unit that preachers and lawyers collected and used as the bases for sermons and arguments. Matthew was one of those who used this form and probably made the later interpretation.

Separating the text from the interpretation is one of the ways to distinguish the teachings of Jesus from the additions of the later church. Those who interpreted earlier texts were not fraudulent authors who composed fiction and attributed it falsely to Jesus. Like modern day exegetes and preachers, these members of the later church tried to explain the teachings of Jesus fairly. They attributed their interpretations to Jesus, because they believed the ideas were his. They were only explaining them more simply.

COMMENTARY

False witnessings, blasphemies. There are eight types of wickedness listed here. This shows that Matthew does not always organize groups of three or seven.

Interpret for us the parable. This is not the first time Matthew included an interpretation to one of Jesus' teachings. There is also an interpretation of the parable of the sower (Matt 13:18-23) and the wheat and the weeds (Matt 13:36-43). The "parable" involved is the unit, Matt 15:2-11, with words taken principally from the two chreias at the beginning and end of that unit. The discussion to be continued is not the subject of the Pharisees being rejected but the question in the final chreia which introduces the subject of becoming common.

Things that make the person common. The things listed here were not defiling, which in Jewish concepts are Levitical, liturgical, and not acts of the will. This prompts twentieth century readers to realize that the discussion here is about things that make holy people common rather than things that defile. Touching corpses and having leprosy are among the things that defile. Whatever makes the holy people pagan makes them common. Some Jews would hold that eating with pagans or Jews who are not rigorously observant of liturgical rules are deeds that make Jews or Christians common. The Pharisees apparently thought eating with unwashed hands was one of the things that made people pagans.

Does not make the person common. This reenters the expression begun at the second verse in the chapter-unwashed hands. Matthew has composed a small sermonette, based on the chreia of 15:1-3, in basically the same way that Hermogenes and other Greek rhetoricians taught:

1) First, the homiletician should praise the speaker briefly.

2) The thesis of the chreia should be presented. This did not mean just to quote the saying but to expand and clarify it.

3) The third step should praise further the speaker who said this, telling what a wise man he was, etc.

4) He should then develop the cause the chreia exemplifies.

5) The interpreter should next attack the subject from the opposite direction, showing what would happen if the advice were not taken seriously.

6) After that, the interpreter should illustrate the chreia from analogy or parable.

7) It is also good to give an illustration to support the point of the chreia.

8) Finally, the interpreter should set forth an exhortation that it is to the

benefit of the hearer to be convinced by the arguments of the speaker.[7] Matthew used four of these steps in the formation of his homily of Matt 15:1-20.

In this homily Matthew (2) quoted the chreia, expanding it to suit his legal belief of the requirements of proof. (4) He developed the cause he understood the chreia to exemplify, namely the Pharisees' support of monastic vows and Jesus' refutation (6 and 7). The interpreter illustrated his argument, using first three proof texts together with their interpretations (Matt 15:4, 8-9 plus 5-6) and a poetic proverb (Matt 15:11) plus its interpretation (Matt 15:15-20). This is one of the primary ways in which the later church added to the teachings of Jesus in the NT. It is a method preachers use in pulpits still today. The art of homiletics should not be mistaken for composition of fiction or a willful distortion of the text, unless, of course, it is.

TEXT

21When Jesus left from there, he went away into the regions of Tyre and Sidon.
22Now look! a Canaanite woman came out from those mountains, and she cried out, saying,

Matthew	First Testament
"Have **mercy** upon me, Lord, son of David. My daughter is badly possessed of a demon," 23but [Jesus] did not answer her a word. When his disciples had arrived, they asked him, saying, "Dismiss her, because she is crying after us." 24In reply he said, "I was sent only to the lost sheep of the house of Israel." 25Then after she came she worshiped him, saying, **"Lord, help me,"** 26but he said in response, "It is not good to take the children's bread and throw it to the dogs." 27Then she said,	**Help me, Yahowah, my God**! Save me according to your **mercy** (Ps 109:26).
"Yes, Lord, for even the **dogs** eat from the crumbs that fall from their lord's table." 28Then Jesus answered and said to her, "Woman, your faith	You shall not bring the salary of a harlot or the wages of a **dog** into the house of Yahowah your God (Deut 23:18).

[7]Hermogenes, "Progymnasmata," L. Spengel, Rhetores Graeci in three vols. (Leipzig: Teubneri, 1853, 1854, 1856) 2, iii, pp. 6.19-7.10. See further Buchanan, Jesus: The King and his Kingdom (Macon: Mercer, c1984), pp. 70-71.

is great. Let it be to you as you wish," and her daughter was healed from that hour (Matt 15:21-28).

TECHNICAL DETAILS

Bultmann called this unit an apophthegm,[8] but that does not say much. An apophthegm is a narrative, either succinct or lengthy, that contains one or more sayings. It could be as small as a chreia or it could be 20 times as long. It could be a quotation of one person or a dialogue, as is the case here.

COMMENTARY

Regions of Tyre and Sidon. These were seaport cities just north of the northern boundary of Joshua's kingdom. They were cities that had been considered gentile and hostile. Ezekiel had strong words of condemnation for them (Ezek 25-26). This is the only instance when Jesus is reported to have traveled outside of the territory belonging to Joshua's kingdom. This does not mean Jesus never ventured farther north. Matthew organized his literature to conclude with Jesus as an antitype of the old Joshua. Therefore Matthew did not picture Jesus in Syria or Lebanon, even though he could easily have walked there from Galilee.

Came out from those mountains. The Ladder of Tyre is at the shore of the Mediterranean Sea at the border between Joshua's kingdom and Lebanon. Immediately to the east of the Ladder of Tyre arises a tall range of mountains. According to the report, the woman came down to the shoreline from these mountains to see Jesus. The Canaanites continued to exist in Israel long after the Israelites had conquered their country and tried to expel them. They were among those called "sojourners of the land." These were some of the people Jews wanted to evict from the territory.

Lord, Son of David. When people came to Jesus asking for healing, they never addressed him as Son of God, Son of Man, or Messiah. They always called him "Son of David" (Matt 9:27; 20:30). This may be because Solomon was addressed as son of David, and he was believed to be not only wise, but a great healer (TSol 20.1). This legend may have led people to think any son of David could heal, or at least the Messiah, son of David. See further commentary on Matt 9:27 and 12:23. "Lord" was a title of respect used for kings and also for other dignitaries.

---

[8]R. Bultmann, The History of the Synoptic Tradition tr. J. Marsh (New York: Harper and Rowe, 1962), p. 38.

Did not answer her a word. This means that at first he strictly ignored her, hoping she would leave.

Dismiss her. Murphy-O'Conner renders this passage, "Release her," meaning "set her free from her burden of worry."[9] He argued that the disciples were encouraging Jesus to help the woman rather than dismissing her without assistance. This is a possible interpretation.

Lost sheep of the house of Israel. The lost sheep were the Jews and possibly the Samaritans who were being assimilated among the gentiles and were not observing their religious practices. Jesus seems to have directed his attention to the wealthy male Jews who had become wealthy by collaborating with the Romans. He asked them to do a right-about face, return to the Jewish fold, and give all of their money to the nationalist movement to regain the Kingdom of Heaven. These "lost sheep" were also sometimes called "dead." Restoring the lost sheep to the fold had the same meaning as "raising the dead" or "restoring them to life." The house of Israel was sometimes applied only to Samaria, sometimes only to Judah, and sometimes to the entire Solomonic kingdom. This means, in any event, that Jesus did not think his assignment was extended to any of the non-Jewish gentiles.

Tyre and Sidon were not very far from Nazareth in Galilee. This is coherent with an earlier report where Jesus commissioned his apostles not to go to any gentile cities or to the Samaritans, but only to the lost sheep of the house of Israel (Matt 10:5-6). Cook argued against any suggestion that this was a pro-Jewish statement. He said Matt 10:5-6 and 15:24 "really represent the end of a reasoning process, and not the beginning."[10] In Cook's opinion Matthew's plan throughout was to show that Christianity was originally pro-Jewish, but this was only to show that Jews rejected Jesus, forcing Christians to move to the gentiles. He obtained his proof for this argument--not from Matthew, but--from Acts:

> Paul was . . . testifying to the Jews that the Christ was Jesus. And when they opposed and reviled him, he shook out his garments and said to them, "Your blood be upon your heads! I am innocent. From now on I will go to the Gentiles" (Acts 13:46).[11]

Cook also failed to notice that when Paul went to the gentiles, he went to the Jews of the diaspora, fulfilling the requirements of the Day of Atonement.

---

[9]J. Murphy-O'Conner, "The Structure of Matthew XIV-XVII," RB 82 (1975):382.

[10]M. J. Cook, "Interpreting the 'Pro-Jewish' Passages in Matthew," HUCA 54 (1983):142.

[11]Cook, "Interpreting," pp. 141-42. Other arguments of Cook will be discussed in this commentary in relationship to Matt 5:17-20; 10:5-6; 13:57; 15:24; 22:8; 24:14; 28:19-20, and the conclusions.

Paul was convinced that the death of Jesus was an adequate gift to pay the debt of the Jews to God. That which was necessary to complete the process of atonement was that Jews must become reconciled to one another. Paul and the Jerusalem apostles divided up the universe among themselves to accomplish this task. Peter, James, and John would undertake the territory of the promised land, and Paul would go to the diaspora. After 11 years, he completed this task in the entire region of Asia Minor and was prepared to go on to Rome. He could never have evangelized all of the gentiles in Asia Minor in such a short time as that. Rabbis called those in the promised land, "circumcised," circumcised or not and those in the diaspora "uncircumcised," circumcised or not. Cook was misled by the word "gentile" into assuming that "gentiles" could mean nothing except non-Jews.

Throw it to the dogs. In this context "the children" were the children of Abraham. Most people know that. That which is not well known is that the term "dog" refers pejoratively to a gentile.[12] The origin of this expression is older than Deuteronomy:

> There shall not be a feminine prostitute (kid-eh-sháh, קדשה)
> from the daughters of Israel;
> there shall not be a masculine prostitute (kah-dáysh, קדש)
> from the sons of Israel.
> You shall not bring the wages of a harlot (zoh-náh, זונה)
> or the salary of a dog (kéh-lev, כלב)
> into the temple of the Lord your God (Deut 23:17-18).

The cult of the religious feminine prostitute who was also called a harlot, was outlawed, but the term was not limited in its metaphorical use to sacred prostitution in worship. It described the faithlessness of Israelites who mingled with gentiles and their ways of worship. The law also prohibited practicing the cult of the male prostitute who was also called a "dog." Another illustration is this:

> You shall not eat any meat from an animal that dies of itself.
> To the stranger (gayr, גר) within your gates it shall be given--
> or, sell it to the foreigner (nah-kreé, נכרי),
> because you are holy to the Lord your God (Deut 14:21).

A different version of the same basic law is:

[12]For example R. H. Gundry, Matthew (Grand Rapids: Eerdmanns, c1994), pp. 314, who said this passage "did not contain a slurring reference to Gentiles."

You shall be holy men to me. Flesh in the field, torn by beasts, you shall not eat. To the dog (kéh-lev, כלב) you shall throw it (Exod 22:30).

The targum (Neofiti) interpreted this verse as follows:

You shall be holy men to my name. **Flesh torn from a wild beast**, killed in the field you shall not eat. To the dog (kéh-lev-ah, לכלבא) **you shall throw it**, or to the foreigner (la-nak-rée-yah, לנכרייה), son of a gentile, who is like a **dog, you shall throw it.**

Saints were forbidden to eat flesh from beasts found dead in the field, whether the beast died of itself or was torn by other beasts. Both of these belong to the same category and are forbidden by Ezekiel (Ezek 22:30). Deuteronomy says it should be given to the stranger or sold to the foreigner. Exodus says it should be thrown to the "dogs" which seems to be just an insulting way of saying it should be given or sold to gentiles. Even though the term "dog" was used insultingly to refer to gentiles, the dog in ancient Judaism was not a hated beast.

Dogs were known for being friendly, faithful, and dependable guards.[13] The term was initially applied to masculine prostitutes as a tribute rather than an insult. The masculine prostitute was recognized and honored within the cult for his faithful service to the deity.[14] When Israel tried to root out the practice of sacred prostitution from its community, the terms "harlot" and "dog" were both used metaphorically in contempt. In the sacred cult of prostitution the mingling of the male and female prostitutes with believers was sexual. Israelites and Jews used these terms to describe Jews and gentiles who mingled with each other socially and in business, implying that they also mingled sexually. The term "dog" seems to have been used as a synonym for foreigner quite early and continued through NT times.[15]

---

[13]See W. G. Lambert, Babylonian Wisdom Literature (Oxford: Clarendon, 1960), pp. 193-205; PesiqR 52a; NatHist 8.6 (140); Tob 6:1; 11:4; Praem, 15 (89).

[14]The inscription from the temple of Astarte at Larnaka referred to "dogs" and "young ladies" as those employed by the temple (see H. Donner and W. Röllig, Kanaanäische und Aramäische Inschriften Wiesbaden: Harrassowitz,1966-68], 3 vols., 37:CIS I 86 AB; pl. XII; KI Nr. 29; NSI nr. 20). The "dogs" were male prostitutes. See further Buchanan, The Consequences of the Covenant (Leiden: Brill, 1970), pp.184-89.

[15]H. Koester, "The Purpose of the Polemic of a 'Pauline Fragment,'" NTS 8 (1961/62):319-20, not knowing the use of the term "dog" in Jewish circles, mistakenly said, "The insulting address'dogs,' should not be used as an indication of the identity of the opponents. However, it must be kept in mind that this word was one of the strongest invective terms possible. This means that the deliberate aim of the polemics here is not to describe the opponents, but to insult them." Koester should have explained how the term "dog" got to be such an insulting word if it had no

Enoch insulted foreigners whom he called "dogs, eagles, and kites" who devoured the Israelite sheep (1 Enoch 90.4; cf. also 89.42-49 where dogs were Philistines). In an undated letter from one Jew to another, the writer said he had sent the letter with "dogs" who would tell the recipient about it. He assured the recipient that under the present conditions their going to someone about something would not be as though they had gone to a church of idol worship, because there was no Jew there.[16] The "dogs" who would tell the recipient about something were obviously people. The church of idol worship was evidently a Christian church. The Jews in correspondence had to deal with gentiles or Christians because there were no Jews nearby, but they did not like it, and, like Rabbi Judah, described them disrespectfully as "dogs," even as they used their services to deliver these messages.

Even though the term "dog" originally referred to a masculine prostitute, it was a gentile woman who came to Jesus asking that her daughter be healed. By the time of Jesus the term was applied to gentiles in general. The woman's request prompted the reply, "It is not good to take the children's bread and throw it to the dogs."[17] Pseudo-Clement, a Jewish Christian author, in reference to that passage, said it was not lawful to heal the gentiles who were like dogs, because they ate various kinds of food (common food--not approved by dietary laws). This anti-gentilic author justified Jesus' decision to heal the Syro-Phoenician's daughter, however, by claiming that when she replied that she wanted the crumbs that fell from the table, this meant to Jesus that she was living like the sons of the kingdom and therefore received healing. Had she continued to live like a gentile (dog), Pseudo-Clement maintained that Jesus would never have healed her (Clem. Hom. 2.19).

Didache said those who had not been baptized were "dogs" who should not be allowed to partake of the Eucharist (Did 9.5).[18] During a year of scarcity Rabbi opened the store house of groceries and announced that those who had studied scripture might enter. A certain man shoved his way in and asked for food. When Rabbi asked if he had studied the scripture or the Mishnah, he said he had not. Then Rabbi asked why he should give him food. The man said Rabbi should feed him as the dogs and ravens were fed. Rabbi gave him food, and he left, but afterwards Rabbi's conscience bothered him because he had given his bread to a man without learning. Later, however, his conscience was relieved

---

identifying significance. See also D. W. Thomas, "Kalebh 'dog': its Origin and Some Usages of it in the OT," VT 10 (1960):410-27.

[16] W. H. Worrell (ed.), Fragments from the Cairo Genizah in the Freer Collection (New York: MacMillan, 1927), III, 4, 13-15 (pp. 19, 21).

[17] W. S. McCullough, "Dog," ID (New York, c1962), I, 862, thought "dogs" in Matt 15:26//Mark 7:27 means non-Jews.

[18] Buchanan, Consequences, pp. 185-88.

when he learned that the man was Rabbi Jonathan ben Amram, a man learned in scripture and mishnah, but one who answered as he did because he had vowed that he would never derive benefit from the honor paid to the Torah (bBBat 8a).

There is no way that this reference to "dogs" can be understood as being anti-Jewish, as Cook holds. Christians today are embarrassed by this account, but 2,000 years ago it was considered unethical from Jewish and Christian standards not to be segregationistic. It is impossible to believe in a doctrine of election, claiming to be the only chosen people, and not also be partisan to an apartheid doctrine. Chosen people do not expect to treat themselves or to be treated by others as "common" people. The idea that the chosen people should be fed first or be the only ones fed is no new doctrine. Scholars have often compared this narrative to the story in which Elijah demanded the woman of Zarephath to use her last morsel of bread to feed Elijah. That story concluded with Elijah providing adequately for this woman in her poverty (1 Kings 17:8-16). Here, like Elijah, Jesus healed the daughter of the woman he insulted.

This experience was not the beginning of a gentile mission, either in the mind of Matthew or of Jesus, as some scholars assume. Whenever a "gentile" mission began it began being addressed to Jews in the diaspora. This is not reported in the Gospel according to Matthew, but the Jews in the diaspora were traditionally in communication with the Jews in Palestine. Jesus probably had programs functioning throughout his mission that were directed to the Jews in the diaspora. In his experience there had been faithful children of Abraham in the East and the West who could be counted on to participate in the Kingdom of Heaven when it was obtained. They were probably already supporting his program financially. This is all conjecture, of course, but there are some reasons for thinking this might have been so. Paul began his ministry to the diaspora no later than 40 I.A. (death of Aritas). At that time there were already Judaizing Christians in Asia Minor and Rome. The missionary effort to the diaspora must have begun very early.

TEXT

Matthew	First Testament
29After Jesus left there he went alongside the Sea of Galilee, and after he had gone up into the mountain he sat down there. 30Many crowds came to him having with them lame, **crippled, blind, speechless**, and many others. They threw	Look! Your **God** will avenge; the retaliation of **God** will come and save you. Then the eyes of **the blind** will be opened, and the ears of the deaf will be opened.

them to the ground at his feet, and he healed them [31]so that the crowd was astonished to see **the speechless** speaking, **the crippled man** well, the lame walking, and **the blind** seeing,

Then **the crippled man** will leap like a deer, and the tongue of **the speechless** will sing (Isa 35:4-6).

Yahowah will take away from you every sickness; he will not inflict upon you any of the evil diseases of Egypt, but he will put them on all who hate you, and you shall destroy all of the people that the Lord your God will give over to you (Deut 7:15-16).

so they **glorified the God of Israel.**

Look!
The glory of the God of Israel came from the east, and the sound [of] his [arrival] was like the sound of much water [running], and the land shone with his **glory** (Isa 43:2).

TECHNICAL DETAILS

On the basis of Isaiah 35 Jesus was pictured here as the one to introduce the new age when the land would be restored to the chosen people. The Isaianic prophet spoke at a time when he already knew that the Jews had made a treaty with Cyrus of Persia, whereby they would provide him with the intelligence he would need to enter Babylon and capture it during a feast when Babylonians would be drunk, and Cyrus, in turn, would assist the Jews in returning to Jerusalem and reestablishing their presence in the promised land.[19] The Isaianic prophet expected all of the miracles would be performed on that occasion that had been performed for Moses when he led the Hebrews out of Egypt, and also for Joshua, preparing the way for the Israelites to enter and conquer Palestine.

When Jesus was shown performing the miracles the Isaianic prophet promised, this meant that Jesus was the new Moses, the new Joshua, and the new Zerubbabel who would again restore the promised land, and the contemporary Jews would again be avenged by God, working through his Messiah. The healing miracles showed Jews where they were in the cycle of time. If the miracles were happening, all of the other associated events related to the conquest of Canaan by Joshua and the restoration of the land by Zerubbabel would soon fit into the chronological pattern. The concluding point was the glorification of the God of Israel. Ezekiel referred to the glory of the God of Israel when the land was to be

---

[19]For support of this interpretation see Buchanan, New Testament Eschatology: Historical and Cultural Background (Lewiston: Mellen, c1993), p. 177, fn 36.

restored, and the temple would function again. The smoke that went up to heaven like a pillar from the temple showed that the Lord was present there. Ezekiel saw the glory of God only in a vision; when the land would be restored the vision would become a reality.

Even if Jesus had never performed these miracles, the later church that believed he was the Messiah would have assumed that he performed them, because they believed the doctrine that all prophecy was prophesied only for the days of the Messiah. These were the days of the Messiah; therefore Jesus must have performed the miracles prophesied by Second Isaiah.

COMMENTARY

Alongside the Sea of Galilee. Geographically this statement is not complete. He did not just leave Tyre and Sidon and arrive at once at the Sea of Galilee. He left Tyre and Sidon, traveled many miles, and then walked alongside the Sea of Galilee. From the mouth of the Litani, north of Tyre, he might have gone up the Litani valley to the valley between the Lebanon and Anti-Lebanon mountains. From there he could have walked south down the valley to the headwaters of the Jordan and followed them to the northern shore of the Sea of Galilee. It is not clear from this narrative whether Jesus walked along the eastern or western shore of the sea, but in the next unit of this chapter Jesus reportedly left from that side of the sea to cross over to Magdana or Magdala,[20] a city north of Tiberias on the west side of the sea. This means Jesus went along the eastern side of the Sea of Galilee.

He sat down there. Before he reached the Sea of Galilee, Jesus stopped at one of the mountains in Lebanon. Mountain scenes are important to biblical history. There are strategic mountains where religious experiences took place. Mount Sinai where Moses received the contract; the Mount of Transfiguration; Mount Zion. Jesus went from the wilderness into the mountain from which he delivered the Sermon on the Mount; the devil took Jesus up into a high mountain to tempt him. There were mountains nearby to Tyre and Sidon, but the multiplication of the loaves from one of these mountains was intended, theologically, to remind the reader of these other mountain scenes. According to one of the rabbinic writings, the Lord told Aaron to go and meet Moses in the wilderness, so Aaron went to meet him on the mountain of the temple of Yahowah (tohr bayt móhk-du-shah, טור בית מוקדשא), TgNeof Exod 4.27). The targumist intentionally confused Mount Sinai here with Mount Zion. Paul seems to have made the same intentional confusion (Gal 4:24-25).

The fact that this event was placed immediately after the healing of the Canaanite woman's daughter suggests that Matthew understood Jesus to have sat down on a new Mount Sinai, because rabbis argued that on basis of scripture that

[20]For a discussion of the problems of the identification of this city see Gundry, Matthew, p. 322.

all the Israelites who were gathered at Mount Sinai were physically healthy. **All the people saw** and **all the people answered** (Exod 19:8) meant there were no blind or dumb among them. The text also said, **we will do and we will hear** (Exod 24:7). This means there were no deaf people there. It also said, **they stood at the base of the mountain** (Exod 19:7). Therefore none of them was lame (Mek Bahod 9.14-20).

Many crowds came to him. Crowds accompanied Jesus throughout the gospel. They are not always the same people, and they do not always reflect the same attitude, but they are part of the program. Here they are positively related to Jesus, coming to him for help.[21] As in other instances they were astonished at his healing powers. Comber said Jesus was appealing to the crowds to side in with him and the disciples rather than the Pharisees.[22]

He healed them. This was reported on the basis of Second Isaiah.

TEXT

Matthew	First Testament
32After Jesus had called his disciples, he said, "I have compassion on the crowd, because already they have remained with me three days, and they have nothing to **eat**. I do not want to dismiss them **hungry**,	He afflicted you, made you **hungry**, and then he made you **eat** manna (Deut 8:3).
33lest they perish on **the way** [home]." His disciples said to him,	You shall remember all **the way** which Yahowah your God has led you these forty years
"**From where in the wilderness** will	**in the wilderness** (Deut 8:2).
	From where am I to have meat to give all **this** people (Num 11:13)?
we obtain as many **loaves** [as are necessary] to satisfy so large a crowd as **this**?" 34Then Jesus said to them,	A man came from Baalshalishah, and he **brought** to the man of God **loaves** of the first fruit, twenty

[21]See W. Carter, "The Crowds in Matthew's Gospel," CBQ 55 (1993):54-67.

[22]J. A. Comber, "The Verb Therapeuo in Matthew's Gospel," JBL 97 (1978):431-34.

"How many **loaves** do you have?" They said, "Seven, and a few fish." [35]Having ordered the crowd to recline on the ground, [36]he took the seven **loaves** and the fish, blessed

barley loaves and a sack of fresh grain. [Elisha] said, "**Give** [it] **to the people** and **let them eat.**" His servant said, "**How can I** set this before a hundred men?" [Elisha] said,

[them], broke [the loaves], and **gave [the food] to the** disciples, and the disciples [gave them] to the crowds.

"**Give [it] to the people and let them eat**, for thus said Yahowah, '**Eat and have some left.**'" He set [it] before them.

[37]**They** all **ate and were satisfied**, and

You will eat meat, **and** in the morning **you will be satisfied** with bread, and you will know that I am Yahowah, your God (Exod 16:12).

They ate and there was

that which was left over of broken pieces they picked up were seven baskets full.

some left over, according to the word of Yahowah (2 Kings 4:42-44).

[38]Those who ate were **4,000 men**, not counting women and children. [39]Then [Jesus] dismissed the crowds and got into the boat and went to the mountains of Magadan.

Moses said, "There are **600,000 people on foot** in whose midst I am, and you say, 'I will give them meat and **they will eat for a month**'" (Num 11:21).

TECHNICAL DETAILS

Like other Jewish and Christian editors, Matthew organized his material so that units that discuss the same topic are placed together. Here he introduced another narrative that dealt with the provision of bread here because he had just finished a narrative with a discussion about whether or not bread should be fed only to the children or also to the dogs. Knackstedt raised the question about the integrity of the two reports of multiplying loaves (Matt 14:13-21 and 15:21-39). Is this a double report of a single event or were there two feedings involved? He concluded that both are historic events that came from different traditions.[23]

Knackstedt is not the first or the last to raise questions about these two reported miracles. Hagner, noticing that very similar wording was used in both narratives, thought at least one was non-historical.[24] Scholars have often

---

[23]J. Knackstedt, "Die Beiden Brotvermehrungen im Evangelium," NTS 10 (1964):309-55.

[24]D. A. Hagner, Word Biblical Commentary: Matthew 14-28 (Dallas: Word Books, c1995), pp. 440-50.

wondered and speculated about the two times when Jesus is reported to have fed the multitude in the wilderness. Why did Matthew report a very similar event twice? There are two possible reasons for this:

1) Repetition did not seem to be much of a problem to early Jews and Christians. In a Jewish Midrash, like Sifra, for example, after the commentator introduced a narrative in relationship to one verse of Leviticus, because it seemed relevant, if he came to another verse that seemed to need the same illustration, just a few verses later, he introduced the very same narrative again with no changes. They did not have footnotes in those days to refer the reader back to an earlier use of a literary unit. Matthew followed the same principle, which is one of the reasons there are doublets in this gospel. In chapter 14 Matthew placed the narrative where he did because it dealt with 1) a wilderness place, 2) a crowd of people, 3) Jesus' compassion, and 4) the subject of dismissing the crowd. In chapter 15 Matthew inserted basically the same story because it was associated with 1) bread, 2) compassion, 3) a dismissal. Coincidentally, he was also able to place the two feedings in antitypal order to fit with two feedings in Deuteronomy.

2) The second explanation deals with typology. Since Matthew was trying to match all of the important events in the Hexateuch with material from the life of Jesus, it was necessary for him to account for two feedings in the wilderness. On one occasion the people were hungry, and Moses tried to buy food for them from Sihon. Sihon refused to sell, so the Hebrews conquered the land and took cattle and booty, thereby having adequate provisions to feed the multitude (Deut 2:26-35). On another occasion, Moses brought down manna from heaven to feed the group (Deut 8:1-10). Matthew matched these two feedings with two antitypal feedings: Matt 14:15-21 and Matt 15:29-39. In the Fourth Gospel there is only one report of the multiplication of food, because there was an antitype of only one multiplication of barley loaves by Elisha (John 6; 2 Kings 4:42-44). Only in the Fourth Gospel is Jesus reported to have multiplied barley loaves. Matthew was following the typology of the Hexateuch and John was following the typology of Elijah-Elisha miracles.

The two narratives reported in Matthew are very similar to one another, differing only in such details as the number of baskets full of pieces of bread left over and the number of people in the crowd. Both narratives seem to reflect scattered words from two of the feedings in the wilderness, the manna and the quails, as they appear in Exodus, Numbers, and Deuteronomy, as well as from the story of Elisha multiplying the loaves. The story in chapter 14 is more closely related to the Elisha narrative than chapter 15, which is closer related to the books of the Torah. The authors of both Matthaean narratives were apparently acquainted with all of the related stories about provision of food.

COMMENTARY

Compassion on the crowd. As in the situation for the previous feeding, when Jesus had compassion on a crowd that meant he provided healing and food. Just above he had healed the Canaanite woman's daughter, and here he gave food for the multitude. The crowds did not always reflect a positive attitude toward Jesus. Here he had compassion on them. Later they called for his crucifixion (Matt 26:47).

Lest they perish on the way. This is a midrash on the Torah passage referring to the way in the wilderness where the Lord led the Hebrews for 40 years. Here it mentions the way home from their meeting in the wilderness.

They all ate and were satisfied. This is a midrashic report, based on the promise of Exod 16:12.

CHAPTER SIXTEEN

RELATIONSHIP BETWEEN MATTHEW AND THE HEXATEUCH

Matthew	Deuteronomy
Jesus promised that some who were standing there would not die before they saw the Son of man coming into his kingdom (Matt 16:24-28).	Children of Israel to cross the Jordan "this day" and receive the promised land (Deut 9:1-6).

TEXT

16:1The Pharisees and Sadducees arrived. Tempting, they asked him to show them a sign from Heaven. 2He, in replying, said to them,

> [When it is evening you say, "(Tomorrow will be) fair weather, for the heaven is red." 3In the morning, "Today will be stormy for the heaven is a gloomy red." On the one hand you know how to discern the face of the sky, but you are not able (to discern) the signs of the times.]

4An evil and adulterous generation looks for a sign, but a sign will not be given it except the sign of Jonah." Leaving them he went away.

TECHNICAL DETAILS

The bracketed portion (Matt 16:2b-3) is omitted by several manuscripts (B,**ℵ**,sy^{sc},Or̊,H) and contradicts the teaching of the chreia which said that there would be no sign. The teaching preserved in the chreia is much more likely to be a true teaching of Jesus than the addition. The bracketed verses constitute a midrashic addition. With variations the chreia is recorded four times in the gospels (Matt 12:38-39; 16:1-2a, 4; Mark 8:11-12; and Luke 11:19).[1] The following points are required for a responsive chreia:

1) The general context identifies the speaker as Jesus.
2) The situation that prompted him to speak is given.
3) The response of the speaker is quoted, and
4) it is very succinct.

If anyone expected Matthew to have organized his materials chronologically that person would be puzzled to find here the Pharisees and Sadducees demanding a sign from heaven in the text that follows another unit where Jesus was reported as having just healed the Canaanite woman's daughter and multiplied the loaves. There is further incongruity in the interpretation of the chreia which was inserted internally (Matt 16:2b-3). This interpretation contradicts the chreia. The one says Jesus would not give a sign, but the other presumes that anyone who could not understand the signs that were given would be very stupid.

This is the way Matthew organized his material. Both the chreia and the addition deal with discerning signs, so Matthew put them both together, even though they contradict one another. Matthew tried to organize his material so that they fit into a hexateuchal pattern and also so that materials of the same kind or subject were kept together. The words, "Leaving them he went away," is an editorial addition made to relate teachings to activity.

COMMENTARY

Pharisees and the Sadducees. These members of different sects were not in agreement among themselves, but they often appeared in the same crowds that gathered around Jesus. Both were asking for a sign from heaven. This meant that they wanted Jesus to do something before their eyes similar to one of the miracles of Moses, Elijah, or Elisha. That would prove to them that Jesus was the antitype of one of these prophets.

For the heaven is red. This is an interruption to the chreia, whose answer appears in Matt 16:4. Before there were satellites from which it is possible to photograph the earth, learn which way the jet streams flow, and view other things that influence weather, the only way people had of predicting weather was to notice which way the wind blew, the color of the sky at sunrise and sunset, and other vague and imprecise methods. These were often wrong, but people trusted them more than they trusted methods of predicting future international events. These methods were not very accurate because they were only signs. When signs are all the data available, however, they were even admitted into court as evidence.

---

[1]See further Buchanan, Jesus: the King and his Kingdom (Macon: Mercer, c1984), pp. 226-27.

In the same way that ancients watched signs to learn the future weather, they also observed cycles of time. There were certain seasons when rain was expected and others when there would almost never be a cloud in the sky. They watched the weather and the seasons, year after year, to learn to anticipate the weather in future years. They also studied events of history as they cycled between prosperity and famine, between war and peace. They thought they could study these closely and anticipate how events would happen in the future.

Quintillian said a sign provides suggestive probabilities but is not adequate in itself to prove a case in court. Probable evidence is called a sign (signum, σημεῖον). It is the task of the advocate to strengthen or weaken the validity of signs, depending on their effect on his client's case. Just because there is a blood stained garment does not prove there was a murder; a woman is not an adulteress just because she was seen associating with men (Quin 5.9, 8-15). Quintilian also shows many other instances of ways one might decrease or increase the value of a sign in court.

The signs of the times. As in court, also in religion "signs" in NT times were very important, but not completely convincing for all people. That which some people considered a sign, others did not. As with the stock market, today, there were many disagreements about the meaning of the signs. In NT times people thought time moved in predictable cycles, each cycle following earlier cycles in order and in events. Just as seasons followed one another in predictable sequence, they believed national events were also predictable on the basis of past events. There are still investors who think the stock market moves in predictable cycles. Ancient prophets studied the sequence of events very carefully, just as authors of almanacs and cycle conscious investors do today. The events that interested Jewish prophets were events that occurred just prior to good fortune events, like the Exodus from Egypt, the conquest of Canaan, the return of the Jews from Babylon, and the Hasmonean victory against the Greeks. The past cycles were not exactly identical. The Egyptian cycle lasted more than 500 years. The Hasmonean cycle, only about 75. The "wilderness" period in the Egyptian cycle continued for 40 years. The Hasmonean "wilderness" period lasted only 3 1/2 years. Prophets who matched their current cycles with the Egyptian cycle did not always synchronize with the Hasmonean cycle. Therefore eschatological prophets disagreed. When Jeremiah was prophesying that Babylon would come and take the Jews captive, contemporary prophets promised continued peace and security. People read the same signs differently.

These were not the kinds of signs that anyone performed. The signs the Pharisees and Sadducees should have been able to read were the daily events and their relationship to the cycles of time. They were signs that prophets had predicted and that would take place before the judgment or at the beginning of the new age. Ezek 47, for example, said that in the new age there would be trees in the Kidron Valley, bearing fruit all the year around. Therefore one of the signs people wanted to appear was fresh fruit on fruit trees out of season. Zech 14 said that on the judgment day the Mount of Olives would split in two and part of it would move one way and part of it would move another, leaving a huge canyon in between. Therefore people watched to see if the Mount of Olives had moved (See comment on Matt 21:18-22).

The instruction that Matthew has organized here as a teaching of Jesus is that there were many signs which anyone who was observing could see. It should not have been necessary for anyone to ask about it. Weather in the Near East is more predictable than in many places of Europe and United States. During the summer, there is almost always a clear sky and no rain. During the winter there are many clouds and much rain. It does not vary as much as some other places. Nevertheless, it is not infallible.[2] Neither are the signs of the times.

A sign will not be given. The sign under discussion here is a different kind from those under observation in the pericope above. The sign Jesus refused to give was one he would instigate by jumping off the pinacle of the temple or making water come out of a rock.

Gibson correctly noticed that there was a conflict between Jesus' refusal to perform a sign and the facts reported of signs that he actually performed. He reported the type of signs that were given in thc FT, such as Jonathan and his armor bearer depended on the verbal reaction of the people at the fortress to decide whether the two them should go up and take the fortress. They judged this to be a sign from heaven (1 Sam 14:9-10). There were also false prophets in NT times who promised signs, such as the opening up of the Jordan for the followers to pass through or the magic overthrow of the walls of Jerusalem just as the walls of Jericho collapsed before Joshua. These were imitations of earlier national miracles, and they all failed. Therefore, Gibson argued, it was Mark, after the events of the false prophets, who composed this disclaimer of Jesus because of the unpopularity of signs.

This was a well-researched analysis of a serious problem. It overlooked, however, two items of data: 1) This pericope is an expanded chreia, and very likely contains the words of Jesus. 2) There is the possibility that Jesus never did perform those miracles attributed to him. In this conflict between the reported miracles and the saying, Gibson challenged only the saying, but never the miracles. It is the teachings of Jesus, however, especially in chreias and parables that can best be tested, and not the actions. The tested sayings are the most likely to be valid. Since a) earlier leaders reported in scripture performed signs; b) Jews believed everything that is in the world is in the scripture; and c) all prophecy was prophesied only for the days of the Messiah; d) they also believed these were the days of the Messiah. e) Therefore, Jesus must have done all of these things, even if no one witnessed them, because they were predicted in the scripture.

---

[2]At the Shechem excavation, near Nablus, Jordan, in 1957, it rained hard for about an hour. The oldest Jordanian in the group said he had never before seen it rain in July. It was so unusual that Jordanians at first denied it. They called it a heavy dew.

Gibson thought Mark (or Matthew) added the saying; either author or his sources might instead have added the miracles. The solutions offered here, and those offered by Gibson, are both conjectural attempts to deal with the conflicting facts.[3]

TEXT

[5]When the disciples arrived at the other side [of the sea], they forgot to take bread. Jesus said to them, [6]"Watch out and protect yourself from the leaven of the Pharisees and the Sadducees." [7]The [disciples] discussed among themselves [how this answer was related to them] saying, "We did not take bread." [8]When Jesus found out, he said, "Why do you discuss among yourselves, men of little faith, because you do not have bread? [9]Do you not understand nor remember the five loaves of the 5,000 and how many baskets you received? [10]Nor the seven loaves of the 4,000 and how many baskets you received? [11]How is it that you do not understand that I was not talking to you about loaves? Protect yourselves from 'the leaven' of the Pharisees and the Sadducees." [12]Then they deduced that he did not say to guard themselves from the leaven of bread, but from the teaching of the Pharisees and Sadducees.

TECHNICAL DETAILS

Verses 9 and 10 were clearly added after the two wilderness feedings had already become part of the gospel. Some editor added these two verses, knowing that the other two had already been reported and were part of the readers' knowledge. In fact it is possible that the only words of Jesus are contained in Matt 16:5-6. The rest seems to be homiletic interpretation.

COMMENTARY

Protect yourselves from the leaven. This is the beginning of an inclusion (Matt 16:6). The end is summarized in Matt 16:12. In between is the unit. The importance of the leaven metaphor is that leaven is very infectious. It is not necessary to add yeast to flour to make it leavened. It has only to be moistened to be considered leavened. For Passover, it is important to have flour that has not been leavened. Therefore care must be taken that no moisture reaches the wheat from the time it heads out until the flour is moistened just before the bread is put into the oven. There must elapse only 18 minutes between the time the flour is moistened until the unleavened bread is taken out of the oven. Most Jewish bakers can manage this operation within 11 minutes. If any flour is accidently moistened or becomes moldy the contents of the entire container must be discarded. Vessels that can hold moisture must be broken. If a small bit of leavened flour falls into

---

[3]J. Gibson, "Jesus' Refusal to Produce a 'Sign,'" JSNT 38 (1990):37-66.

a pot of dough, 60 times as large as the leavened flour, the whole is considered leavened. The dough must be discarded and the pot must be broken (bPes 30a).

Because leaven is considered infectious, it was used metaphorically to describe political or religious movements. When Jesus warned against the leaven of the Pharisees and the Sadducees, he meant that these groups were busy propagating their doctrines everywhere. Like leaven, they were corrupting the nation. Rabbis complained to the Lord,

> Master of the ages, it is revealed and known to you that we want to do your will. Who is hindering? The leaven that is in the dough and subjection to the gentiles. May it be your will that we may escape from their hands (bBer 17a).[4]

All except Matt 16:5-6 of this entire unit have probably been homiletically added to the document, following the multiplication of the loaves, because it had to do with bread, just as those two narratives did. The incident was created to provide the editor an opportunity to explain to the reader the metaphorical meaning of the expression "leaven of the Pharisees and of the Sadducees." The discussion was probably not a historical event. Both Jesus and his disciples would have known the metaphorical significance of leaven.

Do you not remember the five loaves? This unit was written after Matthew 12 and 15 had been composed and organized into the entire Gospel. This was written by someone, like Matthew, and placed intentionally after those two events had been reported.

You do not understand? Reminiscent of Isaiah's complaint, **You really hear, but you do not understand. You really see, but you do not know** (Isa 6:9; cf. also Jer 5:21).

TEXT

13When Jesus came into the regions of Caesarea Phillipi, he asked his disciples, saying, "Who do people say the Son of man is?" 14They said, "On the one hand, some [say] John the Baptist; others [say] Elijah, and [still] others say, Jeremiah or one of the prophets." 15He said to them, "Who are you telling [people] that I am?" 16Simon Peter said, "[I tell them that] you are the Messiah, the Son of the God of life." 17Jesus answered and said to him,

---

[4]Buchanan, Jesus, pp. 213-14.

Poetry

Blessed are you, Simon Baryóhna,
because flesh and blood has not revealed [this] to you
but my Father who is in heaven.
18I say to you, "You are a rock,
and upon this rock I will build my church,
and the gates of Hades will not overpower it.
19I will give you the keys of the Kingdom of Heaven.
Whatever you bind on earth will be bound in heaven,
whatever you release on earth will be released in heaven."

Midrash

Matthew	First Testament and Targum
16Simon Peter said, "[I tell them that] you are the Messiah,	In the place where it is said to them, "You are not my people," it will be said to them,
the Son of the God of life." 17Jesus answered and said to him,	**"the sons of the God of life"** (Hos 2:1).
	My soul thirsts for God, for **the God of life** (Ps 42:3).
"**Blessed** are you, Simon Baryóhnah, because flesh and blood has not revealed [this] to you but my Father who is in heaven. 18I say to you,	Look! A **stone** will be set in Zion, a tested **stone** a precious corner foundation **stone** will be laid (Isa 28:16).
'You are a **rock**, and upon this **rock**	Look to the **rock** [from which] you were chisled, to the quarry [from which] you were dug. Look to Abraham your father, to Sarah who bore you, for [when he was] one, I called him, and I **blessed** him and multiplied him (Isa 51:1-2).
	Moses spoke into the ears of all the **church** of Israel the words of this song (LXX Deut 32:1).
I **will build my church**, and	He **will build** a temple to **my** name, and I will establish the throne of his **kingdom** to the age (2 Sam 7:13).

the gates of Hades

I will leave with my days shortened;
the rest of my years will be counted
in **the gates of Sheol** (Isa 38:10).

They cried aloud to the ruler of all power, begging with an appearance, for mercy upon those, who were already standing **at the gates of Sheol** (3 Macc 5.51).

will **not overpower**
it.

"They have fought with you, but they have **not overpowered you**, because I am with you," said Yahowah "to rescue you" (Jer 1:19).

19**I will give you the keys of the Kingdom** of Heaven. Whatever you bind on earth will be bound in heaven, whatever you release on earth will be released in heaven.'"
20Then Jesus warned his disciples that no one should say that he was the Messiah.

I will give the key of the house of David on his shoulder.
He will open and no one closes, and he will close and no one opens (Isa 22:22).

TECHNICAL DETAILS

It is obvious from the texts organized above that Matt 16:17-19 is both a poem and a midrash. This could hardly be composed this beautifully by simply adding little editorial bits to some other text. The midrash shows that Peter is given the antitypal position of a new Abraham, the rock from which the new Israel would be hewn. He would receive the keys and have the authority of a new Eliakim. Like Eliakim, he would rule over the house of David, the Kingdom of Heaven. He would be blessed like Abraham, and his posterity would increase. This poem was obviously composed by an ardent member of the Petrine branch of the Christian church.

Kingsbury, like many others, presumed that Mark was the earliest gospel and was one of Matthew's sources.[5] The two-source hypothesis presumes that Mark and "Q" were sources for Matthew and Luke. According to this notion, neither Matthew nor Luke ever saw one another's work, and Mark never used either of the other gospels. This poses problems:

---

[5]J. D. Kingsbury, "The Figure of Peter in Matthew's Gospel as a Theological Problem," JBL 98 (1979):69.

1) There are several agreements in this passage between Matthew and Luke against Mark: Matt 16:14; Luke 9:19 **and** (δὲ), Matt 16:15 **he says to them** = Luke 9:20 **He said to them,** Matt 16:16; Luke 9:20 **but** (δὲ), **he said**, and **of God**. Matthew and Luke also agree in omitting the following Markan words: Mark 8:27 **to them**, Mark 8:28 **to him, saying, ". . .**, and Mark 8:29 **to them**, **(ho)**, and **to him**. This constitutes an amazing amount of coincidental agreement between Matthew and Luke against Mark, both in additions and omissions. There are some words in Mark that agree with Matthew against Luke and others that agree with Luke against Mark. These phenomena would make best sense if Mark were considered the third, rather than the first, gospel.[6] Even scholars who assume Markan priority think this Matthaean pericope in its present form is more primitive than the Markan parallel.[7]

2) The majority of the unit is unique to Matthew (Matt 16:17-19), and furthermore the unique section coheres both in content and poetic rhythm with the portion that is part of the triple tradition.[8] The following parallels point out part of the unity.

Matthew 16:13-16	Matthew 16:17-19
Who do you say that I am?	I say that you are . . .
Simon Peter answered and said, "You are the Messiah."	Jesus answered and said, . . . "You are Peter."

Gundry argued strongly against Cullmann's notion that Matt 16:17-19 is out of place. Cullmann said it would make more sense at the last supper in relationship to Luke 22:31-34. Gundry held that these verses would be more out of place there than in their present location. He further argued that these verses were not composed by the later church.[9]

---

[6]P. Parker, "A Second Look at the Gospel before Mark," JBL 100 (1981):389-413, and The Gospel before Mark (Chicago: The University of Chicago Press, c1953), pointed out many other reasons for thinking Mark was third rather than first. See also B. C. Butler, The Originality of St Matthew (Cambridge: Cambridge U., 1951).

[7]W. D. Davies and D. C. Allison, Jr., A Critical and Exegetical Commentary on the Gospel according to Saint Matthew (Edinburgh: T & T Clark, c1991), pp. 602, 605.

[8]For the Greek poetic balance see Butler, Originality, p. 132.

[9]R. H. Gundry, "The Narrative Framework of Matthew xvi 17-19," NovT 7 (1964):1-9.

COMMENTARY

The regions of Caesarea Phillipi. This was an abrupt move. The last report of Jesus was said to be at Magdala, which is along the sea shore just north of Tiberias on the west side of the sea (Matt 15:39). Suddenly he appeared in the Golan Heights, at the southern end of the Anti-Lebanon mountains. There was not a great distance between Magdala and Caesarea Phillipi, but no mention was made of the move.

Who do people say the Son of man is. The Son of man in the Fourth Gospel was to be glorified (John 13:31), and Jesus was identified with the Son of God who was to be glorified. Jesus here was considered both the Son of man and the Son of God. Also in Matt 16 Jesus was identified with the Son of man and the Messiah, the Son of the God of life.[10] First Enoch identified the Son of man with the righteous One (1 Enoch 46.3) and the chosen One (1 Enoch 48.2-6), both of which were names for the Messiah (1 Enoch 48.10). The elect One and the Son of man are in parallel (1 Enoch 49.2) and identical (1 Enoch 49.4). Charlesworth correctly concluded that

> the Elect One, the Righteous One, the Messiah, and the Son of man are different titles for the same messianic and eschatological figure.[11]

Medieval Jewish scholars identified the Son of man with the son of David. For example,

> After that the Messiah son of David will come with a cloud, as it is said, **One like a Son of man will come with the clouds of heaven** (Dan 7:13), after which it is written, **And to him will be given dominion, glory, and a kingdom** (Dan 7:14). He will kill

[10]E. Schweitzer, "The Son of Man," JBL 79 (1960):119-29, refuted those who thought the Son of man was not a title given to Jesus or used by Jesus when speaking of himself. Schweitzer, however, thought Jesus identified himself with the suffering Son of man. It was the later church that changed this role to one coming with the clouds. That probably was not required. When Jesus identified himself with the one like a Son of man in Daniel, he probably identified himself with the entire historical and mythical reality, relating himself to Judas the Maccabee and the clouds of heaven.

[11]J. H. Charlesworth, "From Jewish Messianology to Christian Christology: Some Caveats and Perspectives," Judaisms and their Messiahs, ed., J. Neusner (Cambridge: Cambridge, 1987), p. 240.

> the wicked Armilos, as it is said, **With the breath of his lips he will kill the wicked** (Isa 11:4).[12]

"Armilos" was a code name for the Jewish Antichrist. He represented Rome and Christians, the author's greatest enemies. The Messiah, son of David, was the Son of man who would destroy these enemies in military battle. Predicting the order of events that would take place in the near future, the medieval Jewish author of this portion of "The Secrets of Rabbi Shimon ben Yohai," said,

> Then the messianic king will sprout forth there, as it is said, **He comes with the clouds of heaven** (Dan 7:13), and it is written after it, **to him will be given the sovereignty** (Dan 7:14).[13]

Rabbi Judan was commenting on Ps 2:7-8, **You are my Son.** He interpreted that passage by quoting also from the reference to the Son of man who came with the clouds of heaven (Dan 7:13-14). Both of these texts promised the land or the kingdom as a possession. Rabbi Judan then concluded that all of these good promises would be fulfilled in the Messiah (Mid Ps 2.9 #14b). His deduction presumed that the Son of Man, the Son of God, and the Messiah were all different names for the same office.

Here the messianic king was identified with the Son of man in Dan 7:13. The title "Son of God" was a designation often given to kings in the ancient Near East. The pharaoh of Egypt was called the son of Re; Alexander the Great was called the son of Zeus. Solomon was called God's son (2 Sam 7:13-14). The Messiah was also called "the Son of God." This would be expected, because a messiah in Judaism was understood to be either a high priest or a king. Jesus was called the Messiah because he was expected to function as the ruling king over Palestine.

In one of the recently published Dead Sea Scrolls, Daniel was pictured as interpreting a vision for the king. The content of the vision is not preserved in the fragment. In his interpretation, however, Daniel said that the future would bring war and consequent depressions among nations. After this another king would arise, The text follows:

---

[12]From "A Legend of Rabbi Ishmael," tr. by Buchanan, Revelation and Redemption: Jewish Documents of Deliverance from the Fall of Jerusalem to the Death of Nahmanides (Dillsboro; sold by Mercer U. Press, c1978), p. 446.

[13]Tr. by Buchanan, Redemption, p. 403.

He will be called the Son of God (baráh dee áyl, ברה די אל); Son of the Most High (oo-vahr ahl-yóhn, ובר עליון) they will call him (4Q246 2.1).[14]

This Son of God was to be a great king. All of his ways would be true, and he would judge the land in truth. During his reign the sword would perish from the land, and peace would reign. Every province would serve him. The great God would make war in his behalf, and the peoples would be given into his hand. His government would be a government of the age.[15] Peuch thought this document came from Hasmonean or pre-Hasmonean times. It shows some of the expectations of a messiah and some of the names attached to him. Some of which were also assigned to Jesus. Since this Dead Sea Scroll passage is a commentary on Dan 7, the exegete who composed the unit considered the Son of man in Daniel to be the same as the term "Son of God" and "Son of the Most High." In this chapter of Matthew, Jesus was called "Messiah," "Son of the God of life," and "Son of man," all of which were Jewish designations for a king.

To use the term "Messiah" freely as a title for Jesus, where Romans or their sympathizers could hear, would have ensured his death. Romans knew that a messiah was one who expected to rule the country and throw out the Romans. Therefore Jews used other code names that were synonymous with the Messiah. Such names were "servant," "holy and righteous One," and "Author of life" (Acts 3:13-15). One of these code names was "Son of man." Jews knew what a Son of man was. This term identified Jesus with the Son of man in Dan 7, to whom the kingdom was given. In Daniel this probably was a mythical name for Judas the Maccabee. Jesus used the title "Son of man" as a code name for the Messiah.[16]

Maimonides said, "This is that which was said with [respect to] the Messiah, **With the clouds of heaven there came one like a Son of man**" (Dan 7:13).[17] The question reported in Matt 16:13 was a coded way of asking who people were saying that the Messiah was.[18] There was more than one

---

[14]The Hebrew of this text is taken from E. Peuch, "Fragment D'une Apocalypse en Arameen (4Q246=pseudo-Dan^{d}) et le 'Royaume de Dieu,'" RB 99 (1992):107.

[15]Peuch, "Fragment," p. 107. See the entire article, pp. 99-131.

[16]On this see further, Buchanan, To the Hebrews (Garden City: Doubleday, c1972), pp. 38-51.

[17]Maimonides, "Epistle to Yemen," Buchanan (tr.), Redemption, p. 100.

[18]R. Bultmann, Theology of the New Testament tr. K. Grobel (New York: Charles Scribner's Sons, 1951), p. 9, held that Jesus never thought of himself as the Messiah. He only pointed ahead to the eschatological Son of Man. He thought the Messiah was not the same as the Son of man and that Jesus' messiahship began with the resurrection (p. 25). This interpretation overlooks the expressions both in Judaism and Christianity that identified the Messiah with the Son of man, and it fails to explain how Jesus attracted the kind of following he attracted if he was not playing the

pretending Messiah at almost any time. After the death of Herod the Great, for example, three pretending messiahs appeared and immediately had at their disposal organized troops to lead against the Romans. These messiahs were Judas, Simon, and Athrongaeus, and within 50 days all Judaea had become a scene of guerrilla warfare (War 2.55-65). Prior to that time there were Jews who thought each of these pretenders was the true Messiah, and Jews were following each of them subversively.

Medieval Jews expected the Messiah who came with the clouds of heaven to rule on earth--the whole world:

> He will bring forth [Menahem Ben] Amiel, the Messiah, son of David from prison, for **he will go out from prison to rule** (Eccles 4:14). He will mount him on a cloud, as it is said, **He will come with the clouds of heaven** (Dan 7:13). . . . He will rule over all the countries, and he will be given the kingdom, the glory, and the greatness (cf. Dan 7:14).[19]

Rabbi Hama Ben Hanina said,

> The Son of David will not come until the despicable (hah-zoo-láh, הזלה) kingdom ceases from [ruling] Israel, as it is said, **I will cut off the despicable ones**[20] (hah-zal-zal-eém, הזלזלים) **with pruning hooks** (Isa 18:5), and it is written after it, **In that day gifts will be brought to the Lord of armies of a people that is stretched and bald** (Isa 18:7; bSan 98a).

The disciples were Jesus' emissaries or "fishers of men." They were the ones who mingled with the people, preached to them, spoke to them, argued with them, and recruited some of them for the program. They also functioned as his scouts and occasionally reported back to Jesus all the things that had happened and the things they learned. This meeting at Caesarea Phillipi was ostensibly one of those administrative occasions. Jesus was asking for a news report: "What were the people saying." Of course the people were expecting a messiah. "Who did they think he was?" Peter told him. Then he asked Peter what he, Peter, was telling them about Jesus. Peter said he had been telling them that the Son of man was none of these other biblical heroes but Jesus, himself, who was the Messiah,

---

role of the Messiah.

[19]The text is taken from Cairo Geniza, reported by Marmorstein, "Le Signes du Messie," REJ 52 (1906):176-86. tr. Buchanan, Redemption, p. 505.

[20]The word rendered "despicable ones" really means "shoots," but the rabbi who interpreted this text wanted to insult the Romans, so he gave it a meaning he wanted, based on a word with a similar sound.

the Son of the God of life. In response, Jesus said the apostles had better keep this secret for a while longer.[21] Pamment acknowledged that the Son of man in Matthew was Jesus, but she argued that the Son of man was more than that. It was a representative figure, something like the corporate personality of which Manson spoke.[22] There is nothing in the text that indicates that the "Son of man" was a corporate or representative figure. Jesus was the Son of man as an antitype of the Son of man in Dan 7, but not an antitype of the Saints of the Most High.

Jeremiah or one of the prophets. Dahlberg was puzzled by the appearance of Jeremiah here. Jeremiah does not appear in any of the synoptic parallels. When he checked he observed that Jeremiah was also mentioned twice more in Matthew (Matt 2:17; 27:9). He noticed also that Jeremiah believed that God made him as a "fortified city, and iron pillar, and a bronze wall over all the land" (Jer 1:18-19). This is compared with Matthew's Peter, "a rock" upon which the church would be built.[23] In Judas the Maccabee's famous battle against Nicanor and his troops, he had a vision of Onias. Onias also had a vision of Jeremiah providing Onias with a special golden sword by which he was promised that he could defeat the enemy. This sword was given to Judas who used it victoriously in the battle in which Nicanor was killed (2 Macc 15:11-16).

Who do you say that I am. Delorme said,

> It is strange that it should be Jesus who asks: "Who do you say I am?", and not the disciples who ask: "Tell us who you are".[24]

Jesus did not ask his disciples who they thought Jesus was, but rather what did they tell the people when they were discussing messianology with them. The discussion here was about talk, not simply about opinion. This was not a strange thing for Jesus to ask. He was asking for a report when the apostles returned from one of their missions. He wanted to know what other people were saying and also what the disciples were telling them. After he learned what they had been saying, he told them to stop telling people that he was the Messiah. He

---

[21]G. Bornkamm, Jesus of Nazareth, tr. I. and F. McLuckey (London: Hodder and Stoughton, c1960), p.176-78, said that even though the term "Son of man," was found in Jewish sources, some of these usages could, "without a doubt" be traced back to Jesus himself.

[22]M. Pamment, "The Son of Man in the First Gospel," NTS 29 (1983):116-29.

[23]B. T. Dahlberg, "The Typological use of Jeremiah 1:4-19 in Matthew 16:13-23," JBL 94 (1975):73-75.

[24]J. Delorme, "Intertextualities about Mark," S. Draisma (ed.), Intertextuality in Biblical Writings (Kampen: Uitgeversmaatschappij J. H. Kok, 1989), p. 40.

probably thought this was not the appropriate time to go public with his program. He did not ask them to stop thinking he was the Messiah.

Simon Peter answered. Allison has shown that Peter and Cephas were one and the same person. The person described by one name in the scripture describes also the other.[25]

The Son of the God of life. The medieval Hebrew text reads, "You are the Messiah, which translates into Greek, Kreés-toh, (קריסט"ו), the Son of the God of life which is coming at this age."[26] "This age" here means "the messianic age." Since Jesus was the Messiah, the age in which he lived was the Messianic age, which was to be followed shortly by the age to come.

Because this passage in Matthew is poetry, that which is understood, but not written down is, "I tell them [you are the Messiah]." The Messiah was the Son of God and king by definition. Nathaniel confessed, "Rabbi, you are the Son of God; you are the king of Israel" (John 1:49). Martha said to Jesus, "You are the Messiah, the Son of God" (John 11:27). A king was understood to be God's apostle on earth. He was the one from whom the people could receive God's word and action. He was a legal agent of the Almighty. The expression, "God of life," is often rendered the "living God," as the Greek too thay-oó too zóhn-tos (τοῦ θεοῦ τοῦ ζῶντος) suggests, but the Hebrew is eloh-heém khah-yeém (אלהים חיים), the "God of life." The God of life was the God who was bound by contract to the chosen people.

Both the titles, Son of man and Son of God, occur more times in Matthew than in any other synoptic gospel. Matthew refers to the Son of man 33 times and the Son of God 12 times (Matt 2:15; 3:17; 4:3, 6; 8:29; 14:33; 16:16; 17:5; 26:63; 27:40, 43, 54).

Simon Baryóhnah. Baryona probably does not mean "son of John" or "son of Jonah," as many scholars have thought.[27] Baryona is a title applied to zealots or terrorists. It means Simon the zealot. The word Bar-yóh-nah (בריונא) means an outcast, or a zealot. One of these reportedly sneered at the king's purple coat (ExodR 30.18). Another was described as one who threw rocks at the governor of the city, cursed the magistrate, and said that if anyone would show him where the governor of the city lived that he would show the governor justice (ExodR 30.11)! A nephew of Rabban Johanan ben Zakkai was called Abba Sikra (אבא סקרא) which means "Father of the dagger bearers." He was also called the head

---

[25] D. C. Allison, Jr., "Peter and Cephas: One and the Same," JBL 111 (1992):489-95.

[26] So G. Howard, "The Pseudo-Clementine Writings and Shem-Tob's Hebrew Matthew," NTS 40 (1994):624.

[27] Gundry, Matthew 1-7 (Grand Rapids: Eerdmans, c1994), p. 332, for example.

of the Baryóhni (בריוני ריש) (bGit 56a). Rabbis called the zealots who fought in Jerusalem before it was burned Baryóhni (bGit 56a, 56b).

I will build my church. According to Porter,

> Πέτρος, a masculine noun, is the name given to Simon, but it is usually interpreted to mean a 'stone.' Πάντα κινῆσαι πέτρον, means 'to leave no stone unturned,' (Euripides, Her 1002. Cf. Sophocles, Oed. at Col. 1595), where it means a boulder used for marking boundaries. Although πέτρα is a feminine noun, it is often used for a mass of rock (Euripides, Ion 936: πέτρα κεκρόνια, 'the Acropolis'). 'You are Πέτρος (a name for an individual male and a single stone) and upon this πέτρα (firm foundation of stone) I intend to build my church.'[28]

Most interpreters have rendered this, "You are Peter" or "You are Rocky," assuming that at this point Jesus gave Simon a new name. He may simply have used the word "rock" as a description of his character in relationship to the name he already held, "Peter."

Wilcox has made a thought-provoking proposal. He noted that the term "rock" in the FT refers to God, rather than a human being. In later literature it applies to the Messiah or king. For example, as an interpretation of Ps 118:22, "The rock which the builders rejected has become the head of the corner," the rabbis said,

> The child whom the builders abandoned has appeared among the sons of Jesse and merits becoming a king and ruler" (TgJon Ps 118.22).

They took the rock to mean David. Correspondingly, Wilcox thought the rock on which the church should be built would be Jesus.[29] This requires an assumption that the text was originally in Hebrew or Aramaic and misleadingly translated into Greek.

In Greek the most reasonable assumption is that the rock was Peter, and since Peter was one of the apostles he was legally identical to Jesus, so if Peter was the rock, so was Jesus. Peter was not a king like David, but like David and Jesus, he had the legal authority to speak in behalf of God. The later Petrine branch of the Christian church assumed that the authority was given to Peter and

[28] So S. E. Porter, "Vague Verbs, Periphrastics, and Matt 16:19," Filologia Neotestamentaria 2 (1988):156-57).

[29] M. Wilcox, "Peter and the Rock: A Fresh Look at Matthew XVI.17-19," NTS 22 (1975):73-88.

transferred to the bishops (DidasApos 9.27), and even the anti-Petrine statement in Matt 16:23 presumes a favorable attribute to Peter that it was composed to negate. Fuller said that these were not the words of Jesus, but the additions of the later church.[30] Fornberg thought Peter was here conceived as some kind of successor to the high priest. The rock was an antitype for the temple rock and the keys of the Kingdom were the new temple keys. The church was to be the antitype for the temple.[31]

This confession of faith indicates that Peter was a special apostle of Jesus. Matthew lists Peter first among those Jesus called to be his disciples (Matt 4:18). He was also listed first among the 12 who were commissioned as apostles (Matt 10:2). He alone was the basis for the continuing church. It is probably true that the church continued because Jesus had organized a group of authorized agents to act in his name and with his authority. With these trained leaders, who had been supplied with Jesus' most important teachings in the form of chreias and parables, and with a sound financial basis upon which to continue the program Jesus had begun, the church continued as an apostolic movement. Peter was certainly one of those apostles responsible for the continuance of the church, but so were Paul, James, and John, and others.

This poem was composed by members of the Petrine sect of Christianity, out of respect for their founder. There is no need, however, to assume that this was written late just because the word "church" was mentioned. There were communities that were called "the many," (hah-rahb-beém, הרבים), "the assembly" (yáh-khad, יחד), or "the called out" group (kah-háhl), קהל) in Judaism in pre-NT times. The Greek translation for the Hebrew kah-háhl (קהל) in the LXX was ehk-klay-seé-ah (ἐκκλησία), the same word rendered "church" in this passage. This word also means the assembly or the "called out" group. It could have been the name given to the group while Jesus was still alive.[32] The church was established by authorized apostles who formed a legal corporation in the name of Jesus, the Messiah. Had Jesus and his original apostles not been acquainted with the proper legal offices and forms necessary for agency and corporation, the body of Christ would probably have been concluded with the death of Jesus, but one of the basic rules of a corporation is that it is immortal. Members within the corporation may all be replaced, but the body continues as a legal fiction, having all of the legal authority in court that an individual might have.

Not everyone has the authority or ability to build a church or a temple. According to 2 Sam 7:13 God told David that his son, Solomon, would be the

---

[30]R. H. Fuller, "The 'Thou Art Peter' Pericope and the Easter Appearances," McCormQuart 20 (1967):309-15.

[31]T. Fornberg, "Peter--The High Priest of the new Covenant," EastAsiaJournTheol 4 (1986):113-21.

[32]So also Hagner, Word Biblical Commentary: Matthew 14-28 (Dallas: Word, c1995), p. 471.

one who would build a temple to God's name. Rabbis thought the servant of Isaiah was also the Messiah (TgJon Isa 52.13), and that he would build the temple (TgJon Isa 53.5). The fact that Jesus planned to build a new church suggests that he expected to be not only the Son of man, as Peter confessed, but also the new Solomon, the Messiah, and Son of God. These are all different names for the same office. The midrashic allusions in this poem show that Peter was the new Abraham, and Peter's successors would be blessed as Abraham's children were; the church was the new temple Christ would build; Peter had the kind of authority a son of David had; and the new house of David was the Kingdom of God. This does not mean that the early church instantly became pro-Petrine. There never has been one church or one Judaism. With a religion that is based on a doctrine of election there has never been an agreement among the saints on who, precisely, were the elect. Many different sects claimed that privilege at the same time, and each one for itself alone. While the Petrine church claimed Peter as the rock, the new Abraham, and the one through whom Christ would build his new church, there were also Paulinists, Jacobites, and others who disagreed.

The gates of Hades. The term, Hades, never occurs in the FT. It is a Greek concept of a region under the earth ruled by Pluto. When people died they were supposedly taken to the shore where a boat took the righteous to the Isles of the Blessed and the sinners to Hades. Here the expression, "gates of Hades" is given, as Allison and Jeremias argue, to refer to all the forces and powers, demonic and political, that might attempt to destroy the church.[33] There are some problems with the expression "gates" that "overpower." Gates normally do not overpower; they either close or open. Their role is rather passive. Why was the term "gates" used at all? Many suggestions have been made. None of which is satisfactory. Sometimes "gates" of a city are used to refer to the entire city.[34] Somehow the image intended is that of Hades, surrounded by a wall with gates. It is set against the Kingdom of Heaven, which also has walls and gates. These two kingdoms are opposed to one another, and Peter has the keys to the gates that unlock the Kingdom of Heaven.

The keys of the Kingdom. The archangel Michael was also held to be the one who controlled the keys to the Kingdom of Heaven (3 Bar 11.2). When Isaiah prophesied that Eliakim would succeed his father on the throne he said the Lord would clothe him with royal garments, place a [staff] of authority in his hand, and put the key of the house of David on his shoulder. He would be given authority to open and no one could close, to close and no one could open (Isa 22:20-22). Keys are ordinarily related to doors, so the image is of a king with

[33]Allison, Matthew, pp. 632-33.

[34]J. Marcus, "The Gates of Hades and the Keys of the Kingdom (Matt 16:18-19)," CBQ 50 (1988):446-47.

keys who is able to open and close doors. The "doors" Eliakim would open and close, however, did not swing on steel hinges. This was a metaphor showing the unique power that Eliakim received when he became king. He could not only pardon and punish, but he could tax or remit taxes, declare war or establish peace; he could make or cancel laws.

The targum to this passage says the key of the house of David would be placed in Eliakim's hand rather than on his shoulder. One of the rabbis interpreted the role of Eliakim in Isa 22 as a teacher, "All [students] sit before him and learn from him; whatever he opens no one closes" (Sifre Deut 32.25, 138a).

The term "key" was used metaphorically. There were "keys of knowledge" (Luke 11:22), "keys of death and Hades" (Rev 1:18). It was no physical object that King Eliakim carried on his shoulder, but the responsibility of the government, just as Isaiah prophesied of the new king, "The government shall be upon his shoulder" (Isa 9:6). Pseudo-Clement called the traditional word of truth the "key of the Kingdom of Heaven" (Recog 54). When the temple burned, Baruch reported that the priests confessed that they had not been trustworthy, so they hurled the keys up to heaven for the Lord to control (AbothRabN 4; ParJer 4.4-5). Rabbi Jonathan said there were three keys which the Lord would not entrust to any agent: 1) the key of the womb, 2) the key of the tombs at the resurrection of the dead, and 3) the key of rain (Mid Ps 78.5 #173b). When the early Petrine church claimed that Jesus gave Peter the keys of the kingdom they were asserting their belief that Peter had the authority that had earlier been given to Jesus. It was Peter, rather than James or John, who was really the new successor to Jesus. He alone would be Christ's legal agent.

Whatever you bind on earth. With the authority that was symbolized by the keys was given also the power to bind and loose. Also in the Book of Revelation an angel had a key to the pit and a huge chain with which to bind Satan. After Satan had been bound for 1,000 years he was to be released (Rev 20:1-7). When Satan, the devil, or the demons were bound the chosen people were released; when Satan, the devil, or the demons were released, the chosen people were bound. When the disciples were given apostolic authority they were authorized to throw out unclean spirits (Matt 10:1). This was the same as having authority to bind the demons (Matt 18:18).[35]

Ancients had a custom of preparing bowls, about the size of cereal bowls by writing incantations in them that were designed to bind certain demons to prevent them from acting against certain people. These bowls were then sealed with pitch, joining two bowls together so that one formed a lid for the other, and all of the demons would be sealed inside and thereby be unable to function. They were bound inside by this magic. The angels in the Book of Revelation who poured out curses against people on earth may have unsealed these bowls,

---

[35]See R. H. Hiers, "'Binding' and 'Loosing': The Matthaean Authorizations," JBL 104 (1985):233-50, for the binding and loosing of demons.

releasing the demons who had been bound. The voice that came from heaven, ordering the angels to pour out the wrath of God which had been bound by the bowls (Rev 16:1-2) was apparently God, who, of course, had the power to bind and loose.[36]

Josephus said that when Alexandria became queen of Judah, she made peace with the Pharisees. In so doing she allowed them complete freedom to recall from exile whomever they chose and to exile whomever they wished. They could both release and bind (loó-ain teh kai des-maín, λύειν τε καὶ δεσμεῖν) (War 1.111). They had legal authority both to punish and to pardon. Josephus told of the destructive way in which Pharisees exercised their authority, killing however many Jews they wished. Matthew held that the Pharisees and scribes had keys to the kingdom, and they used them only to lock people out (Matt 23:13). The targumist did not expect someone in authority to forgive sins gratis. He assumed that the good or evil works a person did constituted the deciding factor that would obtain forgiveness for one's sins or retain this guilt for the sinner until the Day of Judgment when guilt would be acknowledged and punished. Good works might cancel evil works in the heavenly record.

In secular context, binding and loosing can mean releasing or putting into prison, freeing, or killing. It is a merismus expression used to include all punitive or rewarding authority. Peter, according to this text, was given the same authority the Pharisees had, only his authority was over the Kingdom of Heaven which would take place in the age to come. His judgment determined which of the parties to the contract would be admitted into the new kingdom when the land was restored. Since Peter held divine legal authority God was obligated to confirm Peter's decisions. This means he functioned as God's legal agent or apostle who acted in the name of, at the authority of, and at the responsibility of his principal, who, through Jesus, was God. He had the same authority as the judges whom Moses appointed (Deut 1:15-17).[37] Peter's authority was believed to have been extended to bishops who had the power to bind and loose, punish and pardon (DidasApos pp. 55, 96 [Oxford, 1929]). Binding and loosing included pardoning criminals or punishing them. Those to be punished would not be admitted into the sinless Kingdom of Heaven.

This passage is not the only witness to binding and to releasing authority. Also in Matthew's gospel, Jesus is reported as having said to his disciples, "I tell you under oath, whatever you bind on earth will be bound in heaven, and whatever you release on earth will be released in heaven" (Matt 18:18). The expression "in heaven" can mean either in the skies where the treasury of merits and demerits are kept or "by Heaven," "through the instrument of Heaven," or "by

---

[36]See further Buchanan, The Book of Revelation: Its Introduction and Prophecy (Lewiston: Mellen, c1993), pp. 398-402.

[37]See further J. D. M. Derrett, "Binding and Loosing (Matt 16:19; 18:18; John 29:23)," JBL 102 (1983):112-17. See also H. W. Basser, "Derrett's 'Binding' Reopened," JBL 104 (1985):297-300.

God." Apostles were all legal agents of Jesus and therefore had authority to speak in the name of Jesus, at the responsibility of Jesus, and in his behalf. Since Jesus was the principal, and the apostles were agents, they all had power of attorney to act in his behalf, and their action was considered valid. The fact that they were legal agents meant that they had authority to bind and loose in behalf of the principal. Since Jesus was also an agent of God, that which the apostles did was legally done by God. Their judgment was legally God's or "Heaven's" judgment. This dialogue between Peter and Jesus was really a dramatization of Peter's apostolic authority. The followers of the apostle John or any other apostle could be expected to accept the same authority for him.

Say that he was the Messiah. This probably means that they should not say any more that he was the Messiah, because Peter, when asked what he had been saying, responded that he already had been telling people that Jesus was the Messiah (Matt 16:17). Other disciples had probably been giving the same testimony, and Jesus evidently suspected that before, but once this hunch was confirmed by Peter's confession, Jesus warned them to stop this part of their program. After all, he had already attracted the attention of Herod (Matt 14:1-2).

TEXT

Matthew	First Testament
[21]From that time on Jesus began to show his disciples that it was necessary for him to go away to Jerusalem, to suffer many things from the elders, chief priests, and scribes, to be killed, and to be	Come, let us return to Yahowah, for he has torn, and he will heal us. He has struck, and he will bandage us. After two days he will revive us;
raised on the third day.	**on the third day** he will **raise** us that we may live before him (Hos 6:1-2).
	Look! I will open your graves and **raise** you from your graves, my people, and I will bring you to the land of Israel. You will know that I am Yahowah when I open your graves and **raise** you (Ezek 37:12-13).

TECHNICAL DETAILS

One of the good NT texts (Bezai [D]) has, instead of "on the third day," "after three days." Both of these readings reflect dependence upon Hos 6:2. The readings other than Bezai are closer to Hosea's Masoretic text. This is the first anticipation of the passion narrative in the Gospel of Matthew. Others are 17:22-23; 20:17-19; 26:2).

COMMENTARY

Go away to Jerusalem, to suffer. It is difficult to judge whether Jesus really taught precisely this way or whether this was added by the later church, after he had suffered. It is quite likely that Jesus taught his disciples something like this sometime in his ministry, probably after the death of John the Baptist. Like other Jews of his day, he undoubtedly knew there were two scriptural passages showing what was required to be counted as righteousness. One of these was Phineas for his zeal in killing foreigners and mingling parties to the contract (Num 25; Ps 106:31-32), and the other was Abraham for his faith (Genesis 15).

Before the death of John, Jesus and John probably planned to raise an undercover army, overthrow Rome, and become the new king and high priest of the land. They both would have believed that this was God's will, and they were fulfilling the requirements of the scripture. Once John was killed, however, their plan was frustrated, and Jesus probably restudied the scripture and watched for signs from Heaven to direct his campaign. What then was the role of the Messiah? Was he to fight like Joshua, David, and the Hasmoneans, or was he to suffer like the servant in Babylon? His struggle over these things is reflected in the temptation narratives and in the Gethsemane report. Disciples probably went to Jerusalem prepared to engage in warfare. There were probably hundreds of secret troops, armed, and ready to fulfill the commands. They were probably stationed in strategic places, ready for final directions which would have reached them through coded signals.

Jesus, however, probably had some reservations. He wanted to be sure that his actions were in agreement with God's will. He apparently went to Jerusalem prepared for two possibilities, depending on his direction from God. He was looking for clues that the time had arrived for God to restore the kingdom. If any of these had appeared, he probably would have carried out his planned strategies. The disappointment came when there was no ripe fruit on the fig tree in the Kidron Valley. That was a bad sign. Since he received no sign directing his action, he finally accepted the antitype of the servant of Isaiah. Because he believed that all of these cyclical, typological events were predestined, he knew that whatever the future held, it would be necessary to fit the preplanned form. It might be necessary for him to go to Jerusalem, not to rule, but to suffer.

In either event the Son of man might be expected to suffer. The first Son of man, Judas the Maccabee, led the Hasmonean Rebellion against the Syrian Greeks nearly 200 years earlier. Judas was successful in his efforts to gain control of the temple after the famous battle of Beth-horon, but he later suffered and died in his conflict with the foreigners at the Battle of Berzetho (Ant 12.420-34). As an antitype Son of man, Jesus might have reasoned that suffering and death was part of the requirement of his office, if not because he was the new Son of man, then because he considered himself also to be the antitype of the Suffering Servant of Isa 52-53. At least by the time of Matthew the Messiah was called the king, the Son of God, the Son of man, and the Suffering Servant. Whether or not it was at the hands of the chief priests and scribes or the Romans, it was necessary for Jesus to go to Jerusalem and there suffer and possibly be killed.

To be raised on the third day. This phrase clearly was quoted from Hos 6:2, and it has obviously had some influence in establishing the doctrine of resurrection. Since all prophecy was prophesied only for the days of the Messiah, and since there is nothing in the world that is not in the scriptures, it would be normal for followers of Jesus to have studied the scriptures after his death to learn what was prophesied concerning a messiah who had been crucified. Hosea said God would revive the parties to the contract after two days, and on the third day he would raise them. This was evidently prophesied only for the days of the Messiah, in the judgment of the early church, and the one to be raised was the Messiah. Another prophecy that might have influenced the text is Ezekiel's prophecy of the Valley of Dry Bones. The spirit breathed on these bones and they came together, were covered with flesh, and stood erect as a mighty army (Ezek 37:1-11).

Paul seems to have had Hos 6:2 in mind when he said, "He was raised on the third day, according to the scriptures" (1 Cor 15:4). This was not the only proof Paul gave for believing in the resurrection, but it was certainly an influential one, and it was a normal conclusion on the basis of accepted exegesis of NT times. According to gospel reports, Jesus was not really raised on the third day but on the second day, or after two nights and one day, from Friday night to Sunday morning. This, however, was close enough to satisfy apologetic Jews and Christians. It was not nearly so far off as Daniel was with his 490 years that were really only 422.

TEXT

[22]Then Peter, after he had taken [Jesus] [aside], began to rebuke him, saying, "[May God be] gracious to you, Lord! This shall not be for you!" [23][Jesus], however, after he turned, said to Peter, "Get behind me, Satan! You are a stumbling block to me, because you do not consider the things of God but the things of human beings."

COMMENTARY

This shall not be for you! A firm oath of refusal, such as the following:
Far be it from me! Far be it if I should swallow up or destroy (2 Sam 20:20). **Far be it from me, Yahowah, that I should do this!** (2 Sam 23:17). As Plummer said of Peter,

> If he is first in rank and first in confession of faith, he is also first in tempting, and first in denying, his Master.[38]

Get behind me, Satan. Disciples and followers were always expected to follow behind their teachers and leaders. When, according to the report, Peter started to correct Jesus, taking issue with him, he was acting like an equal or even a superior, so Jesus told him to take his proper place as a subordinate. The same author who pictured Peter as Jesus' primary apostle to whom he entrusted the authority of punishing and rewarding, including and excluding people from the Kingdom of Heaven, can hardly have written at the same time a claim that Jesus rejected Peter and called him "Satan." The one who received revelations from God would not be accused of being Satan by the same author. This verse is a later addition made by some anti-Petrine Christian.

The things of God. This says that Peter really did not have any legal authority to speak in behalf of God as an apostle. It was not the heavenly Father who revealed this to Peter; it was flesh and blood (contra Matt 16:17). Evidently this is part of the anti-Petrine addition.

TEXT

24 Then Jesus said to his disciples,
"If anyone wants to follow me,
let him deny himself,
let him take up his cross,
and let him follow me,
25 for whoever wants to save his soul will lose it,
but whoever loses his soul for my sake will find it" (partial doublet in Matt 10:39).

COMMENTARY

If anyone wants to follow me. The word "follow" is a walking term. It is sometimes used in this gospel to report someone actually traveling on foot, but it also has a legal or metaphorical meaning. One of the Hebrew words for law is "halakah" (hah-lah-káh, הלכה) which means that observing the law was a way of walking or conducting one's life. The first label given to Christians was "the way," meaning the way or road on which people walked. A student who "followed" a teacher is one who learned the teacher's law and observed it. He walked in the same path as his teacher. Jesus invited disciples to follow him.

---

[38]A. Plummer, An Exegetical Commentary on the Gospel according to St. Matthew (London: Stock, 1909), p. 234.

Let him deny himself. "Let him deny himself what?" the reader asks. The answer is probably that he should deny his present legal identity. He should give up his family, his political and economic position, his property and money, his community status, political offices, and reputation--all of those good things that set him off in the community as a person of rank and status. All of that constitutes his "self." A person's death was only considered a demise. The body decayed, but all of the rest of one's existence was transferred legally to the heirs, and they constituted his continuing life. When a man joined a monastery he was required to give up all of this. This was another way of saying that he denied himself. He would have no continuing existence outside of the monastic community.

Let him take up his cross. This commandment made before the crucifixion of Jesus could not have meant, "Let yourself be crucified." The cross or chi (X) in Greek looks like the last letter of the alphabet in Hebrew in ancient script. This is the tau (ת), which does not look like a chi today. This commandment is related to Ezekiel's narrative (Ezek 9:1-4). The Lord commanded that some destroyers should be sent through the city of Jerusalem to kill every person there, with one exception. First, a man with a pen and an ink well should go through and mark all those who lamented the sins of Jerusalem. The destroyers should spare these, because these were the righteous. In Rev 14:1-5, these segregated saints who were to be spared were specified as monks who had not defiled themselves with women. They were not to be crucified, but they wore the mark of the cross on their foreheads. This seems to be the nature of those whom Jesus asked to wear the mark of the cross. Those who followed Jesus were the ones who took vows of poverty, celibacy, and obedience. They gave up all of their legal and secular claims to status, accepted the mark of the monastic order, and followed Jesus, fulfilling the teachings he instructed.

Whoever wants to save his soul. Matt 16:25 is a chiasm. This is a well-known Semitic form based on the Greek chi (=X). The X is made by drawing a line between the two words "save" and the two words "lose."

The soul seems to be that legal part of a person's being that distinguishes him or her. It is the name, family, position, rank, wealth, identity, and other things of importance which people have if they are blessed. The person who treasures this and wants to keep it cannot be a member of a monastery.

Will lose it. The pronouns in this saying are tricky. The soul that a person loses by trying to save it may not be the same identity. He gives up his membership in the secular community so that he can have membership in the monastery. That is one possibility, but there are others. It may mean that the person who tried to build up and preserve his secular status in this gentile age would lose that very identity when the administrations changed. When the kingdom came, and Romans were overthrown, all of the Roman leaders would be out of work if they were allowed to live at all.

Whoever loses his soul. In the new age when the Jews/Christians ruled, those monks who had given up their status in the gentile government and community would all hold key positions. When powers change, the spoils belong to the victors. Those who had been first in the old administration become last when their enemies rule. Monks would lose their souls in the Roman kingdom, but they would find them in the Kingdom of Heaven.

TEXT

26For what will it benefit a man
if he gains the whole world
but forfeits his soul?
Or what will a man give
in exchange for his soul?

COMMENTARY

If he gains the whole world. Many Jews in Jesus' time held important positions in the Roman government, business, industry, and shipping. When Jesus asked these leaders to take all that they had and give to the community that called itself "the poor," he was asking them to give up a great deal. Nevertheless, he was able to persuade some of these to do just that. Like Jesus, they became convinced that the cycle of times was just about to change. If the Jews were going to be the new world rulers, it would be important to be a Jew at that time. People paid huge prices to become Roman citizens. Suppose a person became a wealthy Roman citizen and then there was no Roman government? How would all of this benefit him?

What will a man give? In ancient society, there were few individual values. People were known by their family, their community, their country. In such a situation life would be tragic if a person had no country, family, or identity. For all of this, people willingly fought and died. Few would want to put their souls on the market.

TEXT

Poetry

27For the Son of man is about to come
in the glory of his Father
with his angels,

and then he gives back to each
according to his work.[39]

Midrash

Matthew	First Testament and Other Jewish Literature
27For **the Son of man is about to come** in	Now look! With the clouds of heaven one like **a son of man was coming** until he reached the Ancient of Days, and he was brought near before him. To him was given the
the glory of his Father	governing authority, **the glory**, and the kingdom (Dan 7:13-14).
with his angels, and	Then Yahowah God **will come**, and all of his holy ones with him (Zech 14:5).
	The kingdom, the governing authority, and the greatness of the kingdom under all heaven will be given to the people of the holy ones (saints or angels) of the Most High (Dan 7:27).
Then he **gives back to each according to his work.**	To you, Lord, belongs contract faithfulness, for you **pay back to each according to his work** (Ps 62:12).
	If you say, "We did not know this," does not the one who tests the minds understand? The one who guards your soul knows, and he **returns to a person according to his work** (Ps 24:12).
28I tell you under oath that there are some standing here who will not	If you exist (fueris) you will see; if you are alive you will often be

[39]C. F. Burney, The Poetry of our Lord (Oxford: Clarendon, 1925). p. 142, fn. 1, concluded that the Matthaean form was the earliest form, and Mark was secondary.

taste death until they see the Son of man coming in his kingdom.

amazed, because the age is speeding through swiftly (4 Ezra 4.26).

COMMENTARY

The glory of his Father.[40] This is a coded and religious way of saying that the Messiah was about to take his place on the throne of David at Jerusalem. This is the reason why it was important to be on the right side when the powers change. Jesus thought they were about to change. It was not something for which they might wait a whole lifetime and then never experience. The new Son of man would be an antitype of the Son of man in Dan 7. That Son of man came up to the Ancient of Days to receive dominion, glory, and the kingdom at the same time the Greeks were being driven out of Palestine, and Judas the Maccabee was in charge of the new government. With the new Son of man would come the same events and consequences. Rome would be forced to back off, and the Messiah would appear before the Ancient of Days, his Father, in glory, and be awarded control of the Palestinian government.

Dan 7 does not seem to tell about the Son of man coming with his angels, but it tells of the **saints of the Most High** (kah-dee sháy el-yoh-neén, קדישי עליונין). These "holy ones of the Most High" could also be understood as heavenly angels. When the Hasmonean Son of man received his governmental authority, the Jewish people also received their governmental authority. Judas was the leader, and they were the citizens. Judas and his contemporary Jewish supporters all received the kingdom together. According to Dan 7:14, 18, Judas and the holy ones of the Most High received their judicial award from the heavenly court together. Since Jesus expected the same things to happen again, he expected to come with his contemporary holy ones of God before the Ancient of Days, his heavenly Father, and then he and they would both receive the judicial award which meant there would be a new Beth-horon victory, and new temple cleansing, and a new Hanukkah.

He gives back to each. It was probably with careful intent that the poet picked up the word "give" that was used in relationship to a person's soul, in the previous verse, and repeated it as the function of the Son of man. Here is the reminder that there would be a judgment before the new administration would be installed. Part of the function of a king is to act as judge. He gives good rewards to those who helped him to acquire possession of the country. He punishes those who stood in his way or opposed his plans. When Judas the Maccabee began to expel the Greeks, one of the first things he did was to have Jason, the high priest, killed, to retaliate for the works Jason had done. His works for which Judas paid him back was killing 60 of the khah-see-deém (חסידים). When Judas and his troops

---

[40]On this see Buchanan, To the Hebrews, 38-51.

came to a town called Emphron, they first asked permission to go through the town. The people there blocked all their gates and entrances against Judas, so he and his troops broke down the gates, entered the town, killed the males, burned the town, and went through over the tops of the dead bodies (Ant 12.345-49). That is the way leaders responded to opposition in NT times.

Who will not taste death. This meant that Jesus expected the Son of man to come and drive out the Romans during the lifetimes of the people standing there. This has been a problem to exegetes who do not like to admit what this obviously says. There is no provision here for a distant "eschaton" that should be anticipated 2,000 years later.

CHAPTER SEVENTEEN

MATTHEAN PARALLELS TO THE HEXATEUCH

Matthew	Deuteronomy
Jesus **went up to the mountain** with Peter, James, and John. **He returned to find the** disciples unable to heal a boy possessed of demons. Jesus **was angry**, because the disciples lacked faith. Said **prayer** could move mountains (17:1-20).	Moses **went up to the mountain** to receive the commandments. **He returned to find the** Israelites worshiping a golden calf. Moses broke the tablets **in anger**. **Prayer** for Aaron and the people (9:9-29).
	"You are the **sons** of the Lord your God." Rules for giving tithes for the temple and for Levites and others who did not have land (14:1-28).
Procedure for dealing with a man who had sinned within the community. If he did not listen, the sin was to be confirmed by **two or three witnesses**. If he refused to listen even to the church he was to be excommunicated. "Wherever two or three are gathered in my name, there I am in the midst of them" (18:15-20).	Procedure for dealing with a man who had broken contract. At the evidence of **two or three witnesses**, he should be put to death. Provisions made for judges and priests to see that justice was rendered (17:1-13).

COMMENTARY

Matthew has used Deuteronomy so thoroughly that some scholars think that the entire gospel is a Deuteronomy, just as others think the entire gospel is a new Genesis. In addition to formal quotations there are more than 100 allusions and implied references in Matthew to Deuteronomy--even more explicit references than from Isaiah or the Psalms (Deut 13, Isa 10, Ps 9).[1] Both of these have overlooked the hexateuchal outline in Matthew, but both have noticed these important Torah contacts.

TEXT

Matthew	First Testament and other Jewish Literature
17:1 After **six days** Jesus took Peter, James, and his brother John, and he brought them to a high **mountain** [where they could be] alone.	**Moses** went up to the **mountain**, and a **cloud covered** the **mountain**, and the glory of the Lord dwelled in a **tent** on Mount Sinai, and the **cloud covered** it **six days**, and God called to Moses out of the midst of **the cloud . . .** (Exod 24:15-16).
2 Then he was transformed before them, and **his face shone** like the sun, and his clothing became white as the light.	When he came down from the **mountain Moses** did not know that the skin of **his face shone**, because he had been speaking with God (Exod 34:29).
3 Now look! **Moses** and Elijah appeared to them, talking together with him. 4 Then Peter answered and said to Jesus, "Lord, it is good for us to be here. If you want, I will make here three **tents**--one for you,	**In the cloud** of glory of my Shekinah I made the children of Israel live in something like **tents** at the time I brought them out, redeemed, from the land of Egypt (TgNeof Lev 23.43).
one for **Moses**, and one for Elijah." 5 While he was still talking, Look! A shining **cloud overshadowed** them, and look! a voice from **the cloud**	You shall live in **tents** for seven days; all who are native to Israel will live in **tents** (Lev 23:42).
	The **cloud covered** the **tent** of meeting, and the glory of Yahowah filled the dwelling, and **Moses** was not able to enter the **tent** of meeting,

[1] Statistics are from T. Brodie, "Fish, Temple Tithe, and Remission: The God-based Generosity of Deuteronomy 14-15 as one Component of Matt 17:22-18:35," RB 99 (1992):698-99. For the Genesis hypothesis see B.T. Viviano, "The Genres of Matthew 1-2: Light from 1 Timothy 1:4," RB 97 (1990):31-53.

	because the **cloud** and the glory of Yahowah dwelled **over** it (Exod 40:34-35).
was speaking:	The Lord said to me, "You are **my son.** Today I gave you birth" (Ps 2:7).
"This **is my beloved son**	**He said,** Daniel, **beloved** man,
in whom I **am well pleased.**	Here **is my** servant, whom I support, my chosen one, **in whom** my soul **is well pleased** (Isa 42:1).
Pay attention to him."	**Pay attention to** the words I **am speaking** to you. **Arise and** stand [before me] (Dan 10:11).
	The Lord your God will raise up a prophet of your brothers from your midst. **Pay attention to him** (Deut 18:15).
6When the disciples heard [that], they fell upon their **faces**	I was [sent] trembling on my **face,** with my face to the ground. Now look! A hand **touched** me and raised me to my hands and knees (Dan 10:9-10).
and were terrified. 7Then Jesus came, **touched** them,	When Aaron and the Israelites saw Moses, look! The skin of his **face shone, and they were afraid** (Exod 34:30).
and **said,** 8"**Arise and** **do not be afraid."**	He **said** to me, **"Do not be afraid,** Daniel" (Dan 10:11).
When they **raised** their **eyes** they **saw** no one except Jesus, himself, alone.	I **raised** my **eyes and** **saw**--Now look! A man dressed in linen (Dan 10:5).

TECHNICAL DETAILS

This unit has parallels both in Luke and Mark, and there are several of the so-called "minor agreements" of Matthew and Luke against Mark. Both have the following words that Mark omitted: **his face** (Matt 17:2; Luke 9:29), **look, Moses and Elijah**, and **him** (Matt 17:3; Luke 9:30), **he said** (Matt 17:4; Luke 9:33); **while he was talking**, and **them** (Matt 17:5; Luke 9:24), **saying** (Matt 17:5; Luke 9:35), and **they were afraid** (Matt 17:6; Luke 9:34). These two have also agreed to omit the following words in Mark: untranslatable article ton (Mark 9:2) and **. . . very, such as no bleacher on earth is able thus to bleach them** (Mark 9:3). These facts provide problems for those who subscribe to the two-source hypothesis.

The reader has only to observe the number of bold face words in the two textual columns above to realize that Matthew has composed a midrash based primarily on references to Moses on the mountain (Exod 24, 34, and 40; Deut 18) and Daniel's vision (Dan 10), with a few references to Psalms and Leviticus. The case was made still stronger with a text from the prophets and another from the Psalms, one from a suffering servant passage and the other from an enthronement psalm. This Matthean midrash was artfully composed in the belief that all prophecy was prophesied only for the days of the Messiah. The author had no historical data at his disposal to prove to him that this event actually happened. The narrative was doctrinally deduced. Like the vision of Dan 10, this was a vision.[2]

There are many textual variants in all three synoptic gospels. Some have the plural ("let us make"), and some omit "if you want." O'Callaghan finally accepted the Matthean text as most nearly original, including the singular "I will make."[3] Carlston argued that this is a misplaced resurrection narrative.[4] Pedersen called Jesus the "one who bears the revelation" (Offenbarungsträger) and noted the coherence of this revelation with those at the baptism, temptations, the confession of Peter at Caesarea Phillipi, the passion, and the confession of the Roman officer at the crucifixion.[5]

---

[2]J. Murphy-O'Conner, "The Structure of Matthew XIV-XVII," RB 82 (1975):379 observed the close literary relationship between Matt 17:6-9 and Dan 10:9-14.

[3]J. O'Callaghan, "Discusión en Mt 17,4," Bib 65 (1984):91-93.

[4]C. E. Carlston, "Transfiguration and Resurrection," JBL 80 (1961):233-40.

[5]S. Pedersen, "Die Proklamation Jesu des Eschatologischen Offenbarungsträgers (Mt xvii 1-13)," NovT 17 (1975):254. The Apokalypse of Peter 1.19-21 expanded homiletically on this text, picturing Jesus scolding Peter as he did at Caesarea Phillipi, and identifying his ideas with those of Satan.

COMMENTARY

Six days. Why six days rather than three or ten? Luke 9:28 has eight. The reason is simple. This midrash was designed to picture Jesus as a new Moses. When Moses was on the mountain to receive the commandments the cloud covered the mountain for six days. The author of this midrash used words and phrases from Exod 24, some of which involved the "six days."

Peter, James, and his brother John. When Moses went up Mount Sinai, he took with him Aaron, Nadab, and Abihu, and the 70 elders. Later he left the elders and went ahead with just the three. Finally Moses was pictured on the mountain top alone (Exod 24:9-18).

To a high mountain. Most modern scholars think this took place on Mount Hermon (modern Golan Heights).[6] Hagner correctly held that it would not have been Mount Tabor, because that was the scene of a Roman military camp at the time (War 2.573; 4.54-55).[7] The mountain, however, may have appeared in the text as a midrashic necessity rather than a historical and geographical one. It is obvious to anyone who sees this narrative in comparison with the FT and targum passages listed here that this pericope was composed in conscious imitation of the revelation of God to Moses on Mount Sinai. The scene was on a mountain; there was a cloud that covered them; the voice of God came from the cloud; the face of Jesus shone just as Moses' face shone when he came down from the mountain; and six days were involved in the story just as at Sinai where the cloud hovered for six days. When the voice came from the cloud it spoke in scriptural terms, using texts from the law, the prophets, and the Psalms. Like the children of Israel who saw that Moses' face shone, the disciples were also afraid when they saw that Jesus' face shone.

His face shone like the sun. This is an antitype of Moses, whose face shone after he had been with God on the mountain and in the cloud. There is a remote possibility that "the sun" alluded to the sun disk with its divine significance, just as it did in "The Song of Deborah" after the victory of the Israelites against Sisera: **Thus may all your enemies perish, Lord, but his friends, like the sun [disk], rising in its power** (Judges 5:31)! Allison has shown that the claim that some leader's face shone was originally attributed to Moses and was continued through

[6] A. Plummer, An Exegetical Commentary on the Gospel according to S. Matthew (London: Stock, c1920), p. 238.

[7] D. A. Hagner, Word Biblical Commentary: Matthew 14-28 (Dallas: Word Books, c1995), p. 492.

the ages to be attributed to various Jewish and Christian leaders.[8] Enoch said the light of the Lord shone on the faces of the holy, righteous, and elect (1 Enoch 38.4).

His clothing became white as light. This gives the impression that his clothing changed color while he was wearing it. This is an important reference to the Ancient of Days whose clothing was white as snow (Dan 7:9). The Ancient of Days was God. The one whose clothing became white was God's legal agent.

I will make here three tents. The word for tents is σκηνάς (skenas) which is a loan word from the Hebrew shah-káyn, (שכן) which means to dwell in tents. The Hebrew noun for this is sheh-kee-náh (שכינה). It is a wilderness term, taken from the nomadic way of life when people lived in tents, and the Lord was thought also to live in the tent of meeting. The glory of the Lord was said to dwell in a tent (wa-yish-kóhn, וישכן) on Mount Sinai (Exod 24:16), and the presence of the Lord was associated with the tent of testimony (Exod 33:7-11).

Tents were normally associated with the Feast of the Tabernacles. After Solomon dedicated the temple, and when Nehemiah reestablished the temple in Jerusalem, this was a feast during which Jews recalled an earlier time when God dwelled in the tent of meeting in the wilderness. Jews anticipated the gathering of the dispersed Jews to the promised land when the glory of the Lord would again appear, and the cloud would be revealed as it had been originally disclosed to Moses (2 Macc 2:7-10). This was all part of the background of tradition and text upon which this Matthean unit was composed. When all of these midrashic details are considered, Del Agua is probably correct in holding that this is not a report of a historical event, but rather a composition based on texts.[9] It was customary for Jews and early Christians to express their convictions in midrashic form, visions, or both. Christian convictions about Jesus and his authority as a Messiah were told in relationship to his baptism (Matt 3), the confession of Peter (Matt 16), the transfiguration (Matt 17), and the scene at the cross (Matt 27).

Pedersen suggested that instead of the Feast of the Tabernacles, the image of the tents might instead allude to the presence of God in the tent of testimony in the wilderness (Exod 33:7-11; Sir 24:4, 8). This was the means by which God dwelled with his people. The word of God which was revealed in the scripture and in the tent was superseded by the legal agency of Jesus, when God's word became flesh and made his presence known to his people (John 1:14). Also on the

---

[8]W. D. Davies and D. C. Allison, Jr., A Critical and Exegetical Commentary on the Gospel according to Saint Matthew (Edinburgh: T. & T. Clark, c1991) II, pp. 692-93.

[9]A. Del Agua, "The Narrative of the Transfiguration as a Derashic Scenification of a Faith Confession (Mark 9:2-8 Par)," NTS 39 (1993):340-54.

Mount of Transfiguration the tents were replaced by Jesus and the voice from heaven announcing that Jesus was God's beloved Son.[10]

One for Elijah. Elijah was not the major figure in this transfiguration scene, but he represented the prophets, and together with Moses, the entire scripture was represented. One of the texts found among the Dead Sea Scrolls said that the books of the Torah were the tent of the king, and the books of the prophets were the peace offerings (CDC 7.14-20). Scripture, however, is not all Elijah represented. He was taken up into heaven without having to face death, so his name here added authority to the testimony (2 Kings 2:9-12), and he also had a special eschatological significance. He was the one who was to come before the great and terrible day of Yahowah (Mal 4:5); he was traditionally expected to announce the coming of the Messiah; he was expected to appear at Passover time and share in the Seder meal. He was also identified with John the Baptist who had announced the Messiahship of Jesus.

A shining cloud overshadowed them. The cloud had the same significance for the Israelites that the sun disk had for surrounding nations. It was the symbol of the deity's presence, and it assured kings of God's victory for them in battle. Some ancient stone art work shows the king coming home in victory procession from battle with the sun disk in the sky just above and before him. For the Israelites, the cloud or the angel was present to provide this confidence. For Moses the cloud showed that God was present in the provision of the commandments; for Jesus this showed that God approved his mission, and the voice from the cloud assured the trio that God had chosen Jesus as his son or the Messiah. In Matt 16 **Peter** confessed that Jesus was the Messiah; in Matthew 17, **God** testified that Jesus was the Messiah.[11] Clouds were used in other cultures with the same significance. For example, Homer portrayed the gods using haze to provide an exit for people from the scene (Iliad 3.380-81; 20.444; Odyssey 7.15).

The Shekinah or the real presence of God was visible in the temple where a bonfire was kept burning day and night (Isa 4:5). In the day time it seemed like a pillar of cloud that reached heaven. At night the blaze was visible. When the cloud could be seen mixed with fire it would appear as a shining cloud. This would relate the appearance of God at Sinai with the presence of the Shekinah on the temple mount at Zion.

My beloved Son. This is a title given to the king as he was enthroned. It was meant to identify Jesus as the Messiah. The same announcement was also made at Jesus' baptism (Matt 3:17). In both instances Jesus was described as the

---

[10]Pedersen, "Proklamation," pp. 257-58.

[11]See further Buchanan, Biblical and Theological Insights from Ancient and Modern Civil Law (Lewiston: Mellen, c1992), p. 105.

beloved son of God and also the Isaianic servant in whom God was well pleased while also alluding to Daniel as the "beloved" man.

Pay attention to him. This translates the words that in Greek and Hebrew literally say, "hear him." The word "hear" also means "obey," with the implication that those who really hear will obey. For that reason this is translated more strongly. Paying attention means one hears attentively. These words were taken from the passage in Deuteronomy where Moses promised that God would raise up after him a prophet like him. Whenever that prophet appeared the Israelites were instructed to pay attention to him. Here the words appear in a passage designed to show that Jesus was the new Moses, the Messiah, and the Isaianic servant. There is also this Deuteronomic proof text from Moses himself that referred to Jesus as the prophet like Moses. Like Daniel before the divine messenger, Jesus' disciples were exhorted to pay attention.

They fell on their faces. When Moses came down from the mountain his face shone and the people were afraid. This is an antitype of the revelation of the commandments on the mountain. Daniel also fell trembling with his face to the ground when he heard the divine messenger speaking. While Jesus' face shone the disciples' faces were pointed to the ground in fear. This is the approved position of defendants in court after all of the arguments have been presented to the judge. If the judge asked the defendant to arise and stand up, facing the judge, this was a good sign that the defendant would receive a favorable verdict. In this case, Jesus touched the disciples and told them not to be afraid but to arise. This was the positive command the disciples needed. The disciples had placed themselves in the worshipful position of defendants as soon as they realized that Jesus was the new Son of God, the Messiah, the prophet Moses promised would come after his death.

Jesus, himself, alone. In Josephus' homily on Deut 24:5-6, he pictured Moses on the mountain with Eleazar and Joshua and the 70 elders. He first dismissed the elders, then Joshua and Eleazar, and he went alone away from the weeping Israelites. Then, when he was alone and at a distance, a cloud suddenly appeared and covered him. Then he disappeared from their sight (Ant 4.325-26). This is almost precisely what the Exodus text says. The transfiguration narrative reported here in Matthew shows some typological similarity to Josephus' narrative about Moses. It is not placed chronologically or structurally in such a typological position as to imply that this Matthean narrative reports Jesus' death, but there are very close antithetical similarities between Matthew's transfiguration narrative (Matt 17:1-8) and the execution narrative (Matt 27:32-54), as Allison has astutely observed:

> (3) The transfiguration narrative has a remarkable twin of sorts in the account of Jesus' execution, 27.32-54. In the one, a private epiphany, an exalted Jesus, with garments glistening,

stands on a high mountain and is flanked by two religious giants from the past. All is light. In the other, a public spectacle, a humiliated Jesus, whose clothes have been torn from him and divided, is lifted upon a cross and flanked by two common convicted criminals. All is darkness. We have here pictorial antithetical parallelism, a diptych in which the two plates have similar lines but different colours.[12]

TEXT

[9]While they were coming down from the mountain, Jesus commanded them, saying, "Tell no one the vision until the Son of man has been raised from the dead."

COMMENTARY

Tell no one the vision. There is still a relationship between these words, like the passage just before them, to Daniel 10, where Daniel was told that the vision he had received did not apply to immediate events but to a time in the future.

This is the fourth time Jesus is reported to have warned people not to tell anyone something. Two of the times were related to healing miracles (Matt 8:4; 9:30). The last two were related to the Son of man. One of these warned the disciples not to disclose his messianic claim (Matt 16:20), and the other is this one, warning not to tell about the vision. Not all of these make sense all by themselves, but the total suggest that Jesus was conducting a secret movement. All of this vision took place in the minds of the disciples. While they were together with Jesus something happened to convince them that Jesus was not only of the same class as Moses and Elijah; he was the one who surpassed and survived them. The six days he supposedly spent with these three apostles was probably time spent discussing Jesus' role in the current events. Here Jesus shared with these three his identification with Moses as the great law giver, John the Baptist's function as the new Elijah, and Jesus' role as the new Son of God. Because messianic movements were subversive and secret, it was important that the disciples not tell anyone these new insights they had just learned.

Raised from the dead. This is the second time that Matthew reported the expectation that the Son of man would be raised from the dead. The first followed Peter's confession (Matt 16:21), and this one followed God's confession. Matthew put this expectation in the narrative where Jesus was related to Elijah who had been raised into heaven, but that happened without his having died. It seems probable that Matthew composed this narrative after the event--after Jesus had both been killed and raised from the dead. Matthew's warning that the disciples should

---

[12]Allison, Matthew, p. 706.

not tell anything about it was his way of explaining why no one ever knew that Jesus had made such a prediction as this.

TEXT

Matthew

[10]Then the disciples asked, saying, "Why, then, do the scribes say it is necessary for **Elijah** to come first?" [11]He answered and said, "**Elijah,** on the one hand, **will** come and **restore** everything, but on the other hand, [12]I tell you that **Elijah** has already come and they did not recognize him but

did with respect to him **whatever they wanted** [to do]. So also the Son of man is about to suffer by them." [13]Then the disciples deduced that he spoke to them about John the Baptist.

First Testament

Look! I am sending you the prophet

Elijah before the great and terrible

day of the Lord, and he **will restore** the hearts of the fathers to the children and the hearts of the children to the fathers (Mal 4:5 [MT3:24]).

No beast stood before him, and no one could succeed from his hand. He **did whatever**
he wanted [to do], and he became great (Dan 8:4).

Then a great king will arise and he will rule from a great government, and he **will do whatever he wants** [to do] (Dan 11:3).

The one who comes toward him **will do whatever he wants** [to do], and no one will stand before him (Dan 11:16).

COMMENTARY

It is necessary for Elijah? This is a stylistic way of introducing a subject. On the question of saying the sheh-máh, Rabban Gamaliel said it might be said as late as the beginning of dawn, but the scholars said, "Until midnight." Then the question arose, "Why did the scholars say, 'Until midnight?'" Since both the scholars and Rabban Gamaliel were famous legal authorities, why was there this disagreement? The dogmatic answer that followed was that everything decreed "until midnight" might be extended to dawn (mBer 1.1), but no answer was given to the question, "Why?" Here in Matthew, Jesus reportedly gave an answer to the question asked.

In typical Matthean organization, the items relating to Elijah are all put here together. First, Elijah appeared with Moses on the Mount of Transfiguration. Then Jesus' resurrection was mentioned to relate it to Elijah's ascension. The question was raised about Elijah appearing before the Day of the Lord. Justin's version (Dial 49) said, "Our Christ said to those [the scribes] who say it is necessary for Elijah to come before the Messiah . . ." Justin evidently understood "first" to mean "before the Messiah" and also that the Messiah would come on the Day of the Lord. Elijah would appear before both.[13] In medieval Jewish literature, Elijah was often pictured either with the Messiah[14] or in relation to the resurrection of the dead.[15]

Jews of NT times believed that events occurred in a certain prescribed order. This order could be discerned through a careful study of the scriptures and of the cycles of time. Malachi had said Elijah would come before the Day of Yahowah (Mal 3:23). This means that he would come first--before the Messiah. The Messiah would not arrive until the way was prepared for him by the prophet Elijah. It was necessary for things to happen in this order.

Elijah, on the one hand, will come. There was an important shift of tenses. The FT, on one hand, predicted that which would happen in the future. Jesus, on the

---

[13]J. Taylor, "The Coming of Elijah, Matt 17, 10-13 and Mark 9, 11-13: The Development of the Texts," RB 98 (1991):117, following J. A. T. Robinson, "Elijah, John and Jesus: An Essay in Detection," NTS 4 (1957):263-81, argued that Mark 9:12 identified Elijah with the Son of man, but that is probably not the way Mark intended it to be understood. Some of Mark's abbreviations of Matthew are so succinct that they do not make sense. For example, in the temptations narrative, Mark said the angels came and ministered to Jesus (1:13) without saying why such a ministry was necessary. He also told of a man who went away on a journey, leaving a watchman in charge, expecting him to be watching whenever he returned, any time of the day or night, any time in the future (Mark 13:34-37), without ever sleeping. This is the summary of two parables in Matt 24:42-25:15. One of these was about a man who went away on a journey and expected the man in charge to have kept the business functioning well during his absence. The other is a parable of ten virgins who were expected to be watching for the bridegroom whenever he came, during one night only. Both of these are reasonable, but Mark's summary is not. Taylor's notion that Mark's version of Elijah's relationship to the Son of man must mean that Matthew used Mark at this point is not required for an understanding of the difference between Matthew and Mark. Mark probably meant 1) on the one hand Elijah would come before the Messiah and restore all things, just as the scribes said, and 2) on the other hand the Son of man would suffer just as it was written about him (Mark 9:12)--two statements, two people. This does not mean the Son of man was identical to Elijah, according to Mark. Mark over abbreviated his sources.

[14]For examples in English see Buchanan, Revelation and Redemption: Jewish Documents of Deliverance from the Fall of Jerusalem to the Death of Nahmanides (Dillsboro: Western North Carolina Press, c1978; sold by Mercer U. Press), pp. 123, 229, 247, 250, 290, 313, 328, 360, 369, 372, 374-75, 384, 412, 416, 425, 449, 453, 518-19, 533, 554-55.

[15]Buchanan, Redemption, pp. 404, 474, 539.

other hand, interpreted the scripture in terms of what had already happened in his day. There was no longer a need to look to the future arrival of Elijah. John the Baptist had already come.

The medieval Hebrew text has "Elijah will come, and he will save all the age." This is an interpretation of Mal 3:23, **He will restore everything**. To restore everything meant to change everything to the way it was when David and Solomon were in power. This would save the entire age or to renew the Davidic-Solomonic age. John the Baptist was trying to fulfill the prophecy that was made by Malachi concerning Elijah. He was attempting to lead Jews to repentance so that the Kingdom might be restored. In this way he was trying, not to save the current common age, but to save the age [to come].

The Son of man is about to suffer. Taylor noted that Bezae and several texts of the Old Latin version place this clause (12b) after 13. Matt 17:12b seems to interrupt the flow of the argument. Justin omits it (Dial 49). Taylor may be right in arguing that it is a later intrusion,[16] but even if so, the intrusion is coherent with the rest of the message. The first Son of man was Judas the Maccabee (Dan 7). Judas led the guerrilla war against the Syrian Greeks for more than 3 1/2 years. He was killed in battle before the Davidic kingdom was fully established. That happened about 20 years after the death of Judas. Since Jesus was the new Son of man it was reasonable to believe that, like Judas, he also would have to suffer before the Kingdom would come. It was not necessary for someone to have to wait until after Jesus' death to consider the necessity for him to suffer.

Whatever they wanted [to do]. In Dan 8:4 it was the Persian king who did whatever he wanted to do. Cyrus came from the North, took Babylon, and expanded his country in all directions. Before Alexander (the goat) moved eastward, the Persians had very little comparable resistance. They had the military power to do whatever they wanted.

Matthew here used the same expression that the author of Daniel employed to describe great foreign leaders who conquered the entire area east of the Mediterranean Sea before the Romans moved east and overthrew them (Dan 8:4; 11:3, 16). This was to identify Herod Antipas and his following with other foreign powers who once ruled Palestine. Typologically, the Herods were the new Seleucids. The current Romans and their local agents ruled Palestine the way the earlier Persians and Syrian Greeks did, and John was the victim of that kind of treatment.

The disciples deduced. The Greek here is soon-áye-kan (συνῆκαν). It means "they put together" the clues he had given them in code and understood his hidden message. It was then that the disciples began to understand the whole concept:

1) Jesus was the Son of man in whom God was pleased;

---

[16]Taylor, "Elijah."

2) John the Baptist was the new Elijah who preceded the Messiah, and like Moses, had now vanished from their sight; and

3) There was a predestined amount of suffering ahead for Jesus, just as there had been earlier for Judas the Maccabee, the Son of man referred to in the vision of Dan 7.

This was the point of the vision that was dramatized on the mountain. That which probably happened on that mountain was that Jesus spent six days sharing his insights with his three most trusted apostles. The "transfiguration" that took place was that they understood clearly for the first time precisely how Jesus understood his role in the current events and the will of God. This probably involved some extensive Bible study and comparison of the signs of the times with events that had happened in Jewish history. The insights involved not only the idea that Jesus was the new Judas the Maccabee, but also that he was the new Moses, and John the Baptist was the new Elijah. Rabbis had similar expectations:

> After this, congregation of Zion, your iniquities will be paid [in full]. Then you will be saved at the hands of the messianic king and Elijah, the high priest (TgJon Lam 4.22).

About John the Baptist. The answer to the question about Elijah was that John the Baptist was the new antitype of Elijah. Through the person of John the Baptist Elijah had already come. This means all the preparation necessary for the coming of the Messiah had been fulfilled. First, Peter confessed Jesus was the Messiah (Matt 16:17); second, God confessed it (Matt 17:5); and third, Jesus told that the events predestined to happen before the arrival of the Messiah had taken place, meaning that Jesus was the Messiah, and the Passover during which the restoration would take place would be the next one.

TEXT

14 After they **had come** down **to** the crowd, a man **came to** him, fell on his knees before him 15 and said, "Lord, have mercy upon my son, because he is deranged and has [this affliction] badly. Many times he falls into the fire and many times into the water, 16 and I have brought him to your **disciples**, but they **were not able to** heal him." 17 **Jesus** answered and **said**,

Matthew	First Testament
"Oh, faithless **and perverse generation!** 1) How long will I be with you? 2) How long can I endure you? 3) Bring him here to me."	It is a twisted **and perverse generation** (Deut 32:5).

1) [18]Then **Jesus** commanded him,
2) and the demon went out from him,
3) and the child was healed from that hour.

TECHNICAL DETAILS

Sterling examined this pericope in comparison with Mark 9:14-29 and Luke 9:37-43a. He noticed in this narrative in the triple tradition numerous agreements exist between Matthew and Luke against Mark. Committed to the two-source theory he could not consider the possibility that Luke had used Matthew or vice versa nor that Mark could have used either of the other synoptics. Therefore, he conjectured an oral source that Matthew and Luke both used as well as Mark. He also observed a typical Markan introduction and conclusion showing that Mark had edited some document. He further concluded that Jesus was actually an exorcist and that this was a true narrative of a historical event.[17] Burney noticed that Matt 17:17 is poetry.[18]

Matthew and Luke agree in having the following words, either exactly or as synonyms, that are not in Mark: **a man**, (Matt 17:14; Luke 9:38), **saying, because** (Matt 17:15; Luke 9:38), **replying, Jesus said, and scattered** (Matt 17:17; Luke 9:41), **here** (Matt 17:17; Luke 9:42), **Jesus commanded**, and **the child was healed**" (Matt 17:18; Luke 9:42).

The following detail was either added by Mark or omitted by both other gospel writers "coincidentally": **and scribes arguing with them. Suddenly all the crowd, when they saw him, were surprised, and they came up to him and greeted him. Then he asked them, "What are you arguing about with them?"**(Mark 9:14-16). . . **them** (Mark 9:19).

After he had fallen to the ground, he rolled around, foaming. Then he [Jesus] asked the father, "How long has this happened to him?" He said, "From childhood, and many times it has thrown him into fire and into water to destroy him, but if you are able, help us and have mercy on us." Jesus said to him, "[What is] this,'If you are able!' All things are possible to the one who believes." At once the father of the child cried out, "I believe. Help my unbelief." When . . . he saw the crowd gathering . . . he said to it, "Dumb and deaf spirit, I command you to come out from him and never to enter him again." After it cried and convulsed him many times, it left. [The child] became like a corpse, so that the multitude said that he had died, but Jesus, after he had taken his hand, he raised him and he stood up (Mark 9:20-27).

---

[17]G. E. Sterling, "Jesus as Exorcist: An analysis of Matthew 17:14-20; Mark 9:14-29; Luke 9:37-43a," CBQ 55 (1993):467-93.

[18]C. F. Burney, The Poetry of our Lord (Oxford: Clarendon, 1925), p. 66.

There are enough agreements among the three gospels to identify the story as a report of the same event. There are too many agreements between Matthew and Luke against Mark, both in addition and in omission to allow for the hypothesis that Matthew and Luke had no access to one another except through Mark and the hypothetical "Q." It would make more sense to presume 1) either that all three used the same source. In which case Mark omitted parts and added still more narrative to give the story life-like detail or 2) he included more of the source than the other gospel writers. It is not reasonable to assume that Matthew and Luke used the same source as Mark and agreed, coincidentally, to omit exactly the same part that Mark accepted. If the same source that Mark used was somehow used by the other two, then one of them must have chosen how to edit it and the other would have to have copied from the one who did. The least complicated theory would be to presume that Mark developed his narrative freely, using both Luke and Matthew. From this narrative only, the relationships among the gospels are very conjectural. As in many instances among the synoptic gospels, it is not clear how these relationships came into being, and in most cases it is not very important.

COMMENTARY

Faithless and perverse generation. These are basically the same words with which Moses addressed the Israelites just before he was to be separated from them, and they were to go ahead into the promised land without him. Jesus pictured himself in the same situation, asking, "How long will I be with you?" Since Moses was addressing the whole nation of Israel, Jesus was probably speaking to the crowd, rather than to the disciples. Because the faith of the father of the child was involved, Matthew has changed the quotation wording of Deuteronomy from "twisted" to "faithless." Paul encouraged the Philippians to be "blameless and innocent children of God, without blemish in the midst of **a twisted and perverse generation**" (Philip 2:15).

That which Matthew implied Mark spelled out clearly, blaming the people who wanted healing for being perverse, because Mark held that Jesus told the father that all things were possible to one who believed. Once he said that he believed, the father was no longer faithless but believing. Then his son was healed. This puts all of the blame on the person who comes seeking health, and gives all of the credit to the person who might do the healing. If healing takes place, the healer gets the credit; if it does not, the proposed recipient is blamed for his or her faithlessness. According to Matthew, Jesus did not demand a confession of faith. He simply healed the boy because he needed healing. In the verses that follow, however, Jesus told the disciples that it was their lack of faith, rather than the boy's father's, that kept them from being able to heal the boy.

The demon went out from him. Mark elaborated extensively on the way the demon left and the corresponding reaction of the child. Matthew simply said the demon left, and the child was healed. In antiquity there was the widespread belief that demons caused sickness. If the demons were driven out the illness would be gone. Modern medicine relates sickness to germs, bacteria, and other scientific terms, but the reaction of the patient is the same as it was years ago. He or she is afflicted with some bodily ailment that prevents normal activity and would like to be made well.

TEXT

[19]Then the **disciples came to Jesus** [when he was] alone and said, "Why **were**
we not **able** to cast it out?" [20]He said to them, "Because of your little **faith**. I tell
you under oath, If you have **faith** as a grain of mustard seed,

Matthew	First Testament
you will say to this **mountain**, 'Be moved from here [to] there!' and it will be moved, and nothing will be **impossible** for you."	Then the Lord will go out and fight those nations as on the day when he 1 on the day of battle. On that day his will stand on the **Mount** of Olives whi across from Jerusalem on the east, an **Mount** of Olives will be split in two, the east and from the west, and there w a great valley with half the **mountain** t north and half to the south (Zech 14:3

TECHNICAL DETAILS

This interpretation of the healing narrative is a midrash in which the homiletician built his commentary on the following words: 1) come to, 2) Jesus, 3) disciples, 4) faith, and 5) ability.

COMMENTARY

[When he was] alone. This is the beginning of a new unit. It is a commentary on the miracle narrative that ended with the healing of the child, but it first picked up the last word of the transfiguration narrative, where Jesus was left alone. According to Matthew, there were many times when Jesus coached the disciples in their work of being fishers of men. At these times, they asked him questions that the Pharisees or disciples of John had asked them, and he gave them stock answers to use when these occasions happened again. According to Matthew they expected to be able to cast out demons, because Jesus, when he appointed them to be his apostles, gave them legal authority to preach, cleanse lepers, and drive out demons (Matt 10:7-8).

Faith as a grain of mustard seed. This statement does not imply that the disciples did not or could not have this much faith but only that a small amount of faith was necessary to perform miracles. That which is understood, however, is the attack in the previous narrative that Jesus made to the "faithless generation," which may have included the disciples. The afflicted person was not blamed for his lack of faith, but his father seems to have been. This is not the same conclusion as that reached by Mark.

The exclamation, "faithless generation!" seems not to have been directed to the disciples alone, but, according to Matthew, it certainly included them, because they were unable to cast out the demon. The logic of this claim was legal. Jesus was God's apostle, and therefore he could speak and act with the authority of God. The apostles were his legal agents, so they also were authorized to act with God's authority, in his name, and in his best interests. Since God could do whatever he wanted to do, it would seem logical to presume that his legal agents could also do whatever he wanted them to do. The only stumbling block was knowing whether or not God wanted this or that done.

You will say to this mountain. This may be a claim that the apostles were capable of bringing about the day of the Lord, when all the nations would be gathered against Jerusalem for battle (Zech 14:1-2; also Joel 3:9-21 [MT4:9-21]). The mountain about which Jesus was speaking was apparently the same mountain of which Zechariah spoke, namely the Mount of Olives, just across the Kidron valley from the temple area in Jerusalem. Matthew has put this story together with other mountain scenes, like the Mount of Transfiguration, and the mountain where Peter confessed that Jesus was the Messiah.

The mountain where Peter and Jesus held their discourse was the only mountain that was identified. This was Caesarea Phillipi in the Golan Heights. Following Matthew, geographically, Jesus and the disciples were still in the Golan Heights when he was transfigured and when he said they could move "this mountain" if they had faith. In its original context, however, the mountain which Jesus said could be moved was probably the Mount of Olives. Matthew, however, has not shown either Jesus or the disciples moving from the Golan Heights to Jerusalem or back to Galilee where the next pericope took place. He may not have paid any attention to the geographical location of the mountains. In his systematic way of putting things together that apply to the same subject, he may have related this mountain scene to the Mount of Transfiguration scene just because they were both mountain scenes.

TEXT

[22]While they were congregating in Galilee, Jesus said to them, "The Son of man is about to be betrayed into the hands of men, [23]and they will kill him,

Matthew	First Testament
and on the third day he will be raised," and they were deeply pained.	After two days he will revive us, **On the third day he will raise** us up, that we may live before him (Hos 6:2).

COMMENTARY

While they were congregating. At the time of feasts, groups gathered together and made the trek to Jerusalem jointly. This was a customary practice (mBik 3.2; tBik 2.8; Luke 2:44; LamR 1.17, 52).[19] After the Roman taxation of Quirinius, groups were formed, not only for companionship, but to form resistance movements at the feasts. They came armed, ready for battle if the opportunity offered itself. Galilee seems to have been the center where the troops were forming. They may have been organizing with the expectation that Jesus would lead them in war.

They will kill him. In Dan 7, the Son of man was the plaintiff in the divine judgment scene. To him was given the kingdom, power, and glory. This is the future that Jews who followed Jesus expected to be the final result of his leadership. The idea that he would fail and be killed was a very remote consideration. After the crucifixion, however, some said, "But we had hoped that he was the one who was about to redeem Israel" (Luke 24:20). Since they believed that Jesus' goal was the restoration of the promised land under Jewish leadership, they were not expecting him to be killed. This narrative may have been written after the event by the later church which deduced that Jesus must have foreseen this possibility.

There is the other possibility, however, that, after the death of John the Baptist, Jesus was forced to reanalyze the role of the Messiah. Was he to lead a war, following the example of Phineas and the Hasmoneans, or was he to suffer like the servant of Isaiah and Moses, following the faith of Abraham? He may have discussed both possibilities with his disciples and have waited for a sign from Heaven to tell him which of these alternatives to take. He probably did not choose between the alternatives until he noticed that the fig tree in the Kidron Valley did not bear fruit out of season as Ezekiel promised (Matt 21:18-20).

---

[19]So also S. Safrai, Die Wallfahrt im Zeitalter des Zweiten Tempels (Neukirchen Vluyn: Neukirchener Verlag, 1981), pp. 121-27; D. J. Verseput, "Jesus' Pilgrimage to Jerusalem and Encounter in the Temple: A Geographical Motif in Matthew's Gospel," NovT 36 (1994):109-11.

On the third day . . . raised. The belief in the resurrection was firm among many Jews from the time of the Hasmoneans. Since all prophecy was expected to be fulfilled in the days of the Messiah, and these were the days of the Messiah, Jesus may have expected to have been killed and raised, according to the scripture, or if he did not, after his death it would have been easy for the early church to have presumed that he thought that. This text from Hosea was probably the basis for Paul's claim that, "he was buried, that he was raised on the third day, according to the scriptures" (1 Cor 15:4; see also Matt 20:17-19).

They were deeply pained. This is an expression that was used again in Matt 26:22, 37.

TEXT

24After they had come to Capernaum, those who collected the didrachma [tax]
came to Peter and said, "Your teacher pays the didrachma [tax], does he not?"
25[Peter] said, "Yes." After he had come into the house, Jesus set out to correct
him, saying, "How does it seem to you, Simon? From whom do the kings of the
land (or earth) take taxes or tribute? From their sons or from the foreigners?
26After he had said, "From the foreigners," Jesus said to him, "Then the sons are
free."

COMMENTARY

They had come to Capernaum. Capernaum seems to have been the residence of Jesus and his disciples. The house mentioned in Matt 17:25 was probably a monastery to which they all belonged. From this base Jesus contacted the disciples who were in the fishing industry somewhere around the Sea of Galilee. Here is the place where the disciples would have gathered when they came back from their missionary tours and made reports to Jesus. Here is where he would have held the banquets for his new recruits. It is probably here where the tax assessors came to ask if Jesus paid the didrachma taxes.

He had come into the house. The subject is not clear. Was it Jesus or Peter who came into the house? Either Peter was already there, and Jesus entered or vice versa. At any rate it seems apparent that both Peter and Jesus were at home there in Capernaum, supporting the supposition that there was a monastery at Capernaum where both Jesus and Peter lived, as well as the other disciples. The RSV correctly translates this clause, "When he came home . . ." As in other places in the Gospel according to Matthew, Peter is the official person who took care of such details as this.

Your teacher. It was not unusual for a messiah to be also a teacher in Judaism. Just before the death of Herod two legal scholars and teachers (so-fis-taí, σοφισταί), Judas and Mattathias, encouraged their students to chop down an image of a Roman eagle which they held was against the Torah (War 1.648, 50, 55-56; Ant 17.151-55). Herod had them all put to death for this deed. There was national lamentation over their deaths, because the masses considered Judas and Mattathias to be important national and religious leaders (War 2.9-11). Judas the Galilean, one of the messianic pretenders who led battles in the war against Rome (66-70 I.A.), was called a legal scholar (War 2.118, 433). This was also true of Menahem (War 2.445). Legal scholars and teachers were the ones who were considered most capable of leading the nation. They knew the law and had the respect of the people. The law that they knew was the Torah which they believed should be the law of the land. These teachers were not teaching their disciples philosophical gems to entertain their imaginations. They were teaching political action and leading military rebellions against Rome.

Kings of the land. This expression is usually translated, "The kings of the earth," and both translations might make sense in this context. First we will present the argument for the "land," and secondly we will present the arguments in favor of translating it "The kings of the earth."

1) If this was the temple tax, then it has an ancient history, going back to the wilderness (Exod 30:11-16). It was assessed as long as the temple stood. When Romans burned the temple Vespasian required Jews to continue paying this tax, but instead of its being used for maintenance of the temple it went to Rome's coffers (War 7.218) and was used to support a Roman temple. Because it supported a pagan temple, Jews and Christians would have resisted this tax forcefully, if this pericope had been written after the fall of Jerusalem. It is unlikely that later Christians would have falsely attributed to Jesus a casual willingness to pay the tax, but there is no certainty that this was the tax involved.

This tax was taken on the land of Palestine, it may have referred to the taxes kings, like David, Solomon, and the Hasmonean kings levied. Since Jesus was the Messiah and expected to be made king, it would seem as though he should follow the same ruling on this matter as other Jewish or Israelite kings. Did the kings, themselves, pay taxes, or did they assess taxes on others? If Jewish kings taxed others, did they tax other Jews and Israelites or did they tax foreigners who needed their country as a buffer state or needed to transport merchandise across it? Although Jews complained bitterly that they were being oppressed by taxation, most of the time, they paid only 10% to 20% for all state and temple taxes. In NT times, most Romans were being taxed about 40% During their heaviest taxation, during the days of Solomon, Israelites were forced to work two months a year to pay their state taxes. That is about 17%, and Jews and North Israelites referred to this as if it were slavery and motivated by the devil. Because of its strategic location, Palestine has never had to pay most of its national cost of existence. This has been paid by other countries--the foreigners.[20]

Brodie thought the whole discussion of a temple tax here was an intended antitype of the rules of the temple tithes in Deut 14. Hagner argued for the temple tax, and said this narrative must have been written before the fall of Jerusalem (70 I.A.). He said if this had been a Roman tax, Jesus' decision to pay it would have been an offense to the Jews.[21]

2) Cassidy argued that the expression involved always refers to the "kings of the earth" when used in the FT (Ps 2:2; 89:27; 148:11). Therefore it must have that meaning here, and the tax must be a civil tax levied by the Romans. Following Wallace's study on the subject of Roman taxation he learned that Romans levied many taxes on their provinces, some of which would were merismoi. Some of these were as small as two drachmae. If people voluntarily failed to pay one of these taxes, the government sent people out to collect it. Cassidy thought this was the tax that was called to Jesus' attention, and he might be correct.[22] Both translations and interpretations are possible.

Then the sons are free. Either the citizens of the land are free, or the kings and their sons are free. In either case, Jesus was not required to pay the taxes[23] assessed, and possibly his apostles were also free. He may even have intended that all Jews were to be free. Under his administration all taxes would come from Rome or other surrounding nations that needed this land as a bridge or a buffer. The didrachma tax was customarily paid in NT times. This is evident from the fact that after the fall of Jerusalem Vespasian decreed that the didrachma tax would continue to be paid, but to Rome rather than Jerusalem (War 7.218). From their inferior position, Jews at that time had little choice but to pay.

TEXT

[27]"But in order that we not make them stumble, after you have gone to the sea,

---

[20] S. Mandell, "Who Paid the Temple Tax When the Jews were under Roman Rule?" HTR 77 (1984):223-32, argued that not all Jews paid either the temple tax or the didrachmon tax imposed by the Romans. The Roman tax was imposed on those who supported the temple and the war. She thought this meant the rabbis alone paid it. She identified the rabbis with the Pharisees. Some of her sources were Josephus (Ant 18.312-13), Seutonius (Dom 12.2), and Dio Cassius (Epit 66.7.2).

[21]Hagner, Matthew, p. 510.

[22]R. J. Cassidy, "Matthew 17:24-27--A Word on Civil Taxes," CBQ 41 (1979):571-80.

[23]On the question of the type of tax under consideration here, see Cassidy, "Matthew 17:24-27," pp. 571-80. W. Horbury, "The Temple Tax," Jesus and Politics of His Day (ed. E. R. Bammel and C. D. F. Moule (Cambridge: Cambridge U., 1984), p. 283, thought the term "sons" meant Israelites in general. Verseput, "Geographical Motif," p. 113, disagreed.

throw a hook, and the first fish which comes up, take, and after you have opened its mouth, you will find a stater. Take that and give it for me and you."

COMMENTARY

Not to make them stumble. When Jesus was trying to avoid Roman authorities and their agents, he did not intend to call attention to himself by fighting the question of taxes. John had been killed by getting involved in a problem of the ethics of Herod. Had he ignored this problem for a while until his and Jesus' plans had been well advanced, the designed program would have succeeded better. Jesus chose not to make the same mistake. This was a political judgment.

The first fish. There is something fishy about this story. The best that can be done to understand it is to conjecturee changes or translation possibilities. One possibility suggested by Schwarz was to translate the Greek into Aramaic. In Aramaic as in Hebrew the word "mouth" (pohm, פום, Aramaic, or peh פה, Hebrew), as an idiom, can have a different meaning. For example (luh-pohm, לפום) means "according to," "in order that," or "after." The Hebrew word for "open" (pah-takh, פתח) may also refer to opening the shop or the market to make something available for sale (Amos 8:5). It has the same basic meaning of "sell." Schwarz then suggested that the passage has been poorly translated from a Semitic language into Greek. Originally the commandment was to go to the sea, catch a fish, sell it, and with the money obtained to pay the tax.[24]

Homeau suggested that the story is geographically out of place. Originally it was associated around the Dead Sea where there are no fish. This would be consistent with Jesus' anti-tax position, and it would be a coded answer.[25]
This verse may also have been added to neutralize the message of Jesus on taxes. After the Bar Cochba defeat it was wise for both Christians and Jews to appear to be loyal Roman supporters. After that both Jews and Christians had to edit their texts to pass Roman inspection (see Sifre Deut 33:3, Piska 344.143b). Then someone may have changed the text to give the impression that Jesus advocated payment of taxes. Jesus may originally have said that Peter should not pay taxes until he had caught a fish with a stater in its mouth. This is a coded way of saying he should never pay it. If that was the original meaning, it has surely been changed since then, and the final form is confusing.[26] It is not likely that the entire pericope was composed by the later church and attributed to Jesus.[27]

---

[24]G. Schwarz, ΑΝΟΙΞΑΣ ΤΟ ΣΤΟΜΑ ΑΥΤΟΥ? (Matthäus 17:27)," NTS 38 (1992):138-41.

[25]H. A. Homeau. "On Fishing for Staters: Matthew 17:27," ExpTim 85 (1974):340-42.

[26]For another inconclusive interpretation see H. Montefiore, "Jews and the Temple Tax," NTS 11 (1964):60-71.

[27]See H. Montefiore, "Jesus and the Temple Tax," NTS 10 (1964):60-71.

CHAPTER EIGHTEEN

MATTHEAN PARALLELS TO THE HEXATEUCH

Matthew	Deuteronomy
Forgiveness required of a brother offended. If he does not forgive he is to be given strict justice without mercy (18:21-35).	Justice should be rendered fairly and the offender punished to purge the evil from the community. Eye should show no pity (18:9-19:21).

TEXT

18:1In that hour the disciples came to Jesus, saying, "Who, then, is greatest in the Kingdom of Heaven?" 2After he had called to [them] a child, he stood it in their midst 3and said, "I tell you under oath, if you do not repent and become as the children, you will not enter the Kingdom of Heaven."

TECHNICAL DETAILS

Wenham called attention to the many agreements between Matthew and Luke against Mark evident in Matt 18:1-6 and parallels. He claimed that these agreements

> may not prove a literary relationship between Matthew and Luke, but at least they indicate that Matthew and Luke had non-Marcan traditions at various points.

He thought the Markan parallel was secondary to the source which he modified.[1]

This literary unit is a responsive chreia. 1) The situation that prompted the

---

[1]D. Wenham, "A Note on Mark 9:33-42/Matt. 18:1-6/Luke 9:46-50," JSNT 14 (1982):113-18. Quotation is from page 113.

speaker to speak is given; 2) the response of the speaker is given; 3) the identity of the speaker is given; and 4) the entire unit is very brief.

COMMENTARY

Greatest in the Kingdom of Heaven. This probably means, "Who will have the chief seats? Who will be the members of the highest court? Who will be governors over the individual tribes of Israel? Who will be the prime minister? Who will be the top general of the armed forces?" The disciples, of course, assumed that they were Jesus' closest associates and should be the first to receive high appointments.

If you do not repent. In two other chreias, Jesus is reported to have said, "If you do not repent, all of you will likewise perish" (Luke 13:3, 5). The fact that these teachings are reported in responsive chreias supports the likelihood that Jesus actually taught repentance. This is also supported by Jewish tradition. Repentance was a necessary ingredient for efficacy on the Day of Atonement. Jews and early Christians believed that the Kingdom would come whenever Israel was atoned for all of its sin. The basic things that Jews had to do in preparation for that day were: 1) Repent of all their sins; 2) bring to the altar the prescribed sacrifice that the law stipulated to pay for this offense; 3) become reconciled to their fellow sectarians. This meant going to that person and doing whatever was required to obtain his forgiveness. 4) God would forgive the individual's sins, so that the believer was as free from sin as a child born that day. Jesus said this type of sinlessness was required for entrance into the Kingdom of Heaven.

Become as the children. Most scholars think this means Jesus wanted the disciples to become meek, humble, and dependent as children,[2] and there is some basis for that opinion. Jesus later said they should humble themselves like the child he used as an illustration. These disciples had once been leaders and prominent businessmen. Jesus chose them because of their ability, not their meekness. Monastic living, however, was not conducive to having many leaders. Members had taken vows of poverty, chastity, and obedience. This was not always an easy adjustment, even though the disciples understood that the monastic life was temporary and would be discontinued as soon as the Kingdom came, but there was probably another dimension to childlikeness.

No matter how many laws a child under 12 years of age broke, he or she was legally innocent. The father was responsible for the child's behavior until the bar mitzvah at the age of 12 or 13. When Israelites sent spies to examine Canaan to learn whether or not they would be able to take the country by military force, ten of the spies brought back a bad report, saying it would be impossible to do

---

[2]A. Plummer, An Exegetical Commentary on the Gospel according to St. Matthew (London: Stock, 1909), p. 249.

so. Because of their lack of faith, the men of that generation were cursed. God said none of the men of that generation (20 years of age or older) would enter the promised land except Joshua and Caleb--those who brought back a good report (Deut 1:39; Num 14:29-30).[3] The adult males were the ones legally responsible for the decisions made at that time. The toddlers (those of pre-bar-mitzwah age) and the sons (those who had passed their bar mitzwah) would enter.

The men were responsible, but the minors were not. The sons had some responsibilities but the toddlers were the children who were legally innocent. They were the ones who finally entered Canaan with Joshua, and the children of Jesus' day, antitypes of wilderness children, would also be the ones who entered the Kingdom of Heaven. Adults that could enter along with them would be those who, like Joshua and Caleb as well as the children, were legally free from prosecution in court. In order to become like the children they had to qualify for atonement on the Day of Atonement. Fowl was correct in thinking that becoming like children was not becoming humble, but he missed the legal significance of the expression.[4] The Kingdom of Heaven would not come until Jews had been reconciled to one another and had qualified for forgiveness on the Day of Atonement. It was not "unself-consciousness" that Jesus wanted to develop but freedom from guilt. This meant they had to become legally innocent, like children before their bar mitzwah.

Enter the Kingdom of Heaven. This meant to "enter into life" (Matt 18:8-9; 19:17) or to "enter into the joy of your Lord" (Matt 25:21, 23). This happened to the children of the wilderness generation when they entered into Canaan.

TEXT

4Whoever, therefore, humbles himself as this **child**, this is the greatest one in the Kingdom of Heaven, 5and whoever receives one **child** such as this in my name receives me, 6and whoever causes one of these **little ones** who believe in me to **stumble**, it would be beneficial for him that a donkey millstone be hanged around his neck, and he be drowned in the waves of the sea. 7Woe to the world because of the **stumbling blocks**, for it is necessary that **stumbling blocks** come, but woe to the man on account of whom the **stumbling blocks** come. 8If your hand or your foot makes you **stumble**, chop it off and throw it from you, for it is better for you to enter into life maimed or crippled than to have two hands or two feet

---

[3]On this see Buchanan, "The Old Testament Meaning of the Knowledge of Good and Evil," JBL 75 (1956):114-20.

[4]S. Fowl, "Receiving the Kingdom of God as a Child: Children and Riches in Luke 18:15 ff.," JNTS 39 (1993):153-58. He thought it meant becoming "single-minded, unrelenting [in] pursuit of an object of desire" (p. 158). This was a teaching of Jesus, to be sure, but not the point of the expression.

and be thrown into the fire of the age. [9]If your eye makes you **stumble**, pick it out and throw it from you, for it is better for you to enter into life with one eye than with two eyes to be thrown into gehenna of fire.

Matthew	First Testament
[10]See that you do not despise one of the least of these, for I say to you that their angels always see the face of my Father in heaven. [12]How does it seem to you? If a certain man has 100 **sheep**, and one of them becomes **lost**. Will he not leave the 99	With whom have you left the small flock [of sheep] there in the wilderness (1 Sam 17:28? I have gone astray like a **lost sheep**. **Look for** your servant, because I have not forgotten your commandments (Ps 119:176).
on the mountains and go	I will bring them to their land, and I will herd them **on the mountains** of Israel (Ezek 34:13).
look for the one that is **lost**? [13]And if he finds it, I tell you under oath he will rejoice over it more than over the 99 who did not get **lost**. [14]Thus it is not the will of my Father in heaven that one of these **little** ones perish.	I will **look for the lost**; I will restore those that have been pushed away; I will bind up those [with] broken [bones] (Ezek 34:16).

TECHNICAL DETAILS

Matthew began this unit with a chreia and concluded it with a parable. The chreia, parable, and all the sayings in between consist of the materials Matthew had that were related to the same subjects. These were related to one another in a catch-word system. Initially, the chreia mentioned the **child**. This called Matthew's attention to **little ones** and **the least of these**. One of the sayings Matthew had in his collection mentioned both **little ones** and **stumbling**. Therefore, Matthew placed this pericope here where it followed the last unit of chapter 17 where the tax was paid to avoid causing the tax gatherers to stumble. He also introduced other material that dealt with stumbling. Matt 18:1-14 is a well organized unit, framed by an inclusion. At the beginning is a reference to children (Matt 18:3) and at the end, the little ones. Matthew put this all together at one time, as a midrash on the chreia as Greek rhetoricians said should be done.

Matt 18:5 agrees with Luke 9:48 against Mark 9:27 in his use of the words **whoever receives** and **child.** They both agree in omitting the words **not me** and **but**. Matt 18:7 agrees with Luke 17:1 against Mark in the words **the stumbling blocks come**, and **woe to the, on account of whom**, and **come.**

COMMENTARY

Humbles himself as this child. Answering the question of the child and entrance into the kingdom, Matthew believed this referred to the humility of the child, but Jesus more than likely emphasized the legal innocence required of disciples, as all children were, according to Jewish law. His disciples became like children, legally, whenever they repented, asked for, and received forgiveness (John 3:1-10; Gerim 2.5; bYeb 46a, 48b; CantR 8.2, 5).[5]

Whoever receives one such child. The child was treated here as if it were a legal agent for Jesus. To receive a person's agent was the same as receiving the person himself or herself. Monasteries raised other people's children as well as orphans, even though they fathered no children. They had no hostility to families or children; they kept themselves celibate so that they would not defile God's holy place. This indicates that Jesus encouraged his followers to accept orphan children and raise them in his name.

One of these little ones. Rabbis said,

> If there is no joy in heaven over the death of the wicked, how much more [is there no joy] over the righteous (Mek Shirata 1.70-71).

In its original context this parable was probably directed to the Pharisees rather than the disciples. The disciples were the ones Jesus called "children." The Pharisees thought the tax collectors and other wealthy businessmen who did business with Rome were wicked, and they would have remembered the scripture, **with the destruction of the wicked there is rejoicing** (Prov 11:10), but Jesus did not call these businessmen "wicked." He referred to them as "children."

The little ones in Matthew were not the little children, chronologically. They were legally little children. They were those who were new in the faith. They had been recently baptized. Usually this reference is given to the tax collectors and other upper class Jews who had newly reached the conviction that they should give all they had to the community, and leave their families and positions

---

[5]See further Buchanan, The Consequences of the Covenant (Leiden: E. J. Brill, 1970), pp. 201-20.

to become leaders in the Christian community. Even though they were middle aged or older, these men were classed as children in the faith. Dealing with degrees of advancement in the faith, the author of First John made distinctions among the "little children" (1 John 2:1), "young men" (1 John 2:13), and "fathers" (1 John 2:14).

The "little children" had been forgiven; the "young men" had overcome evil; and "the fathers" were those who were learned and knew the One from the beginning. Jesus' disciples, who had once been prominent business leaders, had become little children in the faith. This was hard to do, and it is probable that many began this program only to back off later and return to their former lives. Those who encouraged monks to return to former lives were the ones who made them stumble.

Matthew misunderstood the term "little ones." He thought they were the same as the children, so he put the teachings about children and little ones together. Luke has the parable of the lost sheep in the context of Jesus defending the tax collectors and sinners against the attacks of the Pharisees (Luke 15:1-7). In that context, the sinners and tax collectors were clearly the "little ones" whom Jesus defended. Recognizing what important businessmen these sinners had been, the Gospel of Thomas refers to the lost sheep as the largest sheep of the flock, the one loved by the shepherd more than all of the rest (logion 107).

A donkey millstone. The donkey millstone is the upper millstone, a huge, heavy rock, that was carefully chiseled from volcanic rock and constructed so that a wooden "tongue" could be inserted in two places at opposite sides of the circle. Then a bolt could be put through the hole in each place to hold the tongue securely to the upper millstone. At the ends of each of these two tongues a donkey was tied, and the two donkeys were made to go around in circles so that the upper millstone would turn around over the top of the lower cone shaped millstone and grind the wheat. If the tongues were not secured to the upper millstone, there would be these two holes in the stone through which one end of a rope could be tied. The picture offered here is that the other end would be looped around the person's neck. If this heavy stone were then thrown into the sea, it is obvious that it would sink, and the person tied to it would sink as well.

Angels in heaven. This is similar to the belief of the Ahura Mazda religion. Those believers thought there was an angel (fravashi) in heaven for every believer on earth. The angel would stand before God in the heavenly court and intercede in behalf of the individual for which he was responsible. This warning was that Pharisees and others should be careful about despising the tax collectors (the little ones), because they, like other Jews, had guardian angels who could intercede for them against their accusers in the heavenly court. Should the Pharisees cause one of these new recruits to fall back into his old vocation the Pharisees would be severely punished--death worse than drowning.

Your hand or your foot. In the Sermon on the Mount, this saying does not include "the foot" (Matt 5:30). The original context for this is the Sermon on the Mount. Matthew used these sayings again here just because the word "stumble" was used, and he wanted to keep a list of all of the sayings on the same topic together. He added "the foot" to the saying, but Matthew evidently did not understand the importance of the saying in the Sermon on the Mount. There the hand that masturbated would defile the monk and cause him to stumble, ritualistically. The same is true of the eye which could stimulate nocturnal emissions, but the foot does none of these things that could cause defilement, so it is not included in the Sermon on the Mount. Matthew added the word "foot," possibly because it is the foot that stumbles, physically. Anyone who would be willing to chop off his hand should also be willing to chop off his foot, but here the context does not relate it to committing adultery as it does in the Sermon on the Mount (Matt 5:27-30).

Scholars have often wondered why Matthew has some teachings in two places in his gospel. The answer is very simple: he followed the same editorial policies the rabbis followed. They classified things of the same topic together, and they had no cross-references or footnotes, so they just repeated a teaching as many times as necessary to keep all topics together. An example of this is evident in a Mishnaic tractate called Erubin, which is a nine chapter tractate on the topic of the áye-roov (עירוב). Orthodox Jews were forbidden to travel more than 3,000 feet away from their property on the Sabbath. Many times they needed to travel farther, especially to walk to the synagogue, so they had to develop legal fictions to permit such travel. One of these was the erub. If a Jew walked 2,000 cubits (3,000 feet) on the day before the Sabbath, he could place there some food and claim that as the border of his property. Then, he could walk to his erub on the Sabbath and after that an additional 3,000 feet. This enabled him to walk 6,000 feet on the Sabbath. The entire tractate, Erubin, gives the laws related to the erub. In the midst of all these laws is the following discussion about a caravan camp: If a caravan should camp in a valley, and the fence that surrounded it was made from cattle harness, they were permitted to move around inside the circle only if the fence was ten hand breadths high and there were not more breaks than construction.

> Every opening that is up to ten cubits is permitted, because it is like a gate. More than this is forbidden. They surround [the camp] with three ropes [in parallel], the second higher than the first, and the third higher than the second, only there must be three handbreadths between one rope and the next. The measure of the ropes [all three together] in thickness is more than one handbreadth so that the whole [fence] is ten handbreadths [tall]. They may surround the camp with [a fence of] reeds, but there must be three handbreadths between one reed and the next. [These are the rules] they spoke with reference to a caravan, according to Rabbi Judah, but the scholars say they did not speak with respect to caravans [in general] but only to the [one] existing [situation]. Any partition that does not have both perpendicular and horizontal [reeds] is no partition, according to Rabbi Jose bar Judah, but the scholars say [only] one of the two [is required]. There are four things permitted in camps: 1) [Campers] may collect wood from anywhere; 2) they are exempt from washing hands, 3) [they are exempt] from the laws of demai produce, and 4) [they are exempt] from [preparing] the erub (mErub 1.8-10).

The editor evidently had this unit in his possession when he compiled the tractate on Erubin. This unit really belonged under the heading of camps or caravans, but it also included at the end, this one word, "Erub." Therefore the unit also belonged here. The editor did not take just the last sentence from the unit and discard all the rest. He used the whole set of rules as he found them. Matthew was more selective than that; he did not include the whole Sermon on the Mount in chapter 18, but he did use parts of it again in other parts of his gospel.

Enter into life. This has the same meaning as "entering the Kingdom of Heaven" (Matt 5:20; 7:21; 18:3; 19:23; 23:13; 25:10).

Will he not leave the 99. If he were really herding a hundred sheep in the mountains of Judah or Israel, the answer to this question is, "No!" No good shepherd would leave 99 sheep unattended to look for one. If he did, he would find the 99 lost when he returned. Many scholars[6] have been very inventive in their defense of the shepherd who left the 99 sheep unattended on the mountains. He could not really have left them in danger, could he? But this is to miss the point of the parable. Jesus was not trying to give instruction on sheep care. He was speaking in coded language about lost tax collectors who got involved in business with the Roman government rather than a sheep that got lost on the hillside.

The one that is lost. The Gospel of Thomas (107) has a variant version of this parable. In that document the sheep that was lost was the largest of the flock, and he was the one whom the shepherd loved more than the entire flock of 99 other sheep. Petersen argued that the Gospel of Thomas version is the original and that it is not gnostic. He further insisted that the large lost sheep was all Israel.[7] He identified this one sheep with the entire flock of Ezek 34.[8] This Matthean pericope is clearly related to Ezek 34, but for Ezekiel the lost flock constituted all of the Jewish exiles who had been pushed off the land. It was not only one sheep that was lost.[9] According to Matthew (10:6; 15:22-24; 18:11), Jesus was greatly concerned for the Jews who had been unfaithful and should be restored to the faith. It was called "raising the dead." This meant being restored to the rest of the flock. Among these were the wealthy businessmen who had compromised their nationalism by engaging in business with Rome. Some of these were the tax collectors and sinners. The wealthy men who became Jesus' apostles were some of the most prosperous people in Palestine. That may have been the reason Thomas identified them with the largest sheep. According to the Gospel of Truth 31.35-32.9, the entire flock was on the left hand of the shepherd until the one lost sheep was found. Then all 100 moved to the right, implying that the salvation of the 99 depended on the one. By arguing that the one large sheep that was lost represented all of Israel Petersen ignored the 99 who were also members of the flock of Israel. The Lord's flock did not include those outside the contract, the non-Jews.

---

[6]For example, see J. Jeremias, The Parables of Jesus tr. S. H. Hooke (New York: Scribners, c1963), p. 133; M. J. Lagrange, Evangile selon Saint Luc (Paris: Gabalda, 1941), p. 147; F. Bussby, "Did a Shepherd Leave Sheep upon the Mountains or in a Desert? A Note on Matthew 18:12 and Luke 15:4," ATR 45 (1963):93-94; and K. E. Bailey, The Poet and the Peasant (Grand Rapids: Eerdmans, c1976), pp. 149-50.

[7]W. Petersen, "The Parable of the Lost Sheep in the Gospel of Thomas and the Synoptics," NovT 23 (1981):137.

[8]Petersen, "Lost Sheep," pp. 132-33.

[9]Petersen, "Lost Sheep," p. 145, also noted verbal relationships between the Medieval document, Exodus Rabba 2.2 and the Lukan version. He concluded from that that Luke was dependent upon Exodus Rabba. If there was any dependency it would have been Exodus Rabba's dependence on Luke.

Those who knew their scripture recognized the words of the Psalmist who had gone astray and was pleading with the Lord to go look for him and rescue him, because he was one who knew the commandments and was well worth saving (Ps 119:176). The tax collectors were in the same situation. In addition to Ezek 34, readers might also recognize the reference to the time David left his flock of sheep in the wilderness to come down to the battle to help the Israelites in their conflict against the Philistines (1 Sam 17:28).

The 99 who were safely in the fold, needing no care, deliverance, or repentance represented the Pharisees, who are otherwise pictured in parables and chreias as "righteous," "healthy," "wheat," etc. If the wilderness where the sheep had been left was the same as the field with both weeds and wheat and the field where there is buried treasure, then we are talking about the promised land, the place where the Kingdom of Heaven[10] was expected to function as soon as the Romans were driven out. There seems to have been little danger of the Pharisees going astray there. They were the ones who thanked God that they were not like other men. Jesus conceded their righteousness many times, maybe satirically, but nonetheless, he started the argument with the same presuppositions as the Pharisees. Since that was the case, then, how should this Jewish sinner be treated in the promised land? The Pharisees would exclude him, whereas Jesus argued that he should be brought back into the fold which was part of Jesus' recruitment program. Rabbis thought the Lord had the same feeling about the Israelites that Jesus did. They held that the Lord sent Moses down to look after the Israelites, because he said, "If a single individual of them would fall--Look! It would be to me as if all of them [fell]" (Mek Bahod 4.62).

TEXT

Matthew	First Testament
15If **your brother** sins, go, **correct** him between you and him alone. If he will listen to you, you have gained **your brother**, 16but if he will not listen, take with you **one** or **two** more, so that	You shall not hate **your brother** in your heart, you shall surely **correct** your fellow citizen and not bear sin because of him (Lev 19:17). **One** witness shall not **stand** against anyone. For any iniquity or for any

[10]J. Klausner, The Messianic Idea in Israel, tr. W. F. Stinespring (New York: MacMillan, 1955),p. 235, said, "The Hasmoneans were influenced by a strong faith that the hour had come for the 'kingdom of heaven,' that is the kingdom of the God of heaven, to be revealed to the world and the kingdom of Greece to fall." Klausner seemed to think the Hasmoneans did not achieve their goal, because they did not destroy all Gentile nations and rule the entire world. Had they succeeded in doing that they would have acquired the Kingdom of Heaven. See also Buchanan, Jesus: The King and his Kingdom (Macon: Mercer U., c1984), pp. 145-47.

at the mouth of two witnesses or three
every **word shall stand**, [17]but if he disregards them, tell the church. If he disregards the church, let him be to you as the gentile and the tax collector.

sin in which he transgresses.
At the mouth of two witnesses or at the mouth of **three** witnesses the **word shall stand** (Deut 19:15).

COMMENTARY

If your brother sins. This is the text of Vaticanus (B) and Sinaiticus (א). Bezai (D) and some other late texts add "against you," presuming that the sin would not concern a brother if he himself was not injured by the act. The witness involved, of course, might be the one offended, but that is not the only possibility. Monks were concerned for maintaining a sinless community as well as obtaining justice for themselves. That fact might effect the interpretation of this text, because this seems to refer to monastic ethics, which is directed to brothers. The goal of the community was to be sinless and to lay up works of supererogation to remove the sins of Israel. Therefore it was not considered fault-finding to call a brother's attention to his sin. This allowed him an opportunity to repent and make forgiveness possible on the Day of Atonement. The plan was to keep these faults at as low a key as possible. As in the Sermon on the Mount the goal was for the case to be settled out of court (Matt 5:25). Cases should not be taken to the highest court that could be settled locally. The first step, then, was to talk about it with the sinner himself. If he repented, then the case received no further attention. If it did not then further steps were necessary. This would be true whether the witness was also the one offended or not.

There is a text of NT times that may show dependence upon this Matthean passage. It at least reflects the same spirit and logic. It also shows the same motivation for confrontation. Instead of vindication the goal is to remove sin from the community and establish reconciliation and peace.

> You shall love one another from your heart. If anyone sin against you, speak to him [about it] in peace. Drive out the venom of [your] hatred, and do not harbor deceit in your soul. If, after he has admitted [his sin] he repents, forgive him, but if he denies [it], do not argue with him lest, after he has taken oaths, you sin doubly (TGad 6.3-4).

Take with you one or two more. This was standard legal procedure. It required two or three witnesses to condemn a person in court (Deut 19:15). In any judgment case where reconciliation could not be achieved between the two people directly involved it was necessary to find some outsiders who might evaluate the case more objectively than the participants of the dispute. The monastery whose document was preserved in a cave alongside the Dead Sea ordered,

> Also let a man not bring a case against his neighbor before the many that has not been tried before witnesses (1QS 6.1).

This was to prevent frivolous cases from being brought to superior courts. The same procedure was applied to the debtor who needed to be reconciled before the Day of Atonement. Rabbi Isaac said the debtor should go to the creditor with money in the palm of his hand and offer to make restitution. If he refused to be pacified Rabbi Chisdah said he should come to him three times with three people each time. Each time he should ask for forgiveness before the witnesses. Rabbi Jose ben Chanina said he should ask for pardon no more than three times. If the creditor has already died the debtor should bring with him ten people to the grave of the deceased and confess his sin against the deceased (bYoma 87a). Ten people constitute a minyon, the number required to make up a congregation.

Tell the church. If he disregards the witnesses, the case has to come before the entire congregation--at least ten male adults. This is the equivalent of the Dead Sea monastery's group called "the many." This was the group that had taken on itself the responsibility of being a sinless, redeeming remnant for Israel. It would function as the court of last appeal. The accuser in this case was to present the case first to the individual, then to two or three, and only after that, would he take the situation to trial before the whole community. This was to avoid shaming the sinner publicly if it were not necessary.

As a tax collector and a gentile. The congregation acted as a civil court, and it was authorized to excommunicate the sinner from this apartheid community. Gentiles and tax collectors were equally alien to Matthew, even though Jesus defended the tax collectors against the Pharisees. In the eyes of Matthew becoming like a tax collector or a gentile was as far from being included in the sinless community of the contract as was possible. Monks worked arduously to keep their community sinless so that their monastery might be a place where the Lord would condescend to dwell.

Other sects also had rigorous rules that were required. Their goals and logic were basically the same. Any member who sinned by breaking the law could be excommunicated. For example,

> Everyone who rejects these laws in agreement with all of the laws that are found in the Torah of Moses will [not] be reckoned among all the sons of truth, because his soul has rejected the foundations of righteousness. Because of his rebellion let him be sent away from the presence of the Many (4Q266.5-7).

The segregation of members of this sect from those who were excommunicated was very great. The commandment continues:

> Those who transgress them [God's true laws] you will curse, but we are your redeemed people, the sheep of your shepherding. You [God] curse their transgressors, while we uphold [the law]. The one who was excommunicated leaves, and [as for] the man who eats with him or greets the one who was expelled or associates with him, the matter will be recorded by the Mebaqqer, and his punishment will be assigned (4Q266.13-16).

Those who believed that the congregation to which they belonged was the only means of salvation were terrified by the thought of excommunication. They could not just join another church, as would be done today. Extra ecclesiam salus non est meant that very church to which they belonged.

Like Matthew, the Pharisees thought the tax collectors were traitors and no closer to communion with God than gentiles. Neither one had the pro-gentile bias that some scholars hold.[11] Jesus disagreed with the Pharisees on their attitude toward the tax collectors, so it is unlikely that this sentence was part of Jesus' statement. It is not coherent with the teachings of Jesus reflected in the chreias and parables. This may have been composed by Matthew or by some other author who held the same opinions as Matthew.

The fact that Matthew did not force his own anti-gentilic, anti-tax collector point of view into Jesus' parables and chreias shows his integrity and respect for Jesus' words. The recognition that there is a difference of view point between Jesus and Matthew should prompt scholars to give greater credence to the words of Jesus reported by Matthew than would be the case if there were only one opinion reported.

TEXT

Matthew	First Testament
[18]I tell you under oath whatever you bind on earth will be bound in heaven, and whatever you release on earth will be released in heaven. [19]Again I tell you under oath, "If two of you agree on earth concerning any matter, whatever they ask it will	Sing and rejoice, daughter of Zion, because, look! I am coming, and **I** will dwell **in your midst**, says Yahowah (Zech 2:14; RSV 2:10). You will eat and be satisfied, and you will praise the name of

[11]For example see K. W. Clark, "The Gentile Bias in Matthew," JBL 66 (1947):165-72. For an opposing position see D. C. Sim, "The Gospel of Matthew and the Gentiles," JSNT 57 (1995):19-48.

happen to them before my Father in heaven, [20]for wherever two or three are
gathered together in my name, there **I am in their** midst."

Yahowah, your God who has performed miracles with you. My people will not be ashamed for the age, and you will know that
I am in the midst of Israel (Joel 2:26-27)

I heard him speaking to me from the temple . . . "The place of my throne and the place of the footstool of my feet where **I** will dwell **in the midst** of the children of Israel for the age" (Ezek 43:6-7).

TECHNICAL DETAILS

The pericope deals with two subjects: 1) authority both of the apostles and of the church, and 2) the numbers two and three, both in relationship to witnessing in court and to the formation of a valid congregation. These verses continue the subject just before. The church had the authority to expel sinners from the community, but members were required to go through proper procedures to get this done. Once due process requirements were met, the church was authorized to act. Furthermore, the church had apostolic authority. It spoke in behalf of God; that which it decreed was God's decree. This was the same authority given earlier (Matt 16:18) to Peter. The fact that it is given here to the church suggests that Peter earlier symbolized the Petrine church.

COMMENTARY

Whatever you bind on earth. This is the same authority that was given to Peter (Matt 16:19). Here it is given to all of the apostles. This is apostolic authority.

In the midst. The real presence of the Lord among his people was believed to be in the tent of meeting in the wilderness or in the holy of holies of the temple. There a bonfire was kept burning day and night and was visible in the day time through the pillar of smoke and at night in the pillar of fire which went up to heaven from the sacred place on earth. This was called the Shekinah. Israelites wanted God's presence in their midst, because with his presence they were assured that they could eat and be satisfied, their land would be restored, and gentile nations would be converted to Judaism. Then the contract Jews had made with the Lord would be fulfilled, and Jews would not be ashamed again.

Wherever two or three. When the temple was not in existence Israelites and Jews had to find other ways to recognize and justify the presence of God in their midst.

On the basis of legal concepts Jews looked for God's presence in their contract and through legal agents. Since a legal agent is legally identical to the principal who sent him, these are the legal terms by which God could be legally present.

Rabbi Hananiah said that if two sit together, not speaking the words of the Torah this would be the seat of the scornful (Ps 1:1), but if they were speaking words of the Torah (the contract) then the Shekinah would be in their presence (Mal 3:16; mAboth 3.2; Sifra, Kodashim #4.8, 89a). Following the text of Deut 19:15, two witnesses constituted the smallest number valid for punishment in court (mAboth 3.2).

The Psalmist prayed to the Lord, asking that he answer him at an acceptable time (Ps 69:14). Then rabbis asked the question, "When is an acceptable time?" "In the hour when the community prays" (bBer 8a).

In this chapter Matthew brought together as many teachings that related two or three with authority as he could: 1) First there was the quotation from Deuteronomy, 2) then there was the case of witnessing to a brother's sin, 3) the third dealt with the authority of two brothers in prayer, 4) and the fourth dealt with the legal authority of two or three brothers acting in Jesus' name. Orthodox Jews still today require ten undefiled adult males to be present to constitute a congregation valid for prayer. The idea that ten comprise a congregation is as old as Genesis. When Abraham interceded with the Lord to save the city of Sodom, he first asked the Lord to save the city for 50 righteous people; when he could not find 50, he reduced the number to 45, 40, 30, 20, and ten, but when he was not able to find ten righteous people in the city, he stopped interceding for a congregation (Gen 18:22-33). Rabbis had different prayers that could be said for different numbers of people, but the smallest number that could recite a common grace was three (mBer 7.1-4).

Through a legal agent a person could be legally present when he or she was physically absent. The same is true today. A person's legal agent was considered legally the person himself or herself (mBer 6.5). Since Jesus appointed the 12 to be his apostles, they were recognized as agents of Jesus, functioning with his authority and in his name. They assumed that Jesus could make any request he wanted of God, and God would grant it. Therefore, if two of his apostles agreed that something was in the best interests of the church, they were authorized to ask for it and expect that the request would be granted. They also believed that Jesus was legally present wherever two or three of his apostles were gathered together. Legally he was present with every single apostle, but communally two or three were required to comprise a congregation.

It was not out of character to stage the conditions of prayer according to the legal standards for witnesses in court. The word "prayer" is the proper term to use in court even today. That which the plaintiff asks of the judge or jury is called his or her "prayer for relief." Prayers are addressed to God in the heavenly court in the same way that prayers are addressed to human judges or juries in civil or criminal courts today.

TEXT

Matthew	First Testament
[21]Then Peter came and said to him, "Lord, how many times can my brother sin against me, and I forgive him? **Seven times?**" [22]Jesus said to	**Seven times** a righteous man falls and rises (Prov 24:16).
him, "I do not say to you, '**seven times,**' but **seventy-seven times.**"	Cain is avenged **seven times**; Lamech [will be avenged] **seventy-seven times** (Gen 4:24).

COMMENTARY

My brother. In typical Jewish and Christian editing style Matthew has put together his collection of narratives dealing with one topic. The narrative above dealt with the brother who had sinned. Here again the topic deals with "brother" and "sin."

How many times. This was a reasonable question to be raised in a community that set out to be sinless. On the one hand, sinlessness required that the unrepentant sinner be expelled, so that the rest of the community could be sinless. On the other hand, it was necessary for one brother to forgive another brother who repented, so that the community could continue to be sinless, but what should the community do with the brother that kept on sinning and kept on repenting? The rabbis answered this question by saying that if a man said he would sin and repent and sin again and repent, he would be given no chance to repent (mYoma 8.8). Rabbi Jose ben Judah said if a man commits a transgression, he can be forgiven up to three times, but the fourth time he will not be forgiven. This is proved by the text, **For three transgressions of Israel--and for four I will not turn it away** (Amos 2:6; bYoma 86b).

Jesus' response here is clearly related to the discussion in Genesis. When Peter asked if he should forgive his brother seven times as an antidote to Cain's vengeance seven times, he completed the thought of the Scripture passage--Not seven times as in the case of Cain but 77 times, as in the case of Lamech. The turn around came in turning vengeance into forgiveness. The limitation here was against intentional sinning to be followed by intentional repenting. Jesus did not say how the community should treat the one who sinned with malice afore thought, planning to repent over and over again. From the standpoint of the other brother, at least, he should be treated as if his sin was not intentional and his repentance was sincere. Jesus said there should be no end to the number of times one brother forgave another.

Jews and early Christians believed that they were in "exile" from the promised land under their own messianic king for one reason only: they had sinned, breaking the contract with the Lord. Therefore the Lord had divorced them (Deut 24:1). He would not make a new contract with them and restore them to the promised land until they had completed their sentence, serving enough time in "prison" to pay for their crimes. One of the Dead Sea Scrolls tells what God must have thought, according to the author's opinion:

> They have rejected my laws;
> their soul has scorned my torah.
> Therefore I have hidden my face from them
> until they pay for their iniquities (ישלמו עוונם) (4Q389.5-6).

There was still another possible way by which the Lord might restore his people to the promised land. He could forgive their iniquities. If this were to happen it would take place according to the rules of the Day of Atonement. On the Day of Atonement Jews understood that God would forgive the sins members of the contract community had committed against him, but atonement would not be complete until all believers had become reconciled to onc another. Therefore, it was necessary both for the sinner to repent and try to obtain reconciliation and for the one against whom he had committed the crime to forgive and become reconciled to the sinner. Either the criminal or the person against whom he sinned was able to prevent atonement from taking place. If atonement could not take place, then Israel would remain in its sin, and the Kingdom would not come. Since the coming of the kingdom was the highest goal of such monasteries as these, every nerve needed to be extended to remove sin from the midst of the land.[12] Matthew organized his material so that forgiveness was related to mercy as the following parable shows.

Rabbi Eliezer told his students that they should repent one day before their deaths. They then asked how they could know when that day would be. He responded that they could not. Therefore they should repent every day, realizing that they might die the next day. This meant they had to live every day in repentance (bSab 153a). Forgiveness and repentance are two opposite aspects of reconciliation. Both are necessary and both are basic doctrines of Judaism and Christianity.

TEXT

[23]Because of this, the Kingdom of Heaven is like a human king who wanted to settle accounts with his servants. [24]As he was beginning to undertake [the project], a man who owed [him] 10,000 talents was brought to him. [25]Since he did

[12]On this see further the commentary on Matt 5:23-24.

not have [any money] to pay, the lord commanded him to be sold, together with his wife and children, and all that he had be given [to the king]. 26Then the servant fell down and prostrated himself before him, saying, "Be patient with me, and I will pay you everything." 27The Lord of that servant was merciful and released him and forgave him the loan. 28That servant, however, went out and found one of his fellow servants who owed him 100 denaria. He seized him, choked him, and said, "Pay [me] that which you owe!" 29Then, his fellow servant fell down and appealed to him, saying, "Be patient with me, and I will repay you," 30but he was not willing. Instead, he went away and threw him into prison until he paid the debt.

31Then his fellow servants when they saw the events that took place, were very deeply pained. They came and related to the lord all the things that had happened. 32Then his lord called him and said to him, "Wicked servant! All that debt I forgave you, since you begged me. 33Was it not necessary for you to have mercy on your fellow servant just as I had mercy on you?" 34Then his lord became angry and handed him over to the torturers until he would pay back all that he owed him. 35Thus also my heavenly Father will do to you, if each of you does not forgive his brother from your heart (Matt 18:23-35).

COMMENTARY

The Kingdom of Heaven is like a human king. Many rabbinic parables begin with the statements: "To what can this be compared?" "To a king of flesh and blood, who . . . " The term "human king" probably has the same connotation in Greek as the rabbinic expression "a king of flesh and blood," which means a human king, sometimes specifically a gentile king. God was frequently compared to a great human king in rabbinic parables, and it probably has the same significance here.

Breukelmann correctly noticed that there are three scenes in this parable: 1) the servant and the banker, 2) the two servants, and 3) the servant and the banker.[13]

Worshiped him. Scott said, "'worshiping him,' is something no Jew would ever do."[14]That is an overstatement. He should have said that Jews were forbidden to worship gentiles. Actually, some Jews have worshiped foreign leaders. This was standard court etiquette. For example, the Jewish king, Antigonus, worshiped the Roman general, Sossius (War 1.353)

---

[13]F. H. Breukelmann, "Eine Erklärung des Gleichnisses vom Schalks Knecht: Matthäus 18.23-35," Parresia Karl Barth zum 80th Beburtstag, ed. E. Busch (Zurich:EVZ Verlag, 1966), pp. 261-87, followed by B. B. Scott, "The King's Accounting: Matthew 18:23-34," JBL 104 (1985):433-34.

[14]Scott, "Matthew 18:23-34," p. 437.

Commanded him to be sold. In antiquity a person who did not pay his obligations could be sold into slavery. His wives and children were all considered his property and could also be sold, just as his other property, to pay the debt (Diogenes Laertius, Bion [4.47]; Isa 50:1; Amos 2:6). Rabbis said that a man was authorized to sell his daughter, and he himself might be garnisheed and sold to pay for anything he has stolen. A woman was not allowed to be sold to pay for what she had stolen, but the text does not say that she could be sold for a debt that her husband incurred. Since he could sell his daughter, he may have been allowed to sell his wife also. Then if he were also sold, his family would probably be sold at the same time (mSot 3.8).

Forgave him the loan. The discussion here is not just about a loan, but about a loan that could not be repaid. Therefore it was a debt. As in courts today, many crimes could be settled in civil courts in terms of financial settlements. On the same legal basis, in NT times the word "debt" often referred to the national debt in the treasury of merits. It was a crime that had not been corrected and justified. Jews and Christians were conscious of the great debt they had run up because of their sins, and they often spoke of them in hyperbolic terms. How could all of this be repaid? Micah asked, **With what shall I come before the Lord? Will the Lord be pleased with thousands of rams, with 10,000 rivers of oil?** (Mic 6:6-7). The understanding of the Day of Atonement theology, however, was that once each Jew was reconciled to his fellow citizen, Jews had a chance that God would forgive the debt of their sin against them.

Patte missed the painful cost of forgiveness:

> By forgiving, one does not lose anything. On the contrary, one gains something, and indeed something very good: one gains a brother and therefore the possibility of enjoying the presence of Jesus in their midst.[15]

The person who forgives loses the opportunity to recover his or her loss. If this is a financial debt, it can no longer be collected. If it is a criminal injury, forgiveness prevents the offended person from taking the case to court and receiving just compensation. Forgiveness is not cheap.

10,000 talents. A talent was about 75 or 80 pounds weight in silver. The largest unit of silver was a talent, and the largest number used in antiquity was 10,000, so this was intentionally hyperbolic to show the contrast of sums. Derrett[16]

---

[15]D. Patte, The Gospel according to Matthew: A Structural Commentary on Matthew's Faith (Philadelphia: Fortress Press, 1987), p. 255.

[16]J. D. M. Derrett, Law and the New Testament (London: Darton, Longman, and Todd, c1970), pp. 38-39.

argued that the Matthean parable is not exaggerated but makes sense, just as it is, in Near Eastern business of 2,000 years ago. People were sold into slavery to pay debts and servants who were tax collectors dealt in huge sums of money. They collected a lot and had large overhead expenses. Therefore, 10,000 talents was not an exorbitant figure. Josephus, however, said the taxes from Coele Syria, Phoenicia, Judaea, and Samaria totaled only 8,000 talents (Ant 12.175; cf. also 17.317-20), so it is not likely that one of the tax collectors in Judaea or Samaria alone would have been working with so much capital that he could have expected to earn enough in one year to pay this back.

De Boer thought the parable was unreasonable, so he set about the task of rewriting it. He changed talents to denarii, and king to person. He also omitted the references to selling a family into slavery. All of these were "redactional" additions that Matthew made to an original parable that made sense, according to De Boer's reconstruction.[17]

Derrett would have been right in saying that the servant was asking his employer only for an extension on the loan, if this had not been a parable; and De Boer was correct in thinking that the amount of the loan was excessive but, like other parables, it is not necessary that every detail of the parable cohere statistically with business practice. That was not the primary point. The point was that the employer who was also the creditor forgave the servant an extensive debt[18] and the amount was probably made in hyperbolic proportions to dramatize the huge indebtedness in contrast to the small loan of the other servant. Furthermore, it was forgiven--not just deferred. The parable as it now exists in Matthew's gospel makes better sense as a parable of Jesus than it does as a redacted parable of Matthew.

The lord. A normal title of address for a king.

A hundred denarii. A denarius was the wage for a common laborer for one day. Therefore 100 denarii represented a little more than three months' wages for a common laborer--not an impossible amount to be repaid in time. Forgiveness is a fiscal term, just as reconciliation is a fiscal term. By using a fiscal parable to interpret the message of atonement, Jesus took the treasury of merits for granted. Just as bankers could reconcile accounts by forgiving debts, so Christians could become reconciled to one another by forgiving sins. In Pharisee-tax collector terms, it was the Pharisee who would not forgive. Jesus compared him to the debtor who owed 10,000 talents to God and would not forgive his fellow Jew 100 denarii or even wait for him to pay back. According to Atonement Day theology,

---

[17]M. C. De Boer, "Ten Thousand Talents? Matthew's Interpretation and Redaction of the Parable of the Unforgiving Servant (Matt 18:23-35)," CBQ 50 (1988):214-32.

[18]About 600,000 times as large as the loan he refused to forgive. So A. H. M'Neile, The Gospel according to St. Matthew (London: MacMillan, 1915), p. 169.

the tax collector could not be forgiven on that day unless the Pharisee would forgive him his sin and chose to be reconciled to him. The Pharisee realized this, but Jesus reminded the Pharisee that he, too, was a debtor and suggested that a just God would not hold the Pharisee innocent on the judgment day if he refused to be reconciled to the tax collector.

All that debt I forgave you. This parable about debts and debtors is related to the commandment in Exod 22:25-27. In the case of the creditor who demands an unfair amount of security, requiring the debtor to suffer, then the Lord will hear. In this parable the king was the judge, the creditor, and a legal agent of the Lord. When the king heard of the injustice this was legally the same as if God had heard. If the creditor was unjust, the debtor had a right to complain (to cry out) to the judge, and the judge would hear his case--**I will hear, because I am compassionate** (Exod 22:27).

Like the parable of the Pharisee and the tax collector (Luke 18:9-14), this is a Day of Atonement parable. The rules for the Day of Atonement require 1) that the appropriate gift be brought to the altar, 2) that the one who brought the gift have all of his sins against his fellow citizen reconciled, and 3) that God forgive the sins committed against him. In this case a sinner came to God on the Day of Atonement, but his gift was either non-existent or it was inadequate to cover his many sins. He begged for forgiveness, which God was willing to grant--but on condition! The condition was that he become reconciled to his brother. Since he was unwilling to do that, his many sins were not forgiven.[19] All of this came as an answer to the question, "How many times shall I forgive my brother?"

---

[19]Buchanan, Jesus: The King and his Kingdom (Macon: Mercer U., c1984), p. 232.

CHAPTER NINETEEN

MATTHEAN PARALLELS TO THE HEXATEUCH

"Now it happened when Jesus had finished these sayings, he went away from Galilee . . ." (Matt 19:1).

The transition sentence in Matt 19:1 should indicate the end of one section and the beginning of another, but it does not. There are several more chapters in the Book of Deuteronomy, which might be dismissed if that were the only problem. Since it is not possible to provide a parallel to everything in the Hexateuch, the editor or author of Matthew might have followed the outline up to a certain point and then moved on into another book, such as Joshua. But the section beginning with Matt 19:2 does not parallel the first part of the book of Joshua as might be expected from the previous pattern. Neither does this section properly fit under a new category. Because of the summary statement in Matt 19:1, Bacon decided that this was the end of Jesus' discourse on church administration,[1] so he began with Matt 19:1b to organize a new subject heading which he called "Division A. Jesus in Judaea. Chh. 19-22."[2] The material from Matthew 19:1b-20:15, however, is really very similar in content to that found in Matt 17:22-18:35. The section from Matt 20:17-22:46 consists of a unified division which includes further things Jesus did before he began the great discourse which began with Matt 23:1. The discussion of Jesus' moving into a different geographical area in Matt 19:1 was continued in Matt 20:17. Furthermore, Matt 19:20-20:16 continues in proper sequence to resemble the continued parallel material in the Book of Deuteronomy, as is indicated below:

---

[1]B. C. Bacon, Studies in Matthew (New York: H. Holt & Co, c1950), pp. 304-307.

[2]Bacon, Studies, p. 308. See also Buchanan, Typology and the Gospel (Lanham: University Press of America, 1987), pp. 54-58.

Matthew	First Testament
Questions concerning marriage, including questions of divorce and celibacy (Matt 19:2-12).	Questions about the rules of conduct between husbands and wives, including the question of divorce (Deut 21:15-17; 22:13-30; 24:1-5).
Decision of a man who came to Jesus and wanted life of the age [to come]. Could not accept the terms of the contract (Matt 19:16-20).	Exhortations and warnings; promises and condemnations for those who become parties to the contract and either keep the contract or break it. Those who keep it will have life, and those who break it will have death. They have the decision to make (Deut 26:1-30:20).
Parable of the kingdom. A landlord who found idle people in the market places; he took them to his vineyard to work and gave them full wages against the opposition of other workers (Matt 20:10-16).	The Lord found Israel in the wilderness. He led him out and overcame his enemies, promising Jacob his allotted heritage (Deut 32:10-43).

Matt 13:54-20:16 constitutes a division in the Gospel of Matthew that resembles the Book of Deuteronomy both in order and content. The principal problem is that the "transition" sentence that was used to indicate the end of the books of Exodus and Leviticus does not come at the end of the division. This may indicate that the verse has been misplaced in copying or that the material following Matt 19:2 has been added later in between the divisions without transferring the transition sentence to conclude the new additions. If this was so, however, the person who made the additions made them in the proper sequence so as to complete the omitted portion of the Book of Deuteronomy.

TEXT

Matthew	First Testament
19:1 Now when Jesus finished these words, he went away from Galilee, and he came to the regions of Judaea **on the other side of the Jordan.** 2 Many crowds followed him, and he healed them there.	You will inherit it, that which Moses the servant of Yahowah has given you **on the other side of the Jordan** from the east (Josh 1:15).

When all the Amorite kings that were **on the other side of the Jordan,** on the west side, and all the Canaanites which were alongside of the [Mediterranean] Sea heard that Yahowah had dried up the waters of the Jordan before the Israelites until we had crossed over, their hearts melted (Josh 5:1).

When the kings who were **on the other side of the Jordan** in the hill country and on the plain and all the shoreline of the Great Sea . . . heard, they gathered together to fight with Joshua (Josh 9:1).

COMMENTARY

The other side of the Jordan. Mark, like most contemporary scholars, thought the "the other side of the Jordan" referred only to the other side of the river from Palestine, so his text has the addition of an "and." "He came to the mountainous regions of Judaea and the other side of the Jordan" (Mark 10:1). Mark did not think Jesus could both be in Judaea and the other side of the Jordan at the same time. In so doing, he followed the LXX, which made the same correction, probably for the same reason. Matthew used the term "beyond the Jordan" three times:

1) The first was when Jesus settled in Capernaum, alongside the Sea of Galilee, in the mountains of Zebulun and Nephthali, on the west side of the Jordan, Matthew thought of this as the fulfillment of the prophecy from Isa 8:23 which also mentioned Zebulun, Nephthali, the way of the sea, beyond the Jordan, and Galilee of the gentiles (Matt 4:13-15). Here the expression "beyond the Jordan" evidently is described from the eastern side of the Jordan.

2) At the end of the same chapter, however, Matthew told of people who followed Jesus from Galilee, the Decapolis, Jerusalem, and beyond the Jordan (Matt 4:25). It seems here as if the perspective was from the Palestinian side of the Jordan.

3) The third use of the expression is the one involved here in Matt 19:1. From Matthew's two previous usages it is apparent that Matthew could use the expression to mean either side of the Jordan, and some kind of context will be needed to determine its meaning here.

There are four bases on which Matthew might have made the claim that Jesus went on the other side of the Jordan to the mountains of Judaea (Matt 19:1):

1) Since the 2 1/2 tribes settled east of the Jordan, Matthew might have claimed that region as part of Judaea, from the standpoint of the kingdom, and

2) Matthew may have understood that Jesus left Galilee for Jerusalem, without giving any attention to the region east of the Jordan. He nowhere mentioned any location through which Jesus went east of the Jordan. He left Galilee and went beyond the Jordan to the mountains of Judaea (Matt 19:1). There follow nearly two chapters of teaching, and then Jesus appeared in Jericho, ready to leave, as if he had been there all the time that he was teaching (Matt 20:29).

3) Slingerland thought this meant that Matthew was composed by someone who lived east of the Jordan, and therefore always thought of Judaea as being on the other side of the Jordan.[3] There is still a fourth way to consider the role of this peculiar expression in chapter 19.

4) Consistent with his hexateuchal form, however, Matthew followed Joshua at this point. Joshua entered Palestine at Jericho. From the Book of Joshua Matthew learned that "the other side of the Jordan" was structured from the geographical position of the east side (miz-rákh ha-shéh-mesh; מזרח השמש) of the Jordan. That which was on the other side was the mountains and the Great Sea. That is the place where the Canaanites and the Amorites lived (Josh 5:1). The expression, "the other side of the Jordan," could be used from either side. When describing the eastern border, Joshua reported the geographical locations "from the east" (miz-rakh; Josh 12:1, 2). The western border was shown "in the region of 'beyond the Jordan' westward" (be-áye-vehr ha-yor-dáyn yah-máh; בעבר הירדן ימה, Josh 12:7). The early chapters of Joshua, however, that were related to the geographical area around Jericho, identified "the other side of the Jordan" with Canaan. From Matthew's point of view that was Judaea, so when Jesus taught at Jericho he was both in Judaea, and he was "in the region of 'beyond the Jordan'" (Josh 12:7) at the same time.

From Matt 19:2 to Matt 20:28, the concentration has been on Jesus' teaching rather than on his traveling. He was either stationed at Capernaum while all of this teaching was taking place (Matt 17:24), or else it was done at Jericho (Matt 20:29). Matthew has no travel narrative to cover this section as Luke does. According to Matthew when Jesus left Galilee "to the regions of Judaea" he was on his way to Jerusalem (Matt 20:17). It is not clear which route he took, but according to Matthew's typology, Jesus had to enter Judaea at the same place Joshua had entered years before. That meant he had to cross the Jordan at Jericho (Matt 20:29). Therefore his route was organized for him to cross the Jordan in Galilee, and go south toward Judaea in Trans-Jordan territory and then enter Judaea at Jericho. The reason Matthew did not spell this out specifically may have been his desire to follow Joshua carefully in this area, using the term "the other side of the Jordan" exactly the way Joshua did while directing the new Joshua to Jericho, implying that which he did not say. Since he did not say it, however, we

[3]H. D. Slingerland, "The Transjordanian Origin of St. Matthew's Gospel," JSNT 3 (1979):18-28.

can not be sure that our conjecture is accurate. That which is factual is that Jesus was described as moving from Capernaum to Jericho while imitating Joshua.

He healed them there. This is not the introduction to a series of healing miracles. There are no miracle stories in chapter 19 nor in chapter 20 until Jesus had reached Jericho (Matt 20:29). This was just a passing summary statement to cohere with the dividing statement: "After he had finished these words."

TEXT

Matthew	First Testament
[3]Then the Pharisees came and tempted him, saying, "Is it lawful [for a man] to divorce a woman for any reason?"[4]He answered by saying, "Have you not read that the Creator from the beginning **male and female he created them?"** [5]Then he said further, "For this	God created man in his image. In the image of God he created him. **Male and female he created them** (Gen 1:27).
reason **a man shall leave his father and mother and be bound [legally] to his wife, and the two shall become one flesh**, [6]so that they are no longer two but one.	Therefore, **a man shall leave his father and** his **mother and cleave to his wife, and they shall be as one flesh** (Gen 2:14).
Therefore that which God has joined, let a man not separate."	
[7]They said to him, "Why, then, did Moses command [a husband] to give [his wife] **a certificate of divorce, and sent [her]** away?" [8]He said to them, "Moses [made a concession to your hard heart and] permitted you to divorce your wives, but from the beginning it was not so, but [9]I tell you, 'Whoever divorces his wife except for a problem of offense, and marries another, commits adultery.'"	If a man takes a woman and marries her. If she does not find favor in his eyes, because of some sexual problem, he will write for her **a certificate of divorce**, put it into her hand, **and send** her out of his house (Deut 24:1).

COMMENTARY

To divorce his wife? Matt 19:3-12 is a further explanation of a teaching shown in Matt 5:31-32. There have probably been divorce laws as long as there have been marriage ceremonies. In ancient marriage laws there were contained the terms for divorce. This discussion on divorce begins with the statements about divorcing a man's wife and conclude with the same topic. This makes the entire narrative a unit, with an inclusion at the beginning and the end. This question may have been directed to Jesus at a time when the question of divorce was an important theme of discussion in Palestine. Herod Antipas had just divorced the daughter of King Aretas to marry his brother's wife, Herodias (Ant 18.109-12). The Pharisees may have been tempting him to criticize Herod as John the Baptist had done. That might have been politically dangerous.

Male and female he created them. Jesus may have followed the same logic as Paul, that the law of Moses was secondary to the teaching of Genesis (Gal 3:17). Sahlin conjectured that this initially read **Male and female he created one**. In Greek it originally had instead of "them" an alpha (α.), meaning "one." This Greek alpha, then was misunderstood by later scribes as an abbreviation for the pronoun "them" (ow-toós, *αὐτούς*). Black examined 37 texts for which scholars had conjectured emendations. He concluded that only one had merit--this one.[4] For all the rest Matthew's text makes best sense as it has been preserved.

Be bound [legally] to his wife. The marriage ceremony was a legal contract in which vows were taken, and witnesses were present. The vows involved curses called down against the parties involved if the conditions of the contract were broken by any party. The woman agreed to be subject, and the man agreed to love the woman, meaning he would provide for her adequately (Col 3:18-19).

The two shall become one flesh. This is probably a euphemism for sexual intercourse. Following the ceremony the two should begin to raise a family. In ancient Judaism, Christianity, and Islam there were laws decreeing the frequency and also the terms and times of abstinence from intercourse. There were also severe penalties for anyone who committed adultery.

That which God has joined. Since it has been commanded in Genesis how people should act in relationship to marriage, this action is taken in accordance with God's own word. The witnesses and the court were also functioning as God's legal agents in the ceremony. Since the witnesses agreed to the legal contract it was the same as if God had personally joined them. The court that would enforce the contract also acted in God's behalf, so, legally, it would be God who would bring down the curses upon them if they should break the contract.

---

[4]D. A. Black, "Conjectural Emendations in the Gospel of Matthew," NovT 31 (1989):12-14.

Let a man not separate. There is no mention here of a woman divorcing her husband, because in early Judaism a woman did not have that authority. She was only a part of the contract between two fathers who negotiated for her to be the wife of one of the father's sons. She was not commanded to love her husband, because she had no voice in the contract and few legal rights. She was only required to be subject, and her husband agreed to love her, meaning he would provide for her needs the way her father had done previously.[5]

According to Josephus Jewish law did not permit a woman to initiate a divorce, and a divorced woman was not permitted to marry again if her first husband did not consent to it (Ant 15.259). When the husband gave his wife a certificate of divorce the document specified which men she might marry. If he specified individuals, this was not valid, but if he prohibited her from marrying one of his or her close relatives, a slave, a gentile, or anyone with whom she might function as a prostitute, the conditions were valid. He might give no conditions at all but simply say she was free to marry anyone she chose (mGit 9.1-3), but Josephus was right in saying that she had to have the permission of the husband who divorced her before she could remarry. Jesus did not say that there were laws that prohibited the woman from remarrying; he simply held that such a remarriage involved adultery.

The legal picture has changed considerably since then. Today, a woman not only is permitted to divorce her husband--with his consent or without it--but she has legal rights and opportunities to provide and love. Therefore she is also required to promise to love her husband. Love is a legal term that is closely associated with contracts. It has more to do with responsibility than with feeling. The husband who broke a marriage contract still was required to meet the financial conditions of the contract for divorce. This was part of what it meant to swear that he would love his wife.

Why, then, did Moses command. This introduces an argument also used by Paul. Paul noted that God made a contract with Abraham before Moses or his law existed. Therefore God's promise to Abraham happened before Moses and took precedence over Moses' law that required circumcision (Rom 4:9-16). Here Jesus argued that before there was a Deuteronomy God made no arrangement for divorce.

Except for a problem of sexual offense. Matthew understood this offense to be some kind of sexual disqualification, because he rendered ahr-váht mentioned by Deuteronomy as por-náy-ah (πορνείᾳ). No one any longer knows of what this problem consisted. It definitely was not adultery, because a woman could be stoned to death for that. Jesus was following the demand in Deuteronomy which said a man might divorce his wife if he was dissatisfied with her because of some problem of offense (ahr-váht dah-váhr, ערות דבר). The Hebrew expression

---

[5]See further Buchanan, Biblical and Theological Insights from Ancient and Modern Civil Law (Lewiston: Mellen, c1992), 74-87.

translated here, "problem of offense" occurs only twice in the entire FT. In Deuteronomy 23 there is a list of observances required in a military camp. There must not be any man there with damaged testicles, no bastard, no Moabite, Egyptian, or man who has had a nocturnal emission the night before. Members of the camp were commanded to take care of all toilet needs outside of the camp. All of this was summarized as ahr-váht dah-váhr (ערות דבר) that were not allowed to occur in a military camp, because the camp had to be kept holy, a place where there were no women and where the Lord could walk and overthrow Israel's enemies.

The ahr-váht dah-váhr (ערות דבר) which a man found in his wife was apparently something that made her seem more offensive than most wives. She may have had longer or more frequent menstrual periods, some urinal or bowel problem, or something like that, but it is not clear what it was. In the NT it was rendered by a Greek word that has often been translated as "harlotry" (πορνεῖα), but that word also has a broader meaning.

Malina examined all of the relevant biblical usages of the term por-nay-ah (πορνεία) and discovered that it had a wide range of meanings, including idolatry, mixed marriage, sterility, or just any conduct that is prohibited by the Torah.[6] This provides a broader spectrum from which to judge the reasons a Jew was allowed to divorce his wife. Jensen further examined the subject and contended that Christians were not held to the precise limitations of the Torah. Paul used the term por-nay-ah to be the opposite of self control, and sometimes identified it with uncleanness in general (ah-kah-thar-seé-ah, ἀκαθαρσία).[7] Tobit used the term to mean passion (Tob 8:7).

Jews in NT times may have known precisely what this offense really was, and monks might have given it a more unsavory connotation for their own reasons, just as they called masturbation "adultery" (see commentary on 5:32). Witherington thought the offense was incest,[8] but if there had been an incestuous marriage, the groom would have known that in the first place. Whatever the undesirable quality was it seems to have been something about which the groom was uninformed until after the marriage was over.

There is a famous argument between Rabbis Shammai and Hillel on the proper interpretation of Deut 24:1. Most scholars hold that the disagreement was whether or not divorce was permitted at all, but that seems not to be the point. The text is as follows:

---

[6]B. Malina, "Does Porneia Mean Fornication?" NovT 14 (1972):10-17.

[7]J. Jensen, "Does Porneia Mean Fornication? A Critique of Bruce Malina," NovT 20 (1978):161-84.

[8]B. Witherington, "Matthew 5.32 and 19.9--Exception or Exceptional Situation?" NTS 31 (1985):571-76.

The house of Shammai say, "A man shall not divorce his wife unless he finds in her an ahr-váht dah-váhr (ערות דבר), as it is said, **If he finds in her an arvát davár**" (Deut 24:1). The house of Hillel, however, say, "Even if she spoils his soup, as it is said, **If he finds in her an arvát davár**" (Deut 24:1). Rabbi Akiba says, "Even if he finds another woman more beautiful than she is, as it is said, **It will happen if she does not find favor in his eyes**" (Deut 24:1; mGit 9.10).

The argument here is not whether the three rabbis will accept the legislation of Deut 24:1 or not. The question is, what is the meaning of the ahr-váht dah-váhr? Shammai said the only basis for a divorce allowed by Deut 24:1 was the ahr-váht dah-váhr. That is precisely what the text says, but Shammai did not say what it meant. Hillel said that expression allowed a very wide interpretation, including spoiling his soup, but he did not say that Deut 24:1 could be ignored. The mishnaic text does not say that Shammai disagreed with Hillel's interpretation. Rabbi Akiba even interpreted the second half the sentence on the basis of the first half. What does it mean to divorce a woman on the basis of ahr-váht dah-váhr? The first part of the sentence says the woman does not find favor in his eyes. This is the ahr-váht dah-váhr about which Deut 24:1 spoke, according to Rabbi Akiba, and he held that this was what Shammai insisted it was necessary to observe. Although many scholars assume that the offense was "unchastity" or "indecency," none of these rabbis thought ahr-váht dah-váhr was a sexual offense. This interpretation has been transferred into the Mishnah from Matthew.[9]

Jesus also acknowledged that Deut 24:1 allowed husbands to divorce their wives on the basis of ahr-váht dah-váhr. Either Jesus or Matthew translated the offense by a sexual Greek term, but Jesus did not argue against divorce on the basis of Deuteronomy. Instead he appealed to another text (Gen 2:24).

Marries another commits adultery. There are two verbs in the protasis of this sentence: "whoever divorces . . . and **marries** another." This seems to assume that divorce for any reason except ahr-váht dah-váhr constitutes adultery. It is against the law of Deut 24:1. If, however, a man obtained a legal divorce, permitted by Deut 24:1, he would still be guilty of adultery if he married another woman. Wenham compared this sentence to Matt 7:1, which has the closest structural relationship to Matt 19:9, and reached the same conclusion. He concluded, on the basis of Matt 5:31-32, that divorce itself was adultery.[10]

---

[9]For example D. R. Catchpole, "The Synoptic Material as a Traditio-Historical Problem," BJRUL 57 (1974/75):93.

[10]G. J. Wenham, "Matthew and Divorce: An old Crux Revisited," JSNT 22 (1984):95-107; and "The Syntax of Matthew 19:9," JSNT 28 (1986):17-23.

Adultery was considered to be sexual intercourse with someone else's marriage partner. According to the law, a man who had divorced his wife was no longer responsible for her. He might marry another without being considered an adulterer. In fact men in those days were allowed to have more wives than one, and it was not considered adultery, because husbands were responsible for all of their wives, and had undertaken the legal responsibility for all of them. According to te rabbis, the woman who was divorced was free to marry another man (mGit 9.3). But if no other man chose to marry her, she would have had no means of support unless her father was still alive, and she could go back to him. Possibly she had an older brother who would accept her as a financial obligation, but she had very little opportunity to earn an honorable living. If the problem was that she was not able to produce children, she would not be in great demand as a wife for someone else. Jesus may have thought the man should continue to care for her even though she was infertile, and he could solve his heritage problem by marrying someone else at the same time. At any rate he considered marrying someone else after divorcing one wife to be adultery.

There are several variants at the end of this discussion. Some texts add, "makes her to become an adulteress" (moi-khee-yoo-tháy-nah-ee, μοιχευθῆναι) (BDΦlal); some add, "and the divorced woman, after she marries, commits adultery" (moi-kháh-tah-ee, μοιχᾶται) (P25BCΘ). The text without these additions follows ℵDalitsy. These additions carry the argument further and say the man who divorces his wife forces her to become an adulteress, so his guilt is greater than if he had just become an adulterer himself. In both cases, the remarriage was treated as if the first had not been dissolved. Since the scripture said **the two shall become one flesh** (Gen 2:24), it will always be one flesh. Legal divorce or not, any future sexual activity would be done while still joined by God to the first wife or husband.

Jesus was not the only or even the first Jew to object to divorce. The Torah Scroll (11QT) consists of a group of rules intended to be enacted in the new age, after the common era of gentile rule came to an end. The basic source of these rules was Deuteronomy. Deuteronomy, however, was not followed uncritically. Parts of Deuteronomy were omitted or replaced with something else. Some of the omissions were Deut 23:18-19; 24:1-4; and 25:5-10. The editor of 11QT evidently did not approve of Deuteronomy's rules about the sexes or in divorce. He also objected to polygamy (11QT 57.17-18; also CDC 4.19-5:5).[11]

The contract that God made with his people at Sinai was a marriage contract. Therefore admonitions that apply to this contract are easily confused with advice dealing with marriage among members of the community. One of these possibilities for confusion is the frequently quoted admonition against divorce by Mal 2:13-16. The wife of a believer's youth may refer to the Jew's traditional

[11]On this see Y. Yadin, The Temple Scroll (Jerusalem: Israeli Exploration Society, 1983) I, pp. 356-57 and M. Wise, "The Teacher of Righteousness and the High Priest of the Intersacerdotium: Two Approaches," RevQ 14 (1990):605.

religion. The marriage contract that would be broken in this divorce would be the contract that God made with his people at Mount Sinai. Those who broke this contract would bring upon them the curses of the contract (Lev 26).

All of this means that the relevant term, both in the Greek of Matthew and of the underlying Torah passage, cannot be confined to the meaning "adultery." Further, since a woman convicted of adultery would receive the death penalty rather than divorce, the justification for divorce in Matthew clearly is not adultery.

TEXT

10His disciples said to him, "If this is the situation of a man with a wife it is not beneficial to marry." 11He said to them, "Not all can accept this logic, but [only] those to whom it is given, 12for there are eunuchs who have been thus from their mother's womb; there are eunuchs who have been made eunuchs by men; and there are eunuchs who have made themselves eunuchs on account of the Kingdom of Heaven. Let the one who is able to accept [this logic], accept [it]."

COMMENTARY

It is not advantageous to marry. Both Catchpole[12] and Dungan[13] correctly held that Jesus opposed divorce. The final solution to the problem of divorce, according to the disciples who had heard the argument up to that point, was not to marry. Jesus concurred, but said celibacy was not possible for all. Those who could remain celibate, should do so. This is the same judgment as that of Paul:

> I say to the unmarried and the widows, "It is good for them if they remain as also I am, but if they are not able to remain celibate, let them marry, for it is better to marry than to be burned [with passion]" (1 Cor 7:8-9).

Not all can accept this logic. The word rendered "can accept" is choh-roó-sin, (χωροῦσιν). It is the same word used in the last sentence "able to accept." The word means "make room," "give way," "separate," "advance," "succeed," "go forward," "hold," etc. The way in which people advance or succeed in this context is to give up marriage and become celibate. Not all are able to be this self-disciplined.

Eunuchs for the Kingdom of Heaven. It is possible that Jesus meant here that those who took vows of celibacy, which, in effect, made themselves eunuchs,

---

[12]Catchpole, "Synoptic Material," p. 106.

[13]D. L. Dungan, The Sayings of Jesus in the Churches of Paul (Oxford: Oxford U., 1971), p. 89.

because they could no more have intercourse than men who had been emasculated.[14] There is some evidence, however, that the meaning was more extensive than that. There were pious monks who were willing not only to chop off their hands and pluck out their eyes (Matt 5:29-30; 18:8-9) to avoid ritual defilement but who had themselves castrated so that they could no longer have nocturnal emissions or be tempted into any other kind of sexual defilement. One such monk was Origen who had himself emasculated for this purpose. Wisdom of Solomon praised the celibate woman who bore no children, but kept herself undefiled and the man who became a eunuch and had done nothing lawless "with his hands"[15] (Sol 3:13-14).

Deuteronomy said that a man with damaged sexual organs could not be admitted into the assembly of the Lord (Deut 23:1). Josephus interpreted this to mean that Jews should shun eunuchs because they had deprived themselves of their virility (Ant 4.290). Rabbis discussed at great length the guilt of a man who became sterile, either by accident or by intention, whether he was young or old (bSab 110b). The Deuteronomic restrictions on eunuchs is in conflict with the Levitical demand for ritual purity. Scholars have resisted the plain meaning of this passage. One was Blinzler, who, nevertheless thought this statement was a genuine word of Jesus.[16]

Quesnell followed DuPont in arguing that "making oneself a eunuch" was a metaphorical statement that meant remaining celibate after a divorce.[17] It was not to be taken literally. Plummer thought that it was improbable that Jesus taught this. He did not think it was reasonable for a person to teach, on the one hand, that marriage was indissoluble, was intended that way from the beginning of creation, and then advocate celibacy.[18] There are other teachings of Jesus, however, indicating that he did teach celibacy, such as his denial of his mother and his reminder to his apostles that they should have no father on earth. His apostles were those who had left brothers, sisters, fathers, mothers, and children for Jesus' sake

---

[14]So P. Farla, "'The Two Shall Become One Flesh,'" S. Draisma (ed.), Intertextuality in Biblical Writings (Uitgeversmaatschappij: J. H. Kok - Kampen, 1989), p.70, says, "They have chosen to be eunuchs for the sake of the kingdom of Heaven. . . . The word castration can only be applied to the second group of eunuchs" [i.e. those who have been made eunuchs by others].

[15]Possibly meaning that had not masturbated.

[16]J. Blinzler, "Jesus and his Disciples," Jesus in his Time, ed. H. J. Schultz (Philadelphia: Fortress, 1971); "Eisin Eunouchoi. Zur Auslegung vom Mt 19.12," ZNW 28 (1957):254-70.

[17]Q. Quesnell, "'Made Themselves Eunuchs for the Kingdom of Heaven' (Mt 19,12)," CBQ 30 (1968):335-58.

[18]A. Plummer, An Exegetical Commentary on the Gospel according to S. Matthew (London: Stock, c1909), pp. 259-60.

(Matt 19:29). Daniel concluded that Jesus was speaking of the Essenes.[19] The Essenes had monks in their order, to be sure, but they were not the only ones. Jesus seems also to have approved of celibacy.

TEXT

[13]Then they brought to him children, so that he might put his hands on them and pray, but the disciples warned them [to stay away]. [14]Jesus, however, said,

"Permit the children to come to me
and do not prohibit them,
for of such as these is the Kingdom of Heaven." [20]

Then after he had laid his hands upon them he went away from there.

COMMENTARY

This unit is a chreia. 1) The speaker was identified--Jesus. 2) The situation that prompted the speaker to speak was given--people brought children to Jesus. 3) Jesus' response was given--he permitted them to come, and 4) the unit is very brief.

<u>The disciples warned them [to stay away]</u>. The disciples evidently thought Jesus was too important a person and had too many important things to do to be bothered with children. This was before the time when politicians attracted votes by kissing children.

<u>Is the Kingdom of Heaven</u>. Typologically, the children of Jesus' day were like the children of the wilderness. Since they were not yet of bar mitzwah age, let alone adults, they were not responsible for the decision made by the adults because of the bad report brought back by the spies. Therefore the curses that applied to the adults (Deut 1:29) did not apply to them, and they were the ones who finally entered the promised land under the leadership of Joshua, forty years later. Likewise the children in the new Joshua's (Jesus') day were innocent of the sins of such adults as the Pharisees, the scribes, the elders, and the Herodians. The Kingdom of Heaven here is an antitype of the Land of Canaan into which Joshua led the survivors of the wilderness generation. The new children would become the new heirs of the new Land of Canaan. Montefiore overlooked the importance of the Kingdom of Heaven in the message of Jesus when he said,

---

[19]C. Daniel, "Esséniens et Eunuques," <u>RevQ</u> 6 (1966-67):353-79.

[20]This is a little poem with the first two lines as a couplet and the third as a justification or summary.

At such a time, it is obvious that the only really important thing is the "salvation" of the individual. "Society" is about to break up altogether. Again, Jesus is thinking of the individual case.[21]

Rabbi Joshua, commenting on the passage, **You are standing today--all of you . . . your children** (Deut 29:9), asked why children were brought, since they were not mature enough to make adult decisions. His answer was that parents brought them to increase the reward of those who do the Lord's will (Mek Pisha 16.55-57). Later rabbis said that when the Shunammite's son died the Shunammite ran to Elisha for help, but Gehazi tried to drive her off. When Elisha found out, he said to let her come, and he sent Gehazi to her home to revive her son (ExodR 19.1).

TEXT

Matthew	First Testament and Josephus
[16]Now look! After he approached, one said to him, "Teacher, what **good** shall I do in order that I might have life of the age?" [17]He [Jesus] said to him, "(Why do you ask me about **the good**? There is one who is **good**),	For a **good** acquisition I have given you; do not abandon my Torah (Prov 4:2).
	The one who misdirected the righteous in an evil way will fall into his own pit, but the perfect will inherit **good** (Prov 28:10).
but if you want to enter into **life keep the commandments.**" [18]He said to him, "Which ones?"	Let your heart cleave to my words; **keep my commandments and live** (Prov 4:4).
Jesus said, "**You shall not murder; you shall not commit adultery; you shall not steal; you shall not bear false witness;**	**You shall not murder; you shall not commit adultery; you shall not steal; you shall not bear** against your neighbor **false witness** (Exod 20:12-13).

[21]C. G. Montefiore, Rabbinic Literature and Gospel Teachings (New York: KTAV Publishing House, Inc., 1970), p. 282.

[19]**Honor your father and mother;**

Honor your father and your mother (Exod 20:12).

You shall not avenge or hold a grudge against your fellow citizen; **you shall love your neighbor as yourself.** I am Yahowah (Lev 19:18).

and **you shall love your neighbor as yourself."**

[20]The young man said to him, "All these things I have kept. What do I

One of those reclining, by the name of Eleazar, who had a bad disposition, taking pleasure in conflict, said, "Since you have asked to know the truth, **if you want to be** just, give up the priesthood and be satisfied only to rule the people" (Ant 13.291).

still lack?" [21]Jesus said to him, **"If you want to be**

perfect, go away, sell all your possessions, and give [them] to the poor, and you will have treasure in the heavens. Then come and follow me." [22]When the young man heard the word, he went away pained, for he was accustomed to having many possessions.

the **perfect** will inherit **good** (Prov 28:10).

COMMENTARY

What good shall I do? Like other good Jews, this man wanted to be sure he would belong to the ruling community in the age to come. This man already was alive, physically. He already lived in the current age, but he was talking about legal life as a member of the community of God's chosen people in the age [to come] (zoh-áyn ai-óhn-ee-on, *Ζωὴν αἰώνιον*). Life in the age [to come] was not "eternal life," as most translations render this term.[22] Life in the age to come meant living as a citizen on the land of Palestine after the gentile rulers had been driven out, and the land was ruled by Israel's own messianic king. Life in the age to come was that which Jews had been promised as an inheritance (Matt 19:29), just as Palestine was considered to be the promised land. Those who lived in the Kingdom of God (Matt 19:23) would live on the promised land when the Davidic kingdom was renewed (Matt 19:28). They would enter into this life just as the followers of Joshua entered into Canaan during the conquest of that nation.

---

[22]So Plummer, Matthew, p. 263.

According to the Gospel of Phillip gentiles do not die, because they have never believed the truth, so they have never lived. Since they have never lived, they cannot die (4). The same author said that baptism was great, because the people who receive it would live (87). Charette noted that in Matthew "life" often had the same meaning as "The Kingdom of Heaven," because people entered into life just as they entered into the Kingdom of Heaven (Matt 5:20; 7:21; 18:3; 19:23; 23:13). "The two terms, 'kingdom' and 'life' are effectively synonymous; they both denote a final state of blessedness."[23]

The word ai-óhn (αἰῶν) renders the Hebrew oh-láhm (עולם), and was used in Jewish concepts to mean "age" or "era." It was not a part of life in a different world but of this world. It was a unit of time. The current time was called "this age," and was normally considered a common or bad age, because Jews and/or Christians were living under the rule of some other country or power. When that was the case they looked forward to life of another age, one that would follow this age on this earth on the promised land, one that Jews and/or Christians would rule. Since Jesus was expecting to be the new king of Israel, the man was asking to belong to the community which he would govern after the nation became liberated from the Romans. He thought this was a privilege that people would have to earn by doing something special. Jesus did not discourage that concept. He only made the demand higher than the man was prepared to fulfill.

Why do you ask me? Plummer followed Mark and Clement (Hom 18.3) taking this to mean the good is God.[24] "The good" might also mean "the Torah."

Keep the commandments. The commandments were the rules Jews understood to be their part of the contract they had with the Lord. The reason they were under the rule of a foreign power was that the Lord was punishing them for having broken the contract. Life in the new age would also be ruled by the contract made with the Lord. If Jews ever learned to keep all of these rules the land would be restored and the age to come would come.

Which ones? Since the FT contains hundreds of commandments, he asked for more precision. Jesus specified some of the so-called "ten" commandments. There are really only nine of these. There are ten in the Samaritan list, which includes one more--the commandment to worship and offer sacrifices on Mount Gerizim. It is easy to understand why Jews omitted that one. In order to justify calling the nine, "ten," Jews separated the first commandment from its interpretation and called the interpretation number two. Jesus here listed only five, omitting the

---

[23]B. Charette, The Theme of Recompense in Matthew's Gospel (Sheffield: JSOT Press, c1992), p. 80.

[24]Plummer, Matthew, pp. 264-65.

commandments 1) to worship only the Lord, 2) to keep from taking the name of the Lord in vain, 3) to keep the Sabbath day holy, and 4) to avoid coveting.

Love your neighbor as yourself. The word "love" in biblical concepts did not mean simply feeling kindly or something like that. The term was part of the contract Jews and Christians had with the Lord. When the Jews and Christians loved the Lord they kept the contract. When the Lord loved Jews and/or Christians he kept his side of the contract. Lovers were people or nations who lived in some contractual relationship with each other. When men married women, they agreed to love them, which meant they would provide for them adequately. To love someone the same way you loved yourself meant to provide for the other person's needs as well as you provided for your own. The only people who really fulfilled this commandment were monks who pooled all of their resources and cared for one another equally. People could love without liking one another, and they could like one another without loving. Monks took vows of poverty, celibacy, and obedience. This meant they were obligated to love, even if they found living together difficult.[25]

All these things I have kept. Some texts say, "from youth" (D) or "from my youth" (CKpl). This is a scribal addition taken from Mark 10:20, but it makes no sense for a young man to speak of his youth in the past tense. Mark called this person a rich man, Luke called him a ruler, Matthew called him a young man, so modern Christians call him a rich, young, ruler. According to Matthew's account he was young and also had many possessions, so Mark was accurate in interpreting this to mean he was rich.

If you want to be perfect. Being perfect is not precisely the same as being just or righteous, but they are both terms recognized in courts of law. They differ only in the matter of degree. When John Hyrcanus was confronted by Eleazar, he was asked if he wanted to be just. That meant he would be righteous in terms of the law. He would be one who had committed no misdemeanors or felonies.[26] Being perfect has the same meaning in a more rigorous sense. The context of John Hyrcanus was one of public legal approval with the rigorous Pharisee legalists. Jesus used the term "perfect" in a still more demanding context of monastic ethics. The word "perfect" in Western scientific concepts is a hypothetical term that is never reached in reality and is not applicable to human beings. Human beings can be affectionate, caring, kind, thoughtful, or mean, but they cannot be

---

[25]On the meaning of love see Buchanan, The Consequences of the Covenant (Leiden: Brill, 1970), pp. 290-305.

[26]See further K. Berger, "Jesus als Pharisäer und Frühe Christen als Pharisäer," NovT 30 (1988):235.

"perfect" in twentieth century terms. Scientists speak of a "perfect circle" or a "perfectly straight line," but they have never seen one.

In NT terms "perfect" meant one who kept all of the rules of the community. Every member of good standing in a community was considered "perfect." Those Jews of Jesus' day who were perfect were the monks. They took vows of poverty, celibacy, and obedience. When Jesus told the young man that he should love his neighbor as himself he was saying almost the same thing as if he had commanded him to be perfect. It was only the monks who were either perfect or were those who loved their fellow monks as themselves. See further the comment on Matt 5:48. Jesus had invited the young man to join his monastic group, taking all he had and giving it to the monastic community called "the poor."[27]

Rabba ben Abbahu told would-be proselytes first to go and sell all they had and then come and become proselytes (bAbodZar 64a). The purpose of this may have been to be sure the proselytes had nothing idolatrous in their possession. Another possibility is that they were volunteering to enter a monastic community where all of their money would become property of the group. It is not likely that the rabbi intended to accept the proselytes only on the condition that they were bankrupt of money.

Jews who once considered entering the Community of the Rule and then changed their mind received the following judgment from the council whose members considered themselves perfect:

> Everyone who refuses to enter the [ways of Go]d so as to walk in the stubbornness of his own mind, will not be accepted by the [com]munity, because his soul has rejected its truth by turning aside from the knowledge of righteous traditions and the one who restores his life. He will not be counted among the righteous people, and his knowledge, his ability, and his wealth will not be brought into the council of the community because of the defense of his evil designs and defilements (1QS 2.24-3.2).

Plummer thought the idea of giving up all of a person's money was ridiculous: "It is quite certain that our Lord could not have meant that either he or any one else can win eternal life by any such act."[28] He thought these were not anything Jesus might have said. He did not realize how important monasticism was to the early formation of the Christian church.

You will have treasures in heaven. Jews of NT times, including Paul, believed in a treasury of merits whose records were kept in heaven. Giving all of one's possessions to a community dedicated to establishing the Kingdom of God would

---

[27]See further Buchanan, Jesus: The King and his Kingdom (Macon: Mercer, 1984), pp. 171-90.

[28]Plummer, Matthew, p. 267.

certainly be considered meritorious. Since both Jews and early Christians believed that they were then living under the rule of a foreign power because their national account in the heavenly treasury was overdrawn, those who were seriously trying to gain possession of the land were also trying to cancel all of these debits by balancing them with merits.[29]

TEXT

[23]Then Jesus said to his disciples, "I tell you under oath, 'A rich man with difficulty will enter the Kingdom of Heaven.' [24]Again I say to you, 'It is easier for a camel to enter through the eye of a needle than for a rich man to enter the Kingdom of God.'" [25]When the disciples heard, they were very much surprised and said, "Who, then, can be saved?" [26]Jesus looked [at them] and said,

Matthew	First Testament
	Thus said Yahowah of armies, "If it is marvelous in the eyes of the remnant of this people in those days, also is it miraculous in my eyes?" said Yahowah of armies (MT Zech 8:6).
With men this **is impossible**; **with God** all things **are possible**.	Thus says the Lord almighty, "Even if it **is impossible** before the remnant of this people in those days, it will not be im**possible with me**, will it?" says the Lord almighty (LXX Zech 8:6).

COMMENTARY

A rich man to enter the Kingdom of God. Scholars have tried to explain this in some possible way. For instance they have said that the low gate in Bethlehem is one where a human being or a donkey might enter, but not a camel unless it were to get on its knees and crawl through. This is cute homiletics, but that is not what is meant here. Jesus was speaking hyperbolically. The disciples understood correctly, he meant a rich man could not make it. This is an exaggerated way of saying that which he said just before, "A rich man with difficulty will enter the

---

[29]On this see further Buchanan, Jesus, pp. 223-52.

Kingdom of Heaven."[30] A medieval rabbi, Rabbi Jassa, apparently acquainted with this idiom from the NT, said that if Israel presented to the Lord an opening to repentance, no bigger than the eye of a needle, the Lord would widen it so that wagons and carriages could pass through (CantR 5.2; see also bBer 55b).

Who, then, can be saved? Since a camel under no circumstances could enter through the eye of a needle, then no rich man could be saved. This aroused the anxiety of the apostles, all of whom were probably rich before they chose to join Jesus' program, and they hoped to be richer when the Kingdom came. The term "salvation" for a nation meant it was delivered from some oppressor. For an individual, it meant being a citizen of a saved nation.

With God all things are possible. This is clearly one half of a couplet formed on the basis of LXX Zech 8:6. This not only provides a nice poetic unit to remember, but it also reminded those listeners who knew their scripture of the context in Zechariah. Those who had returned to the land and not found it so grand and beautiful as they expected were discouraged, but Zechariah reminded them of the still blessed future. The Lord promised that he would again return to Zion and re-establish the city of Jerusalem. There would again be old men and little children in the streets of Jerusalem. Although all of this seemed impossible in the current circumstances, Zechariah reminded them that God was able to do what the returning Jews in Palestine could not do. The same was true of rich people who wanted to enter the Kingdom of Heaven. It is clear from the parallel use of the terms Kingdom of Heaven and Kingdom of God that they are terms that have the identical meaning. The word "Heaven" is a term used for God to avoid blasphemy that might occur if the real name were misused. The expression, "Kingdom of God," occurs in Matthew only here, in Matt 12:28, and 21:31, 43).

TEXT

Matthew	First Testament
27Then Peter in reply said, "Look! We have left everything and followed you. What, then, will there be for us?" 28Jesus said to them, "I tell you under oath, that you who have followed me, in the rebirth, when the Son of man will sit on his glorious throne, you yourselves will also will sit upon **the** twelve **thrones**	Our feet are standing in your gates, Jerusalem . . . There the tribes, the tribes of Yahowah go up . . . For there **the thrones** are set for

[30]So also Plummer, Matthew, p. 269.

judging the twelve tribes of Israel. [29]Everyone who has left houses, brothers, sisters, father, mother, children, or fields for the sake of my name, will receive many times more and will inherit life of the age.

judgment, **thrones** of the house of David (Ps 122:2-5).

[30]Many first ones [now] will be last [then],
and [many who are] last [now will be] first [then]."

COMMENTARY

We have left everything. "Everything" was not just a hypothetical term. It meant that they had left property and family to follow Jesus. They had cast their lot with Jesus; if he won, so would they. If he failed they also would lose all that they forfeited to follow him. That which prevented the young man from becoming perfect so as to enter the Kingdom of Heaven had not kept them.[31] They had taken vows of poverty, celibacy, and obedience--but not forever. This was a temporary measure they accepted as a necessary means of gaining control of the Kingdom of Heaven. They expected the ages to change within their lifetimes.

What, then, will there be for us? This is the real crux of the matter. The apostles were not interested in this question abstractly. If the young man could not enter, how about them? Some scholars think of this as a foolish and selfish question, but Jesus apparently did not. Charette, who observed the many instances in Matthew where rewards and punishments were promised, concluded that this question was a very natural one.[32]

In the rebirth. Josephus used this expression to describe Judah after the exile (Ant 11.66). Sim presumed that all Jewish and Christian thought had to fit into a linear concept of history, so he argued that the rebirth involved a complete destruction of the cosmos. All heaven and earth would pass away.[33] Burnett, however,

---

[31]T. E. Schmidt, "Mark 10.29-30; Matthew 19:29: 'Leave Houses . . . and Region'?" NTS 38 (1992):617-20, suggested that instead of "fields" the disciples left the region and traveled somewhere else. He said, "Since the disciples had left little, it would be presumptuous to use the word 'all,'" (p. 617). Therefore Luke omitted the word, but we have no evidence to contradict Matthew's assertion that they had formerly been rich, owned a great deal, and forfeited it all to follow Jesus. This is what all monks did. They did not just walk away; they gave up their status, families, and possessions. See further Buchanan, "Jesus and the Upper Class," NovT 8 (1964):195-209. The context prefers the translation "fields" to "lands."

[32]Charette, Recompense, p. 113, fn. 2.

[33]D. C. Sim, "The Meaning of παλιγγενεσία in Matthew 19.28," JSNT 50 (1993):3-12.

thought that the word rendered "rebirth" had a wide variety of meanings, everything from the creation of a new cosmos to the rebirth of an individual. In Matt 19:28, however, he correctly held that it was synonymous to "the age to come," which is the Markan and Lukan parallel (Mark 10:30//Luke 22:30). He mistakenly understood "the age to come" to mean eternal life.[34] Geyser said,

> The Palingenesia is exactly what it says in its twelve tribe context in the throne logion: the "recreation" of the twelve tribes. In exactly this meaning the word is used by Flavius Josephus, Ant. XI.iii.9: "the restoration of Judah".[35]

The Greek word literally means "becoming again." This means that some one or some thing would become again what he, she, or it had once been. Partially based on Josephus (Apion 2.218), Derrett thought this expression in Matthew referred to the resurrection,[36] and that may be implied, but it is not required. A nation that once was could be reborn and reestablished, and that might be called a resurrection, but there are other names that are also applicable.

Being reborn or born again was a legal expression. A person might be physically born only once, but the same person could be adopted into another family, join another religious sect, become a citizen of another country, and be considered "born again." This person would have a new identity after such a rebirth.[37] When a nation ceased to exist, it was thought to be dead. It could be born again when it was reestablished as an independent state. This involved making a new contract with the Lord as Jeremiah promised (Jer 31:31). That was the "rebirth" about which Jesus reportedly spoke. It had the same meaning as a national renewal.

In similar contexts "renewal" or "establishing anew" was used in relationship to the establishment of the kingdom under Israelite leadership. After Saul defeated the Ammonites, Samuel agreed to go with Saul and the people to Gilgal to establish anew the kingdom (wah-nikh-dáhsh shahm hah-mah-loo-káh, ונחדש שם המלוכה) with Saul as king (1 Sam 11:14-15). When Second Isaiah promised the Jews that the Lord was about to do something new (Isa 43:19), the plan was to restore the twelve tribes on the land under Davidic leadership.

---

[34] F. W. Burnett, "Παλιγγενεσία in Matt. 19:28: A Window on the Matthaean Community?" JSNT 17 (1983):60-72. Burnett's many suggestions for assuming later editing of this manuscript do not seem necessary.

[35] A. S. Geyser, "Jesus, the Twelve and the Twelve Tribes in Matthew," Neotestamentica 12 (1978):16.

[36] J. D. M. Derrett, "Palingenesia (Matthew 19:28)," JSNT 20 (1984):51-58.

[37] On the legal significance of being born again see Buchanan, Insights , pp. 10-17.

Jubilees said the Lord had four places on earth: 1) the Garden of Eden, 2) the Mountain of the East, 3) Mount Sinai, and 4) Mount Zion which would be sanctified in the new creation (Jub 4.26). Mount Zion was the center or the navel of the earth (Jub 8.19). In relationship to the Lord's promises that he would send the messianic king, give his children the land, fulfill his oath, bring the end, redeem his people from captivity, and comfort his people, the rabbis taught that generations were afflicted according to their iniquities.

> Said the holy One blessed be He, "In that hour I will create it [the generation who has suffered for its quota of sins] anew, and it will suffer hardships no more, and I will give you your land" (PesiqR 84a; see also (31.146b).

In a similar context of promises that the Lord would restore the kingdom was also the promise that the messianic king, the Son of man, would come.

> Said the holy One blessed be He, "I am obligated to make him a new creation. Therefore it says, **Today I have given you birth**" (Ps 2:7; Mid Ps 2.14b).

The translation of Onkelos promised the Israelites, "Yahowah will bless them alone in the age which he will renew" (TgOnq Deut 32.23). TgJon quoted the Lord,

> "I am the God of the contract of the age at the beginning," said the Lord. "I am the God appointed to renew the age for the righteous" (TgJon Jer 23.23).

Rabbi Tanhuma anticipated the time when the Lord would destroy the wicked from the age and make the righteous a new creation and give them breath (Noah 12, 19a).

Baruch promised that after the building of Zion had been destroyed, it would again be renewed and completed for the age [to come] (2 Bar 32.4). That would happen when the Mighty One renewed his creation (2 Bar 32.6). In the vision of the vine that destroyed the last cedar of the forest, the interpretation explained that the last cedar was the fourth kingdom. When its decreed time of existence was over, then the rule of the Lord's Messiah would be revealed (2 Bar 39.7). The Sibyl who pictured a future international scene foresaw a celestial conflagration on earth, a new phenomenon (SibOr 5.211-12). This did not do away with all nations, however, much less the cosmos. India, Ethiopia, and Corinth would be destroyed, but Persia would have peace, and the Jews would continue to dwell in peace around the city of God at the center of the earth (SibOr 5.206-54; see also 1QS 4.16-17, 25). Ezra asked what would happen to the souls that died before the Lord renewed his creation (4 Ezra 7.75). After a detailed answer, the Lord promised that at the last times there would be for Israel Paradise, the tree of life, the future age, the city rebuilt, and a rest appointed (4 Ezra 8.52). These were all expectations that were to take place on the earth.

Will sit on his glorious throne. The Son of man is a code term for a king.[38] It was customary for kings to sit on glorious thrones. This is an antitype of Judas the Maccabee in Dan 7. The throne on which Judas sat was the royal throne in Jerusalem. The new Son of man was expected to sit on the same glorious throne. The days of the Messiah, the rebirth, or the age to come were all expressions of the future good days Jews anticipated. Rabbis said that there would be no proselytes accepted during the days of the Messiah, because the days of the Messiah would be like the days of David and Solomon (bYeb 24b). There were no proselytes accepted in the days of David and Solomon. This means that the rabbis thought the Son of man would sit on his glorious throne in Jerusalem just as David and Solomon did.

Dupont studied Matt 19:28 together with Luke 22:28-30 and Matt 25:31. He correctly argued that all of these were intended to be related to the last judgment.[39] Only Matt 25:31, however, deals directly with the judgment. This is before the establishment of the Kingdom of Heaven. At this time the Son of man will judge first between his participants and his enemies. Then he will judge among his own people, those who should have supported him. This is the judgment mentioned in Matt 25. It is after that judgment that the Kingdom of Heaven would be established in the "new birth." Then the Son of man would sit on his glorious throne at Jerusalem, and the government would be established. At that time the leaders would be chosen and appointed to their various thrones. This is the situation described here in Matt 19:27-29.

Everyone who has left houses. Not just the apostles but everyone who sacrificed painfully to support the program Jesus led would be remembered and blessed generously in the age to come when Jesus sat on the throne in Jerusalem. The apostles had left everything for Jesus. Patte noted that there was no mention of a wife.[40] He thought that this meant that the apostles had not given up their wives. This is not the only possibility. Either they were celibate or they had wives, as Peter had, and also left them temporarily to follow Jesus. Rabbis said

---

[38]For defense of this see Buchanan, To the Hebrews (Garden City: Doubleday, 1972), pp. 38-51. C. Berger, "Die Königlichen Messiastraditionen des Neuen Testaments," NTS 20 (1973):19, overlooked some important data when he concluded that the Son of man title had nothing to do with Christological titles.

[39]J. Dupont, "Le Logion des Douze Trônes (Mt 19,28; Lc 22:28-30)," Bib 45 (1964):355-92.

[40]D. Patte, The Gospel according to Matthew (Philadelphia: Fortress Press, c1946), p. 273. A few texts (א, CKX and Syr.Cur) add "or wife," but that is not necessary to make sense of the passage.

that a man's wife was his house (mYoma 1.1). If he left his house, he left his wife. This did not mean, however, that this was a permanent divorce. In times of war the ancients left their families for the season to fight, but they returned when it was time for the crops to be planted. During times of war, those like Uriah, were obligated to stay away from their wives to be sure that defilement would not enter the battle field (Deut 23:9-14; 1 Sam 21:4-5; 2 Sam 11:6-17).

Judging the twelve tribes of Israel. If there had been any question about which kingdom Jesus was talking, the point is clear here. In the wilderness Moses appointed judges to assist him in his work (Deut 1:9-18). The rabbis took this to mean that in the promised land there would be twelve courts of the twelve tribes and that Moses would be the supreme judge over all of them (pSan 19c). The term "judge" was used to mean both judging cases in court and also ruling. The judges that governed tribes before the time of Saul were people like Gideon, Barak, Deborah, and others. Against this background, Jesus might have meant that the twelve apostles would sit on governing thrones in separate cities, each one ruling a tribe.

The other possibility is that they would be members of the great court in Jerusalem where the king would be the chief justice and the apostles would be assistant justices. According to the Torah Scroll the king of Israel in the new age was expected to have twelve leaders of the people, twelve priests, and twelve Levites as assistant judges who would sit together with him in judgment to assist him in making decisions (11QT 57.11-15). In such an arrangement as this, the apostles would probably have been classed as the "leaders of the people" (ahn-sháy ahm-móh, אנשי עמו). In any case, their offices would take place on earth on the very land that was promised to the children of Abraham whose capital city was Jerusalem.

All of this discussion is related to the young man who wanted to have life of the age [to come]. Jesus interpreted this to mean he wanted to enter into the Kingdom of Heaven which is the same as the Kingdom of God. In a discussion that compared the apostles to the young man, his possible reward with their possible rewards, Jesus spelled out his intentions clearly, using national terms, such as "renewal" which meant renewal of the Davidic kingdom, and the twelve tribes, which meant the twelve tribes of Israel, located on the promised land. The apostles would sit on real thrones judging real people on specific parcels of land within the Davidic kingdom. At the same time, Jesus as the Son of man would sit on his glorious throne in the same nation, undoubtedly at the capital city of Jerusalem. In this context it is obvious that the Kingdom of Heaven or of God about which this discussion began was the kingdom ruled by David and Solomon. This country was called the Kingdom of God, and its capital city was called the city of God. The citizens of this nation were called the chosen people of God, and the king was called the Son of man and the Son of God.

Even Boring, who many times referred to the eschaton as "the end of history," here also called this the eschaton,[41] but it was obvious, even to him, that this was not the end of history. It was the end of foreign rule over the promised land. More and more scholars are beginning to realize that Jesus was somehow related to a political movement. There are too many indications in scripture to be ignored. For example, Trumbower began his discussion with the text from Acts 5:35-39, where Rabbi Gamaliel was reported to have compared the work of Jesus to the things done by Theudas and Judas, two political leaders who were killed as subversives. Although Trumbower did not consider the author of Acts to have been an objective historian, he thought that author had sources and an obvious apologetical point of view. He would not have introduced these two zealots into comparison with Jesus if his readers had not already known that this comparison had been made.

The author of Acts tried to use this comparison to show that Jesus was superior to those other messianic pretenders. Trumbower found the comparison valid. Jesus and Judas were both Galileans who became involved with the political activities of Jerusalem, and both were popular speakers who may have sparked revolutions but neither led them. Theudas and Jesus both attempted to reenact signs: Theudas tried to become a new Joshua and open the waters of the Jordan near Jericho, whereas Jesus tried to fulfill the prophecy of Zechariah by riding into Jerusalem on a donkey. Trumbower concluded that

> the speech of Gamaliel may help us to be more confident when locating Jesus in the Jewish eschatological politico-religious realm of Judas the Galilean and Theudas.[42]

Will receive many times more. Meaning many times more than they gave up originally. He was reminding them that their sacrifice was really a good investment (cf. also Matt 5:12).

Inherit life of the age. These words return the reader to the beginning of the discussion when the young man asked how he might obtain life of the age (Matt 19:16). This expression here concludes the discussion, forming an inclusion of all of the material in between. Matt 19:30 seems to be an editorial addition. "Inheriting" was a frequently used Jewish term. Jews and Christians both considered it their right to inherit good things, including the promised land. The term "inherit" was not simply a passive term which meant people waited until someone

---

[41] M. E. Boring, The Continuing Voice of Jesus (Louisville: Westminster-John Knox, c1991), p. 229.

[42] J. A. Trumbower, "The Historical Jesus and the Speech of Gamaliel (Acts 5:35-9)," NTS 39 (1993):500-517. This quote is from p. 517.

died to leave them wealth. One of the ways ancients "inherited" was by military conquest, such as the military invasion of Canaan by Joshua.

Many first ones [now] will be last [then]. This is, on the one hand, a poetic unit called a chiasm. You can form a Greek letter chi, which looks like an X by drawing lines to join the two words "first" and "last." On the other hand it is also the beginning of a literary unit called an inclusion. The same verse is repeated in Matt 20:16, enclosing the verses in between as the unit. The teaching involves the political changes that will take place when administrations change. Those who were leaders in the current administration would be replaced, and those who held minor positions in the current administration would hold high offices. To the victors belong the spoils. This disturbed the Pharisees who were enjoying the chief seats they were holding in the current administration, and they wanted these positions for themselves in the future. They realized, however, that Jesus had already selected for his cabinet men who had formerly been tax collectors, had mingled with Romans in business, and had only recently shown serious devotion to the nation of Judah.

According to this passage in Matthew 19, Jesus embraced an eschatology where he would be king over a nation, sitting on a throne. His disciples would also sit on thrones, governing the tribes of Israel. That means Jesus would be king over the same land. Burnett mistakenly understood the Greek expression *αἰῶνος* to mean "eternal," rather than "age," so he insisted that the two promises: 1) life in the age to come, and 2) key offices in the new kingdom were unrelated. He did not believe that the disciples were promised any earthly positions of authority.[43] These two promises are more closely related than he realized. It was in the age to come, in the Kingdom of God, where the disciples were promised official positions on earth. The age to come was a future age on the promised land, but the faithful did not expect that they would live there forever.

[43]Burnett, "Matt 19:28," p. 63.

CHAPTER TWENTY

MATTHEAN PARALLELS TO THE HEXATEUCH

The belief that the fifth division of the Book of Matthew ends at Matt 20:16 rather than Matt 18:35 is further confirmed by the content of the material beginning with Matt 20:17, which parallels the beginning of the Book of Joshua. The transition sentence (Matt 19:1) says Jesus went from Galilee, along the territory beyond the Jordan, until he came to Judah in the mountain region. There is no further mention of the territory in which he ministered until after Matt 20:17, where he was on his way to Jerusalem--a natural follow-up from Matt 19:1. This further suggests that at one time Matt 19:1 was followed immediately by Matt 20:17, whether the verses in between were added later or not.

Matthew	Joshua
Jesus prepared to enter Jerusalem; he instructed the twelve to be ready. James and John asked to be made chief officers (Matt 20:17-28).	Joshua prepared to enter the land; he instructed the officers to be ready (Josh 1:1-18).
Jesus sent two messengers from Jericho to prepare (Matt 20:29-21:7).	Joshua sent two spies to Jericho to prepare for the invasion (Josh 2:1).

TEXT

20:1 For the Kingdom of Heaven is like a man [who is] a property owner who
went out early to hire laborers for his vineyard. 2 After he had agreed with the
laborers [to pay them] a denarius a day, he sent them into his vineyard. 3 When
he also went out about 9 A.M. he saw others standing in the market, idle, 4 and
he said to them, "Also you go into the vineyard, and whatever is just I will give
you," 5 and they went. When he went out again at noon and at 3 P.M. he did the
same, 6 and about 5 P.M., after he went out, he found others standing, and he
said to them, "Why are you standing here the whole day, idle?" 7 They said to

him, "Because no one has hired us." He said to them, "Also you go into the vineyard."

[8]When it was evening, the Lord of the vineyard said to the superintendent,
"Call the laborers and pay them the wage, beginning from the last [and continu-
ing] to the first. [9]Now those who had come at 5 P.M. received a denarius each.
[10]When the first ones came, they thought that they would receive more, but they
received also a denarius each. [11]When they received [their wages] they complained to the property owner, saying, [12]"These last ones worked [only] one hour
and you made them equal to us, who bore the burden of the day and its heat."
[13]He answered one of them and said, "Friend, I did not treat you unjustly. Did
you not agree with me [to work all day for] a denarius? [14]Take that which is
yours and leave! I want to pay this last one as also you. [15]Is it not lawful for me
to do what I want with the things that are mine? Or, is your eye evil that I am
good?"

[16]Thus the last   will be first
and the first,   last.

COMMENTARY

A man [who is] a property owner. This parable is very similar to one in DeutR 6.2. The word translated here "property owner" is literally "despot of a house"(oik-oh-des-pó-tay, *οἰκοδεσπότῃ*). This is the Greek equivalent of the Hebrew báh-ahl hah-báh-yet, בעל הבית, "lord of the house." The rabbis said a shop keeper was a "lord of the house" (mBMetz 3.11). This was evidently a term used for many kinds of independent business managers. The "lord of the house" here was a man who owned and managed a vineyard, so he should be called a "farmer," "nurseryman," or something like that.

Laborers for his vineyard. This parable seems not to have been directed to the apostles as Allen and Hagner thought.[1] Instead, it is more likely to have been aimed at the Pharisees.[2] Although the parable includes those who began work at 9:00 A.M. (the third hour), noon, 3:00 P.M., and 5:00 P.M., the people in the parable who are most directly discussed are only those who came to work promptly at 6:00 A.M. and worked all day, in comparison with those who came at 5:00 P.M. and worked only one hour. Patte asked if this procedure of going out and getting still more workers was a sign of the employer's compassion in

---

[1]W. C. Allen, A Critical and Exegetical Commentary on the Gospel according to St. Matthew (New York: Scribners, 1925), p. 214; D. A. Hagner, Word Biblical Commentary: Matthew 14-28 (Dallas: Word Books, c1995), p. 572.

[2]So also J. Jeremias The Parables of Jesus tr. S. H. Hooke (New York: Scribners, 1972), p. 38.

providing work for the unemployed.[3] That was beside the point. Jesus was not talking about employees, really. His real message effected the Pharisees and the tax collectors. Those who worked all day long for an agreed upon wage[4] were the Pharisees who had always kept the law and had expected that God would fulfill his contract with them and give them back the land. According to the parable Jesus, as the employer, went to the Pharisees first and only addressed the tax collectors when the work was not being completed by the Pharisees. The attitude of the Pharisees here is very similar to their attitude reflected in the prodigal son, where they played the role of the older brother. The contrast between the Pharisees and the tax collectors is shown in many parables--The Prodigal Son, The Two Sons in the Vineyard, The Wheat and the Weeds, and The Arrogant Pharisee in the Temple. This is one more.

About 5:00 P.M. he went out. Those who began working just before the payment time were the tax collectors who had only recently accepted Jesus' call and invitation to work for the Kingdom of Heaven. In the eyes of the Pharisees, these were not just the people who loitered all day; they were working against the kingdom, in the judgment of the Pharisees. They should not even be allowed to work this late in the day. They had been identifying themselves with the gentiles. When the judgment day came, let them perish with the gentiles! It would not be fair for them to be admitted into the Kingdom of Heaven without having worked for it all along.

Beginning with the last. Like other parables, this narrative has a hidden meaning. Jesus was not really talking about laborers in the vineyard, but Jews, working on the promised land. The contrast is with only two groups, the first and the last. The other groups were included just to build up the drama. The first to begin working to lay up treasures for Israel were the Pharisees. They were the ones who bore the burden of the day and its heat. The last to enter were the rich tax collectors whom Jesus had recruited. The Pharisees objected to their being admitted; Pharisees complained that it was unfair for the hated tax collectors to gain the same conditions as they themselves received. Jesus not only admitted these liberal Jews into the kingdom. He chose them as apostles. They were to be members of his cabinet. It seemed evident to the Pharisees that when the kingdom came, these men would be Jesus' chief advisors. They came last in time, but they would be first in status. There is nothing in this situation to suggest that the ones who were coming last were the gentiles.[5] At the time most of this Matthean

---

[3]D. Patte, The Gospel according to Matthew (Philadelphia: Fortress Press, 1987), p. 274.

[4]The standard wages for an unskilled worker for one day was one Denarius. So also Tob 5:15.

[5]As J. Dupont, "La Parabole des Ouvriers de la Vigne (Matthieu, XX 1-16," NouvRevThéol 79 (1957):785-97, suggested.

material was being composed the gentiles had not become an issue in Palestine. That came after Paul's mission and the fall of the temple in 70 I.A.

With the things that are mine? Jesus' argument was that the employer was free to spend his money any way he wanted, so long as he fulfilled his agreement. He agreed only to allow the Pharisees the admission for which they had worked. They behaved like the elder brother (also the Pharisees) who had stayed home and worked while the younger brother left home and spent all of his money wastefully (Luke 15:25-30). Jesus allowed the tax collectors the same admission terms, even though they came in late. There was no labor union in those days to interfere with management's negotiation. In ancient Near Eastern monarchies, kings could do as they pleased. In the parable the employer was to be compared to a king or the Messiah in the Kingdom of Heaven.

Or is your eye evil. For the meaning of an evil eye see the commentary on Matt 6:22.

The last shall be first. In the parable, the laborers who came to the vineyard last were the first to be paid, and those who came first were the last to be paid. The statement summarizes the poetic verse (Matt 19:30) which introduced the parable. The two statements form an inclusion showing the limits of the unit. Matt 19:30 is more closely related to Matt 20 than to Matt 19. Both verses (Matt 19:30 and 20:16) were probably later editorial additions, and probably had further implications. In the kingdom, the tax collectors who were the most lowly in the religious status would not only receive their pay first but they would also have the highest positions in the Kingdom of Heaven, and the Pharisees who had the highest status in this age would be lowest in rank in the Kingdom of Heaven. The parable itself, however, teaches only that all would receive the same wages, but that the last would receive theirs first so that the first could see what happened and comment on it. The parable was structured specially to provide a setting to bring up this argument. Some texts (CKDθpllattsy) add, "For many are called but few are elected" (Matt 20:16+).

It was not God, but Jesus, who was the hero in the parable. As the Messiah, he had the right to decide who would be admitted into his kingdom when the kingdom came. The Pharisees agreed that it was near the end of the age; the Kingdom would soon come. They had no suspicion that God would reverse Jesus' decision. The Messiah was a monarch, the legal agent of the Lord. If he allowed these tax collectors into the kingdom, they would be admitted. Therefore Pharisees were trying to persuade Jesus to change his mind beforehand. This was not just idle speculation or nit-picking philosophy. This had evidently been a continuing conflict that Jesus had with the Pharisees in justifying his efforts to include the tax collectors in the coming Kingdom of Heaven. Other Jewish writings later expressed the view that all Israel would have a place in the age to come (mSan 10.1) and that all would be equally treated at that time (4 Ezra 5.42). That is not precisely the teaching of Jesus, but this parable teaches that tax collectors would have equal advantages in the Kingdom of Heaven. Other teachings indicate that they would even have preferred positions which is indicated by the fact that they were already associating with Jesus and receiving positions of leadership.

There is a parable about laborers in rabbinic literature:

> He told a parable: To what can the matter be compared? To a king who hired many laborers, and there was there one laborer, and he did his work with him many days. The laborers entered to receive their pay, and that laborer entered with them. The king said to that laborer, "My son, **I respect you** (Lev 26:9). These many who have done with me little work, and I give them small wages, but I have to reckon with you a large sum."
>
> Thus the Israelites were requesting their wages before the Lord, and those 45 nations were requesting their wages before the Lord. The Lord said to the Israelites, "**I respect you** (Lev 26:9). These nations of the world have done with me little work, and I give them a small wage, but [as for] you, I have to reckon with you a large sum, therefore it is said, **I respect you**" (Lev 26:9; Sifra Lev 26.9, 111a).

TEXT

17When Jesus was about to go up to Jerusalem, he took the twelve aside by themselves, and on the road he said to them, 18"Look! We are going up to Jerusalem,
and the Son of man will be betrayed to the chief priests and scribes, and they will
condemn him to death. 19They will hand him over to the gentiles

Matthew	First Testament
to mock, whip, and crucify, **and on the third day he will be raised.**"	Come, let us return to the Lord. He has torn, and he will heal us; he has struck, and he will bind us up. After two days we shall live, **and on the third day he will raise us, and we shall live before him** (Hos 6:2).

COMMENTARY

We are going up to Jerusalem. From ancient times, people have said they have gone up to Jerusalem. From the coastal plain or from Jericho, of course, people go up topographically to reach Jerusalem, but the expression also has a theological meaning. Jerusalem is held to be the navel of the universe. Even though the adjacent mountain, the Mount of Olives, is taller than Jerusalem, Jews and early

Christians would say they went up from the Mount of Olives to Jerusalem, when they actually went down, topographically. They also said they went up to Palestine from any place on the earth, no matter the altitude of the place from which they came.

The Son of man will be betrayed. This is the third time in the gospel that the passion was predicted (also Matt 16:21; 17:22). Since he was well versed in scripture, it is reasonable to assume that Jesus could have considered his trip to Jerusalem to have ended as indicated here and for him to have interpreted it as God's will. It would be just as logical for later Christians to have deduced that he had reasoned this way, since that is the way it actually turned out.

On the third day he will be raised. In the FT passage, Hosea, probably from Judah, had condemned North Israel for separating itself from Judah and making treaties with other nations. Hosea called this relationship with other nations "harlotry." He urged Israelites to return to the Lord their God [in Judah] and David their king [in Jerusalem] (Hos 3:5). He lamented that Israel had been a bad influence on Judah (Hos 4:15), so that Judah was also stumbling, and both Israel and Judah were sick and wounded (Hos 5:13). Because of their sin God himself would punish both Israel and Judah (Hos 5:13-14), but after he had punished them both with wounds and afflictions, Hosea promised that, if they would return to God, God would restore them. He had torn them apart, but he would bind them back together again. He would restore them to life and raise them up again (Hos 6:2).

Hosea here was speaking about the united kingdom that had been divided. The restoration to life and the resurrection was intended metaphorically to mean the restoration of the nation to unity and strength. Hosea was no more speaking about individual resurrection than Ezekiel was when he told of his vision of dry bones that were restored to life. The interpretation was, **Then he said to me, "These bones are the whole house of Israel"** (Ezek 37:11). It is normal in midrash, however, for a later author to interpret an earlier text in a way that best suited the local situation of the interpreter's day. Just because Hosea and Ezekiel referred to the restoration of Israel and Judah in terms of resurrection and restoration of life does not mean later interpreters were bound to that meaning for the texts involved.

By the time of the Hasmoneans (2d century B.I.A.), Jews took passages like those from Hosea and Ezekiel to mean that those righteous individual Jews who had died for their nation would be raised up, physically, and permitted to live in the new nation after the enemy had been driven out. By NT times, the belief in the resurrection of dead individuals was a widely accepted doctrine, and Paul argued that Jesus was raised on the third day, according to the scriptures (1 Cor 15:4). The scriptures upon which this belief was based was Hos 6:2, **On the third day he will raise us up.**

TEXT

[20]Then the mother of the sons of Zebedee came to him with her sons, prostrating herself and requesting something from him. [21]He said to her, "What do you want?" She said to him, "Declare that these two sons of mine may sit, one at your right hand and one at your left in your kingdom." [22]Jesus answered and said, "You do not know what you are asking." [Speaking to the sons, he said], "Are you able to drink the cup that I am about to drink?" They said to him, "We are able." [23]He said to them, "On the one hand you will drink my cup, but to sit on my right and on my left is not mine to give, but it is for those for whom it has been prepared by my Father."[6]

COMMENTARY

The mother of the sons. Matthew seems to have been protecting these two apostles. Mark identified them and presented them as making their own requests. This Matthean narrative may have been written while the two sons were still alive and the author chose not to expose them to insults and accusations. Mark, on the other hand, may have written from a different location at a later time, when it would no longer damage the young men. Mark always pictured the twelve in an unfavorable light, whereas Matthew never damaged the apostles. This may mean that Mark wrote later and closer to Pauline territory, or that he simply had a different point of view concerning the apostles. These are only conjectures.

One on your right hand. The request is clear. The apostles' mother expected Jesus to become king of the new kingdom, ruling Palestine from Jerusalem, and she wanted her sons to be in top positions in the new administration. These two sons seem to have been among the top three leaders among the apostles. Peter was the only one who may have ranked above them. They were apparently requesting Jesus to place them above Peter. Although the mother began the request, her sons were also there and in perfect agreement with her wishes. After the mother had made the request, Jesus directed his questions to the sons. According to Mark, the mother was not involved. Plummer was of the opinion that Matthew was the more accurate of the two, but there is really no way to know.[7]

---

[6]There are many indications in the scriptures for thinking that it was normal for the king to be thought of as God's son and God to be held as the king's father. E.g., 2 Sam 7:5-16; Ps 89:4-5, 20-38, and 1 Kings 11:36. See further D. C. Duling, "The Promises to David and their Entrance into Christianity--Nailing Down a Likely Hypothesis," NTS 20 (1973):55-77.

[7]A. Plummer, An Exegetical Commentary on the Gospel according to St. Matthew (London: Stock, 1909), p. 277.

Drink the cup that I am about to drink. Burney noticed that the Markan parallel to Matt 20:22-23 (Mark 10:38-39) is a well-balanced parallel poem. Matthew has omitted the second half of each of the couplets.[8] In other places, such as Matthew 10, Mark has used only a few lines of a poem that is much longer in Matthew. There must have been a poetic source used by both Matthew and Mark, which one sometimes quoted precisely and sometimes the other. The direction would not go both ways if Matthew used only Mark or Mark used only Matthew. This is a metaphor for the kind of life expected. The seer was speaking about the treatment Rome had given Jews and the future situation hoped for Rome when he said,

> Give back to her as she has given, and double the doubles according to her works, in the cup which she mixed [for others] give her double (Rev 18:5-6)!

The seer was not talking about drinking a real liquid drink; he was talking about punishing Rome twice as much as she punished others. In the same way Jesus was telling his apostles that the way ahead was a rough one, filled with dangers (Ps 75:8: Isa 51:17). It would not be all sweetness and light, living in a lovely palace in luxury. Could they endure this kind of life? They said they could. Jesus said they would get their chance, and they probably did, but he did not give out assignments for these offices in advance.

Is not mine to give. Since Jesus was the Messiah, God's legal agent, that which he did was done in the name of, in behalf of, and at the responsibility of God. When Jesus selected his disciples it was assumed that this was done with God's approval. If Jesus should have chosen to give the sons of Zebedee the chief seats it would mean that God had given them these positions. To avoid interfering, however, Jesus may have meant that when the time came he would draw straws to see who would have the chief seats. This is the way the disciples replaced Judas with Mathias (Acts 1:26).

TEXT

24When the ten [other apostles] heard, they were angry about the two brothers.
25Then Jesus called them to him and said, "You know that

> those who rule over the gentiles lord it over them,
> and the great ones exercise authority over them.
> 26It is not this way with you, but
> whoever among you wants to become great let him be your servant,

---

[8]C. F. Burney, The Poetry of our Lord (Oxford: Oxford U., 1925), p. 63.

[27]and whoever among you wants to be first, let him be your slave.
[28]Just as the Son of man did not come to be ministered to but to minister
and to give his soul a ransom for [the] many."[9]

COMMENTARY

Whoever among you wants to be first. This is monastic ethics. In some monasteries every member was held to be equal. The monks functioned as a legal family, with the ones who were strong helping those who were weak, the young members taking care of the old members as if they were their children. Of course, the apostles assumed that their monastic life would come to an end when the Kingdom of Heaven was established, the proper priesthood installed in the temple, and there was no longer a separate place required in which the Lord might dwell. When that happened, the disciples would be able to renew their family lives, and take up political positions in the government. Jesus refused to allow them to give up their monastic plans too quickly. Until the kingdom came, the monastic administration was in force, and they were expected to think and act like monks.

To give his soul a ransom for [the] many. The Son of man in Daniel was the mythical name given to Judas the Maccabee. He finally died for his country, but he first became the effective military leader and national ruler that made him go down in history as a great Jewish hero. The Messiah in NT times was expected to be the antitype of Judas and to function as he had. The suffering servant of Isaiah was the one who gave his life as a ransom for "the many," meaning the Jewish nation. Here either Jesus or Matthew interpreted the future religious role of Jesus as an antitype of the suffering servant, but he called himself the Son of man, so these two concepts were put together here.

Jesus was not only the antitype of Judas, who died for his nation, but also for Moses who was the servant of the Lord who offered his life and community membership in behalf of the sinful people of the wilderness (Exod 32:32). A basic Jewish and Christian belief was that God would not restore the kingdom until the people had paid double for all their sins (Jer 16:18; Isa 40:2). Another basic belief was that merit could be transferred from individuals to the community. Rabbis said that just as the Day of Atonement atoned, so also the death of the righteous atoned (LevR 16.1 #20.12, 20b-c).

It was because the people had not paid the fines they had earned that Jesus volunteered to pay for the sins in their behalf. This was part of the logic of the

---

[9]Burney, Poetry, p. 64, observed that this was poetry both in Mark and Matthew. This suggests that both Matthew and Mark used the same source, and both copied these verses faithfully. In the earlier verses (Matt 20:22-23), however, Matthew abbreviated his source.

Day of Atonement. Even after this had been done, Jews and later Christians would still have to be forgiven for all of their sins against other believers and become reconciled. Therefore Jesus urged people to repent, so that the Kingdom of Heaven could come (Matt 4:17).

Powell observed that this was the basic plot of Matthew's gospel. The gospel began with the interpretation of Jesus' name as meaning he would save the people from their sins (Matt 1:21). Later, he was reported to identify his mission as that of calling sinners, rather than righteous (Matt 9:13). Here his ministry was repeated as that of giving his soul as a ransom for the many (Matt 20:28). He had to go to Jerusalem to suffer and be killed so that he could become a ransom for the many.[10] Jesus probably considered submissive death as an alternative way to provide salvation for the Jews, but this final decision would not have been made until he saw the fig tree in the Kidron Valley not bearing fruit out of season. The apostles apparently were not in agreement with his unwillingness to lead a revolution at that particular feast, but after his death, they quickly understood the act in terms of suffering servant theology. It is quite likely that Jesus and his apostles had discussed the two alternative ways of restoring the Kingdom. That would have been a reasonable consideration after the death of John the Baptist.

TEXT

[29]While they were going out from Jericho a great crowd followed him. [30]Now look! two blind men were seated alongside the road. When they heard that Jesus was going past, they cried out, saying, "Lord, have mercy upon us, son of David!"[11] [31]The crowd warned them that they should keep still, but they cried out more, "Lord, have mercy upon us, son of David!" [32]Then Jesus stood up, called them, and said, "What do you want me to do for you?" [33]They said to him, "Lord, [we wish] that you would open our eyes." [34]Jesus had compassion and touched their eyes, and they received their sight at once and followed him.

COMMENTARY

Going out from Jericho. This is now in the "Joshua" section of the Book of Matthew. Jesus crossed the Jordan at Jericho, just as Joshua had done many years earlier.

---

[10]M. A. Powell, "The Plot and Subplots of Matthew's Gospel," NTS 38 (1992):195.

[11]K. Berger, "Die Königlichen Messiastraditionen des Neuen Testaments," NTS 20 (1973):22-28, has accurately noticed that the terms "Son of David," "Son of God," and "King of the Jews" are all synonyms. The title "Son of God" is a well known title for a king. Although it was sometimes also used later to refer to a magician, this does not justify Berger's conclusion (p. 43) that the political characterizations of messianology as typically Jewish are invalid.

Have mercy upon us, son of David. There Jesus was recognized as the son of David, which was one of the titles in Palestine for a king. Jesus demonstrated that, like King Solomon, son of David, he was the Messiah by the miraculous healings that he performed, fulfilling the prophecy of Isaiah that "the eyes of the blind will see" (Isa 35). Antitypically he was the new Joshua at the beginning of the conquest in the new Kingdom. Solomon was the first son of David who became king; he was also a legendary wise man who could heal. People came to him asking for mercy. He then drove out the demons, and the people were healed. Other people also healed in his name, as son of David. See further commentary on Matt 9:27 and 12:23.

CHAPTER TWENTY-ONE

MATTHEAN PARALLELS TO THE HEXATEUCH

Matthew	First Testament
Israelites shouted, "Hosanna!" as Jesus with his disciples entered Jerusalem (Matt 21:8-27).	Joshua was exalted in the sight of Israel as the people under his leadership entered the land (Josh 3:1-4:24).

CHAPTER COMMENTARY

TEXT

21:1 Now when they drew near to Jerusalem, and they came to Bethphage at the Mount of Olives,

Matthew	First Testament
then **Jesus sent two** disciples, 2 **saying** to them, "Go into the village opposite you, and at once	Now **Joshua**, son of Nun, **sent two** spies from Shittim, secretly, **saying**, "Look at the land and Jericho" (Josh 2:1).
you will find **a donkey** and **a colt** with her. **Untie** them and lead [them] to me, 3 but if anyone says to you, 'Why [are you doing this],' you will say, 'Their Lord has need,' and	The sceptre will not depart from Judah nor the ruler's staff from between his feet, until Shiloh **comes**, and the peoples declare him innocent. He **ties** to a vine **a donkey**, to a vine branch its **colt** (Gen 49:10-11).

at once he will send them.[4]" This happened in order that that which was spoken by the prophet might be fulfilled, saying,	
[5]**Say to the daughter of Zion, "Look! Your king is coming to you,**	**Look!** Yahowah has announced to the border of the land, "**Say to the daughter of Zion, 'Look! your savior is coming'**" (Isa 62:11
	Greatly rejoice, **daughter of Zion;** shout, **daughter of Jerusalem! Look! your king will come to you**, innocent and delivered is he,
meek and seated upon a donkey, and upon a colt the foal of a beast of burden	**meek, riding on a donkey, and upon a colt, the foal of a donkey** (Zech 9:9).

COMMENTARY

Bethphage at the Mount of Olives. Bethphage means "the house of unripe figs."

Jesus sent two disciples. Jesus here was playing the role of the antitype of Joshua, who approached the land, but first sent out two spies to search out the land and prepare for the entrance of the Israelites. This also occurs at the beginning both of the Book of Joshua and at the beginning of the "Joshua" section of the Gospel of Matthew.

Their Lord has need. This statement was expected to communicate enough to the owner to allow the donkey to be released for Jesus' use. Either "their Lord" meant "their owner," or it meant "the Messiah." If it meant the latter, almost any Jew would allow his or her beast to be used to bring the Messiah into the holy city. If it were the former, it would be permitted only if there were certain understandings. If the people who saw the donkey being untied did not know who the real owner was, were not the real owners themselves, or did not belong to the same sect as Jesus they should normally have resisted the activity. If, however, they were members of the same sect and considered Jesus to be the administrator and lord of all their possessions this kind of generosity would be understandable. This is especially true of a monastery in relationship to monastic members of the same order from another city. Monastic hospitality allowed this kind of sharing for members of the same sect. Boers was unacquainted with the way secret, underground, nationalistic movements work. He thought this whole program was historically impossible. Therefore he said it was a miracle story, composed on the basis of Zech 9:9.[1]

The directions given to the disciples are those that would make best sense for a previously planned event. There were some local people there who knew Jesus was coming and would have the necessary beasts of burden there waiting for him.

Your king is coming. This is not only a quotation from Zechariah; it also refers back to Gen 49, alluding to Shiloh who was coming and to Isa 62, anouncing salvation, which accompanies the restoration of Jerusalem, the land, and the renewal of the contract with Yahowah. It was necessary for the king to come before the Kingdom could come. Collins was correct in saying that this is the first time that Jesus was referred to as a king. Prior to that he called himself a Son of man, which had the same meaning to those who knew Dan 7. It was not until the public entrance into Jerusalem that the term "king" was used openly. This was Jesus' parousia.

Collins presumed from that that Jesus had played the role of a prophetic herald of the kingdom prior to this time, but that at this moment changed from a herald of the kingdom to that of the king who brings in the kingdom.[2] The change that took place was just as important as that but it was different. Jesus did not change his concept or role at all by entering Jerusalem in fulfillment of Zech 9:9. Prior to his entrance Jesus was a messiah in hiding, an undercover leader. This does not mean that he was hidden from before the creation of the world like the Son of man in 1 Enoch, although Christians probably made that claim, too (1 Enoch 48.6). The hiding which Jesus was doing was during his lifetime on the land of Palestine. He was keeping "that fox," Herod, from knowing about his plans (Luke 13:32). His leadership was as secret as he was able to keep it. The messianic secret was not just the literary plan of the Gospel according to Mark. It was the way underground movements had to be organized. Jesus communicated by parables and scripture passages that only the educated Jews would understand. During that time he told his apostles that there would be a time when that which he had told them in secret they would shout from the housetops. That would happen when he had determined that the time was ripe to bring his secret movement out into the open. That was his parousia. It happened when he entered Jerusalem and refused to keep the response of the crowd quiet.

Seated upon a donkey. When Jesus rode into the holy city on a donkey, this was a sign to all who knew Zechariah that he was the expected Messiah, the king who would soon rule over the promised land. This was to come as a fulfillment of the prophecy in Zechariah. In Zechariah the king was to come to Jerusalem after the

---

[1]Boers, Jesus, pp. 86-87.

[2]J. J. Collins, The Scepter and the Star (New York: Doubleday, c1995), p. 206.

surrounding cities and states had been taken and had become subject to Judah just as the Jebusites became subject to David when he first conquered the city of Jerusalem. After the wars had been fought, the king would ride into Jerusalem in peace, triumphant and victorious (Zech 9:9), after the enemies had been driven out of Judah and north Israel. The king Zechariah expected would rule the entire promised land,

> **from sea to sea,**
> **and from the river to the end of the land** (Zech 9:10).

This means the territory **from** the Dead **Sea to** the Mediterranean **Sea**, which is the same area as that between **the** Jordan **River** and **the end of the** promised **land** to the west, that touching the Mediterranean **Sea**.

Blenkinsopp said that Jesus' entry into Jerusalem was his messianic and royal parousia. The quotation from Zechariah shows it was a messianic parousia. His association with the Mount of Olives and his cleansing of the temple were all indications that Jesus was openly declaring himself to be the new Messiah.[3] That is what a parousia is. Prior to this time Jesus had been moving around Palestine in a secretive and refugee fashion. During this time, the disciples were asking Jesus, "When will these things take place, and what is the sign of your parousia and the end of the [pagan or common] age?" (Matt 24:3). He gave his answer to this when he rode a donkey into the holy city.

TEXT

[6]After the disciples had gone and had done just as Jesus commanded them, [7]they led the donkey and the colt and they placed their robes upon them and he sat upon them. [8]The [members of a] great crowd spread out their own robes in the road, and others cut off branches of the trees and spread them in the road.

Matthew	First Testament
[9]The crowds who went ahead of him and those who followed him cried out, saying,	Sing to Yahowah a new song, his praise in the congregation of the saints. Let Israel rejoice in his deeds, let the sons of Zion be glad with their king (Ps 149:1-2).
Hosanna! to the son of David.	Please, Yahowah, **save please** (hoh-shee-áh nah, הושיע נא) if you will! Please, Yahowah, make [us] suc-
Blessed is he who	ceed, if you will! **Blessed is he who**

[3]J. Blenkinsopp, "The Oracle of Judah and the Messianic Entry," JBL 80 (1961):55.

comes in the name of the Lord. Hosanna! O [you] in the heavens

comes in the name of Yahowah (Ps 118:25-26).

Now, Yahowah, our God, save us, please (hoh-shee-áh-nu-nah, הושיענו נא), from his [the king of Assyria] hand (2 Kings 19:19).

The woman of Tekoah spoke to the king. She fell on her face to the ground and worshiped [David]. Then she said, "**Save** (hoh-sheé-ah, הושיעה), O king" (2 Sam 14:4).

COMMENTARY

And he sat upon them. The idea of Jesus riding on the backs of two beasts at the same time is ridiculous, but Matthew was often very exact in his interpretation of FT texts. In Zechariah, this was a couplet, with the second line saying in other words the same thing that the first line had said. The two names were to be understood poetically rather than accumulatively. The colt was the same as the donkey. In Semitic thought a farmer might be called the "son of a farmer," or one might say that his father or mother was a farmer. The animal was called by two names to avoid being redundant. The conjunction (*καί* = ו) should either have been omitted or understood as "even" in translation:

a donkey,
even a colt, the offspring of a donkey.

Matthew, however, mistakenly took the conjunction to mean there was both a donkey **and** a colt, so Jesus had to be placed on both, in his judgment.[4] When Matthew's method of composition is exposed, it becomes clear that this pericope was composed by someone who forced a historical account to fit into prophecy. He may not have been a witness of the event himself. Matthew may have deduced this report from the Books of Genesis and Zechariah and his belief

---

[4]R. H. Gundry, Matthew: A Commentary on his Literary and Theological Art (Grand Rapids, c1982), p. 409, argues that the colt just followed along after its mother as the mother was the beast that carried Jesus. This is the way things usually were done, but Matthew said he rode on "them"--both of them! This is the kind of exegesis McCasland called Matthew's habit of "twisting" the scriptures. R. Bartnicki, "Das Zitaat vonn Zach IX, 9-10 und die Tiere im Bericht von Matthäus über dem Einzug Jesu in Jerusalem (Mt XXI, 1-11," NovTest 18 (1976):161-66), was of nearly the same opinion. He thought that there were two beasts there, a mother and her colt, and that Jesus rode on only one, but the author of the text wrote it so that scripture would be exactly fulfilled.

that Jesus was the Messiah. He may have known in general that the event occurred, and Jesus may actually have entered Jerusalem on a donkey to show the people of Jerusalem that he was the one about whom Zechariah and Genesis prophesied, but Matthew filled in the details on the basis of scripture. Since these were days of the Messiah, and since all prophecy was prophesied only for the days of the Messiah certainly these messianic passages were fulfilled by Jesus. All Matthew had to do was report these convictions in narrative form.

Frenz tried to make this whole event about the donkey and its colt seem reasonable. He noted that it would be important to bring the colt with the mother. Otherwise both the mother and the colt would become nervous and bray, thus upsetting the program. It was the colt, Frenz argued, upon which no one had previously sat, not the mother. He presumed that the colt had not yet been weaned. If so it would have been too small to be a beast upon which a grown man would ride. Although donkeys are strong beasts, even a grown donkey is small.[5]

Jews were well aware of the prophecy of Zechariah and studied it carefully in relationship to the anticipation of the Messiah. Rabbi Joshua said that if the people were worthy, then the prophecy of Daniel (which was fulfilled by Judas the Maccabee), would be fulfilled again: **[Look! One like a son of man is coming] with the clouds of heaven** (Dan 7:13). If the people were unworthy, the prophecy of Zechariah would be fulfilled when the Messiah came: **[Look! Your king comes to you meek] and riding upon a donkey** (Zech 9:7; bSan 98b). Both were conditional prophecies, but there was no condition about the fact that the Messiah would come. The only question was the way of his appearing.

There was no need for a colt to come along so far as transportation was concerned, but it was necessary for the fulfillment of prophecy. Matthew had two intertexts at his disposal. The first was Gen 49:10-11. This predicted that when Shiloh came to to claim the ruler's scepter at Jerusalem he would "tie his colt to a vine, his donkey's offspring to a vine branch." This was only one animal, poetically referred to twice. When Zechariah prepared his prophecy, he based it on this passage. He understood "Shiloh" to be the new Messiah, the king that would come to Zion. When he came, of course, he would enter Jerusalem, as Genesis promised with "a donkey, a colt the foul of a beast of burden." When Matthew composed this historical account, he wove these texts into his report. He even went further than Zechariah did in his dependence upon Genesis 49:10-11. According to Matthew, Jesus sent the apostles to find these beasts of burden, and he said that they would be "tied," just as Genesis reported (Gen 49:11: Matt 21:2).

Cut off branches. They probably did not cut off branches of fig trees or cedar trees and lay them in the road for Jesus to have to ride through. This kind of brush would have created a real obstacle to travel, but palm leaves are soft fern-like branches, sometimes eight feet long. They are large, but also flat and as soft as straw. It had the hospitality significance of people rolling out a red

[5]A. Frenz, "Mt XXI 5-7," 13 (1971):259-60.

carpet on which Jesus could travel, but they also had a symbolic significance. Palm leaves were symbols that were as strongly nationalistic to Jews as the shamrock is to the Irish or the various tartans are to the Scots. Jews were coming to a national feast, singing one of their national anthems as they marched in procession, and Jesus was the expected Messiah. This was his parousia.

The crowds who went ahead. It was customary in antiquity for people from a town or city to go out to meet any dignitary who entered the town. Then they would accompany him into the city or town. This was done when David returned from a victorious battle against the Philistines (1 Sam 18:6-7). Martha went out to meet Jesus when he came to her home (John 11:20). Paul looked forward to a Jubilee call when the Lord would descend and all the faithful who were still alive would go out to meet him (1 Thes 4:16-17). The people of his town went out to meet Rabbi Eleazar when he approached the village (bTa'an 20b). There are many other instances of this in rabbinic literature and also classical Greek and Latin literature.

Hosanna. Hosanna, in Hebrew, means, "Save, please!" or "Save, if you will!" It was directed to two listeners, 1) Jesus, as "the son of David," and 2) God, as the one "in heaven." Some translators render this "Hosanna in the highest," which is an attempted literal translation of the Greek, hoh-sahn-náh en tois heepsís-tous (ὡσαννὰ ἐν τοῖς ὑψίστοις) (Matt 21:9). A better translation is, "Save, please, you in the heights!" Words like "Heaven" or "[the One] in the heights" were used euphemistically to avoid the pronunciation of the divine name. Saying, "the One in the heavens," is like saying, "the holy One blessed be He," or "the One who formed the heavens and spread out the earth." It is the euphemistic translation of "Yahowah." The Hebrew Ps 118:25 is אנא יהוה הושיעה נא (ah-nah-Yahowah-hoh-sheé-ah nah) ("Please, Yahowah, save, if you will!") The people were not in the heights, singing, "Hosanna!" They were staying on earth, singing "Hosanna" to God, the one in the heavens. According to Did 10.6, a post-communion prayer included the words, "Hosanna to the God of David," which has the same meaning.

Jews addressed their pleas for salvation both to the Messiah and to God. The Messiah was the king, the legal agent on earth of God in the heavens. As the Lord's legal agent, everything the king did was done in the name of the Lord, who was the principal. The king would act in such a way as to deliver his people, but this would be the act of God, because the legal agent is legally identical to the principal. He acts in the name of the principal, in the interests of the principal, and at the responsibility of the principal. The term, "Hosanna," was used mostly in direct address, either to a king (2 Sam 14:4) or to God (Ps 118:25-26).[6] Boers thought this entry story was unhistorical. He added,

---

[6]For a somewhat similar analysis see M. H. Pope, "Hosanna: What it Really Means," BAR 4 (1988):16-25.

> If Jesus' entry was anything like the one described in the account, the conclusion that he had been a messianic pretender would have been inescapable.[7]

That appears to have been the intent. This was Jesus' parousia. The people who followed Jesus in the parade may have been Jews who were coming as they did every year to the feasts, but there may have been a larger crowd than usual because the apostles had previously gone out into the Jewish cities and towns announcing the coming of the Kingdom of Heaven (Matt 10), perhaps at this feast. This would have drawn a larger crowd than usual. That may be the reason the Pharisees were anxious and asked that the disciples keep still (Luke 19:39). The crowd may have been large enough to appear threatening to peace loving Jews and Roman leaders. Prior to this time Jesus had taught the crowds in code and kept his plans and activities secret. Jesus told his apostles that the time would come when that which they were then whispering they would shout from the housetops (Matt 10:27). Disciples had been asking when all of this would take place. What would be the sign of his coming and the end of the Roman age (Matt 24:3). The entry into Jerusalem seemed to have been the time.

Blessed is he who comes in the name of the Lord. Blessings for messiahs were normal responses of Jews to messiahs. One medieval Jewish blessing for the Messiah was:

> Blessed be the righteous shoot, and blessed be his parents and teachers, and blessed be the people who come with him, and blessed be the men who obey him. Blessed be Yadod the God, the God of Israel, his God who had blessed him [with] a blessing of the age [as] his blessing for from [this blessing] all will exist.[8]

A woman from the crowd reportedly called out to Jesus: "Blessed be the womb that bore you, and blessed be the breasts you sucked" (Luke 11:27). When Jesus entered the holy city many Jews were prepared to decorate his way and offer him blessings.

Jews all over the Roman Empire were looking forward to "the coming one," the Messiah who would come, recapture the promised land, overpower the Romans, and rule the civilized world. One poet said,

> A holy prince will come and hold a scepter over the entire world for all ages as time moves swiftly on. Then there will be unyield-

---

[7]Boers, Jesus, p. 89.

[8]Abraham Abulafia, "The Book of the Sign." Hebrew text from A. Z. Aescoly, Messianic Movements in Israel (Jerusalem: Bialik, 1917, 1956), p. 205.

> ing anger against the Latin men. Three [Anthony, Lepidus, and Octavian] will destroy Rome with piteous fate (SibOr 3.49-52).

After he had analyzed the militant expectations and activity of pretending messiahs of NT times Collins said,

> To be sure, a real life messiah needed more mundane weapons than the breath of his mouth. But the violent destruction of the wicked is a standard element in the repertoire of the Davidic messiah.

Collins further doubted that Jesus' followers would have given him the title of Davidic messiah after his death, knowing all of its associations with political inflamation if there were no factual basis for this identification.[9] He also observed correctly that it is easy to see how Jesus' entry into Jerusalem might have been instrumental in causing his crucifixion by the Romans.[10]

TEXT

10After he had entered Jerusalem, all the city was excited, saying, "Who is this?"
11Then the crowds said, "This is the prophet, Jesus, the one from Nazareth of Galilee."

COMMENTARY

The city was excited. Cities do not become excited; people do. The word here rendered "excited" really means "shaken violently." It is the same word used to describe an earth quake or a terrible storm. It means the news stirred up a terrific amount of excitement. Jews knew all about messiahs. They had been taught from childhood to expect the Messiah who would come and liberate the nation. Now the report was that the Messiah had entered Jerusalem.

The one from Nazareth of Galilee. This was not just anyone. This was the prophet, the one from Galilee, about whom they had heard in secret conversations, but now that which had been told in secret was going to be shouted from the house tops! This was his parousia.

Patte accurately noticed that there are two groups of people associated with the triumphal entry of Jesus into Jerusalem. The people from the city of Jerusalem who were surprised at Jesus' arrival and the crowds, who evidently came

---

9Collins, Scepter, pp. 203-204.

10Collins, Scepter, pp. 206-207.

along with Jesus into Jerusalem.[11] The crowds probably consisted of pilgrims who were coming to the feasts and supporters who wanted to participate in any messianic excitement that might follow. They were not disappointed. One of his first activities after he entered Jerusalem was to move into the temple area. The report in Matthew of the events in the temple area (Matt 21:12-13) is more extensive in the Markan parallel, which will receive special attention here.

SYMBOLIC MONEY-CHANGERS IN THE TEMPLE?[12]

J. Neusner and E. P. Sanders have directed scholarly attention to Mark 11:15-19 and its parallels. Sanders used this pericope to demonstrate his belief that this was the most trustworthy report of any of Jesus' teachings and actions, and Neusner presumed its historical validity while conjecturing that on this occasion Jesus repudiated Jewish temple sacrifice and intended to substitute for the tables in the temple the Eucharist table as a means of obtaining atonement.[13] These are bold claims and prompt a further analysis of the relevant passage:

THE TEXT

Mark 11:15-19	First Testament
[15]After he had entered into **the temple**, he began to throw out the **sellers and buyers in the temple**. He overturned the tables of the money changers and the chairs of those who sold pigeons.	There will not be a **trader** again **in the temple** of the Lord of armies on that day (Zech 14:21).
[16]He would not permit anyone to carry a vessel through the temple, [17]and he began to teach and he said to them, "Is it not written,	I will bring them [the foreign proselytes] to my holy mountain, and I will make them happy in my house of prayer, accepting on my altar their burnt offerings and their sacrifices, for **my temple shall be called a house of prayer for all the peoples** (Isa 56:7).
My temple shall be called a house of prayer for all the nations?	

[11]D. Patte, The Gospel according to Matthew (Philadelphia: Fortress Press, c1946), p. 286.

[12]Parts of this essay originally appeared as "Mark 11:15-19: Brigands in the Temple," HUCA 30 (1959):169-177. The basic point of that essay was later developed and enclosed as part of another article: "Symbolic Money-Changers in the Temple?" NTS 37: (1991):280-90. It is basic to a correct understanding of this passage of scripture.

[13]E. P. Sanders, Jesus and Judaism (Philadelphia: Fortress, 1985), 61-76, and J. Neusner, 'Money-Changers in the Temple: The Mishnah's Explanation', NTS 35 (1989):287-90.

But you have made it
a cave of
brigands (spáy-lai-ohn lays-tóhn,
σπήλαιον λῃστῶν). [18]Then the chief
priests and the scribes heard, and
they tried to find out how they might
destroy him, for all the crowd was
surprised at his teachings. [19]When
evening came they went out of the
city.

Has this **temple** which is called by **my** name become **a cave of brigands** in your eyes (Jer 7:11)?

TECHNICAL DETAILS

This is obviously a composite unit. Verses 18 and 19 are not contained in Matt 21:12-13. The words, "They were surprised," is a typical Markan summary phrase used 4 other times in the gospel (Mark 1:22; 7:37; 10:27; 11:19).[14] Verse 19 is an editorial sentence, composed of words found elsewhere in Mark. Verse 16, "And he would not allow anyone to carry anything through the temple," is an isolated halakhic recollection, different from the ordinary gospel material, and probably added later.[15] It was either unknown to or omitted by Matthew, Luke, and John. The Fourth Gospel (John 2:13-17) contains a story of the cleansing of the temple which does not conclude with a reference to the "cave of brigands." John may preserve an earlier tradition of the temple cleansing to which Mark appended the later tradition (Mark 11:17) of the cave of brigands. The further facts that this verse begins with a typically Markan introduction eh-díd-ahs-ken (*ἐδίδασκεν*) (Mark 1:21; 4:2; 9:31; 10:1) or áyrk-sah-to did-áhs-kayn (*ἤρξατο διδάσκειν*) (Mark 4:1; 6:2, 34; 8:31) and that Luke provided this passage a separate introduction may indicate that Mark 11:17, like Mark 11:16, was at one time independent from the rest of the pericope.

THE CLEANSING

Although Sanders thought the cleansing incident was the most reliable report of Jesus' actions and teachings in all of the gospels, there are reasons to doubt its historicity. It is difficult to imagine how such an event as this could

---

[14]See further Buchanan, Typology and the Gospel (Lanham, New York, London, University Press of America, c1987) 78-79.

[15]A similar halachic passage is mBer 10.5: "He may not enter into the temple mount with his staff, sandal, his wallet, or with the dust upon his feet, nor may he make of it a short by-path; still less may he spit there."

have happened in the temple area, in exactly the way it has been reported, without any further repercussions. The temple was also the national treasury and the nation's best fortress. Josephus said there were two fortresses that controlled Jerusalem. One guarded the city itself and the other, the temple. Whoever mastered these two fortresses held the nation in his power (Ant 15.247-48). When Eleazer, Simon, and John were fighting to gain control of Jerusalem, the foremost goal of each was to gain and keep possession of the temple area (War 5.5-38). It is not likely that the nation's treasury and best fortress was left without military guard. Would military policemen, without reacting, allow a man or group of men to come into this strategic, defended area and start an upheaval which involved driving people out of the building and overturning the furniture? Josephus reported that the Romans were specially alert to revolutionary movements among the Jews at feasts. With the long history of conflict associated with feasts at Jerusalem against which Rome was well prepared, how could Jesus have been allowed to have walked away unmolested after this turmoil had taken place (Mark 11:19)?

1) One explanation is that the incident may have been much more violent than has been reported. If Jesus had come in with a sizeable army and successfully taken control of the temple by overpowering the military guard, then he might have walked away safely.[16] This would bc coherent with his entrance into Jerusalem as a parousia. If this were the case, it would come as no surprise to discover that the church after the second revolt of the Jews against Rome (32-35 I.A.) might have found it, for security reasons, necessary to revise the narrative so that the Romans would not think of Jesus or his followers as insurrectionists. The idea that Rome censored such literature as that produced by Christians and Jews is supported by the following Tannaitic narrative:

> Once the [Roman] government sent two officials and said to them, "Go and become [false Jewish] proselytes, and examine the Torah of the Jews, what its nature is." They went to Rabban Gamaliel at

[16]So also M. Hengel, Was Jesus a Revolutionist? (Philadelphia,1971) 16-17. D. Seeley, "Jesus' Temple Act," CBQ 55 (1993):263-83, followed Buchanan, "Symbolic Money-Changers in the Temple?" NTS37 (1991):280-90, almost entirely. Seely objected, however, to the suggestion that any military involvement was possible on the basis that there "was no tradition of the Messiah marching against the temple" (p. 276). A messiah did not have to march against the temple in order to be involved in a military conquest. Conquering the temple would have been considered an act of agression against the temple. It would have been thought of as an act of defense, necessary to liberate the temple from the heathen. One of the first things Judas the Maccabee did after his famous victory at Beth-horon was to take control of the temple fortress and cleanse it. During the war of A.D. 66-70, nationalists fought mightily against one another to control the temple fortress. First it was in the hands of Eleazar, but later it was taken by John (War 5.1-10, 248-54). Both of these were messianic pretenders. When the Romans fought against the Jews in this great war, they realized that they had to secure the temple to control the city (War 5.357). This does not mean Jesus actually led a military force to take control of the temple, but it means that possibility can not be dismissed out of hand on the basis of tradition.

Usha, and they read the FT; they studied the Mishnah, midrash, halachot, and haggadoth. When they left they said to them [the rabbis], "All of your teachings are good and admirable, except for one item. Stealing from a pagan is permitted, but from a Jew it is forbidden, but we shall not disclose this matter to the government" (Sifre Deut 33.3, #344. 143b).

It was partly because of Rome's censoring that Jews and early Christians used code terms, like Babylon for Rome, Edom for Rome, and Persia sometimes for Rome and sometimes for Parthia (bYoma 10a).[17] Had this "temple cleansing" really been a military confrontation, it would also not be difficult to imagine why the Romans thought it was necessary to have Jesus crucified after the disturbance had taken place. The account that now appears in the gospels, however, does not make sense in the Jerusalem situation during Jesus' ministry. Others have also found problems with the story as it is in its present context.

Trocme thought Jesus probably cleansed the temple, but not in the context in which the gospels report. He thought it took place much earlier, so that there was no official account of the incident. He believed that this was the immediate cause of Jesus' crucifixion,[18] but he strongly resisted Carmichael's claim that Jesus played a revolutionary role in this action.[19] Hamilton thought that if all Jesus did was preached the Kingdom of God as a future kingdom not of this world, there would have been no basis for the Roman government to have crucified him. He thought Jesus really had no political intentions, but that the Romans might have thought that he did when he interfered with the financial business of the temple.

The temple was the national bank where Jews kept their money stored. Millions of dollars worth of money was stored here. That is the reason kings plundered temples; they wanted all of this wealth (2 Macc 3:10-11). Kings controlled national banks, so any attempt of Jesus to take over the bank would imply that he was leading a revolution to become king.

The capital of Galilee at one time was Sepphoris, the city where the royal bank was located. The term Josephus used to identify this bank was "the royal table" (bah-sil-i-káne trá-ped-zahn, βασιλικὴν τράπεζαν) (life 38). The word for "table" is the same as that used in Matt 21:12 to identify the tables Jesus over-

[17]See further S. Krauss, Persia and Rome in the Talmud and Midrashim (Jerusalem, 1948) [Hebrew], 27.

[18]E. Trocme, 'L'expulsion des marchands du Temple', NTS 15 (1968) 1-22.

[19]E.Trocme, 'Jesus-Christ et le Temple: eloge d'un naif', Revue d'Histoire et de Philosophie Religieuses 44 (1964) 245-51; J. Carmichael, 'Jesus-Christ et le Temple', Nouvelle Revue Francaise 12 (1964) 276-95.

turned (tra-péd-zas, τραπέζας).[20] This seems to mean that Jesus interfered with the national banking system where money changers were located. Although Hamilton said that Jesus did this without any military force, that would have been difficult to accomplish.

Sabbe assumed the event was historical, but he argued that the various gospels used the narrative to suit their own peculiar literary and theological needs.[21] Medner argued that the selling of sheep and oxen was unhistorical and that the Johannine account was a reworking of the Matthean narrative.[22] Buse did not raise the historical question but concluded that all gospel accounts were dependent upon an earlier source.[23]

Roth thought that Jesus was actually living out the fulfillment of prophecy. In his opinion Jesus took the word here translated "trader" to be literally "Canaanite," and was ridding the temple of foreigners (Zech 14:21). Roth also called attention of the Dead Sea Scroll which commented on Exod 15:17-18 and Deut 23:4. That commentator argued that the temple would be a place for the Lord's holy ones, but no Ammonite, Moabite, bastard, alien, or sojourner would enter the sanctuary in the age [to come]. Strangers would not desolate the place as they had done formerly (4QFl 1.5). Roth held that Jesus was cleansing the temple area so that it could be undefiled as the prophets thought it should be in the last days [of the evil era]. He did not consider what kind of a force Jesus would need to perform this function.[24]

None of these scholars considered the possibility that the story was written after the crucifixion by the later church for apologetic reasons, but that is also a possibility.

2) The second possibility is that Jesus never cleansed the temple at all. This is the alternative Seeley favored.[25] Seeley's arguments are good, and he may be correct in holding this alternative, but he dismissed the military alternative too easily. He said, ". . . there was no tradition of the Messiah marching

---

[20]N. Q. Hamilton, "Temple Cleansing and Temple Bank, " JBL 83 (1964):364-72.

[21]M. Sabbe, 'Tempelreiniging en Tempellogion', Collationes Brugenses et Gandavenses 2 (1956):289-99.

[22]S. Medner, 'Die Tempelreinigung', ZNTW 47 (1956) 93-112. Neusner, however, has refuted this.

[23]I. Buse, 'The Cleansing of the Temple in the Synoptics and in John', ExpTim 70 (1958):22-24.

[24]C. Roth, "The Cleansing of the Temple and Zechariah xiv 21," NovTest 4 (1960):174-81.

[25]D. Seeley, "Jesus' Temple act,"CBQ 55 (1993): 276-83. A. Plummer, An Exegetical Commentary on the Gospel according to S. Matthew (London: Stock, c1909), p. 288, considered the possibility that there were actually two cleansings--one at the beginning of his ministry, following the Fourth Gospel, and other at the end, according to the synoptic gospels. This is not very likely.

against the temple."[26] In the eyes of Jesus and his supporters he would not have been marching against the temple. He would have been liberating it from foreign control the way Judas did before he had it cleansed.

During the first war with Rome (66-70 I.A.) Josephus said Menahem acted like a king and a tyrant (War 2.434, 441-42). Eleazar made plans to attack him in the temple (War 2.443-45). Josephus did not tell the Romans that Menahem had messianic pretensions when he behaved like a messiah. That would not have been prudent. Josephus did not call Eleazar a messiah either, but Eleazar took control of the temple area (War 5. 5) as leader of the zealots there. John fought Eleazar, leader of the Sicarii (War 7.275), and captured the temple area (War 5.98-105). Josephus did not call either Eleazar or Simon a messiah, but he said Simon had such devoted followers that any one of them would have died for him (War 5.309). When he finally surrendered, Simon appeared wearing the royal robes of a king (War 7.29). None of these royal pretenders who engaged in battle in and around the temple area thought of himself as attacking the temple, and they all seemed to be messianic pretenders. Had Jesus led a military force into the temple area he would have belonged to a long messianic tradition. Horsley also showed the numerous messianic movements that Josephus called by other names, but he thought Menahem was the only real messiah who belonged to a dynasty.[27]

There are more indirect allusions to dynasty than Horsley noticed. When Josephus told of the three messianaic pretenders to the throne after the death of Herod the Great, he said one was Judas, son of Hezekiah; another was Simon. Both of these had Hasmonean names. The third was Athrongaeus who acted like a king, was a strong, courageous man, who was a good administrator and had brothers who were also good leaders. Josephus spoke of him desparagingly as a "mere shepherd." He had many royal qualities and was pretending to the throne, but obviously lacked something, in Josephus' opnion. He did not come from a royal family--either Hasmonean or Davidic! This means the other two did (War 2.56-65). Josephus described the capture of Machaerus by the Romans by telling how the Romans first siezed the leader of the fortress, whose name was Eleazar, a Hasmonean name, and he came from a very distinguished and numerous family (War 7.204). When he was captured those in the fortress lamented extensively and bargained with the Romans for his release, agreeing to surrender the fortress if his life were saved (War 7.196-209).

The famous family was probably Hasmonean, although the Hasmonean Josephus would not have said so. These are the kinds of subtle allusions Josephus made about the dynasties to which zealotish leaders belonged, but there is an

---

[26]Seeley, "Temple Act," p. 276.

[27]R. A. Horsley, "Menahem in Jerusalem: A Brief Messianic Episode among the Sicarii--Not 'Zealot Messianism'" (NovTest 27 (1985):334-48).

alternative interpretation of the passage, reporting Jesus' action in the temple. It does not involve any military action on Jesus' part. This is the one Seely chose.

Jews of NT times expected the Messiah to perform the heroic deeds that earlier leaders had done. Hezekiah (2 Kings 18:1-6; 2 Chron 29:3-19) and Judas the Maccabee, had each cleansed the temple (Ant 12.316-22). When Jews gained complete freedom from the Syrian Greeks (141 B.I.A.), Simon, Judas' older brother, drove out the Greeks, cleansed the fortress that was on the temple grounds and took up residence there. This event was accompanied by celebrating with palm branches and music (1 Macc 13:49-53).

Since all of these cleansed the temple area, it would have been reasonable for contemporaries to have deduced that the Messiah also cleansed the temple. This is all the more probable since this narrative also shows that Jesus entered with a procession of palm branches and also fulfilled the prophecy of Zech 9:9. The temple narrative reportedly fulfilled the prophecy of Zech 14:21, **And there shall no longer be a trader in the house of the Lord of armies on that day**. Since all prophecy was prophesied only for the days of the Messiah (bBer 34b), and these were the days of the Messiah, there could have been no question in the minds of committed Christians that something like this must have taken place. With such doctrines as these prevailing it would not have taken a great deal of creativity to compose a narrative to fit the supposed facts. One Jewish poet of NT times asked God to send to his people the Messiah, the son of David, to rule the tribes of Israel as its righteous king. When God sent his Messiah, the Messiah was expected to cleanse Jerusalem, so that it would again be holy (PssSol 17.30-32).

If Jesus never cleansed the temple at all but instead this event had been attributed to him from the necessity of the doctrines and messianic expectations, it is easy to understand why there are differences between the Johannine and the synoptic accounts of this supposed event. The midrashic author may have known that Jesus entered Jerusalem as he did to fulfill the prophecy of Zech 9:9. He may have conjectured that Jesus also fulfilled the prophecy of Zech 14:21, so he reported his belief.

It is impossible to prove that either of these suggestions was a reality, but either one is reasonable enough to cast doubt on the "unassailable facts" of Sander's "bedrock" position and the indisputability of his claim to the historicity of the gospel report as it now exists. It also shows the problems that anyone, such as Sanders, faces who tries to reconstruct the life of Jesus on the basis that this is the soundest historical report in all of the gospels. Sanders' task becomes still more difficult when he tries to prove that this was a non-military, historical event that was intended to have only a prophetic, symbolic significance.[28]

[28]Sanders apparently reached his confused conclusion by applying the decisions of three other scholars: 1) N. A. Dahl had said historical study of Jesus should begin with the one known historical fact: Jesus was crucified. 2) M. Smith said historical Jesus study should take account of his reported actions as well as his teachings. 3) N. Perrin began his historical Jesus research

Although it is difficult to say with confidence from a distance of 2,000 years what Jews might or might not have understood as symbolism, Neusner may have been correct in saying that Jews other than Jesus' disciples would not have understood any symbolic or prophetic significance to such an act as the one reported.[29] If any symbolism was intended, how could anyone know what it was? Creating a disturbance in the national treasury and fortress does not provide an unequivocal, prophetic, symbolic message such as walking around wearing a yoke of slavery (Jer 27:2-13; 28:10-16), for example. When FT prophets acted symbolically, they also spoke so that no one had any question about the message they intended to illustrate.

There is no message in Mark 11:17 to suggest that Jesus wanted his hearers to understand that the temple would be destroyed, as Sanders and Neusner claim. Conjectured messages of the symbolism intended have to be imported from other texts and contexts. As Evans has shown, if Jesus had prophesied the destruction of the temple, as Sanders holds, the authors of the gospels would not have been expected to suppress a prophecy that seemed to have been fulfilled in 70 I.A.[30] Military guards would have been poorly trained if they treated an upheaval like the event reported as if it were nothing but a harmless prophetic symbol foretelling the destruction of the temple a generation later.

In the Fourth Gospel, the text is associated with the demand for a sign, and Jesus reportedly answered that if they destroyed this temple he would raise it in three days. He was not reported as saying either that he would destroy the temple or that it would be destroyed. He only told what he would do if it were destroyed. The text also explains that Jesus was talking about the temple of the body (John 2:18-21). The more allegory there is mixed with the narrative, the less likely it is to be historical. Neusner agreed with Sanders that the cleansing of the temple was a symbolic act. He differed from Sanders in that he thought this symbolic performance was intended for the disciples alone to understand. He believed that Jesus was trying to demonstrate to his disciples his belief that the temple sacrifices should be replaced by the Eucharist, the tables of the money changers for the Eucharist table.[31]

---

by finding just one small teaching that he thought was valid and deduced all of his account by comparing that which was coherent with that one teaching. Sanders put these altogether to formulate his basis for historical Jesus reserach.

[29]Neusner, 'Money-Changers,' p. 289.

[30]C. A. Evans, 'Jesus' Action in the Temple: Cleansing or Portent of Destruction,' CBQ 51 (1989) 238.

[31]Neusner, 'Money-Changers', 290. Evidently the money-changers had tables (τραπέζος) and chairs, but Jesus regularly banqueted with his disciples and others on the floor in a reclining position (Matt 9:10-13; Mark 2:15-17; Luke 5:29-31). This is the report of the Last Supper as well (ἀνέκειτο, Matt 26:20; ἀνακείμενων, Mark 14:18; ἀνέπεσαν, Luke 22:14; ἀνακείμεννος,

If, however, Jesus had wanted only the disciples to understand this message it would not have been necessary to have made a public spectacle of the instruction. Jesus could have told the apostles privately without posing a threat to himself from the Romans.

Furthermore, if Jesus had intended to substitute the Eucharist for sacrifices, the author of the Clementine Recognitions was unaware of it. Writing after the fall of Jerusalem, he mentioned several times that sacrifices had been superseded and that Christians were commanded to discontinue sacrificing. The institution, however, which replaced sacrifices for obtaining atonement was not the Eucharist but baptism (Recog 1.39, 54, 55, 64), according to that Jewish-Christian author. According to Paul and some texts of Luke, Jesus told the disciples to continue celebrating the Passover in remembrance of him (1 Cor 11:23-26; Luke 22:19), but he did not say that the Eucharist replaced the sacrifices in the temple or that their celebrations would be efficacious for atonement. The authors of the Book of Hebrews and First John both held that Jesus' death functioned as an atonement offering, but there is no direct claim in the NT that Jesus intended to substitute the Eucharist for sacrifices. Neusner may have known some extra-biblical literary evidence for his hypothesis, but he neglected to include it in his article.

Evans has correctly shown that any symbolic message intended would have to reflect known tradition to be understood. Nowhere in the scripture or related literature is there an expectation that the Messiah would destroy the temple, but on the other hand, there are many passages that teach the corruption of the priesthood and the expectation that the Messiah would cleanse the defiled temple.[32] From this evidence he concluded that if Jesus had acted in a symbolic way, he would have intended a symbolism different from any suggested either by Sanders or Neusner. Jesus would have meant that he was fulfilling the messianic expectations that the Messiah should cleanse the temple of its defilement and economic corruption as other Jewish leaders had done before him. Evans did not raise this question, but the examples he gave for deciding which symbolism Jesus intended would apply just as well for arguing that the narrative was not historical at all but had been attributed to Jesus by the later church on the basis of messianic expectations and fulfillment of prophecy.

John 13.23). It is from a reclining position that it was possible for the other disciple whom Jesus loved to be at his bosom, the place of highest honor (John 13.23). The exchange of "table for table" is homiletically attractive but realistically not as nearly perfect as it would be if the transfer had been made in the Western world in the twentieth century.

[32]Passages Evans used as examples are from Isaiah, Micah, Hosea, Jeremiah, Ezekiel, Lamentations, Zephaniah, Zechariah, Malachi, Jubilees, Testament of Levi, 1 Enoch, Psalms of Solomon, and the Testament of Moses. Evans, "Action," pp. 248-56.

THE MIDRASH

NT scholars have not always recognized the way authors have used FT in forming their literature, but the methods were standard and well accepted. Some important beliefs were the following: 1) Everything that is in the world is in the scripture; 2) all prophecy was propesied only for the days of the Messiah; and 3) two or three witnesses are required to prove a case in court.

This last rule was followed carefully by the author of Matthew, especially, who "proved" arguments over and over again by providing two parables, two chreias, or two FT passages. The author of the small midrash (Mark 11:17) in this pericope found two necessary prophecies that could apply to his own time. The first was from Second Isaiah who claimed that the Babylonian gentile who had embraced Judaism could go to Jerusalem with the Jews who were returning and be accepted on the same terms as if he had been born in Palestine.[33] The temple was not limited to the worshipers who were local or born into Judaism. It was to be called a **house of prayer for all the peoples** (Isa 56:7). Earlier, Jeremiah had been distressed by the sinful behavior of the men of Judah. They stole, murdered, committed adultery, perjured themselves, worshiped foreign gods, and then expected God to deliver them, because they worshiped in the temple (Jer 7:1-11). Jeremiah asked in the name of the Lord, **Has this temple which is called by my name become a cave of brigands** (Jer 7:11)?

The author of this midrash noted the difference between the claim of Second Isaiah and the situation lamented by Jeremiah, so he wove these passages artfully into a sentence that would apply to his day. The significance of the fact that the word used for "brigand" here is not klép-tays (κλέπτης), a thief, but lays-táys (λῃστῆς), a highway robber or brigand, has been known for more than 30 years.[34] This was precisely the term Josephus used to describe the insurrectionists that fought against Rome in the war of 66-70 I.A. When Herod was made king of the Jews his first assignment was "a campaign against the cave dwelling brigands (eh-peé toos ehn tois spay-laí-ois hor-may-to lays-tás, ἐπὶ τοὺς ἐν τοῖς σπηλαίοις ὥρμητο λῃστάς who were infesting a large area and inflicting on the inhabitants evils no less than those of war" (War 1.304). Strabo used the term λῃστήρια to describe the Hasmonean troops that overpowered the Syrian Greeks (Strabo 7.16,2.37-40). Rabbis also used the term as a loan word to describe soldiers ליסטיא, ליסטיות, etc.; bSan 46b; GenR 48.6; bAbodZar 25b; pTa'an 68d; bBBat 92b; bKetub 58a; bKid 11a; et alia).

---

[33]Rabbis were not in complete agreement on this. Sifre Deut (26.3; # 299) said the proselyte was prohibited from offering first fruits. mBik 1.4 said the proselyte would be allowed to bring his gift, but he could not make his declaration. Maimonides said he could do both (Code 7.6,4.3).

[34]See further Buchanan, "Mark 11:15-19: Brigands in the Temple," HUCA 30 (1959):169-77; "An Additional Note to "Mark 11:15-19: Brigands in the Temple," HUCA 31 (1960):103-105.

To learn the intended meaning of the midrash, it is necessary to learn how the author updated the scripture and to what situation it applied. When was the temple a cave of brigands or a zealot stronghold? Barabbas was described as one who participated in an insurrection (Mark 15:7). Luke said, in a chreia, that Pilate mingled the blood of the Galileans with their sacrifices (Luke 13:1-2). This seems to have been an otherwise unrecorded incident that took place in the temple area. So long as this is considered, the period of Jesus' ministry must be left as a possible candidate for the Sitz im Leben of Mark 11:17, even though there is no direct evidence that the zealots controlled the temple during Jesus' ministry.

A more likely possibility, however, is the First Revolt of the Jews against Rome in 68-70 I.A. At that time the zealots unquestionably had control of the temple mount, and might have been accused of having made it a "cave of brigands" or a zealot stronghold (War 4.147-61). Josephus said they made the sanctuary (*τὸ ἅγιον*) a place of tyranny, and the temple of God itself had become a fortress (*φρούριον*) (War 4.151). This seems to be the most likely situation to explain the origin the midrash in this pericope. After the fall of Jerusalem, some Christian, who opposed the action of the zealots in Jerusalem formed this midrash, using two FT texts to prove that the zealotic action was wrong.

CONCLUSIONS

The relevant paragraph upon which both Sanders and Neusner appealed contains five verses: 1) Vs 16 is a separate halachic sentence; 2) vs 17 is a midrash that probably reflects an origin after 68 I.A.; 3) vss 18-19 contain typical Markan editorial and summary passages that are unnecessary to the content of the paragraph. Only vs 15 reports the cleansing of the temple upon which, with its synoptic parallels, both Sanders and Neusner appeal as being the most likely historical report in the message of the entire gospels. Since this sentence has been put together with another verse that is probably post 68 I.A. in composition, the editing, at least, and possibly the composition of the individual fragments of this pericope would have been done after the fall of Jerusalem in 70 I.A.

There are many questions raised about the authenticity of this as a historical symbolic event. There are at least two reasonable ways in which this sentence can be explained besides claiming it as a historical report of a symbolic action. 1) It could have been a much more violent report than is now preserved, having been edited after the fall of Jerusalem by the later church. If this were the case it would not have been intended as a symbolic prophecy to communicate any special message either to the disciples or other observers, either about the later fall of Jerusalem or the later interpretation of the Eucharist. It would have been an act of aggression intended to result in the control of the temple area. The following crucifixion of Jesus supports this possibility, and the composite nature of the paragraph suggests some kind of serious editing.

2) The other possibility is that it might never have happened. It could have been created by the later church in the first place. If this were true, it would be

a weak place to look for valid data for historical Jesus research. The amount of fulfilled prophecy and messianic expectations met by this paragraph suggests a midrashic composition. Methodologically, Sanders has claimed to base his study

> primarily on facts about Jesus and only secondarily on a study of some of the sayings material.[35]

He held that

> . . . in the present work emphasis will be placed on unassailable facts about Jesus.[36]

He considered the activity of Jesus in the temple

> "as the surest starting point for our investigation."[37]

Sanders said,

> The conflict over the temple seems deeply implanted in the tradition, and that there was such a conflict would seem to be indisputable.[38]

Sanders' plan was to "found the study on bedrock, and especially to begin at the right point."[39] These are desirable goals. A researcher should never work with anything less than bedrock, unassailable facts, and indisputable arguments, if this is possible. Unfortunately historians often have to accept something less and deduce the possible or probable from that. This study has shown that the pericope about the temple cleansing lacks some of the qualities Sanders claimed for it, and there are serious questions raised about the conjectures of the symbolism given both by Sanders and Neusner.

---

[35]Sanders, Jesus, 5.

[36]Sanders, Jesus, 17.

[37]Sanders, Jesus, 61.

[38]Sanders, Jesus 61.

[39]Sanders, Jesus, 10. Sanders may have been drawn to this beginning point by N. A. Dahl, 'The Problem of the Historical Jesus' Kerygma and History, tr. and ed. C. E. Braaten and R. A. Harrisville (New York: Abingdon, c1962) 138-71. Dahl correctly said, "There is a point in the life of Jesus which is unconditionally established. That is his death" (157). Although the story of the cleansing is reported close in time and geography to the death of Jesus, it is far less secure from the standpoint of literature and history.

Scholars might think at least twice before overlooking the content of the sayings material contained in chreias and parables[40] and accepting instead the bold conjectures of Sanders and Neusner as the surest starting point from which to begin research about the historical Jesus or the most likely interpretations of the relevant narrative.[41]

THE MATTHEAN PARALLEL TO MARK 11:15-19 IS MATTHEW 21:12-13

TEXT

Matthew	First Testament
12Then Jesus entered into the temple and threw out all those who bought and sold in the temple, and he upset the tables of the money changers and the chairs of those who sold doves, 13and he said to them, "It is written,	The gentiles who join themselves to Yahowah to minister to him love the name of Yahowah, to his servants--everyone who avoids defiling the Sabbath and keeps contract--I will bring them to my holy mountain, and I will make them happy **in my house of prayer**. Their whole burnt offerings and their sacrifices will be accepted at my altar, for
My temple will be called a house of prayer, but you have made it	**my temple will be called a house of prayer for all the** peoples (Isa 56:6-7; see also Isa 60:7-10).
a cave of brigands."	Has this house which is called by my name become **a cave of brigands** in your eyes (Jer 7:11)?

COMMENTARY

Who bought and sold in the temple. Derrett thought this activity was prompted because Jesus had observed that the temple was defiled with the uncleanness of leprosy and therefore should be torn down and rebuilt.[42] In antiquity many tem-

---

[40]For an examination of chreias and parables as a basis from which to begin historical Jesus research see Buchanan, Jesus: The King and his Kingdom (Macon: Mercer U, 1984), 43-82.

[41]This essay is an update of an earlier article, Buchanan, "Symbolic," 280-90.

[42]J. D. M. Derrett, "No Stone upon Another: Leprosy and the Temple," JSNT 30 (19878):3-20.

ples, including Jerusalem, were not only temples. They constituted the main, last stand, fortress of the nation and the national treasury. Temple banks were found all through territories of Greece, Egypt, Babylonia, and Asia Minor. There were famous temple banks at Delphi, Ephesus, Delos, and Olympius. This was also true of the temple at Jerusalem which held at least 400 talents of silver and 200 talents of gold while the Syrians ruled Jerusalem.[43] When Heliodorus came to Jerusalem to confiscate this wealth, the temple priests prayed for his failure (2 Macc 3:15). Hamilton correctly answered those who thought that Jesus was opposed to the temple itself,

> This could not have been the case, since those who had been closest to Jesus in his ministry continued afterward in their post-Easter faith "day by day attending the temple" (Acts 2:46). The national treasury was considered holy, and Jews objected strenuously when the non-Jew, Pilate, used these national funds for national projects, such as constructing an aqueduct (War 2.175).

For anyone to come into a temple and take it over by simply tipping over a few tables and chairs seems impossible. The abomination of desolations referred to in Daniel was the time Antiochus entered Jerusalem with troops and plundered the temple, taking all the gold vessels, furniture, and money (Ant 12.248-50). When the Hasmonean war became costly for Antiochus IV he went to Persia where there was a rich temple to Artemis which he wanted to conquer and plunder so that he could pay his military expenses, but the local people defended it strongly and drove him out of the city (Ant 12:354-57). He finally died there.

Antiochus' father, Antiochus the Great also met his death in the East where he was trying to plunder a temple to take its wealth to pay his military expenses. Temples were normally well defended, and kings wanted to capture them to rob them of their treasures. Sander's conjecture that this was only a symbolical act that Jesus did with the full awareness and permission of the military guard is fictitious. It would require a sizeable military force to take over such a fortress and national treasury. Anyone who tried to create a riot by "symbolically" turning over the merchants' tables in the treasury would have been arrested, in all probability, if he did not have a very strong military defense with him.

Both Matthew and Luke agreed against Mark in holding that the temple cleansing occurred on the same day as the triumphal entry into Jerusalem. Mark 3:20-21 reported the temple cleansing the following day.

---

[43]So 2 Macc 3:10-11. See also N. Q. Hamilton, "Temple Cleansing and Temple Bank," JBL 83 (1964):366.

A house of prayer. Matthew's anti-gentilic tendency prevented him from including Isaiah's entire quotation, which read, "A house of prayer **for all the gentiles,**" as Mark 11:17 has it.[44]

TEXT

Matthew	First Testament
[14]**The blind** and **the lame** came to him in the temple, and he healed them. [15]When the chief priests and the scribes saw the	Then the eyes of **the blind** will be opened, and the ears of the deaf, unstopped. Then **the lame** one will jump like a deer, and the tongue of the dumb will sing (Isa 35:5-6).
miracles that he did and **the children** who cried out in the temple and said, "**Hosanna,** to the son of David," they were angry [16]and said to him, "You hear what these are saying don't you?" Jesus said to them, "Yes. Have you never	Let the Israelites be glad in his deeds; Let **the children** of Zion rejoice in their king (Ps 149:2). Please, Yahowah, **save please** (Ps 118:25). The woman of Tekoah spoke to the king. She fell on her face to the ground and worshiped. Then she said, "**Save,** O king" (2 Sam 14:4).
read, **From the mouths of infants and babies I have provided praise?"** [17]Then he left them and went to Bethany, and he spent the night there.	**From the mouths of infants and babies I will provide praise** because of your enemies (LXX Ps 8:3).

[44]See further Buchanan, "Brigands," pp. 169-77.

COMMENTARY

He healed them. According to 2 Sam 5:8 the blind and the lame were not permitted to enter the temple. Nevertheless, Isaiah said the blind would receive their sight and the lame would leap like deer. Of course, Isaiah did not say that this would take place in the temple, but it was in the scripture. It had been prophesied by the prophet Isaiah; therefore, according to Matthew, it must have happened. All prophecy was prophesied only for the days of the Messiah. Since Jesus was the Messiah, he must have done that which the prophet prophesied. It was only a matter of determining when or where Jesus healed the lame and the blind. According to Matthew's doctrine, there could be no question that it was done. Whenever ancient historians based their history on doctrine, modern readers should question the historical accuracy of the account.

Children cried out in the temple. This was given to provide Matthew another opportunity to justify actions by the fulfillment of scripture. Since Jesus was praised, it must have been prophesied that he would be praised. It was only in the LXX version that he could find the proper basis for this praise. Since that came from the children, the author supposed that there were also children in the temple, even though children would not have been allowed in the temple itself. These actions must have taken place, if at all, in the temple grounds.

Went to Bethany Most texts say, "went out of the city to Bethany," but Sinaiticus and the medieval Hebrew Text omit these words.

TEXT

18Early the [next] morning after he had gone into the city, he was hungry, 19and
he saw a fig tree along the way; he came to it; he found nothing on it but leaves;
and he said to it, "No longer will any fruit come from you in the age [to come]."
Then the fig tree suddenly dried up. 20When the disciples saw [it], they were surprised and said, "How [could] the fig tree be dried up suddenly?" 21Jesus answered and said to them, "I tell you under oath, if you have faith and do not
doubt, you will not only do that [which happened] to the fig tree, but even to this
mountain you will say, 'Be taken up and thrown into the sea,' and it will be
done, 22and everything which you ask in prayer, believing, you will receive."

TECHNICAL DETAILS

No one has ever explained the narrative about the fig tree incident in a way that is pleasing to Christians. Jesus seems to have behaved as if the tree was personally responsible for its condition. This seemingly impulsive behavior on Jesus' part seems less than mature, and the idea that it could happen seems ridiculous.

In the following picture, the ancient road which separates the area with trees and bushes from the field is probably the road on which Jesus walked as he came down to Kidron Valley from the Mount of Olives. It was there that he found the fig tree that had no ripe fruit at Passover time. The picture was taken from the Kidron Valley.

SCHOLARLY REACTIONS

There have been very few scholarly reactions to this passage of scripture, especially in recent journals.[44] Many failed to deal with the problems of this passage. Edward Schweitzer avoided the issue by neglecting comment on the entire passage,[45] and Albright and Mann said it was impossible to know "what historical background lies behind the narrative of these verses."[46] Gundry allegorized the passage, saying that Jesus was not looking for figs on a tree but "fruit

[44]I have checked all issues to date of New Testament Abstracts and all issues of Zeitschriftenschau für die Bibelwissenschaft und Grenzgebiet for the past twenty years to find articles on these verses. Only the articles mentioned were relevant to this topic.

[45]E. Schweitzer, The Good News according to Matthew (Atlanta: John Knox, c1975), 408-409.

[46]W. F. Albright and C. S. Mann, Matthew (Garden City: Doubleday, 1971), p. 260.

of faith and good works on the tree of Jerusalem."[47] He also thought that Jesus was looking for "green winter figs" which had not ripened before the tree lost its leaves in the autumn.[48] Bartsch thought this was a symbolic miracle intended to instruct the nearness of the passion and resurrection.[49] Münderlein also took the event to be a symbolic teaching, comparing the contemporary Jews to unfruitful trees.[50]

Sabourin also followed Victor of Antioch in saying this was an acted parable which Jesus used to set for the judgment that was about to happen to Jerusalem.[51] McLaughlin said Jesus was angry because the tree was deceptive:

> So the fig tree was not punished for not having fruit primarily but for falsely professing to have it.[52]

Trench said,

> We must first ask ourselves here, how should our Lord, knowing, as by his divine power he must, that there was no fruit upon that tree, have gone to seek it there?[53]

Smith denied all of the modern means used to justify Jesus' action. He finally said there was none, but that the situation would make more sense if it were assumed that the story was related to the Feast of Tabernacles rather than Passover season. In the Autumn the figs would really be ripe. At that time Jesus might be justified in looking for ripe figs. Smith conjectured this event really

---

[47]Gundry, Matthew, p. 416.

[48]Gundry, Matthew, p. 417.

[49]H. W. Bartsch, "Die 'Verfluchung' des Feigenbaums," ZNW 53 (1962):256-60. Bartsch's major point was his attempt to prove that Bultmann was wrong in considering the Matthean version of this pericope to be original and the Markan unit secondary. He correctly noted that the Markan version was much like a chreia, but he failed to note that Matthew's was nearer to that form, lacking the interpretive comment, "For it was not the season for figs."

[50]G. Münderlein, "Die Verfluchung des Feigenbaumes (Mk XI.12-14)," NTS 10 (1963/64):94-104.

[51]L. Sabourin, The Gospel according to St Matthew (Bandra, Bombay: St. Paul's Press, c1982), p. 765. J. P. Meier, Matthew (Wilmington: Glazier, 1980), p. 237, and A. W. Argyle, The Gospel according to Matthew (Cambridge: University Press, c1963), p. 159, followed the same course.

[52]G. A. McLaughlin, Commentary on the Gospel according to Saint Matthew (Chicago: The Christian Witness Co., 1909), p. 293.

[53]R. C. Trench, Notes on the Miracles of our Lord (New York: Fleming H. Revell, n.d.) p. 463.

happened in the Fall. Christians stopped celebrating the Feast of Tabernacles after the fall of Jerusalem in 70 I.A. Then Mark would have transferred the story to Passover which was not the season for figs. This means that Mark was written later than 70 I.A.[54] This would still leave Jesus looking rather petulant for cursing a fig tree when he found someone had picked the figs before he got there.

Robin said that Jesus probably did not curse the fig tree at all. Instead he quoted from Mic 7:1-6, and the disciples misunderstood his quotation as a curse.[55] Meyer said Jesus saw the tree had leaves so he naturally expected to find fruit, and when there was none he was disappointed,[56] but Rabbi Shimon ben Gamaliel said normally 50 days elapsed between the time when fig leaves appear and the time when there was green fruit. Other rabbis said there was either 40 or 50 days between the time of the first appearance of leaves until the trees bloomed; it took another 40 or 50 days for the green fruit to appear and still another 40 or 50 days until there was ripe fruit--a total of about 120 to 150 days from the first appearance of leaves until there would be ripe fruit (pSheb 35d). Rabbis also told of a certain owner of a fig tree who used to get up early and pick figs before the worms got into them. He not only knew the right season to pick figs but also the correct time of day (CantR 6.2, #2.2).

Since Jesus was a native Palestinian it is reasonable to assume that Jesus also knew there should normally be several months between the first leaves and the first ripe fruit. Therefore he should not have been deceived by the leaves into thinking there was fruit on the tree, ready to eat. Tasker said, "some fruit usually appeared on the fig tree before the leaves,"[57] but gave no evidence for his belief. Slater held that Jesus would not have expected new, fresh figs that early in the year, but the leaves had already appeared, and he probably expected the tree to have some of the previous season's fruit left over from the year before.[58] Hyvernat said there were figs that remained on the tree after the leaves had fallen. Any such figs as these could easily be shaken off, and it is unlikely that these would have continued to hang on the tree, unpicked or ungleaned, after the new leaves had appeared, especially in a country where gleaners were allowed to

---

[54] C. W. F. Smith, "No Time for Figs," JBL 79 (1960):315-27.

[55] A. de Q. Robin, "The Cursing of the Fig Tree in Mark XI. A Hypothesis," NTS 8 (1961/62):276-81.

[56] H. A. W. Meyer, Critical and Exegetical Hand-Book to the Gospel of Matthew (New York: Funk & Wagnalls, 1884, c1970), p. 366. Meyer listed other scholars who followed Chrysostom in holding that Jesus was not fooled by the tree, but he only acted as he did to provide the occasion for a miracle.

[57] R. V. G. Tasker, The Gospel according to St. Matthew (Grand Rapids: Eerdmans, c1961), p. 201.

[58] W. F. Slater, St. Matthew (Edinburgh: T. C. & E. C. Jack, n.d.), pp. 263-64.

pick the fruit left after the tree had been shaken once (Deut 24:20). Some figs ripened in June, but the largest harvest of figs came in August.[59] Grundmann followed Lohmeyer in thinking that this was a pious personal legend.[60]

Johnson correctly said, "The story has raised many questions in the minds of the readers." He asked, "Was it like Jesus to curse the fig tree, particularly if, as Mark 11:13 says, 'it was not the season for figs'?"[61] Patte said, "But such a violent use of power against a fig tree seems out of character for Jesus."[62] Neither scholar, however, found a satisfying answer to the problem.[63] This is where the problem is left unless some new insight is found. The solution may have been with us all the time, residing in the text of the FT.

LITERARY QUESTIONS

Bartsch was correct in observing that the Markan version is very much like a chreia.[64] The Matthean version appears to be a responsive chreia that has been expanded, and the Markan version expanded still more.[65] A responsive chreia is a literary form distinguished in the following ways: 1) A speaker or actor is identified, 2) the situation that prompted the speaker to speak or the actor to act is given, 3) a summary of the speaker's saying or the actor's action is given, and 4) the entire unit is very brief. The Matthean chreia is as follows:

1) The context shows that the speaker was Jesus.
2) The situation that prompted him to speak was as follows:

---

[59]H. Hyvernat, "Fig and Fig-Tree," The Jewish Encyclopedia, V, p. 382.

[60]W. Grundmann, Das Evangelium nach Matthäus (Berlin: Evangelische Verlaganstalt, c1968), p. 450-52.

[61]S. E. Johnson, The Gospel according to St. Matthew (New York: Abingdon, c1951), p. 506.

[62]Patte, Matthew, p. 292. Patte later strained to relate this story to the tenants (Matt 21:34-35, 41-43) since the latter did not pay rent when it was due. He said, "the servants are sent while it is not quite 'the time of fruit'" (p. 299). M. -J. LaGrange, Evangile selon Saint Matthieu (Paris: Gabalda, 1948), pp. 404-405, also had more questions than answers.

[63]Even the church fathers failed to understand the scriptural promises behind this passage. See S. Thomas Aquinas, Commentary on the Four Gospels, collected out of the Works of the Fathers (Oxford: Parker, 1841), pp. 716-20.

[64]Bartsch, "Verfluchung," pp. 256-60.

[65]B. Charette, The Theme of Recompense in Matthew's Gospel (Sheffield: JSOT Press, c1992), p. 134, noted that Mark modified the story by adding "if by chance" he might find figs and "it was not the season for figs." That was done because Mark saw no reason for Jesus expecting figs at Passover time.

"Early the [next] morning after he had gone into the city, he was hungry, and he saw a fig tree along the way; he came to it; he found nothing on it but leaves;"

The summary quotation is:

3) "No longer will any fruit come from you in the age [to come]."

4) The entire unit is brief.

Mark made the addition, "For it was not the season for figs," and Matthew and Mark (11:20) both reported that the tree dried up, but these statements are not a part of the chreia. When the chreia is compared with 28 other chreias and 38 parables in the gospels, it seems coherent with other teachings of Jesus.[66] It belongs to a Palestinian setting around Passover time. There is nothing in the chreia to suggest a later date or a different location. There is an extensive collection of evidence showing the reliability of chreias in reporting fairly events relating to great teachers or leaders, so we cannot rule out the possibility that Jesus himself actually cursed the fig tree.[67] No matter how the literary form came into existence, however, there is the problem of making sense of the report. How can the event be explained? The answer to this question is so easy that it should have been noticed long before now.

THE MOOD OF THE TIMES

Jesus and his disciples, like other Jews before, during, and after NT times, seemed to be confident that they were living in the last days of the old Roman age. According to the gospels, some thought Jesus was the one who would redeem Israel (Luke 24:21). Jesus reportedly said there were some of his hearers who would not die before the kingdom came (Matt 24:34; Mark 13:28-30). He also assured his disciples that within their own lifetimes they would sit on 12 thrones governing the 12 tribes of Israel (Matt 19:28). Jews reached these conclusions on several bases:

1) They thought history would be repeated. That which had happened after the exile in Egypt, the exile in Babylon, and the exile under the Syrian Greeks would happen again under the exile to the Romans. They studied carefully the events that were supposed to take place at the very end of the old common age before the kingdom came. They thought they were close to the time when the

---

[66]For a list of these literary forms in the gospels see Buchanan, Jesus, pp. 45-74, 127-28, 165, 221, 238-39.

[67]Buchanan, Jesus, pp. 45-74, 127-28, 165, 221, 238-39.

ages would change. At any moment their whole situation would be different. The first would become last and the last, first. The cycle was predestined to turn over into the antitype of the age of Solomon, Nehemiah, and the Hasmoneans, so Jews were looking everywhere for signs of the end of the age.[68]

2) The second base is really an extension of the first: A new redemption would be like the redemption from the Greeks reported by Daniel. If Jews could only identify parts of the current history with parts of the last 3 1/2 year period of Daniel's calendrical account, they could tell where they were in the cycle and when the 3 1/2 years would be over.

3) The third point is that Jews believed that all prophecy was prophesied only for the days of the Messiah (bBer 34b), and those were the days of the Messiah. This is probably what was meant by the statement, "All the prophets and the law prophesied until John" (Matt 11:13). That was when the messianic age began, so Jews had only to read all of the prophecies related to the changing of the ages and look for signs they could identify with these events to learn how close Jews were to the crucial change. Matthew interpreted many events in the life of Jesus as current fulfillments of FT. Luke thought Jesus was the one through whom Isaiah 61 was fulfilled (Luke 4:21). These methods of calculating the time of the end of Jewish exile were applied many times throughout Jewish history, from the Jubilee following the North Israelite captivity (Isa 27) until the present day.[69] There are many indications that these were also applied at the time of Jesus.

UNFULFILLED PROMISES

Fresh Figs at Passover. As reported, both the fig tree incident and the promise to be able to move mountains took place in the Kidron Valley, as Jesus and the apostles were returning to the temple area from their overnight lodging in Bethany. This was a crucial time, just before Passover, and a critical place, between the Mount of Olives and the temple area at Jerusalem. While they were all seated near the Kidron Valley on the Mount of Olives, disciples asked Jesus when all these expected things would take place. What would be the signs that could prompt Jesus to declare his position openly? When could they shout these secrets

---

[68]On cycles of time and eschatological expectations see Buchanan, Jesus, pp. 253-83; on Sabbatical eschatology see Buchanan, The Consequences of the Covenant (Leiden, Brill, 1970), pp. 9-18. The term "sabbatical eschatology" has been recognized, accepted, and used by such other scholars as A. Y. Collins, "Numerical Symbolism in Jewish and Early Christian Apocalyptic Literature," Aufsteig und Niedergang der Römischen Welt, II.21.2, 1228-29, S. Bacchiocchi, "Sabbatical Typologies of Messianic Redemption," JSJ 17 (1986):153-176, and R. M. Johnston, "The Eschatological Sabbath in John's Apocalypse: A Reconsideration," AUSS 25 (1987):39-50.

[69]See further Buchanan, Revelation and Redemption: Jewish Documents of Deliverance from the Fall of Jerusalem to the death of Nahmanides (Dillsboro: sold by Mercer U. Press, c1978), passim.

from the roof tops (Matt 10:27)? When would the end of the Roman age take place, followed by the succeeding messianic age (Matt 24:3)?

Jesus may have been looking for such signs as these himself. Those Jews who calculated the end of the Roman era, studied, primarily, FT that dealt with promises related to the end of the "captivity." These were Jeremiah, Ezekiel, Second Isaiah, Zechariah, and Daniel. Since all prophecy was prophesied only for the days of the Messiah, and these were the days of the Messiah, Jesus and his disciples had only to read all of the prophecies related to the changing of the ages and look for current signs related to these events to learn how close they were to the crucial change. Two of the great prophets of change were Ezekiel and Zechariah. Ezekiel prophesied that in the new age the Kidron Valley, between the Mount of Olives and the temple area, would carry a stream of the water of life from the temple that would run all the way down through the Wadi Qumran to the Dead Sea.[70] The valley that led to the Dead Sea from the temple area was probably the one Joel called the Valley of Shittim (Joel 4:18). On both sides of this stream there would be trees bearing all kinds of fruit every month of the year, so there would be no time which was "not the season for figs," as Mark noted (Mark 11:13) was the case when Jesus approached the fig tree. Citizens of Palestine would never be without fruit for food (Ezek 47:1-12). One anonymous Medieval Jewish scholar thought these would be the trees Second Isaiah said would clap their hands (Isa 55:12). When these things happened the Messiah would come announcing good news to Israel.[71]

That which Jews of NT times expected to take place at the introduction of the new age was not the normal but the miraculous. They did not expect things to be as they normally had been in the old age under Roman control. One of the first miracles of the new age would be fresh fruit all the year around in the Kidron Valley. Jesus evidently expected to see some of the signs of change at that particular feast. One certain sign available for checking the calendar was the condition of the fruit trees near the Kidron stream. If they produced fruit out of season, the new age had already begun. The text said that Jesus looked for figs when he was hungry (Matt 21:18). He may have been, but that was not the main reason he wanted ripe figs to appear on that tree just before Passover. This was a strategic sign that would determine his future activity.

When Jesus found no fruit he was understandably disappointed, so he cursed the fig tree. Since it did not produce fruit of the new age at that time, Jesus asked that it not be one of the trees blessed with the ability to bear fruit out of normal season "in the age [to come]" (ays ton ai-óh-nah, *εἰς τὸν αἰῶνα*) (Matt 21:19). That was the curse. According to the chreia, Jesus did not ask that the tree dry up. That was a later addition, employed by a later scribe who misunderstood the curse and misinterpreted it to prove that Jesus' curses were effective.

---

[70]See W. R. Farmer, "The Geography of Ezekiel's River of Life," BA 19 (1956):17-22.

[71]Buchanan, Redemption, p. 542-43.

Not only the gospel writers but the NT seer and later rabbis expected Ezekiel's promise to be fulfilled in the new age. The seer thought that in the new age the river would flow at Jerusalem where the Garden of Eden would be restored, and there would be fruit trees on its banks (Rev 22:1-2). Another early seer envisioned himself being taken to the Lord's Paradise where fruit trees would be flourishing, bearing fruits, with their roots from an immortal land [probably Palestine]. These fruits were watered by the river of gladness [probably the river in the Kidron Valley], and the area around was the land of life of the age [to come] (OdesSol 11.15-16). Among the proofs that Saadia Gaon gave that salvation was destined to come to Israel was the promise given in Ezek 47:1-12. Whenever this prophecy was fulfilled then the land would be restored and salvation would take place.[72] This was also part of the scripture expected to be fulfilled at the national redemption according to the "Book of Zerubbabel."[73]

Miracles and Mountains. Another miracle expected at the change of the ages was foretold by Zechariah. Zechariah had promised that on the judgment day the Lord would stand on the Mount of Olives, and the mountain would split in two, part of it moving north and part of it moving south (Zech 14:4). Like other faithful Jews, Jesus probably expected this to happen, because this is what was said in the Lord's word. If the disciples had faith they could hasten the judgment when this mountain would move. Then **the Lord would come, and all of the holy ones [would come] with him** (Zech 14:5). According to Matthew Jesus, as the Son of man, expected to come into his glory bringing all of his angels with him (Matt 25:31), and thought he could ask his Father, and God would send him more than 12 legions of angels (Matt 26:53). This shows Jesus' familiarity with the relevant passage in Zechariah, according to Matthew.

While Jesus and his disciples were in the Kidron Valley, Jesus told them that if they had faith they could command "this mountain" to move, and it would. This mountain was obviously the Mount of Olives, the place where Jesus had spent the night, the mountain adjacent to the Kidron Valley where Jesus tested the fruit tree, and the very mountain where the disciples asked Jesus about signs of the end of the age (Matt 24:3). The judgment day was to take place just at the end of the common gentile age and the beginning of the holy Jewish age to come. The Judgment Day was expected to take place on New Year's Day, and according to the old Pentacontad calendar, New Year's Day was the first Sunday after Passover.[74] The time when Matthew reported Jesus and his disciples to have discussed these things would have been very close to the time when judgment should

---

[72]Buchanan, Redemption, p. 58.

[73]Buchanan, Redemption, p. 380.

[74]H. and J. Lewy, "The Origin of the Week and the Oldest West Asiatic Calendar," HUCA 17 (1942-43):1-152a; J. Morgenstern, "The Calendar of the Book of Jubilees," VT 5 (1955):34-76.

have taken place, according to Jewish eschatology. The mountain should have moved, and the trees should have borne fruit out of season. The place was also very close to the place where all these things were expected to take place when the ages changed.

Postponed Optimism. When signs like these did not occur, Jesus evidently became convinced that this was not the feast at which the Kingdom of Heaven would be restored.[75] While people continued to ask Jesus when the ages would change and what signs he would give to prove it, he could never tell them for sure in Galilee, because the signs of the changing of the age would all appear around Jerusalem. He also had to wait until the judgment day that would occur just after Passover. Nevertheless, he had to prepare for that eventuality. The calendrical signs pointed to this feast, so he sent his apostles out to get everyone ready to act if the signs confirmed his expectations. There was consequently a large group in parade on Palm Sunday, and he came riding in on a donkey to announce his parousia to those who had eyes to see and ears to hear. The Pharisees understood the code and tried to subdue it. All of Jerusalem would have been excited, and the apostles could hardly wait. Then the signs did not appear as they were expected. Everything that had been planned had to be postponed.

This was a disappointment to the apostles, who apparently expected Jesus to initiate some action to take possession of the kingdom at that particular feast. They had hurried all over Judah, Galilee, and Perea, preparing Jews for this particular feast. What a let down! It was only after they were sure that he would not lead some rebellion against the Romans that Judas betrayed him, and Peter denied him, but Jesus refused to act without God's approval, and God had not given a sign. If the fig tree had produced fresh, ripe fruit at Passover time when Jesus looked for it; if the mountain had moved to announce the Judgment Day; and if the holy armies had come down from heaven to support Jesus' movement (Zech 14:5; Matt 25:31; 26:53), Jesus probably would have acted as the apostles anticipated, but that was not the case.

Since no sign had been given at this feast, Jesus promised that it would happen before the next Passover. Maybe the sign would come near the time of popular Judaism's New Year's Day or the Day of Atonement, as it had for Judas the Maccabee. In any case, there was not much time left in this Roman age, in Jesus' judgment, but there still was some. His new revision of time tables was that the age to come would begin before the next Passover which he and his apostles would celebrate in the new Kingdom of his Father (Matt 26:28-29).

One of the time lines which calculators of the end of the common era followed was the typology of Dan 7. Between the defilement of the temple and the cleansing was 3 1/2 years. Based on some unknown event in the temple that Jesus thought was the typological equivalent of the abomination of desolations by Antiochus Epiphanes, Jesus was counting. He may have thought that three years had

---

[75]See further Buchanan, Jesus, pp, 247-52.

passed since that event. This Passover would surely be the year when there would be a new Battle of Beth-horon and the temple would be cleansed. He expected fruit in the Kidron Valley out of season to confirm that deduction. When that failed, he thought there was another half year left. The new age would begin before the next Passover, so they would have to wait again.

It may have been after the cursing of the fig tree that Jesus told the parable of the unproductive fig tree. It had grown for three years and produced nothing. The question was: should they cut it down and give up the program entirely. The answer was, "No." Fertilize the tree, cultivate it well, and wait one more year. If then it failed to produce it could be cut down (Luke 13:6-9). This meant that if there was no sign from heaven before the next Passover he would admit that his calculation was mistaken, but he would not lead a military movement at this Passover, and he would not lead any movement without a sign from Heaven.

CONCLUSIONS

The author of Matthew seemed to think there was not anything abnormal about Jesus expecting fresh fruit at Passover time in the Kidron Valley. Like the author of Rev 22:1-5, the author of The Book of Zerubbabel, Rabbi Saadia Gaon, and other religious Jews, the author of Matthew was familiar with Jewish expectations and their understanding of biblical texts. The author of Mark was probably the first to express surprise. At Passover, of course, there would be no ripe figs on the fig tree, and Mark explained why--because that was not the season for figs (Mark 11:13)!

Scholars ever since have had difficulty with this passage, because they did not know how important FT was to Jews and early Christians for an attempt to understand what God had in mind for them in the future. It is clear that Matthew thought there was nothing abnormal about Jesus' action. This means Matthew or one of his sources might have composed this pericope and attributed it to Jesus. Another possibility is that Jesus might have actually cursed the fig tree and told the disciples that if they had faith they could make the Mount of Olives move. Although there is no proof that this was a historical report there are some arguments in its favor.

The fact that the report was contained in a chreia that was expanded in a way that is different from the meaning of the chreia itself shows that the interpretations were later additions by someone other than the author of the chreia. The additions--but not the chreia--were composed by the later church. This is typical of midrash and the normal use of chreias as texts. This alone speaks for the validity of the chreia report. Another consideration is the content: Why would any Christian in the later church compose this chreia after the fall of Jerusalem in 70 I.A., falsely showing Jesus to have become angry and have taken out his violence on a fig tree? The fact that some members of the church did not like the character portrayal is shown by the addition whereby later editors "corrected" the content of the curse and the emphasis of the pericope. The scribe who made this interpretative addition did not want people to think Jesus was a false messiah who was mistaken in his expectations, so he added a sentence to show that Jesus' curse was different but effective. The kingdom did not come, but the tree withered and died.

This study has added two new considerations to the data necessary for interpreting Matt 21:18-22.

1) It has recognized the limitations of the literary unit, the chreia, and

2) it has taken into account the expectations that the prophecies of the FT would be fulfilled in the days of the Messiah. Christians may not like this solution any more than previous suggestions, but there is a strong argument in its favor. It makes sense in terms of normal Jewish beliefs and expectations in Jesus' time and geographical situation without resorting to any kind of allegory or moralistic defense.[76]

COMMENTARY

I tell you under oath. Literally this says, "Amen! I say to you" (Matt 21:21), but "Amen," was a court term used when taking oaths, so the force was that of an oath. (See Num 5:1-22; bSheb 29b).

To this mountain you will say. During the crusades Jewish and Christian eschatology was high. Both expected the land soon to be restored to them. Jews had developed precise expectations related both to Ezek 47 and to Zech 14. They expected the Mount of Olives to split in two with part of the mountain moving south and part, north. The crevice in between would become a wadi through which water might flow. The water that came out from the temple area, as Ezekiel prophesied would then run both ways: Part of the water would run around the north side of the city and down one of the wadies, like Beth-horon, to the Mediterranean Sea. The rest of the water would flow eastward, down the Valley of Shittim, to the Dead Sea. This would become the river that would have trees producing fruit every month of the year. The other stream would be called Soter (savior in Greek). At the resurrection, the waves of the Mediterranean Sea would wash all of the bodies of Jews that had died in the sea up this river to the Mount of Olives.[77] These details may have varied from those anticipated by Jews and Christians of NT times, but they were based on the same kind of logic.

Everything which you ask in prayer. This message was directed to Jesus' authorized apostles, those who had been commissioned as Jesus' legal agents. Not only

[76]An earlier form of this exegesis was published in "Withering Fig Trees and Progression in Midrash," C. A. Evans and W. R. Stegner (eds.), The Gospels and the Scriptures of Israel (Sheffield: Sheffield Academic Press Ltd., c1994), pp. 249-69.

[77]Buchanan, Redemption, pp. 371, 380.

prayer, but everything that they did was to be done in the name of God, in behalf of God, and at the responsibility of God.

TEXT

[23]After he had entered the temple, the chief priests and the elders of the people came to him, while he was teaching, saying, "By what authority do you do these things? Who has given you this authority?" [24]Jesus answered and said to them, "I will also ask you one word, and if you tell me [the answer], I will also tell you by what authority I do these things: [25]'The baptism of John, from where was it? From Heaven or from men?'"[78] They held a conference among themselves, saying, "If we say, 'from Heaven,' he will tell us, 'Then why did you not believe him?' [26]If we say, 'From men,' we are afraid of the crowd, because they all hold that John was a prophet." [27]Then they answered Jesus and said, "We do not know." So he said to them, "Neither will I tell you by what authority I do these things."

TECHNICAL DETAILS

Gundry noted the well constructed chiasm in Matt 21:24:

a) I will ask
  b) you
    c) I also
      d) one word
      d') which if you tell me [the answer]
    c') I also
  b') you
a') I will tell you by which authority I do these things.[79]

---

[78]This was admittedly a sharp retort on the part of Jesus reported here, but it takes more than "a ring of authenticity" to prove that these were the ippsissima verba Jesu. How does anyone distinguish a "ring of authenticity" from any other ring. Harvey continued his confident claim, "It has a brilliance and aptness which can only be original--and indeed commentators are almost unanimous in regarding it as an unimpeachable utterance of Jesus" (A. E. Harvey, Jesus on Trial (Atlanta: John Knox, c1976), p. 31. Harvey did not say why he thought Jesus was the only one capable of making brilliant and apt utterances.

[79]Gundry, Matthew, p. 420.

COMMENTARY

Chief priests and elders. The targumist was probably speaking of these leaders when he said,

> I told them to perform justice, but they have become oppressors; [I told them to] perform merits, but they have increased debts [in the treasure of merits]" (TgJon Isa 5.7).
>
> The priest and the scribe are drunk with old wine (TgJon Isa 28.7). All priests and scribes were called "robbers of money" and "fraudulent servants" (TgJon Jer 8.10).

By what authority do you do these things. These words both introduce and conclude this unit. The words that perform this function are called parts of an inclusion. This is the second time Jesus' authority was questioned. At one point he was asked whether he received it from God or from Beelzebub. At that point he accused the questioners of blaspheming God by doubting the function of the Holy Spirit (Matt 12:22-32). Jesus was acting like a messiah, and he could not have been a messiah unless he had been anointed. There was probably a secret anointing ceremony at the so-called baptism of Jesus by John. This was how he obtained his authority, but no one wanted to say that openly when there were eavesdropping Romans around.

The baptism of John, from where was it? Here Jesus associated his own authority with that of John who had baptized him and possibly anointed him in secret. Jesus implied that he had received his authority from John. If John's authority was valid then so was Jesus' authority. John was so popular with the masses that when Herod lost a battle with the Arabian King Aretas and his army, people said this was God's punishment to Herod for having killed John the Baptist (Ant 18.116-119). John's baptizing was to provide forgiveness of sins for those who were repentant--not to provide all the people baptized with any kind of authority. When he "baptized" Jesus, however, the Spirit came upon Jesus, just as the Spirit had come upon Saul and David when they were secretly anointed. After his "baptism" Jesus was treated as if he had the authority of a messiah, a legal agent of God. It is possible that John also anointed Jesus, but that no one called it an anointing to protect him from the Romans. His answer to the chief priests and elders reminded them that John was a legitimate priest who had the authority to anoint Jesus. It was the anointing rather than the baptism that gave Jesus authority from God.

From Heaven. A euphemism. It means, "From God."

TEXT

[28]How does it seem to you? A man had two sons. He came to the first and said, "Son, go out today and work in the vineyard." [29]He, by way of reply, said, "I will, Sir," but he did not go out. [30]After he had come to the second, he said the same. But, replying, [the second son] said, "I do not want to." Later, after he had repented, he went away [and worked in the vineyard]. [31]Which of the two did the will of the father?" [The chief priests and elders] said, "The last one." Jesus said to them, "I tell you under oath that the tax collectors and harlots will precede you into the Kingdom of God."

COMMENTARY

A man had two sons. This parable is found only in Matthew, but there is a Lukan parable of the same theme--a man had two sons. The Lukan story is a lengthy and well-known parable of a man who had an older son and a younger prodigal son. The younger brother went away from home, lived among the gentiles (called "hogs"), spent his money and was left in need of kah-sháyr, (כשר) food that was approved by orthodox Jews. He would even have been glad to have food sold at a pagan meat market, but he had no money with which to buy it. He finally returned home and was gladly received by all except the older brother who refused to enter the same house with him (Luke 15:11-32).

It is important for judging reliability that one of these stories occurs only in Luke and the other only in Matthew. This means that they came from different traditions. It is not a situation in which one was copied from the other and modified. They are two definite and separate parables, but they are enough alike that the same basic teaching is central to both. This makes the probability that Jesus taught something like this much greater than if both stories were in only one gospel or if they were enough alike that someone might have copied one from the other.

By using this theme of a father with two sons Jesus showed his skill and clever wit in debate. In NT times, Jews were personified as Jacob, and Romans, as well as Roman collaborators like Herod, were called Esau or Edom. Probably every Jew knew the story of Jacob and Esau. Esau was the older brother, but he was not as clever or as unprincipled as Jacob, so his younger brother tricked him out of his just inheritance and his father's blessing. The Lukan parable followed the Genesis typology more closely than Matthew's parable. Like Jacob, the prodigal son went away into a far country, and like Jacob, the prodigal son returned repentant and received forgiveness (Gen 28, 32, and 33). The Lukan typology of the forgiven Jacob, however, did not find the new Esau forgiving. It was the father who forgave--not the elder brother.

The clever way in which Jesus prepared the story of the prodigal son and the older brother and the two sons and the vineyard was to reverse the story. Jacob had managed to manipulate his father in such a way as to obtain Isaac's blessing as well as the heritage of Esau and then leave to go into a far country. Like the prodigal son, however, Jacob returned from the far country and took over the heritage. His children became heirs of the entire promised land (Gen 25:19-34; 27:1-28:22; 32:1-33:20; 35:1-15). So the prodigal son became the new Jacob, and the Pharisee became the new Esau. In Matthew the new Esau was identified with the chief priests and the elders. In Luke the Pharisees constituted the new Esau. The Jacob-Esau story provided the intertext for both of these parables.

Son, go out today and work in my vineyard. This parable is now worked into a whole dialogue which makes it difficult to separate clearly. The question, "Which of the two did the will of the father?" may not be a part of the original context. The same is true of the following repartee: "They said, 'The second.' Jesus said to them, 'I swear to you that the tax collectors and harlots will precede you into the Kingdom of God'" (Matt 21:31). Perrin[80] followed Jeremias,[81] who followed Plummer mistakenly, in using one of the weakest texts, one that represents the first son as declining the invitation but later repenting and working in the vineyard. The argument is that if the first brother had accepted, the father would have had no reason to approach the second brother at all. There are two basic weaknesses with this argument apart from the textual support:

1) This assumes that the father needed only as much work done in the vineyard as one could do. Therefore, if the first son consented, the father would not have asked the second, but the story gives no basis for that assumption at all.

2) All of these interpretations presume that the parable was expected to make sense in and of itself. But this is not always the case.

The parable was a vehicle to communicate some message other than the actual events of the story. Sometimes this is done even if it strained or distorted factual history a bit to make the parable fit the narrator's needs. Matthew has placed this parable in a context in which Jesus was defending the second brother,

---

[80]N. Perrin, Rediscovering the Teaching of Jesus (New York: Harper & Rowe, c1967), pp. 118-19. Both Perrin and Jeremias were followed by J. Roloff, "Das Kirchenverständnis des Matthäus im Spiegel seiner Gelichnisse," NTS 38 (1992):346, who identified the disobedient son with Israel and the obedient son with the heathen who became Christians later, assuming that the parable did not come from Jesus but from the later church. See also J. R. Michaels, "The Parable of the Regretful Son," HTR 61 (1968):15-26.

[81]J. Jeremias, The Parables of Jesus, tr. S. H. Hooke (New York, Scribners, c1955), p. 125. So also Meyer, Hand-Book, pp. 360, 368-69 and J. Weiss, Die Schriften des Neuen Testaments Göttingen: Vandenhoeck & Ruprecht, 1907) I, pp. 363-64. Michaels, "Regretful Son,"pp. 25-26, noted that there was still a third variant: The first son refused and then worked; the second consented but then did not work. Nevertheless, the second was considered the obedient one. Michaels rendered the passage "repented and went," "regretfully went away." Michaels conjectured that this was the original version, overlooking the two sons theme in the Hebrew Scripture. This text he said, if not simply the result of a careless scribe, reflects pro-Pharisaism in the early Matthean church.

who was identified with the tax collector and the harlot (Matt 21:31) against the attacks of the chief priests and elders (Matt 21:23) or the chief priests and the Pharisees (Matt 21:45). Although this is the work of the editor, even if separated from its present context, the content of the parable itself suggests an intended context that poses some such situation. Historically, the Pharisees, chief priests, and elders did come first and they did agree to keep the law, which was doing God's work. Historically, the tax collectors (also called harlots) did break the law before they repented.[82]

It was only after Jesus had begun his recruitment program that some of the tax collectors and sinners began to repent, give up all they had, and follow Jesus. Therefore the parable was designed to show their relationship. Since Jesus asked the tax collectors to give up all of their possessions, while the Pharisees were giving only their tithes, Jesus was in a position to compare the Pharisees unfavorably to the tax collectors. The Pharisees were not working in the vineyard the way the tax collectors were doing. They said they would, but they did not; the tax collectors said they would not, but they repented and did. That was the situation, and Jesus made the parable fit his needs.

Although Jeremias acknowledged that the parable is not now in its original context,[83] he agreed with Dodd[84] in identifying the first brother with the religious leaders of the day and the second brother with the sinners and tax collectors. Most scholars agree with the identification.[85] Plummer also rejected the interpretations of those early church fathers who thought the older son represented the Jews, and that they should be considered the first to reject the Father's will because they rejected Jesus, the Messiah. The second son who first rejected the Father and then repented and accepted Jesus represented the gentiles.[86] He correctly held that there is no thought here of Jews and gentiles.

Later after he had repented. Like Jacob at Peniel, the younger son repented, came, and worked in the vineyard, meaning the tax collectors repented and came to Jesus and worked in his program of trying to restore the Kingdom of God to

---

[82]For the metaphorical use of harlot" to mean "liberal Jew," see Buchanan, Consequences, pp. 184-89. R. Augstein, Jesus the Son of Man, tr. H. Young (New York: Urizen Books, 1977), p. 134, was not acquainted with such Jewish customs, so he referred to Jesus' "apparent companionship with gluttons, boozers, and whores."

[83]Jeremias, Parables, pp. 80, 125.

[84]C. H. Dodd, The Parables of Jesus (London: Nisbet, 1952, 1960), p. 120.

[85]P. Dausch, Die Drei Alteren Evangelien (Bonn: T. Hansstein, 1932), p. 284; Meyer, Matthew, p. 368; Plummer, Matthew, p. 295; Weiss, Schriften I, p. 364.

[86]Plummer, Matthew, pp. 294-95. There are still scholars, like D. A. Hagner, Word Biblical Commentary: Matthew 14-28 (Dallas: Word Publishers, c1995), p. 617, who identify the elder son with Israel and the younger son with the church.

the chosen people. The Lukan prodigal son story pictured the younger son returning home, poor. Jacob had returned to the promised land, and he got as far as Peniel, at the border of the land, before he sent his wealth to his brother Esau, entering the land poor. There may have been tax collectors who spent all of their wealth in riotous living, and finally became poor, but the tax collectors who followed Jesus had taken all of their wealth and had given it to the the community called the "poor" (see Luke 19:1-10). When they confronted the Pharisees, chief priests, and elders as followers of Jesus, however, they were legally poor. These evidently would not have agreed with the chief priests and elders or with the Pharisees with whom Jesus was in conflict.

I tell you under oath. See commentary on Matt 24:1-2.

Tax collectors and harlots. Some rabbis said that if an orthodox Jew (khah-váyr (חבר) became a tax collector he would be pushed out of his community, and could not be trusted as long as he was a tax collector. If, however, he gave up his tax collecting, he could be readmitted and trusted with all of the orthodox rules (tDem 3.4 [49]). This, however, was not the position of the Pharisees.

A harlot is an insulting name for any Jew who mingles with gentiles in business or society. It implies that the Jew who was called a harlot was mingling sexually with gentiles. Jesus mingled with these wealthy male Jews and persuaded some of them to give all of their money to the cause and order he supported.

Which of the two did the will of the father? It was the Pharisees, the chief priests, and the elders who considered themselves, typologically, to be the true sons of Jacob. It was they who called the tax collectors Esau and Edom. Jesus told a parable that put the tax collector in the role of Jacob who had tricked his older brother out of his inheritance and his blessing. The Pharisee was shown as the older brother, in this case, who had been left out of the celebration. More than that, this was the older brother's own doing. Esau just was not as smart as Jacob, or as unprincipled, but the Pharisee still had a chance to belong to the celebration, too. If he did not enter, of course, it seemed that the tax collector, to whom the Pharisee referred as Esau, was really Jacob, and he displaced the Pharisaic Esau. Like Jacob of old the tax collector would receive the inheritance and all of the blessings.

Will precede you into the Kingdom of God. Just as in the Lukan parable, in the story of the two sons in a vineyard, it was the second son who actually worked in the vineyard who was identified by the Matthean editor as the tax collectors and harlots who would precede the Pharisees, chief priests, and elders into the kingdom.[87] The people with whom Jesus was in conversation were the chief priests and the elders (Matt 21:23) or the chief priests and the Pharisees (Matt 21:45). These officials objected to Jesus' acceptance of the tax collectors and other wealthy businessmen who had repented and had become zealous supporters of his program. Those called "harlots" were not feminine prostitutes, as Patte assumed.[88] They were masculine, liberal Jews. They mingled with gentiles--not sexually--but in business. In defense of these who had repented, Jesus said they would enter the Kingdom of God before the chief priests and elders.

Also in the parable of the prodigal son, who, like Jacob of old, went away into a far country before he repented and returned, the prodigal son played the role of the tax collector in the parable. The older brother functioned as a Pharisee. Scholars, like Abel, who thought the oldest son represented Israel and the second son, the gentiles, were mistaken.[89] There is not much basis for accepting Lowe's suggestion that the youngest son represented the followers of John the Baptist. It is true that tax collectors came to John when he preached, but it is also true that Jesus was notorious for his following of tax collectors[90] and for his conflict with the Pharisees.

TEXT

Matthew	First Testament
[32]For John came to you **in the way of righteousness**, and you did not believe him. The tax collectors and the "harlots," however, believed him, but you, when you saw [tax collectors believing] did not even repent later so as to believe in him.	I will walk **in the way of righteousness** (Prov 8:20). **In the way of righteousness** is life (Prov 12:28).

[87]J. D. M. Derrett, Law in the New Testament (London: Darton, Longman, & Todd, c1970), pp. 16-18, noticed the importance of the two brothers theme in the Hebrew Scripture and discussed the relationship of the older brother to the younger brother in law and in practice, but he failed to see the clever way in which Jesus turned the tables with this theme.

[88]D. Patte, The Gospel according to Matthew (Philadelphia: Fortress Press, c1946), p. 297.

[89]E. L. Abel, "Who Wrote Matthew?" NTS 17 (1970/71):149.

[90]M. Lowe, "From the Parable of the Vineyard to a Pre-Synoptic Source," NTS 28 (1982):258.

COMMENTARY

John came in the way of righteousness. John and Jesus both came (Matt 11:18-19). Righteousness is a legal term. A person is righteous who has received a verdict in court of "not guilty." He or she had not broken any laws. So far as any report of John is recorded, this was the case. He was a very careful, law observing Jew.[91] Jesus had come to him to be baptized "to fulfill all righteousness" (Matt 3:15). Plummer thought this personal righteousness of John did not apply here. The point was that John taught righteousness as the way to God (Matt 22:16).[92] One of these does not exclude the other. John was brought into the discussion here, because the story began with him in Jesus' response to the chief priests and elders (Matt 21:24). The fact that he was reintroduced means this is the end of the unit. The two references to John constitute an inclusion.

Tax collectors and "harlots" believed. "Harlots" were not women. This term was used metaphorically and insultingly to refer to Jews who mingled socially and in business with gentiles. The tax collectors were insulted as if they also mingled sexually with foreigners. Even before Jesus began his association with this group, members came to John, and John taught them, even though they were not law observers at all. Luke reported this association in greater detail. Luke said they came to be baptized, asking what they should do. John did not ask them to give up their positions, but he said they should not take any more taxes than were required by the Roman government (Luke 3:12).

You did not even repent later. When people, including tax collectors, were coming to John from all the surrounding area, they were baptized. The Pharisees and Sadducees also came to the baptism, but there is no report that they were baptized (Matt 3:7).[93] They did not even repent after they saw the tax collectors repent and become baptized. This may have been the situation about which Jesus spoke here. Jesus further spelled out the way in which the chief priests and elders were like the older son. In the Lukan story, the older son refused to join in the celebration upon the father's invitation (Luke 15:28), and in the Matthean account, the older brother never did go and work in the vineyard (Matt 21:29). Therefore they were like the older brother, Esau or Edom. They voluntarily left themselves out of the inheritance. Old Jacob was a schemer and a cheater, but he later repented, repaid his brother, Esau, for his offenses, and was forgiven; his sins were

---

[91]Meier was puzzled by this statement: "What exactly 'in the way of justice' means is not clear." There is nothing puzzling about it. John observed all of the dietary, cleanliness, and other rules stipulated in the scripture. J. P. Meier, "John the Baptist in Matthew's Gospel," JBL 99 (1980):401.

[92]Plummer, Matthew, p. 295.

[93]The RSV is probably in error in its translation of Matt 3:7. See the commentary on that verse.

atoned (Gen 33:11-17).[94] The tax collectors and other wealthy businessmen who had followed Jesus had been sinners, but they also later repented and made atonement. In earlier times Esau forgave his brother, Jacob, after he repented, but the chief priests, elders, and Pharisees refused to forgive their brothers the tax collectors and other minglers after they had repented. Since they were never reconciled, they could not be forgiven on the Day of Atonement (Luke 18:10-14).[95]

TEXT

Matthew	First Testament
33 A man was a landlord who **planted**	You brought a **vine** out of Egypt. You drove out the nations and **planted** it (Ps 80:8).
a vineyard, put a fence around it,	Now I will sing to my beloved a song about my **vineyard.** My beloved had **a vineyard** in a fertile place on a hill. **He put a fence around it**, fortified it, and planted a vine cover.
dug a wine press, built a tower, rented it out to tenants, and went away. 34 When the time of harvest approached, he sent his servants to the tenants to collect his rent. 35 Then the tenants seized the servants. Some they whipped, some they killed, and	Then he **built a tower** in its midst and **dug a wine press** in it. He waited for it to produce grapes, but it produced thorns (LXX Isa 5:1-2).
others they **stoned.** 36 Again he sent different servants, more than at first, and they did the same to them. 37 Afterward he sent them his son, saying, "They will respect my son." 38 When the tenants saw the son, they said among themselves, "This is the heir.	Let me sing to my beloved a song to my beloved about his **vineyard**. My beloved had **a vineyard** on a very fertile hill. He **dug** it, cleared it of **stones**, and **planted** it with **vines**. He **built a tower** inside. He also **hollowed out a wine press**. He expected it to produce grapes, but it produced bad grapes. Now Jerusalemite, man of Judah, pass judgment between my

[94] See further Buchanan, "Wandering Toward Home," Pulpit Digest March/April, 1993:69-72.

[95] A. Ogawa, "Paraboles de L'Israël Veritable? Reconsidération Critique de Mt. XXI 28 - XXII 14," NovT 21 (1979):126-27, thought Matthew composed Matt 21:32 and redirected the offense to the Jews rather than just the leaders.

Come, let us kill him, and we will have his inheritance." [39]Then they seized him, threw him out of **the vineyard**, and killed him. [40]Now, when **the lord of that vineyard** comes, **what will he do to** those tenants? [41]They said to him, "He will utterly destroy them, and he will rent out the **vineyard** to other tenants, who will pay him his rent on time."

vineyard and me.
What [more] should be done still

with my **vineyard** than I have done? Why have I expected it to produce grapes, but it produced bad grapes? Now I will tell you **that which I will do to** my **vineyard.** I will remove its hedge, and it will be burned; I will break down its wall and it will be trampled . . . for **the vineyard of the Lord** of Armies is the house of Israel (MT Isa 5:1-5, 7).

[42]Jesus said to them, "Have you never read in the scriptures:

> **The stone which the builders rejected--**
> **This one has become the head of the corner.**
> **It is from the Lord,**
> **and it is surprising in our eyes** (Ps 118:22-23);

Matthew 21

[43]Because of this I tell you, 'The **Kingdom of God** will be taken from you and

given to a nation [that] produces its fruit.' [44][Whoever falls upon this **stone** will be crushed, and the one on whom it falls **it will shatter**]."

First Testament

In the days of those kings the **God** of heaven will raise up **a kingdom,** which for the ages will not be overthrown, and its government **will** not **be left to** another **people.**

[the **stone** of Nebuchadnezzar's dream, 2:34] **It will shatter** and finish off all these kingdoms and it will stand for ages (Dan 2:44).

The **kingdom**, the government, and the greatness of the **kingdom will be given to the people of the saints of the Most High** (Dan 7:27).

TECHNICAL DETAILS

The integrity of the unit. This narrative is called a parable (Matt 21:33). It has been placed here because it is about a vineyard, as was the previous parable about the two sons who had been asked to work in a vineyard. Like other Jewish authors, Matthew organized things together that had something in common with each other. The intertext from Isaiah 5, seems to be partially from LXX and partially from MT, or else Matthew used a text no longer available. Matthew got the word "stone" from MT and the word "fence" from LXX, or he used a text that had both terms.

This is one of the most difficult units to analyze in the Gospel of Matthew.

1) It is uncertain who the dramatis personae are.

2) There is no assurance that it is a complete, unedited unit. It is possible that Matt 21:43-44 is a separate unit.

3) The word "you" (Matt 21:43) might have been a revision of an earlier different pronoun. Here possibilities will be offered and probabilities suggested, but readers may choose alternatives different from those recommended here.

The most candid appearance is that Matt 21:33-41 is a parable, and Matt 21:42-44 is an interpretation, including a Psalm and a midrash on Dan 2:44. This observation, however, will require some justification. Another example of confusion of subjects in Matthew is reported in Matt 23:37-39:

These three verses also seem composite. Matt 23:37 is poetry; Matt 23:38-39a is prose, but Matt 23:39b is poetry again. The pronouns and verbs are confused. According to this text, Jesus first addressed Jerusalem directly, then changed the pronoun to the third person, "sent to her." Then he reported that he wanted to gather your (singular) children but you (plural) did not want [it done].

37Jerusalem, Jerusalem, the one who kills the prophets
and stones the ones sent to her,
how many times I wanted to gather your children
in the same manner as a bird gathers her nestlings under her wings,
but you did not want [it done].

38Look! your house will be left [a wilderness] 39for I tell you. You will not see me from now on until you say,

Blessed is he who comes
in the name of the Lord.

The composite nature of the passage may also explain the confusing "you" in Matt 21:43. If this is understood to have been initially written in a context that was addressing the gentiles, and that Matthew wove it into another context without changing the pronouns, then this entire midrashic narrative (Matt 21:33-45) is one of those subversive, fifth column messages that was designed for those who had ears to hear. The ones who recognized the FT passages involved and understood Jewish hopes and code could understand the message. Because the message was hidden, it survived all Roman inquisitions and censorship. This explanation is contingent upon the word "if." Just because it is a possible way of interpretation does not prove that it is the correct one. Readers may prefer some other analysis.[96]

Synoptic relationships. The Markan version of this narrative is shorter than the Matthean version. Since Tagawa presumed the Markan priority, he thought Matt 21:43 was a Matthean addition to the Markan text. There are problems with the assumption that Mark was the source for Matthew and Luke. One obvious problem is that there are several words in Matthew which do not appear in Mark but which agree verbatim or nearly verbatim with the Lukan parallel: **parable, a man, planted a vineyard** (Matt 21:33; Luke 20:9), **the tenants** (Matt 21:35; Luke 20:10), **and** (Matt 21:37; Luke 20:13); **when** [the tenants] **saw** (Matt 21:38; Luke 20:14), **threw out . . . killed** (Matt 21:39; Luke 20:15), **now** (Matt 21:40; Luke 20:15); **when . . . heard** (Matt 21:45; Luke 20:16); **whoever falls upon this stone will be crushed, but the one upon whom it falls it will shatter** (Matt 21:44; Luke 20:18), and **the high priests** (Matt 21:45; Luke 20:29). Both Matthew and Luke also agreed to omit: **those** (Mark 12:7), **him** (Mark 12:8), and **after they had left him they went away** (Mark 12:12).

According to the two source hypothesis Matthew and Luke both used Mark and a hypothetical "Q" source as bases for their documents. Matthew never saw Luke, and Luke never saw Matthew. On this theory, how do you suppose Matthew and Luke both coincidentally made exactly the same verbal additions and omissions when they revised Mark's text? The answer, of course, is that the theory is flawed, and scholars like Tagawa made some faulty assumptions.[97] Mark probably was not the earliest gospel, and "Q" is only a conjectured document. That hypothesis is not necessary for the understanding of the message in Matthew.

COMMENTARY

Planted a vineyard. In addition to the intertext from Isa 5, the author of Matthew also used Ps 80 which identified the vine with the Israelites whom the Lord brought out of Egypt and planted. The field where the vines were planted was the promised land. Using the same metaphor as Isa 5, the Psalmist described in agricultural terms all the things God had done for the Israelites to make them happy on the land. He cleared the ground of gentiles so that the vine could extend its branches to the Mediterranean Sea on the one side and the Jordan River on the

[96]Patte, Matthew, p. 298, recognized that there was more than one possible identification for the dramatis personae here.

[97]K. Tagawa, "People and Community in the Gospel of Matthew," NTS 16 (1969/70):161.

other. Then he blamed the Israelites for breaking down the walls that surrounded this vineyard (Ps 80:8-13). Charette correctly held that the word "plant," as it was used here, is a theological concept. Planting a nation has the same basic meaning as "inheriting," or "entering" in relationship to the promised land.[98]

In the Isaiah parable, the landlord was the Lord, and the vineyard was Palestine. The tower was probably Jerusalem. The gospel parable probably continues with the same dramatis personae. This parable is more complex than any other parable attributed to Jesus, but it is simplified by the discovery that it is a unified midrash. It is found, not only in all three gospels, but also in the Gospel of Thomas with some variations among these sources.

Isa 5 was a warning to Judah and Israel against their unfaithfulness. Authors of scripture and midrashim, however, often took texts out of context and gave them different meanings from those which were originally intended. One scriptural example of this is Jer 6, which is a prophecy against the cities of Judah, urging the people to flee, warning of the evil that would come from the north against them, bringing war against Jerusalem. This country that would come from the north would act as an agent of the Lord, punishing his people. Jer 50 is a warning to flee from similar threat of a north country, coming as an agent of the Lord, bringing destruction, but this time the destruction was prophesied--not for Judah, but--to Babylon, as punishment. The theme is the same, but the characters have changed. Isa 53 pictures the servant as one who suffered in behalf of Israel. The targum on this chapter translated the text so freely that the servant was identified with the Messiah who would make the gentile nations suffer.[99]

This is what the midrashic author did with Isa 5. He could do this because the following beliefs were accepted: 1) Everything that is in the world is in the scripture. Therefore that is the only place to look for data. 2) There is no before and after in scripture; 3) all prophecy was prophesied only for the days of the Messiah; and 4) these were the days of the Messiah. Instead of being directed against Judah and Israel, here the tenants were interpreted to be Roman agents and the son as Jesus, the Messiah. The fact that this midrash pictured Jesus as having been killed means that the midrash was either formed or revised by the church after Jesus' crucifixion.

Put a fence around it. This phrase apparently comes from the LXX. It is not a part of MT. It seems to have been implied in the Hebrew passage from Isaiah which said that they cleared the area of stones. Normally when farmers cleared a field of stones, they piled the stones on the border of the field to make a fence.

---

[98]Charette, Recompense, p. 44-45.

[99]See further the introduction of this commentary, volume I, p. 4.

He rented it out to tenants. The question is the identification of the tenants. In Isa 5 and Ps 80, the tenants were the Israelites who had been brought out of Egypt and allowed to inherit the land of Canaan.

Matthew has brought together composite materials that are related to one another. There are first two parables about vineyards (Matt 21:28-41); second, a quotation from Ps 118:22-23 (Matt 21:42); third, this warning:

> 43Because of this I tell you, "The **Kingdom of God** will be taken from you and **given to a nation** [that] produces its fruit.44 [Whoever falls upon this **stone** will be crushed, and the one on whom it falls **it will be shattered**]."

This is followed by an editorial comment telling the reaction of the Pharisees and chief priests to the two parables (Matt 21:45-46). Matthew probably did not compose any of this portion of Matt 21. He probably found Matt 21:43 in another unit where the message was addressed to the gentiles, threateningly. Matt 21:44 is lacking in some texts. It appears to be an expansion of Matt 21:43 by someone who recognized its relationship to Dan 2:44. Both verses (Matt 21:43 and 44) are lacking in the other synoptic gospels. Matthew's typical organization methodologies are evident throughout Matt 21:33-44.

The most normal way to read Matt 21:43 is to assume the message was directed to the chief priests and Pharisees mentioned in Matt 21:45, but Matt 21:43-45 is a midrash on Dan 2:44 which is against gentiles, not Jews, and it is **a nation** rather than "the nations," which is involved.[100] Gentiles in biblical thought are almost always mentioned in the plural. Lowe noticed the incoherence between the message of Matt 21:43 and the rest of the Gospel, assuming that it was directed against Jews. He could explain this incoherence only by assuming that it was a later addition made by some other editor. He may have been right in thinking that it was not composed by the same author as the preceding parable, but he failed to see the importance of the reference to Dan 2:44 and 7:27 in the same verses. It is only the identification of the word "you" that is incoherent. This is not the only place where Matthew's pronouns are confused. He seems to have woven his sources together without changing pronouns to make all passages coherent. Another example of that practice can be seen in Matt 23:37-39.

Some they whipped, some they killed. This dramatized the abuse Jews suffered at the hands of the Romans from the time of Herod until the fall of Jerusalem in 70 I.A. This was the same kind of treatment Jews had received earlier from the Syrian Greeks during the reign of Antiochus Epiphanes. Stoning was performed within the Israelite community for blasphemy (Exod 19:13; Lev 20:2, 27; 24:14, 16, 23). This act was done by hurling a person over a cliff and dropping large

---

[100]Charette, Recompense, p. 137, thought "the nation" was "supra-national." There is no hint from the text for this meaning.

stones upon him or her. This mode of killing was probably used in this parable because the word "stones" appeared in the Isaiah passage. The verbs, "whipped," "killed," and "stoned," were used for rhetorical effect. The main point was not the type of murder employed but the fact that the local people were abused and killed.

They will respect my son. The son in this parable was the Messiah. He was the son of the king, and the king in this parable was God. Lowe recognized this, but then identified the son with John the Baptist, forgetting that John was a priest's son--not a king's son.[101] He was to be the priestly Messiah--not the royal Messiah. The Son of God was not a priestly role; it was the title for a king.

The stone which the builders rejected. At this point the author changed from Isa 5 to Ps 118, still commenting on the word "stone." The tenants who rejected the messengers became the builders who rejected the stone that was basic to construction. Although the metaphor changed, the message did not. This situation still decribed the promised land under the control of the Romans. It was "out of square," a subject nation without its own king or its own government. Failing to recognize the function of the stone in Daniel's prophecy caused Lowe to identify the stone with John the Baptist.[102]

Swaeles noted the reference here to Daniel.[103] He related Matt 21:43 with the fifth kingdom in Dan 2:44 which would not pass away or be transferred to another people. In Nebuchadnezzar's dream a statue was set up which symbolized the four pagan nations that ruled Israel from 586-164 B.C. Then a rock was created without the work of human hands and crushed the statue to pieces (Dan 2:31-35). This rock is the fifth kingdom which becomes decoded as the Hasmonean kingdom of Judah. In Matt 21:42 the rock which the builders rejected, which became the head of the corner, is to be identified with the fifth kingdom. This kingdom would shatter the Roman "statue." The "vineyard" would be taken from Rome and given to this fifth kingdom--a nation that would produce fruit. The antitype of the Hasmonean kingdom in Jesus' day was the Davidic kingdom under messianic rule. The antitype of the fourth kingdom of Daniel was the Roman empire in Jesus' time.

The head of the corner. This is not a corner stone placed in the foundation. It is a stone that is slightly out of parallel, and it is placed somewhere in an arch over a doorway or window with other stones that are perfectly rectangular. This

---

[101]Lowe, "Vineyard," p. 258.

[102]Lowe, "Vineyard," p. 258.

[103]R. Swaeles, "L'Arriere-fond Scripturaire de Matt xxi.43 son lien avec Matt xxi.44," NTS 6 (1960):310-13.

slightly distorted stone is necessary for the arch. Without this one stone the arch could not hold itself against gravity. In arches that are hastily made, these stones are placed at the very top of the arches and are recognizable. In arches that are skillfully and artfully made it is not possible for the ordinary human being to recognize with human eyes the stone that is the head of the corner, because it could be placed anywhere within the arch. This was the gospel message of the narrative. Even though Palestine seemed useless at the time the midrash was being composed, the hope was that the future would be better. Although Palestine appeared to most to be a part of a rock heap, Jews and early Christians believed it was destined to rule the entire western world--that which Rome governed at the time.

The Kingdom of God will be taken from you. The promised land was initially taken from the Canaanites which God expelled before the Israelites because the Canaanites had defiled themselves (Lev 18:24, 28). Leviticus warned that God would also throw out the Israelites if they failed to keep the laws God commanded. Possession of the promised land was never an unconditional guarantee. Any people that succeeded in taking it as a possession and failed to keep God's contract would be expelled.

The Kingdom of God in Matt 21:43 is the vineyard of Matt 21:41. Vs 43 is an interpretive verse, explaining what the vineyard of the parable symbolizes. In the Isaiah passage, that which was destroyed was the vineyard, probably anticipating the destruction of Palestine. In Matthew, the vineyard was unharmed; it was the "tenants" who were destroyed. The vineyard in both cases is Palestine, free from foreign control. It was in the hands of the Romans when the Matthean parable was composed. Jews looked forward to the time when God would take it away from the Romans and give it back to the Jews, just as the same kingdom was taken from the Syrian Greeks and given to the people of the saints of the Most High in the heavenly court scene of Dan 7:27. The nation that would bear fruit is the typological equivalent of the people of the saints of the Most High.

Given to another nation. In the opinion of Jews of NT times, Palestine was the land God had promised to Jews for an inheritance. The promised land was not always in possession of Palestinian Jews, but Jews did not think that it was ever the inheritance that God intended for the gentiles. Whenever other larger nations used this land, either as a land bridge for merchandise to move from the North and East to the West and South or as a buffer state against other nations that were enemies, they were expected to pay taxes to the Israelites as rent for using the land as a thoroughfare. Following the imagery of the narrative, foreign nations who paid rent were tenants. Jews believed they should receive enough money in this way to finance their entire government so that Jews themselves would not need to pay taxes at all. In Jesus' time, however, the "tenants" were abusive, and Rome (the tenants), instead of adequately financing Palestine by paying "rent," in fact, collected taxes from the heirs, the rightful owners of the vineyard.

When the FT references to Isaiah, the Psalm, and Daniel are pointed out, it becomes obvious that this narrative is midrashic. The author first used the parable in Isaiah, which he expanded to suit his purposes. Then he quoted a part of a Psalm that referred to a corner stone. This stone was put there to match the word "stone" in MT Isa 5. It also called his attention to the stone in Dan 2 which destroyed the image of the pagan king. Jesus is quoted as saying that the kingdom of God would be taken from the gentile kings that then controlled it and given to another nation, namely the Jewish nation, and the pagan kingdoms would be shattered by this Jewish nation just as the Greeks were shattered by the Maccabeans mentioned in Daniel. This homily says that the Kingdom of God was going to be reestablished on the promised land as it was during the time of the Hasmoneans. The chosen people would again receive their inheritance.

Lowe held that Matt 21:43 was incoherent with the rest of the passage, so he argued that this was a later editorial addition.[104] He may have been partially correct, but the question is, "How did it get that way?" Part of the same verse supplements and supports the rest of the midrash very well. The only problem is the identification of the people addressed. Matt 21:33-42 is in the third person. Matt 21:43 alone, by only one word, contradicts the rest of the passage.

The passive voice is used here to avoid using the name of God and thereby possibly blaspheming his name. A Jewish parable would not make sense teaching that God would take the land away from the Jews who did not actually possess it and give it to the Romans who already had it under their control.

Everything stated above is coherent and true to Jewish thought form in NT times. The midrash is well developed; the inheritance is always the promised land in Jewish thought; the use of the scripture is normal; and the message is addressed to Jews. Then there appears the change of interpretation to apply it to the Pharisees and chief priests, who are the ones to whom the narrative is addressed. This poses problems, and none of the solutions is satisfactory.

1) One solution is that offered by Crossan, who presumed at the outset that the tenants who were being evicted were the Palestinian Jews, and the new tenants would be the gentiles. Nearly the same position was taken by Kingsbury, who thought the parable was directed against Israel.[105] This is the position also taken by Cook, who believed that the whole Gospel according to Matthew was anti-Jewish.[106] Crossan edited the text to remove all scripture texts, destroying all of the midrashic implications, and arriving at a narrative very much like the parable in the Gospel of Thomas (93.1-24). Instead of a midrash he called the text

---

[104]Lowe, "Vineyard," p. 261.

[105]J. Kingsbury, "Rhetoric of Comprehension in Matthew" NTS 41 (1995):68.

[106]M. J. Cook, "Interpreting 'Pro-Jewish' Passages in Matthew," HUCA 54 (1983):142. For an analysis of his arguments see the commentary on Matt 5:7; 10:5-6; 15:24; 13:57; 22:8; 24:14; and the conclusions.

as it now stands an allegory; once all of the texts are removed, he called it a parable. Some other assumptions he made are that "in parable analysis . . . such stories must be true to life,"[107] and that those sayings that are Jesus' own words can only be detected through dissimilarity. That means his teaching must be different from anything in contemporary Jewish teachings or the contemporary church. These assumptions are not valid, so his interpretation is mistaken.

The parables of Jesus do not make sense without knowing his code. It is not true to life that mustard seeds grow up and become trees, nor can an ordinary hired day worker sell all that he has and have enough money to buy a field in which he worked. If Jesus taught only things different from or dissimilar to those of anyone around him, and in no way reflected the teachings of earlier Jews or later Christians no one would have understood his teachings. Crossan was evidently unacquainted with the methodology of midrash, because he thought the FT texts on which this pericope were built were later additions.

Following Trilling, Ogawa argued that the tenants were the Jews, and the nation that produced fruits was the church. God took the Kingdom of God from the Jews and gave it to the Christians.[108]

2) A second solution is offered by Kingsbury. Without editing the text Kingsbury also treated the parable like an allegory, but the important point of his study was his claim that Matthew, like Mark for Wrede, had a messianic secret disguised within his gospel. Dividing the gospel into three parts, Kingsbury noted that in the first part the messages from heaven came only to Jesus; in the second part, the disciples were the only ones who learned that Jesus was the Son of God; in the third part it became public knowledge, and there first of all in the parable of the wicked husbandman.[109]

Even if this had not been part of Matthew's plot there is a necessary secrecy in any under cover movement. The parables of the leaven and the mustard seed both disclose through code the subversive character of a movement that slowly, quietly, mysteriously grows until its greatness becomes known, and it is too late to stop it. It is because it was a secret movement that the disciples needed to ask when this waiting period would come to an end; when would Jesus make his public announcement, his parousia? Jesus had to be identified through code as the Son of man, because Romans also knew that titles like Son of God, Messiah, and Lord were given to pretending kings. Jesus' messiahship had to be kept secret. To the extent that Matthew reflected that situation accurately to that extent he was

---

[107]J. D. Crossan, "The Parable of the Wicked Husbandman," JBL 90 (1971):455-62. The quotation is from p. 459.

[108]A. Ogawa, "Paraboles, pp. 136-39.

[109]J. D. Kingsbury, "The Parable of the Wicked Husbandmen and the Secret of Jesus' Divine Sonship in Matthew: Some Literary-Critical Observations," JBL 105 (1986):643-55.

fair to the nature of the movement. As soon as the secret of Jesus' messiahship became public knowledge, the Romans moved into action and had him crucified.

Kingsbury thought God was the owner; Jesus was the son; the tenants were Palestinian Jews; and the Christian church would be the new tenants. The parable was composed by Matthew after the fall of Jerusalem, and it does not represent the teaching of Jesus.

3) A third possibility is that of the Newells. They identified the tenants with the Galilean zealots, supported by poor Jews, religiously resentful of Roman ownership of the land. These zealots fought the Romans and tried to take the land away from them. In the end their situation was worse than before. They thought Jesus taught this parable to suppress the zealots. In Newells' judgment, the son involved was a foreign prince.[110] It would seem strange, indeed, for Jesus, who was trying to establish the Kingdom of Heaven to have supported the position of the Romans and considered them to be the true owners of the vineyard. If Jesus had really been pro-Roman the Romans would never have crucified him. The further notion that Matthew would have preserved a parable in which the son played the role of a foreigner also seems unlikely.

4) A fourth solution is to presume that Jesus changed his audience in the middle of the narrative. Instead of speaking about the gentiles, he suddenly spoke to the gentiles when he said "You." This also seems unlikely.

5) A fifth possibility is that proposed by Lowe. He thought Matt 21:43 was a later addition by an anti-Jewish gentile, and that the initial tenants were Palestinian Jews.

6) A sixth suggestion is the one proposed here. It is that Matt 21:43-44 once had an independent existence in a context addressed to gentiles. It was inserted here unchanged, because the verses were otherwise consistent with the teaching of the parable. Matthew frequently put together units that did not exactly fit without changing them. For example, in chapter 6 the term, "you," is used frequently, but is first in plural and then it switches to singular, and so it goes, back and forth throughout the the chapter from singular "you" to plural "you." These lines were not all composed by the same author. They were put together from different sources without correcting the number. Matthew probably did the same with Matt 21:43-44.

Following this possibility, God was the one who owned this "vineyard" (=Kingdom of God) under the agency of the chosen people, and he could be counted on to punish the Romans, sooner or later, and take Palestine out of their hands. Then it would be given to another nation, namely the chosen people in Palestine free from foreign rule and under the rule of its own Jewish Messiah. The "you" involved here does not represent the Jewish leaders,[111] or the Jews

---

[110]J. E. and R. R. Newell, "The Parable of the Wicked Tenants," NovT 14 (1972):226-37.

[111]As Tagawa, "People," p. 161, thought.

in general,[112] but the foreign nation, Rome. A similar teaching is reported in rabbinic literature:

> You [Pharaoh] sin against your people [Israel] and your nation [Egypt], and in addition, yourself. The kingdom will be taken from you and given to another nation (she-tis-ta-káyl ha-mal-choót mi-máy-kah. Yi-ta-noón le-oo-máh a-ché-ret, שתסתקל המלכות ממך יתנון לאומה אחרת, CantR 2.7, 1).

This medieval document may have been influenced by this earlier gospel teaching. In this pericope, the nation involved was Israel. This nation lived in Egypt as a distinct, identifiable group. With the Exodus, this nation was taken from under Pharaoh's dominion and given to the land of Canaan where Israel developed as a nation after it left Egypt.

7) A seventh possibility is that the chief priests and Pharisees were so closely allied with the Romans that the Pharisees were thought to have the kingdom in their own hands. Whenever it would be taken from the Romans it would also be taken from the chief priests and the Pharisees. This possibility would require no editing or change of audience. It would not be anti-Jewish, as Lowe, Crossan, Cook, and Kingsbury thought, but it would be anti-Roman and at the same time anti-Pharisaic and anti-chief priests. Readers may analyze the above possibilities and accept whichever one makes most sense to them.

The one who falls upon this stone. This entire sentence (Matt 21:44) is a midrash added later as a small commentary on the stone. It is in Washingtoniansis and several later manuscripts but not included in Bezai, Irenaeas, Origen, and some later texts. This whole unit, from Matt 21:42-44, seems to be a collection of materials that are only slightly related to the previous and succeeding sections and do not seem integral to the unit.[113] Nevertheless, Matt 21:42-44 was added to clarify the parable and show its relationship to Daniel and the rock that was divinely created. Rome was the one who would fall against that "rock" and be shattered (Matt 21:44), just as the rock in Daniel crushed all of the pagan kingdoms that enslaved Jews after the fall of Jerusalem in 586 B.C. These kingdoms fell against the Hasmonean kingdom when they were crushed.

---

[112]E. A. Abel, "Matthew," p. 151. He also thought the nation that would bring forth fruit constituted the gentile Christians.

[113]For an understanding of the social and economic situation against which this parable was composed, see M. Hengel, "Das Gleichnis von den Weingartneren Mc 12:1-12 im Lichte der Zenopapyri und der rabbinischen Gleichnis," ZNW 59 (1968):1-39. Hengel concluded that this parable did not need a post 70 I.A. date. See also Derrett, Law, pp. 296-309; and Newells, "Wicked Tenants,"pp. 226-37, noted that Jesus did not criticize the goal of the tenants--only their methods (p. 236). It seems to have been directed against the zealots who were using force for their land reform (War 2.426), according to Newells.

TEXT

45When the chief priests and the Pharisees heard his parables they knew that he was speaking about them. 46While trying to seize him, they feared the crowd, since they took him to be a prophet.

COMMENTARY

The chief priests and the Pharisees. This is the final part of an inclusion that begins with the chief priests and elders in Matt 21:23. The Pharisees are not mentioned in the beginning listing, but they are identified in the Lukan parable on two sons. The early church, at least, associated the Pharisees with the elders, chief priests, and scribes. In two instances Matthew has "Pharisees" (Matt 21:45; 22:15) where Luke has "chief priests and scribes," and Luke mentions "Pharisees" (Luke 5:17) where Matthew has "some of the scribes" (Matt 9:3) or "chief priests and scribes" (Luke 19:39 //Matt 21:15). The chief priests were servants of Rome in NT times. The Pharisees were some of the chief judges at the time, and evidently interpreted the law in ways that suited the Romans. Therefore they were classed with those who whipped and killed the "owners" of the "vineyard."

After the chief priests and the Pharisees. These words constitute a later interpretation of the parable. They were added to give the narrative a new meaning and are not part of the parable itself. The leaders mentioned understood the parables to mean the government they ruled would be taken from them, and Jesus would select a new group of leaders, probably the tax collectors to rule the Kingdom of God. The chief priests and Pharisees here are typological correspondences to the "elders of the people and its princes" who burned the vineyard (Isa 3:14).

They feared the crowd. This is the third time Matthew told of the protection the crowd offered against the governmental authorities (Matt 14:5; 21:26; 21:46).

CHAPTER TWENTY-TWO

TEXT

Matthew	First Testament (not quotations)
[22:1]Again, Jesus answered and spoke to them in parables, saying, [2]"The Kingdom of Heaven is like a man who is a king, who prepared a wedding for his son. [3]He sent his servants to call those who had been invited to the wedding feast, but they did not want to come. [4]Again he sent other servants, saying, 'Tell those who have been invited, "Look, my meal is ready; my bulls and fatted animals have been slaughtered; and all things are prepared.	King Hezekiah planned a huge Passover feast, and he invited all the Jews and Israelites to come. He sent couriers throughout all of Israel and Judah with letters from the king and his officials, as the king ordered (2 Chron 30:17). Hezekiah gave 1,000 bulls and 7,000 sheep for offerings, and the officials gave the assembly 1,000 bulls and 10,000 sheep (30:24).
[5]Come to the wedding feast!"'	Couriers urged the Israelites, begging them to serve the Lord by coming to the Passover at Jerusalem, so that his fierce anger may turn away from the people (30:9).
But they rudely went away, one to his own field, another to his place of business, [6][and the servants seized the rest, treated them dishonorably, and killed (them). [7]Then the king became angry, and after he had sent his troops, he destroyed those	Instead of accepting the invitation from the king, Jews and Israelites laughed at the couriers and jeered them (30:10).

murderers and burned their city]. [8]Then he said to his servants, 'The wedding feast is ready, and the invited ones were not worthy. [9]Go, then, to the secondary roads, and whomever you find, invite to the wedding feast.' [10]When those servants had gone out into the ways, they brought together all whom they found, evil and good, and the bridal chamber was filled with those reclining."

Some people came, and they celebrated the Passover, but were not sanctified. Nonetheless Hezekiah prayed that God would pardon them, and they were admitted (30:17-20).

TECHNICAL DETAILS

These verses seem to be patterned after the experience of Hezekiah on that special Passover, although it is not written midrashically. Special words are not used in both narratives. Hezekiah's banquet was held, but there were not nearly as many guests as he hoped would be there. Matt 22:6-7 interrupts the narrative and may have been added later.[1] The basic parable makes sense as one of the parables of Jesus. It is coherent with all of the rest of his parables, and it contains nothing that reflects a period later than the crucifixion. This intruded passage, however, enters the picture abruptly without fitting into the context. So the servants seized the rest. What servants? the rest of what? This passage was taken from some other context by a later editor and forced into this parable. These two verses are usually held to refer to the fall of Jerusalem in I.A. 70, and maybe they do, but there are problems with that assumption as well. At that time only the temple was burned--not the city. According to Hagner,[2]

> Even if one nevertheless feels compelled to understand the words as an allusion to the destruction of Jerusalem, this hardly demonstrates a post-70 date for the Gospel. Jesus is shortly to prophesy the fall of the city (24:2-26), and thus the present passage could itself be an anticipation of the future rather than post eventum.

---

[1]So also A. Ogawa, "Paraboles de L'Israël Véritable? Reconsidération Critique de Mt. XXI 28 - XXII 14," NovT 21 (1979):139-40. Also S. Pedersen, "Zum Problem der Vaticinia ex eventu (Eine Analyse von Mt. 21,33-46 par.; 22:1-10 par.)," ST 19 (1965):167-88, followed K. H. Rengstorf in believing that 22:6-7 might come from an independent source telling about the capture of a city.

[2]D. A. Hagner, Word Biblical Commentary: Matthew 14-28 (Dallas: Word Books, c1995), pp. 628-29.

All of that would be true if the city involved is Jerusalem, but that is not the only possibility. The author of these two verses (Matt 22:6-7) may have anticipated the future burning of the city of Rome, rather than Jerusalem. Many Palestinian Jews would have rejoiced at the burning of Rome, as they did when it burned in 69 I.A. At that time the Jerusalem saints cried "Hallelujah!" because God had judged and avenged the blood of his servants. They were glad when they saw the smoke of Rome's burning going up for ages of ages (Rev 19:1-3). As soon as God burned the city of Rome, the saints at Jerusalem made plans for the wedding of the Lamb (Rev 19:6-8). In Matthew also the wedding of the Messiah was planned together with the destruction of the city (of Rome) (Matt 22:1-10).

If, on the other hand, the author of these verses referred to the city of Jerusalem, then the editor would probably have been a Paulinist or someone else in the diaspora who thought the fall of Jerusalem was an act of God in punishment for the Palestinian Jews.

The main parable was based on the events surrounding Hezekiah's attempt to unify the tribes of Israel, making the North Israelites subject to Jerusalem as they had been in the days of Solomon. After the temple had been cleansed Hezekiah, a king, sent messengers out to cities and towns all over Judah, inviting all to attend the Passover feast in Jerusalem. Many people laughed and mocked the messengers when they came with invitations (2 Chron 30:10). There was no amount of persuasion that would convince them to come. Nevertheless, there were some who came, but they had not been sanctified, so the priests and Levites had to sanctify them before they could participate (2 Chron 30; Ant 9.261-67).

To those who had ears to hear, the experiences Jesus was facing in trying to free the nation and bring about a messianic banquet constituted an antitype of Hezekiah's attempts to unify Israel and Judah for a national Passover. Hezekiah was not very successful, and Jesus was also having difficulties. That is the point of the parable. The Lukan parallel (Luke 14:16-24) omits any reference to a king, but, following Chronicles, the king is a figure that is inherent to the parable, so it is not obvious, as Bacon thought, that Matthew's parable is secondary to Luke's.[3] It is only verses six and seven that might reflect a post 70 I.A. date, and that is far from certain.

This parable might fit into the context of the commission of the apostles to visit the cities in Palestine with the exception of the Samaritan and gentile cities and announce the coming of the Kingdom of Heaven (Matt 10). This mission was probably conducted in secret and might have alerted Jews to the potential events that might take place in Jerusalem on the next Passover feast.

COMMENTARY

Spoke to them in parables. The words, "Having answered," does not mean Jesus was answering somebody's question. This is a standard Semitic introduction. It

[3]B. W. Bacon, Studies in Matthew (New York: Henry Holt and Co., c1930), pp. 65-66.

is part of a sentence that is an editorial comment, informing the reader that chapter 22 contains more parables than one.

A king who made a wedding. In this parable, God filled the role of a king, and the banquet was for the Son of God, a role to be filled by the Messiah, who would be king of Israel immediately following the messianic banquet. Bornkamm thought Matthew's version of the parable was secondary to that of Luke. Matthean additions included the "lurid" features such as the king, the marriage feast, the maltreated servants, and the king's troops sent out to burn the city. Bornkamm recognized many of the code meanings for Matthew's parable, but he assumed the shorter the parable the more nearly original. That does not follow. The purpose for which parables were composed was to communicate code messages to those who had "ears to hear."[4]

Lowe's suggestion that the son was John the Baptist also overlooks a few points. John was a priest's son, destined to be the priestly Messiah--not the Davidic Messiah who would rule Israel as the Son of God.[5] The only way a priest could be a Son of God would be to become also the king, like the Hasmoneans--not as a Davidic king.[6] The relationship between John and Jesus did not fit the Hasmonean pattern. John was nowhere in the gospels called the Son of God; it was not John but Jesus who was tempted by the devil and asked to perform the kind of miracles a Davidic messiah was expected to perform.

He sent his servants. See also Matt 21:34. At a time when there were no telephones, telegraphs, e-mail, faxes, TV, or outer space missiles, the only way to communicate with anyone in a distance was either to go yourself or to send a messenger. Kings normally had many messengers that managed their governments for them in distant places, just as large business magnates, government leaders, and leaders in commerce do today.

Come to my wedding feast. With the exclusion of the bracketed section (Matt 22:6-7), this parable tells of only one event, a wedding feast for a prince. The king first sent his servants to tell the people they would be invited when everything was ready, so this invitation would not come as a surprise. Then, after everything was prepared, the servants went again to these same people to tell them to come, assuming that they would be ready. In parabolic code, the wedding feast was intended to refer to the wedding contract which the Lord made with the

---

[4]G. Bornkamm, Jesus of Nazareth tr. I and F. McLuckey (London: Hodder and Stoughton, c1960), p. 18.

[5]M. Lowe, "From the Parable of the Vineyard to a Pre-Synoptic Source," NTS 28 (1982):259-60.

[6]See the text for 4Q246.2, 1, which identified Alexander Jannaeus as a Son of God in chapter 3 of this commentary.

Israelites under the leadership of Moses. Jews and Christians of NT times looked forward to the renewal of the contract under the leadership of their own messianic king, as Jeremiah promised (Jer 31:31). Whenever the contract with the Lord was renewed, there would be a new messiah who, if he had not already been anointed in secret, would be anointed and there would be a contract liturgy at the banquet (Rev 19:7-9), probably like the one Jesus celebrated with his disciples (Matt 26:26-29). Jesus, and not John, became famous for his banquets where he ate with tax collectors and sinners. John was very careful abouts dietary laws and would not have attended these banquets. As the Messiah, Jesus was legally identified with God, and it was Jesus, rather than John, who sent his apostles out to recruit followers, inviting them to the "messianic banquet." Matthew obviously used sources, no one knows how many, but one of them was not the pre-Matthean source which contained parables about John the Baptist, as Lowe conjectured.[7]

One to his own field. This parable had as intertexts not only the biblical report of Hezekiah's Passover feast but also the biblical report of Gideon's adventures. The people invited did not laugh as the Israelites did at Hezekiah's invitation, but they all made the same kind of excuses that Gideon accepted (Judges 7:2-7 and Deut 20:5-9) when they were offered by soldiers to exempt themselves from military service, so that only the committed would be involved in war. These may have been included in the parable intentionally to give the listeners, who had ears, the clue that the wedding about which he was speaking came only after the war was over, and the land was restored, and the people invited offered excuses allowed in the rules of holy warfare.[8] The result was that Jesus, like Gideon and Hezekiah, was left with a relatively small number of shock troops with which to begin "the birth pangs of the Messiah."[9] Ogawa thought this parable was composed to explain the fact that Jews did not accept the gospel.[10] Kingsbury thought it was a parable against Israelites. It was a message to Jews in Israel. This was a mistake. Those who responded by coming to the banquet were Jews, and those who refused and ridiculed the project were Jews. Jesus lived among the Jews in Palestine, and nearly all of the people in his audiences were Jews. The

---

[7]Lowe, "Vineyard," pp. 257-63.

[8]L. Schottroff and W. Stegemann, Jesus von Nazareth-Hoffnung der Armen (Stuttgart: Kohlhammer, c1978), p. 131, failed to notice the Deuteronomic origin of these excuses, so they held that the excuses ". . . can be understood as nothing else than fish . . . there are no reasonable excuses for the refusal [italics theirs]. These may also have seemed foolish to the Romans. That was the intent.

[9]For the use and meaning of this expression, see Buchanan, Revelation and Redemption: Jewish Documents from the Fall of Jerusalem to the Death of Nahmanides (Dillboro: West North Carolina Press, 1978; sold by Mercer U Press), pp. 20, 23, 282, 310, 319, 533, 583, 585.

[10]Ogawa, "Paraboles," p. 149.

parable was not directed against Israel or Jews as a nation or a people.[11] The parable does not have to be dated late enough to make Kingsbury's conclusion feasible.

Invited to the wedding feast. Jesus was not willing to stop at the point where Gideon limited his forces. Jesus invited those still less qualified, and these came.[12] This is one of the many parables of Jesus in which two groups of people were involved. The first group, like the first son in the vineyard, or the elder brother when the prodigal son returned, was invited but did not come. The second group, composed of those who had been invited only as a last resort, were like laborers who came at 5:00 p. m. to work in the vineyard, or like the second son who did not want to work in the vineyard but finally repented and worked. The second group was like the younger son who returned home and attended a feast held in his honor.

This parable, then, seems to be another one of those attacking the Pharisees and justifying the admission of those tax collectors and other businessmen who were invited after the Pharisees had made excuses. In this parable, it was the Pharisees who were chosen first but the tax collectors who actually attended the feast. The image of a feast may also have been used to give a different slant to the criticism of Jesus' eating with tax collectors[13] and "harlots." If the Messiah had not been anointed before in secret, like David and Saul, then at the messianic banquet the Messiah would be anointed, and the new contract would be confirmed. The second, follow-up, invitation after a first announcement may actually have followed a pattern of Jesus' program. He first sent his apostles out to announce the imminence of the kingdom, expecting later to send them out again to bring in the new recruits.

Jeremias correctly observed that in the Lukan narrative, the servant was sent out a third time, probably to the Jews in the diaspora (called gentiles) after the tax collectors proved not to be enough to fill the places. Jeremias may have been correct in holding that this was an addition of the later church to include

---

[11]J. Kingsbury, "Rhetoric of Comprehension in Matthew," NTS 41 (1995):369.

[12]E. Linnemann, Jesus of the Parables, tr. J. Sturdy (London: SPCK, c1966), pp. 25, 89-91, did not see this, so she did not think the host solved his problem of embarrassment by letting down his standards. Therefore she conjectured that the first one planned to come, but not on time. The main problem was not the host's embarrassment. It was the need to fill the ranks, and the real topic was not a wedding but a war, not guests, but recruits.

[13]D. O. Via, Jr., "The Relationship of Form to Content in the Parables: The Wedding Feast," Int 25 (1971):178.

conditions that were not part of the situation when Jesus was recruiting followers.[14] This does not say, however, that Jesus had no contacts with the Jews of the diaspora. He probably did, but Matthew did not report it. Luke's summary account of this activity is the only report we have. The rapidity with which Christianity spread among the Jews in the diaspora suggests that diaspora Jews were involved in Christianity from the beginning.

Both the Matthean and Lukan version of this parable were designed to alert Jews and/or early Christians to the belief that there would soon be a rebellion, and every soldier would be needed and prepared. This would be the revolt intended to recover the promised land and renew the wedding contract with the Lord. No one knew just when that would happen. There were people ready to lead the movement when the time was ripe. Now things were quietly being organized behind the scenes. Some day there would be a surprise movement when all of these underground actions would come out into the open. That would be the parousia, when the Messiah would become known. Until then everyone should be on guard.

Palmer, telling of this victory-feast, said apologetically, "the king is Messiah, of course, and his battle is with sin." This "of course" is not obvious from the text alone.[15] This parable was not anti-Jewish, as Cook argued.[16] The invitation to the "wedding feast" was sent only to Jews. Some accepted and some did not. Those who were "worthy" were Jews, and those who were not worthy were also Jews. Cook may have been misled in his analysis by scholars like Ogawa and Kingsbury who also thought that those who were unworthy were the Jews. If so, he should have criticized the twentieth century interpreters rather than the text of Matthew.

TEXT

[11]When the king entered to see those reclining, he saw there a man who was not wearing a wedding garment. [12]He said to him, "Friend, how did you enter here without a wedding garment?" [The guest] was silent. [13]Then the king said to the servants, "After you have tied his feet and hands, throw him out into outer darkness. In that place, there will be weeping and grinding of teeth,

[14]for many are invited
but few are elected."

---

[14]J. Jeremias, The Parables of Jesus tr. S. H. Hooke (New York: Scribners, 1992), p. 64. A. Plummer, An Exegetical Commentary on the Gospel according to Matthew (London: Stock, 1909), pp. 300-301, also held that the Lukan version included the gentiles, but he did not think the Lukan parable and the Matthean parable were divergent reports of the same parable.

[15]H. Palmer, "Just Married, Cannot Come," NovT 18 (1976):245.

[16]M. J. Cook, "Interpreting 'Pro-Jewish' Passages in Matthew," HUCA 54 (1983):141.

COMMENTARY

A man without a wedding garment. The expression, "garment" or "clothing," was often used idiomatically to mean something that was not literally clothing. For example the "garment of salvation," the "robe of righteousness" (Isa 61:10), the "garment of life" or "garments of glory" (1 Enoch 62.15).

Many scholars have failed to notice that this is a different parable from the one just before. Patte, for example, thought this was the second part of one parable. In his judgment the person who came without a wedding garment was to be faulted because he was probably given a chance to go home and get one, but he did not bother.[17] Jeremias presumed that the garment involved was not a special wedding garment but rather a clean, freshly laundered, garment. He further presumed that the person was given enough time to have his clothes laundered before the banquet.[18] The text does not mention that. Failing to distinguish the two parables has forced scholars to invent excuses and conditions that are not part of the parable or question the justice of a king who would ask people to come as they were and then complain about their preparation. This is not a necessary problem once it is clear that there are two different parables involved, and they originated from separate situations.

Because the messianic banquet was associated with the renewal of the contract with the Lord, Jesus probably used the parable to encourage Jews to be prepared at any moment for the reestablishment of the promised land, the renewal of the contract, and the expulsion of the Romans from the land. This would all happen together.

In the later church, however, the wedding garment was related to baptism. St. John Chrysostom invited those coming to be baptized to come as those being invited to a wedding feast and to a royal banquet, where, without cost, the one receiving baptism would receive a wedding garment.[19] Pseudo-Clement said baptism was a wedding garment (Recog 4.25). Members of the Essene sect also attended meals dressed in special white garments which they put on after they had bathed (War 2.127-31). Since they were communally organized, the "free" garment belonged to the whole group. Early Christians may also have provided the initiate a white garment when he was baptized, which was called the wedding garment. Only after baptism was the initiate allowed to share in the holy meals or the Eucharist with the rest of the community. Should anyone attempt to attend the

---

[17]D. Patte, The Gospel according to Matthew (Philadelphia: Fortress Press, c1946), p. 304. Plummer, Matthew, p. 303, called this second parable an appendix to the parable which Matthew attached to the other parable.

[18]Jeremias, Parables, pp. 187-88.

[19]See Hom 8.23; T Levi 11.9-10; 15.8; 21.2; Hermas, Sim 8.2, 3-4.

Eucharist or one of the holy meals without having first been baptized and having a "wedding garment" he or she would have been expelled.

This may have been the meaning of this "riddle." It was intended to warn against trying to receive communion without first being baptized. Jeremias[20] correctly held that this was a later addition, partially because there is no known custom that required a wedding garment at a wedding in NT times. Jeremias and Via thought Matthew added it to the other parable to correct the impression the other parable left that almost anyone was welcome to our Christian celebration. That is probably not necessary. Both in NT and Rabbinic literature, editors tended to put under one heading all the material related to that subject, even if it was very remotely related. Here are two parables about wedding and wedding guests, so they were put together, but not carelessly. Since the original parable was made to typologize Hezekiah's plans for a national Passover, this parable was added in such a way as to supplement it. Those who came to Hezekiah's Passover were not sanctified, so they had to be ritually cleansed before they could participate. This parable was placed in its present position to complete the picture (2 Chron 30; Ant 9.261-67). This is consistent with Matthew's methods of typology, biblical interpretation, and organization. There is no psychologizing needed to explain the fact.

Both of these wedding banquet parables were appreciated not only by Christians, but rabbis evidently knew both parables, probably found them both together in the Gospel of Matthew, and worked them both intertextually into one parable. The following is a medieval talmudic and a Tannaitic account.

> Rabbi Yohanan ben Zakkai told a parable about a king who invited his servants to a banquet without appointing a precise time. The wise [servants] dressed themselves properly and sat at the door of the palace of the king. They said, "Is anything lacking in the palace of the king?" The foolish ones of them went to their places of work. They said, "Can there be a banquet without preparation?" Suddenly the king requested [the presence] of his servants. The wise [servants] entered, properly dressed. The fools entered wearing dirty clothes. The king was happy to meet the wise, but he was angry to meet the fools. He said, "These who have dressed themselves properly for a banquet may sit down, eat, and drink. Those who have not dressed themselves properly for a banquet may stand and watch"(bSab 153a).

> There were brigands who entered the palace of a king, destroyed his possessions, killed the king's family, and destroyed the king's

[20]Jeremias, Parables, p. 65. R. Augstein, Jesus the Son of Man tr. H. Young (New York: Urizen Books, 1977), p. 242, did not know how parables were classified, so he ridiculed the ethics of someone calling in people off the street and then demanding proper garments for the occasion.

> palace. Later the king sat in judgment over them [the brigands]. He put some of them in jail; he killed some of them; crucified some of them; and then took up residence in his palace. Afterwards his reign was known in the age (Mek Shirata 10.44-48).

Weeping and grinding of teeth. This is a typical Matthean expression (Matt 8:12; 13:42; 22:13; 24:51; 25:30). It means the people will be embarrassed and sorry for their condition. They will lament and punish themselves. They will be excluded from the nation which God has chosen to receive blessings. This was an especially severe punishment in antiquity where individuals were hardly known. People were identified as members of families and communities.

Many are invited, but few are elected. This summary sentence may apply to both parables or to just the last one. It was at the last banquet where one of the invited ones was rejected. It neither says nor means that "all" are called, as some scholars suggest. The summary was intended to fit the messages of the parables. The first messengers went only to a select group. The second group of messengers invited all they could find, but in no instance was there any intention of inviting all of the people in the world to the banquet.

TEXT

15Then the Pharisees held council how they might trap him in logic. 16They sent
to him their disciples with the Herodians, saying, "Teacher, we know that you
are true; you teach the way of God in truth; and you do not care about anyone,
for you do not look at the face of people [when you pass judgment]. 17Therefore,
tell us, what do you think? Is it permissible to give taxes to Caesar or not?"
18Jesus, knowing their evil [intent], said, "Why do you test me, hypocrites?
19Show me a contemporary coin used to pay the tax." They brought him a denarius. He said to them, 20"Whose is this image and engraving?" 21They said, "Caesar's." Then, he said, "Give to Caesar the things that belong to Caesar, and to
God the things that belong to God." 22When they heard, they were astonished,
and they left him and went away.

COMMENTARY

How they might trap him. The word here translated "logic" is lóh-goh (λόγῳ), which could also be translated "word" or "speech." It means that they were planning to cross-examine him and try to get him to incriminate himself by disclosing something he wanted to be kept secret.

They sent to him their disciples. Rather than debating with Jesus, themselves, they commissioned their disciples to undertake this task.

Is it permissible? This question was designed to put Jesus in a dangerous spot. The disciples of the Pharisees brought with them Herodians who were strong Roman supporters. There were zealots in every gathering who believed that no Jew should pay taxes to Rome, and they were prepared to kill any Jew who did. If Jesus had said Jews should give taxes to Caesar, zealots would have killed him; if Jesus said they should not, the Herodians would have reported him, and the Romans would have killed him. Jesus seemed to have no way out of this situation.

The things that belong to God. Plummer did not appreciate the feelings Jews had toward Roman taxation. He said,

> The tribute to Rome was not a gift; it was the payment of a debt: and it was no impediment to the discharge of any obligation to God.[21]

Jews did not think of Roman taxation as the payment of a debt. They did not feel indebted to Rome at all, and Jesus in this narrative did not imply that they were. So? What did he say? Should they pay taxes or not? The answer was non-committal. He did not say that money for taxes was something that belonged to Caesar. Neither did he define what belonged to God. The text says of the questioners, "They were surprised," or, perhaps better, "they were non-plussed." They left having failed in their commission.

TEXT

[23]On that day, Sadducees [who] say there is no resurrection, came to him, [24]saying, "Teacher, Moses said,

Matthew	First Testament
	When two **brothers** live together,
'If anyone dies **without having**	and **one of them dies without having** a son, the wife of **the dead man** shall not become the wife of a
children	stranger, outside [the family].
his [the dead man's] brother shall marry his [the dead man's] **wife**	**Her brother-in-law shall** come over her, **take her as a wife,** and perform the duties of her brother-in-law. The first son which
and **raise** offspring for his [the	she bears he **shall raise in the name**

[21]Plummer, Matthew, p. 305; see also R. H. Gundry, Matthew (Grand Rapids: Eerdmans, 1994), p. 442-43.

survivor's **brother.**' [25]Now there were among us seven brothers. After the first married [the dead man's wife],

of the dead man. He shall not blot out his name from Israel (Deut 25:5-6).

he died, not having left the wife of his brother offspring. [26]Likewise the second and the third, up to the seventh. [27]After all [the brothers] died, the woman died. [28]In the resurrection, then of which of the seven will she be the wife, for all have had her [as a wife]?" [29]By reply Jesus said to them, "You go astray, not knowing the scriptures nor the power of God. [30]In the resurrection they will neither marry nor be married, but they are as the angels in heaven. [31]Concerning the resurrection, have you not read that which has been said to us by God, saying, [32]**I am the God of Abraham, the God of Isaac, and the God of Jacob** (Exod 3:6)? He is not the God of the dead but of the living." [33]After they had heard, the crowds were amazed at his teaching.

COMMENTARY

Raise offspring. This is the second question put to Jesus in an attempt to embarrass him. The first question was asked by the Pharisees. This second question was asked by the Sadducees. These were the two sects that gave Jesus the most trouble. Here they are lined up, one after the other. It was the Sadducees who did not believe there was a resurrection. They also did not believe that the prophetic writings were the word of God. Therefore they quoted as scripture only from the Pentateuch. The rule they quoted from Deuteronomy was one known as the levarite commandment. It required a surviving brother to marry the wife of a deceased brother if the deceased brother had died childless (see Gen 38:8). The first child of this marriage did not legally belong to the man who fathered him, but to the deceased brother. This was to prevent the deceased brother's name from being blotted out and forgotten in Israel.

Not only in biblical but in Roman law it was assumed that a person lived on in his posterity. When a man stopped breathing only his body came to an end; his life continued--his wealth, property, reputation, community position, offices, status, debts, and everything else that was identified with him was legally transferred to his heirs, just as his ancestors continued to live through him. These were all blessings that were continued from one generation to another to keep life and family together legally. Both the Sadducees and the Torah apparently agreed with this concept. Sects whose convictions were limited to these alone were not likely to produce many celibate groups, because that would allow no way for life to continue. For them procreation was basic to continued life.

Plummer thought the resurrection required new life after the physical body had perished.[22] Jewish doctrine has not assumed that the two beliefs are

[22]Plummer, Matthew, p. 306.

completely separate. Today, Orthodox Jews are buried on the mountain that was once the Mount of Olives so that their bodies will be there to be raised in the new age when the Mount of Olives would be split into two parts. The effort to have their bodies preserved would seem to be Sadducean, but their burial on the Mount of Olives presumes a belief in the resurrection of the physical body. Christians and Jews have never been unified in their beliefs about the resurrection.

Of which of the seven? Assuming, of course, that life in the age to come, after the resurrection, would continue as in this age. People would work, earn money, marry, have children and grand children, and carry on routine duties. The picture is of eight people in the new age--one woman and seven men--each of whom had once been her husband. In the age to come would she belong to the first one only? Would they draw lots for her? What would be the situation? The Sadducees assumed that there was no just answer and that therefore God would never allow a resurrection to take place.

They are as angels of heaven. This seems to indicate that Jesus believed the standard life in the resurrection would be monastic. Only monks were those who, as a class, lived without marriage. The description of people in the resurrection as like angels of heaven means they will be celibate. The only angels who married were those who fell and sinned, having had intercourse with women. Their indulgence was the cause of the flood (Gen 6-8). Jesus had concluded his discussion on levarite marriage, holding that it was profitable not to marry, although some were not able to accept celibate demands. Others, however, like Origen, made themselves eunuchs for the Kingdom of Heaven (Matt 19:10-12). This was an even greater demand than celibacy, but it was for the same purpose--to keep an undefiled camp, so that the Lord could be present. The 144,000 elect ones on Mount Zion were celibate, not having defiled themselves with women (Rev 14:1-4).

If Jesus really belonged to a celibate community, he seems also to have believed that the age to come would be only for celibate males. There are many indications that Jesus belonged to a monastic group. One of the clues for believing that Jesus was a member of a monastic group is the rejection he showed his mother. He never displayed any affection to her or called her "Mother." In fact, he denied that she was. At the wedding of Cana, when she addressed him, he replied, "Woman, what do we have to do with each other?" (John 2:4).

When those around him told him his mother and brothers had come to see him, he replied, "Who is my mother? and who are my brothers?" Then, pointing to his immediate followers, he said, "Look! My mother and brothers" (Matt 12:46-50). This implies that Jesus had rejected the mother who had given him birth and transferred his family loyalty to another group which included those around him just as other monks did. On another occasion a woman from the crowd shouted, "Blessed is the womb that bore you and the breasts that nursed you!" This a figurative way of offering a blessing for Jesus' mother, but Jesus rejected it just as he rejected his mother and brothers when they came to see him. He responded. "Rather, blessed are those who hear the word of God and keep it" (Luke 11:27-28).[23] In both cases, Jesus reminded the people around him that he no longer had any allegiance to the family into which he had been born. At the cross he said to his mother, "Woman, look! your son," and indicated someone else (John 19:26).

There is no report of Jesus mentioning his own father, and that is not surprising. He told his disciples to call no man father on earth (Matt 23:9). Since the disciples had rejected their families, they must live as if their original family never existed. Their only father was God; their only brothers were members of the order; and their family loyalty was transferred to another group. The Lord's prayer, taught to Jesus' apostles, addressed God as "Father" (Matt 6:9). The celibate community governed by the Rule of the Community (1QS6.10) referred to its members both as "neighbors" and "brothers." When Jesus gave directions for the terms by which people could join his group, he said, "If anyone will come to me and does not hate his father, mother, children, brothers, sisters, and even his own soul, he cannot be my disciple" (Luke 14:25-26).

This measure seems severe to many Protestants but not to rigorous monastic orders. The same requirements were made of members governed by the Community Rule. These rules governed whom the members of the sect should hate and whom they should love. They were to love all the sons of light--the members--and hate all the sons of darkness--all the rest, including former family members (1QS 9). Jesus insisted that he did not come to bring peace but division. He would separate father from son, mother from daughter, mother-in-law from daughter-in-law (Luke 12:51-53). Prospective followers of Jesus were not allowed to postpone their commitment until they had fulfilled the commandment to honor their parents by caring for them while they lived and burying them respectfully after they had died. Those outside the group, called, "dead," were given the responsibility of burying corpses of others who were considered dead while they still breathed (Matt 8:21-22). Followers were to break with their families and join a community that displaced the family. This was evidently a celibate, communal, masculine group. Of course there are those scholars, like Kümmel, who think that this verse proves that the kingdom is angelic and heavenly.[24]

The God of Abraham. The only times that the designation, Abraham, Isaac, and Jacob, were listed together, were to tell of Yahowah (Exod 4:5; 1 Kings 18:36;

[23]This is an allusion to Exod 24:7: **We will do and we will hear [the law].**

[24]W. G. Kümmel, Verheissung und Erfüllung (Zürich: Zwingli-Verlag, 1953), p. 83.

1 Chron 29:18) or in a context referring to the promised land (Gen 50:24; Exod 33:1; Lev 26:42; Deut 34:4; 2 Kings 13:23 and Ps 105:8-11).[25]

The Sadducees had expected Jesus to give scriptural support for his belief from the Book of Daniel, which they rejected, but he responded with a quotation from the Torah, which could be interpreted to mean that Abraham, Isaac, and Jacob still existed. This implied that they had been raised from the dead.[26] The Sadducees, like the Pharisees, came expecting to out-wit Jesus, but they all left amazed at his response. To the Sadducees, who conjectured a ridiculous situation, Jesus responded that there would be only monks in the age to come. That would exclude the marrying Sadducees. Although many scholars assume against the evidence that the rabbis were all Pharisees,[27] the famous Rabbi Yohanan seems to have affirmed the Sadducean position. He said that the end of a man was death, the end of a beast was slaughtering. He expressed no hope in a resurrection. He said anyone was blessed if he grew up in the Torah--not prophets and writings as well--labored in the Torah, pleased his maker, and grew up with a good name and left the world with a good name (bBer 17a). He also referred to the Pharisees in the third person, indicating that he was not one of them (mYad 4.6).

TEXT

[34]When the Pharisees heard that [Jesus] had silenced the Sadducees, they gathered together. [35]One of them, a lawyer, asked him a question to test him: [36]"Teacher, which is the great commandment in the law." [37][Jesus] said to him,

Matthew	First Testament
You shall love the Lord your God with your whole heart, with your whole soul, and with your whole mind. [38]This is the great and first	**You shall love Yahowah your God with all your heart, with all your soul, and with all your** might (Deut 6:5).

[25]Noted by B. Charette, The Theme of Recompense in Matthew's Gospel (Sheffield: JSOT Press, c1992), p. 69, fn 3.

[26]D. M. Cohn-Sherbok, "Jesus' Defense of the Resurrection of the Dead," JSNT 11 (1981):64-73, ridiculed the idea that this was acceptable rabbinic logic. If he had only read a little rabbinic literature, he would have seen many weaker arguments than this. It is true that this would not be satisfactory proof on the basis of twentieth century rhetoric, but it satisfied Jews of NT times. For example, when Moses said, **Tomorrow I will stand on the top of the hill** (Exod 17:9). According to Rabbi Eleazar of Modiim, "**The top** these are the deeds of the fathers. **The hill** these are the deeds of the mothers" (Mek Amalek 1. 94-98). By what logic did Rabbi Eleazar appeal to reach that conclusion? There was none, but Rabbi Eleazar was a famous rabbi, and his declaration was preserved among the Tannaitic midrashim. This is not an isolated case.

[27]For an analysis of the sects see Buchanan, The Consequences of the Covenant (Leiden: Brill, 1970), pp. 252-72.

commandment. [39]A second like it is

you shall love
your neighbor as yourself. [40]On these two commandments hang all the law and the prophets.

You shall not rise up, and you shall not bear ill will against the citizens of your people, and **you shall love your neighbor as yourself**. I am Yahowah (Lev 19:18).

TECHNICAL DETAILS

Matt 22:34-40 is paralleled both in Luke and Mark. Contrary to the supposition that there are only minor agreements between Matthew and Luke against Mark, the following terms occur in Matthew and Luke but not in Mark: **a lawyer, tempting** (Matt 22:35; Luke 10:25), **teacher** (Matt 22:36; Luke 10:25), **in the law**, and **and** (Matt 22:36; Luke 10:26). The following words occur in Mark but not in the other synoptic gospels: **Jesus**, and **Hear, Israel! The Lord our God is one Lord, and** (Mark 12:29-30). This is a striking number of agreements against Mark both in "additions" and "omissions" to be coincidental.

COMMENTARY

Silenced the Sadducees. Jesus had already outwitted the Pharisees. Then he silenced the Sadducees. Here the Pharisees try again, employing a lawyer to be their spokesman.

You shall love. Loving in biblical terms was a legal concept. Therefore it could be commanded. Contrary to many scholars, it was not a term dealing so much with feeling as performance. Quell[28] said that there was an inner paradox of attempting to apply a non-legal word in a legal direction. Hence a statement like, **And you shall love your neighbor as yourself,**

> although couched in a legal style of the usual demand, and containing the legally very closely circumscribed term ([ráy-ah] רע) [neighbor], is not really a legal statement [emphasis added], because the attitude denoted by the word is one of natural feeling [emphasis added] which cannot be legally directed.[29]

Quell assumed that "love" referred to a spontaneous feeling, and therefore concluded that it could not properly be commanded, even though it was. Because

[28]G. Quell, "Agapao [A]," TWNT 1, p. 24.

[29]Quell, "Agapao," p. 24; Lev 19:18. S. R. Driver, ICC, A Critical and Exegetical Commentary on Deuteronomy (New York: Scribners, 1916), pp. 91, 94-99, without mentioning the problems directly, emphasized both the inward, intense affection involved and also the duty to render service to the Lord. He dealt with fear and service in much the same way.

his method was wrong, his conclusions are erroneous. Quell began with an arbitrarily chosen definition of love and then tried to explain biblical usage on the basis of his non-biblical definition. The beginning point should have been a recognition of love as something that can be commanded, as it actually had been in the Bible. The unknown quantity is the effect of the commandment when it was obeyed.

Moran[30] held that love could be commanded both in Deuteronomy and in non-canonical texts dealing with contract or treaty relationships. Lohfink[31] concurred with Moran and said the same kind of love was meant in Hos 9:15. Joshua urged the Hebrews to love the Lord their God (Josh 23:11). Deuteronomy commanded them to love the Lord their God with all their heart, soul, and might (Deut 6:5), and further instructed them to keep the Lord's charge, his statutes, his ordinances, and his commandments always (Deut 11:1)--which apparently meant the same as loving God (See also Ps 31:24[23]). Israelites were also commanded not to take vengeance against other Israelites, but rather to love the stranger who sojourned in their territory (Lev 19:18), remembering that they themselves once sojourned in Egypt. The Lord commanded Hosea: "Go love a woman . . . " (Hos 3:1). In response Hosea bought the woman for 15 shekels of silver and a homer and a lethech of barley and made her dwell with him under his jurisdiction (Hos 3:1-2). There is no indication that affection was a part of the requirement or fulfillment.

These commandments in the FT are too many and too direct to be dismissed as mistakes or faulty communication. Furthermore, in one instance loving had the same meaning as not taking vengeance; in another it meant the proper way to treat a stranger; in a third it meant buying and providing for another person. These did not deal primarily with either the Lord's or the Israelites' feeling but with the way they were expected to behave. To love the Lord with all one's mind meant with all mental skills; with all his soul meant with all his contractual loyalty, being willing to surrender life in the world (among the pagans) for life in the contract community; with all his strength meant with all of his wealth (Sifre Deut 6.5 #32 [73a]). The monks of the Community Rule (1QS) interpreted loving God (Deut 6:4) to mean "searching" the scriptures. Stauffer[32] said,

> The love of God for Israel (Deut 7:13) is not impulse but will; the love of God and for neighbor demanded of the Israelite (Deut 6:5; Lev 19:18) is not intoxication but act.

30W. L. Moran, "The Ancient Near Eastern Background of Love of God in Deuteronomy," CBQ 25 (1963):77-87.

31N. Lohfink, "Hate and Love in Osee 9:15," CBQ 25 (1963):417.

32E. Stauffer, "Agapao, [C]," TWNT 1, p. 38.

Believers were to love in deed and truth--not in speech only (1 John 3:18). The commandment to love the neighbor as oneself is a summary of other commandments relating to the neighbor. The corner of the field and part of the fruit crop should be left for the neighbor; his property must not be stolen; and he must not be cheated in business or overworked. His wages should be paid day by day. He must not be abused or injured. He must be judged fairly. His neighbor must not hate him, cause him to sin, or bear anger against him. All of this is involved in loving the neighbor (Lev 19:9-18). These rules were all delegated in the masculine gender, because women did not have the same rights then that they do now. Naomi could not claim her family property in Judah until she had a male heir in whose name it could be taken (Ruth).

The commanded love of the FT was continued in the NT (Matt 19:19; 22:37; Mark 12:31, 33; Luke 10:37; Rom 13:8-10; Gal 5:14), although that will not be demonstrated here.[33] The important point here is the relationship of love and marriage contracts to law. Paul admonished wives to be subject to their husbands and commanded husbands to love their wives (Col 3:18-19; Eph 5:25, 28, 33). The later Pauline interpreter compared the love a husband had for his wife to the love Christ showed to the church when he gave himself up for her (Eph 5:25). Giving may have been closely allied with loving. Paul may even have only reminded couples of the vows they took when they entered into a marriage contract together.

When Solomon became king, Hiram, king of Tyre, sent servants to Solomon, because Hiram had loved King David, which meant that Hiram had supported David in international situations, probably under the terms of a treaty. The supporters of Pashur the prophet (Jer 20:6) and the supporters of Haman (Esth 5:10, 14; 6:13) were called "lovers." Jerusalem's lovers were the counts and political leaders from whom she might have received help before her destruction.[34] Israel's lovers were Egypt and Assyria (Hos 7:11; 8:9-13; Ezek 23:5), with whom Israel had made treaties for mutual military support. The pessimistic wisdom writer noted that the rich man had many who loved him (Prov 14:20), meaning those who stood by to support him, because it was to their own advantage. In these contexts, love was more closely related to international treaties (which involved trade agreements and the terms by which one nation would support another nation in times of national crises) than to any emotional upsurge of feeling. It was also a legal relationship that existed between a slave and his master whereby the slave could expect to have his material needs met by the master who loved him and the master in turn expected work from the slave who loved him.

These love relationships had more to do with economic or military advantage than with feelings or affection, although one did not necessarily exclude the

---

[33]For a more extensive discussion on the legal force of love in the Bible see, Buchanan, Consequences, pp. 290-305.

[34]Lam 1:2, 19; see also Jer 22:20; 30:14; Ezek 16:33; 23:22.

other. Such love could be commanded, required, and enforced in court, regardless of the feelings involved. The contract relationship that the Lord had with his people had been taken with an oath as part of a contract, and therefore the people could expect him to fulfill his bargain no matter how angry he became with them. Those who belonged to the community with whom the Lord had made a contract were destined to receive the promises of the contract fulfilled. They were the ones loved by the Lord and therefore they were called beloved.[35]

You shall love your neighbor. Words like "sons of your people," "citizens," "neighbor," and "brothers" are all terms that apply to other members of the community with whom Jews or Christians were bound in contract relationship. These were the people to whom this commandment applied. This commandment was fully carried out only in monastic communities where all members gave all they owned to the community, and all received for use the necessities of life from the same community. Every monk loved his fellow monk of the same order as himself, because he and his brother had the same access to the same possessions. If one had food and clothing so did the other.

On these two commandments. To love God was to keep his commandments, which constituted upholding the contract. Loving one's neighbor meant seeing that all that the neighbor's needs were met as well as your own. Those who were faithful in this respect automatically kept all of the other demands of the scripture.

Allison observed the frequency that the dual command occurred in early Jewish and Christian literature. Philo said there were two sets of five commandments, the first was directed to God and the second to the neighbor (Dec 50; 106; 108-10; 121), and that the decalog was a precis of the entire Mosaic law. Like Philo Josephus held that there were two tablets of stone which Moses brought down from the mountain with five commandments on each (Ant 3.101). Justin (Dial 44) and Ireneus (AdvHaer 4.16, 3) made the same claim. Loving God (Deut 5:6) and loving the neighbor (Lev 19:18) is a commandment that also occurs in Aristides Ep 15.3-5; Tertullian, AdvJud 4; Gregory of Nyssa, VitMos 2.48; and Benedict, Regula 4.2-7. The precis of the law in the ten commandments with two divisions in two tablets supported by two scripture texts seems to have been well attested.[36]

---

[35]For a good bibliography see J. W. McKay, "Man's Love for God in Deuteronomy and the Father/Teacher-Son/Pupil Relationship," VT 22 (1972):426-435. McKay was in agreement with Buchanan, Consequences, pp. 290-305, that love from the point of view of a father or teacher demanded disciplining; from the position of the son or pupil it required obedience.

[36]D. C. Allison, Jr., "Mark 12.28-31 and the Decalogue," C. A. Evans and W. R. Stegner (eds.), The Gospels and the Scriptures of Israel (Sheffield: Sheffield Academic Press, c1994), pp.270-78.

Moo said, "Love is the greatest commandment, but it is not the only one."[37] Jesus did not think of this law as only one among many. He intended these two commandments to be the complete summary of all of the law and all of the prophets, because it included the entire contract made by Moses at Sinai between Israel and God. Those who kept all of the contract loved both God and their fellow parties to the contract. Loving meant keeping the contract, and it did not apply to those outside of the contract. It was not for humanity in general but only to God and the neighbor, God and the brother, God and the fellow party to the contract.

Donaldson found a rabbinic passage that seemed to him very similar to the passage attributed to Jesus here:

> What is the smallest portion of scripture from which all essential regulations of the Torah hang (תלויין)? "In all your ways acknowledge him, and he will direct your paths" (Prov 3:6).[38]

But Donaldson then wondered

> why Matthew would use such a characteristically rabbinic formulation in such an anti-Pharisaic passage, and to such unrabbinic ends.[39]

This provided a problem for Donaldson because of two of his assumptions:

1) He presumed that the rabbinic literature was composed by Pharisees and represented the Pharisaic point of view, but there is not much evidence for this conclusion. There are only five passages in the entire Tosephta and two in the Mishnah that even mention the Pharisees. None of these praises the Pharisees. The famous Rabbi Johanan b. Zakkai referred to the Pharisees in the third person, as if he were not one himself (mYad 4.6-8), and he held positions that are more closely identified with the Sadducees than the Pharisees (tBer 3.25; tSab 1.15; tYad 3.25; tSot 15.11; tYad 2.20 mSot 3.4; mYad 4.6-8.

2) He also assumed that Matthew was composed after 70 I.A. and that Jesus' teaching on which commandments the entire Torah hung was intended for both Jews and gentiles. Except for a very few possible additions after 70 I.A. most of the Gospel according to Matthew makes good sense written before 70 I.A., and there is no reason to suggest that Jesus included non-Jews in his concept of neighbors.

---

[37]D. J. Moo, "Jesus and the Authority of the Mosaic Law," JSNT 20 (1984):11.

[38]T. L. Donaldson, "The Law that Hangs (Matthew 22:40): Rabbinic Formulation and Matthaean Social World," CBQ 57 (1995):689.

[39]Donaldson, "Hangs," p. 694.

Matthew's negative attitude to the Pharisees is coherent with the description given also by Josephus. Both of these accounts are more offensive than the attitude reflected in the chreias of Jesus, but there is more basis for thinking that they represent accurate pictures of the Pharisees than rabbinic literature does.[40]

TEXT

[41]While the Pharisees were gathered together, Jesus asked them, [42]saying, "How does it seem to you concerning the Messiah. Whose son is he?" They said to him, "David's." [Jesus] said to them, [43]"How then does David in the spirit call him 'Lord,' saying,

> [44]**The Lord said to my Lord, 'Sit at my right hand**
> **until I put your enemies under your feet'** (Ps 110:1)?

[45]If, then, David calls him 'Lord,' how is he his son?" [46]No one was able to answer him a word, nor did anyone dare to ask him any question any longer from that day on.

COMMENTARY

The Pharisees were gathered. This is put in relationship to verse 34, where the Pharisees were gathered together. This editorial note was intended to show that they were still there gathered.

How, then does David . . . call him 'Lord'? In the spirit does not mean "in a visionary state," as some scholars have held.[41] Rather, it means "through the Holy Spirit" or "in the word of God." This is a periphrastic way of saying "in the scriptures." It was presumed that David wrote all of the Psalms and that as God's legal agent he acted as God himself when he wrote. Therefore a quotation from Psalm 110 was a quotation from David as well as a quotation from God. Since all prophecy was held to be prophesied only for the days of the Messiah, it was presumed also that the "him" mentioned in Psalm 110 was the Messiah whom God would make to sit at his right hand. Because the Messiah was God's legal agent, legally equal to God, it was considered proper to call the Messiah, "Lord," but a king would hardly refer to his own son as "Lord." Therefore, Jesus reportedly reasoned, David's son could not be the Messiah.

Nevertheless, it was customary for Jews to call their king "the son of David," "the Son of God," "king," "Messiah," and "Lord." This was probably one of those puzzles for which Jews found no answer and that circulated widely.

---

[40]Buchanan, Consequences, p. 266.

[41]Gundry, Matthew, p. 451.

Matthew just added it to his collection of arguments that made the Pharisees look foolish. It probably was not spoken by Jesus and did not raise the question about the authenticity of Jesus' parentage and the validity of his messiahship. If it had, the Pharisees would have used it to his disadvantage. This was like asking if the almighty God could create a stick with one end or make a rock so big that he could not lift it. It could be addressed just as well to any other Jewish sect. This would be an especially clever question for someone who advocated a king from the Hasmonean line to ask someone who thought the true king could only come from David's line.

From the time of David and Solomon it was assumed that the divine right of kings should descend through the Davidic dynasty. In the second century B.I.A., however, the Hasmoneans succeeded in overthrowing the Syrian Greeks and regaining control of the Solomonic empire. They called themselves priests and kings, although they were Levites. They used Psalm 110 to justify their position, and they may have used this question as an instrument to refute the Jews who thought they were not entitled to their position. If Jesus actually said this which has been attributed to him, it suggests that Jesus himself was from the Hasmonean line rather than the Davidic. This would concur with the argument in Hebrews claiming that he was the high priest of the age. Jesus also called himself the "Son of man" which was the name given to Judas the Maccabee in Dan 7. After all it was David and Zadok who were entitled to be king and high priest. The testimony is mixed, and there is no certain way to judge which evidence is correct. The testimony of the birth narratives in Matthew and Luke claim Jesus as a Son of David. One of these claims has been inaccurately attributed to him.

CONCLUSIONS

Chapter 22 was dedicated to the task of presenting Jesus as the wise man who was able to repudiate all of his attackers. First he showed the Pharisees how foolish they were (Matt 22:1-22). Then his attention was directed to the Sadducees who tried to entrap him (Matt 22:23-33). When the Sadducees failed, the Pharisees tried again (Matt 22:34-40). The chapter concluded with this last question being one which Jesus turned to the Pharisees that left them without an answer (Matt 22:41-46). The discussion concluded after Jesus had answered all of his questioners well, and with them unable to answer even one of his questions.

CHAPTER TWENTY-THREE

TEXT

23:1 Then Jesus spoke to the crowds and to his disciples, 2 saying, "Upon Moses'
bench the scribes and Pharisees have sat.

Matthew	First Testament
3 **Everything**, then, **whatever** they **say, do and keep** (poi-áy-sah-teh kai tay-ráy-teh, ποιήσατε καὶ τηρεῖτε), but according to their works **do** not **do**, for they **say** but **do not do**."	**Everything which** the Lord has **said**, we will **do, and** we will **obey** (LXX poi-áy-so-men kai a-koo-só-meh-thah ποιήσομεν καὶ ἀκουσόμεθα; MT nah-ah-sáy weh-nish-máh, (נעשה ונשמע) (Exod 24:7).

COMMENTARY

The crowds and to his disciples. This chapter seems unequivocally addressed to the disciples and the crowds. It was spoken about the Pharisees, but not to them. The information in the chapter, however, sometimes seems to be directed to the Pharisees, themselves. Matt 23 is not just a continuation of the parable of the wicked tenants, as some have thought. The wicked tenants were the pagan Romans. Those being attacked in Matt 23 are Jewish leaders and sectarians. This is one side of an inner family dispute.

On Moses' bench. Moses' bench was no ordinary chair. It was a chair where a judge would sit when pronouncing judgment. It was a prestigious chair, once occupied by Moses, and then occupied by Joshua, the elders, the prophets, the men of the great synagogue, and in Jesus' time, it was occupied by Pharisees (mAboth 1.1). A similar bench is the cathedra where the pope might sit when he makes an infallible judgment. It is legally infallible, because the pope is a monarch. His bench constitutes the highest court in the system. No one can take his decisions to a higher court for correction.

The same is true of Moses' bench. Those who sat on Moses' bench were the judges, members of the national Sanhedrin. Theirs was a great responsibility. Rabbis referred to the Sanhedrin as the "eyes of the congregation" (CantR I.15 #2). They also said that the decree of Heaven is whatever the Beth Din (the court) decides (TgJon Ruth 3.18). In one of Zechariah's visions the seven lamps were interpreted as **the eyes of Yahowah; they go back and forth in all the land** (Zech 4:10). The eyes of the Lord on the promised land would have been either the judges or, more likely, Jewish intelligence agents, those spies who would report secret crimes. In any case the eyes represented the judicial system. If some offense was committed unintentionally, away from the eyes of the congregation so that it could not be brought before the courts, then the community was required to perform certain prescribed ritualistic acts to get the sin atoned and the offense blotted out from the community's heavenly record (Num 15:24). It was the task of those who sat on Moses' seat to see that all crime was punished or pardoned so that Israel's sin might be forgiven on the Day of Atonement. According to Matt 23, this was an important function. The leaders involved deserved all of the cooperation Jews and early Christians could provide.

The scribes and the Pharisees have sat. The past tense of this verb provides problems of interpretation. Does it mean that they no longer sit there but that they did at one time? One possible solution to the problem is that this text was originally composed in unpointed Hebrew, and the word for "sat"(ישב, yah-sháhv) could be pointed either as a finite verb, past tense (yah-sháhv), or as a participle, present tense (yoh-sháyv). In that case the Greek translator may have misunderstood the participle to have been a past tense finite verb. The reason this seems to be a possibility is that the scribes and Pharisees were being criticized here for their behavior, not their ancient history. People are less likely to be criticized for crimes that they once committed than for crimes they are still committing.

Garland said that if scholars demanded that this aorist be given a past tense force and this rigor were applied throughout the NT

> it would raise an even more vexing question about the current status of Jesus who 'formerly sat' at the right hand of God (cf. Mk. 16:19; Heb. 1:3; 8:1; 10:12 and Rev. 3:21).[1]

In his attack against anyone who thought Matthew was pro-Jewish, Cook asked,

---

[1]D. E. Garland, The Intention of Matthew 23 (Leiden: E. J. Brill, 1979), p. 47.

> How can this passage [Matt 23:2] be construed as pro-Jewish when it introduces thirty-four verses of denunciation of the scribes and Pharisees?[2]

This is not a difficult question to answer for anyone familiar with the early Jewish and Christians sects and their behavior. With all of the early conflicts in Judaism among the various sects, it seems strange for Cook even to suggest that any Jew who took issue with another Jewish leader or sect of Jews was to be considered for that act anti-Jewish. To hold such a position as that one would have to call the great Rabbi Yohanan ben Zakkai anti-Jewish. He was evidently not a Pharisee himself, because he referred to the Pharisees in the third person, and he spoke critically of the Pharisees on one of their interpretations (mYad 4.6). Rabbi Joshua also accused the Pharisees of wearing out the world (mSot 3.4). Sadducees criticized Pharisees on several points (mYad 4.6-7), but they were not anti-Jewish. A Galilean Jewish heretic also criticized the Pharisees (mYad 4.8). According to Cook's logic Rabbi Yohanan ben Zakkai, the Sadducees, and the particular Galilean Jewish heretic mentioned would all be anti-Jewish. Today, in the U.S.A. an American does not have to be anti-American to criticize either the Democrats or the Republicans, and a Reform Jew who criticizes an Orthodox Jew is not thought to be anti-Semitic. Why would a Jew in antiquity who criticized one sect have to be anti-Jewish?

Jesus was a national leader, so were the chief priests, some of the Pharisees, and some of the scribes. He criticized them and they criticized him. None of these represented all of Judaism, except, perhaps, Jesus, on the basis that he was the Messiah, and, like other kings, was therefore a representative of the people. These were all Jews and leaders, carrying on inter-Jewish debates. None of them can justly be called anti-Jewish. Neither can Matthew be considered anti-Jewish for reporting the conflicts among Jewish sects.

Do and keep. This is clearly a midrash on Exod 24:7 as an antitype of the response the people gave to Moses when he brought the ten commandments to the Israelites. The introduction prepares the reader to expect that. Moses was understood to be God's legal agent. His words had the authority of God. He functioned as a judge, as did the scribes and Pharisees. They were members of the Sanhedrin, and their words carried legal authority, so it was wise to follow their teachings. The criticism given here was not with their authority or their office, but only with their performance. This is not the only time Matthew has given an antitype of Moses giving the commandments and the Israelites accepting them. The Hebrew terms, nah-ah-sáy weh-nish-máh (נעשה ונשמע) mean, literally, **We will do and we will hear** [or obey]. The Sermon on the Mount concludes with

[2] M. J. Cook, "Interpreting 'Pro-Jewish' Passages in Matthew," HUCA 54 (1983):144. For other analyses of Cook's article see the commentary on the relevant passages (Matt 5:17-18; 10:5-6; 15:24; 21:43; 22:8; 23:37; 24:14; and the conclusions).

the observation, "Everyone who **hears** these my words and **does** them is like a wise man who built his house upon the rock" (Matt 7:24; also see 7:26). Following the parable of the sower comes the conclusion: "Now the one who has sown on the good ground--this man is the one who **hears** the word and understands, and he bears fruit and **does** (poi-áy, ποιεῖ) (produces) one, 100, one, 60, and another, 30" [measures or times as much as planted] (Matt 13:23). Jesus said, "Rather, 'Blessed are those who **hear** the word of God and **keep** it'" (Luke 11:28). Paul said, "It is not the **hearers** of the law who are righteous before God, but the **doers** of the law are justified" (Rom 2:13).

TEXT

4For they bind heavy and large burdens,
  and they put [them] upon the shoulders of men,
but they do not want [to use] their finger
  to move them [off their shoulders].
5All their works they do to be seen by people,
for they make their phylacteries wide,
  and they enlarge their fringes.
6They love the first seats at banquets,
  the first seats in the synagogues,
7the greetings in the marketplace,
  and to be called by others, "Rabbi."

8But you are not called, "Rabbi," for one is your teacher, and you are all brothers. 9Do not call [anyone] on earth your father, for one is your Father, the heavenly one. 10Do not be called "leader," because one is your leader, the Messiah. 11The greater among you will be your servant.

12Whoever	exalts himself	will be humbled,
and whoever	humbles himself	will be exalted.

COMMENTARY

They bind heavy and large burdens. The words "and large" are omitted in many texts, but belong to the Sinaiticus and the medieval Hebrew text.[3] This means that they assess heavy fines and prison sentences. As members of the Sanhedrin, these judges had authority to bind or loose; they could put people in prison or release them from prison. They could make punishments for offenses either light or heavy. Jesus complained that these officials were unusually severe in their demands. This was not always the case. When Rabban Gamaliel was chief justice,

---

[3]So G. Howard, "A Note on Codex Sinaiticus and Shem-Tob's Hebrew Matthew," NovT 24 (1992):46.

there was a shortage of sacrificial animals at the feast, so the vendors charged excessive prices that the poor people could not pay. When this was called to Gamaliel's attention, he at once reduced the kind and number of sacrifices required by one half. This action immediately brought down the prices.

They do to be seen by people. Fringes and phylacteries are necessary instruments for daily worship for the pious Jew. The criticism given here is not that the Pharisees used them, but that they used them ostentatiously to show people that they were religious. Jesus encouraged Christians to pray and fast in secret (Matt 6:5-6; 16-18). Pharisees and scribes had positions of great status. It was normal for them to be given chief seats at banquets and synagogues. Like most other people, they liked recognition that went with their offices. Those who did good works, like the Pharisees, and received the normal recognition for their accomplishments already received their rewards for their virtue, so there would not be additional merits recorded in the heavenly treasury. Monks, however, were dedicated to the purpose of increasing merit in the heavenly treasury. Therefore, they avoided receiving earthly rewards. They prayed and fasted in secret. They turned the other cheek and walked the second mile so that there would certainly be works of supererogation.

They make their phylacteries wide. These were part of their religious apparel (Exod 13:9, 16; Deut 6:8; 11:18; Num 15:38).

To be called by others, "Rabbi." Verses 4-7 seem to form a unit. It concludes with the comment on being called "Rabbi." Verses 8-12 constitutes a homiletical comment on this one verse, discussing the way the apostles should respond to such titles as this.

The title "rabbi" is a legal term of status. It was applied to judges. The term means "my great one." For centuries judges in every society have been treated with more respect than almost anyone else in the community. From the time that Moses appointed his first subordinate judges and told them that their judgment was the judgment of God (Deut 1:17), judges have been recognized as legal agents of the Lord. Like kings they were allowed to be called "gods," because of this legal agency. The Psalmist resented their arrogance and reminded them that even though they were called "gods," they would die like other human beings (Ps 82:6-7).

People rise when judges enter the court room and in English tradition refer to them as "your honor" or "your worship." Judges in Israel were addressed as "rabbi." The fact that Jesus prohibited the disciples from accepting this title implies that they were sufficiently competent in the field of law to consider the title applicable. In the monastery, however, all members were brothers, so there was no special title, except for the leader. By avoiding titles of prestige, the disciples were laying up treasures in heaven. The title "father" was not applied to priests in NT times, but it was a title for the dean of a court. Otherwise, it was applied to the masculine heads of families. Monks, however, had denied their parents, taken vows not to recognize them or provide for them; therefore, they did not even refer to them by their legitimate family names. Jesus refused to recognize either his mother or his brothers and sisters (Matt 12:46-50). Disciples were to live by the same rules.

Whoever exalts himself will be humbled. Jesus is not reported as having reminded the sons of Zebedee of this policy when they came with their mother asking for chief seats in the Kingdom. Rabbis said, "He who humbles himself, the holy One blessed be He raises up, and the one who exalts himself, the holy One blessed be he humbles" (bErub 13b). Jesus and the rabbis agreed. Jesus used the passive voice to avoid misusing the divine name. The rabbis used a descriptive title for the same purpose. Both meant, "God will humble the one who exalts himself or herself."

TEXT

13 Woe to you, scribes and Pharisees, [you] theater actors!
You close the Kingdom of Heaven before men.
You, yourselves, do not enter,
and you do not allow the entering ones to come in.

COMMENTARY

Woe to you, scribes and Pharisees. "Woe" means "It will be hard on . . ." This sounds imprecatory, and it probably is. Early Jews and Christians were not always kind to one another. They sometimes threatened or warned one another. There has been in-fighting among Jews, Christians, Samaritans, and between sects of these groups from the very beginning. To get a reminder of the way some Jews and Samaritans talked to one another reread Amos. Amos was a Jew speaking to Samaritans. He called their worship "transgression" (Amos 4:4) and said that God hated their feasts and solemn assemblies (Amos 5:21).

Woes were said, sometimes threateningly in anger, and sometimes kindly in sympathy. For example there were woes against the women of Jerusalem who were pregnant when the battle would be fought there. If it were in winter it would be very difficult; if it were on the Sabbath, people could not walk more than 2,000 cubits (Matt 24:19). These would be hard times, and no one was glad about it. Reportedly, Jesus foresaw the stumbling blocks (betrayals) that were coming, and thought they were predestined. None the less he said, "Woe to the man through which these stumbling blocks are coming" (Matt 18:7). It would be better for that man (Judas) if he had never been born (Matt 26:24). This was not a curse; it was more like a lament. When Jesus said, "Woe to you, Chorazin! Woe to you, Bethsaida!" (Matt 11:21), however, he probably meant that as a warning that there would be vengeance upon these towns for their non-cooperation. In the

FT there were woes of lament, like Isaiah's "Woe is me for I am lost! I am a man of unclean lips, and I live in the midst of a people of unclean lips" (Isa 6:5). There are also woes to the bad shepherds who abandon their flocks. These are accompanied by curses against them (Zech 11:17). Sometimes woes are cries of distress and sometimes warnings of evil consequences either in this age or in the divine judgment.[4]

Theater actors. The word "hypocrite" in ancient Greece was applied to a person who played a role on a stage. Such a person tried to appear as someone else. Like other movie stars, these actors played one role at one time and another role at another. The character that the audience saw was not the real character of the actor. The Pharisees were called "theater actors" as an insult. This was a popular insult among early Jews and Christians, usually applied to one who was thought to be insincere or to be going through his forms to gain the applause of the audience. Garland said hypocrites

> do not necessarily pretend to be better; they wrongly believe they are better, just as the Pharisee considered himself better than the publican in Luke 18:9-14.[5]

It was a more descriptive insult than "snake" or "descendant of a scorpion," but it was an insult, nonetheless. Garland compared the insult to other Jewish insults: A good judge was one who searched the Torah for truth and justice. Hypocrites searched for deception or "smooth things." They were prophets of falsehood (1QH 2.15-16; 2.31; 2.18; 4.9; CDC 6.6-7; 7.14).[6]

The ones being insulted here were the scribes and the Pharisees, Jewish officials and sectarians. If these words actually came from the lips of Jesus they were not attacks on Jews by Christians or gentiles, as many scholars have presumed. These were attacks on Jews by Jews. In Jesus' time there was no Christianity. Jesus was a Jew and he spoke to Jews in Palestine. There were only various sects of Judaism. Insults like these were made among Jews both before and after NT times. Christians also continued the practice among themselves, one Christian sect offending another sect. Neither Jews nor Christians should deny this; it is part of our history. Neither Jews nor Christians have experienced shortages in their vocabulary of insults. We might try to reduce it rather than accuse each other or defamation.

---

[4]See the extensive analysis of Garland, Intention, pp. 64-90.

[5]Garland, Intention, p. 102.

[6]Garland, Intention, pp. 104-110.

You close the Kingdom. The woes against the Pharisees seem to be promises of evil consequences for them on the day of judgment. The evil they were doing at the time Jesus was reported to have spoken would be avenged by God on that day. They were closing the circle of the elite, making the apartheid still more restrictive, just as the Pharisees did during the rule of Queen Alexandra. This limited citizenship in the Kingdom of Heaven so that others who might be admitted would be excluded. The ones that the Pharisees wanted to exclude were the tax collectors whom Jesus recruited. Because the Pharisees and scribes were unwilling to forgive these wealthy people who had mingled with the Romans, Jesus said the Pharisees themselves would be excluded. They were preventing those who were already preparing to enter into the Kingdom from being admitted.

Paul was speaking about the Jews in Judaea when he said they were trying to keep the Pauline Christians from speaking to the gentiles so that they could be saved (1 Thess 2:18-19).

TEXT

> 15Woe to you, scribes and Pharisees, [you] theater actors!
> You travel overseas and dry land to make one proselyte,
> and when it happens, you make him a worse son of Gehenna than
> you are.

TECHNICAL DETAILS

Matt 23 has no verse 14 that is well testified by the sources.

COMMENTARY

You travel over sea and dry land. At least since the Assyrian and Babylonian captivities, Jews and North Israelites have been engaged in international commerce. Jewish merchants have traveled widely, and in their travels they have been active proselyters. In NT times there was a Jew by the name of Ananias who instructed King Izates of Adiabene in Judaism. When he considered becoming a proselyte, Ananias told him that it was possible for him to do so without becoming circumcised (Ant 20.41). There evidently was a very successful program of conversion going on in NT times. Some scholars estimate that Jews constituted 10% of the Roman population in those days. Paul worked so arduously and effectively with the Jews of the diaspora that other Christians continued his conversion activity very successfully. Jews have also continued to make proselytes, sometimes openly and sometimes secretly, depending upon the social and political situation of the time and area. It is not clear here whether Pharisees were attacked for their work of making proselytes of gentiles who would become Jews in the process or whether they were more concerned to make proselytes of Jewish members of other sects. It was probably both, but they would have been more successful, if, like Paul, they had begun with those who were already trained in Judaism. Pharisees, then, would be distinguished for their effort in strengthening the size and power of their own sect within the Jewish community.

A worse son of Gehenna than you are. This is the kind of insult a member of one sect would hurl at another. Given the premise 1) that God has a chosen people, 2) that you alone belong to the true group of chosen people, 3) you automatically conclude that all others are not chosen and therefore are sons of Gehenna rather than sons of the kingdom (Matt 8:12). Of course other sects attribute the same destiny to the members of your sect.

TEXT

16Woe to you, blind leaders who say,
"Whoever swears by the altar [has done] nothing, but whoever swears by the gold of the temple, has taken a valid oath.

> 17Fools and blind people! Which is greater,
> the gold or the temple which sanctified the gold?"

[You] also [hold that]
18whoever swears by the altar [has done] nothing, but whoever swears by the gift which is upon the altar has taken a valid oath.

> 19Blind people! Which is greater,
> the gift or the altar that sanctifies the gift?
> 20Whoever, then, swears by the altar
> swears by it and all that is on it,
> 21and whoever swears by the temple
> swears by it and the One who dwells in it.
> 22Whoever swears by Heaven
> swears by the throne of God
> and the One who is seated on it.

TECHNICAL DETAILS

In the above passage there are several parallel statements: Verse 16 is parallel with verse 18; verse 17 and 19 are parallel; verses 20, 21, and 22 are all parallel.

COMMENTARY

Woe to you, blind leaders. Paul was speaking to the Jewish Christians at Rome when he said, "Since you are persuaded that you are a guide to the blind . . .

while teaching others will you not teach yourself" (Rom 2:19, 21)? In an editorial addition to a chreia, Matt 15:14 says, "They [the Pharisees] are blind leaders of the blind. If the blind lead the blind, they will both fall into a ditch." This insult seems to be a Matthean expression rather than a teaching of Jesus.

By the gift which is on the altar. The altar was the "holy of holies" or the most holy place, and everyone who touches it becomes holy (Exod 29:37), but some held that the gift on the altar was holier. This kind of nit-picking, legalistic detail sounds Pharisaic, and seems incoherent with the Sermon on the Mount which commands a pious Jew not to swear at all (Matt 5:33-37). People in NT times, however, did take vows, and they were upheld. Jesus was reported to have accused the Pharisees of upholding vows of monasticism on the basis of the gift on the altar: "You say, 'Whoever says to his father or his mother, "[by the] gift [on the altar] [may the following unexpressed curses come upon me] if you receive any benefit from me," he will not honor his father or his mother'" (Matt 15:5-6).

Some rabbis said that if someone used substitute terms in a vow, such as "like the altar," "like the temple," or "like Jerusalem" the vow is as valid as if he had used the term "Korban"--the gift on the altar (mNed 1.3).

Swears by the temple. The One who dwelled in the temple, of course, was God. In an a fortiori argument, medieval rabbis said,

> If the altar, which is but one of the ornaments of the house of the sanctuary, is built of twelve stones, how much more so the [entire] house of the sanctuary, which is the praise of Israel, the praise of those above and those below, and the praise of the holy One blessed be He.[7]

Jewish, Christian, and Moslem sects have often disagreed on technical liturgical forms, each one thinking that it alone performs the ritual correctly and that the other is excluded from God's grace because it omits or adds some detail of form. The most reliable literary forms in which the teachings of Jesus are preserved show Jesus in conflict with the Pharisees--not on details of form but on the treatment to be rendered to the tax collectors and other liberal Jews who engaged in business with gentiles. These legalistic and ritualistic details do not cohere with his teachings.

---

[7]Buchanan, Revelation and Redemption: Jewish Documents of Deliverance from the Fall of Jerusalem to the Death of Nahmanides (Dillsboro: Western North Carolina Press, c1978; sold by Mercer U. Press), p. 535.

TEXT

[23]Woe to you, scribes and Pharisees, [you] theater actors! You give a tenth of mint, dill, and cumin, but you have abandoned the more important parts of the law--judgment, mercy, and faith. These things it was necessary to do without neglecting those [smaller details]. [24]Blind leaders! [You] who strain out the gnat, but swallow the camel.

COMMENTARY

A tenth of mint, dill, and cumin. The author of this unit has neatly balanced three small items--mint, dill, and cumin with three important virtues--judgment, mercy, and faith. Mishnaic rules require that Jews who want to discard the leaves of vegetables to lighten loads on their carts or baskets must first give a tenth of the value of the leaves before throwing them away (mDemai 3.2). If a Jew bought vegetables and decided to return them and receive the money he paid for them, he must first pay the tenth on them before he returns them. Once they become his possession he is responsible for giving the tenth (mDemai 3.2).

Pharisees and scribes were very careful to fulfill the exact requirements of the law. They gave the full tenth which the law commanded, but no more. Like other monks, Jesus asked followers to give all that they had and said that their righteousness had to exceed that of the Pharisees if they were to enter the Kingdom of Heaven. The rabbis were more exacting than the law, which required only grain, wine, and oil to be tithed (Deut 14:22-23).

Judgment, mercy, and faith. The logic was as follows: 1) Israel could not receive the kingdom so long as it was still in sin. 2) Israel had a huge debt in the treasury of merits and demerits. 3) Pharisees were only doing that which was required, which only kept from adding more demerits to the record. 4) This procedure would never cancel the national debt. Ergo, Pharisaic righteousness was inadequate for entrance into the Kingdom of Heaven.

Strain out the gnat. In Aramaic the word for camel is gahm-láh (גמלה) and the word for gnat is kahl-máh (קלמה). This comparison was an intentional play on these words. The metaphor of straining liquid to remove impurities is clearly a hyperbole, but it makes its point. The gnat was the impurity that they wanted to strain out. This metaphor was used to describe their legal policies. The Pharisees were careful about minute details of the law, but they overlooked the most important ones, in the judgment of the author of this section of woes. The comparative importance of the ones they observed to the ones they omitted is like that between a gnat and a camel in size. The ones that were so obvious that a strainer was not needed to discover them were the ones they ignored.

TEXT

[25]Woe to you, scribes and Pharisees, [you] theater actors! Because you cleanse the outside of the cup and platter, but the inside is full of plunder and incontinence. [26]Blind Pharisee! Cleanse first the inside of the cup, in order that its outside may be clean.

COMMENTARY

The outside of the cup and platter. Mishnaic law requires that all vessels be distinguished, the inside from the outside (mKel 25.1). Rabbis and scribes were the judges and lawyers of NT times. They represented the legal system. Rabbis required people to cleanse only the side of a vessel that had been defiled. If the inside became defiled it was not necessary to cleanse the outside and vice versa. They argued about the amount of a vessel that was outside and inside. This depended on how many rims the jar had and which one was the highest in altitude. In most cases the outside was that which was defiled, because it could be touched most easily. Rabbis even made a distinction between the cleanliness of the outside of a vessel and that of the handles by which it is lifted. One could be unclean without the other (mKel 4.4; 25.7-8).[8] If anything unclean, such as an unclean insect or reptile or anything that has touched something dead, falls into a vessel, then the vessel itself is unclean and must be broken (Lev 11:33; Sifra 54c-55c). Some of these rules are still observed by Arabs in the Near East. Arabs are able to drink from a vessel that looks like a teapot without a handle by holding the vessel above their heads and pouring water from its spout into their mouths. They can do this without spilling a drop. In that way they can drink from a vessel that is clean inside without anxiety about the cleanliness of the outside. If someone makes a mistake and allows the spout to touch his or her lips, it is assumed that the vessel is unclean also on the inside, and the vessel is broken at once.[9]

The inside is full of plunder. The translation "plunder" for the Greek har-pah-gáys (ἁρπαγῆς), does not adequately translate the image. The har-pah-gáys (ἁρπαγῆς) here refers to the dirt and sludge that settles to the bottom of a vessel. Rabbis said that a vessel was "clean" if the outside was cleaned, since the inside is not touchable by defiling contacts, like hands and furniture. According to this report, Jesus challenged the logic of that purity law, but that was not the real

[8]See also J. Neusner, "First Cleanse the Inside," NTS 22 (1976):486-95.

[9]The common cup Jesus used with his disciples at the Last Supper was probably one of these. Near Easterners would have been shocked at the idea of all drinking from the same chalice. The chalice was introduced into the service of communion in the Roman Catholic Church when the priest alone drank the wine, and he had the kind of chalice a king would have used, but it was not shared with the community.

point of discussion here. He compared defilement of dishes to defilement of the character of the Pharisees, who were famous for their outward display and claim for status. Paul said,

> He is not a Jew who is one outwardly, nor is he circumcised who is circumcised outwardly, in the flesh, but he is a Jew who is one secretly and circumcised of the heart, in the spirit, and not in the letter (Rom 2:28-29).

TEXT

Matthew	First Testament
27Woe to you, scribes and Pharisees, [you] theater actors! You are like whitewashed tombs--on the one hand, you appear beautiful, but from within you are full of dead bones and all **uncleanness**, 28so you appear to men just from the outside, but from the inside you are full of hypocrisy and lawlessness.	Everyone who touches a corpse, the body of a man who has died and does not purify himself defiles the tabernacle. That person will be excommunicated from Israel, because the water of purification has not been sprinkled over him. He is **unclean**, and his **uncleanness** is still upon him (Num 19:13; cf. Num 6:6; 19:16).

COMMENTARY

Whitewashed tombs. According to the Lukan parallel, the problem was with unmarked tombs. Dead bodies were believed to defile all people who touched them or were under the same roof as corpses. Those who touched corpses or entered caves where corpses were stored were defiled and were required to be sprinkled with the ashes of the red heifer on the third day and on the seventh day in order to be undefiled on the eighth day after corpse defilement. A person defiled who was not cleansed was required to be excommunicated (Num 19:11-22). If the tombs were not marked, people could walk over them without knowing it and become defiled. If they did not know they were defiled they would not act to have themselves cleansed. Therefore, rabbis decreed that graves should be marked and made visible (mMaasSh 5.1). This was to prevent accidental defilement.

According to Matthew, the problem was with the overdecoration of tombs. Rabbis said tombs in a cemetery used to be marked with lime, so that they would be painted white (bBKam 69a; mMaasSh 5.1). Even plowed fields were supposed to be marked if graves had been lost within its borders (bMKat 5b). If tombs were sufficiently decorated they would not seem to be tombs at all, and people would not realize that they were defiled when they entered the caves in which these corpses were stored.

Full of dead bones. In both the Matthean and Lukan account the point of concern was not the tombs, but the Pharisees. The Pharisees, who were the judges, were entrusted to distinguish between the things that were clean and those that were defiling, as well as people who were sinful and those that were righteous. In actuality, however, they were themselves as unclean as corpses who would defile multitudes of people by their deception, but they were not marked! Whitewashed tombs were attractive but deceptive. The Pharisees were also externally attractive and received respect. They wore white gowns to be distinguished for their purity, but their outward appearance misled people into thinking that they were not defiled, even though they were, so they were destroying the sanctity of the holy people. This was not only legally so, but metaphorically so. These lawyers were not only defiled, but lawless. The concern here was primarily the deceptive character of the Pharisees rather than their liturgical defilement.

TEXT

[29]Woe to you, scribes and Pharisees, [you] theater actors, because you construct the tombs of the prophets, decorate the graves of the just, [30]and say, "If we had been in the days of our fathers, we would not have been those who share in the blood of the prophets." [31]In this way you act as witnesses against yourselves that you are sons of those who murdered the prophets, [32]and you fill up the measure of your fathers. [33]Snakes, descendants of scorpions! How can you flee from the judgment of Gehenna?

COMMENTARY

Woe to you, scribes and Pharisees. Scribes were lawyers by profession. Pharisees were members of a Jewish sect. Josephus said that before the Jewish Roman war of 66-70 I.A. the Pharisees constituted the largest of the Jewish sects in Palestine. He said there were 6,000 members in comparison with the Essenes, which he reported to have 4,000 members. The only places where Pharisees can be confidently identified are in the works of Josephus and the NT. In both documents Pharisees are pictured as zealous, law-abiding religious leaders who were able to get themselves into positions of political power and influence. Rubenstein presumed that the Pharisees wrote all of the rabbinic literature. Since there are teachings of humility and passive ethics in rabbinic literature, he concluded that Matthew's report of the Pharisees is inaccurate and unfair.[10]

Matt 23 may be unfair in its account of the Pharisees. It certainly is tendentious, but Rubenstein's basis for describing the Pharisees is unsound. There are only six references to the Pharisees in the entire Mishnah//Tosephta, and three of these describe the Pharisees negatively, while the other three are neutral.

---

[10]R. L. Rubenstein, "Scribes, Pharisees and Hypocrites, A Study in Rabbinic Psychology," Judaism 12 (1963):456-68.

None of them shows the Pharisees in a favorable light. Rabbi Yohanan mentioned the Pharisees in the third person, implying that he was not a Pharisee. It is unlikely that such a large body as the Mishnah//Tosephta should not describe the Pharisees at all favorably if it were completely composed by the Pharisees. Therefore it is not a valid methodology to pick only the passive, humble references in the rabbinic literature as a basis for defining the Pharisees. It is also unreasonable to assume that all twentieth century Jews are descendants of the Pharisees.

Rabbinic literature was composed by whatever Jewish scholars survived the fall of Jerusalem in 70 I.A. These rabbis were not from Palestine alone, and were not from any one sect. The literature itself was carefully edited after the Bar Cochba Revolt to remove all anti-Roman, openly zealotish, nationalistic teachings. This was necessary for survival within the Roman Empire. Christians had to edit their literature in the same way. The Dead Sea Scrolls provide the only unedited extant Jewish literature written in NT times. This makes it difficult to learn precisely what a sect like the Pharisees was in pre-70 I.A. Judaism.

For many years Christians have attacked contemporary Jews as heirs of the Pharisees, and Jews, accepting the accusation, have used rabbinic literature to oppose the attack. Since the term "Pharisee" is so seldom used in Tannaitic literature, the Jews might have had a stronger defense if they had denied that they were the successors of the Pharisees. Instead they accepted the Christian analysis as being correct without analyzing the data accurately. Like Christians they erroneously assumed that the Pharisees had composed all rabbinic literature, and they looked in rabbinic literature for data to refute Christians. From these materials Jews tried to show that the teachings of Jesus against the Pharisees were unfair. In such a large amount of legal literature as there is in the Medieval Jewish collection, it is not hard to find material to support almost any position if a person carefully picks and chooses. In this way Christians and Jews have argued against each other in relationship to the Pharisees on a false basis. Both Jews and Christians should now give up our prejudicial tendencies and analyze Pharisees and Jesus' conflict with them on the basis of available literature in antiquity.[11]

Bear witness against yourselves. Witnessing is a court term. Many cases in court require two or three witnesses to prove a case. In this situation the Pharisees provide the witnesses needed by the prosecution, when the Pharisees themselves are the defendants.

Construct the tombs of the prophets. This pericope is included at this point in the chapter, because it belongs to the same subject--tombs.

[11]H. Merkel, "Jesus und die Pharisäer," NTS 14 (1967/68):194-208, refuted those who have said that Jesus was not really in conflict with the Pharisees but very much like the Pharisees himself. He insisted that Jesus genuinely opposed the Pharisees.

Fill up the measure of your fathers. Before his conversion, Paul persecuted Christians, thinking that by so doing he was filling up the measure of virtue. Later Paul accused the Jews in Judaea who were doing the same things of "filling up the measure of their sins" (1 Thess 2:16). The same Greek term is used here for filling up the measure of sins that is also used for the fulfillment of prophecy.

The sins of the fathers were to descend to the children to the third and fourth generation (Exod 20:5; 34:7; Num 14:18; Deut 5:9). This means that children bore the guilt of their parents. This guilt would accumulate like debts until the account was overdrawn. Jesus here was speaking to the children who inherited the guilt of their fathers and added more to it. It was the Pharisees who were continuing the sins of their forefathers. To be faithful the Pharisees should have been paying off the debts their forefathers accumulated to clear the family and national reputation, but they were not. Instead they were persecuting the prophets of their day, just as their fathers had done in years gone by. They were filling up the measure of sinfulness.

This attack seems not to have been directed toward the Jews in general who, some time in the ancient past, had opposed such prophets as Jeremiah. These famous prophets were not murdered. The reference here seems to have been to ancestors of the Pharisees themselves. These were accused of having murdered prophets. There is no record of Pharisees ever having killed prophets, but they had a murderous history, and some of the people they killed may have been those whom the people considered to be prophets, even though they are now unknown.

The reference may have been to the time of Queen Alexandra, successor of Alexander Jannaeus, who controlled the nation by allowing the Pharisees to do as they pleased, since they had so much influence among the people. This happened less that a century before the time of Jesus. These fathers of the Pharisees had committed their murders fewer than four generations before the contemporaries of Jesus. They reenacted the situation dramatized in the Book of Esther when the Persian king gave the Jews permission to kill any of their enemies that they chose.[12] The difference was that, according to Esther, Jews then killed numerous enemies--all of whom were non-Jews.

During the time of Queen Alexandra, the Pharisees killed many of their enemies--all of whom were Jews. They killed so many people that the national leaders came to Queen Alexandra, pleading for safety and relief. Josephus said,

> After having escaped the dangers of war they were now being killed like cattle at home by their enemies, and there was no one to redress their injuries (Ant 13.412).

These events were probably not forgotten, and the great grand-children of the victims still hated the great grand-children of the ancient Pharisees who killed

---

[12]This event is still celebrated by modern Jews as the Feast of Purim every year.

their ancestors. If these had been the words of Jesus he would not have been the only one to have called the Pharisees insulting names for this behavior. This hatred was not instigated by later Christians or gentiles; it developed within the Jewish community itself.

The quotations from Paul's letters that use similar insulting language were not directed to the Pharisees but either the Jews in general in Judaea or the Jewish Christians in Rome. There are enough similar terms in Matt 23, Rom 2, and 1 Thess 2:17-20 to suggest literary dependence.[13]

The transfer of guilt to heirs was not a unique factor in biblical law. When Roman citizens died the heirs not only received their property and land. They continued the life of the deceased in civil affairs, as well as their legal and social existence. From a legal point of view the fact of death was removed. Maine argued,

> But Ancient Law, it must again be repeated, knows next to nothing of individuals. . . The life of each citizen is not regarded as limited by birth and death; it is a continuation of the existence of his forefathers, and it will be prolonged in the existence of his descendants.[14]

When Jacob negotiated Esau out of his birth right, this was the oldest son's first share of the property. When he tricked Esau out of his blessing, this was probably the family status, position, and other distinctions that continued the existence of his father. They were passed on to Jacob through a legal ritual that had the same force as a written contract. Once the blessing had been given to Jacob it could not be retracted and given instead to Esau. All of this means that the Pharisees of Jesus' day were held responsible for the murders the Pharisees had committed many years earlier.

Snakes, descendants of scorpions. Snakes are not, objectively, descendants of scorpions. Snakes are descendants of snakes, and human beings are neither, but these are not objectively accurate descriptions. They are insults, intended to offend rather than describe. The author not only intended to insult contemporary Pharisees but to insult their ancesters who lived in the time of Queen Alexandra. Christians have called other respectable gentiles "dogs" and "pigs" (Matt 7:6; 2 Peter 2:22; Mark 7:27-28). Jews have called other upper class, male, celibate Jews "harlots" (Matt 21:31-32). Jews have accused Samaritan women of being menstruants from their birth, and Samaritans returned the insults. It is never wise to mistake religious or political insults for descriptive facts. No one should be

---

[13]So also M. D. Goulder, Midrash and Lection in Matthew (London: SPCK, 1974), p. 165.

[14]H. S. Maine, Ancient Law (London, c1901, 17th), pp. 186-90; (U.S.A: Dorset, c1986), pp. 149-51.

surprised or shocked when reading or hearing insults from Jews or Christians involved in adverse discussions. It is a part of the tradition that has continued across the years.

The judgment of Gehenna. Gehenna was initially the Valley of Hinnom, south of Jerusalem. It was the place where Jews offered human sacrifices to pagan gods (Jer 7:30-31). During the Middle Ages at least, it took on extensive theological dimensions. Satan was believed to be the prince of Gehenna.[15] It was identified with Sheol and Hades. Faithful Jews would rejoice (Isa 61:10) when they were delivered from Gehenna.[16] Gehenna is the place of the dead wicked gentiles and Jewish idolaters. Without repentance wicked gentiles and Jewish idolaters would go there and never recover.[17] Idolaters were destined to be "rewarded" in Gehenna which has fire, sulfur, darkness, and gloom,[18] although some sources hold that all Israelites will be forgiven and allowed to enter the Garden of Eden; all gentiles will burn with fire in Gehenna. There is no anger compared with the judgment of Gehenna.[19] Rabbi Akiba has been quoted as saying that when Jews in the Garden of Eden were saying the Kadesh, those Jews in Gehenna who said, "Amen!" would be rescued at once and admitted into the Garden of Eden. Gehenna would open its gates at the brook of Joshua.[20] Gentiles would be burned in Gehenna; Jews would pass through Gehenna without being burned; Jewish transgressors would spend one year in Gehenna before they were raised into the Garden of Eden.[21]

The Garden of Eden is at the Lord's right hand; Gehenna is at his left.[22] There would not be any gentiles in the Garden of Eden.[23] Jewish theology was closely tied to geography. The Garden of Eden was placed within the walls of Jerusalem. All of the righteous Jews of the world would be contained within these walls. Outside the walls was Gehenna. There all dead of the gentiles would be burning in torment. The Garden of Eden and Gehenna were so close to one

---

[15]Buchanan, Redemption, p. 72.

[16]Buchanan, Redemption, p. 77.

[17]Buchanan, Redemption, p. 154.

[18]Buchanan, Redemption, p. 348, 447.

[19]Buchanan, Redemption, p. 476-77, 486.

[20]Buchanan, Redemption p. 405.

[21]Buchanan, Redemption, p. 406, 444-45.

[22]Buchanan, Redemption, p. 551.

[23]Buchanan, Redemption, p. 554.

another that those who were in Gehenna would be able to hear the Jews inside the walls of Jerusalem reciting the Kadesh, and the righteous inside the walls of Jerusalem could hear the wicked crying in torment in Gehenna (Luke 16:19-31). No consideration was given to the size of the areas or the number of people who would be crowded into them.

When Matthew threatened the Pharisees with the tortures of Gehenna, he was associating them with gentiles and idolaters. Jeremiah accused only Jews of the pagan practices at Gehenna, but they were those who had learned the practices from gentiles.

TEXT

Matthew	First Testament
34Because of this I send to you **prophets**, wise men, and scribes. Some of them you kill and crucify; some of them you whip in your synagogues and pursue from city to city,	**From the** sins of her **prophets**, the
35until all the **innocent blood is poured out** upon the land **from the blood of innocent** Abel until the **blood of [innocent]**	iniquity of her priests who **poured out** in her midst **blood of innocent** (Lam 4:13).
Zechariah, son of Barachiah, whom you murdered between the temple and the altar. 36I tell you under oath, all these things will come upon this generation.	The word of Yahowah came to **Zechariah, son of Barachiah**, son of Ido the prophet (Zech 1:1).

COMMENTARY

Because of this. Because the Pharisees had committed so many sins over such a long period of time, the record of sins which had accumulated was being held against the nation, so that the Kingdom could not come. This is the reason God sent prophets, wise men, and scribes. Their role was to add virtue to the treasury of merits and in that way balance the budget.

Prophets, wise men, and scribes. Although Lamentation criticized the prophets and priests of being frauds, Matthew considered them virtuous. This group of professional leaders to which Matthew referred comprised the ones who had been paying off the national debt. It was by their virtue that the demerits in the heavenly record were being cancelled. Prophets in the first century were people trained to compare current events with earlier cycles of time to determine how long Jews still had to wait until the end of the gentile age. Wise men were probably judges or elders--those who had an office or reputation for giving good counsel. Scribes were lawyers, trained in rhetoric and public speech. Josephus said there were many "false" prophets who were predicting deliverance from the Romans right up to the time when the temple burned (War 6.285-87). There had also been prophets, wise men, and scribes in earlier times.

Some of them you kill and crucify. The mass crucifixion, to which Josephus referred, was performed by Alexander Jannaeus who had 800 prominent Jewish leaders crucified on one day. While these men were hanging on crosses, he had their wives and children killed before their eyes (Ant 13.279-80). It is not known whether Alexander Jannaeus was a Pharisee or a Sadducee. This possibility can only be deduced. His father, John Hyrcanus I, was first a Pharisee, but later became a Sadducee (Ant 13.295), so scholars have generally assumed that Hyrcanus's son, Alexander Jannaeus, was also a Sadducee, but Josephus never said to which sect Alexander belonged. If he had chosen to be a Pharisee, and encouraged his mother at his death bed to support this group, then Matthew's accusation that Pharisees had crucified prophets, wise men, and scribes, may have been based on this mass crucifixion of Jews (Ant 13.401-403).

Alexander told his mother that the Pharisees had caused him to come into conflict with the nation. This may mean that there were Pharisees among the 800 who were crucified, and therefore the living Pharisees wanted vengeance. This may mean that Alexander was not a Pharisee, but that is not certain. The fact that the Pharisee, Josephus, failed to mention that Alexander was a member of another sect could be taken as evidence that he was a Pharisee and that Josephus did not want to be associated with him and acknowledge him as a Pharisee. Of the 800 Jewish leaders killed, it is unlikely that they were all members of one sect. Alexander probably killed Sadducees, Pharisees, and Essenes, indiscriminately, on that fateful day when he crucified 800 men and their families. The Pharisees were the most influential of the sects, but they may not have been the only ones who hated Alexander Jannaeus. Jews of Matthew's time may have held this crucifixion against the Pharisees for many years, even though Pharisees themselves hated Alexander for the deed. If he had been a Pharisee, the non-Pharisaic Jews would still have blamed them. In any event the non-Pharisees would have remembered and resented the cruel tortures the Pharisees applied to non-Pharisees after the death of Alexander Jannaeus when his mother was queen.

This analysis is not proof; it is only a deduction; but it is one explanation for the accusation that Pharisees crucified prophets, wise men, and scribes, when crucifixion was a Roman punishment not used by Jews in Jesus' time.

Some of them you whip. This is an echo from the counsel given to the apostles as they were sent out: "In their synagogues they will whip you" (Matt 10:17). In NT times synagogues were evidently used as courts as well as places of worship. Both in Roman and in Jewish courts, in NT times, judges allowed whipping to take place, either as punishment or as a means of forcing a confession. Earlier scripture allowed Jews to be whipped as many as 40 times, according to the decision of the judges (Deut 25:1-3). Rabbis said at least three judges were required to make a decision to whip someone, but Deuteronomy required only one (mSan 1.2). Whipping was done with a person tied to a pole, the chest was bared, and he was whipped with a leather whip (mMak 3.12).

"When they pursue you in this city flee to the next" (Matt 10:23). Early Christians probably suffered some of the humiliation expressed here. The Pharisees were accused of inflicting this abuse. Matthew argued that instead of benefiting from the merit of these good people, the Pharisees added still more sins to that accumulated by their ancestors. Prior to his conversion Paul was one of those zealous Pharisees who considered himself to be fulfilling God's will when he persecuted Christians (Gal 1:13-17; Col 3:5; Acts 23:6). Paul later complained about the Jews in Judaea who killed both Jesus and the prophets, and drove the Christians out (1 Thess 2:15). Pharisees probably treated other Jews of different sects the same way.

Until the blood of [innocent] Zechariah. There were two Zechariahs who could be candidates for this description. There was a Zechariah, son of Jehoiada, the priest. At a time when the people were worshiping idols, Zechariah criticized them. In response the people stoned Zechariah to death in the court of the temple (2 Chron 24:17-22). This Zechariah was a righteous priest and he was killed in the temple area, but his father's name was not Barachiah.

There was another Zechariah who was called "the son of Baris" by Josephus. Baris is closer to Barachaiah than Jehoiada, but it is not perfect, either (War 4.335-344). During the last days of the war (ca. I.A. 69), when the zealots had control of the temple, zealots accused Zechariah of betraying the state to the Romans. This was in response to his criticism of the zealots. He was tried in court and found innocent or righteous. zealots really accused him for two reasons: 1) because he opposed their cause and 2) because he was rich, and they wanted to confiscate his wealth.

When the court failed to reach their desired verdict, two zealots took the law into their own hands and killed Zechariah there in the temple area. Therefore he qualified as one whose blood had been shed between the sanctuary and the altar. Both Zechariahs had their blood poured out in the temple area; both were righteous. The son of Baris was closer to the time when Matthew may have composed his gospel than the time of Zechariah son of Jehoiada and his memory would have been more vivid in the mind of the author. Both would qualify as distant contrasts to the innocent Abel. The Zechariah reported in Chronicles, which now is classified as the last book in the Bible, can be contrasted in time with Abel who is reported in the first book.[24] On the other hand the Zechariah

---

[24]This is a suggestion made by D. A. Hagner, Word Biblical Commentary: Matthew 14-28 (Dallas: Word Books, c1995), pp. 676-77.

who was killed by zealots, could also be contrasted in time from the first century I.A. with the innocent Abel, shed at the beginning of the human race--a long time earlier. Neither one can be absolutely identified as the person about whom Matthew spoke.

This unit is an interruption to a long harangue against the Pharisees, but this is not directly said of the Pharisees. This passage may have been added after 70 I.A., but that is not a required solution. In any event it was put in the position it is because it was of the same tenor as the harangue against the Pharisees. There is no external evidence that the people who murdered either of the Zechariahs were Pharisees, but the subject was murder of innocent people, so some editor put it in the same category as these other evil events.

Will come upon this generation. Since iniquities accumulated against the third and fourth generation in the treasury of merits and demerits, either Jesus or Matthew or both thought that the sins had just about reached their limit. This very generation would have to pay them, just as the first generation of Jews in Babylon had to pay for the sins of their fathers.

TEXT

37Jerusalem, Jerusalem, the one who kills the prophets
and stones the ones sent to her,
how many times I wanted to gather your children
in the same manner as a bird gathers her nestlings under her wings,
but you did not want [it done].

Matthew	First Testament
38Look! your **house will be left a wilderness**	If you do not obey these words, I hereby swear, said Yahowah, that this **house will be a wilderness** (Jer 22:5).
	Zion **will become a wilderness,** Jerusalem, a desolation (Isa 64:9).
39for I tell you. You will not **see me** from now on until you say,	If I find favor in the eyes of Yahowah, then he will bring me back and **let me see** both it [the ark of the contract] and his dwelling (2 Sam 15:25).
	Please, Yahowah, save, if you will;

Blessed is he who comes in the name of the Lord.	please, Yahowah, make us succeed, if you will. **Blessed is he who comes in the name of Yahowah** (Ps 118:26).

COMMENTARY

The one who kills the prophets. This may be a complaint against the zealots who killed Zechariah or those Pharisees who killed numerous Jewish leaders during the time of Queen Alexandra. Josephus reported Zechariah as a righteous man, but he did not say he was a prophet. He said, however, that there were many prophets in Jerusalem right up to the time when the temple burned who promised that Jews would soon be released. Those who killed Zechariah, of course, were all killed in the war. Pharisees were also accused as those who killed and crucified prophets (Matt 23:34). This poem was probably composed separately from the harangue against the Pharisees and added here because it also deals with murdering prophets. Matthew regularly organized his materials so that the reports dealing with the same subject were put together.

Another Jewish poet said,

Blow the trumpet in Zion,
the holy trumpet of Jubilee.
Stand up on high, Jerusalem,
and see your children gathered
from the East and the West
by the Lord (PssSol 11.1, 3).

This passage may also have been intended to remind the reader of the time David fled from Jerusalem when Absalom attempted to overthrow David and become king. David crossed over the Kidron stream to the Mount of Olives and the wilderness, weeping (2 Sam 15:23-30). This passage in Matthew pictures Jesus weeping over Jerusalem as he left it, expecting possibly to return, as David did.

Stoning the ones sent to her. The passive voice was used with the verb "sent." This was to avoid the blasphemous use of the sacred name. It meant "Stoning the ones God sent to her."

I wanted to gather your children. This suggests that Jesus was in Jerusalem many times, trying to organize its citizens, but they were not interested. We do not know how many times Jesus was in the holy city. The only report is the one where he entered triumphantly, riding on a donkey during his parousia.

When the great Jubilee trumpet sounded (Isa 27:13), the Lord was expected to gather together all of the Jews and Israelites that had been driven off the land and scattered among the gentiles (Deut 30:3-4; Neh 1:9; Ps 106:47; 107:3;

Isa 43:5; 54:7; 56:8; 66:18; Jer 29:14; 31:8, 10; 32:37; Ezek 16:37; 20:34, 41; 28:23; 29:13; 36:24; 37:21; 39:27; PssSol 11.1, 3).

This poem (Matt 23:37) may have been a claim made after Jerusalem had been destroyed by the Romans. Some later Christian may have thought that Jesus could have prevented this if the people had only followed him when he was trying to gather them together. One of the expectations of the Messiah was that he would gather the exiles together from all of the countries where they had been driven and bring them all back to Jerusalem. Jews asked,

> Why should the messianic king come? What will he have to do [for Israelites]? He will gather the Jewish exiles (GenR 98.9).

Look! your house will be left [a wilderness]. The word "a wilderness" does not occur in Sinaiticus and several other texts. Omitted, this might mean, "Your house will be abandoned," meaning abandoned by God. (See War 6.288-309; 2 Bar 8.2; Ezek 8:6). The word "wilderness" may have been added later to concur with Jer 22:5 (leh-khahr-báh, לחרבה) or it may have been original. If the word is included, this is the warning Jeremiah gave to the king of Judah in the name of the Lord. He warned him to judge fairly, avoiding exploitation of the widows and orphans, and the shedding of innocent blood. This was placed here in relationship to the innocent blood of Zechariah that had been shed. If this pericope had been composed after the fall of Jerusalem in 70 I.A., the author of this midrash thought that the Lord had allowed the temple, "the house," to be abandoned because of the wicked deed of the zealots to Zechariah.[25] Like the previous paragraph that reported the fate of Zechariah, this comment may have been made after Zechariah had been killed. Its composition may also have been made after the temple had been burned and Jerusalem had fallen, but the latter possibility is not a certainty. The Dead Sea Scrolls show that there were Jews of NT times who thought the temple at Jerusalem was defiled and no longer a suitable place of worship. They could have predicted its destruction, or even thought of it as a wilderness while it was standing.

The defilement of the temple also reminded Jews of the event nearly 200 years earlier when Antiochus Epiphanes defiled the temple so that pious Jews had to abandon it, and they assumed that God also abandoned it. They could not worship in this defiled temple for 3 1/2 years. During this time it was left desolate, and the defilement was called an "abomination of desolation" (Isa 64:9: Dan 12:11). Although the desolation of the temple was bad news for the Jews of NT times, it was also good news. It assured them that they were only 3 1/2 years away from the end of this wicked era.

---

[25] A. Plummer, An Exegetical Commentary on the Gospel according to St. Matthew (London: Stock, 1909), pp. 324-25, on the basis of Enoch 89 thought the "house" was Jerusalem rather than the temple.

When David fled from Jerusalem in the way of the wilderness, Zadok and all of the priests brought the ark of the contract and came with David, bringing the ark back into the wilderness, away from Jerusalem. David blessed the priests and told them to return the ark to the city (2 Sam 15:24-29). All of these historical events should be considered in determining the message of this passage.

You will not see me from now on. Van der Kwaak takes the words hé-ohs ahn (ἕως ἄν) to be conditional. Instead of meaning "until" they should be understood as "unless."[26] He also thought that the "many times" (ποσάκις, poh-sa-kis) implied that Jesus had visited Jerusalem many more times than have been reported in the gospels.[27]

This verse is clearly out of place. If these are really the words of Jesus, he seems to have made this complaint early in his ministry, threatening not to enter Jerusalem again until the Jerusalemites recognized him as the Messiah by saying "Blessed is he who comes in the name of the Lord,"[28] but according to Matthew this was already done in Matt 21:9!

When David fled from Jerusalem he sent the priests with the ark of the contract back to the city, saying that he would not see it again unless he found favor in the eyes of Yahowah and would be returned to the city (2 Sam 15:25-26). This verse may have been placed here to parallel David's departure from Jerusalem. He was soon returned after that experience.

These three verses (Matt 23:37-39) seem composite. The pronouns and verbs are confused. Jesus first addressed Jerusalem directly, then changed the pronoun to the third person, "sent to her." Then he reported that he wanted to gather "your"(s.) children but "you"(pl.) did not want [it done].

Garland placed the texts of 1 Thess 2:15-16 alongside those of Matt 23 in the following way to show their relationship:

1 Thessalonians	Matthew
They killed both the Lord Jesus and the prophets.	killing the prophets (vv. 31, 34)
They persecuted us out.	Killed, crucified, scourged, and persecuted from city to city (v.34)

---

[26]H. Van der Kwaak, "Die Klage über Jerusalem (Matth. XXIII 37-39)," NovT 8 (1966):169-70. D. C. Allison, "Matt. 23:39 = Luke 13:35b as a Conditional Prophecy," JSNT 18 (1983):75-84, made the same basic interpretation, saying that when the people bless him then the Messiah will come.

[27]Van der Kwaak, "Die Klage," p. 157.

[28]Van der Kwaak, "Der Klage," pp. 165-66, concurred that the one who was coming would have been the Messiah.

They displeased God and opposed men by hindering the preaching of the Gentiles.	Cf. 23:13, they shut the kingdom to men.
They fill up the measure of sins.	Fill up the measure of your fathers! (v. 32)
God's wrath has come upon them.	All righteous blood upon you (v. 36 cf. vv. 37-39)

MATTHEW AND THE PHARISEES

There are many puzzling things about Matt 23. It is by far the most angry text in the Gospel according to Matthew. It is directed--not against the Jews in general, but--against the Pharisees by some other Jewish sect or some other Jew. There is an apparent textual relationship between Matt 23 and 1 Thess 2, which has traditionally been accepted as a genuine letter of Paul. How did all of this come about? No one can do more than conjecture the historical background of this chapter, but the following data should be considered:

1) Jesus was in conflict with the Pharisees over the admission of repentant tax collectors and other prominent businessmen who had become wealthy through their associations with the Romans. This is apparent in the chreias and the parables, which are the most reliable units of literature for determining the teachings of Jesus. They are clever, but not basically name calling or offensive. They picture the Pharisees as voluntary antitypes of Esau, as people who come down from the temple on the Day of Atonement unforgiven, and as those who had blasphemed the Holy Spirit.

2) There are editorial statements that have been added to some of the chreias related to Jesus that were probably added by Matthew. This suggests that the person who organized the Gospel according to Matthew did not like the Pharisees and added insults to Jesus' sayings against the Pharisees.

3) The most severe, name-calling attack against the Pharisees is found in chapter 23. Although it is attributed to Jesus it is more coherent with the editorial additions in the rest of the gospel than it is to the chreias and parables of Jesus. This attack is a nit-picking, legalistic attack that is not related to the tax collectors and sinners. It is an offensive attack against the Pharisees in general.

4) The behavior of the Pharisees in the nation of Israel during the time of Queen Alexandra was so vicious and murderous that anyone related to the victims of their murders would hate them and would need to express hostility in some such literary way as this.

5) The basis of this chapter might have been written any time within the fourth generation after the Pharisees had committed their abominations during the first century B.I.A. During this period the descendants of those Pharisees who were friends of Queen Alexandra would be held responsible for the sins of their ancestors. Instead they were filling up the measure of their ancestors' sins. This document may have been written before Jesus began his mission; it was certainly

composed before I.A. 70 when the temple was burned, because the author still discussed parts of the temple by which it was possible to take vows.

6) Christians were being persecuted by Pharisees before 40 I.A. One of these Pharisees was the Apostle Paul. When he wrote 1 Thessalonians he evidently had this anti-Pharisaic document before him. While he was still a Pharisee he probably had learned of the anti-Pharisaic manuscript. At that time he probably would have wanted it suppressed, but later he employed it for a different purpose. Like Paul, Matthew may have updated this document to make it apply to the experiences of early Christians.

7) Matthew tried to organize his materials so that materials related to one subject were placed in one section of the gospel. Jesus actually was in conflict with the Pharisees, so Matthew felt free to add further insults to the words of Jesus. He also took the occasion to add this early anti-Pharisaic document to his gospel.

8) This is not an anti-Jewish or anti-Semitic document. It reflects an inner family conflict. Even those who updated the essay to apply it to Christian experiences were themselves Jewish Christian editors. During the first century I.A. all Christians were considered Jewish sectarians. They had been reared and trained in Jewish sectarianism. They learned from other Jewish sectarians how to debate with other Jewish sects.

The Greek word for sectarians is hai-reh-tis-taí (αἱρετισταί), a word that has become anglicized as "heretics." Each sect thought of itself as the true Israel and all other Jews as sectarians or heretics. Those who called the Pharisees insulting names did not think for a moment that the Pharisees were the true Jews; they thought that they were. When they insulted the Pharisees they were only insulting the heretics. They would have been horrified to be told that they were anti-Jewish when they insulted Pharisaic heretics.

All of this took place prior to general, deep conflicts between Jews and gentile Christians. This division began with Bar Cochba's abuse of Christians during the second Jewish Roman war (I.A. 132-35). At that time Bar Cochba punished severely those Jews who did not deny and defame Jesus as the Messiah (Justin, Apology 1.31, 6; HE 4.8, 4). When Bar Cochba's cause had been lost, Christians who had been tortured dissociated themselves from their torturers. This, however, happened many years after Matt 23 had been written.

CONCLUSIONS

The conclusions reached here are not above criticism. Like every other analysis of Matt 23, this analysis involves a lot of conjecture. Each reader should judge for himself or herself the most likely solution of these problems. The available data is given here for consideration, together with possible conclusions.

CHAPTER TWENTY-FOUR

TEXT

24:1Then Jesus left the temple, and he went away, and his disciples came to him to show him the buildings of the temple. 2He answered and said to them, "Do you see all these things? I tell you under oath that there will not be left here one stone upon another that will not be destroyed."

Matthew	Fourth Ezra
3While he was seated on the Mount of Olives, the disciples came to him [while they were] alone, saying, "**When will these things be, and** what is **the sign** of your public appearance and the end of the age?"	**When these things happen, and the signs** which I showed you before take place, then my son will be revealed, whom you saw as a man ascending . . . he will stand on the top of Mount Zion (4 Ezra 13.32-35).

TECHNICAL DETAILS

Matthew began this chapter in continuity with the previous chapter. Matt 23 concluded with Jesus lamenting over Jerusalem, and predicting that the temple would be left desolate. Chapter 24 began with Jesus and his disciples on the Mount of Olives, overlooking the temple area in Jerusalem and with Jesus predicting that one stone of the temple would not be left on another. The corner stone mentioned at the end of chapter 23 suggested the stones that would not be left one on top of the other.

COMMENTARY

I tell you under oath. Berger has correctly noted that the expression, "Amen, I say to you," is an expression used in apocalyptic literature by people in authority and as oath expressions. Associated expressions are, "I command you, " or "I hereby testify to you."[1] The promise given by God to Abraham in LXX Gen 22:17 was reexpressed in the Testament of Abraham as, "Amen, I say to you" (TAbr 8.7; cf. also 20.1-2). Rabbis said the word "amen" was an oath term as in Num 5:22.

Not be one stone left upon another. This sounds as if it were prophecy after the fact of the destruction of the temple in 70 I.A., but there is another possibility. In the temple scroll, found among the Dead Sea Scrolls, is reported the expectation that the temple would be destroyed completely and rebuilt square. Rabbis thought the servant of Isaiah was also the Messiah (TgJon Isa 52.13), and that he would build the temple (TgJon Isa 53.5). It is difficult to estimate how many Jews of Jesus' time had similar expectations. It is possible that Jesus also held this belief, although it is far from certain. Tannaitic Rabbis said that the temple was given conditionally.

> The Lord told Solomon, **This house which you are building, if you walk in my statutes, practice my traditions, and keep all of my commandments to walk in them, then I will uphold my word with you which I spoke to David your father** (1 Kings 6:12). But if not, **This house will be high, [but] everyone who passes will be astonished and whistle. They will say, Why has Yahowah acted this way to this land and this temple** (1 Kings 9:8; Mek Amalek 4.136-41).

The temple at Jerusalem had been started about 20 B.I.A. by Herod the Great. It was completed during the seventh decade I.A. Although it was much larger and more beautiful than Solomon's temple, Jews hated Herod, and many refused to worship there because they thought it was pagan. That is probably why some Jews thought it must be replaced. This did not mean, however, that they expected history to come to an end at the same time, as Patte thought,[2] but it meant that Jews were expecting a new age with a new contract and a new temple. The idea that Jesus or any other messianic pretender would anticipate the destruction of Jerusalem by a foreign power is ridiculous. Why would anyone lead a national movement with the goal of national destruction? Jews were

---

[1]K. Berger, "Zur Geschichte der Einleitungsformel 'Amen, ich sage euch,'" ZNW 63 (1972):45-75.

[2]D. Patte, The Gospel according to Matthew (Philadelphia: Fortress Press, c1946; 1987), p. 334.

looking forward to victory and liberation. They knew, of course, that this would involve a bitter war, like the one the Hasmoneans fought against the Syrian Greeks, but, like the Hasmoneans, they expected to win. They thought the tribulation was worth the risk.

While he was seated on the Mount of Olives. The Mount of Olives was directly east of the temple mount. This picture was taken from the temple mount facing east. Jesus and his disciples were reportedly seated somewhere on this hill, overlooking Jerusalem. The ancient road leading to the temple area from the Mount of Olives is seen at the right of the picture. This is the road Jesus would have taken as he walked from the Mount of Olives to Jerusalem.

[When they were] alone. The most important things that happened between Jesus and his apostles happened when they were together, alone. It was then that Jesus taught the apostles the parables and other teachings that they conserved in chreias. Like fishers of men, they went out into the cities and told of the Kingdom possibilities and plans to Jews singly and in groups. Then they returned to Jesus and reported their success and adventures. They answered his questions and discussed problems with him. It was in small groups where the apostles learned Jesus' hopes and plans. This was just one of many group meetings.

When will these things happen? Ever since Jews lost sovereign control to the Romans,[3] they looked forward to the time when they would again gain control of the promised land. They studied the cycles of time. They tried to match the order of events in their own time with those of an earlier time, especially those times when Israel was prospering.

Josephus was the famous historian who wrote about the events that happened to the Jews during the first century I.A., but he omitted the period that would be the most important to historians today for explaining how and when things happened just before the ministries of John the Baptist and Jesus. He interrupted his history after Herod's son Archelaus had been deposed and his territory turned into a Roman province. At this time Judas of Galilee led a rebellion, which Josephus mentioned (War 2.117-118). He then told of the sects of the Jews (War 2.119-166). He summarized the events of 20 years in one short paragraph (War 2.167-68). Then, instead of returning to the same period, he continued his story (War 2.169) during the last of the reign of Pilate (26-36 I.A), after the crucifixion of Jesus. If we only knew more about the 20 years Josephus omitted, we might deduce the events that Jesus and his apostles were studying more accurately. It was during the unreported 20 years that John the Baptist and Jesus began their activity.

Approximately three years before the Last Supper, there must have been an event that seemed to many to be the antitype of the defilement of the temple by Antiochus Epiphanes, because the apostles expected a new Hanukkah after the Passover they were attending when Jesus was crucified. It may have been an event like the one described in a chreia when Pilate mixed the blood of the Galileans with their sacrifices (Luke 13:1-3). The excitement of the apostles was high at the last Passover. They must have had some reason for thinking they were nearing the last days of the tribulation. They were within the 3 1/2 year period after the defilement of the temple. So they were asking Jesus, when, specifically, would these anticipated things happen.

Your public appearance. The word translated here "public appearance" is pahr-oo-seé-ah (παρουσία). It was used in the Hellenistic, secular world to describe the arrival and appearance of a king. Like Saul and David, Jesus was probably anointed in secret at his baptism, and he was recognized by some Jews as the new Messiah. He was a king in hiding. His followers were looking forward to the time when he would function openly as a king on his throne from Jerusalem. This public appearance would be his parousia. Since the primary purpose of Jesus' program was to change the status of the nation among the nations of the world, the open conflict with Rome seemed inevitable. The question the apostles asked at this meeting was always at the forefront of their thinking. It was the highest topic on their list of priorities.

---

[3]This began with the time Pompey entered the temple in 63 B.I.A. and was completed with the taxation of Quirinius in 6-7 I.A.

The expression "second coming" is not found in the gospels. It would have been out of place anytime during the life of Jesus. This appeared first in the works of Justin (Trypho 40; Apol 1.52). During the time of Jesus the expression, parousia, did not refer to a second coming but rather the event expected to take place when the Messiah, who had been organizing a movement underground, came out in the open with his threats against the enemy power. For Jesus, that would have been his entrance into Jerusalem, antityping the prophecy of Zechariah.

The end of the age. The expression, "the end of the age," was used originally to describe the last of the Greek age of rule over Palestine. It was later used to anticipate the antitype of the end of the common era under the control of Antiochus Epiphanes. That end began when Antiochus defiled the temple. There followed a 3 1/2 year period between the desolation of the temple (ca. 168 B.I.A.) until the temple was rededicated by Judas the Maccabee (ca. 164 B.I.A.). This was not the end of time or the world as Patte, Walvoord, Plummer, and others supposed.[4] It was the beginning of the end of the pagan age and the beginning of the holy age when Jews would again have their own national leader and were free to worship in their own temple that was not under foreign control.

TEXT

[4]In reply, Jesus said to them, "Watch out lest anyone lead you astray, [5]for many will come in my name, saying, 'I am the Messiah,' and they will lead many astray. [6]You are about to hear wars and reports of wars. Watch out that you do not become disturbed,

Matthew	First Testament
for **it is necessary** for [all these	But there is a God in heaven who reveals mysteries, who has made clear to King Nebuchadnezzar **what things are necessary** at **the end** of the days (LXX Dan 2:28).
things] to **take place**,	God in heaven reveals mysteries and he will make known to King Nebuchadnezzar what **will be** in the last days (MT Dan 2:28).

[4]A. Plummer, An Exegetical Commentary on the Gospel according to St.Matthew (London: Stock, 1909), p. 329; D. Patte, The Gospel according to Matthew (Philadelphia: Fortress Press, c1987), p. 334, 336; J. F. Walvoord, "Christ's Olivet Discourse on the End of the Age. Signs of the End of the Age," BibSac 128 (1971):316-26.

	A great God has made known to the king what **will be** after this (Dan 2:44).
but **the end**	How long until **the end** of the fantasies (Dan 12:6)?
is not yet. 7**Nation** will rise up **against nation**	In those times there was no peace for the one going out or the one coming in, for there were great disturbances over every inhabitant of the lands, and they were cut into pieces, **nation against nation**, and city against city (2 Chron 15:5-6).
and **kingdom against kingdom**. There will be famines and earth- quakes everywhere. 8All these things are the beginning of the birth pangs. 9Then they will turn you over **for** **torture**, and they will kill you. You	Each man will engage in war with his brother and each man with his neighbor, city against city, and **kingdom against kingdom** (Isa 19:2). There will be a time of **tribulation** (Dan 12:1).
will be hated by **all the gentiles** because of my name.	**All the nations** will come from surrounding areas, and they will congregate there . . . I will sit there and I will judge **all the** surrounding **nations** (Joel 4:11-13). Yahowah will scatter you among **all the peoples**, from one end of the earth to the other (Deut 28:64). At the time of the end the king of the south will advance toward him, but the king of the north will storm him with cavalry, chariots, and many ships. He will enter countries, and he will come into the glorious land. He will flood in and pass through.

[10]Then many **will stumble.**"	Myriads **will stumble** (Dan 11:40-41).

COMMENTARY

The warnings given here are the kind people might expect if they were doing something offensive and aggressive. People sometimes hate and kill innocent people, but it is not the normal expectation. The acquisition of extensive hatred usually requires notoriety caused by action that involves many people. This, however, is the expectation taught as doctrine among Jews of NT times, because these were the kinds of events that took place during the 3 1/2 year period between the defilement of the temple and its restoration under the leadership of Judas the Maccabee. Taylor argued that the persecutions described in Matt 24:9-13 must reflect the persecutions of Nero,[5] but that is not decisive. Christians and Jews did not wait for Nero to become revolutionaries. From the time of Herod's death, at least, Jews, and later Christians, were involved in sabotage and guerrilla warfare against Rome. Rome dealt with these in various ways, but normally in ways Jews and Christians called persecution.

In reply Jesus said. Literally, "having answered, Jesus said" (ah-poh-krí-thays ho Yay-soós áy-pen, ἀποκριθεὶς ὁ 'Ιησοῦς εἶπεν). This is a Greek way of translating the Hebrew, "he answered and said" (ענה ואמר, ah-náh wuh-ah-már). This Hebrew idiom does not require answering anyone. Mark probably rendered the same Hebrew, "he began to say" (áyrx-ah-toh lég-ayn, ἤρξατο λέγειν) (Mark 13:5).

In my name. At first sight that would seem to mean that some would say, "I am Jesus," or "I am sent by Jesus to be the Messiah." There is a more likely possibility. It would presume that Jesus accepted the name "Messiah." He had already been anointed. Anyone other than Jesus who claimed messiahship was usurping a name that belonged to Jesus, because that was a title and designation that was reserved only for him.

I am the Messiah. There were leaders of rebels who appeared before the time of Jesus, and many came after the time of Jesus, each claiming to be the Messiah, but Josephus did not report either that they came in Jesus' name or that they were messiahs. One of them gathered troops of Egyptian Jews, led them across the border from Egypt into the wilderness. He promised to show them great signs of deliverance there, but Roman forces interfered with their designs. Another promised to make the walls of Jerusalem fall before him the way Jericho's walls fell for Joshua, but the Romans also stopped him (Acts 21:37-38; War 2.259, 433-56;

[5]J. Taylor, "'The Love of Many Will Grow Cold': Matt 24:9-13 and the Neronian Persecution," RB 96 (1989):352-57.

6.285-87). Rabbi Akiba thought Bar Cochba was the Messiah (pTa'an 4.7 #68d), and Hagner correctly held that Bar Cochba is the only one reported to have made a claim to messiahship.[6] He claimed that he was the Messiah, and he led a war for 3 1/2 years to obtain the right to sit on the throne at Jerusalem and rule the promised land. Other leaders were not actually called messiahs in any extant literature, but they acted as Messiahs. They had the same goals and methodology that Bar Cochba had. These were the people about which Jesus spoke. After 70 I.A., and especially after 135 I.A., all of these attempts had failed, and the Jewish and Christian believers had good reason to question the counsel of other Messiahs.

You will hear about wars. Broer correctly said that the time of the mission of the disciples (Matt 10:23; 23:34) and the beginning of the woes are the same time.[7] These were all events that were expected to occur before the end. If Jesus had not thought that he was living within the last 3 1/2 years of the old age he would not have sent the apostles out to prepare everyone for the end of that age. All of these events predicted in Matt 24 were experienced during the Maccabean Rebellion. Jews of NT times thought they were living in the same part of the cycle of time. Since the 3 1/2 year period, known as the "tribulation" or "the birth pangs of the Messiah," was one of serious military conflict between Judas the Maccabee and the Syrian Greeks, later Jews were prompted to think every time there was a war that the defeat of the Romans was at hand. This was one of the signs that they were in the same place in the cycle of time as Judas was just before the first Hanukkah. The medieval Rabbi Abina said, "If you see the kingdoms at war, one against the other, watch for the footsteps of the Messiah" (GenR 42.4). It was when other nations were distracted with international conflicts in other geographical areas that Jews took the opportunity to rebel. The Matthean message cautioned against such temptations.

It is necessary. Jews of NT times believed events in history were predestined. God had designed everything to fall in a certain sequence. Just as spring followed winter, and autumn followed summer, so historical events were destined to fit into a cycle in a certain pre-arranged order. The way Jews could tell what was going to happen next was by studying earlier cycles of time to learn the details.

Beginning of the birth pangs. "Birth pangs" was the title given to the 3 1/2 year war fought between the Hasmoneans and the Greeks. It was also called the "tribulation" or "the fantasies," referring to the fantastically wicked things that Antiochus did to the Jews between the time of the defilement of the temple by

---

[6]D. A. Hagner, Word Biblical Commentary: Matthew 14-28 (Dallas: Word Books, c1995), pp. 690-91.

[7]I. Broer, "Redaktionsgeschichtliche Aspekte von Mt 24:1-28." NovT 35 (1993):226.

Antiochus IV and the rededication of the temple by Judas the Maccabee.[8] This was the period that finally came to an end with the restoration of the promised land to the Jews. Later generations of Jews and Christians who thought they were nearing the end of the gentile age expected events to take place similar to those that happened during that typological period. The author of this apocalypse cautioned his readers that wars, famines, and eruptions of nature were signs, to be sure, but they were only signs of the beginning of this 3 1/2 year period. Believers still had some time to go before the temple would be cleansed, and the kingdom would come. During this time believers should not do anything rash.[9] Jesus himself watched for other signs that he trusted, such as the prophecy of Ezek 47 being fulfilled by fig trees producing ripe fruit out of season. Jews should not engage in warfare until they were sure that God was directing the battle.

They will turn you over for torture. This is a practice that was often followed in ancient courts. Whenever one lawyer thought a defendant or witness was lying, he might ask the judge to apply torturing practices upon him or her. This meant whipping the witness or putting the witness on the rack to be tortured until he or she confessed. Herod the Great often put people on the rack when he was suspicious of them for some reason. This was the practice the divine judge reportedly applied to Job. Early Christians were often taken to court, where they might be forced to take oaths to pagan deities. If they refused they were assumed to be lying. Their refusal to take oaths evoked severe punishment, torture, and even death. The promise that they would be turned over to torture meant they would be taken to court and accused. This torture was a part of the tribulation promised by Dan 12:1. The same word that is here translated "torture" is often rendered "tribulation." These are synonyms. In Daniel the time of tribulation or torture was the Hasmonean Revolt which lasted 3 1/2 years before the temple was cleansed.

---

[8]Plummer, Matthew, pp. 330-31, correctly said that the Greek used here can just mean "pains," without the connotation that birth would follow. The context of this term in relationship to Dan 7 makes it clear that these pains were the bad news that preceded the good news. Things had to get this bad before they could get better.

[9]There is no Matthean parallel in chapter 24 for Mark 13:9-13. This is paralleled in Matthew 10:17-22. Many scholars, like Thompson, "Historical Perspective," presume that Mark was the earliest gospel, so they have to explain why Matthew would have taken this unit from Mark and placed it in chapter 10. They usually agree that Matthew was a good editor, and fit it into a place where it was more coherent. Actually, it would have been very difficult for Matthew to have taken a verse of poetry, which Mark included in his prose account, and composed an entire 14 verse poem around it that matched the meter and content as well as Matthew is thought to have done.

In most of the synoptic parallels the evidence could go either way, judging from the individual pericopae alone. Here, however, the evidence all points to the priority either of Matthew or a source that Matthew copied without change. This does not solve the synoptic problem, but it points up one of the problems with the two source hypothesis.

You will be hated by all the gentiles. There were many gentiles in Palestine, most of them concentrated in certain cities--Tiberias, the Decapolis, Gaza, and Caesarea. Whenever there was any kind of conflict between the Romans and the Jews in Palestine, these gentiles could be counted on to side with the Romans. They were called "sojourners" in the Book of Revelation. Nationalistic Jews thought of them as subversive forces within the nation. If a Jewish insurrection should break out, these gentiles would hate the Jews and try to sabotage them. This is the most probable identification of the gentiles who would hate Palestinian Jews, but there are other possibilities. Judah was an active party in international commerce and military events.

This may be a reference to the gathering of the nations at the Kidron Valley to fight with the Jews there. This great battle is anticipated by Ezekiel (Ezek 39), Zechariah (Zech 14:1-15), and Joel (Joel 3 [M 4]). The hated nations probably do not include Israel, as Stanton suggested.[10] See further 4 Ezra 7.37; 2 Bar 72, and 1 Enoch 62. Because there were hostile relationships among various Jewish sects in NT and other times does not mean that negative statements made to some Jews can be applied to all. It is necessary first to check all of the FT passages used in their contexts before determining whether the anger is directed to the Jews in general, the gentiles in general, or only certain sects of Jews or Christians.

Many will stumble. The Greek skahn-dah-lis-tháy-son-tai (*σκανδαλισθήσονται*) renders the Hebrew yi-kásh-ay-loo (יכשלו), **will stumble**, but the Hebrew is rab-bóht (רבות), rather than rab-beém (רבים), **many**, and means "myriads, tens of thousands," rather than "many," as the LXX rendered it. This is an easy confusion and mistranslation. Most of those who stumbled and fell were not Jews, although the battles took place in Palestine between the Egyptians and the Syrian Greeks (Dan 11:40-41). At that time there were wars and rumors of war, but Antiochus III finally overthrew the Egyptians and took control over Palestine.

Matthew, however, used this intertext in a way that differed from that of Daniel. He took the LXX translation of "many" rather than the Masoretic text of "myriads," and, instead of warring superpowers, he used it to refer to the Jews who compromised and submitted to the gentile rule. Those who stumbled and fell were believers who might go astray from their traditional faithfulness. Matthew seems to have understood this "stumbling" to mean they became unfaithful and betrayed one another, but that was probably not the meaning of the report in Daniel (Dan 11:41). A civil war or a war that takes place on the land of the participants will have certain predictable events. There will be hardship, heroism, and sabotage. People who once were enthusiastic will become discouraged and retreat. There is always a certain amount of plundering and profiteering. People can successfully break more laws than usual without getting caught.

---

[10]G. N. Stanton, "The Gospel of Matthew and Judaism," BJRUL 66 (1983-84):275.

TEXT

They will betray one another and hate one another. [11]Many false prophets will arise and lead many astray. [12]Because lawlessness will be increased, the love of the many will grow cold, [13]but the one who endures to the end will be saved. [14]This gospel of the kingdom will be proclaimed in all the [Roman] world as a testimony to the gentiles.

COMMENTARY

They will betray one another. These were the people who would stumble. They were believers who were normally faithful, but under the crises described, they would give up their loyalty. They would betray one another to the enemy; their love for "the many," i.e., the Christian community to which they belonged, would grow cold as lawlessness increased. As in other critical situations, there would be a few who remained faithful in the midst of lawlessness. These were like the ones marked with a cross on their foreheads (Ezek 9:1-5) or the followers of the Lamb (Rev 14:1-5). These would be saved.

The term "saved" was used by mystery cults as a synonym for membership (Diogenes Laertius 6.59). Those who were members were saved. That may be part of the meaning of being saved here. It may mean that these are the ones who were faithful through persecution and constitute the faithful remnant. Even if they were killed they would be raised as citizens of the reestablished community. In a context of war, however, it may mean those who survive all of these crises will be saved and permitted to live in the new Kingdom of Heaven after all of these birth pangs were over.

This gospel of the kingdom. From the Babylonian captivity in the sixth century B.I.A. the gospel that was sent to Jerusalem was that Darius the Persian king was about to conquer Babylon and when he did, he would release all of the Babylonian Jews to return to the promised land, free from foreign rule. Jews probably knew this, because they were involved in a plot with Darius to arrange a surprise take-over of Babylon during a feast when Babylonians were drunk and were not prepared to defend the city. This plan required careful intelligence work in Babylon before the event took place. The plot was good news to Jerusalem and from the Jews in Babylon; it was bad news for the Babylonians.

This gospel was the one proclaimed in NT times, when Rome ruled the Mediterranean world from Spain to India. Some scholars assume that the word this makes the reference indicate the document Matthew was writing,[11] and they may be right. This gospel of the kingdom may be a subtle allusion to the

---

[11]R. H. Gundry, Matthew (Grand Rapids: Eerdmans, 1994), p. 480; T. Brodie, "Fish, Temple Tithe, and Remission: The God-based Generosity of Deuteronomy 14-15 as one Component of Matt 17:22-18:35," RB 99 (1992):699-700.

reference from Deut 28:58: **"If you do not take care to perform all the words of this Torah which are written in this book . . ."** (cf. Deut 28:61; 29:20, 26; 30:10; 31:9, 24). In that case this gospel would refer to the Gospel of Matthew, just as this Torah or this book refers to the Book of Deuteronomy (cf. Matt 26:13), but this gospel does not have to refer to a document. It might be the good news of that particular time as over against the gospel in the time of Second Isaiah. The oi-koo-méh-nay (*οἰκουμένῃ*) was the "whole [Roman] world" into which the gospel would be proclaimed to the Jews of the diaspora.

Jeremiah had prophesied earlier that Jews would be driven off the land and out of the "house" (temple), because God had divorced them and annulled the contract made between the Lord and his people (Deut 24:1). Jeremiah also promised, however, that after the Jews had worked off their assigned prison sentence, and in so doing paid double for all of their sins, then God would make with Israel a new contract (Jer 31:31). At that time the diaspora Jews would be returned. The gospel which Second Isaiah announced to Jerusalem was that the prison sentence was over. It was also the same gospel that was announced to the Jews in the entire Roman world. Just as Isa 27:13 promised that there would be a great Jubilee trumpet blown to announce the return of the North Israelites to their homes from their exile in Assyria, so the good news of the return of the Jews to the promised land would be announced throughout the Roman world. The gospel was that the time had come when the land would be restored to the chosen people; the new contract was about to be confirmed; and the Jews of the diaspora would be allowed to return to the promised land.

Paul evidently believed that it was necessary to proclaim the gospel to all the world before the end could come, because he had set out to do exactly that. He first proclaimed the gospel to the Jews in Asia Minor; then he prepared to go to Rome and from Rome to Spain and probably circle (kúk-loh, *κύκλῳ*) around the North African coast of the Mediterranean Sea until he returned to Jerusalem (Rom 15:18-29).

A testimony to the gentiles. The testimony to the gentiles probably had a two-fold purpose: 1) It would tell the Jews among the foreign nations that the land had been restored, and they could return to Jerusalem, and 2) it would amaze the heathen in foreign nations when they learned what God had done for his people. When the coastlands would see they would tremble in fear (Isa 41:5). This would be good news to Zion (Isa 41:27) which would become a light to the gentiles (Isa 42:6; 49:6), because the Lord would have comforted his people and redeemed Jerusalem (Isa 52:7-9). The Lord would treat Egypt as a pawn to be used to pay for Jewish ransom (Isa 43:3). The city of Jerusalem would be rebuilt and the exiled Jews would be set free (Isa 45:13). Gentiles would become envious and jealous. They would all bow to Yahowah and confess him (Isa 45:23). Jews would become so powerful that their promised land would have to be expanded to the end of the earth (Isa 49:6, 19-21). Jews would possess the heathen as slaves (Isa 54:3); foreigners would do all of the menial work (Isa 61:5), while

Jews would consume the wealth of the nations (Isa 61:6). Then gentiles would beg Jews to allow them to come with them to Jerusalem, because they would learn that God was with the Jews (Zech 8:23). This is the gospel of the Kingdom that Matthew said would be preached to all the gentiles, and Cook said this was anti-Jewish! What would he call anti-gentilic?[12] All of this would happen after the gospel had been preached, and then the end of the common era would come. When this age of heathen rule came to an end, the holy age to come would begin.

TEXT

Matthew	First Testament
Then **the end will come.** [15]Therefore	**Its end will come** with a flood, and to **the end** there will be war, decreed desolations. He will make a treaty with the many for one week [of years], and for half a week [of years] he will stop the meat and grain sacrifices. On the wing of abominations will come a desolater until **the decreed end** is poured out on the desolater (Dan 9:26-27).
	[As for] you, Daniel. close up the words, and seal the book until the time of **the end** (Dan 12:4).
when you see **the abomination of desolations**, which was spoken by	From the time of the removal of the continual burnt offering and the provision of **the abomination of desolations**, 1290 days (Dan 12:11).
Daniel the prophet, standing in **the holy place**, let the reader understand,	The people of this prince who is coming will destroy the city and **the holy place** (Dan 9:26).
	Then those who oppressed you will come to you bowed down. Those who despised you will prostrate themselves at your feet. They will call you the city of the Lord, **the holy** One of Israel (Isa 60:14).

[12]M. J. Cook, "Interpreting 'Pro-Jewish Passages' in Matthew," HUCA 54 (1983):142.

COMMENTARY

Then the end will come. The quotations from Daniel here show that Matthew expected the same kind of end that Daniel expected. Following the Daniel typology, he believed that Christians at that time were living at the very place in the cycle of time where Jews had been living at the beginning of the Hasmonean rebellion against the Greeks. Ever since the death of Herod the Great there had been guerrilla warfare, off and on, led by pretending kings who hoped to throw off the yoke of the Romans and reestablish the Hasmonean or Davidic kingdom. That would happen when the times of the evil age were fulfilled (Tob 14:5).

The end expected by the Hasmoneans in the second century B.I.A was the end of the Greek domination--not the end of the world or of history, as Thompson presumed,[13] or the end of time, as Patte thought.[14] Matthew, likewise, expected the end of the Roman rule to be followed by the Kingdom of Heaven under the Christian Messiah, Jesus. In the meantime, Christians were living out the "birth pangs"--the 3 1/2 year war with Rome, before these tribulations came to an end, during the Messianic era. It was to be followed by the Kingdom of Heaven. All of this was decreed by the prophet Daniel as God's word and could be expected to be fulfilled in predestined order.

The abomination of desolations. In Daniel, this was Antiochus IV Epiphanes, the Greek king who plundered the temple of Jerusalem (168 B.I.A.), which was also the national treasury, took all of its valuable contents, and enforced Hellenistic religion on the Jews. He even entered the holy of holies in the temple, defiling it so that it could not be used for Jewish worship (see 1 Macc 1:43-63). The holy place in Matthew was the temple, as it was in the time of Antiochus Epiphanes. Jerusalem was the holy city, and Palestine was the holy land, which was sometimes called the holy place (2 Macc 2:18). The context here, however, directs us to the temple.

The defilement of the temple was terribly offensive to Jews, and it was the event in Jewish history that set off the Maccabean Rebellion that finally gained freedom for the Jews. This was the bad news that preceded the good news. The birth pangs of the Messiah began at that time and continued for 3 1/2 years. Jews of that time did not realize it but they were nearing the end of the common era when gentiles ruled their land.

In NT times, the antitype to Antiochus Epiphanes might have been one of the Herods or Roman procurators who enforced order in Palestine and controlled the high priest's garments, so that he could not conduct services without Roman

---

[13]W. G. Thompson, "An Historical Perspective in the Gospel of Matthew," JBL 93 (1974):256, following T. J. Weeden, Traditions in Conflict, pp. 72-73.

[14]Patte, Matthew, p. 336.

approval. It was good news to learn that the new Antiochus Epiphanes had defiled the temple in the Roman cycle of time, because that meant that there could be only 3 1/2 years--a time, two times, and half a time--left before the temple would be cleansed and the land would be restored. Following the predestined order of temporal cycles the defilement of the temple had to precede the cleansing and the new Hanukkah. The bad news was predestined to be followed by good news, in their opinion.

Let the reader understand. This is a clue to tell the believer that the author was writing in code, and there was a clue given which could be understood by anyone who knew Jewish customs and scripture. The clue given here was an allusion to Antiochus Epiphanes' defilement of the temple. The author indicated that the situation in which he and the reader lived was very similar to the one described by Daniel. That defilement was followed by Judas Maccabee's victory and all the good things that came after.

TEXT

Matthew	First Testament: MT and LXX
16Then those who are in Judaea, let them **flee to the mountains**, 17and	He [Mattathias] and his sons **fled to the mountains** and left whatever they had in the city (1 Macc 2:18).
	You shall **flee** by the valley of my **mountain** (Zech 14:4).
	Flee from the midst of Babylon; leave the land of the Chaldeans (Jer 50:8).
	Refugees will escape, and they will be in **the mountains** (Ezek 7:16). **Flee** for safety, people of Benjamin, from the midst of Jerusalem (Jer 6:1).
anyone **on the roof**, let him not go down to take the things out of his house.	What's the matter with you? Why have all of you gone up **to the roofs**? You are full of shouting, noisy city, joyous town! Your slain were not slain by the

sword; they are not killed in battle (Isa 22:1-2).

[18]**The one that is in the field,** let him not turn back to get his garment. [19]Woe to those women who are pregnant and those who are nursing babies in those days. [20]Pray that your flight may not be during the winter or on the Sabbath.

The one that is in the field will die by the sword, and the one that is in the city, famine and pestilence consume (Ezek 7:15).

COMMENTARY

Flee to the mountains. This was to fulfill the prophecy of Zechariah. At the time when the land would be restored, Zechariah said that first there would be a terrible conflict around Jerusalem. The city would be taken, houses looted, women raped, and half of the residents would be taken into exile. Then the Lord would fight those gentiles. He would split the Mount of Olives in two, making a great valley, going east and west. Then those in Jerusalem could flee through that valley to escape the city and get to the mountains (Zech 14:1-5).

This was not anything of "allegorical significance," as Brown suggested.[15] This was practical advice for those who lived in Jerusalem during a war. Since this was held to be the antitype of the end of the Syrian Greek era, and the 3 1/2 year period between the defilement and the rededication of the temple (168-164 B.I.A.), it was obvious that the reenactment of the Maccabean Rebellion would have to take place soon. The period anticipated was not simply a persecution of one sect of Judaism or Christianity by another. The antitype of this expected period was a vicious war. It would be like the guerrilla war led by the Hasmoneans.

Although Jerusalem was well fortified, it was not impregnable. Natives of Palestine were normally more successful fighting guerrilla fashion outside of the city. At one time Judas was surrounded by Syrian Greeks under the leadership of the general, Lysias. It was a Sabbath year;[16] so there was not a grain crop to refill the granaries, and the siege had gone on for a long time. Judas had very few supplies left. Many of the inhabitants fled. The situation for Jews inside Jerusalem was grim, but at that moment there was a threat of a civil war back in Syria, so Lysias was forced to leave. This alone saved the city (Ant 12.375-88).

It is not necessary to conjecture that this was composed post-70 I.A. Jews during the time of Jesus thought they were living in the time cycle reported in

---

[15]S. Brown, "The Matthean Apocalypse," JSNT 3 (1979):10.

[16]Knowledge of this report may have prompted the author of the pericope in Matthew 24 to consider the dangers posed by the Sabbath in time of war.

Daniel. They were in the last years before there would be a new Battle of Beth-horon, a new cleansing of the temple, and a new restoration of the promised land. Before this deliverance took place and the new age began Jews would have to live through a tribulation like that during the reign of Antiochus Epiphanes. They would have to be surrounded by the enemy while they starved inside Jerusalem. At such a time as this, many would flee to the mountains, as Judas' contemporaries had done. Anyone who fled from Jerusalem would run toward the mountains; that is the only place where they might hide.

Judaea has many mountains and caves which have provided seclusion for guerrillas ever since the time Saul hid from David in one of these caves. From the mountains of Judaea the Hasmoneans led the rebellion that finally restored the Solomonic kingdom to the Jews. Elijah hid in these mountains, and Jews of NT times found them to be very handy hide-outs.

Anyone who needed to flee to the mountains from the streets of Jerusalem would be ill-advised to try to hurry through the narrow, crowded streets. During a feast, when the city streets are crowded with merchants and foreign guests, any disturbance can cause a stampede when thousands of people can be killed (<u>Ant</u> 20.111-112).

<u>Anyone on the roof</u>. There were supposedly 3,000 people on the roof when Samson pulled out the pillars that supported it (Judges 16:26-30); King David was walking on his roof when he spotted Bathsheba taking her bath on another roof nearby (2 Sam 11:2). Still today roof tops in Jerusalem are mostly constructed of concrete. People hang out their laundry, fly kites, and haul things in donkey carts on Jerusalem roofs (cf.

Acts 10:9-10). Those who are on the house top are wisely urged to move from roof to roof until they are out of the city without getting mixed up with the mob.

The one in the field. This seems to refer to a laborer who has left his outer garment lying on the ground or hanging on a post or tree while he worked. The danger would be so great that he should forfeit his garment rather than his life, running toward the mountains from the very place he learned of the impending disaster. This was the procedure followed by those who accepted Mattathias' challenge to resist the Syrian Greeks.

Woe to the women who are pregnant. In time of war, these would find it difficult to run, so they would probably be caught by the enemy and killed. This is what happened when the Jews of Gishala tried to flee at night to Jerusalem. The fastest and strongest of the men made it; the children and women could not keep up, so the Romans caught up with them and killed them all (War 4.106-115). When, according to Matthew, people should have been fleeing from Jerusalem, the people of Gishala fled toward Jerusalem. Most of them did not succeed in reaching the holy city. Most of those who did were killed by the Romans later.

Pray that it not be in the winter. Matthew is not an anti-Sabbatical gospel. This document presents a situation that presumes the inhabitants would be impeded by the Sabbath in their flight from the city, and they were not criticized for having such orthodox feelings as these. According to Matthew Jesus argued with Pharisees about legitimate behavior on the Sabbath, but he did not suggest that it be abandoned.[17] In Jerusalem it is nearly always rainy or snowy in winter, making flight through the mud difficult and mountain climbing up slippery slopes nearly impossible. On the Sabbath Jews are permitted to travel only 2,000 cubits (3,000 feet) away from their home or city. From Jerusalem, this would permit people to travel only as far as the Mount of Olives. These warnings apply to real situations that would effect people trying to escape by foot from the areas of Judaea and Jerusalem. The crisis considered is not the end of the world, time, or history, but a frightening military conflict.

The debate over the extent to which Matthew's community observed Sabbath regulations may apply to this situation[18] only to the extent that Matthew accepted this document into his gospel. It probably was not the Matthean community specifically for whom this was written, nor for the disciples alone,[19] but for all those who would be in Jerusalem when the war would be in a critical stage. This prophecy may have been composed before the gospel was compiled--whenever that was. This unit might have been one of the early Jewish or Christian sources composed earlier and accepted by the compiler of this gospel. Jews from all over the diaspora returned to Jerusalem, so that there were almost always visiting Jews there, and the ones who came were mostly observant Jews. Some of these, at least, as well as the local residents would have been too carefully observant to break Sabbath rules, even in case of war. Because this was so, the author called attention to the kinds of danger that lay ahead, especially for pregnant women, small children, and Sabbath observers.

TEXT

Matthew	First Testament
	At that time Michael, the great prince, who stands over the children
21 then there **will**	of your people will stand up. It **will**
be great tribulation, such as has	be a time of **tribulation such as has**
not happened from the beginning of	**not happened from the** origin of the

17 R. K. McIver, "The Sabbath in the Gospel of Matthew: A Paradigm for Understanding the Law in Matthew," AUSS (1995):231-43.

18 Reported by E. Kun-Chun Wong, "The Matthaean Understanding of the Sabbath: A Response to G. N. Stanton," JSNT 44 (1991):3-18.

19 Patte, Matthew, p. 339.

the world **until that time** and will ever be.

nation [Israel] **until that time**. At that time your people will escape--all who are found written in the book (Dan 12:1).

COMMENTARY

The tribulation described in Daniel was that which happened in Palestine between 168-164 B.I.A. This was the 3 1/2 year period from the time the temple was defiled until the first Hanukkah, after Judas the Maccabee won an outstanding victory against the Syrian Greeks at Beth-horon. This period is sometimes called the "Birth pangs of the Messiah." Since the author of this Matthean apocalypse thought Christians were at that time facing the same point in the cycle of time, he expected the kind of hardship that went with the Hasmonean rebellion. This was composed in the future tense, but the next verse switches to the past tense to tell how things were with the Hasmoneans.

TEXT

22If those days had not been shortened, no flesh would have been saved, but because of the elect, those days will be shortened.

COMMENTARY

If those days had not been shortened. The author here was speaking historically in the past tense. This was the way it was when Daniel reported it (Dan 12:1). The tribulation before the Beth-horon victory was the worst that had ever been. Jews were finally saved from that event, because God had paroled the Jews and shortened their punishment time for good behavior. If God had not interceded, none of the Jews would have survived.

Jeremiah promised that Jews would be in captivity until they had paid double for all of their sins. That was the normal fine for non-payment of debts. The expectation that the days would be shortened does not mean that the days would be shorter than 24 hours each, but that the prison sentence or captivity would be reduced because of the generosity of the One who threw them into captivity. The Semitic idiom "shortening days" meant shortening the number of days, the length of time involved. For example, the targumist said that Naomi's sons, Mahlon and Chilion died young, i.e., "their days were cut short" (it-keh-tah-oo yo-may-hohm, אתקטעו יומיהום), because they married foreign wives (TgJon Ruth 5).

No flesh would be saved. This does not mean that no person in the whole world would survive, but the discussion is limited to the residents of Jerusalem. No

Jews living in Jerusalem would have survived that Hasmonean war if God had not been merciful and reduced the punishment.

Because of the elect. The narrative suddenly shifted to the future tense. The future began in verse 21. The prophet said it would be in the future just like it was in the past. Then he told how things were in the past, during the Hasmonean Revolt (Dan 12:1; Matt 24:22a). At that time the punishment was shortened. Then, in Matt 24:22b, the author returned to the future tense. Just as it was with the Hasmoneans years earlier, so it would be with the author's contemporaries. They could count on God shortening the prison sentence again because of good behavior. The good behavior was performed by the elect who performed works of supererogation.

The elect are God's chosen people. They are his favored few for whom he is expected to work miracles, win wars, and provide generously. From statements like this Christians and Jews have formulated the doctrine of election. This is a doctrine that is accepted by every sect of Jews and Christians. It is an apartheid doctrine responsible for many bloody wars and for prejudicial treatment of the non-elect. All Christians and Jews should reexamine the ethics of this doctrine. It is a self-isolating belief that limits the association of the saved with the non-saved (i.e., members and non-members), forcing self-designated Jewish and Christian ghettos throughout the world. It justifies much abusive treatment of those who are not believed to be the elect and favored people of God.

In one of the early Jewish prayers, the author asked that the times of Jewish aid not be cut short, since Jews were God's chosen people (2 Bar 48.19-20). After all they had been meritorious, not having mingled with the gentiles (2 Bar 49.23). It was because of this doctrine that the Pharisees accused Jesus of mingling with "harlots," an insulting name for gentiles.

TEXT

Matthew	First Testament
[23]Then if anyone says to you, "Look! Here is the Messiah!" or, "There!" do not believe, for many	
false Messiahs and	If there
[24]false **prophets will arise** and they	**arises** in your midst **a prophet** or a
will **give you** great	dreamer of dreams and he **gives you**
signs and miracles so as to lead	a **sign or a miracle** and the **sign** or
astray, if possible, even the elect,	**miracle** which he has
[25]look! I have told you in advance.	
[26]If, then, they **say** to you, "Look!	spoken to you, **saying**, "Let us walk
He is in the	after other gods," which you have
	not known, and "Let us serve them,"

wilderness," do **not** go out [or] "Look! He is in the store rooms," do **not** believe, 27for just as lightning goes out from the East and appears as far as the West, thus it will be with the public appearance of the Son of man.

you shall **not** pay attention to that prophet or to that dreamer of dreams, for the Lord your God is testing you to find out whether you love the Lord your God with all your heart and with all your soul (Deut 13:2-4).

COMMENTARY

False prophets will arise. Deuteronomy also said that if a prophet arose and told what would happen in the future, Israelites should not believe him until it had happened. Then they should recognize him as a true prophet (Deut 18:15-22). Here, however, Deuteronomy said that even if the person prophesied accurately and gave signs and wonders to prove his validity, if he advocated following other gods, Israelites should still not follow him. Such events were only temptations to find out whether or not Israelites were really faithful to the Lord. Against this same theme, using some of the same words, Matthew warned against those false prophets who indicated that there was some other Messiah. He classified them in the same category as false prophets and idolaters whose motive was to lead believers astray. Because prophesying is not a profession that is 100% accurate, prophets often disagree about the meaning of the same signs. At the same time there sometimes occur two or more prophets giving different advice (1 Kings 22:10-28; Jer 6:14). Whichever prophet's prophecy is fulfilled in the future is considered a true prophet. The others are false.

He is in the wilderness. After the Israelites escaped from Egypt they spent a whole generation in the wilderness, preparing themselves to conquer Canaan. After that the wilderness was always thought of as a place of refuge. Since it was the step just before the conquest, Jews went back to the wilderness, hoping to begin the conquest of Canaan again. Josephus said there were many leaders who claimed divine inspiration and lured Jews into the wilderness, promising them signs of deliverance. One of these was an Egyptian Jew who, following the typology of Moses, led 30,000 people into the wilderness, promising that he would move from there to the Mount of Olives from which place he would overthrow the Roman garrison. Felix took this meeting seriously and sent out his cavalry and infantry to meet the group. Some were killed and others taken captive by the Romans (War 2.259-63; Ant 20.188).

A Jewish leader, named Theudas, encouraged the members of a large crowd to take their possessions and follow him to the Jordan River. There he promised that he would make the waters part, as Joshua had done, to provide easy passage into the promised land. The Roman procurator, Fadus, however, preempted the experiment with his cavalry. He killed many, took others prisoners, and beheaded Theudas (Ant 20.97-98).

Even after Jerusalem had been destroyed, Masada had been taken, and the temple at Heliopolos had been plundered, a certain Egyptian Jew, named Jonathan, led followers out into the wilderness, promising to show them signs and miracles. When Catullus, governor of Libyan Pentapolis, heard of the exodus, he sent his cavalry and infantry to put an end to the plan (War 7.437-41). Things like this happened so often that Christians were warned not to go out to the wilderness in response to the report that the Messiah was there showing great signs (Matt 24:24-26). It was in the wilderness that the crowds threatened to take Jesus and make him king (John 6:15).

From the East and appears as far as the West. The Greek word for east (ah-nah-taw-lóhn, ἀνατολῶν) also means "rising," probably because the sun rises from the east. This is related to a passage from Numbers

> A star stepped forth from Jacob; a staff arose from Israel.
> It beat down the corners of Moab, and crushed all the sons of Seth.
> Edom became an inheritance; Seir, his enemy, became an inheritance;
> and Israel did valiantly (Num 24:17).

The Greek translated this passage, "A star will rise (ah-nah-tah-láy, ἀνατaελεῖ) from Jacob; a man will stand up from Israel." The "star" and "staff" in Numbers probably allude to David who conquered all the territory of Moab and Edom. In the Dead Sea Scrolls, the "star" came to be a title for the Messiah. The word "arise" also was used as a designation for the Messiah. Therefore this use of the word "east" by Matthew may mean that the Messiah would arise and pass over the land, swift as lightning to the west, taking all the territory with him just as Alexander the Great did many years earlier.

Jews have always depended on outside help in all of their military programs. The last of the Hasmonean kings, King Antigonus, was placed on the throne by the Parthians, who came from the east, overthrew Herod, and reestablished the Hasmonean kingdom. In the seventh decade I.A. the Parthians fought a bitter battle with the Romans and won. Shortly after (69 I.A), when Vespasian withdrew his troops from Jerusalem to settle the civil war in Rome, Jews expected the Parthians to come to their aid again and help them drive out the Romans. Unfortunately for the Jews, Vespasian had previously made a treaty with the Parthians whereby they agreed not to invade Palestine while Vespasian was occupied with a civil war in Rome.[20]

Before the destruction of Jerusalem, however, Jews were hoping, and making plans, to overpower the Romans in the west with the aid of the Parthians

---

[20]See further Buchanan, The Book of Revelation: Its Introduction and Prophecy (Lewiston: Mellen, c1993), pp. 420-32.

from the East. Whenever that happened, the Son of man would appear, as Antigonus had done before, and take his place on the throne at Jerusalem. This was a reversal of the direction of the goat (Dan 8:5-8) who traveled eastward from the west at great speed. That was Alexander the Great.

The public appearance of the Son of man. This refers to the time when this secret, underground movement would have enough strength to make a public appearance and lead an open rebellion against the Romans, just the way Judas the Maccabee did with the Greeks.

TEXT

Poetry

[29]The sun will be darkened,
and the moon will not shed its light,
The stars will fall from heaven,
and the powers of heaven will be shaken.[21]

Midrash

Matthew	First Testament
[28]Where the body is, there the eagles will be gathered. [29]Immediately after the tribulation of those days,	Look! The day of the Lord is coming--cruel wrath and fierce anger, to make the land a desolation, and to destroy its sinners from it, for **the stars of heaven** and their planets **will not** give their **light.**
The sun will be darkened, and the moon will not shed its light.	**The sun will be dark** when it rises, **and the moon will not shed its light** (Isa 13:9-10).
The stars will	**The sun and moon will be darkened** and **the stars will** gather in their **light**. The Lord from Zion will roar; from Jerusalem emit his voice.
fall from **heaven**, and **the** powers of **heaven will be shaken.** [30]Then will appear the sign of the	**The heaven** and the earth **will be shaken** (Joel 3:15-16).

[21]C. F. Burney, The Poetry of our Lord (Oxford: Clarendon, 1925), p. 66 noticed the poetry in these verses.

Son of man in **heaven**. Then all the	All the **heavenly** troops will rot; the **heavens** will be rolled up like a scroll and all their **troops will fall** as the falling of a leaf from a vine or from a fig tree (Isa 34:4).
	They will look at the one whom they stabbed (Zech 12:10) . . . and
tribes of **the land will mourn**, and	**the land will mourn** (Zech 12:12).
they will see **the Son of man coming with the clouds of heaven** with power	Look! **With the clouds of heaven** one like a **Son of man comes**; he came to the Ancient of Days, and he was presented before him. To him [the Son of man] was given the
and much **glory**.	government, **glory**, and a kingdom (Dan 7:13-14).

TECHNICAL DETAILS

There has been much scholarly discussion about the relationship between Matt 24:29-31 and 25:30-31 and Did 16.6-8. There are many verbal similarities between the Matthean passages and those in Didache. Some scholars have suggested that both passages go back to a common source. That may be true, but it cannot be proved. Assuming that this Matthean passage is dependent upon Mark, Kloppenborg thought he had to relate only the Matthean words that were not found in Mark to make a test. He said,

> If, on the other hand, we find only Special Matthean material [i.e. not found in Mark] without elements of either Matthean redaction or Marcan tradition, dependence of 16 6-8 on Matthew would be rather unlikely, since the Didachist scarcely could have borrowed from Matthew in such a discriminating fashion.[22]

This would be no problem for those who were not tied to Markan priority. Comparing only Matthew with Didache, it appears quite likely that Didache used Matthew. We do not know whether Didache had access to Mark or not, and it is only guess work to think that we know how discriminating anonymous copyists may have been 2,000 years ago. Fortunately this argument is not very important for determining the meaning of the Matthean text.

---

[22]J. S. Kloppenborg, "Didache 6 6-8 and Special Matthaean Tradition," ZNW 70 (1979):57.

COMMENTARY

Where the body is. In the Near East animals, like donkeys, cattle, and dogs, sometimes die and are left out in the open desert. There these carcasses lie and swell without the appearance of a single vulture in the sky. Then, the carcass breaks open, and all at once the vultures come from everywhere. In a very short time, nothing is left except bones. Some of these vultures might be eagles, but not very often. The picture given here is parabolic. The eagles probably are not false disciples, as Patte suggested.[23] It is the Romans who had the eagle as a national symbol. The Romans are caricatured as the eagles, and the body is probably Jerusalem.

Many scholars presume this message was prophesied after the event, and they believe the event involved was the war of 66-70 I.A. between the Jews and the Romans. Matthew, however, did not need the historical event to describe the gathering of "eagles" around Jerusalem. Ezekiel, Zechariah, and Joel all prophesied that the gentiles would all be gathered to Jerusalem to try to destroy the city and the Israelites. Matthew assumed, of course, that those prophecies would be fulfilled, and the gentiles who would gather would be the Romans who ruled all of the gentile nations from Spain to the Euphrates. There were Roman troops stationed at Jerusalem from the time of Herod the Great (38-4 B.I.A.) until the city was destroyed in 70 I.A. Local citizens thought of them as vultures from the very beginning. At many of the feasts there were military skirmishes in Jerusalem. At one time, at least, Pilate mixed the blood of Galileans with their sacrifices in the temple area (Luke 13:1). Cestius stationed his Roman troops on Mount Scopus during a Jewish feast (66 I.A.). When he moved his troops away, the Jews followed with arms and fought the Romans all the way down the canyon of Beth-horon, defeating them. This was the beginning of the great war that brought Vespasian and Titus to Jerusalem, where they surrounded the city twice and finally captured it (70 I.A). They finally stripped it as bare as an animal carcass in the wilderness picked by the vultures.

This literature was written, however, before Jerusalem had been stripped bare. Jews were expecting it because it had been prophesied. It would be preceded by the tribulation which was an antitype for the conflict between the Greeks and Jews, led by Judas the Maccabee. Every Jew in Jerusalem knew how that conflict turned out, and they expected this one to turn out the same way. After only 3 1/2 years the Greeks were defeated, the temple was cleansed, and Jews celebrated their first Hanukkah. Before December of I.A. 69, hopes in Jerusalem were high. Jews had many troops in Jerusalem, and enough supplies to last for years. This tribulation had already lasted two years. The prophesied 3 1/2 years could last only 1 1/2 years more. This tribulation would soon end.

Vespasian had withdrawn Roman troops to settle a civil war in Rome, and Rome was in distress with its Capitol buildings burning. Everything looked

---

[23]Patte, Matthew, p. 340.

promising for the Jews in Jerusalem. Jews thought this tribulation would soon be over, and "immediately after. . ." things would be better.[24] It would not have made any sense for anyone to have written this prophecy after John had burned the grain supplies in Jerusalem, and Titus had returned and completed the acquisition. The eagles had gathered, just as the Syrian Greeks had gathered around Jerusalem years before, but the last word had not been said. The prophecy was still waiting to be fulfilled. That prophecy might have been made any one of several times after the taxation of Quirinius (6-7 I.A.).

Mark 13, on the other hand, may have been finalized after 70 I.A., because he replaced the words "Immediately after the tribulation" by "After that tribulation" (Mark 13:24), as if it was a special tribulation that had happened in the past.

After the tribulation. This means after the 3 1/2 year period of warfare before the temple is dedicated, following the typology of Daniel 7.

The sun will be darkened. When the ten commandments were given at Mount Sinai (Exod 19); when Deborah and Barak's troops overpowered Sisera (Judges 5); when Joshua was deeply engaged in battle, the forces of nature came to the rescue of Israel, and the Lord spoke through thunder, rain, lightning, and earthquakes. He made the sun stand still (Josh 10:12-14) and the waters of the sea and the River Jordan to separate. He raised the waters of the Brook Kishon, and **the stars in their courses fought against Sisera** (Judges 5:21). With this typological background it is normal to expect these forces to appear again to guarantee victory for God's chosen people. This text was composed when Jews still expected them to happen again--before 70 I.A.. Throughout the Gospel of Matthew these natural phenomena are intended to direct the reader to remember the same signs on Mount Sinai when God made a contract with his people. Jews of NT times were anticipating the restoration of the land and the reestablishment of the contract. All of these signs were good news to the believer.

The sign of the Son of man in heaven. Glasson may be correct in holding that this should be the "standard" of the Son of man. The discussion here is about a Son of man coming into his glory. Whenever that happened, of course, he would establish his standard, sit on this throne, and rule the country with his scepter.[25] The sign, however, might also, or instead, call the reader's attention to Dan 7, which is a mythical court scene that was held in heaven. First the defendant (Antiochus Epiphanes, "the little horn") was given a death sentence. Then the

---

[24]B. W. Bacon, Studies in Matthew (New York: Henry Holt and Co., c1930), p. 69, thought "after the tribulation" meant after the sufferings of the church, but the church was nowhere mentioned in this context.

[25]T. F. Glasson, "The Ensign of the Son of Man (Matt XXIV.30," JTS 15 (1964):299-300.

plaintiff (Judas the Maccabee, "the Son of man") was given the kingdom, ruling power, and glory that comes with leadership of a nation. Only the mythical judgment took place in heaven; the earthly ramifications took place in Palestine when Judas won the Battle of Beth-horon, had the temple cleansed, and initiated Hanukkah. Matthew obviously expected a new heavenly judgment scene to take place and a new Son of man to take his place upon the throne at Jerusalem.

The tribes of the land will mourn. The tribes that mourn are the 12 tribes of Israel. The tribes are the tribes of the Land of Palestine rather than the tribes of the whole earth.

They will see the Son of man. The tribes of the land would not see the Son of man on the clouds any more this time than they did during the time of the Maccabees. Dan 7 described mythically a heavenly court scene that was seen only in a vision. That which was seen on earth was the victory of the Palestinian Jews over the Syrian Greeks in military battle. Jews of NT times were not expecting to see the Son of man in heaven, either. They wanted to see earthly manifestations of this heavenly court scene. If they could see the Romans defeated in a major battle at Beth-horon this would be evidence enough to convince them that the Son of man was appearing in heaven before the Ancient of Days.

The new Son of man would not appear as an antitype in the heavenly court in front of the Ancient of Days in Heaven until there was 3 1/2 years of war, and all of these other events had also taken place on earth. Broer was also correct in saying that these events were not prophesied ex eventu.[26] This was not written after the war of 66-70 I.A. was over as if it were prophesied. The destruction of Jerusalem and the temple were not necessary for these events to be prophesied. Anyone who was convinced that he or she was reliving the tortures of the Maccabean Revolt would expect that all of these difficulties would precede the restoration of the land.

With the clouds of heaven. The Aramaic of Dan 7:13 is im-ah-nah-nay shah-máh-yah (עם ענני שמיא). The word rendered "with" was translated by Matthew as ep-peé (ἐπί) ("on," "with," "against") and by Mark 13:26 and Luke 21:27 as en (ἐν) ("in,"). The variation of the preposition is not significant. The importance is that the Son of man would come in association with the clouds. The clouds symbolized God's presence, just as it did when Moses was on Mount Sinai and Jesus was with three of his apostles on the Mount of Transfiguration.

---

[26]Broer, "Mt. 24:1-28," p. 229.

TEXT

Matthew	First Testament and other Jewish literature
	It will happen in that day that
[31]He will send his messengers with **a great trumpet,**	**a great ram's horn** will be sounded, and those who are perishing in Assyria and those who have been pushed off into the land of Egypt will come, and they will worship Yahowah on the holy mountain in Jerusalem (Isa 27:13).
	When the age which is beginning to pass away is sealed, the books will be opened before the face of the firmament, and everyone will see it at the same time (4 Ezra 6.20).
	The trumpet will sound loudly, which, when all hear, suddenly they will be frightened (6.23). It will happen that all who will be left from all these things which I have foretold to you will be saved and will see my salvation and the end of my age (4 Ezra 6.25).
and they **will gather**	If your pushed off ones will be at the end of **heaven, from** there Yahowah your God **will gather** you, and from there he will take you. Yahowah your God will bring you to the land which your fathers inherited, and you will inherit it (Deut 30:4-5).
the elect **from the four winds and from** the corners **of heaven** until their corners.	"Ho! Ho! Flee from the land of the North," says Yahowah! "For I have scattered you like **the four winds of heaven.** Ho! Escape to Zion, you who dwell with the daughter of Babylon" (Zech 2:10).

32From the fig tree learn the parable: When already its branch becomes tender and the leaves sprout, you know that the harvest is near. 33Thus also you, when you see all these things, you know that it is near--at the gates. 34I tell you under oath, "This generation will not pass away until all these things take place.

35Heaven and earth will pass away,
but my words will not pass away."

COMMENTARY

He will send his messengers. The word translated "messengers" is ang-éh-loos (ἀγγέλους), which is a general term. It may mean earthly, human messengers, or it may mean angels, heavenly messengers. The trumpet shows that Matthew expected a replay of the first Jubilee after the North Israelites had been taken into captivity to Assyria. On the basis of Sabbatical logic, they should have been allowed to return after 50 years in captivity. When Israelites borrowed money from fellow Israelites they were not required to pay interest, but if they could not repay the principal within the contracted time, they had to work off the obligation at half wages. This meant they were required to pay back in work twice as much as they had borrowed. If, however, the Sabbath year came around before they had paid back their obligation, the creditor was required to release them anyway. If they sold their land to obtain money, the land had to be returned to the family on the Jubilee year.

When Assyria captured North Israel and took its leaders captive into Assyria, the Israelites believed that God had done this as punishment for their sin. They considered their sins to be debts which they had to work off at half wages, but they expected to be released on the Jubilee year when not only would the slaves be set free but the land would be restored, according to Deuteronomic and Levitical rules. It was just before that time that Isaiah expected the Lord to sound a great ram's horn to call the North Israelites home (Isa 27). Matthew believed that Jews and Christians were approaching a great Jubilee year, and they could expect the sound of the ram's horn very soon.

Gather the elect. When the Israelites and later the Jews were exiled from their land into Assyria and Babylon, they believed that the Lord had "pushed" them off the land and sent them away. This meant that the Lord had annulled the marriage contract he had made with his people at Sinai and divorced them. The rule for divorce was that a man who wanted a divorce from his wife was required to give her a written document saying that was the case and send her out of his house. When the Assyrians and Babylonians took control of Israel and Judah, they burned both of the temples involved. This meant to the faithful that the Lord had sent them out of his "house," and scattered them among the nations (Jer 28:26).

But, on the basis of Deuteronomy, Jeremiah promised that, after they had paid double for all their sins, the Lord would restore their fortunes, gather them from all the places where he had driven them, bring them back to their own land, and institute the marriage contract he had made with his people (Jer 29:13-14; 23:5-8; 30:18-24; 31:1-39; 33:6-22). This was according to the rules both of Sabbath and Jubilee justice and divorce and remarriage. This is what Matthew expected to happen in his day. It was part of the legal requirements of Jubilee. Since the rules were part of God's contract and were considered God's word, believers could expect that God would uphold his word on these points.

When the branch is tender. Fig trees do not start to have tender branches and sprouting leaves just before the harvest of figs, but they begin to sprout and grow just before the harvest of grain, in April or May. The point of this argument is that farmers in the Near East know the normal progression of time. It works in cycles; there is a sowing time before harvest; grain ripens before olives or grapes. It happens that way every year. Therefore farmers are never taken by surprise. They always know how far away from harvesting of the various crops they are. According to Matthew, Jesus thought the cycles of time were just as predictable.

Anyone who studied the things that happened just before Joshua invaded Canaan, just before Ezra and Nehemiah returned, or just before the temple was cleansed by Judas the Maccabbee should recognize that they were living at that very moment in a situation just like one or more of those. Everything was happening properly and in normal order. Jubilee was just about to occur, and Jews were just about to see the Son of man coming with the clouds. That which Hasmonean Jews saw at that time was not the heavenly court scene but the victory at the Battle of Beth-horon and the cleansing of the temple. When the Son of man ascended to the clouds again, the Jews hoped to see a new victory in battle with Rome and a new cleansing of the temple.

This generation will not pass away. This sentence is a close parallel to Matt 5:18. "All these things" means all the things mentioned in Matt 24:2-3 and detailed extensively in Matt 24:4-32. They were mentioned here again to form an inclusion between Matt 24:2 and Matt 24:35. So the harvest is very near--at your gates. Just how long is that? How long would it be before the trumpet would sound and the Son of man would come with the clouds? Probably within 3 1/2 years, because they believed they were right then in the period of the tribulation or the birth pangs of the Messiah. At the very longest, it would take place within the lifetimes of that very generation.

Apologists have used some very fancy logic to explain why this did not really mean what was said, but that is simple pleading. It was a mistaken expectation, that is all there is to it. It is foolish to avoid facts. Kidder, for example, argued that "this generation" is subsequent to the fall of Jerusalem in 70 I.A. and presupposes a long delay before Christ's second coming.[27] This overlooks the

---

[27]S. J. Kidder, "This Generation in Matthew 24:34," AUSS 21 (1983):203-09.

kind of prophecies made in NT times on the basis of typology. Kidder noted a chiasmic structure in this form:

Signs on Earth (24:6-8): wars and rumors of wars; nation against nation and kingdom against kingdom; famines, pestilences, and earthquakes.	False messiahs and false prophets (24:23-28)
False messiahs (24:5)	Signs in heaven (24:29): sun darkened, moon not giving light, stars falling, powers of heaven shaken.

Kidder demonstrated that this small chiasm is part of a larger well balanced structure into which Matt 23:36, "Amen I say to you that all these shall come upon this generation," is paralleled by Matt 24:34, "Amen, I say to you that this generation shall not pass until all these things be fulfilled."[28]

Heaven and earth will pass away. This entire verse is omitted by Sinaiticus and also the medieval Hebrew text. This is a separate saying that is unrelated to the rest of the narrative. Matthew put this together with the saying about a generation passing away, because both sayings dealt with passing away, just as he put in chapter 22 the instances when someone tried to silence Jesus by outwitting him with difficult questions, and in chapter 23 he placed several of the woes to the scribes and Pharisees. This is normal organization in Jewish and Christian tradition.

TEXT

[36]Concerning that day and hour no one knows--not even the angels of heaven nor the Son, but the Father only, [37]for just as the days of Noah, so will be the public appearance of the Son of man; [38]for just as in those days they were eating and drinking, marrying and being married, until the day

Matthew	First Testament
Noah **went into the** **house boat**, [39]but they did not know until **the flood** came and took	Then **Noah**, with his sons, his wife, and his sons' wives **went into the house boat** [to escape] from **the flood** (Gen 7:6-7).

[28]Kidder, "This Generation," p. 204.

everything away. Thus also will be the public appearance of the Son of man.

COMMENTARY

Concerning the day and hour. Tannaitic Rabbis said that there were seven things hidden from human beings: 1) the day of death, 2) the day of comfort, 3) the depth of judgment, 4) that from which a person can profit, 5) what is in a person's mind, 6) when the kingdom of David will be restored to its former position, and 7) when the wicked kingdom will be uprooted (Mek Vayassah 6.60-64). The day of comfort is the time after the judgment when the land is restored to the Jews or Christians. The assurance that no one knows when all this will take place is a nice escape hatch. Those who calculate faithfully the sequence of events in comparison with typological events predict precisely when the end will come. It is always near, at the gates, within 3 1/2 years, within this generation, but when these precise dates come and go, calculators can always find refuge in the observation that no one can really know when. It is possible only to know that it will happen, how it will happen, and that it will happen soon. This has always been the hope and the anxiety of Jews and Christians.

Medieval Jewish sages explained their understanding of the way the cycle would function during the last seven years before the Messiah would come:

> The week [of years] in which the son of David come: 1) In the first year, this verse will be fulfilled: **I will provide rain in one city, and I will not provide rain on the other** (Amos 4:7). 2) The second [year], the arrows of famine will be sent out. 3) In the third [year], there will be a great famine. Men, women, and children, khasidim, and men of [miraculous] deeds will die, and the Torah will be forgotten by students. 4) In the fourth [year] there will be satiety and no satiety. 5) During the fifth [year], there will be a great abundance. [People] will eat, drink, and be merry, and the Torah will return to its students. 6) In the sixth [year], there will be voices; 7) in the seventh [year], wars. At the close of the seventh [year], the son of David will come. Rabbi Joseph said, 'Many weeks [of years] have been thus, but he has not come.' Rabbi Abaye said, 'Were there in the sixth [year] voices and in the seventh [year], wars? And were they further in their [prescribed] sequence?'[29]

---

[29]Buchanan, Revelation and Redemption: Jewish Documents of Deliverance from the Fall of Jerusalem to the Death of Nahmanides (Dillsboro, c1978; sold by Mercer U. Press), p. 310.

People like Rabbi Abaye continue to hope against hope that the Son of man who failed to show up according to calculations for the last 2,000 years will probably show up very soon. So they reorganize figures so that days are calculated as if they were years or thousands of years or weeks of years and wait for the prophesy to be fulfilled.

Noah went into the house boat. The word here translated "house boat" is usually rendered "ark." It basically means "box" or "chest." The same word is used for the chest in which the scrolls with the contract between the Lord and his people were kept and the boat that Noah built for his family to live in during the flood. One of these obviously was a chest and the other was a very large "box" made to float. Today we would call it a "house boat." Matthew used this text, because Noah built a house boat in preparation for a flood that no one else thought would ever occur. When it came he was prepared, and no one else was. The flood came without announcement, and the Son of man was expected to come the same way.

The parousia. Plummer said, "Mt.'s whole Gospel is coloured with the conviction that the Second Advent was near and would follow closely upon the fall of the city."[30] The parousia was not the second advent, which was nowhere mentioned in the gospels. The parousia is the open public appearance. Jesus' public entry into Jerusalem with shouts of, "Hosanna!" was probably considered his parousia (Matt 21:6-11) about which the apostles asked (Matt 24:3).

Messiahs in NT times were leading guerrilla bands in hiding. They existed for a long time underground, waiting for the right opportunity to come out into the open and lead an open rebellion. Some examples of these messiahs appeared publicly after Herod the Great's death. After Herod's death, during the short time that it took for Archelaus to go to Rome and gain authority to lead the country (50 days from Passover to Pentecost), three leaders arose very suddenly and led extensive military movements. The bulk of the royal troops, that ostensibly had been loyal to Herod and Rome, deserted to the rebellious movements (War 2.52).

One of these guerrilla leaders was Judas, a Galilean rebel. He broke open the royal arsenals and obtained weapons to arm his troops, and then he began his resistance movement. It seems obvious that he had been working quietly, preparing followers for any opportunity that should present itself (War 2.56; Ant 17.271-72).

Another leader was Simon, one of the royal officers in Herod's kingdom. While pretending to support Herod's government, he had also been organizing a guerrilla movement behind the scenes, probably among Herod's own forces. He was very quickly able to organize troops, burn down the royal palace at Jericho, and destroy many other stately mansions. He was finally killed in a conflict with Roman soldiers (War 2.57-59; Ant 17.273-77).

---

[30]Plummer, Matthew, p. 338.

A third leader was named Athronges. He was a man whose only qualifications, Josephus said, were a strong body, a courageous soul, and four brothers very much like himself. That which he lacked that made Josephus speak of him disparagingly, was a great family name, like one of the Hasmoneans or sons of David. The fact that Josephus singled him out for this pejorative description probably means that these other guerrilla leaders had royal family histories and support.

Athronges suddenly appeared, well organized with troops lined up under different brothers depending on the military engagement. He himself acted like a king, wearing a crown, and making all major decisions. He evidently had a well organized administration, prepared to break out into the open whenever it seemed wise. The goals of Athronges and his brothers as well as his followers had been established long before the death of Herod. He wanted to be king of the nation, to overthrow Herod and his Roman supporters. All of these brothers were finally silenced by the Romans, but before that happened, Josephus said they had made all Judaea a scene of guerrilla warfare (War 2.60-65; Ant 17.276-84).

In the short seven weeks between Passover and Pentecost, these three military movements arose and tried to overthrow the government of Archelaus before he could get control of it himself. Archelaus' departure for Rome seemed to them like a sign from Heaven. Although it happened suddenly, like lightning, or a thief in the night, or Noah's flood, it is more than likely that all three of these men had met many times with small groups of trained followers, who, in turn, had organized still other subordinate groups of Jews who were unhappy with their current regime and were willing to risk their lives and fortunes to change the leadership. These men were probably impatient people who had urged open action many years before action was actually initiated. During that time followers may have asked, "When will these things take place? and what is the sign of your parousia?" This is a conjecture, but there was another leader, a few years later, who also led a movement that never broke out into military rebellion, so far as we know, but there are clues of the secret nature of the movement.

Jesus told his disciples that the beautiful temple at Jerusalem would be destroyed, so that not one stone would be left intact. The disciples asked, "When will these things be, and what is the sign of your parousia and the end of the age" (Matt 24:1-3)? "The end of the age" was a mythical expression related to Daniel, which meant the end of the foreign rule. After some unknown period of secrecy, earlier guerrilla leaders, like Mattathias the Hasmonean, Athronges, Simon, and Judas, finally made their public appearances.

These were the parousiai. A twentieth century example of this took place in Iran. After thirteen years as an exile in France, Khomeini finally flew back to Iran to lead the country, after his secret followers had expelled the Shah. At the time of Jesus' discussion with his disciples, Jesus had not made his plans public. There had been no parousia; the disciples of Jesus were impatient, as were others who tried to take Jesus by force and make him king (John 6:15). When speaking to his disciples, he could employ "the mysteries of the Kingdom of Heaven," but to outsiders, he spoke in riddles.[31] Many scholars have imposed upon this term "parousia" the belief that this was only a public appearance that would take place at the end of history.[32]

TEXT

[40]Then, there will be two in the field: one is taken, and one is left. [41]Two women are grinding with the mill: one is taken, and one is left. [42]Watch, then, because you do not know at what hour the Lord is coming. [43]Know this, that if the landlord had known at which watch the thief was coming, he would have watched and not allowed his house to be broken into. [44]Because of this, you also be prepared, because at an hour when you are not thinking [about it], the Son of man comes.

COMMENTARY

You do not know. These are further examples, like the situation of Noah before the flood, in which people might be taken by surprise. Not all of these situations are clear. In the cases of the two men in the field or the two women at the mill. How will they be taken? Will they die? Will they be drafted into some kind of service? Will they be killed? These are all possibilities but not the only ones. Here the Lord (Matt 24:42) is the same as the Son of man (Matt 24:39), as Kingsbury acknowledged. This does not mean, however, that Son of man is a subordinate title to that of Son of God.[33] They both applied to a Jewish king, a Messiah, a Son of David. Jesus fit all of these titles.

If the landlord had known. Of course, landlords, home owners, or shop owners do not know when thieves plan to break in and rob the places. Watches have to be set up for any possible time, and that is the point of the teaching. The same situation exists with the coming of the Son of man. No one knows when it will happen, so everyone should be prepared for his arrival at any time. Rabbi Eliezer told his disciples they should repent one day before they died. His disciples asked, "Who knows when he will die?" He responded that, of course, no one did, but that is the reason they should repent today, because they might die tomorrow.

---

[31]Buchanan, Jesus: The King and his Kingdom (Macon: Mercer U., 1984), pp. 204-05.

[32]So, for example, H. K. McArthur, "Parousia," The Interpreter's Dictionary of the Bible (New York: Abingdon, c1962), pp. 658-61. McArthur did not seem to notice any incoherence in his understanding that the parousia was to bring an end to history at the same time Christ was expected to usher in the new age (p. 659). Where was the new age to take place if history had already come to an end?

[33]J. D. Kingsbury, "The Title 'Kurios' in Matthew's Gospel," JBL 94 (1975):249-55.

The final result is that they would live out their entire lives in repentance (Mid Ps 90.12 [197a]).

In this parable the landlord is the "lord." The word "lord" can be applied to a landlord, a supervisor, a king, a messiah, or God.

TEXT

46 Who is the prudent and faithful servant whose master has set him over his
household servants so that he would give them their food at the proper time?
Blessed is that servant, who, when his master comes, will find [him] doing just
that. 47 I tell you under oath he will appoint him [as administrator] over all his
possessions. 48 But if that wicked servant says to himself, "My master is delayed,"
49 and he will begin to strike his fellow servants, and eat and drink with drunkards,

Matthew	First Testament and Other Jewish Literature
50 the master of that servant will come / on a day when he does not expect, / and at an hour which he does not know. /	All the curses of this contract will cleave to him, and God will divide him off for wickedness, and
51 Then **he will cut him in two** /	**he will be cut off** from the midst of all the sons of light . . . the scandal
and **cast his lot with** the hypocrites. There will be there weeping and	of his iniquity will **put his lot in** the midst of those who are cursed for ages (1QS 2.15-17).
grinding of **teeth**!	The wicked will see and become angry; and he will **grind** his **teeth**. The desire of the **wicked** will fail (Ps 112:10).

COMMENTARY

Who is the wise. The word doó-los (δοῦλος), rendered "servant" here, has a wide possibility of meanings in Greek. A "servant" was not simply someone who waits tables, cleans house, and does other menial jobs. A servant was anyone in a subordinate position. Context alone defines the person's role. A servant might have been a slave who did unskilled manual work, but he might instead have been a high ranking official, so long as he was still responsible to someone with a higher authority. For instance, a king's ambassador or highest ranking general was a servant. In this parable, the employer, who at that time was called the master or lord, seems to have been some person involved in business who had many middle managers working for him. The "servant" who would either have been faithful or wicked was one who had just been promoted to his first position as supervisor or superintendent in charge of this particular unit. His responsibility was to see that the other employees did their work and received their pay on time. Luke's version calls this particular servant a manager (oi-koh-nó-mos, *οἰκονόμος*), and it is correct, but that does not mean Matthew's version is wrong. One is more precise than the other.

Over all his possessions. The number of business parables Jesus told indicates that he was in communication with wealthy business men who understood what was involved in this kind of administration. Any manager of a large business finds it necessary to delegate authority to subordinate officials. If he or she has been in business very long, she or he has had experience in trusting the wrong people with responsibility. The sooner that is discovered, the less damage will be caused. Therefore employers usually promote employees in steps, letting them prove their ability before advancing them further.

He will cut him in two. This is a rather firm way of saying that he would fire him and let him belong to the unemployed. Two thousand years ago there were no unions to protect employees and guarantee them gentle treatment and the right of due process, so the treatment may actually have been more destructive than would be accepted today,[34] but the subordinate manager was probably not physically cut in two. Many scholars have had difficulty with the idea that a person would be cut in two as punishment for mismanaging a business. Part of the problem is that after he had been "cut in two" his lot would be cast with the hypocrites, as if he were still alive but belonged to an inferior class. There he would be very unhappy and grind his teeth in his embarrassment. Some have tried to amend the text to make better sense of the passage, but Otto Betz noticed the comparable passage in the Dead Sea Scrolls. There the one who had misbehaved was "divided off" or "separated" from the children of light, and he made his lot with the cursed ones. By being divided he was not cut in two but was cut off from the community--excommunicated.[35] The same situation seems to apply to the manager who was "cut in two." The Hebrew word "cut" (cah-ráth, כרת) is used

---

[34]The word rendered "slash to pieces" literally means "cut in two" (dee-kho-toh-máy-say (*διχοτομήσει*). If we understood customs better we would know better how to translate this word in this context. The manager was probably not cut in two by his employer. When God made a contract with Abraham, Abraham prepared for the liturgy by killing some animals and birds, cutting them in two, and walking between the halves with a flaming torch and a smoking fire pot (Gen 15:7-20). This constituted the ritual to conclude a contract. There may have been some reversal of this process to break a contract, but that is just a guess. If this were the meaning, then "cutting in two" would mean he went through a legal formula to fire the servant.

[35]O. Betz, "The Dichotomized Servant and the End of Judas Iscariot (Light on the dark passages: Matthew 24, 51 and parallel; Acts 1, 18)," RevQ 5 (1964/66):43-48. Buchanan, The Consequences of the Covenant (Leiden: Brill, 1970), pp. 305-11.

for making a contract and also for breaking a contract, cutting apart the parties to the contract.[36]

Weeping and grinding of teeth. This is a typical Matthean editorial comment, also found at Matt 8:12, 13:50, 22:13 and 25:30. Those who weep and grind their teeth are not suffering in the flames of hell after death. They are in emotional distress here on this earth. These all have their source in Ps 112:10. Ps 112 distinguished the faithful who would be generous and righteous, fulfilling all of their responsibilities, and would consequently be rewarded with prosperity and happiness in this life. The wicked, however, would behave differently and consequently would be resentful, angry, and jealous, grinding their teeth in their disappointment. This small poem (Matt 24:50-51) is based on Ps 112.

[36]The verb is also used in the same way in the Mari tablets. So M. Noth, "Das altestamentliche Bundesschliessen im Lichte eines Mari-Textes," Gesammelte Studien zum Alten Testament (München: C. Kaiser, 1957; 1966), pp. 142-54. There "qa-ta-lum ha-a-ri-im bi-ri-it X and Y" means "to kill an ass between X and Y." This was a liturgy similar to that which Abraham made with God (Gen 15:4-21).

CHAPTER TWENTY-FIVE

TEXT

25:1 The Kingdom of Heaven is like ten virgins, who took their lamps and went
out to meet the bridegroom. 2 Five of them were foolish, and five were prudent.
3 The foolish ones took the lamps, but they did not take oil with them. 4 The wise
ones took oil in their vessels with their lamps. 5 As the time for the bridegroom
to come was delayed, they all became drowsy, and they fell asleep. 6 In the middle of the night a cry went out, "Look! the bridegroom. Go out to meet him!"
7 All those virgins arose and prepared their lamps. 8 The foolish ones said to the
prudent ones, "Give us some of your oil, because our lamps have burned out."
9 The prudent ones said by reply, "No. There may not be enough for the both of
us. Instead, go to the market and buy your own." 10 While they were going out
to buy oil, the bridegroom came, and those who were ready went in with him to
the wedding chamber, and the door was closed. 11 Later on, the rest of the virgins
came, saying, "Sir, Sir, open for us!" 12 But he, in reply, said, "I tell you under
oath that I do not know you."

COMMENTARY

The Kingdom of Heaven is like ten virgins. The meaning here is not exactly as the words say. This is a typical introductory formula which means, "The Kingdom of Heaven is like a situation in which there were ten virgins who did as follows": The details of a wedding ceremony in NT times against which this parable makes sense are no longer known. The virgins seem to have been waiting at night in the home of the bride to usher in the bridegroom, whereas it is assumed that usually the bridegroom came to the home of the bride's father and took the bride to his own home. Virgins may have been on hand to secure the tokens of virginity to take to the father of the bride to prove that his daughter was a virgin at the time of the marriage (Deut 22:13-21; Isa 64:5; Sifre 117a #234-118a #240). Jeremias held that the lamps involved were not small hand lamps the size of birthday candles, but rather they were torches that would give considerable light and would also consume a large amount of oil.[1] These torches would have been used as street lights to lighten the way of a parade. Part of the reason the details of wedding customs are not apparent in this parable is that the real teaching dealt, not with an ordinary wedding, but with a marriage contract the Messiah would make with his people. The wedding customs, therefore, are intentionally confused with Passover traditions.

They became drowsy and fell asleep. On Passover night Jews were not supposed to sleep while the service was still in process. Since all the people attending the Passover Seder were expected[2] to drink four glasses of wine, there was a strong tendency for people to nap during the service (mPes 10.1). The service included loud singing, games with the children, eating parched nuts and mazza, and other activities designed to keep people awake and counter the effects of the wine (bPes 109a). If some in the group actually fell asleep the group could continue and eat again, but if all fell asleep they were not permitted to eat again. Rabbi Jose ben Halaphta ruled that if people only dozed but did not fall into a deep sleep the Passover program might continue. The question was whether a person was asleep or whether he or she was just dozing. Rabbi Ashi said that if a person was addressed and was able to respond, even though it was incoherently, and later remembered the incident if he were reminded, he was just dozing (bPes 120b). Passover programs were planned to keep people awake, so that the Passover service would not have to be stopped before the middle of the night. Although these virgins are reported to have gone to sleep, there must have been some legal standard by which their sleeping was considered permissible (tPes 10.1; bPes 109a).[3]

Bornkamm, who thought this parable was composed by the later church after the time of Jesus, held that the sleeping of the virgins represented the reaction of the later church to the delay of the parousia. He thought there were some strange things going on at this wedding.[4] He failed to relate the parable to the Passover celebration, so he concluded that the nightly arrival of the bridegroom refers to the "primitive expectation that the end of the world and the Son of man would come at night (Mk 13,33 ff; Lk 12,35 ff; Mt 24,42 ff;--Röm 13,11;

[1]J. Jeremias, "LAMPADES Mt 25:1. 3f. 7f," ZNW 56 (1965):196-201.

[2]This was not a requirement. There were three requirements for the Passover: 1) The Passover lamb, 2) unleavened bread, and 3) bitter herbs. There is no report in the first Passover in Egypt of wine being part of the meal. The wine was probably introduced after the Israelites reached the land, under the influence of the Dionysian festivals.

[3]See further D. Daube, The New Testament and Rabbinic Judaism (New York: Arno Press, 1973), pp. 332-35.

[4]G. Bornkamm, Geschichte und Glaube III (München: Chr. Kaiser Verlag, 1968), pp. 51, 54-55.

1 Thes 5,1 ff; Eph 5,14; Apk 3,3; 16,15)."[5] Patte also said the parable referred to "the kingdom at the end of time ("then") rather than in the present."[6] If this were the end of time there would be nothing to celebrate. The ceremony would be one of lamentation. This parable, however, is not about death and resurrection of individuals.[7] Neither did it visualize the world coming to an end. It was expecting the arrival of the Messiah on Passover night. It was a celebration rather than a mourning or lamentation parable. The Son of man was expected here, as in Dan 7, to be the victorious leader that would usher in the Kingdom of Heaven and renew the contract with God.

In the middle of the night. There are some odd characteristics about this wedding. Why would the bridegroom arrive at midnight? Why does he come to the bride's house when it was customary for the bride to be escorted to his home? A Near Eastern wedding normally takes about eight days. Bornkamm and Ford asked some of the same questions. Into whose home would the bridegroom come? Why was the bride not mentioned?[8] Part of these questions can be answered if the parable is related to a Passover festival, as Strobel has suggested. He noted that this Passover night ritual was known in the early church (Epiphanius, AdvHaer 70.10, 6; 70.12). Jerome said it was a tradition of the Jews that the Messiah would come in the middle of the night when the Passover was being celebrated.

This would follow the pattern of the way the Israelites left Egypt on Passover night as the angel of death (exterminator) passed over their tents because their door posts were marked with the blood of the lamb (Exod 12:3-13). Jerome said that Christians also observed this evening watch until midnight when they celebrated the Lord's Supper, awaiting the coming of Christ. On that night no one was allowed to leave the celebration until the midnight while Christians awaited the coming of Christ,[9] just as Jews awaited the coming of the Messiah on their Passover Seders. Neither early Christians nor Jews, however, expected that the end of the world would come at the same time the Son of man arrived, as Bornkamm thought. He expected that both of these events would happen at night and that Christians were waiting up at night, not only for the Son of man but also for

---

[5]Bornkamm, Geschichte, p. 52.

[6]D. Patte, The Gospel according to Matthew (Philadelphia: Fortress Press, c1946), p. 343.

[7]As W. Schenk, "Auferweckung der Toten oder Gericht nach den Werken. Tradition und Redaktion in Mattäus xxv.1-13," NovT 20 (1978):278-99, thought.

[8]J. M. Ford, "The Parable of the Foolish Scholars," NovT 9 (1967):107; Bornkamm, Geschichte, p. 51.

[9]A. Strobel, "Zum Verständnes von Mt XXV 1-13," NovT 2 (1958):199-227.

the end of the world.[10] Jerome said after midnight the group dissembled and individually went home (MPL 26,192A). They were not surprised that the world had not come to an end, as Bornkamm thought.

Like other parables that do not seem practical, this parable was intended to communicate a message in code. In this parable, the groom was really the Messiah who would come to his bride, which would be the chosen people, the other party to the wedding contract. He would come on Passover night just as Moses came in the middle of Passover night to lead the Israelites out of Egypt. In such a case the people would not be brought to God in heaven, but God would come through his Messiah to the people, and the contract would take place on the promised land. Wedding ceremonies are not normally held on Passover eve, but in this parable the wedding factor was introduced to remind the readers of the renewal of the marriage contract between God and his chosen people. When Jesus actually met with his apostles on Passover night he made a new contract, using Passover elements as means for the contract ritual (Matt 26:28). He was fulfilling the program that was expected of the Messiah if he should come on Passover night.

When the Messiah came he was expected to renew the contract that had been annulled when the people were sent into exile. Frequent allusions to the provisions of the contract together with the coming of the Messiah are made in Jewish and Christian literature in code by describing a wedding or the provision of the contract to Moses at Mount Sinai with its accompanying natural noises. The main character was called a "bridegroom" rather than "the Messiah," so that eavesdropping Romans would not suspect this was part of a subversive movement. Celebrants, however, all knew what was meant by the code word "bridegroom." They also prayed that they would celebrate other feasts in "your city," without mentioning the name, "Jerusalem" (mPes 10.6). These were all coded ways of communicating to those who had ears to hear while keeping the outsiders ignorant of the message involved.

In NT times Jews identified the containers of religious materials by initials rather than names, so that Romans would not suspect that Jews were still carrying on their regular religious practices in secret. If there was only an initial on a jar, Romans would think that was someone's name rather than identification of the contents.

> If someone found a vessel and on it was written a kohf (ק), this meant qohr-báhn (קורבן) (offering). If it was maym (מ), it would be mah-ah-sáyr (מעסר), (tithe). A dáh-leth (ד) is deh-maí produce, and a tau (ת) was for teh-roo-máh (תרומה) (heave-offering) (mMaasSh 4.11).

[10]G. Bornkamm, "Die Verzögerung der Parusie," In Memoriam Ernst Lohmeyer (Stuttgart: Evangelische Verlagswerk, 1951), p. 123.

In many coded ways like this Jews have been able to continue practicing their religions in secret without authorities realizing the subversive intentions of their practices. Communicating in parables was only one method.

Look! The bridegroom! It was customary, not only in Jewish circles, but also in Greek and Roman communities for citizens of a town to go out to meet famous people who entered their village. This was done when David returned from a victorious battle against the Philistines (1 Sam 18:6-7). Martha went out to meet Jesus when he came to her home (John 11:20). The people of his town went out to meet Rabbi Eleazar when he approached the village (bTa'an 20b). There are many other instances of this in rabbinic literature and also classical Greek and Latin literature. Paul looked forward to a Jubilee call when the Lord would descend, and all the faithful who were still alive would go out to meet him (1 Thes 4:16-17). When Jesus entered Jerusalem, riding on a donkey, people from Jerusalem were there to meet him, spreading palm leaves before him. When the cry went out (Matt 25:6) it was the kind of cry that went out before the crowds came to meet Jesus as he entered Jerusalem. If it were midnight when the special guest was expected to arrive, ancient hospitality committees might be expected to meet the guest with torches, even though on Passover night there would be a full moon. On the other hand, if the guest they were expecting was the Messiah, they might have avoided excessive visible ceremony and have the lamps lighted only after the bridegroom entered the house.

This may be one of those parables in which the imagery of the wedding situation was strained a little to make the point that Jesus really wanted to get across. He was not speaking of any ordinary wedding, but of a special renewal of the contract. At this ceremony the Messiah would come to overthrow the Roman authorities and establish the Kingdom of Heaven on the promised land. Every practicing Jew would understand the coded parts of this parable in terms of Passover liturgy. Only the outsiders would be confused.

Jesus had been conducting his entire campaign to obtain the kingdom. He was not only trying to arouse the support of contemporary Jews, but he wanted those already aroused to stand by in readiness for the time when action was required. The contract that the Israelites signed with Yahowah at Sinai was a marriage contract. This contract had been broken, according to Jeremiah, when the Lord sent his people out of his "house" (his temple) and off the land. In Jesus' day Jews were looking forward to a new wedding contract, as Jer 31:31 promised, when the Lord would take them back and live with them in the new kingdom. When the Messiah came to them, the "bride" and all of her attendants should be ready.

The virgins arose. The Passover service was allowed to continue, because the dozing virgins were able to wake up and respond when they were addressed.

The bridegroom came. The virgins had had plenty of time to get oil before they ran out, but they procrastinated. "While they are going out" renders the Greek ahp-ehr-kho-mén-ohn deh au-tóhn (ἀπερχομένων δὲ αὐτῶν). Part of this expression is still used today at Jewish Seders, slightly mispronounced. Today it is called the afikóman, and many Jews may no longer remember its origin. There are different customs in different countries in relationship to it, but it involved some hidden manna, for which children search. Initially it probably involved a search and an expectation that the Messiah, the ahp-ehr-khóm-eh-non, "the coming one," who was hiding, would appear. This would be his parousia. They thought the Messiah would come to them at the Passover feast. This was a secret expectation. They did not want the gentiles to know this was part of their belief, so they made it into a game,[11] so that the doctrine would be remembered, but they coded it so that others would not know the meaning of the game. In this parable the word is used, probably deliberately, to remind the reader that this is a Passover parable, and the Messiah was soon going to come. Therefore they should all be prepared.

The picture given here is one of people trying to buy oil at the market late at night. In the Middle East the shops close when the sun goes down. This points out the fiction element of the parable. Jesus intended the listener to understand the coded meaning he was communicating rather than the logic of the story. The message of this parable is basically the same as the one at the end of chapter 24. The imagery is different. In the parable in chapter 24, the delay for the employer seemed to be a long time, perhaps many weeks or months, and the servant was expected to have been carrying on his assigned duties all that time.

The parable about ten virgins, however, pictures virgins staying up all night with lamps, and they were required to be ready at any moment--during one night only, namely Passover night. Mark gives a compressed version of these two parables told as if it were one, giving the nonsensical picture of a man going away for an indefinite period of time and expecting the servant to be ready when he returned, always awake and watching at any time of the day or night. The vocabulary of Mark's abbreviated version of these two parables (Mark 13:34-36) is almost entirely included in Matthew's version (Matt 24:45-25:12). Matthew's version is reasonable, even if we do not know all of the details about wedding customs involved. Both Matthean parables bear the same message, even though the time involved is different. Those who consider Mark to be the earliest gospel find this problem difficult to explain.[12]

The messianic secret is not only in Mark but also in the other gospels. Like other messiahs, Jesus had an organized group of followers trained and waiting in hiding until the right time came to act. Whenever that happened, there

---

[11]Just as they did with Purim.

[12]Buchanan, Jesus: The King and his Kingdom (Macon: Mercer U. Press, 1984), pp. 123-24.

would have to be both people and oil ready.[13] There were people prepared to accompany the Messiah in his action, and oil was on hand to anoint the Messiah. They needed to be alert especially at Passover time. Near the end of the war between Rome and the Jews (69-70 I.A.) Jews were starving to death, and soldiers confiscated all the food they could find in Jerusalem. (War 5.562-65; mMid 2.6). Even in these extreme conditions, Jews were warned, "Don't damage the oil or the wine" (Rev 6:6). These would be necessary for anointing the Messiah and for the messianic banquet. The oil, the virgins, and the bridegroom were all coded allusions to the restoration of the promised land with its new contract and its new Messiah. Other imagery of the parable was related to Passover night.

The door was closed. Strobel compared this to the closed door of Rev 3:8, 20, where Jesus was pictured at a closed door, knocking and awaiting admission.[14] At Passover Jews have traditionally kept the doors closed, because this has been a secret ceremony. Anyone, like the late virgins, who came after the doors were closed would not be admitted. Participants open the door only at one part of the service to welcome Elijah. They have a cup of wine poured for him. Since Elijah is expected to announce the Messiah, just as John the Baptist announced Jesus, the arrival of Elijah would be the same as the arrival of the Messiah. They are really expecting the Messiah. This is probably the message intended in Revelation, with Christ knocking at the door, when the Passover door was closed, and the Messiah would have to knock for admission. Those who would hear his voice would open the door and admit the Messiah to their Passover meal where the Messiah and the celebrants would feast together (Rev 3:20). This is what both Jews and Christians hoped would happen during Passover/Easter season.

I tell you under oath. See commentary on Matt 24:1-2.

Summary. There are three parables in chapter 25, all of which are judgment scenes. In this parable the door was closed and would not be opened for those who were unprepared (Matt 25:12); in the parable of the talents, the wicked servant who neglected to invest his talent was cast out into outer darkness (Matt 25:30). In the parable of the sheep and the goats, those who failed to support the program of Jesus went away into punishment of the age (Matt 25:46). The same

---

[13]K. P. Donfried, "The Allegory of the Ten Virgins (Matt 25:1-13) as a Summary of Matthaean Theology," JBL 93 (1974):424, missed the live dynamics of the situation to which the parable reacted when he suggested that the virgins who slept really died and would be raised at the resurrection. Donfried (p. 424) followed Stendahl in claiming that the wedding garment symbolized the ethical quality expected of the church. Both overlooked Chrysostom's identification of the wedding garment with baptism (Hom 8.23; TLevi 11.9-10; 15.8; 21.2; Hermas Sim 8.2, 3-4). See further the commentary on Matt 22:11-12. The important imagery here is the Messiah as the groom and the wedding ceremony as a renewal of the contract.

[14]Strobel, "Mt XXV 1-13," p. 209.

message appears in Matt 24:45-51 where the faithful servant does what is assigned to him while his master is away and the wicked servant misbehaves because his master is delayed. The master will reward the faithful servant with greater responsibility, but the wicked servant will be punished and classified with the hypocrites (Matt 24:46-51). There he would weep and grind his teeth in despair. These were illustrations that contrasted good and bad behavior and consequences. It also shows Matthew's organizing ability. He regularly placed materials with the same message together.

TEXT

13Watch, then, because you do not know the day nor the hour. 14For it is like a
man who went on a journey. He called his servants and entrusted to them his
possessions, 15to the one he gave five talents, to another, two, and to the third,
one--each according to his ability. Then he went away on his journey. 16The one
who had received five talents went at once, invested them, and gained another
five. 17Likewise, the [one who had received] two, gained another two. 18But the
one who had received one went out and dug [a hole in] the ground and hid his
master's silver.

19After a long time, the master of those servants came and held a reckoning with them. 20The one who had taken five talents came and brought an additional five talents, saying "Sir, you have given me five talents. Look, I have
gained another five talents." 21His master said to him, "Well done, good and
faithful servant. You have been faithful over a few things. I will set you over
many. Enter into the joy of your master." 22The one [who had taken] two talents
said, "Sir, you have given me two talents. Look, I have gained an additional
two." 23His master said to him, "Well done, good and faithful servant. You have
been faithful over a few things. I will set you over many. Enter into the joy of
your master."

24Then the one who had taken the one talent came and said, "Sir, I knew
you, that you are a hard man, harvesting where you have not sown and gathering
where you have not scattered, 25and, since I was afraid, I went away and hid
your talent in the ground. See, you have your own [talent]." 26Then his master,
in reply, said to him, "Wicked and cowardly servant! You knew that I harvested
where I have not sown and gathered where I have not scattered. 27Then you were
obliged to give my silver to the money changers, and when I came I would have
acquired my [silver] with interest. 28Take, then, the talent from him and give it
to the one who has ten talents, 29for to the one who has [interest] shall be given
everything, and he will abound, but to the one who has no [interest], even that
[principal] which he has will be taken from him. 30Throw the useless servant out
into outer darkness." There there will be weeping and grinding of teeth.

COMMENTARY

To one he gave five talents. A talent weighs about 75 pounds. That much silver multiplied by five is a large sum of money. The story here is told in big business terms. The master or employer was testing the management skills of his personnel to see which he should promote to more responsible positions.

Look, I have gained another five talents. The story does not say how long the master was gone or how long it took these servants to show their investment skills, but interest was very high in those days--sometimes 30-50% per year--so money wisely invested could quickly double itself.

See, you have your own [talent]. Derrett correctly observed that in the investment business, it is much easier to double a large amount of money than a small amount. The one with the one talent would have had to work much harder than the one with the five talents, and that was part of the problem. The one with the one talent felt that he had been slighted, so he sabotaged the program, planning to teach his employer a lesson. The employer had not given him enough capital with which to work, and it was not worth his own time and investment to take the risks involved for a small amount of possible profits he might receive.

Even that [principal]. The technical problem of taking something from a person who has nothing seems illogical, all by itself. In this case none of the three investors had any of their own money to invest. Having nothing means having no interest to add to the principal with which they were all entrusted. Since the one employee had earned no money with his capital his employment was taken from him along with his employer's principal. Like the parable of the trustworthy servant, this parable was addressed to the apostles themselves, and it deals with a personnel problem. Leaders who had once been businessmen and tax collectors would understand all of the implications involved. The difference between their previous occupation and their current responsibilities as subordinate officials in Jesus' campaign is that their positions in the empire had changed.

At one time, they had been top leaders; now they had to take positions that seemed beneath their dignity. Jesus had to remind them in terms of their former business logic in order to keep them using all their skills. Jesus had once called them to give up a great deal to help recover the Kingdom of God. They had been willing then, and the need was as great as ever. There was no time to deal with sabotage within the ranks. They should reserve their sabotage to apply against the Romans. Every single skill, every single coin, and every single moment was needed. The campaign pressures were still on, just as they were when these leaders had first responded. In the monastery they were expected to undertake tasks that seemed beneath their dignity, and this caused friction.

The same kind of logic as applies between principal and interest also makes sense in education. Explaining the relationship between being learned and not being learned, Rabbi Haninah bar Papa said,

> The holy One blessed be does not measure according to the human measure. Human beings fill the empty vessel, but do not fill the full [vessel], but [the method of] the holy One blessed be He is not thus. He fills the full [vessel], but he does not fill the empty [vessel], as it is said, and he said, **If you really hear** (11:13) [literally, "If hearing you will hear"]. [This means] if you are hearing [now], you will hear [in the future], but if not you will not hear [in the future] (bBer 40a).

Rabbis told a parable of "a king who appointed two trustees. One was appointed over a supply of straw, and the other was appointed over a supply of silver and gold. The one appointed over the supply of straw was suspected, and he used to become angry because they had not appointed him over the silver and gold. [The people] said to him, "Fool! if you were suspected over a supply of straw, how will they trust you over a supply of silver and gold?" (Mek Bahod 5.85-89).

I harvest where I have not sown. When a king "harvests" he does not go out in a field with a sickle and cut grain in his own field. He conquers another country and collects booty. He confiscates the gold of the treasury, the way Antiochus Epiphanes did when he defiled the temple at Jerusalem and plundered the national treasury that was kept in the temple. The citizens of the other country had all paid taxes to put gold into their treasury, but when the invading king looted the treasury, he "harvested" where he had not "sown." This was political language.

Throw the useless servant out. This may have meant, "Fire him!" But it may have involved more punitive measures as well.

Weeping and grinding of teeth. This is a typical Matthean editorial comment, also found at Matt 8:12; 13:50; 22:13; and 24:51. These all have their source in Ps 112:10. In that Psalm the one who fears God is contrasted with the wicked person. The faithful person does many good things, among which are giving generously and loaning (Ps 112:5), the way the wicked servant does not. Consequently the faithful person prospers, but the wicked one does not. Instead he becomes jealous, angry, and grinds his teeth in despair. This intertextual Psalm was in the background on which the parable was based. Like the Psalm, the parable concludes with the wicked reaping the results of his wickedness.

The judgment scene of Daniel 7. The following judgment scene is important background for the next parable. After the "beasts" had all been described in succession, the little horn from the previous beast, which represented Antiochus Epiphanes, king of the Greek empire (fourth beast) was speaking extensively. Instead of describing in historical terms the way the Maccabees led the rebellion against the Greeks until Judas succeeded in recovering the temple area and rededicating the temple, the author of Daniel described the whole event mythologically, in theophanic terms, showing the clouds of heaven as God's presence. Judas's victory was explained in terms of his winning a case in court, the verdict decreed was that he should be appointed leader, "like a Son of man," or like a king. The drama reads as follows:

TEXT

Matthew	Jewish Background Sources
[31]**When the Son of man**	**When** they see that **Son of man** (1 Enoch 62.5)
comes to his glory / **and all his messengers with him**, /	Then Yahowah my God **will come, and all his holy ones with him** (Zech 14:5).
then he **will sit on his glorious throne,** / [32]and all the nations will be gathered before him. / Then he will separate them	**sitting on his glorious throne** (1 Enoch 62.5).
	Then my elect One **will sit on his glorious throne** (1 Enoch 45.3).
one from another, / just as a shepherd separates the **sheep** from the **goats**; /	Look! I will judge **one sheep from another**, between rams and male **goats** (Ezek 34:17).
	In those days [the elect One] **will sit on** my **throne** (1 Enoch 51.3).
	You will have to see my elect one how he **sits on the glorious throne** and judges (1 Enoch 55.4).
	He positioned the elect One on **the glorious throne**, and he will judge (1 Enoch 61.8).

[The Lord] gave to him [David] the contract of kings, even **the glorious throne** in Israel (Sir 47:11).

33and he will station the sheep **on**
his right, / but the goats **on the left**.
/ 34Then the king will say to those
on his right, / 34"Come, blessed of
my Father, / inherit the Kingdom
prepared for you / from the
foundation of the world. / 35For I
was **hungry**, and you gave me
[something] to eat, / and I was
thirsty, and you quenched my thirst;/
I was a stranger, and you gave me
hospitality, / 36**naked**, and you
clothed me; / I was sick and you
cared for me, / in prison and you
visited me." / 37Then **the righteous**
will answer him, saying,

I saw Yahowah **sitting on his throne**, and all of his heavenly troops standing alongside of him, **on his right and on his left** (1 Kings 22:19).

Is not this the fast that I have chosen? . . . Is it not to distribute your **food** to the **hungry**, to take the oppressed poor people into your home, when you see **the naked** to **clothe** him (Isa 58:6, 7).

The congregation of **the righteous** shall appear (1 Enoch 37.1)

"Lord, when did we see you **hungry** and we fed you
or thirsty and we gave you [something] to drink?
38"When did we see you a stranger,
and we provided you hospitality,
or **naked** and we **clothed** you?
39When did we see you sick or in prison, and we visited you?"
40Then, by reply, the king will say to them,
"I tell you under oath,
'Whatever you did to one the least of my brothers
you did to me.'"
41Then he will say to those on his left,
"Leave me, you cursed, into eternal fire
prepared for the devil and his angels.
42For I was **hungry**, and you gave me no[thing] to eat;
I was thirsty, and you did not quench my thirst;
43I was a stranger, and you gave me no hospitality;
naked, and you did not **clothe** me,
sick and in prison, and you did not care for me."
44Then they will answer, saying,
"Lord, when did we see you **hungry** or thirsty or
a stranger or **naked** or sick or in prison,
and we did not minister to you?"
45Then, by reply, he will say to them,

"I tell you under oath,
whatever you did to one of these least
you did to me."

Matthew	First Testament
[46]Then **these** [on the left] **will** go away to punishment **of the age [to come]**, / but the righteous **into life of the age [to come].**	Many, sleeping in the dust of the ground **will** rise up, **these to life of the age [to come]** and **these** to disgrace and rejection **of the age [to come]** (Dan 12:2).

TECHNICAL DETAILS

The literary unit. Just as the parable of the talents was based on Ps 112 and concluded with the last verse of that Psalm, to remind the reader of the text on which the parable was based, so this parable concludes with a quotation of the last chapter of Daniel, to remind the reader of the basic intertext. Both of these parables are small homilies.

This latter parable is a poem, and it is one of the most elaborate and extensive of the parables attributed to Jesus. Some would not call it a parable at all. It has the type of imagery one might expect of a parable, and it is coherent with other parables and chreias of Jesus, but it is closer in style, form, and substance to the poem of Matt 10 than any of the parables of Jesus.

It is a unified poem that cannot be reduced successfully, layer by layer, the way Robinson has conjectured.[15] Neither is it true, as Smith argued, that the sheep and goats are merely an incidental simile, so unrelated to the theme that "if anything they confuse the problem to be dealt with."[16] The sheep and goats are as integral to this well-designed poem as any of the animals are in Aesop's fables or the beasts in Dan 7. They symbolize the saints and the sinners in the

[15]J. A. T. Robinson, "The 'Parable' of the Sheep and the Goats," NTS 2 (1956):225-37. The poetic balance is so obvious that I translated this into poetic form before I saw that C. F. Burney, "St Matthew xxv 31-46 as a Hebrew Poem," JTS 14 (1965):414-24, had done the same 30 years earlier. I was delighted to observe that our poetic lines are almost identical. He said, "It is important to remark (for the sake of those who are unacquainted with Hebrew) that I have not in the slightest degree exercised a tour de force in order to produce this rhythmical and rhyming effect in my translation. I have simply translated the Greek as it stands, as literally as possible and in the same order of words" (p. 419). I have taken more freedom than Burney has in translation, holding to the meaning without being as literal. He made two additions that I do not consider necessary. Before he began the translation he assumed that Jesus spoke only Aramaic, so he was surprised to find that this translated back into Hebrew easily, but not into Aramaic (pp. 420-21). On the basis of this poem, he argued that Jesus must have known Hebrew. His original assumption was faulty, because he lived before the Dead Sea Scrolls were discovered.

[16]C. W. F. Smith, "Mixed State of the Church in Matthew's Gospel," JBL 82 (1963):159.

judgment, which is the main point of the parable. Both Cope and Johnson correctly noted that the entire poem is Matthean in style.[17] Johnson rightly classified this as a typical king parable, similar to many in rabbinic literature. If this is not to be classified as a parable, it is at least very parabolic.

Johnson also held, however, that the phrases "Son of man" and "my father" were added later.[18] There is no special reason why this latter assumption is necessary. These words do not break the poetry nor interrupt the thought of the poem, and they are typical Matthean terms. Burney recognized this passage as a poem more than 80 years ago, and he cast it into Hebrew poetry. He tried to translate it into Aramaic, but was unable.[19] The typical Matthean vocabulary and style does not prove that the poem was composed late or by someone other than Jesus. Anyone who translates another work must use his own vocabulary in the translation.

The poem is too carefully formulated to have been composed on the spur of the moment or to have been originally composed for some other purpose and then later changed slightly and readapted. It appears to be a literary unit composed with the intention of using it again and again in a campaign with the same Messiah and with the same king in mind. This is a picture, like the poem of Daniel 7, of a dramatic judgment scene after the battle. The difference is that the Son of man, in this scene, is also the judge who has his accompanying messengers, whereas the divine judgment scene in Daniel pictures the Son of man as the plaintiff receiving his kingdom at the same time the saints of the Most High receive the kingdom. This scene pictures the Son of man after that judgment had taken place, determining who would be accepted as the new saints of the Most High.

Matthew's poem is presented as if the war was over; the Son of man had been enthroned as king and then he was about to pass judgment on the people who had participated in the conflict in some way. Dan 7 was composed after the event, when the Battle of Beth-horon had been won, and the temple had been rededicated. Matthew's poem, however, was used in anticipation of such a victory, warning non-participants of the way things would be after the battle had been won. This is a realistic picture, but it would not make sense composed after 70 I.A. after the battle had been lost, and there was no victory. The later church would have had little reason to place false prophecy in the mouth of Jesus.

---

[17]Smith, "Mixed State," p. 159, fn. 25, also considered the unit to be basically Matthean, even though he approved Robinson's dissection.

[18]S. E. Johnson, "King Parables in the Synoptic Gospels," JBL 74 (1955):39; L. Cope, "Matthew XXV:31-46 'The Sheep and the Goats' Reinterpreted," NovT 11 (1969):32-44.

[19]Burney, "Hebrew Poem," pp. 420-21, from reprint, 1965, pp. 414-24; Cope, "The Sheep," p. 36, 42.

Hutter demonstrated the strong influence Matt 25:31-46 had on the Manachean doctrine of judgment. He said Manis obviously used the text and gave it his own eschatological interpretation.[20]

Historical background. After the final battle of a war, it was customary for the leading general to pass judgment on the fate of the participants. After the fall of Jerusalem, for instance, the Romans separated the surviving Jews and decided which should be given freedom, which should be killed, which were to be sent as slaves into Egypt, and which would be led in procession to Rome (War 6.378-434). After that judgment had been carried out, Titus set up his judgment seat and passed another judgment on those Romans who had shown special valor during the war. These were given special medals, promotions, and financial awards (War 7.2-16).

This second kind of judgment scene is the one the poem of the sheep and the goats pictured. The theme of the parable is "to the victors belong the spoils." This may have been a parable that Jesus trained his apostles to tell many times while they were recruiting others. These "fishers of men" would need hospitality and provision as they traveled through Palestine and possibly into the diaspora, recruiting followers for this new movement. Therefore, Jesus had this carefully prepared parable to suggest to the people to whom his recruiters spoke how it would be with his supporters and his adversaries in the Kingdom of Heaven. At a time later in his program it became evident that not all cities supported his program, so he promised them destruction on the day of judgment. These included his own home town of Capernaum and the neighboring towns of Chorazin and Bethsaida (Matt 11:20-24).[21]

When Judas the Maccabee, nearly 200 years earlier, asked permission to pass through Emphron, people blocked the gates with stones and refused entrance to the troops. In retaliation, Judas laid siege to the city, took it, killed all males, burned the city, and then passed through, walking over the top of all the dead bodies in the road (Ant 12.346-47). The parable of the "sheep and the goats" reflects similar possibilities for non-cooperating villages. The same kind of pressure and seriousness that was evident in the chreia dealing with recruitment is obvious here and seems to point to the same person in a similar situation.

This poem might have been composed by Matthew rather than Jesus. Cope has given some strong reasons for thinking this,[22] but even if this were the case

---

[20]M. Hutter, "Mt 25:31-46 in der Deutung Manis," NovT 33 (1991):276-82.

[21]Dodd said he failed to understand what this meant. It seemed to be expressed in terms of war and social upheaval, but why should Galilean cities be more destructively treated than Tyre and Sidon in the upcoming Roman war. Dodd did not see that Jesus was not saying Roman troops would punish these cities, but that he would. See C. H. Dodd, The Parables of the Kingdom (London: Nisbet, 1952; 1960), p. 82.

[22]Cope, "Matthew 25:31-46," pp. 41-44.

a post 70 I.A. date for its composition is not required. After 70 I.A., all attempts at acquiring a kingdom had failed. There continued to be Jewish uprisings in other parts of the Roman Empire, but there was no longer much hope of overthrowing Rome. All the political, messianic pretenders had failed. It seems very unlikely that Christians would have composed new literature that falsely attributed to Jesus predictions like this that obviously were not fulfilled. It seems much more likely that it was actually delivered at an earlier time, when hopes of victory over Rome were still high. That was at the time Jesus lived, and this parable is coherent with the other parables and chreias attributed to Jesus.

This is not the only judgment scene in the Gospel according to Matthew. There is the separation of the wheat from the chaff (Matt 3:1); the faithful from the hypocrites (Matt 6:2, 5, 16), the wise and foolish builder (Matt 7:24-27), the wheat from the weeds (Matt 13:30), the good from the bad fish (Matt 13:48-49), and the competent from the incompetent employees (Matt 13:14-30).

COMMENTARY

The Son of man comes in his glory. The Son of man was not "the representative of humanity,"[23] as Plummer presumed. The Son of man in Matthew is an antitype of the Son of man in Dan 7 and in 1 Enoch 62. In the Danielic heavenly judgment scene, the Son of man was the plaintiff who was given authority like that of a king. It was not a universal concept. It was a national one. The Son of man was a code name for king, Messiah, or Son of God. (See further in the commentary on Matt 3). Those who come into their offices in glory, and sit on glorious thrones are kings.

All his messengers with him. The word translated "messengers," might also be rendered "angels." It is the Greek translation given for "holy ones" in Zechariah. Since both holy ones and messengers might either be heavenly or earthly, only the context here decides which is meant. In an earthly royal context, the messengers would be the king's cabinet of chief officers. For Jesus this would be his apostles, which is fitting here, because the term "apostle" is one of the synonyms for messenger. The term "angel" is a general term. An apostle is an angel who is commissioned with authority to act in behalf of, in the name of, and at the responsibility of the principal who commissioned him or her. With Jesus as the Son of man, his apostles might be considered his earthly angels who would be with him.

According to Matt 26:53, however, Jesus believed that God would send him 12 legions of angels, if he wanted them. This is a group much larger than the 12 apostles. Both here and in Matt 26, the angels involved are antitypes of the holy ones of Zech 14:5. Some later Matthean texts have "holy ones" instead of

---

[23]A. Plummer, An Exegetical Commentary on the Gospel according to St. Matthew (London: Stock, 1909), p. 349.

"angels" or "messengers" to conform more closely with Zech 14:5. During the Hasmonean Rebellion, three fearful riders of horses with magnificent harness reportedly appeared and overpowered the Greek general, Heliodorus, assisting, in that way, the Hasmoneans in their rebellion against the Syrian Greeks. These were believed to have been sent by God (2 Macc 3:25-29). Jesus may have expected that kind of military support had he received a positive sign from heaven, but when there were no ripe figs on the trees in the Kidron Valley, he made no effort to carry out any action.

On his glorious throne. This envisions the Son of man sitting on the royal throne at Jerusalem after the war had been won, and the Kingdom of Heaven had been established. Just as Jesus was pictured here as the Son of man coming into his glory, sitting on his throne, and judging, so Enoch visualized the Son of man sitting on his glorious throne and judging.[24] Caragounis[25] listed the qualities that were identical in the narratives about the Son of man in Daniel, 1 Enoch, 4 Ezra and the gospels. Most of his qualities were accurate, but a few were not. The Son of man in Daniel, 1 Enoch, and 4 Ezra was not "non-human" as he thought, nor was the Son of man in Daniel a judge, as he was in 1 Enoch. In Daniel he was a plaintiff in the trial where the Ancient of Days was the judge.

None of the characters was ontologically divine as Cargounis believed. Kings were the highest judges in the land, and even subordinate judges were considered legal agents of God, ever since Moses appointed his first assistants and told them that their judgments were the judgments of God (Deut 1:17). The Psalmist called judges "gods, sons of the Most High" (Ps 82:6), although he reminded them that they were still human and would die like other human beings (Ps 82:7).[26] According to Justin Martyr, Jews of NT times expected the Messiah to be a human being, born like other human beings (Trypho, 49.1). Nevertheless, they were believed to have divine authority, because of their offices. Because Judas the Maccabee was not really a king, he was classed as one "like" a Son of man. David, Solomon, and many others were legally God when they ruled, but no human being was non-human or ontologically God. Doeve said,

> This [Matt 25:31] is quite in harmony with Dan vii 13sq.: The Son of Man who receives the מלכותא [kingdom] and the Saints, who receive the מלכותא [kingdom]. But those who are on the right hand of the King, and who correspond to the Saints of Dan. vii 18, are termed "the blessed of my Father." So the Son of Man, who

---

[24]F. H. Borsch, "Mark XIV.62 and I Enoch LXII.5," NTS 14 (1967/68):565-62.

[25]C. C. Caragounis, The Son of Man (Tübingen: J. C. Mohr [Paul Siebeck], 1986) p. 172.

[26]On the relationship among kings, and gods, and heavenly councils see S. B. Parker, "The Beginning of the Reign of God--Psalm 82 as Myth and Liturgy," RB 102/04 (1995):532-59.

has received the Kingdom and the Glory, is at the same time the Son of the Ancient of Days, the Son of God.[27]

All the nations will be gathered. The situation involved here is not obvious. There are two ways to examine the problem: 1) There will be a great judgment involving Judah and the nations in conflict, followed by a secondary judgment of the Jewish participants afterward, or 2) the "nations" include the diaspora Jews who were also participants in the movement. These will be examined in order:

1) The first impression given here is that the Messiah would be so victorious that the surrounding enemy nations would be subject to him, and they would have to wait for his verdict to see how he would deal with them. They would be at his mercy. If they had supported the Messiah's enemies as Edom had done when the Babylonians destroyed Jerusalem (Obad; Ps 137:7-9) they could expect only punishment.

Rabbis said, "The nations of the world will be assembled because of him, as it is said, **The Root of Jesse who stands as an ensign of the peoples. The gentiles will look to him"** (Isa 11:10; GenR 99.8, 185c). World conquest has been part of Jewish and Christian theology for centuries. Alexander the Great enlarged his empire from a small country of Macedonia to include part of India. In his era he seemed to have conquered all of the nations. Rome was only a city state before the time of Hannibal, but in less than 200 years it ruled all of Europe and the East as far as the Euphrates River. Jews and Christians of NT times had visions of becoming as great as that, so mythological judgment scenes included such ideas. The judgment day in Dan 7 was not the judgment of every single battle involved. There had been conflict going on for more than 400 years, and the most recent struggle had lasted 3 1/2 years. The final situation included in the judgment myth was the Battle of Beth-horon and the cleansing of the temple.

2) All of this may be the understood background of this poem of judgment, but the subject of this poem is more complex than that. Although it is related to the great judgment against all the nations, this poem is more local in its application. A legitimate question is: Who were the nations who were gathered before the Son of man in judgment? Cope correctly observed that they were not "the least of these" who were Jesus' disciples. The least were not to stand in judgment. The judgment was centered around the way people treated the least of these.[28]

This poem is closely related to 1 Enoch 62-63, where the Son of man is shown seated on his glorious throne, judging the righteous elect ones from the wicked. Among those facing judgment were the kings, governors, high officials, and landlords that ruled the land. Matthew probably had these in mind when he

---

[27]J. W. Doeve, Jewish Hermeneutics in the Synoptic Gospels and Acts (Assen: Van Gorcum, 1934), pp. 151-52.

[28]Cope, "The Sheep," pp. 36-37.

spoke of the "nations," but that does not mean that all of the nations of the world were gathered together at that judgment. This was probably coherent with Joel who prophesied that enemy nations would be gathered at Jerusalem in the Kidron Valley, where they would be defeated in war (Joel 4:9-21; RSV 3:9-21). The kings and governors involved would have been only those who had ruled the land of Palestine, keeping Jews there in a subject position. This would have been the Caesars, Herods, Pilates, Quiriniuses, and other procurators and governors who had ruled the land--not the earth. For 1 Enoch the elect ones were the Jews, and the wicked were those who oppressed the Jews. They probably included both Palestinian and non-Palestinian Jews. The wicked were probably Palestinian and non-Palestinian gentiles. Matthew may not have understood the same people to have played the same roles in the drama as 1 Enoch, but 1 Enoch was evidently familiar with the text of Daniel.

The "nations" in Matt 25 may not have been the same as the "gentiles" in Matt 10:5 or pagans in general, but Cope was further correct in thinking that the "nations" here were the same as the "nations" in Matt 28. That, however, does not mean that they were non-Palestine gentiles. Gentiles were not expected to win favors in judgment. The disciples who went out as Jesus' messengers did not go to the non-Judaized gentiles--not even to the Samaritans. Neither did Paul. Rabbis said that the expression "uncircumcised" meant those outside of Palestine, circumcised or not. When Paul went out to the uncircumcised (Gal 2:9) he went to the diaspora Jews, those who were already trained in scripture and already expected a messiah. Some of these were circumcised and some were not. If he had not gone to those already trained, he never would have completed his mission in all of modern Turkey in a short 11 years. Jeremiah had promised that the diaspora Jews would be returned to Palestine when the kingdom was restored (Jer 29:13-14).

Sectarian Jews would not have accepted hospitality from pagan gentiles if it had been offered (Matt 10:5-15). Much less would they have asked for it and considered the gentiles guilty for having rejected them. Although the great judgment described here may have understood that all of the pagans were also lined up as goats on the left side, the poem was written for believers to read. It was designed to warn those Jews who were free to help or hinder the campaign of the consequences they might face if they did not cooperate. The fact that these Jews were called "nations" may mean they were diaspora Jews and that this poem applied especially to those outside Palestine as the poem in Matt 10 did not.

Because this early messianic movement which Jesus led was mostly done in secret out of earshot of the Romans, there is no report in the NT about all of the plans and negotiations that went on while the chreias and parables were being told. The diaspora Jews were never completely removed from Palestinian Jews. Many of them came to feasts at Jerusalem every year. After the death of Herod when his son Archelaus came to Rome to have Caesar confirm his position as king to succeed his father, Jews in Rome heard of it, and instantly 8,000 Jews gathered to express their opinions and become as much involved as they could

(War 2.80). When Herod was gaining control over Palestine, Jews negotiated with Parthians to overthrow Herod and reestablish a Hasmonean as king over Palestine, ruling from Jerusalem (War 1.248-270).

There were many Jews in Syria during the Hasmonean Revolt, and they probably were deeply involved in stirring up disarray in the Syrian government there while Judas was extending his borders. Wealthy Jews from Rome, Persia, Parthia, Egypt, and other countries provided financial support for military movements in Palestine. Jesus knew there were loyal Jews in the diaspora who would come from the East and the West to Palestine when the kingdom was reestablished. Luke reports that there was a second group of emissaries sent into the diaspora as part of the recruiting campaign. No later than 52 I.A., when Paul was preparing to move farther west to Rome, there already was a strong Jewish Christian church there. All of these diaspora Jews were called "uncircumcised" and "nations." This judgment poem may have been directed to them.

Brown said that Matthew originally was interested in a mission no farther from Jerusalem than Syria, where the sect moved its center of operations after the fall of Jerusalem, in his judgment. The interest in gentile missions began after the fall of Jerusalem and only slowly developed amid conflict within the community.[29] Nevertheless, he acknowledged that Peter may have had a mission to the gentiles earlier,[30] but Brown overlooked the close diaspora-Palestinian Jewish relationship that existed before the fall of Jerusalem. This judgment scene was effective before the fall of Jerusalem, while Jews still anticipated the defeat of Rome and the reestablishment of the kingdom during their own lifetimes.

Either of the two interpretations given above would explain the situation for which the poem was composed:

1) Either this is the second judgment, directed to the winning side after the judgment against the nations had been completed, or

2) this judgment was designed to include the diaspora Jews who were called "nations." In either case the message was directed to contemporary Jews who could participate in the campaign if they chose to.

The sheep from the goats. Sheep and goats often graze together in the Near East, but it is very easy to distinguish sheep from goats: the goats are almost always black, and the sheep are almost always white. As in Aesop's fables, the animals involved are really people, the sheep supported Jesus' program, but the goats did not. Sheep are obedient followers who depend for their security entirely upon the shepherd, his dogs, and his goats. Goats are independent thinkers. They look out for their own safety. They do not rely only on the shepherd for food. They are capable of acting without guidance. Because of this, shepherds keep a few goats in their sheep fold. When the goats see danger, they run, and the sheep follow

---

[29]S. Brown, "The Matthean Community and the Gentile Mission," NovT 3 (1980):193-221.

[30]Brown, "Gentile Mission," p. 219.

them (Jer 50:8). Because of these differences heretics and pagans are normally classified as goats, and orthodox believers as sheep. Monarchs want citizens who are like sheep; goats usually rebel until they can obtain a democracy. Just as 1 Enoch pictured the Son of man sitting on his glorious throne, judging, so Matthew shows Jesus as the Son of man sitting on his glorious throne, judging--separating the sheep from the goats.

The following picture shows a shepherd, riding on a donkey. He was playing a flute when this picture was taken at 5:00 A.M. from the area near Mar Saba. The sheep are easily distinguished from the goats, because the sheep are white, and the goats are black.

The sheep on his right. In the Near East the distinction between the right and the left is very important. The left hand is the hand of demons. It is used for toilet needs and things of that nature. People eat and shake hands with the right hand. They also raise the right hand for taking oaths. Therefore the favored people are stationed at the right. Such good names as "righteous" and "dexterous" come from the word "right." Pejorative names like "gauche" and "sinister" come from the word "left," showing that these prejudices continue into Western society.

The righteous were those who were expected to inherit the kingdom. The traditional idea that the righteous should inherit the kingdom was as old as Joshua, when he led the Israelites into the Land of Canaan to inherit this promised land. The righteous were not the pagan gentiles, who would not have known that there was a movement going on by which the faithful were expecting to inherit the promised land. Eleazer ben Hyrcanus said the pagans have no share in the age to come (tSan 13.2). First Enoch said there was a special place prepared for the righteous. These were the ones who suffered offense, gave bread to the hungry, clothing to the naked, helped the fallen to rise, and cared for the orphans (2 Enoch 9.1).[31]

The least of these. These were probably those Jews who had only recently become enthusiastic about the kingdom. They were not elders; they were children in the faith, even though they were adults and at that time more loyal than the Pharisees. They were evaluated depreciatively by the Pharisees, but Jesus called and trained them to be his legal agents. They were not the poor and needy, as some scholars have suggested.[32] They had once been rich businessmen and leaders who had given all they had to the monastic community that called itself "the poor." The apostles were the ones who were given authority to function as legal agents for Jesus.

The other possibility is that the name "least" could have been a general term. Jesus evidently had more supporters than 12 in his organization, and they were of varying ranks. Nevertheless, they all belonged to his movement and deserved respect. Whenever someone helped them as they went about their assignments, that person's assistance would be appreciated and recognized.

The logic of considering action done to Jesus' recruiters is the legal concept of agency.[33] In NT times a man's agent or apostle was legally identical with the man himself, just as men and women are today in most Western court systems. In royal terms, a king's ambassadors had the same authority to negotiate in behalf of a king as the king himself. When the Ammonites thought David's messengers were really spies, they shaved off half the beards of each and cut off their garments above their hips and sent them away (2 Sam 10:1-5). This was like treating David himself this shameful way, so David sent Joab to conquer the Ammonites (2 Sam 10:6-14). Jesus indicated by this parable that he would consider treatment of his ambassadors the same way.

When did we see you? Pamment thought the righteous sheep should have known that they were sheep. He was surprised that they were surprised at the judgment. In an attempt to explain this surprise he traced the ethics of Jesus in his teaching

---

[31]See J. M. Court, "Right and Left: The Implications for Matthew 25.31-46," NTS 31 (1985):223-33.

[32]G. Gross, "Die 'geringsten Brüder' Jesu in Mt 25,40 in Auseinandersetzung mit der neueren Exegese," BibLeb 5 (1964):172-80.

[33]Cope, "The Sheep," pp. 39-41, has correctly observed this.

and actions as reported in Matthew and concluded that it was total commitment that Jesus required of the sheep.[34]

Then the king will say. Here the Son of man (Matt 25:31) was not a representative of humanity but a judge and king (Matt 25:34). He would hold all three offices, Son of God, Son of man, and king, at the same time. Didache renders "Son of man," as "the Lord," which is also a name for the Messiah or a king (Did 16.7). Therefore the terms, "king" and "Son of man," were synonymous. This helps to understand the function of the Son of man.

The least of my brothers. Here the ones called the "least" are the Son of man's "brothers." These least were Jesus' legal agents. One of the rabbinic stories is about a king who came to one of the cities of his kingdom where he heard the people complain about the way the king's counsel treated them. The king responded that it was not the counsel about whom they were complaining but about the king himself. Legally this was so. Jesus sent his apostles out as "fishers of men," recruiting followers. In some places they were kindly received, and at other places they were badly treated. Jesus said this was the way these people treated him. Today, when people in foreign countries object to actions taken by the president of the U.S., they damage the embassy and the ambassador or counsel.

Punishment of the age. These were the ones on his left hand. When the war was over, and the Son of man took his place on the throne at Jerusalem, those who had sabotaged the movement would be punished. They would be tortured, become members of work camps, held in prison, or receive some other type of punitive treatment. They could not expect the benefits of the new age that other citizens enjoyed.

Life of the age [to come]. Life of the age to come was existence as citizens of the promised land after it had been taken away from the Romans. Those who belonged to this age were the antitypes of the saints of the Most High of Dan 7. The "sheep" would belong to the age to come. The age to come for Daniel was the Jewish age that followed the defeat of the Greeks by the Hasmoneans. The age to come about which Jesus spoke would be an antitype of this age. It would be the Jewish age of freedom following the expulsion of the Romans from Palestine. Christians had to wait until the time of Constantine before the age to come came.

---

[34]M. Pamment, "Singleness and Matthew's Attitude to the Torah," JSNT 17 (1983):73-86.

CHAPTER TWENTY-SIX

MATTHEAN PARALLELS TO THE HEXATEUCH

Matthew	Joshua
And it happened when Jesus **had finished** these things . . . (Matt 26:1).	When they **had finished** distributing their several territories . . . (19:49).
The last supper with Jesus' disciples in which he inaugurated the new contract (Matt 26:2-30).	The renewal of the contract (24:1-26).
Death of Jesus (Matt 27:27-50).	Death of Joshua (24:29-30).
Joseph buried the body of Jesus (Matt 27:57-60).	Bones of Joseph buried at Shechem (24:32).

The "transition" sentence (Matt 26:1), thought to conclude divisions within the Gospel of Matthew is located here before the end of the gospel and also before the end of the Book of Joshua. But it shows some parallel to Josh 19:49. Josh 19:49 might have been the passage in the Hexateuch that suggested the formula to the author which he then used four additional times in the gospel. The other possibility is that a later scribe moved the verse from its original position--wherever that was--to its present location so that its relationship to Josh 19:49 would be more evident. The events which follow in both books continue in the same sequence as was true also of the fifth division in relationship to the Book of Deuteronomy.

The "Joshua" section of Matthew (Matt 20:17-27:26) began with Jesus in Judaea at Jericho at the very place where Joshua had earlier entered the promised land. Jesus had moved from Galilee across the Jordan so that he could enter the land at the same place Joshua crossed before. The entrance into Jerusalem was very similar to Joshua's entrance into Palestine. Jesus celebrated the Passover just after his arrival into Jerusalem just as Joshua had earlier celebrated the Passover just after his arrival into the land. Since the major objective of Jesus, according to Matthew, was Jerusalem, Jesus' program was not made to correspond in order to that of Joshua (Josh 5:10-12). Instead, Jesus' Passover celebration (Matt 26:2-30) was placed in a position to represent Joshua's renewal of the contract, because it included Jesus' inauguration of the new contract. The prophesied fall of Jerusalem (Matt 24:1-12) might be expected to reflect the fall of Jericho in Joshua,[1] but in sequence it falls closer to the destruction of Ai (Josh 8:1-29), and the fall of Jericho has no direct counterpart in Matthew.

The "transition" sentence does not come at the end of the "Joshua" section of Matthew, but it matches a corresponding quotation in the Book of Joshua. Even such details as the burial of Joseph's bones in a different tomb was reflected by a Joseph in Matthew who placed Jesus' body in a new tomb. Since there was no resurrection in Joshua, Matthew 28 extends beyond the limits of the Hexateuch in the FT.

SUMMARY

This examination has not demonstrated a perfect relationship between the contents and order of events in the Gospel of Matthew and the Hexateuch in the FT, but it would have satisfied those who were already convinced that these were the last days of the evil age. They thought they were in the very position where the Hebrews had been just before the conquest, at the place Babylonian Jews had been just before the invasion of Cyrus into Babylon, and just where Palestinian Jews had been after the temple had been defiled by Antiochus Epiphanes. They were looking for signs that would "prove" their beliefs, and these typologies would have pleased them. The divisions between Exodus and Leviticus and Leviticus and Numbers seem less artificial than Farrer thought them to be. Once these divisions are seen more clearly, a hypothesis seems possible that has at least a little more claim for itself than "likely guesswork."[2]

In review, the Matthean Hexateuch would be divided as follows:

1. Genesis--Matt 1:2-2:15.
2. Exodus--Matt 2:16-7:27 plus transition sentence.
3. Leviticus--Matt 8:1-10:39 plus transition sentence.
4. Numbers--Matt 11:2-13:52 plus transition sentence.
5. Deuteronomy--Matt 13:54-20:16 with transition sentence.
displaced at 19:1.

---

[1]A. Farrer, St. Matthew and St. Mark (Westminister:Dacre, 1954), p. 184, made that identification.

[2]Farrer, St. Matthew, p. 197.

6. Joshua--Matt 20:17-27:60 with transition sentence misplaced at 26:1.
--Resurrection account in Matthew 28.

Bacon's organization of the Matthean Torah is as follows:

Prologue--Matt 1:1-2:23.
1. Genesis--Matt 3:1-7:27.
2. Exodus--Matt 8:1-10:39.
3. Leviticus--Matt 11:2-13:52.
4. Numbers--Matt 13:54-18:35.
5. Deuteronomy--19:1b-25:46.
Epilogue--Matt 26:2-28:20.

Farrer's Hexateuchal "stripes" in Matthew seem to be about as follows:

1. Genesis--Matt 1:1-2:15.[3]
2. Exodus--Matt 5:1-7:27.[4]
3. Leviticus--Matt 10:1-39.[5]
4. Numbers--Matt 12:46-13:58.[6]
5. Deuteronomy--Matt 16:21-18:35.[7]
6. Joshua--Matt 20:29-25:46.[8]

TEXT

[26:1]Now it happened when Jesus had finished [speaking] all these words, he said
to his disciples, [2]"You know that after two days the Passover comes, and the Son
of man will be given over to be crucified. [3]Then the chief priests and the elders
of the people were congregated into the court of the high priest, who was called
Caiaphas, [4]and they held council so that they might seize and kill Jesus. [5]They
were saying, "Not at the feast lest there be a turbulence among the people."

---

[3]Farrer, St. Matthew, p. 182.

[4]Farrer, St. Matthew, p. 183.

[5]Farrer, St. Matthew, p. 183, 90.

[6]Farrer, St. Matthew, p. 184.

[7]Farrer, St. Matthew, pp. 184-85.

[8]Farrer, St. Matthew, p. 184.

COMMENTARY

When Jesus had finished. These are the well recognized words from the transition sentence by which Matthew notified his readers that there was a major division in the book at this point. This example, however, is out of place to mark the end of the "Joshua" section of the book, but it parallels another passage in Joshua that "finishes" something. It may have been moved to make it match the Joshua verse.

After two days the Passover comes. Scholars have argued about the correct date of the last supper of Jesus with his disciples. According to the synoptic gospels Jesus was crucified the day after he had celebrated Passover, but it is illegal in Judaism to execute anyone on a feast day. This does not seem to be as much of a problem since scholars have recognized among the Dead Sea Scrolls a calendar that some sectarians observed that was different from the Roman calendar observed by popular Judaism. Jesus apparently observed this old calendar, so that his Passover was earlier than the Passover of popular Judaism. He was crucified on his Passover but not on the Passover most Jews observed.

Jaubert, who first raised the question of the sectarian calendar, claimed that the calendar would have demanded a Passover celebration on Tuesday, rather than Thursday. This would have allowed more time to pass between the Last Supper and the crucifixion than is usually considered to be the case.

Shepherd objected to this solution, because he said there would not be Passover lambs killed in the temple on two consecutive days.[9] In response to this objection Carmignac argued that Passover lambs could be slaughtered the same way other sacrificial lambs were killed on days other than the legally scheduled Passover.[10]

Shepherd's claim may be true, but sects that observed different calendars and celebrated feasts on different days performed their own sacrifices and did not respect the activities of the temple. One of the sects called itself "a holy temple for Israel and the foundation of a holy of holies for Aaron" (1QS 8.5-6). Shepherd's solution is that Jews in the diaspora probably celebrated Passover on a different day from Palestinian Jews. John followed the Palestinian tradition, and Mark followed the Roman tradition. He assumed that Mark was the principle source for Matthew and Luke. It is true that different Jews used different calendars, but this is evident from literature composed and preserved within Palestine itself. Sects were formed primarily on the basis of calendars used. These were doctrinal questions, not geographical. It is also not likely that the same sect celebrated the same feast on different days. Rabbis report efforts made to

---

[9]M. H. Shepherd, Jr., "Are Both the Synoptics and John Correct about the Date of Jesus' Death?" JBL 80 (1961):123-32.

[10]J. Carmignac, "Comment Jésus et ses Contemporains Pouvaient-ils célébrer la Pâque a Une Date non Officielle?" RevQ 5 (1964):59-79.

celebrate feasts in Babylon at the same time they celebrated them in Jerusalem. Pharisees had people stationed all along the way between Babylon and Jerusalem, sending signals by bonfires from one to the other until the signal reached Babylon (mRoshH 2.2-4).

Given over to be crucified. This appears to be an after-the-fact prediction. Jesus might have realized that at this feast a threat would be made on his life, but it seems unlikely that he would have been able to predict a death by crucifixion. There is, however, one possibility for thinking that he could have predicted his crucifixion. After he had seen that the fig tree had not borne fruit out of season, he realized that this was not the feast at which the Kingdom of God would be established. He had probably pondered many times over the possibility that he might be obligated to fill the role of the suffering Son of man rather than the mighty warrior who would lead a war against Rome.

Israel had obtained the kingdom in the past by two ways: 1) military power, like that of Joshua or Judas the Hasmonean, and 2) suffering, like the Isaianic servant, to pay for the sins of the nation. Jesus was apparently prepared to fulfill either role, whichever God wanted him to play. He was looking for a sign from Heaven to tell him how to act. Once he saw the fig tree that had not borne fruit out of season as Ezek 47 had promised would be the case when the land was restored, he reviewed the function of the lamb that was to be led to be slaughtered. The last official Son of man to rule as king from Jerusalem was the Hasmonean king, Antigonus, who was crucified by the Romans. He was led like a lamb to be slain, and he was slain by crucifixion. Following the same typology, Jesus might expect the same destiny. He was also prepared to continue if he survived. He looked forward to his Passover with his disciples in the Kingdom of Heaven, probably on the next year. Other predictions of the passion are reported in Matt 16:21; 17:22-23; 20:17-19.

Chief priests and the elders. Matthew frequently grouped these two types of people together. The Greek word for "chief priests" is the same as that for "high priest," but there could not have been several high priests at the same time. Josephus also mentioned the chief priests, so there must have been a group of temple officials that were designated as chief priests. They may have been priests who had once served as high priests. According to the report these leaders were making plans to have Jesus killed at the same time the apostles were making plans for their Passover meal with Jesus. Since Rome chose which priests would function as high priests, it should come as no surprise that the chief priests were assisting the Romans in this experience.

Not at the feast. Every year at the times of the major feasts, Jews from all over the world came to Jerusalem to attend the feasts. They also came armed so that if there happened to be a messianic uprising while they were there, they would be prepared for action.

TEXT

[6]While Jesus was in Bethany, in the house of Simon the leper, [7]a woman came to him who had very expensive alabaster myrrh, and she poured it upon his head while he was reclining. [8]When the disciples saw [that], they complained, saying, "Why this loss? [9]For this could have been sold for much and given to "the poor." [10]When Jesus found out [what they had said], he said, "Do not trouble the woman, for she has done a good work to me.

[11]The poor	you have with you	always;
me	you do not have	always,

[12]for when she put this myrrh on my body she acted for the purpose of burying me. [13]I tell you under oath that wherever this gospel is proclaimed in all the world that which she has done will also be spoken for her memorial." [14]Then one of the 12, Judas, who is called the "dagger bearer," went out to the high priest [15]and said, "What do you want to give me, and I will betray him to you?"

Matthew	First Testament
So they weighed out for him thirty pieces of silver, [16]and from then on he was looking for an opportune moment so that he could betray him.	If it seems good in your eyes give [me] my wages. If not, withhold [them]. **So they weighed out [for him] thirty pieces of silver** (Zech 11:12).

TECHNICAL DETAILS

The Markan parallel to Matt 26:11 is as follows:

The poor **you have with you** **always**
And when you want you can do good to them, but
me **you do not have** **always** (Mark 14:7).

The second line breaks the poetry, and Burney observed long ago that even if we had only the Markan text we would almost certainly deduce that the non-poetic line was a later addition, but since we have the poetic couplet in Matt 26:11, all doubt is removed. It is clear that Matthew has preserved the earliest form to which Mark has added an explanatory comment. The same is true of Matt 19:28//Mark 10:27 and Matt 16:35//Mark 8:35.[11]

COMMENTARY

Jesus was at Bethany. Bethany was a village in the vicinity of the Mount of Olives.

The home of Simon the leper. If the man called Simon was actively afflicted with leprosy, being in his house would have defiled the group. It is possible that Simon had this name because of a previous affliction that had since been declared removed.

Expensive alabaster myrrh. This is a rare perfume, and the disciples thought it was very wasteful to pour it over Jesus' head. They did not have so much money that they could afford to be wasteful. After all, they had given up all they owned to build up an adequate financial base for the program they had all undertaken.

A good deed for me. It was too late to complain about the action after it had been done, but Jesus seemed not to have been upset by it instinctively, as the apostles were. This is further evidence that Jesus came from a wealthy home and at one time was accustomed to expensive comforts. Like the disciples, he had given up this wealth for the monastic group that called itself "the poor."

You have with you always. The group that called itself "the poor" may actually have been very well endowed financially. It was called "the poor" because its members owned no money, individually. They had all taken vows of celibacy, poverty, and obedience. Every legally organized body or corporation is by definition immortal. This means that all of its members could be replaced, but the corporation would still exist. Therefore it "always" exists. People could always add to its treasury; it would be there long after Jesus and the disciples had all died. The probability that there was a sizeable treasury administered by the apostles is

---

[11]C. F. Burney, The Poetry of our Lord (Oxford: Clarendon, 1925), pp. 83-87. Burney was a professor of Hebrew Scripture, and he presumed that the New Testament professors were correct in saying that there existed one source, called "Q," which was used both by Matthew and Luke, but not Mark. Since he found these instances where the earliest form clearly belonged to Matthew he deduced that Mark also used "Q." That which is clear is either that Mark used Matthew or the same source Matthew used. If there was a common source Matthew copied it unchanged, and Mark commented on it, making additions that broke the poetry. If Matthew and Mark used the same source it could not have been identical to the hypothetical "Q," because that document, by definition, was one Mark did not use. Burney died in 1925, the very year his book was published and also the year Streeter's The Four Gospels was published. Burney's death may have been one of the reasons Streeter's hypothesis was widely accepted, and Burney's almost completely forgotten.

strengthened by the fact that the community continued after the death of Jesus. The apostles were evidently organized legally as a corporation; they were well financed; and the apostles were legal agents of Jesus. This made the corporation (the body of Christ) immortal, according to law. Judas was probably not a selfish person who was interested only in himself and money. He had probably given all he had to the community called the "poor." He was devoted to the prosperity and success of the community itself.

For the purpose of burying me. All of these points that anticipate Jesus' death and burial have probably been added by the later church in retrospect. Most translators and scholars have rendered the passage about the memorial as "as a memorial to her." The text literally says, "As her memorial." It might have meant that this was her memorial for Jesus. In any case, this has functioned as a memorial to Jesus. He has been remembered, but she has not. Her name has never been mentioned in the gospels.

I will betray him to you. Paul testified independently that Jesus was betrayed (1 Cor 11:23), but all the rest of the betrayal is reported only in the gospels and Acts. There evidently was a betrayal, and Judas was probably the one who betrayed Jesus. The other apostles would have known. After Jesus shocked the apostles by telling them of his experience with the fig tree and his conclusion that he would not lead a rebellion at this point, the apostles probably had some heated discussions among themselves. This was not fair! After all they had done! Judas may not have been the only one who had thoughts of leaving the group. Whenever they missed Judas in the group, the other apostles probably suspected what he was doing. As soon as people recognized the betrayal, they would quickly have thought of Judas as a new Achitophel. As soon as that was done, details from the Achitophel account were mixed with the Judas story, so that now it is difficult, if not impossible to distinguish the history from the midrash. Since many details were deduced from scripture that were dogmatically determined, their historical value is not automatically valid.

Thirty pieces of silver. The historian normally asks at this point, "How did anyone know what Judas and the high priest had said together in private?" If that had really happened, it is not likely that Judas would have told the other apostles that he was doing it. The answer is that they did not really know, but it was accepted apologetic historiography among Jews and Christians of that time to fill in gaps in history from the scripture. Among their working doctrines was the belief that 1) everything that was in the world was in the scripture; 2) all prophecy was prophesied only for the days of the Messiah; and 3) these were the days of the Messiah. Therefore, everything dealing with the betrayal of Jesus must have been prophesied, and a historian had only to search through the scriptures to find which prophecy fit the situation. In that way Matthew found the statement in Zechariah about the silver, and he assumed that was prophesied about Judas.

Thirty pieces of silver was a very low price to expect for betraying the leader of an important resistance movement, but that was the only text the author could find that specified a price for betrayal.

TEXT

17On the first [day] of unleavened [bread], the disciples of Jesus came, saying, "Where do you want us to prepare for you to eat the Passover?" 18He said, "Go to the city, to that [man]--and say to him, 'The teacher says, "My time is near. With my disciples, I will make the Passover at your place."'" 19Then the disciples did as Jesus had commanded them and prepared the Passover.

COMMENTARY

The first [day] of unleavened [bread]. The words "day" and "bread" are not a part of the Greek text. These nouns are implied from the preceding adjectives. Arnott argued that this was not the first day of the feast of unleavened bread but the first day of the unleavening of things, the day when Jews prepared for the feast, by slaughtering the lambs and removing all leavened bread from the house. In preparation for the feast Jesus sent his disciples ahead to make arrangements. The feast would begin in the evening which would be the beginning of the next day. This would concur with the Johannine report (John 11:55-12:1).[12]

Passover was the day to prepare for the feast of unleavened bread. This happened on Nisan 14 (MT between the evenings of the 14th and the 15th) (Exod 12:1-6; Lev 23:5). The next day (Nisan 15) was the feast of unleavened bread. It was to be observed by a holy convocation (Exod 12:16; Lev 23:7-8; Num 28:16-17). Jews were not permitted to eat any leavened bread. All three Torah accounts agree that preparation should be made on Nisan 14 and the feast of unleavened bread should take place on the evening of Nisan 15. The Leviticus and Numbers accounts call Nisan 14 the day of preparation and Nisan 15 the day of the feast of unleavened bread, Exod 12:11 says that the feast of unleavened bread is the Lord's Passover. Jews of NT times had many disagreements about dates for feasts, and sects were formed on the basis of these disagreements. That which is very likely, however, is that Jesus did not follow the same calendar as popular Judaism.[13]

Although this feast has been interpreted around the Passover from Egypt, the custom was established in Canaan long before there were Jews. In ancient times, New Year's Day was the very day Christians now celebrate as Easter, the

[12]A. G. Arnott, "'The First Day of the Unleavened . . .' Mt 26.17, Mk 14.12, Lk 22.7," BibTrans 35 (1984):235-38.

[13]See further R. T. Beckwith, "The Essene Calendar and the Moon: A Reconsideration," RevQ 15 (1991-92):457-66.

Sunday following the first full moon after the Spring equinox. Approximately two weeks before New Year's Day Canaanites destroyed all of the food they possessed, believing it was bad luck to carry over into the new year any food from the old year. The old year ended about two weeks before the new year began. During this period Canaanites ate only unleavened bread, the rest of their food having been destroyed. When Israelites moved into Canaan they accepted the custom of the Canaanites, but they related the practice to their escape from Egypt. When Israelites changed from the old pentacontad calendar to the new Roman calendar, they moved New Year's Day to the autumn and divided the two week period between Passover and New Year's Day, leaving one week between the beginning of the fast and Passover and one week between New Year's Day and the Day of Atonement.[14]

Go to the city--to that one. The expression pros ton dáy-nah (πρὸς τὸν δεῖνα) here rendered "that one" is difficult to understand and therefore to translate confidently. Dáy-nah (Δεῖνα) means "a certain one," "one not named." It could be feminine and refer to "that city." It could also be either neuter or masculine. The only clue to the noun implied is the following pronoun, which has to be either neuter or masculine. Therefore it designates a certain masculine person. The apostles were to go to the city, which was probably understood to be Jerusalem, and there they were to find a certain man. When they found him they should give him the instructions Jesus suggested. The vagueness involved was part of the code used to carry on secret activities.

The disciples understood which man Jesus had in mind. Mark's account is that the disciples were to go to the city and there they would meet a man carrying a water jar. They should follow him to the place where he was taking the water. That is the place where they should plan the feast (Mark 14:13-14). The only **men** who would have carried water in jars in NT times would have been monks. All the rest of the water would have been carried by women. After waiting until they saw a monk, they were directed to follow him to his residence. This would have been a monastery, and there Jesus would have found hospitality. It was probably the only monastery in the area and one that was well-known by Jesus and his disciples.

My time is near. Most scholars assume that Jesus was talking about the time of his death being near. That is only one of the possibilities. He was probably speaking in code to a trusted person who understood what the time was. This may have meant the time for celebrating the Passover (that was certainly near), the time for establishing a new contract, the time for leading a revolt against Rome, or some other time that we can only guess.

---

[14]See further Buchanan, New Testament Eschatology (Lewiston: Mellen, c1993), p. 26, fn. 2.

TEXT

[20]When it was evening [Jesus] reclined with the 12 [apostles]. [21]While they were eating, he said, "I tell you under oath, that one of you will betray me." [22]Being very much disturbed they began to say, each one of them, to him, "I am not the one. Am I, Lord?" [23]In reply, he said, "The one who has dipped with me his hand into the bowl--this one will betray me."

Matthew	First Testament and other Jewish sources
[24]The Son of man **leads** away, just as it is written of him, but woe to that man through whom the Son of man is betrayed.	He was oppressed, and he was afflicted, but he did not open his mouth. Like a sheep **is led** to the slaughter, and like a lamb before its shearers is dumb, he did not open his mouth (Isa 53:7).
It would have been good if that man **had not been born**." [25]Judas, the one who betrayed him said in reply, "I am not the one, am I, Rabbi?" [26][Jesus] said to him, "You have said," While they were eating, Jesus took **the bread**, blessed, broke [it], and **gave** [it] to the disciples, and said, "Take, **eat**! This is my body."	Where then will be the dwelling of sinners . . . **It would have been good** for them **if they had not been born** (1 Enoch 38.2) Moses said to them, "It is **the bread** which Yahowah **has given** you **to eat**" (Exod 16:15).
[27]After he took the cup and after he had given thanks, he gave [it] to them, saying, "Drink from it, all of you, [28]for this is my **blood of the contract which** is being poured out in behalf	Moses took the blood, sprinkled it over the people, and said, "Look! **The blood of the contract which** Yahowah has made with you on the basis of all these words" (Exod 24:8). Also you, in the **blood of** your **contract**, I will send your prisoners, from the cistern that has no water (Zech 9:10-11).

of the many	Yahowah has laid upon him the **iniquity of us all** (Isa 53:6).
for **the forgiveness of sins.** 29I say to you, 'I will not drink from the fruit of the vine from now until the day when I drink with you anew in the Kingdom of my Father.'"	I will make a new **contract** with the house of Israel and the house of Judah (Jer 31:30) . . . for I will **forgive their iniquity and their sin** I will not longer remember (Jer 31:34). Yahowah . . . keeps contractual bond with thousands, **forgiving** iniquity, transgressions, and **sin** (Exod 34:6-7).

COMMENTARY

When it was evening. In Jewish concepts, the day began at evening, when the sun had set. That is when the Passover and the feast of unleavened bread also began.

[Jesus] reclined with the twelve [disciples]. It was customary in the Near East to eat while reclining, resting on mats with a pillow at the head, propped up on one elbow.

As it is written. It was normal to think that all things fit into a predestined cycle and that everything in the cycle was reported in the Scripture. If we knew the scripture that Jesus had in mind we could know what he expected to happen. In Daniel the Son of man is not reported to have died, and that is the only place where the Son of man is discussed. Later rabbis identified the Son of man in Daniel with the suffering servant in Second Isaiah, so it is possible that one of these passages was intended (e.g., Isa 53). Judas the Maccabee, as the first Son of man, was killed in battle as a martyr. He may have been interpreted as the person who was led like a sheep to be slaughtered (Isa 53:7).

A more likely earlier type would have been during the time of Herod the Great. That was the Hasmonean, Antigonus--the last Hasmonean to rule from Jerusalem as king. The Parthians appointed Antigonus, and he ruled for about three years before Herod deposed him and killed him. He was the last of the Hasmonean kings, the Messiah, and therefore the Lamb. Since he was killed by Herod he would have been the Lamb who was slain. He was even crucified. If Jesus thought of himself as another King Antigonus, this would have suggested to him that he would also be crucified. Others whom Herod or his son, Aristobulous, killed were Judas, son of Ezekias, Simon, and Athrongaeus (War 2.55-65).[15]

---

[15]Josephus spelled this man's name Athrongaeus in some places and Athronges in others.

Followers of any of these leaders might have thought of their leader as the Lamb that was led to the slaughter, one who had sacrificed his life for his nation.

The problem with this analysis is that none of these, except Judas, was mentioned in FT, and Jesus said that he would go away as it was written of him--meaning, of course, written in the scripture. Any of these other messiahs, however, could have been interpreted as the fulfillments of Isa 53. The servant in Second Isaiah was believed to have suffered, and through his suffering to have paid off all of the iniquities that had been added to the heavenly debt against the Jewish nation. The Messiah, the Lamb, whatever his identity, was held to be the antitype of the suffering servant. Like the servant, he was led like a sheep to be slaughtered. He had been sacrificed for his nation.

The word hee-páh-gay (ὑπάγει) can mean "die," in which case this would mean "the Son of man will die . . ." Because it comes from the word "lead," it might allude to Isa 53:7 where the sheep is led to the slaughter. If this were the force intended, then Jesus would have meant that he was being led away just as the earlier Son of man, Judas the Maccabee, to be slaughtered like a sheep. This possibility would be greater if the verb were in the passive voice in Greek as in the Hebrew passage in Isa 53. Matthew regularly presented Jesus as being in charge of his future. He knew that which was about to happen to him. He was going to be led--not by the Romans, really, but--by God, and Jesus was in complete agreement with God in the matter of will.

That one had not been born. A rather common expression (1 Enoch 38.2; Strom 3.18; Hom 12.29).

I am not the one. The word "rabbi" was applied either to a teacher or a judge. Shanks refuted Zeitlin's claim that the term was not used in NT times.[16]

Dipped his hand with me. The rules recorded in the Dead Sea Scrolls include the order in which the common meal was performed. First the high priest would put forth his hand, secondly, the Messiah, and after that each person in the order of his dignity (1QSa 2.11-22). Fensham suggested that in the Last Supper, Judas broke protocol by reaching out his hand at the same time the Messiah did.[17] It is possible, however, that Judas was of priestly descent and therefore authorized to reach forth his hand before the Davidic messiah. We can only guess at this.

Blessed and broke it. The blessing he used was probably the same one used still today at Jewish meals: "Blessed are you, Yahowah, our God, King of the age [to come], who brings forth bread from the [promised] land." (ברוך אתה יי' אלוהינו מלך העולם [הבא] המוציא לחם מן הארץ, bah-rookh ah-tah, Yah-

[16]H. Shanks, "Is the Title 'Rabbi' Anachronistic in the Gospels," JQR 53 (1963):337-45.

[17]F. C. Fensham, "Judas' Hand in the Bowl and Qumran," RevQ 5 (1965):259-61.

hoh-wah, ehl-oh-hay-noo, meh-lehk hah-oh-lahm [hah-bah], hah-moh-tsee leh-khem min hah-ah-retz [mBer 6.1]).

This is my body. D. B. Carmichael analyzed first the suggestion of Eisler which was later developed by Daube. She then surveyed works of both scholars and explained the basis for their arguments. It was Eisler who first identified Jesus' saying with the practice associated with the afikomen at Passover. The afikomen is a special piece of bread set aside at the Passover meal. Daube argued that the afikomen is a mispronunciation of the Greek af-ehr-khó-meh-non (ἀφερχόμενος), "the coming one." The coming one was the Messiah which Jews anticipated every Passover Feast. Carmichael followed Daube in thinking that the identification of the wine with Jesus' blood was a later development of the early church after the death of Jesus. It was not a part of the original statement of Jesus.[18] This is not necessarily so. The blood was probably a basic part of the ceremony involved.

Written contracts have been made and signed for thousands of years, but before that, legally binding contracts were made through ceremonies. Maine said,

> No pledge is enforced if a single form be omitted or misplaced, but, on the other hand, if the forms can be shown to have been accurately proceeded with, it is of no avail to plead that the promise was made under duress or deception.[19]

The introduction of written contracts did not put an end to contracts by ceremony. Both methods were in force at the same time--sometimes, as with the marriage ceremony, the ceremony and the written document were involved for the same contract. This has continued to this very day. The following are some ancient biblical examples. According to one report, when God made a contract with Abraham, Abraham brought together various sacrificial animals, killed them and cut each one in two. Then when it was dark, he carried a torch and a smoking pot between the two parts of each animal (Gen 15:7-20). According to another report, this contract was made when Abraham was circumcised.

The liturgy of his circumcision was the sign of the contract (אות ברית, oht buh-reét) (Gen 17:11) that was made to confirm this contract. Like baptism, this liturgy has continued to be performed as the ritual necessary to admit males into the contract community.[20] When Jacob and Laban made a contract after their angry confrontation, they piled many stones in a heap; then they ate a meal

---

[18]D. B. Carmichael, "David Daube on the Eucharist and the Passover Seder," JSNT 42 (1991):45-67.

[19]H. S. Maine, Ancient Law (London, c1901, 17th), pp. 172-73. Reprinted in U.S.A. by Dorset Press, c1986).

[20]See further M. V. Fox, "The Sign of the Covenant," RB 81 (1974):557-96.

their angry confrontation, they piled many stones in a heap; then they ate a meal there, and Jacob said, **This heap is a witness between you and me today** (Gen 31:48). After Joshua concluded a contract between the Lord and the Israelites, he took a huge stone, set it under an oak at Shechem and said, **Look! This stone will be a witness against us** (Josh 24:27).

Ceremonies were designed to imitate, legally, the way something would have been done if it were done physically. For example, it was legally possible to be born again, without a physical death. The person who was to be born again had to be prepared to leave one identity to begin another. Such a ritual sometimes required a person to change garments and be baptized.

When a child is born the mother's water bag is broken and the child comes through the water out into life in the air. When a person was born again a legal ritual was performed which imitated the physical birth. The person was made to be submerged into water and brought through the water of baptism into a new legal life. This new legal life was one in which the baptized people existed as members of a new community and received new identities. That new life began with a legal ritual. This ritual has still further ceremonial significance. It reenacts the passage through the body of water at the eastern border of Egypt, and it also symbolizes death and resurrection.

The person died to his or her old identity, leaving the garments of the old identity on the bank, becoming immersed into the water and coming up a different person and putting on different clothing. In Christian baptism this means being buried with Christ, ceremonially, and raised with Christ from legal death to the glory of the Father, so as to walk in newness of life (Rom 6:4). The change of garments is the ceremonial way of putting off the old man and putting on the new (Col 3:9). People who were baptized did not really die and come to life again physically. The death, resurrection, and new life at baptism are all legal fictions.

Maine said that ancients performed legal actions and conveyances through rituals.

> They are in the highest degree ceremonious; they require a variety of symbolical acts and words intended to impress the business on the memory of all who take part in it. . . . Ancient law uniformly refuses to dispense with a single gesture, however grotesque; with a single syllable, however its meaning may have been forgotten; with a single witness, however superfluous may be his testimony.

Blackstone described an old English liturgy for transferring property, called "livery of seisin":

> And then the feoffor, if it be of land, doth deliver to the feoffee, all other persons being out of the ground, a clod or turf, or a twig or bough there growing, with words to this effect: "I deliver these

> to you in the name of seisin of all the lands and tenements contained in this deed." But if it be of a house, the feoffor must take the ring or latch of the door, the house being quite empty, and deliver it to the feoffee in the same form; and then the feoffee must enter alone, and shut-to the door, and then open it, and let in the others.[21]

English jurists do not know how this ceremony originated. They know only that it is very old. The Livery of Seisin did not originate with the English in the Middle Ages. It is as old as the ceremony through which Boaz required the next of kin to Naomi to contract that he would give up his right as next of kin to purchase Naomi's land and also to purchase Ruth as his wife. In the company of witnesses he took off his own sandal and gave it to Boaz and said, "Acquire it for yourself" (Ruth 4:8). This transferred his rights of purchase to Boaz (Ruth 4:1-9) just as efficiently and completely as property was transferred in England by handing the new owner a clod of turf or a twig from the property. When Jesus broke bread and handed it to his apostles, he said, "This is my body" (Matt 26:26), he probably transferred corporate authority to the twelve just as legally as Ruth's next of kin and the feoffer in England.

The ritual of eating and/or drinking was frequently used to signify something that would be legally internalized and made effective. For example, the suspected adulteress was required to take oaths, but this was not enough. To make the oath legal, she was required to drink the water of bitterness. The priest had previously prepared the water of bitterness by writing the curses involved in a book and then washing off the ink into the water of bitterness. This ritual internalized the curses which would make the woman abort if she had taken the oaths falsely (Num 5:16-23). When the Israelites broke the first contract, Moses made the annulment effective by breaking the stone tablets into pieces (Exod 32:19). In order to destroy the legal ritual of loyalty the Israelites had made with the golden calf, Moses burned the calf, ground the material into powder, put the powder into water, and made the people drink it (Exod 32:20). This made all contracts invalid and enabled Moses to begin again to form a new contract. When a person was murdered, and the murderer could not be identified, the elders of the nearest town were required by law to take a heifer who had never been harnessed and break its neck in a wadi with water in it surrounded by unploughed land. Then they washed their hands over the heifer. This ritual legally absolved the citizens of the town from the guilt of that particular murder (Deut 21:1-9). The liturgy of washing hands was reportedly employed also by Pilate to absolve himself from the guilt of having Jesus crucified (Matt 27:24).

In NT times, as today, corporations were formed. These were given the name of "bodies" (corpora) because they could function legally as existent bodies.

---

[21]W. Blackstone, Commentaries on the Laws of England (Chicago: Callaghan and Co, 1884, 3d ed. rev) II, p. 314.

They could be sued, fined, and taxed, and they could represent themselves in court. Of course, these were all legal fictions, but they were very significant in court. A corporation by definition is immortal and continues even though all of the members of the corporation change. The corporation never dies. Corporations were legally born through ceremonies and contracts,[22] just as people were legally born again through ceremonies and contracts.

There were several other leaders who aspired to become kings in NT times, but none of them left a surviving group of followers that continued after their deaths. After Herod the Great died, Simon, Judas, and Athrongaeus each one had large groups following him, and all were killed, but we have no record that any of them was anointed or left followers who were legal agents and incorporated (War 2.55-79). During the Jewish-Roman war of 66-70 I.A., Josephus was indignant because John and his followers in the temple used the sacred wine and oil. Those elements should have been reserved for anointing the Messiah and for the messianic banquet. The followers of John, however, may have thought of him as the Messiah, used the oil to anoint him, and the sacred wine for the banquet (War 5.564-65). Josephus may have objected only because he did not believe John was the true Messiah. This is only a conjecture, but, even if he had been anointed, he evidently left no legal agents or corporation to continue after his death.

One of the reasons the followers of Jesus continued after his death as the body of Christ is that the body was legally organized so as to make this possible. The disciples of Jesus did not continue as students. After they were adequately trained they became legal agents of Jesus, called apostles in Greek. Furthermore they were probably organized into a corporation before Jesus' death. The legal transference of Jesus' body and blood would have been necessary for the formation of the legal body of Christ even if he had not been crucified. Although we do not have the complete liturgy preserved, the ceremony of the Last Supper implies that a contract was formed and a corporation was organized. After that people could be baptized into the body of Christ, and after they were legal members could participate in a repetition of the incorporation ceremony.

Jesus legally distributed his body and blood before he was captured or knew that he would be crucified. At the Passover meal, he began with a blessing over the bread, probably using the same blessing Jews have used ever since. It was customary to break the unleavened bread as part of the blessing, but Jesus contributed an additional clause to the liturgy: "This is my body" (Matt 26:26), and he distributed it to the apostles, just as Moses' spirit had been distributed to the 70 elders of Israel (Num 11:25). It apparently had the same kind of legal function as Naomi's next of kin giving his sandal to Boaz or the English transferance of property by handing a small portion to the purchaser.

At a normal Passover Seder the bread is broken at the beginning of the service and the blessing over the fruit of the vine near the end, but Jesus had a

---

[22]E. H. Kantorowicz, The King's Two Bodies (Princeton: Princeton U., 1957), pp. 12, 501.

further reason for following this order. It was necessary to form the corporation before he made a contract with it. The contract was between God and the new Israel. Jesus was God's legal agent, so he represented God in this legal action. The new people of God required a legal body to act in its behalf to be party to the contract, so Jesus formed this body of Christ, using the unleavened bread of Passover for his livery seisen. Next he made with this new people of God his new contract, using the fruit of the vine as the livery seisen.

The text does not say, "This is my flesh," because Jesus was not speaking ontologically, but legally. Legally, a "body" is a corporation that has been legally formed by the proper liturgies or contracts. When he said, "This is my body," it had the same significance as when Joshua said, **This stone is a witness** or when Naomi's next of kin handed Boaz his sandal and said, "Acquire it for yourself." The stone was not really a human person who could speak and testify, but once Joshua declared in legal ritual that it was a witness, it fulfilled the necessary ritualistic function of a witness. It had some of the same ritualistic significance of the later English livery of seisin, when something from the object transferred was given from one owner to another. These legal liturgical examples seem to resemble the ceremonial significance of the expression, "This is my body . . ." (Matt 26:26). That would explain why the Christian community is called the "body of Christ." It is a legal corporation that has been properly formed.

After he took the cup. The blessing with the cup was also probably the one still used today at Jewish Passover Seders: "Blessed are you, Lord, our God, King of the age [to come], who creates the fruit of the vine" (ברוך אתה יי אלוהינו מלך העולם בורא פרי הגפן, bah-roókh aht-táh ad-doh-naí, ehl-oh-háy-noo, méh-lehk hah-oh-láhm, boh-ráy puh-reé hah-geh-fen) (mBer 6.1).

According to Daube there is no Jewish liturgy or practice that identifies the wine of Passover with blood. The Passover reported in the Pentateuch shows no use of wine at the Passover feast. This practice was probably added much later after the establishment of the Israelites in Palestine where grapes constituted one of the major agricultural products. Wine was regularly used in Dionysian and Bacchic festivals in the Mediterranean area and may have influenced this change in the Jewish Passover meal.

After the disciples had become apostles the Holy Spirit was legally "in" them, just as the authority of corporation was "in" them when they ate the bread as part of the liturgy for the legal ceremony. The reception of the fruit of the vine as Jesus' "blood" was the liturgy by which the corporation became a party to a contract with God. It is not necessary to suppose that the later church conjectured this ritual after the death of Jesus. It might have been a normal part of a ritual for making a contract.

My blood of the contract. Near the end of the meal Jesus took the fruit of the vine and ordered his apostles, everyone of them, to drink from it. He said, "This is my blood of the contract which is being poured out in behalf of the many for the forgiveness of sins" (Matt 26:28), but he may not have expected his physical blood to be shed at that time. This fruit of the vine was seisen for blood of the contract, just as Naomi's next of kin's sandal was seisin for the purchase of land and a wife. Jesus vowed that he would not drink again from the fruit of the vine until he drank it again with them anew in the Kingdom of his Father (Matt 26:29). He probably expected to celebrate the next Passover with his apostles, in the liberated Palestine. He expected to be alive at that time. The body that was formed through the ceremony of the broken bread was a legal body, a corporation, which transferred part of his authority to his apostles. This blood would have been a valid part of the liturgy whether Jesus' physical blood had ever been shed or not.

The Messiah was expected to provide a new contract, just as Moses had done. When Moses gave the Israelites a contract (Exod 24), the contract he finalized was between God and his people, and it incorporated them and made them a special people. When that contract was later annulled, Moses liturgically broke the tablets, indicating that the contract was no longer in force. Later there was a new ritual and a renewal of the contract (Exod 34). This was all done according to the proper legal rituals. The contract made with the Lord was understood to be a marriage contract. If a man wished to divorce his wife, he had to have a divorce writ prepared, specifying his reasons for the divorce, but this was not enough. There was a ritual involved. He was required to put the writ in her hand and send her out of his house (Deut 24:1; cf. Gen 21:14). When Jews and Israelites were driven out of their respective temples (houses) and sent into captivity in Assyria and Babylonia Jeremiah concluded that God had performed the ritual of divorce. That meant that the contract made in the wilderness (Exod 24, 34) was no longer in force.

When Jesus gave the fruit of the vine to his apostles he said this was his blood of the contract that was poured out for "the many," meaning the parties to the contract. In this ceremony, Jesus, as God's legal agent, initiated a new contract between God and the apostles. The apostles became parties to the new contract only if they all took part in the ceremony. Therefore Jesus ordered all of them to drink of this fruit of the vine (Matt 26:27). It was on Passover night that Jews expected the Messiah to appear, make his parousia, and renew the contract. This Jesus did with his apostles at the same time that he formed them legally into a corporation of Christ. This was the significance of the parable of the bridegroom and the virgins at the wedding contract (Matt 25:1-13).

The likelihood is that the bread and wine ceremony was part of a new contract and also a liturgy to form a corporation through which Jesus would remain with the members of the corporation legally even when he was not physically present. This is supported by the fact that the church continued the ritual. His Spirit was with them legally, and they repeated the ceremony by which the apostles were originally organized into the body of Christ. The "real presence" of Christ is symbolized by the communion wafer, "the body." The wafer is not the ontological presence, but the legal presence. The flame over the altar on liturgical churches is not the ontological presence of God but the ritualistic or legal presence.

This fruit of the vine was the legal blood of Jesus that is part of the contract designed by God. Even though there might not have been a Jewish tradition in Jesus' time which identified the wine of Passover with blood, Zechariah followed Exod 24 in relating blood to the contract. Contracts in antiquity were made valid either in writing or by liturgy. Some contracts required both. Abraham's contract with God required only a liturgy that was performed with a smoking torch and the halves of slaughtered beasts (Gen 15:1-21). The animals that were slain and divided may have symbolized the curses that accompanied the contract and would be applied to either party which would break the contract.[23] The torch and smoking pot which Abraham carried between the pieces probably symbolized the presence of the deity as in the pillar of fire and smoke. Both Abraham and God went through between the parts together, legally, and through that liturgy became parties to the contract made.

When Moses first made a contract between God and the people, he took three leaders of the people and the 70 elders. He then told the people the terms of the contract, and they accepted them. After sacrifices had been made he took half of the blood from the sacrifices and poured it upon the altar. The other half he sprinkled upon the people. As he sprinkled the blood he said, "Look! The blood of the contract" (Exod 24:8). Since the blood was sprinkled on both the people and God's altar it legally bound God and the people to the contract made. Then Moses took the 73 apart where they saw the God of Israel, and they ate and drank (Exod 24:1-11). There are some similarities between the contract made on that occasion and the one Jesus made with his apostles, as they ate and drank and received the blood of the contract.

After the people sinned by making a golden calf, Moses arranged to have a new contract made (Exod 34:10). This contract required the people to observe the terms of the contract that were commanded. If that were done, God promised to keep his terms of the contract which involved 1) forgiving the sins of the people, 2) being present in their midst, and 3) driving out all of the inhabitants of the land that the Israelites wanted to conquer and possess (Exod 34:1-12). This new contract provided the precedent and legal basis for Jeremiah's promise that God would make still another new contract after the people had been unfaithful (Jer 31:31).

When it seemed clear to Zechariah that the land was going to be restored, he related it to the coming of the king into Jerusalem and a fulfillment of the terms of the contract. These terms involved the promise of a return to the promised land where the hostility of nations would be subdued. All the surrounding peoples would be defeated. The entire promised land would be at peace, from eastern borders to the western borders. Then the Lord spoke, according to Zechariah, and either took an oath:

---

[23]So M. Weinfeld, "בריח," TDOT II, p. 262.

1) [I hereby swear] **By the blood of your contract**
2) **I will send your prisoners from the cistern where there is no water** (Zech 9:10-11)

--Or--the Lord may have asserted

Through the blood of your contract or by means of the blood of your contract, **I will send your prisoners . . .**

In the latter case, the blood of the contract would be part of a liturgy that would bring about the release of the prisoners. The contract involved was the one made at Sinai which the Hebrews broke. Therefore this contract was annulled, but it was renewed under the leadership of Moses in the wilderness (Exod 34). Later Jeremiah concluded that when Israelites were sent away to Nineveh as "captives," "slaves," or "prisoners" that this was a sign that the contract had been annulled. He further held that Judah had been less faithful than Israel so that God would also annul its contract and send the Jews away as captives to Babylon (Jer 3:8). He reached this conclusion on the basis of Deuteronomy and Leviticus. Because the broken contract in the wilderness had been replaced by a new contract (Exod 34), Jeremiah concurred with Hosea and further prophesied that the contract broken in his day would also be replaced by a new contract (Hos 2:14-23; Jer 31:31).

According to the contract, these debtor slaves would be released when they had paid double for all their sins. Therefore Zechariah thought the terms had been met, and following Jubilee terms, the captives would be set free.[24] In any case the blood of the contract was used in relationship to a plan to release Jews from their captivity to return to the promised land free from foreign rule and bound by contract with their own king. Later sects of Judaism claimed that the contract promised by Jeremiah had been concluded in their own time. One of these sects resided in Damascus (CDC 7:19; 3:12-20). Another sect was Christianity with Jesus as the new Moses. The author of Hebrews spoke of Jesus as the mediator of a new contract (Heb 9:15), noting that since God had said through the scripture that this was a new contract and that this meant the contract concluded by Moses was old (Heb 12:24). When Paul wrote 2 Cor 3-4 he followed both Jeremiah and Exod 34 as bases for his belief that a new contract had been concluded by Jesus. Matthew was of the same opinion on the same bases.[25]

---

[24]K. R. Schaeffer, "The Ending of the Book of Zechariah; a Commentary," RB 100 (1993):204-210, has argued that the territory Zechariah defined was only Judah; i.e., from the Dead Sea to the Mediterranean Sea and from the lower end of the Jordan to the shores of the Mediterranean Sea. He may be right.

[25]See further Buchanan, "Paul and the Jews," When Jews and Christians Meet, ed. J. J Petuchowski (Albany: State University of New York Press, c1988), pp. 148-60.

Instead of being the blood of your contract, Jesus said it was by his blood of the contract. In the formation of this contract, the liturgy involved eating and drinking. Those who ate and drank at the Last Supper were Jesus, who, as the Messiah was God's legal agent, made the contract in behalf of God, and the apostles who had become the corporation that functioned in behalf of the people. Jesus said this fruit of the vine was **his** blood, liturgically, because he was the mediator of this corporation. This would have been so even if Jesus had not been crucified. In a similar way Moses was the mediator of the earlier contract between God and his people. Part of the liturgy performed to consummate the contract was eating and drinking. Moses, as God's legal agent, fulfilled the role of God, and the chief men of the community became the new corporation governed by the contract, functioning in behalf of the Israelites.

Paul, Luke, and some texts of Matthew referred to the contract Jesus made as "a new contract" (1 Cor 11:25; Luke 22:20). This seems to be an allusion to the contract mentioned in Jer 31 and Exod 34. The blood was related to the first contract (Exod 24) and the one on which Zechariah depended (Zech 9:11). This is further supported by Jesus' entrance into Jersualem, following the prophecy of Zech 9.[26]

Poured out for [the] many. Earlier scriptural contracts were not made with people in general, but with a special group that constituted the parties to the contract. The community party to this particular contract was sometimes called "the many" (הרבים, hah-rah-beém). Both rabbis and NT authors were careless in their use or omission of definite articles. Jesus may have said that his blood was poured out for the many rather than just "many" in general. Contracts are made with certain members. This contract was made with the new chief leaders of Israel in behalf of the community of Israel. This is true whether the correct reading is the many or just "many." In this case "the many" was the body of Christ or the corporation of Christ. Paul complained to the Corinthians because when they came together for their Passover meal some had more than enough to eat and drink but others were hungry (1 Cor 11:17-23). He accused these of not "discerning the body" (1 Cor 11:29). The body to which he referred was evidently the body of Christ, "the many," the parties to the contract in his blood, the corporation in Christ. Those who discerned the body were concerned for the whole body of Christ and therefore would share their food and drink with one another.

For the forgiveness of sins. This phrase may have been part of the corporation ceremony even though it does not seem to be essential to that ritual. It may, instead, have been added later, after the crucifixion to relate Jesus' death to the new contract. It seems to reflect the liturgy of the new contract Moses made with the elders of Israel and the God who was merciful and patient, forgiving transgressions, iniquities, and sins (Exod 34:7, 10). This was after the sin of the

---

[26]See also Buchanan, "Paul and the Jews."

golden calf, and Moses asked God to pardon the people's sin and iniquity and accept the people again as God's heirs (Exod 34:9). This was the intertextual basis for Jeremiah when he promised a new contract which would include the forgiveness of sins.

Many scholars have been disturbed by the theological implications of a system that transfers the punishment for one person's sins to another. For example, Jensen made some very astute and sensitive observations about this kind of justice. On the one hand he said that if God forgave the sins then Jesus would not have had to pay for them. If a mother had two sons, and one of them sinned, how could it clear the guilt of the sinner by punishing the other son?[27]

These are all good questions in modern Western concepts, but the logic of transferring guilt was developed in ancient legal systems, where different assumptions were applied. For example, 1) it was presumed that there were crimes that could be reconciled by the payment of fines or monetary settlements. This would not apply to crimes that required a death penalty, but it would apply to many others. For example, if a man stole someone's cow, the court would require him to repay five cows; if it were a sheep he would have to pay with four sheep; if he were caught with the animal still alive in his possession, he would have to pay double (Exod 22:1). This legal system allows a transfer of concepts from punishment to payment and allows a system whereby crimes could accumulate and their payment be recorded. 2) A second Mediterranean concept of antiquity is that guilt was a community affair, and a sin could require that an entire family, community, or nation be punished to repay for one person's crimes. Maine said,

> But Ancient Law, it must again be repeated, knows next to nothing of individuals. . . The life of each citizen is not regarded as limited by birth and death; it is a continuation of the existence of his forefathers, and it will be prolonged in the existence of his descendants.[28]

This view of life allowed Joshua to have Achan's entire family and all of his livestock stoned to death. Furthermore, all of his possessions were burned for Achan's act of thievery and disobedience (Josh 7:10-26). No one at that time believed that Achan existed alone. He was a member of a family, so the sin would not be removed until the whole family was destroyed. It was part of the philosophy that was extended to the ethnic cleansing of the Amalekites (1 Sam 15:1-35). Children were punished for the sins of their fathers to the third and fourth generation (Exod 20:5; 34:7; Num 14:18). Hostages could be taken,

---

[27]P. Jensen, "Forgiveness and Atonement," SJT 46 (1993):144-45.

[28]Maine, Ancient Law, pp. 152-53.

tortured, and killed as a reconciliation measure between nations to prevent war. Entire communities shared in each member's shame and honor.

This logic allows the transference of punishment from one person within a family to another or from one citizen in a nation to another. From this logic also developed the treasury of merits doctrine. The nation of Israel was being punished by God by allowing foreign nations to rule their land. This meant that Israel was guilty of crimes that had added up until God declared the nation bankrupt. It would have to pay double for all of its sins (Isa 40:1). This meant that members within the nation would have to pay for this national debt through undeserved "taxes" and torture. Therefore, Jesus was willing to have his blood poured out to pay this national debt.

Still speaking in servant terms, Jesus continued to talk of forgiveness together with injury. Just as the Lord had laid on the servant **the iniquity of us all**, so Jesus' blood was being poured out for "the many," a technical term meaning the entire community. The servant bore the sins of the community by suffering and making his death with the wicked; Judas the Maccabee, as the first Son of man, was led like a sheep into battle where he was slaughtered for the community; then Jesus understood his own role as the Son of man to be one of dying in behalf of the community, so that the community's sins might be forgiven and the land restored as it was after the deaths of the servant in Babylon and Judas the Maccabee.

Clement said Jesus' blood was poured out for our salvation. When Jesus did this he "brought the grace of repentance to the whole world" (1 Clem 7.4). That which was required for the Day of Atonement to be effective was:

1) A gift to God to pay for the sins committed;
2) forgiveness and reconciliation among believers.
   When these requirements were met, then
3) God would forgive his people and restore the land.

Christians believed that when Jesus suffered and allowed his blood to be poured out, this provided the necessary sacrificial gift and opened the way for the members of "the many" to repent. Paul said,

> God was in Christ, reconciling the world to himself, not counting their trespasses against them, and entrusting to us the reckoning of reconciliation (2 Cor 5:19).[29]

The trespasses were not counted in this case just as they were forgiven for the sins of the golden calf before the new contract could be made (Exod 34).

---

[29]See further Buchanan, "The Day of Atonement and Paul's Doctrine of Redemption," NovT 32 (1990):236-49.

At this Passover meal Jesus seems to have performed a ritual whereby the apostles who received the bread received also the legal authority by which they became a legal corporation, the body of Christ.

Earlier, according to Matt 10:1 each of these former disciples became legal agents (appointed apostles) of Jesus when he gave them authority to do all of the things he had been doing. Matthew did not describe the ritual by which Jesus transferred his authority to them. He just announced that it had been done. According to John 20:22 the disciples became apostles when Jesus breathed upon them and commanded them to receive the Holy Spirit and with it apostolic authority by which he sent them out to function as ambassadors. This was a legal ritual.

Only those who had been baptized were allowed to participate in this ceremony, but as soon as a person had been baptized and had made all of the other preparations necessary for membership he or she was permitted to participate in the ritual by which members were received into the contract community (1 Cor 10:16; 11:24; Ign Eph 20).[30] It may have been with the ritualistic words, "Take, eat. This is my body," that the baptized person was actually received into the body of Christ. After this ritual the presence of Christ was legally "in" the new member, and the new member became a part of the body of Christ, the Christian corporation. Without a contract and a corporation the church could not have continued. A corporation, however, is immortal. The membership may be completely changed, but the corporation continues as a legal body. In one of the twentieth century Christian churches, the ritual for receiving members into the body of Christ begins, "Dearly beloved, the church is of God and will be preserved to the end of time."[31] These words recognize the legal significance of a corporation.

Sometime, during the ministry of Jesus, he gave the disciples authority to become his apostles, and he formed this group into a corporation which was identified with his body. This may have happened when Jesus commissioned the disciples as apostles and gave them authority as legal agents. At the same time or at some other time, Jesus performed a ceremony by which the group became a legal corporation, the body of Christ. The community that was called "the poor" was immortal; it was with them always, because it had been incorporated. The most likely ceremony by which the corporation was formed was at the last ceremonial supper when Jesus identified the Passover bread as a corporation, the body of Christ, and renewed the contract with the cup.

Although the baptism of Jesus was not directly called an anointing, and the last supper was not called a ritual of corporation, the surrounding events and claims suggest that both of these were implied.

---

[30]See further Buchanan, The Consequences of the Covenant (Leiden: Brill, 1970), pp. 282-90.

[31]Paragraph 1914, "The Order for Receiving Persons into the Church, " The Ritual: A Reprint of Part X Worship and Ritual from Doctrines and Discipline of the Methodist Church (Nashville: The Methodist Publishing House, 1944), p. 457.

The legal details related to the body of Christ and the apostolic authority were very influential in the establishment of the early church. There had been messiahs, such as Athronges, Simon, John, Eleazar, Zadok, and Judas of Galilee. None of the movements that these leaders organized continued after their deaths. Jesus, however, made some very important administrative plans:

> 1) He established a sound financial base. This was done by calling the wealthy to follow him, while giving up all of their wealth to the community;
> 2) He trained a group of followers and gave them apostolic authority;
> 3) He organized a legal corporation that could continue after all the organizing members had died.

What happened to this community after the death of Jesus? Three of the apostles were strategically placed: James in Jerusalem, Peter in Upper Galilee and Syria, and John in Samaria.[32] These three continued as a legal council with authority that met occasionally at Jerusalem. Paul had to deal with these (Gal 2). They had apostolic authority, and he did not, at first. A person is not legally authorized to act in behalf of another as an agent until the other has identified himself as a principal and acknowledged the claimant as an apostle. Since Paul had never seen Jesus in the flesh, his apostolic authority was not acknowledged by the other apostles. Goulder held that the other nine must have scattered themselves around Galilee and established church communities there.[33] That is as good a guess as any. Before a quarter of a century had elapsed they had established churches in Asia Minor and as far west as Rome. This did not happen accidentally as a result of charismatic individuals. This happened, partially, because of a legally well-organized and well-financed community.

Very shortly after the death of Jesus, Paul understood the relationship between the ceremony at the Last Supper and the existence of the church. Paul said,

> The cup of blessing which we bless, is it not a sharing of the blood of Christ? The bread which we break, is it not a sharing of the body of Christ? Because there is one bread, we who are many are one body (1 Cor 10:16-17).

---

[32]Buchanan, "The Samaritan Origin of the Gospel of John," Religions in Antiquity, ed. J. Neusner (Leiden: E. J. Brill, 1970):149-75.

[33]D. M. Goulder, Midrash and Lection in Matthew (London: SPCK, 1979), p. 139.

SUMMARY

This chapter shows that the Last Supper Jesus had with his apostles was very important for the continuance of Christianity. This was no ordinary Passover. The ceremony seems to have been one by which the church as the body of Christ was organized and a new contract was established. The text does not say all of this, but there are some implications:

1) Jesus initiated a new ceremony which he interpreted as a sharing of his blood and his body, when it was really unleavened bread and fruit of the vine. This was evidently a legal fiction. The elements were seisen.

2) The disciples had previously been appointed as apostles with legal authority. This shows that both they and Jesus were acquainted with legal forms.

3) The church survived after Jesus' death and was called corpus Christi, the corporation of Christ.

4) The apostles and Jesus had formed a well administered organization before the Last Supper. It had its own treasury; the apostles had contributed all of their own wealth to the organization that was probably called "the poor." Before the apostles gave their possessions to the community, they owned, in addition to money, houses and lands (Matt 19:29).

5) The church evidently had its origin in the plan and administration of Jesus. He structured a legally sound corporation comprised of legal agents and a financially sound organization.

The number of terms and formulas in the Last Supper that echo parts of the intertextual scriptural passages in which contracts were made indicate that there was a ritual performed at that feast which the apostles understood to be both the establishment of a new contract and the formation of a corporation, the body of Christ:

1) Jesus' entrance into the holy city riding upon a donkey,
2) the term "blood of the contract,"
3) the new Moses eating and drinking with the chief men of the people of Israel;
4) sacrificial blood offered together with unleavened bread (Exod 34:25);
5) promise of forgiveness of sins;
6) the relationship between the contract made and existence in the kingdom.

Matthew also organized his gospel so that the features of Jesus' last days were antitypes of those of Joshua:

1) both sent messengers ahead to prepare for the advance of Joshua;
2) both Joshuas crossed the Jordan at Jericho;
3) both Joshuas renewed the contract;
4) both Joshuas celebrated the Passover shortly after entering the promised land at Jericho.

When I drink it anew in the Kingdom. Van Cangh took this to mean that Jesus would never again participate in earthly feasts, but that he would take part in the feast at the last banquet when the Kingdom of God had come.[34] That is not a necessary interpretation of the passage.

Jews celebrated Passover once every year. Then they drank from the fruit of the vine. The expression "fruit of the vine" was taken from the Passover liturgy. Jesus meant here that he would not celebrate Passover again until the Kingdom of Heaven came. That would be before the very next year. Jesus had evidently been recruiting and working in preparation for the coming of the Kingdom of Heaven for three years. The tribulation, birth pangs of the Messiah, or end of days were to last no more than 3 1/2 years as an antitype of the period from the defilement of the temple until its cleansing by Judas the Maccabee. In Jesus' parable of the fig tree that had not produced fruit for three years, the care taker said it should be cultivated well, fertilized, and allowed one more year before it should be dug out (Luke 13:6-9). Like other parables, the message of this one had nothing to do with fig trees. It was designed to explain the number of years required to bring in the Kingdom. There had already been three Passovers, and both Jesus and his disciples thought this was the very Passover when the Kingdom of God would come, but the fig tree in the Kidron Valley proved that the new age had not yet begun (Matt 21:18-19).

There was probably a lot of discussion among the apostles and Jesus after Jesus reported the condition of the fig tree in the Kidron Valley. The disciples evidently still wanted to continue with their plans. After all, they had gone out to many of the cities of Galilee and Judah alerting people to the approaching Kingdom that would probably take form this very Passover. Like messengers of the king, they had told people to prepare for the wedding banquet and accompanying wedding contract. They told the "virgins" to have their oil prepared and their lamps trimmed. People had followed Jesus into the city spreading palm leaves before him, acclaiming him as the Messiah. They had aroused everyone's hopes. They had been waiting anxiously for a chance to proclaim him from the housetops. How could they back out now?

Jesus, however, was unwilling to proceed without God's clear approval. He was God's legal agent; he held a fiduciary office. He was responsible for acting in behalf of God. Therefore he was obligated to learn what God's will was before he acted. The only way he could learn that was from the scripture and from signs. Without God's acknowledged approval he postponed their plans one more year. He said the Kingdom would come within one more year, or this was a false alarm. The disciples were impatient. It was after that reevaluation of plans that Judas betrayed him, and Peter later denied him. They thought he was not taking the movement seriously.

---

[34]J. -M. van Cangh, "Le Déroulement primitif de la Cene (Mc 14, 18-26 et par.)," RB 102 (1995):224.

At that point Jesus had no plans to die that Passover. He was expecting to live to enter the Kingdom of God within one more year. This was not a planned separation from his disciples as Patte thought.[35] Neither Jesus nor his disciples thought of this as a farewell meal.

In the Kingdom of my Father. This is Palestine, the land of the promise, under the rule of the Messiah, free from any foreign rule. This is the contemporary antitype of the Land of Canaan God had promised the Israelites in the second contract (Exod 34) and also the land promised in the contract proposed by Zechariah (Zech 9).

TEXT

30 After they had sung a hymn they went out to the Mount of Olives. 31 Then Jesus said to them, "All of you will be offended in me tonight, for it is written:

Matthew	First Testament
	Awake, sword, against my shepherd and against the man who is next to me, said Yahowah of armies.
I will **strike the shepherd, and** the sheep of **the flock will be scattered,** 32 but after I have been raised **I will** go before you into Galilee."	**Strike the shepherd, and the flock will be scattered. I will** turn my hand against the little ones (Zech 13:7).

33 In reply, Peter said to him,

> "If all [others] are offended in you,
> I will never be offended."

34 Jesus said to him, "I tell you under oath: This night, before the cock crows, you will deny me three times." 35 Peter said to him, "Even if you need me to die with you, I will not deny you." All the disciples spoke similarly.

COMMENTARY

After they had sung a hymn. The normal hymn modern Jews would sing on Passover eve is "Dah-yáy-noo" (דיינו), "It is enough." The theme of the song is that even if the Lord had left the Hebrews in Egypt, that was all they deserved. If he had left them in the wilderness, that was all they deserved, etc.

---

35 D. Patte, The Gospel according to Matthew (Philadelphia: Fortress, 1987), p. 364.

All of you will be offended. If Jesus had already told the apostles of his conclusions after he saw the fig tree, then they probably had all become offended by the time Jesus was speaking. His description of their future attitudes was not difficult to predict. They had all come to Jerusalem expecting military activity and the restoration of the promised land. This was the goal for which they had all been striving. Their plans had been carefully made and apparently received an effective response from the populace. After the disappointment with the fig tree that had no fruit out of season, Jesus was not prepared to continue with these plans. As soon as they learned of Jesus' change of plans the apostles would have been crushed and then become offended in Jesus. Some would doubt. Others would consider him a saboteur. Judas may have expressed negative feelings openly when he was alone with the other apostles. The apostles were not only offended but also depressed.

At the time this discussion was going on, if it is anywhere nearly accurate, it means that there had been no military activity at that point. The apostles were still expecting it. If there had been a military conflict in the temple where they had successfully taken over the nation's greatest fortress, there would no longer be a chance to back out. They would already have been engaged in war and would then be discussing further military policy. They would have to have placed a huge military force in the temple to contain it and probably would have been inside the temple themselves at that time. If Jesus' whole design depended on a directive from God, Jesus would not have first attacked the nation's most formidable fortress and then looked around to see if there were any ripe figs in the Kidron Valley to tell him whether or not he should begin a war against the Romans. This means that the odds are great that there never was a cleansing of the temple. This was probably deduced later on the basis of scripture and tradition.

The Last Supper seems not to have been a happy experience, not because the apostles anticipated Jesus' death and were sad, but because their plans had been upset. The group was gathered; the contract was made; the corporation was formed; and then the discussion about immediate plans was begun. When Jesus told the apostles that he could not proceed at once, the apostles were apparently very much disturbed. This was a real let-down. It appeared to Jesus as if they would all abandon him and become scattered like lost sheep.

It is written: **I will strike the shepherd**. This prediction was probably written by Matthew after the fact. After the shepherd had been struck, Matthew would have interpreted this as the fulfillment of scripture and presumed that Jesus must have thought of that and predicted it. The term "shepherd" was frequently used in scripture to describe a king or a major general. Just as shepherds lead and defend the helpless flock of sheep, so the king leads and protects the citizens of his land. Romans normally brought out their troops on feast days, because they anticipated some revolutionary movement when Jews from all over the world gathered to celebrate a feast. If the Romans could find the leader, the pretending Messiah, they would try to kill or incapacitate him so that he could not lead a rebellion. That is what they did with Jesus, and as soon as that was done, the apostles ran away. This was not a sudden burst of cowardice on their part. They had just been upset; they were confused about the next step to take. Jesus and his apostles had not yet redesigned their plans. In the midst of this confusion, Jesus was handcuffed and taken away. What should they do? Jesus had just told them about the fig tree. This meant they should not become engaged in military combat. Were they expected to stand around and let the Romans kill them? They ran and were scattered. After the event, Matthew understood this as the fulfillment of the scripture in Zechariah. The disciples were the sheep of the flock who were scattered that Passover night.

<u>Even if you need me to die</u>. This also is probably an after the event discussion that Matthew presumed. All of the disciples affirmed their loyalty, but all failed in the test. This conclusion, however, is not certain. There were disciples who survived the crucifixion, and they may have admitted exactly the way it happened. They may have known of Judas' anger and not have been surprised by his betrayal.

TEXT

36 Then Jesus came with them to a region called Gethsemane, and he said to the
disciples, "Sit here until I go over there and pray." 37 Then, he took with him
Peter and the two sons of Zebedee, and he began to be discouraged and greatly
disturbed. 38 Then he said to them,

<u>Matthew</u>	<u>First Testament</u>
"**My soul is very sorrowful** to the extent of death. Stay here and watch with me."	**My soul is bowed down**. Therefore I will remember you from the land of Jordan, Hermon, and from the small mountain (Ps 42:7).
39 Then he advanced a little and **fell on his face**, praying and saying, "My Father, if it is possible	Abram **fell on his face**, and God spoke to him (Gen 17:3).
	Then Moses heard and **fell on his face** (Num 16:4).
	Moses and Aaron **fell on their faces** before the whole congregation of the Israelite council (Num 14:5).
let this **cup** pass away from me, but not as I wish but as you [wish]."	There is a **cup** in Yahowah's hand . . . all the wicked of the land shall

40Then he came to the disciples and
found them sleeping, and said to
Peter, "Were you not strong enough
to watch with me thus for one hour?
41Watch and pray, that you not enter
into temptation.
The spirit is willing,
but the flesh is weak."

drink [from it] (Ps 75:9).

You [Judah] will drink your sister's [Samaria's] **cup** . . . **a cup** of sorrow and desolation (Ezek 23:31, 33).

42Again a second time he went away
and prayed saying, "My Father, if it
is possible, let **this cup** pass away.
If not [unless] I drink it, let your
will be done." 43After he came again
he found them sleeping, for their
eyes were heavy, 44and he left them
again and went away and prayed a
third time, saying again the same
message. 45Then he came to the disciples and said to them, "Continue
sleeping and get your rest. Look!
The hour is near, and the Son of
man is betrayed into the hands of
sinners. 46Arise, let us go. Look! my
betrayer is near."

The cup [in] Yahowah's right hand will turn over you, and shame [will turn] over your glory (Hab 2:16).

COMMENTARY

A region called Gethsemane. The word Gethsemane means "olive press" from the Hebrew shéh-men (שמן) (olive or oil) and gath (גת) (press). The place where Jesus went with three of his disciples was somewhere on the Mount of Olives, across the Kidron Valley from the temple area. Although institutions that own property on the Mount of Olives claim that Jesus prayed precisely on their property, there is no way anyone can know that. We have to be satisfied with a general idea of the location. This mountain which was covered with olive trees years ago is now a Jewish cemetery.

Jesus went away from the temple area to the Mount of Olives nearby. He had with him only three of his apostles--not enough to defend him against a whole Roman force, as he would have if he had already conquered the temple area and declared open warfare against the Romans. This evidently happened before there was any action taken against the temple.

Sit here until I go over there and pray. The Greek word for "here" is au-toó (αὐτοῦ), which is seldom used in the NT as an adverb, meaning "here" or "there." It is usually a pronoun, meaning "his." It was normal for Jews to continue praying and singing hymns after Passover supper. It was permitted until dawn. Jews are forbidden, however, to continue together or disperse and join in some kind of revelry after the Passover meal (mPes 10.8).

Stay here and watch with me. Watch or guard may be a command to stand guard while Jesus prayed. Support for this possibility is evident in the report that Peter had a sword while he watched, and when military opposition appeared he engaged in conflict with one of the high priest's soldiers, cutting off one soldier's ear. He was probably aiming for the soldier's neck (Matt 26:51; John 18:10). Even with swords, it is clear that the three tired men were not prepared to defend themselves against any sizeable force.

Let this cup pass away from me. The word "cup" is frequently used in the scriptures and later Jewish literature to mean "fortune." There were different kinds of cups: a cup of cursing (TgJon Isa 15.1; 17.1; 21.11, 13; 51.22), a cup of punishment (TgJon Isa 27.3), a cup of consolation (TgJon Isa 40.2), a cup of fury (TgJon Isa 51.17, 22). In asking that this cup pass away, Jesus requested deliverance from the fate that seemed imminent.

Not as I wish, but as you [wish]. This is another way of saying, "Let your will be done on earth as it is in heaven" (Matt 6:10; 26:42). Historians normally ask questions about the historicity of this report. How could anyone know what Jesus prayed? Who was there to listen? Jesus left the apostles to be alone--not to be overheard. Luke said he went away from the disciples about a stone's throw distant (Luke 22:41). There probably was no one who heard Jesus pray, but Matthew knew what prayers were customary for Jews to pray in times of crisis. Prayers for that occasion first asked for deliverance, but finally requested that God's will be done. Since this was customary, Matthew was probably correct in thinking that Jesus also prayed in that way on that occasion.[36]

He found them sleeping. Gundry renders this verse, "So you were able to keep awake with me one hour, weren't you" (Matt 26:40)? [37] The negative ook (οὐκ), normally expects a positive answer in Greek, as Gundry translated, but the context denies it. Peter was found sleeping, not watching. If the translation of Gundry is correct, then it must be understood as satire.

Passover worship was permitted to continue until dawn, so long as the worshiping group remained awake. If they went to sleep, the worship had to stop. The rabbis, then, asked what the condition was that was called "sleep." They concluded that if a person could be addressed and respond, even if the response was

---

[36]D. Daube, "Evangelisten und Rabbinen" ZNW 48 (1967):120-21.

[37]R. Gundry, Matthew (Grand Rapids: Eerdmans, c1994), p. 533.

incoherent, and later when reminded could remember the incident, he or she was not asleep, but only dozing. If, however, someone spoke, and the person could not answer he or she was judged to be sleeping (mPes 10.8). The first two times Jesus checked on his disciples he evidently found them "napping," rather than sleeping, but the third time they were sound asleep, with heavy eyes, so he did not go back again to pray.[38] He simply told them to sleep on and get their rest.[39] Sleep was not a theological motif either here in Matthew or in Mark as some scholars have thought.[40] It was apparently a fact of history.

The Son of man is betrayed. This is a crucial place to use the title "Son of man." The first Son of man was Judas the Maccabee who led zealous guerrilla bands until he had received the kingdom, power, and glory fitting for a king. But Judas, the Maccabee, as the Son of man, also suffered and died for his country. Jesus continued to identify himself with the Son of man right up to the crucifixion. But instead of leading a war the way Judas did, Jesus suffered and died like a sheep led to the slaughter.

Look! My betrayer is near. The Greek for "is near" (áng-ee-ken, ἤγγικεν) is the same term used to say "The Kingdom of heaven is near" (Matt 3:2; 4:17; 10:7); or the harvest time is near (Matt 21:34). This probably means Jesus saw Judas and his supporters coming. The implication throughout this story is that Jesus was omniscient and foresaw everything in advance. Matthew may have intended the narrative to be understood that way, but there is so much omitted of the events that took place that we have to guess how much could have been suspected on the basis also of that which we cannot learn. It seems odd, for example, for him to have identified his betrayer before eating supper with him as a guest and still to have dealt with him philosophically. Most leaders of revolutions who learned of a betrayer would have had him killed immediately, but this may not be as artificial as it seems. There are two factors to examine for an answer to the puzzle.

One point to consider is the likelihood that the apostles objected violently when Jesus told them of his change of plans. Judas may have complained bitterly and arisen from the table and left the group in anger. When he returned with the chief priests and their soldiers, it would not have been hard to deduce what had transpired in the meantime.

The other is that all Jews and early Christians were conquest theologians. Their primary religious goal was to gain possession of the promised land. They

---

[38]On this see D. Daube, The New Testament and Rabbinic Judaism (New York: Arno Press, 1973), pp. 332-35.

[39]Daube, Rabbinic, pp. 332-35.

[40]R. S. Barbour, "Gethsemane in the Tradition of the Passion," NTS 16 (1969/70):235, following H. Risenfeld, Jésus Transfiguré L'Arriére Plan Récit Evangélique de la 'Transfiguration de Notre-"Seigneur (Copenhagen: Munksgaard, 1947), p. 208.

believed they were deprived of this promise because they and their ancestors had broken contract with the Lord, and they would have to be adequately punished before they could regain it. To speed up the process they wanted to punish themselves more so the required amount would be reached sooner. Some followed the zeal of Phineas who obtained the judgment of righteousness by killing the mingling Hebrew and his gentile wife. Joshua used this active way of obtaining possession of the Land of Canaan. Judas the Maccabee also led a movement that resulted in the return of the Davidic kingdom. On the other hand, there was also Abraham who only believed without acting, and it was reckoned to him as righteousness. This was the method of the Isaianic servant that suffered unjustly until the land was restored to Joshua and Zerubbabel. The emotional struggle of Jesus over these points is evident in the reports of the Gethsemane prayer and the temptations in the wilderness.

Jesus was apparently watching for signs from Heaven to learn what it was that the Messiah should do. Should he lead a rebellion, like Judas or Joshua? or should he suffer like the Isaianic servant. One of the signs he could not ignore was the death of John the Baptist. He watched for mountains to move, fruit trees to bear fruit out of season (Matt 21:18-22), and other unequivocal signs that prophecy was being fulfilled, and he was expected to carry it out. As the time of decision drew nearer the evidence seemed to point in the direction of suffering and not in leading a revolution. There may have been many attempts that failed and close escapes that are not reported which led him to think he was expected to suffer like the servant. If this was the case, then he should not add more sins to the balance by retaliating against his apostle, Judas, but rejoice in his sufferings, being sure that his sufferings were all undeserved and would therefore count toward redemption. That which seems evident is that Jesus was willing to fulfill whatever role God wanted him to undertake, once he knew what that was. The prayer at Gethsemane may not have been historical, but the apostles obviously learned from Jesus of the struggle he faced which was later mythicized into this Gethsemane experience.

TEXT

47While he was still speaking, look! Judas, one of the 12, came, and with him a
large crowd from the chief priests and elders of the people with swords and clubs.
48His betrayer gave them a sign, saying, "Whomever I kiss, he is the one. Seize
him!" 49At once, he came to Jesus and said, "Hi, Rabbi," and he kissed him.50
Jesus said to him, "Friend, why are you here?" Then [the crowd] approached,
laid their hands upon Jesus, and overpowered him.

Matthew	First Testament
51Look! one of those who was with Jesus reached out his hand and drew	Everyone who pours the blood of man by man shall his blood be

his **sword**, and struck the high priest's soldier, taking off his ear. [52]Then Jesus said to him, "**Return** your **sword** to its place,	poured, because in his own image God made human beings (Gen 9:6).
for all who **take up the sword**	Look! All you that kindle a fire, **take a sword**; go, fall into the fire which you have kindled and into **the sword** which you **have taken**. From my Memra you have this. You shall
. . **will be destroyed** by the **sword**, [53]or do you think that I cannot	**return to your destruction** (TgJon Isa 50.11).
implore my Father, and he will present me now more than 12 legions of **angels**? [54]How then will the scriptures be fulfilled that it is necessary thus to happen?"	Then Yahowah my God will come, and all his **angels** (keh-doh-sheém, קדשים) with him (Zech 14:5).

COMMENTARY

Friend, why are you here? Matthew has used three different words for "here" in this short narrative, showing his concern for good style: ow-toó (*αὐτοῦ*) (Matt 26:36); hóh-de (*ὧδε*) (Matt 26:38); pár-ay (*πάρει*) (Matt 26:50). It was not out of place for Judas, one of the 12, to be with Jesus. Judas, however, was there, not as a friend, but as one of the members of the hostile group that had come to put an end to Jesus and his mission. Lee has suggested that this is not a question at all, but rather some kind of accusation. He holds that it means something like, "For what kind of a mission did you come!"[41] The Romans would have been interested only in Jesus. Without Jesus, the rest of the apostles could cause no serious trouble, at least at this feast. It was important to the Romans for Judas to be there to identify Jesus. Plummer asked a thought-provoking question? Why was Judas not called into the trial as a witness? [42]

Drew his sword. This was what he was expected to do. He had been appointed to stand guard for Jesus. Even though there was a large crowd, and the disciples were no match for them, like the Maccabees, they were not frightened by numbers. Matthew did not identify this disciple, but John (Matt 18:10) said it was Peter. It was Peter who said that he would be willing to die with Jesus.

---

[41]G. M. Lee, "Matthew xxvi.50 Hetaire, eph' ho parei," ExpTim 81 (1969):55.

[42]A. Plummer, An Exegetical Commentary on the Gospel according to St. Matthew (London: Stock, 1909), p. 375.

Return your sword to its place. Patte said that violence was inappropriate for those who were with Jesus.[43] That seems to have been true, but it was a recent change of attitude. Those who carried swords had been appointed to stand guard over Jesus while he was at prayer. Jesus was apparently wrestling with this question while he was in prayer. The apostles may not have agreed with him and his passive stance. By the time the prayer was over, Jesus had decided it was not God's will that he lead a revolution. He had probably been moving toward this opinion ever since he saw the fig tree not bearing fruit out of season. Although the Lord could save with few as well as with many this worked only when the battle was one God ordained. This response was probably inherent to the text. The next two statements were Matthean additions: 1) Taking up the sword and perishing by the sword, and 2) Jesus' ability to call down legions of angels, the way Judas the Maccabee had done. These were later editorial comments put in by editors who thought Jesus should have said these things to refute the disciple.

Twelve legions of angels. Zechariah had promised that God would come with all of his holy ones (either saints or angels). This would happen when all of the gentiles were gathered around Jerusalem. They would take the city and loot it, rape the women, and half of the city would be taken into exile. At that time the Mount of Olives would be split in two, and many of the residents of the city would flee. Then would be the time when the Lord would come with his angels. He would fight against those gentiles. Then the miracles Ezekiel had promised (Ezek 47) would take place, and a plague like the one that saved the Jews during the time of Hezekiah would occur and destroy all of the enemies gathered (Zech 14:1-15). All of these things were expected to happen together, but they were also to coincide with the promises of Ezekiel that there would be fruit in the Kidron Valley every month of the year. Jesus had already checked this out, and he learned there were no ripe figs in that valley out of season, and the Mount of Olives had not split in two. Therefore he knew this was not the time for all of these things to take place, so he would not call upon the legions of angels he would have summoned if the other signs had been positive.

How then are the scriptures fulfilled. If the well-known scripture of Zechariah and Ezekiel were not going to be fulfilled at this time, then which ones were? This question is consistent in the belief that all things that are in the world are in the scripture. Since this is prophesied, it is destined to be just as it happened. The scripture to which this allusion is made is probably the targum to Isa 50:11:[44]

---

[43]Patte, Matthew, p. 370.

[44]H. Kosmala, "Matthew xxvi.52--A Quotation from the Targum," NovT 4 (1960):3-5.

> Look! All of you who light a fire, who take hold of a sword, go, fall into the fire you have kindled and on the sword which you have taken.

TEXT

[55]In that hour Jesus said to the crowds, "Like a brigand you have come out with swords and clubs to take me. Every day I sat, teaching in the temple, and you did not subdue me, [56]but this whole [event] has happened so that the writings of the prophets might be fulfilled." Then all the disciples left him and fled.

COMMENTARY

Like a brigand. The insurrectionists who fought against Rome up through the war of 70 I.A. were called lays-taí (λῃσταί)--brigands. This was an insulting ascription to those who organized in bands to fight Rome, but in many ways they behaved like a group of highway robbers who held up caravans and plundered their goods. According to this report, Jesus did not belong to that group.

Every day I sat, teaching in the temple. If this was true then there was no cleansing of the temple. Any "cleansing" of the temple would have required a large military force and battle. If Jesus had led such a revolt, there would have had to continue in Jerusalem a military siege. Jesus could not have been casually teaching in the open, peacefully.

The prophets might be fulfilled. This was a strong conviction of Matthew and probably also of Jesus that everything that happened to Jews in that day was prophesied earlier and was predestined to take place. The writings of the prophets understood here were either the works of Second Isaiah and Zechariah, mentioned earlier, or the prophecies from 2 Samuel and Daniel quoted in the following verses.

TEXT

[57]Those who captured Jesus led him away to Caiaphus, the chief priest, where the scribes and the elders had congregated. [58]Peter followed him [from] a distance as far as the court of the high priest, and went inside [the court] and sat down with the servants to see the outcome. [59]The chief priests, however, and the whole Sanhedrin were looking for a false witness against Jesus so that they might kill him, [60]but they could not find many false witnesses coming forth.

Matthew	First Testament and First Enoch
Later, however, two [false witnesses] came forward and [61]said, "This man said, 'I am able to destroy **the temple of God** and within three days **to build [it].'"** Then the high priest stood up and said to him, [62]"Do you answer him nothing? What have	I will establish his kingdom. He will **build a temple for my name**, and I will establish the throne of his kingdom until the age. I will be his Father (2 Sam 7:13-14).
these witnessed against you?" [63]But Jesus **was silent**, and the high priest said to him, "I put you under oath	[As a sheep before its shearers **is silent**, he did not open his mouth. He was taken by oppression and judgment. Who will declare his generation, because he was cut off from
by **the God of life**	**the land of life** (Isa 53:7-8)].
that you tell us if you are **the Messiah**,	Then he said to his men, "It is prohibited to me by **Yahowah** that I should do this thing to my master, to **the Messiah** of **Yahowah**, to put my hand against him because he is **the anointed (Messiah)** of **Yahowah** (1 Sam 24:7).
the Son of God." [64]Jesus said to him, "You have spoken, but I say to you from now	and **he will be my son** (2 Sam 7:12-13).
you will see the Son of man seated on the right hand of Power,	**You will see that Son of man sitting on** his glorious throne (1 Enoch 62.5).
	Yahowah said to my lord [the king], "**Sit on my right hand** until I place your enemies as a footstool for your feet" (Ps 110:1).
coming with the clouds of heaven." [65]Then the chief priest tore his robe, saying, "He has blasphemed! What need have we of witnesses? Look! Now you heard the blasphemy. [66]How does it seem to	I kept watching in the visions of the night. Now look! **With the clouds of heaven** one like **a Son of man came** up to the Ancient of Days and was presented before him. To him was given the power, glory, and the kingdom (Dan 7:13-14).

you?" Those who answered said, "He is guilty of [a] death [penalty]."

67Then they **spat in his face** and socked him. They slapped him
68saying, "Prophesy to us, Messiah! Who is the one who **struck** you?"

I gave my back to **the whippers**, and my cheeks to those who pulled out the beard. I did not hide **my face** from shame and **spitting** (Isa 50:6).

TECHNICAL DETAILS

From the gospel reports there is no account of any of Jesus' followers close enough to these events to have heard the conversation. Where, then, did Matthew get the data for knowing the precise conversation that went on in the high priest's court? He deduced it on the basis of accepted rules. Ancient historians had some doctrines by which they could reproduce the conversations from scriptural texts. The doctrines were these: 1) All prophecy is prophesied only for the days of the Messiah; 2) all things that are in the world are in the scripture; and 3) there is no before and after in scripture. On the basis of these rules an unknown historical event could be deduced by anyone who would check through the scripture until he or she found passages that were somehow related. The author of Matt 26:60-68 composed this midrash on the basis of 2 Sam 7:4-17; Dan 7:13-14; and Isa 53:7-8.

COMMENTARY

The court of the high priest. This may have been just a court yard, an open space associated with the home of the high priest--not an active legal court used by the high priest. There is another possibility. There was a law court of the priests (bayt deén shel koh-hah-neém, בית דין של כוהנים; mKet 1.5, bKet 12b) which evidently was controlled by priests and was the place where priests passed judgment on some matters of defilement.

The whole Sanhedrin. It is not clear exactly how the court of the priests was related to the other civil courts of the land. This was not just a court where priests did the judging. Also at the court of the priests the members of the Great Sanhedrin came and judged the priesthood. They judged the priests to discover whether or not any of them had acquired some blemish or defilement that would prevent them from participating in the Passover (mMid 5.4; tSan 4.7; bPes 80b; bErub 32a).

Within three days to rebuild [it]. At first glance one would think this is sheer hyperbole, or prefer Mark's version. Mark reported that Jesus said he would destroy the temple made with hands and after three days construct another one not made with hands (Mark 14:58). This is a reasonable undertaking. That would have required only that Jesus would have the old temple cleansed the way Judas the Maccabee had the temple cleansed before the first Hanukkah in 164 B.I.A. The old temple was the "temple made with hands." That means it was a profane or pagan temple. Once Judas had it cleansed it was a temple "not made with hands." The temple Herod began constructing about 20 B.I.A. was not completed until about 66 I.A. Jesus did not say he would destroy it, but if it were destroyed, he would immediately rebuild it.

There are many questions here. Kings sometimes did grandiose things. For example Tiberius had granted his friend, Sextus Marius, so many imperial favors that he became fabulously rich. Marius once invited his neighbor to be his guest for a few days. While he was there, Marius had the man's house razed to the ground in one day. On the next day he had it rebuilt on a larger and more grandiose scale. When his neighbor found out what had happened, Marius told him he had done this to show his neighbor the amount of power he had either to ward off attacks from his enemies or to reward kindness of his friends (Dio, RomHist 58.22, 2-3). If Jesus had really made a claim to be able to rebuild the temple in three days, he probably meant to say that when he became king he would have at his finger tips tremendous power, wealth, and authority. (See also John's version [John 2:19]).

There is another significant point to the claim made here. Nathan's prophecy with respect to Solomon was that he would be God's son and that he would build the temple of God in Jerusalem. Since Jesus was the Messiah, God's legal agent, and the anointed king, he must also have had the authority to rebuild the temple. Since the priest considered Jesus guilty of trying to set up a new kingdom, he must have said something in this conversation to justify his opinion. Two of the things that would have given his messiahship away would have been a claim to sonship to God and a claim that he would rebuild the temple. This would mean he would act like a king, like Solomon or Judas the Maccabee. The author of this unit would have obtained one claim from 2 Sam and the other from Daniel. Once the author recognized these passages he had only to fill in the details to reconstruct that vital historical event.[45]

Jesus was silent. In Jewish courts, as in American courts to-day, people were not required to testify against themselves. There was also a motivation on the part of the author to report on Jesus' silence, to show that the scripture in Isa 53 was fulfilled with Jesus identified as the suffering servant who was led like a sheep to be slaughtered, and like a sheep he did not make a sound, or, to use the words of a popular hymn, "He never said a mumbling word."

I put you under oath. In ancient courts witnesses were not regularly put under oath. Only when a person's veracity was questioned did the judge require that he be put under oath. Because most people were afraid of the consequences from the

[45]See further O. Betz, Jesus, Qumran and the Vatican (New York: Crossroads, 1994), pp. 94-101.

gods if they lied under oath to the deity, they sometimes would tell the truth when they would not otherwise. If they maintained the same testimony under oath that they had made before, they were judged innocent. If they refused to testify under oath they were considered guilty (Matt 5:37; 26:63; Quin 5.6, 1-5).[46]

The God of life. The word "life" often refers to a condition of existence on the promised land free from foreign rule. The "land of life" was another name for Palestine. The "dead" are metaphorically those not members of the contract with Yahowah. The God of life, then, is the God who made a contract with the Israelites.

Are you the Messiah. These terms are synonymous. Both the Messiah and the Son of God were titles for kings. The term messiah means "the anointed one." The anointed one was the one anointed as king. Any one anointed as king was God's legal agent, by definition. This means he was legally identical to God. When Jesus was asked whether or not he was the Messiah, the Son of God, he responded by saying that the high priest would see the Son of man coming with the clouds of heaven (Dan 7:13). The high priest then tore his garments, because he understood the code in which Jesus spoke; it was a positive answer. The high priest understood the Son of man to be the same as the Messiah or the Son of God. All three titles were brought into the conversation, according to this midrash. That is why the high priest accused him of blasphemy, but it was not really blasphemous. Anyone who accepted any of these titles claimed to be God's legal agent.

You have spoken. As today, in ancient Jewish courts a person was not required to testify against himself or herself. Jesus' reply may have had that intent, but if that was the case, he was misunderstood. Mark rendered the same answer, "I am." The high priest thought it was a claim to messiahship (Matt 26:65). Catchpole noticed that Jesus' reply to Judas was the same, and it clearly meant, "Yes" (Matt 26:25).[47]

At the right hand of Power. In Dan 7 the establishment of Judas the Maccabee as the nation's divinely ordained leader was mythicized by a court scene where the Son of man came before the Ancient of Days, the judge at that court, and was granted the victory in the trial between Judas and Antiochus, between the Syrian Greeks and the Jews, called the Saints of the Most High.[48] To Judas and the

[46]See further Buchanan, Biblical and Theological Insights from Ancient and Modern Civil Law (Lewiston: Mellen, 1992), pp. 41-43.

[47]D. R. Catchpole, "The Answer of Jesus to Caiphas. (Matt. XXVI.64)," NTS 17 (1971):213-26.

[48]See further Buchanan, Eschatology, pp. 121-59.

saints were given the Kingdom, authority, and glory of home rule. In this scene projected before the high priest, Jesus pictured himself reenacting that earlier court scene and expected the case to end with Jesus as the Son of man, appointed as God's legal agent, holding the chief seat beside the King who was called Power, in this case, rather than the Ancient of Days. The Son of man was a character in Daniel that Jews, such as the high priest, would have known but Romans would not. Romans knew that a messiah or a Son of God was a pretending king and therefore an insurrectionist. A Son of man was also the leader of a revolution but it was a code term.

TEXT

69Peter, however, sat outside, in the court. A maiden came to him, saying, "Were you with Jesus the Galilean?" 70But he denied before all, saying, "I do not know what you are saying." 71After he had gone into the gate another girl saw him and said to those who were there, "This man was with Jesus the Nazoraion." 72Again he denied with a curse, "I do not know the man." 73After a little, those standing [around] came near and said to Peter, "Truly you are also from them; for your speech gives you away." 74Then he began to curse and take oaths, "I do not know the man," and at once the rooster crowed, 75and Peter remembered the word which Jesus had said, "Before the rooster crows you will deny me three times," and he went out and wept bitterly.

COMMENTARY

Jesus the Galilean. There is little question that Jesus was from Galilee. He may not have been born in Bethlehem or lived in Nazareth, but he was acquainted with the region around the Sea of Galilee. This was the first of Peter's denials. Each one was more complete and vehement. The first denial was a simple statement that he did not know Jesus and was not one of his followers.

This man was with Jesus the Nazoraion. Being a Nazoraion was not the same as being from Galilee. Galilee was a geographical location. A Nazoraion was a member of a specific religious sect. Jesus was called the Nazoraion by Matthew. Paul called himself a member of the Nazoraion sect (Acts 25-26). Luke and Mark misunderstood a Nazoraion to be a Nazarene, but there was a Nazoraion sect in NT times. John the Baptist and Jesus reportedly belonged to it. There are still members of this sect in the Fertile Crescent who trace their origin back to John the Baptist. Jewish Christians were still called Nazoraions at the time of Jerome.[49]

He denied with a curse. Oaths and vows were normally taken with curses. The person who volunteered an oath said something like, "By [the name of some deity or religious object], may [the following curses] come upon me, if [I did such and such]." Here Peter called curses upon himself if he knew Jesus the Galilean. This was his second denial in response to a different woman.

Curse and take oaths. The extent of Peter's third denial is not known. This third denial was near the gate and before many people. Gerhardsson, following H. Merkel, thought Peter probably even cursed Jesus, but that is conjecture.[50] According to Matt 10:33, Jesus said he would deny before his Father in heaven anyone who would deny him before men, but the early church assumed that Peter was forgiven for his denial, because he continued to be an important leader in the church. McEleney noted that in Luke's account Peter denied Jesus more than once, but that is not true of Matthew's narrative.[51]

He went out and wept bitterly. Judas went out and hanged himself. Peter had denied Jesus, and he followed only from a distance, but he never separated himself from Jesus or his movement.

---

[49]See further P. Parker, The Gospel before Mark (Chicago: U. of Chicago, c1953), pp. 94-99. Later developments from this sect may be the Nasaraioi and Nazaraioi (Epiphanius, Panarion 18,1.1-3.5; 29,1.1-9.5). See also A. Schmidke, Neue Fragmente und Untersuchungen zu den Juden-christlichen Evangelien (Leipzig: J. C. Hinrichs, 1911), pp. 41-126, 248-49, and J. Thomas, Le Mouvement Baptiste en Palestine et Syrie (Gembloux: J. Duculox, 1935), pp. 37-40, 156-62.

[50]B. Gerhardsson, "Confession and Denial before Men: Observations on Matt 26:57-27:2," JSNT 13 (1981):54-55.

[51]N. J. McEleney, "Peter's Denials--How Many? To Whom?," CBQ 52 (1990):467-72.

CHAPTER TWENTY-SEVEN

TEXT

27:1 Now when it was dawn, all the chief priests and elders of the people held counsel against Jesus so that they might put him to death. 2 They bound him, led him away, and gave him over to Pilate the governor.

Matthew	First Testament and Later Jewish Literature
3 Then Judas, who had betrayed him, saw that he had been judged, repented	Those who acquired them slaughtered them and were not judged guilty (Zech 11:5).
and returned the **30 silver coins** to the chief priests and the elders,	And they weighed out my wages, **30 silver [coins]**,
4 **saying**, "I have sinned, having	and he **said** to me (Zech 11:12).
betrayed **innocent blood**." They said, "What is that to us? You will see."	The kings of Judah have filled this place with **innocent blood** (Jer 19:4).
	Look! Yahowah will appear from the place of his house of Shekinah to punish the guilt of the sojourners of the land upon it, and the land will reveal the **innocent blood** that has been shed in it and will not cover its shame any more (TgJon Isa 26.21).
Then he **threw**	"**Throw** into the treasury the noble price I was paid by them, so I took

the silver [coins]	**the** 30 **silver [coins], and I threw [them]**
into the temple and went away. After he	**into the house of the Lord, into** the treasury" (Zech 11:13).
had left, **he hanged himself.**	When Ahitophel saw that his counsel had not been observed, he saddled his donkey, arose, went to his house and his city, put his house in order and **hanged himself** (2 Sam 17:23).

TECHNICAL DETAILS

This is the seventh of the examples Good noticed. Five of these follow in succession these events: 1) a threatening situation, 2) a departure, and 3) a prophetic text.[1] In this case the threatening situation was the crucifixion and Judas' role in the project. The withdrawal was when Judas left and committed suicide. The prophecy fulfilled was Zech 11:12-13, using the 30 pieces of silver to buy a field.

The entire passage, Matt 27:3-10, is a unit composed by someone who was familiar with Zech 11 as well as Jer 19 and 32. He wove words from these two sources together, quoting Zechariah precisely and alluding to words from Jeremiah into the narrative, rather loosely. Tilborg was correct in saying that the author probably expected the reader to be familiar with both sources and recognize both the quotes and the allusions. Although he used more quotes from Zechariah he presumed the reader would know the context of Jeremiah.[2] Luz was probably correct in claiming that this account is not historically valid, but it is not quite fair to call it "pure redactional fiction" that is "grotesque."[3] The author who wrote this thought he was justified in reporting this as history, because he was able to justify it on the basis of scripture. This logic would not satisfy a twentieth century Western historian, like Luz, but it was composed 2,000 years ago by a Near Easterner who had different rules of historical deduction to follow. Westerners are not required to use the logic of the ancients. We are free to analyze ancient literature in our own concepts. From that point of view this would be classified as more doctrinal than historical, but at the same time we should recognize and sympathize with the motivation and rules of the ancients.

---

[1]The first example was Matt 2:12-15.

[2]S. V. Tilborg, "Matthew 27:3-10: and Intertextual Reading," Intertextuality in Biblical Writings, ed. S. Draisma (Uitgevermaatschappij: J. H. Kok--Kampen, 1989), pp. 159-74.

[3]U. Luz, "Fiktivität und Traditionstreue im Matthäusevangelium im Lichte griechischer Literatur," ZNW 84 (1993):157.

Pilate the governor. Pilate was procurator of Judah at the time Jesus was crucified. Archaeologists have found a stone in the ruins of Caesarea that bears his name. He usually resided at Caesarea on the sea, but at feasts he tried to be at Jerusalem, suspecting that there might be trouble there that would need his attention. Pilate was evidently the Roman official responsible for Jesus' execution, but Matthew blamed the chief priests and elders of the people for initiating the action. It was they who held counsel so that they might put him to death.

It was not out of character for some Jews to report messiahs to the foreign leaders before the messiahs began a military movement. Jewish leaders in foreign countries do not want to be upset in their security. If a Jewish insurrection begins it would probably turn the governmental power against all Jews in the country and the results of such action as this have sometimes been disastrous for Jews.

Jewish messianic movements did not stop with Jesus. There have been scores of identifiable Jewish messianic movements that have occurred during the last 2,000 years. These have all been fifth columnist actions that have not endeared the Jews to the ruling powers. Messianic movements were especially frequent during the Crusades, where some messiahs gathered tens of thousands of soldiers to take part in the Crusade upheaval. These messiahs were trying to get the Christians and Moslems to destroy one another so that they could succeed both and take over the rule of Europe and the Middle East.

Maimonides wrote a lengthy dissertation to the people of Yemen who thought the signs supported the likelihood that the pretender in their community might be a true messiah. Maimonides gave several examples of others who claimed to be messiahs who led military rebellious movements with disastrous results. Maimonides believed the messianic age was near, but that the time was not exactly ripe at that time, and the Messiah the people of Yemen promoted was not qualified. Therefore, the Jews in Yemen should suppress this movement before the gentiles realized what was happening. He gave the Yemenite Jews the folowing advice:

> I advise you with counsel that is good both for you and for him, that he be fettered several days until it becomes public knowledge among all the Gentiles that he is demented. Then circulate the message and publicize it widely among all people. After that, you may free him, and with this you may deliver his soul at the outset, because when the Gentiles hear of him after this position [in jail], the claim will cause them to mock him and refer to him as a madman, which he is.[4]

---

[4]Buchanan, Revelation and Redemption: Jewish Documents of Redemption from the Fall of Jerusalem to the Death of Nahmanides (Dillsboro: Western North Carolina Press, 1978; sold by Mercer U. Press), p. 94. See further pp. 36-204.

When Jesus entered Jerusalem, the crowds announced him as the king who was coming in the name of the Lord. The Pharisees were worried about the consequences of this beginning action, so they tried to get Jesus to caution the disciples and make them stop (Luke 19:39). They were offering the kind of counsel Maimonides gave to the Jews of Yemen. Maimonides said that if the pretender in Yemen were more competent, the people should give him the death penalty rather than suffer the consequences of a military encounter at that time. Had Maimonides lived in Jesus' time he would have agreed with the elders and chief priests in recommending crucifixion. Messianic movements are dangerous.

There is a type of inclusion between the opening chapters of Matthew and the concluding ones. At the beginning, Jesus was recognized as one born to be a king, and the foreign political ruler was Herod who wanted to have him killed. He was recognized as the son of David. Here it was the foreign political leader who was responsible for having him killed, while he was addressed as "king of the Jews," "Messiah," and "Son of God"--all proper titles for a king of Judah. In between these two parts of the inclusion is the entire gospel, picturing Jesus functioning as a messiah, anointed to be king of Israel. It has been impossible, but frequently attempted, to remove all of the political associations from Jesus.

Judas, who had betrayed him. The references to Judas are found only in the gospels, Acts, and possibly 1 Cor 11:23. Paul did not mention Judas by name, but he reported that Jesus had been betrayed on the night of the Last Supper. The story of the betrayal is so heavily dependent on earlier scripture that it is uncertain how much was fact and how much was deduced from scripture. Although it contains legendary features, it is not likely that the entire account was ficticious. The effort to match Jesus' betrayal with that of David by Achitophel was standard typology. The details may have been forced to make things fit, but it is probable that Judas was the one who betrayed Jesus.[5]

Threw the silver [coins] into the temple. When Jesus was captured, the apostles soon vanished. How, then, could later generations know how Jesus reacted to this time of suffering? What happened at the cross? How did Jesus respond, and what were his thoughts and feelings? Without witnesses, Herodotus or Thucydides might have said they did not know. Authors like Matthew and Luke, however, who had been trained in rabbinic research and exegesis, would not have felt so severely limited as historians would have been. They could always look to the scripture to find what had been prophesied.

It was assumed that all evil and wicked people suffered terrible deaths during which time they expressed regret that they had done such evil things as they did and recognized their misfortune as God's just punishment. The logic for this was based on civil court practice. When judges believed defendants were lying

---

[5]I have modified some of my positions since I wrote, "Judas Iscariot," ISBE (Grand Rapids: Eerdmans, c1980-), vol.2, (pp. 1151-1153).

in court they would allow the defendants to be tortured to bring out confessions. Sometimes this worked. Ancient Jews and early Christians believed that God did the same at the death of wicked people. This made them suffer painful deaths when God tortured them until they confessed their sins.

Josephus described terrible deaths of Herod the Great and Antiochus Epiphanes. How then about that wicked Judas who betrayed Jesus? He reminded others of Achitophel, David's trusted spy who betrayed David to Absalom in that rebellion. Once that had been recognized, the apologetic author simply attributed to Judas the evil results that happened to Achitophel. After all, Judas was simply an antitype of Achitophel, and Judas must have lived in the same portion of the cycle of time as Achitophel did. Ergo that which happened to Achitophel must have happened to Judas. The 30 pieces of silver were unrelated to Achitophel, but they were reported in the work of Zechariah, so this prophecy must have been fulfilled in Judas. He threw the silver back into the temple after he had repented.

It is likely that Judas was the one who betrayed Jesus, but it is unlikely that he did it for money, as the Matthean text suggests. Tilborg noted that prices for slaves was between 20 and 200 drachmas; 80 drachmas would be paid for someone between the ages five and 20; 200 would be required for someone between 20 and 60 years of age (Lev 27:1-7). Joseph was said to have been sold by his brothers for 20 sickles of silver, but later tradition expanded the price. The LXX took it to be 20 pieces of gold, and Josephus said it was 2,000 drachmas (Ant. 2.33).[6] To have betrayed a king for a little more than the price of a teen age slave seems ridiculous. The price was obtained from Zechariah rather than known historical data.

A more likely motivation for Judas' action may have been sincere patriotism. His loyalty to his country led him to be disappointed in Jesus. The apostles came to Jerusalem for the apparent reason of participating in a movement to overthrow the Romans and to set up an independent Kingdom of God on the land of Palestine. Plans had been made. Following Jesus' commands (Matt 10) the apostles had made their announcements throughout all of Judah and Galilee. Jews in the diaspora may have been alerted to the possibility of a messianic movement at this particular feast. Mobs of people had come to Jerusalem prepared to fight. Everything was in place until they actually got to Jerusalem, and Jesus found that there were no figs on the tree in the Kidron Valley, as Ezek 47 had promised would be there in the new age (Matt 21:18-22).

This new data put a damper on the whole military movement. Jesus refused to act militantly. He was committed to do God's will, and he depended on the fulfillment of scripture to give him directions. When no directions were given he withdrew his tentative plans. Judas may have considered this to be a betrayal of the apostles' trust. After the apostles had told hundreds of Jews that the Kingdom would come this Passover, then Jesus backed out. It made the apostles look like false messengers or even fools.

---

[6]Tilborg, "Intertextual," p. 167.

The name "Iscarioth" may have been a Semitic form of the Latin, sicarius, which means "dagger bearer." Some Jewish insurrectionists who fought against the Romans in the first century were called "sicarii." The initial vowel of the name could be a prosthetic aleph, often used when semitizing a foreign name. For example: "special" and "especial," "Spanish," and "Español," or "Pharat," and "Euphrates."[7] If Judas had been called "Judas the Terrorist," his action against Jesus would be more easily understood in a potentially military situation.

Innocent blood. Innocent blood is shed whenever an innocent person is unfairly given the death sentence. The "sojourners of the land," often mistakenly called "inhabitants of the earth" by twentieth century scholars, were people of foreign birth or foreign nationality who lived in the land of Palestine.[8] Jews and Israelites believed this land was destined for them alone and all other peoples--Canaanites, Romans, Greeks, Syrians, Arabs, etc.--were intruders whom Jews thought should be expelled. These local residents of foreign loyalty often cooperated with foreign ruling powers, such as the Syrian Greeks and the Romans in suppressing nationalistic rebellions. They constituted a spy group in the land. Therefore they were hated by the patriots, who would like to have engineered an ethnic cleansing of the land. The sojourners had previously helped the Egyptian Pharaoh, Antiochus Epiphanes, Herod, Agrippa, Pilate, and other kings, governors, and procurators in giving the death sentence to local insurrectionists. TgJon Isa 26.21 referred to the innocent blood which the sojourners shed; Jer 19:4 spoke of the blood of innocent citizens which Jewish kings had shed. Matthew told of the innocent Jesus, whose blood had been shed unjustly. The judgment against Jesus was unfair, according to Matthew, and it was corrupted by reward money (Matt 27:6).

After he left he hanged himself. Acts 1:16-20 reported that Judas fell headlong so that his bowels gushed out. This was to teach a lesson that all traitors suffer terrible deaths. The tortures suffered by the wicked at their deaths were considered the beginning of God's judgment. Most of the Book of Job is based on the policy of torturing the defendant until he confessed his sin. No one knows what happened to Judas. His death was reported on the basis of Achitophel's. Since Achitophel hanged himself, Judas must have done the same.

---

[7]See further Buchanan, "Judas Iscariot," ISBE 3, pp. 1151-53.

[8]See further Buchanan, "Sojourners in the Land," The Answers Lie Below, ed. H. O. Thompson (Lanham: University Press of America, 1984), pp. 187-96.

TEXT

Matthew	First Testament
[6]The chief priests, after they had taken the silver, said, "It is not lawful **to put it in the temple treasury,**	**I took the thirty silver [coins], and** **I threw them [into] the house of the Lord, into the treasury** (Zech 11:13b).
since it is a reward for **blood."**	The kings of Judah filled this place with innocent **blood** (Jer 19:4)
[7]After they had taken counsel they [took the money and] bought with it a potter's **field** as a tomb for	Acquire for yourself **the field** which is in Anathoth (Jer 32:7).
foreigners. [8]Because of this,	They have made this place **foreign,** and they have sacrificed in it to **foreign** gods (LXX Jer 19:4)
that field **is called** the **"field of blood"** until this very day. [9]Then was fulfilled that which was spoken through the prophet Jeremiah, saying,	The place **will** not **be called** Topeth again or the Valley of Ben Hinnom, but rather the Valley of Slaughter (Jer 19:6).
They **took the thirty silver [coins], the high price which** they **were paid by** the sons of Israel,	They weighed out my wages, **thirty silver [coins], the high price** I **was paid** by them (Zech 11:13a).
[10]and they gave them for a potter's field,	. . .
just as the Lord commanded me.	**just as Yahowah commanded** Moses (Exod 40:25, 29).

COMMENTARY

A reward for blood. Even the wicked priests recognized that the money they had paid Judas was unclean. Blood money could not be used for ordinary expenditures (tZeb 3.1-3). It was used instead for a burial ground where only foreigners would be buried.

Spoken through the prophet Jeremiah. Scholars have been very creative in explaining how Matthew happened to attribute the following quote from Zechariah to Jeremiah. The most likely theory is that of Tilborg, who noted that the midrash of Matt 27:3-10 is typologically closer to Jeremiah than to Zechariah, even though Zechariah's words were more accurately quoted. The context of Zechariah is quite different from that of Matthew. Whether the prophet is Jeremiah or Zechariah the original author is understood to have been God, who was the principal. The prophet was only the agent through whom God spoke, whether it was Jeremiah or Zechariah. The agent was an instrument for the principal just as a flute is the agent for a musician.

The 30 silver [coins]. There is no certainty that Judas was paid for the betrayal. Matthew composed this narrative on the basis of Zechariah. This was justified, because, according to approved doctrine of early Jewish and Christian rhetoric, 1) there is no before and after in scripture; 2) all prophecy is prophesied only for the days of the Messiah; 3) these were the days of the Messiah; and 4) there is nothing in the world that is not in the scripture. Since Matthew found this passage in Zechariah, and it could be applied to Judas, he applied it and assumed that he was right in doing so.

Paid by the sons of Israel. Matthew blamed the chief priests and the elders more than Judas for the betrayal of Jesus. Zech 11:13 indicates that the coins were paid by "them." The pronoun, "them," of Zechariah was interpreted to be the "sons of Israel" by Matthew. The priests and the elders had spent money they had received from the "tax payers," the Israelites who financed the welfare of the chief priests and elders. It was not their own money. The scripture cursed anyone who took a bribe for shedding innocent blood (Deut 27:25).

TEXT

11Jesus was made to stand before the governor, and the governor asked him, saying, "Are you the king of the Jews?" Jesus said, "You said [that]." 12While he
was being accused by the chief priests and the elders, he answered nothing.
13Then Pilate said to him, "Do you not hear all the things of which they are ac-
cusing you?" 14But [Jesus] did not answer him a single word, so that the governor
was very much surprised. 15At the feast the governor was accustomed to release
to the crowd one prisoner, whomever they wanted. 16At that time they had a notorious prisoner, called Barabbas. 17Therefore, when they had gathered, Pilate
said to them, "Whom do you want me to release to you? Barabbas or Jesus, the
one called Christ?" 18He knew that it was because of envy that they had given
him over. 19While he was seated at the judicial bench, his wife sent to him,
saying, "Do nothing to this innocent man, for I have suffered many things on account of him today in a dream," 20but the chief priests and elders persuaded the
crowds to ask for Barabbas, and that they would destroy Jesus. 21In reply the
governor said, "Which of the two do you want me to release to you?" They said,
"Barabbas." 22Pilate said to them, "Then what shall I do with Jesus who is called
the Christ?" They all said, "Let him be crucified!" 23He, however, said, "Why?

What evil has he done?" They cried out all the more, saying, "Let him be crucified!"

Matthew	First Testament
[24]When Pilate saw that he had not helped at all, but that the disturbance became greater, he took water and **washed his hands** before the crowd,	All the elders of the city nearest to the slain man shall **wash their hands** over the heifer whose neck had been broken in the valley, and they shall testify, "Our hands did not shed this **blood**, and our eyes did not **see** it shed" (Deut 21:6-7).
saying, "I am **innocent** of this **blood**. You will **see**." [25]Then the people	Cursed be anyone who takes a bribe to give a death penalty, [shedding] **innocent** **blood** (Deut 27:25).
answered and said, "His **blood** be upon us and upon our children." [26]Then he released Barabbas, but Jesus he gave over to the torturers to be crucified.	

COMMENTARY

King of the Jews. Here near the end of the Gospel, Jesus appeared before the Roman king, being tried, and later killed, as king of the Jews. This turns the reader back to chapter 2 where the governing authority tried to kill Jesus as the one born to be king of the Jews (Matt 2:2).

[Jesus] did not answer him. According to the rabbis a man was not required to testify against himself in court. This is the precedent for the fifth amendment in the U.S.A. constitution.

Accustomed to release. This custom is never reported by Josephus. This seems like the most unreasonable thing Romans might have done. Many of the people Romans had in prison were there because of their revolutionary activities. At feasts Romans tried to find out who all the pretending Messiahs were and lock them up or kill them so that they could not lead insurrections, because it was at the feasts where revolutions normally broke out. Luke reported that Barabbas was in prison because of his activity in an insurrection (Luke 23:19).

Sometimes Romans were forced to release insurrectionists--not during feasts--in exchange for people whom the insurrectionists kidnapped (Ant 20.208-10), but that did not prove wise, because these prisoners, once released, caused still more mischief.

His wife sent to him. Patte said of Pilate's wife, "It is to someone who is in no way associated with the Jewish leaders that such a revelation is made."[9] That may have been the intent of the author, but we cannot be sure, 2,000 years later, that Pilate's wife had no association with Jews of the first century. There were many Jews in Rome in NT times. Some of them, like Herod Agrippa, were confidents of the Caesars. On the other hand this report may have been fabricated to show Romans that Christians were really faithful Romans.

Jesus, the one called the Christ. Jesus was identified in this passage as "the king of the Jews" (Matt 27:11; 2:2) as well as the Messiah (Christ) (Matt 27:17, 22; 2:4; 16:16). Matthew also called Jesus a leader, shepherd (Matt 2:6), son of the living God, and Son of man (Matt 16:13-15). These are all titles for a king. Allison has shown that Matthew organized his material so as to remind the reader in the last chapters of messages given in earlier chapters. One of the ways he did this was by comparing the death of Jesus with the death of John the Baptist[10]:

John	Jesus
Herod the tetrarch was responsible for John's death.	Pilate, the governor was responsible for Jesus' death.
John was seized (κρατέω, 14:3).	Jesus was seized (κρατέω, 21:46, etc.).
John was bound (δέω, 14:3).	Jesus was bound (δέω, 27:2).
Herod feared the crowds because they thought John was a prophet (14:5).	The chief priests and Pharisees feared the crowds because they thought Jesus a prophet (21:46).

[9]D. Patte, The Gospel according to Matthew (Philadelphia: Fortress Press, c1946), p. 379.

[10]D. C. Allison, Jr., "Anticipating the Passion: The Literary Reach of Matt 16:47-27:56," CBQ 56 (1994):702.

Herod was asked by another to execute John and grieved so to do (14:12).	Pilate was asked by others to execute Jesus and was reluctant so to do (27:11-26).
John was buried by his disciples (14:12).	Jesus was buried by a disciple (27:57-61).

Similar parallels are evident between Matthew 17 and 27, as Allison has shown[11]

The Transfiguration (Matt 17:18)	The Crucifixion (Matt 17:27-56)
Similarities	
"After six days" (17:1)	"From the sixth hour" (27:45)
Three named onlookers (17:1)	Three named onlookers (27:55-56)
Jesus is God's "Son" (17:5)	Jesus is God's "Son" (27:54)
'Εφοβήθησαν σφόδρα (17:6)	'Εφοβήθησαν σφόδρα
Contrasts	
Jesus takes others (17:1)	Jesus is taken by others (27:31)
Elevation on mountain (17:1)	Elevation on cross (27:35)
Private epiphany (17:1)	Public spectacle (27:39)
Light (17:2)	Darkness (27:45)
'Ιμάτια illumined (17:2)	'Ιμάτια stripped off (27:28, 35)
Jesus glorified (17:2-6)	Jesus is shamed (27:27-31)
Elijah appears (17:3)	Elijah does not appear (27:45-50)
Two saints beside Jesus (17:3)	Two criminals beside Jesus (27:8)
God confesses Jesus (17:5)	God abandons Jesus (27:38)
Reverent prostration (17:6)	Mocking prostration (27:29)

What evil has he done? This was a good question. From the available evidence, Jesus had done no wrong. Even if he had plotted a revolution, he had not led one. People are not usually punished for their thoughts but only for their actions.

Let him be crucified! Maccoby suggested that the unmodified Matthean source would have shown the crowds supporting Jesus and only the high priests asking that he be crucified.[12] He noted that the crowds and the Jewish leaders were often shown holding different positions (Matt 21:45; 26:5, 8-9; 27:20; John 7:12,

---

[11] Allison, "Passion," p. 709.

[12] H. Z. Maccoby, "Jesus and Barabbas," NTS 16 (1969/70):56-58.

43; 9:19). He also thought the name Barabbas might come from the words Bar and Abba, meaning "Son of the father," which could mean "Son of God." This would indicate that he was attributed the title by some people who thought he was the Messiah or king.[13]

To this very day. This implies that the author of this narrative wrote a reasonably long time after the crucifixion. The name had continued to be in use from the time of Judas' death until the time the author wrote.

TEXT

27Then the soldiers of the governor took Jesus to the praitorion, and the whole
cohort went with him. 28They led him out, put a crimson officer's cloak upon
him, 29and plaiting a crown from thorns, they put it upon his head, and a reed
in his right hand. They genuflected before him, mocking him, saying, "Hi there,
king of the Jews," 30and they spat on him and took a reed and struck him on his
head. When they had mocked him 31they took off the cloak, dressed him in his
robe and led him away to crucify him.

COMMENTARY

It was not necessary to be present to suspect that some of these things happened. People were often abused as they were given the death penalty. On one occasion, Alexander Jannaeas crucified 800 leaders from Judah at one time. He himself lay in a comfortable situation, drinking wine with his concubines while he had all of the men's wives and children killed before their eyes while they were hanging on the crosses (War 1.97-98). The fact that there is very much in this chapter whose historicity depends on the ability of the author to deduce it from scripture casts doubt on even those passages that seem reasonable. Even though reasonable, they also might have been imagined.

Since they did not know precisely what happened around the cross, authors asked what were the typological possibilities for a person facing the death penalty unjustly? There were two lengthy Psalms expressing the feelings of men in despair, crying out to the Lord. Jesus must have reacted as an antitype to these. Therefore Matthew wove these two Psalms (22 and 69) together to recover this unknown part of Jesus' life. Psalm 22 begins with a cry of despair of one who thought God had forsaken him. In times past Israelites had cried to the Lord, and he delivered them. The Psalmist, however, had become an object of ridicule. People mocked him for trusting the Lord. The Psalmist suffered hunger, thirst, and physical pain. People stabbed his hands and feet, divided his garments among themselves, casting lots. Nevertheless, the author cried to the Lord in confidence, assured that God was not far off. He vowed that he would continue to praise the

[13]Maccoby, "Barabbas," p. 58.

Lord, knowing that God alone ruled over nations and that all the proud people of the earth would have to bow down to the Lord.

Ps 69 describes a man who had become hoarse from crying out; he was sunk into the mire, with no place to stand. Multitudes gathered around attacking him with lies, desiring his death. No one came to his rescue; all his friends had forsaken him; he was given poison for food and vinegar to drink. All of this suffering and embarrassment was because of the Psalmist's defense of the Lord. Therefore, he called on the Lord to come to his rescue, destroy his foes, rescue the Psalmist, and blot out his enemies from the Book of Life. Then the Psalmist would praise the Lord for his salvation. With these two Psalms as the required two witnesses to prove his case, the Matthean mythologist reconstructed the experience of Jesus on the cross.

Quite apart from the scripture, the author might have expected anyone convicted of a criminal offense to be abused before his execution. The Roman citizen and close friend of Tiberius, for example, was later executed. Although he had been given the highest honors of the government and worshiped as a god, when he was led to execution the crowd jeered him and shouted insults at him (Dio, RomHist 58.11, 3). Likewise, when the Roman emperor, Gaius, was murdered, people who had worshiped him as a god previously, then stabbed his corpse and spat on it (RomHist 59.30, 1).

TEXT

[32]While they were going out, they found a man of Cyrenaeus, called Simon. They compelled this man to take his cross. [33]When they came to a place called Golgotha, which is the place called "the skull,"

Matthew	First Testament
[34]**they gave him** wine mixed with **vinegar to drink**, but after he had tasted, he did not want to drink.	They put poison in my food; **for my thirst they gave me vinegar** (Ps 69:22).
[35]After they had crucified him, **they divided his robe, casting lots**, [36]and sitting down they kept him there.	**They divided my clothes** among them; for my clothing **they cast lots** (Ps 22:19).

COMMENTARY

A man of Cyrenaeus. This is the only time this person is mentioned in the NT. There is very little reason to assume it was a conjectured report. It was seen by people from whom Matthew might have learned. It was a customary practice of

Roman soldiers, which Jews deeply resented, to recruit nearby people and force them to do whatever they wanted done. He evidently really carried Jesus' cross.

Vinegar to drink. There were at least two reasons why Jesus was given something to drink, according to the text. 1) When lambs were slain for sacrifice, either on the Day of Atonement or for the daily sacrifice, those involved in the slaughter always gave the lamb a drink from a gold cup (mTam 3.4). Since Jesus was interpreted as a lamb led to be slaughtered, he was expected to have shared some of the exact ritualistic experiences as other lambs to be slaughtered. 2) the reason the author thought Jesus' ritualistic drink was vinegar is that this was the experience of the Psalmist, and Jesus must have been the antitype as a fulfillment of prophecy. The same is true of the division of the victim's garments. These insights came directly from Pss 69:22 and 22:19.

TEXT

Matthew	First Testamemt
[37]They placed over his head his accusation, written, "This is Jesus, the king of the Jews." [38]Then they crucified together with him two insurrectionists (lays-taí, λησταί), one on the right, and one on the left,	
[39]and **those who were passing by** blasphemed him, **shaking their heads** [40]and saying,	All **those who pass by** on the road clap their hands. They whistle and **shake their heads** (Lam 2:15).
"[You] who destroy the temple and in three days build it, **save** yourself. If you are the Son of God, then come down from the cross."	All who see me mock me; they stick out their lips; **they shake their heads**: "He rejoiced in Yahowah;
[41]Likewise the chief priests, together with the scribes and elders, mocking said, [42]"He **saved** others; **him**self he cannot **save**.	let him **save him**" (Ps 22:8-9).
[If] he is the king of Israel, let him come down now from the cross, and we will believe in him.	
[43]**He trusted in God; let him rescue [him]** if **he wants him**, for he said, 'I am God's Son.'" [44]At the same [time] the two insurrectionists who were crucified together with him also derided him.	**He rejoiced in God; let him rescue him**. He will **save him**, because **he wants him** (Ps 22:9).

COMMENTARY

Jesus the king of the Jews. The accusation was placed above Jesus, which means that the cross arms were placed lower than the top of the center pole. This account of these events seems to be a historical report. Activities in which Jesus was involved might easily lead Romans to suspect him of pretending the Davidic crown which meant the overthrow of Rome. They crucified people for things like this. That is why they crucified two insurrectionists with him; Romans thought they were crucifying three insurrectionists that day. Herod and Herod Agrippa were the only two members of the Herodian family who were allowed to be called "king" by Jews in Palestine. These were both appointed by the Romans. There was no room in Roman foreign policy for the establishment of a king of the Jews in Palestine that was not chosen and appointed by Rome.

Two insurrectionists. Instead of "insurrectionists" (λῃσταί), Luke 23:32-33 and the GosPet 4.10 both have "evil doers" (κακοῦργοι). After 70 I.A., and especially after 135 I.A., it was politically dangerous for Jews or Christians in the Roman Empire to be identified with any of the nationalistic Jewish military movements that led up to the two famous wars of the Jews against Rome. Sons of David were enough of a threat to the Romans that after the fall of Jerusalem some were brought to Domitian. They were asked about the Messiah and his kingdom. They told him that the messianic kingdom was heavenly and would happen after the end of the age, so they were released (HE 3.30, 1-4). If Domitian had understood the underlying code and realized that the heavenly kingdom would be installed in Palestine and that the end of the age of which they spoke was the Roman age, he might not have released them.

The fact that John the Baptist, who was killed for his threat to the Romans, was much more closely related to Jesus in the Gospel of Matthew than either Luke or the Gospel of Peter is one of the reasons to date Matthew earlier than either of these documents.[14] It was the later church that modified the documents to make them seem politically innocuous. An evil doer might be also an insurrectionist, but he might not. Matthew was probably composed before this danger was obvious. Therefore Matthew dared to tell the story more accurately and unequivocally.

Earlier the sons of Zebedee, James and John, had asked for chief seats in the kingdom. This meant that they wanted to sit, one on his right and one on his left in the Kingdom of God (Matt 20:31-23). Although these "sons of thunder" may have been insurrectionists before the crucifixion, it was apparently not they, but others, who accompanied him on the cross.

---

[14]For other reasons see A. Kirk, "Examining Priorities: Another Look at the Gospel of Peter's Relationship to the New Testament Gospels," NTS 40 (1994):572-95.

They blasphemed him. People might have done this, but the reason Matthew had for thinking it was done was that he found it prophesied in scripture. All he had to do was fill in the details.

He trusted in God. This was just part of the harassment Matthew thought Jesus experienced because it was reported as prophecy in one of the Psalms.

For he said, "I am God's Son." Donaldson has shown that this paragraph of mocking is the conclusion to a plot woven throughout the Gospel of Matthew. Here the mockers were the brigands (insurrectionists), the passers-by, and the Jewish leaders. They mocked him because he claimed to be the Son of God, and the author here identified "Son of God" with "King of Israel" (Matt 27:40, 42). Throughout the gospel, Donaldson held, there is the conflict between the mockers and Jesus. Satan mocked him at the temptation (Matt 4:3, 6), doubting that he was the Son of God. Pharisees mocked him, doubting the authority by which he cast out demons (Matt 9:34). By the time the reader had become aware of this theme he or she would realize that Jesus really was the Son of God and that the mockers would always be refuted for their mockery.[15]

TEXT

Matthew	First Testament
45 From **noon** until three P.M. it **became dark over all the land**. At about three P.M. Jesus raised his voice, speaking loudly,	There was thick **darkness in all the land** of Egypt (Exod 10:22).
	On that day, said my Lord Yahowah, I will make the sun go down **at noon**; I will **darken the land** during the day time; I will change your feasts to mourning, and all your songs to laments (Amos 8:9-10).
Áye-ly, Áye-ly! lah-máh sah-bakh-tháh-nee which is **My God, my God, why have you abandoned me?** 47 Some who were standing there, when they heard, were saying, 48 "He is calling Elijah." At once one of them ran and took a sponge full of	**My God, My God, why have you abandoned me?** [Why are] you far from saving me? From the words of my groaning (Ps 22:2).
	They gave him with his food poison; and for his thirst they **gave** him

[15] T. L. Donaldson, "The Mockers and the Son of God (Matthew 27.37-44): Two Characters in Matthew's Story of Jesus," JSNT 41 (1991):3-18.

vinegar After he tied it around a reed, he **gave it to him to drink** [49]The rest said, "Let us see if Elijah will come to save him," [50]but Jesus cried out again in a loud voice and gave up the spirit.	**vinegar** **to drink** (Ps 69:22).

COMMENTARY

It became dark. The author of a medieval narrative describing the death of a Samaritan Messiah was apparently acquainted with the narrative telling of Jesus' death. According to that report, when the Messiah Nehemiah was killed by the Romans, he was supposed to have been killed at noon, and all the land became dark at that time.[16] The land involved was the land of Palestine--not the whole earth.

Why have you abandoned me. Rehm argued that the fact that people who passed by misunderstood the word, "My God" (Aye-lee as "Elijah"(Aye-lee-yáh-hoo) proves that these were the very words of Jesus. He actually said these words on the cross.[17] Of course, that is possible, but it is not the only possibility. Even if no one ever heard the expression, Matthew would have "known" Jesus said this, because it was reported in Ps 69:22, and since all prophecy was prophesied only for the days of the Messiah, and these were the days of the Messiah, Jesus must have said this, even if no one told Matthew that he had heard Jesus say this or the response of the people who passed by.

TEXT

Matthew	First Testament
[51]Now look! The veil of the temple was torn in two from top to bottom; the **earth quaked**; and the rocks were split in two.	You will be visited from Yahowah of armies with thunder, **earthquake**, and loud noise, windstorm, tempest, and flaming fire that consumes (Isa 29:6).
[52]The **tombs were opened**,	Look! I will **open your tombs**, and I will raise you from your graves,

---

[16]From "The Prayer of Rabbi Shimon ben Yohai," Buchanan (tr.), Redemption, p. 415.

[17]M. Rehm, "Eli, Eli lamma sabachthani," BZ 2 (58):275-78.

	my people, and I will bring you to the land of Israel (Ezek 37:12).
and many **bodies** of the saints **who had been sleeping were raised.** 53They went out from their **tombs** after his resurrection. They entered the holy city and appeared to many, 54but the centurion and those with him keeping Jesus, when they saw the **earthquake** and the things that had happened, they were very much afraid, saying, "Truly this was God's Son."	Your dead will live; their **bodies will rise.** Those **who sleep** in the dust will jump up and sing (Isa 26:19) Many of those **who sleep** [in] the dust of the ground will jump up, some to life of the age and some to disgrace and contempt of the age (Dan 12:2).

COMMENTARY

The veil of the temple was torn. DeJonge examined the early apostolic and church fathers to learn the best interpretation of this passage. He discovered that there was no universal interpretation.

> Our survey of the material suggests, however, that it is very unlikely that "the" meaning of Matt 27:51a will ever be established beyond doubt.[18]

Here there were prophecies from Isaiah, Ezekiel, and Daniel.

The tombs were opened. There is no reported witness of this event, but that was not necessary. The witness was in the scripture. Once you accept the dogma that everything that is in the world is in the scripture, all that is necessary to reconstruct an unknown historical event is to find two places in the scripture that might prophesy the event, and the case is closed. All the author has to do is to fill in the details. Later rabbis said that the dead would first come to life in the days of the Messiah (pKet 12.3).

Many bodies of the saints. According to this report these saints were raised before Jesus was. Therefore Jesus' resurrection was not a unique experience. Hai Gaon said that at the resurrection a great trumpet would sound, according to Isa 27:13. Then there would be a great earthquake so that all the bones that have been trampled on in the land or have disintegrated and become parts of buildings will be rejoined, as Ezekiel said (Ezek 37). Those who had deformities would be raised with their deformities, so that they could be identified. Then the Lord

[18]M. DeJonge, "Matthew 27:51 in Early Christian Exegesis," HTR 79 (1986):79.

would heal them (Isa 35:5-6; Ps 103:5). This would all take place at Jerusalem.[19] Hai Gaon knew all of this was true, because he found scripture passages that he believed were prophesied only for the days of the Messiah. The Sibyl said that after death the godly would live again on earth (SibOr 4.87). Rabbi Hiyya ben Joseph said that sometime in the future the just would break through the soil and be raised. This would take place at Jerusalem (bKet 111a). This is the reason that the Mount of Olives has become a Jewish cemetery during the last 40 years. Faithful Jews want their loved ones to be there when the resurrection occurs. Rabbi Eliezar said the dead outside the land of Israel would not be raised in the resurrection. Rabbi Elai said that those outside the land of Palestine would be rolled like logs to the promised land where they could be raised. Abaye said there would be underground tunnels through which the corpses could be rolled (bKet 111a).

The centurion and those with him. The importance of the confession of the centurion and those with him is that they would not have been prejudiced. They provide independent witnesses by a non-tendential people. Another similar example is near the beginning of the gospel where there were foreign wise men from the East who acknowledged Jesus as the King of the Jews. Here, near the end, other foreign witnesses acknowledge his royalty. Convinced that Jesus was the Messiah and armed with these two Psalms, the author of this narrative did not at all presume that he was composing fiction. As a good research student, he was simply applying the scripture that was available to him as the only source in the world. These Psalms provided the intertexts he needed to fill in the gaps of unknown history. That which was prophesied there must have been fulfilled in the days of the Messiah, even if there had been no nonscriptural witnesses to see it happen. Like the wise man, Daniel, Matthew knew some mysteries that the pagans did not know. He employed these to reconstruct the past; these same tools could be employed to discern the future.

TEXT

Matthew	First Testament
55There were there many women who had followed Jesus from Galilee, ministering to him. 56Among them was Mary Magdalene, Mary the mother of James and Joseph, and the mother of the sons of Zebedee. 57When it was evening,	

[19]Hai Gaon, "The topic of Salvation," tr. Buchanan, Redemption, p. 126; see also p. 507.

a rich man came from Arimathea, named Joseph, who also himself had been a disciple of Jesus. 58This man came to Pilate and requested the body of Jesus. Then Pilate commanded that [it] be given. 59After he took the body, Joseph wrapped it in clean muslin, 60and he placed it in his own new tomb which he had quarried in the rock, and he rolled a large stone in the door and left the tomb.

Then he made his death with the wicked, with **a rich man** in his death (Isa 53:9).

COMMENTARY

Mary the mother of James and Joseph. Two Marys and two Josephs are mentioned here at the conclusion of the gospel. That may reflect only factual historical reporting, but there is another possibility. Matthew may have placed these names here to match the Mary and Joseph at the beginning of the narrative (Matt 1:18) to form an inclusion. There are other inclusions in the Gospel of Matthew.

A rich man came. This is the only time this expression appears. Jesus had many associations with rich people. It was considered a virtue for Jews to give friends and relatives suitable burials. Scholars have suggested before that the word "rich" was derived from Isa 53:9, describing the suffering servant who **made his grave with the wicked and rich in his death.**[20] The suggestion is thought-provoking: 1) the same word is used; 2) it refers to a grave; 3) it applies to an antitype of a suffering servant. It does not, however, seem to be a midrash on Isa 53. The various words of Isa 53 do not occur in the immediate passage. The subject matter is the same, but the important words are omitted.

A new tomb. There are still many tombs like this in Palestine. They are carved out of soft limestone rock, which is easy to work. Individual tombs often are small caves with doors about two or three feet in height. In front of the door and to one side, parallel with the outside wall a groove is carved into the rock which slopes upward away from the door alongside the wall. Then a wheel is made exactly the right size to fit into that groove. This wheel functions as a door. The

---

[20]W. B. Barrick, "The Rich Man from Arimathea (Matt 27:57-60) and 1QSA," JBL 96 (1977):235-39.

heavy wheel, when not obstructed, rolls downhill in this groove and covers the opening.

TEXT

61Now there was there Mary Magdalene and the other Mary, seated in front of
the tomb. 62On the next day, which is after the preparation, the high priest and
Pharisees came to Pilate, 63saying, "Sir, we have been reminded that that wan-
derer said while he was still alive, 'After three days, I will be raised.' 64Com-
mand, therefore, that the tomb be secured until the third day, lest the disciples
come and steal him and tell the people he has been raised from the dead, and the
last will be worse than the first." 65Pilate said to them, "You have a guard. Go,
make [it] secure, since you know [how to do that]." 66Then they went and made
the tomb secure, having sealed the stone with the guard.

COMMENTARY

Seated in front of the tomb. They were stationed, like the guards before, at the tomb where they could be witnesses.

The high priest and the Pharisees. These had been opponents of Jesus for a long time. Now it was they who made the door of the tomb secure, so no one could question that it was well done.

Lest the disciples come. It was normal for disciples to take great risks to provide proper burial for their master. The disciples of John the Baptist did this for him. After the citizens of Jabesh-gilead learned that the bodies of Saul and Jonathan were disgracefully hanging on the walls of the fortress at Beth-shan, they went out at night and removed the bodies, took them to Jabesh and there performed the proper burial rites (1 Sam 31:8-13).

After three days I will be raised. Paul has, "He was raised on the third day, according to the scriptures" (1 Cor 15:4). The scripture that prophesied the words Paul used for documentation was probably Hos 6:2, **After two days he will revive us; on the third day he will raise us up that we may live before him.**

CHAPTER TWENTY-EIGHT

TEXT

28:1 On the evening of the Sabbath, while it was growing toward dawn, at the first
day of the week, Mary Magdalene and the other Mary came to see the tomb.
2 Look! there was a great earthquake, for the angel of the Lord came down from
heaven, approached [the tomb], rolled back the stone, and sat on it.

Matthew	First Testament
3 His appearance was like lightning,	Thrones were placed, and the Ancient of Days took his seat.
and **his clothes were white as snow**. 4 From [their] fear of him the guards were shaken up and became like dead men.	**His clothes were white as snow**, and the hair of his head, like pure wool (Dan 7:9).

5 In reply, the angel said to the women, "Do not be afraid! I know that you are
looking for Jesus, the one who has been crucified. 6 He is not here; for he has
been raised, just as he said [he would]. Go, look at the place where he lay, 7 and
at once go, tell his disciples that he has been raised from the dead. Look! he goes
before you into Galilee. There you will see him. Look! I have told you."

COMMENTARY

On the evening of the Sabbath. This would probably be at the end of the Sabbath day which concluded in the evening, but that is not certain. The first day of the week began at the same time that the week ended. Op-séh deh sab-bá-tohn (*ὀψὲ δὲ σαββάτων*), in Greek, seems to represent the Hebrew idiom móh-tsee shab-báth (מוצאי שבת). Driver, however, has argued that the passage should be rendered, "The Sabbath had passed, and it was about daybreak." He argued that the reckoning was from day break to day break, following a different calendar,[1] which he held was used in Galilee by some Jews. This question is still pending.

While it was growing toward dawn. This may mean that it was dark, but the Sabbath is normally over while it is still dusk. The women may have gone out to the tomb as soon as the Sabbath was over without waiting until dawn. For many Jewish calendars, the first day of the week had begun, but it was not yet dark. Part of the problem here comes from not knowing which calendar the author used.

Mary Magdalene and the other Mary. These were the women who saw Jesus at the cross. The number of women at the empty tomb differs with the different gospels, but all are consistent in having the same women at the tomb who were at the crucifixion.

Rolled back the stone. This is the same stone that was used to close the entrance two nights before (Matt 27:60). It was a round, wheel-like stone, specially carved for this purpose. It rolled in a track that was purposely made for it. The wheel was at the bottom of the track when the tomb was closed. It required strength to roll it up hill to open the cave. To keep the cave open, it would be necessary to place a block in the track, down hill from the wheel. In the picture given Dr. Dewey Beegle is standing at the opening of the

[1]G. R. Driver, "Two Problems in the New Testament," JTS 16n.s. (1965):327-31. The quotation is from p. 327.

tomb with the stone wheel to his right. The woman at the tomb in the foreground of the picture is Harlene Buchanan. The picture was taken at Tel Hesbon, Jordan.

His clothes were white as snow. This is an intentional allusion to Dan 7, where the Ancient of Days was described just before the heavenly court case was tried between the Jews and the Syrian Greeks, Judas the Maccabee and Antiochus Epiphanes. The angel dressed like the Ancient of Days was to suggest that the angel was an agent of the Lord. White garments meant that he was undefiled. This antitype was designed to indicate that this whole trial of Jesus was a victory for the Jews just as the trial in Dan 7 was a victory for Judas and the saints of the Most High.

He goes before you into Galilee. This should remind the reader of Matt 26:32, "After I have been raised, I will go before you into Galilee." This statement was made to explain why the Petrine Christian activity continued in Galilee. The party of James centered around Jerusalem, and John directed the church in Samaria, but Peter evidently worked in Galilee and Syria.[2] The other disciples may have continued their ministry in Galilee as well.

TEXT

8After they had gone away from the tomb quickly with fear and great joy, they ran to announce to his disciples. 9Now look! Jesus met them, saying, "Hi!" The women seized his feet, and they worshiped him. 10Then Jesus said to them, "Do not be afraid. Go and announce to my disciples so that they might go away into Galilee. There they will see me."

COMMENTARY

Jesus met them, saying, "Hi"! Jesus gave the women no new information. He simply repeated the announcement of the angel. His greeting to the women was a familiar Greek greeting. The 16th century translation of this was, "Hail!" But in the 16th century, "Hail!" was a normal greeting. Today people seldom greet each other that way. "Hi!" is the nearest twentieth century American equivalent.

Do not be afraid. This statement was literarily designed to form an inclusion of the entire gospel. In the first chapter the angel of the Lord removed Joseph's anxiety by telling him not to be afraid (Matt 1:20). Before Jesus was born the angel announced to Joseph that he should not be afraid, and then, after his death, the angel appeared again to offer the same comfort.

[2]Buchanan, "The Samaritan Origin of the Gospel of John," Religions of Antiquity, ed. J. Neusner (Leiden: E. J. Brill, 1970):149-175.

TEXT

[11]While they were going, look! Some of the guards, having come into the city, announced to the chief priests all the things that had happened. [12]After they [the chief priests] had been gathered together with the elders they took counsel and gave an agreed upon amount of silver to the soldiers, [13]saying, "Say 'His disciples came during the night and stole him while we were sleeping.' [14]If this is heard by the governor, we shall persuade [him], and we shall make you blameless." [15]Then they took the silver and did as they were taught, and this word is being told among the Jews until this very day.

COMMENTARY

His disciples came. It is not easy to persuade soldiers who have been employed to guard something to say they slept while they were supposed to be guarding. Soldiers get killed sometimes when they are found sleeping on duty. Most scholars have assumed that this story is a fictional defense composed to defend the apostles against attacks and doubts raised by the Jews. In defense of the historicity of this narrative Craig argued that the events may have happened exactly as they were told. Contrary to the opinions of most scholars, Jesus may actually have prophesied his resurrection after three days. Luke and John may not have heard of the story, because it was not widely told. Craig argued that just because some of these explanations seem absurd does not prove that they were not true. If people knew of historical facts that were good arguments they would have preferred telling facts to composing fiction. If there had been no empty tomb the Jews would not have had to find an explanation for its being empty. The story must have originated in Jerusalem, said Craig, and if so local people would have corrected these statements if they had been erroneous. If there had been no guard at the tomb Jews would not have had to say either that he had fallen asleep or that he had been bribed. Craig's defensive explanations sound very much like the defenses in the story itself.[3] Luz considered this entire account to be fiction.[4]

Told among the Jews. This implies that at least this sentence was composed a long time after the event, but the story was still being told. There were obviously two accounts of the empty tomb. Disciples said he had been raised and later appeared to them; other Jews said his body had been stolen.

The story is told of the body of R. Akiba after he had been killed. Romans would not allow his body to be buried, but they kept it in prison with a guard to defend it. The prophet Elijah came in the form of a priest and told Rabbi Joseph

[3]W. L. Craig, "The Guard at the Tomb," NTS 30 (1984):273-81.

[4]U. Luz, "Fiktivität und Traditionstreue im Matthäusevangelium im Lichte griechischer Literatur," ZNW 84 (1993):158.

that Rabbi Akiba lay dead in prison, so the two of them went, found all the prison guards asleep and the gate open, so without any interference, they took his body, carried it all night to Antipatris. There they found a cave with a lamp in it. They placed the corpse there and left the cave. As soon as they left the cave, the lamp lighted itself and the cave closed up (Mid Prov 9.2, 31a).

TEXT

16The twelve disciples went into Galilee, to the mountain where Jesus commanded them [to go]. 17When they saw him, they worshiped, but some doubted. 18Jesus came and spoke to them saying,

Matthew	First Testament and Other Jewish Literature
All authority has been given me in heaven and **on earth**. 19Go, therefore, and make disciples of	To him **was given** ruling **authority**, glory, and the kingdom, and **all peoples**, nations, and [peoples of all] languages will serve him. His ruling **authority** will be a ruling **authority of the age**, which will not change, and his kingdom [one] which will not be destroyed (Dan 7:14).
all the gentiles, baptizing them in the name of the Father, the Son, the Holy Spirit,	Thus said Cyrus, king of Persia, "**All** kingdoms **of the earth** Yahowah, the God of heaven, **has given me**, and he **has commanded me** to build for him a temple in Jerusalem which is in Judah" (2 Chron 36:23).
20**teaching them**	**These things which I am commanding you** today shall be on your minds, and you shall **teach them** . . . (Deut 6:6).
to keep all the things **I have commanded you**. Now look!	You shall **keep** the commandment, the statutes, and the customs, which **I am commanding you** today, to do them (Deut 7:11).

Let us go up and fight, according to **all that Yahowah, our God, has commanded** us (Deut 1:41).

I am with you all the days until the end of the age.

I will be their [God] for the age, and **I will dwell with them for the age [to come] until [the end of that age]** . . . I will create my temple for my dwelling **all the days**, according to the contract which I made with Jacob at Bethel (11QT 29:7-10).

I am the God of Abraham, your father, **Do not be afraid for I am with you** and I will bless you and multiply your seed (Gen 26:24).

Look! **I am with you**; I will protect you wherever you go, and I will return you to this land (Gen 28:15).

I will be with you, and this will be a sign to you . . . you will serve God on this mountain (Exod 3:12).

Just as **I was with Moses I will be with you;** I will not fail you nor abandon you (Josh 1:5).

TECHNICAL DETAILS

This Matthean unit is a clear midrash on Dan 7:14 and 2 Chron 36:23. Jesus is portrayed here as the new Son of man and the new leader of the return from Babylon. This concluding passage in Matthew was also based on the concluding verse of Second Chronicles. It called attention to the release of the Babylonian Jews who were taken captive. In keeping with sabbatical eschatology and in fulfillment of the prophecy of Jeremiah, Cyrus made an announcement pass through the land providing release of the captive Jews. He also gave permission to the Jews in Persia to return to their land, and reconstruct the temple at Jerusalem, just as Lev 25:10-17 commanded for Jubilee observance.

The last verses of Second Chronicles is a midrash based on two passages--one from the prophets (Jer 25:12-13) and one from the Torah (Lev 25:10-17). The Chronicler interpreted these texts as having been fulfilled through the return of the Jews to the promised land and the construction of the temple on a new

Jubilee. The author of this conclusion in Matthew also used other texts--one from Chronicles which heralded the return of the captives to the promised land, one from Daniel which told of the victory over Antiochus Epiphanes and the cleansing of the temple, and others from Deuteronomy that Moses received from God at Mount Sinai. Still other texts taken from Genesis, Exodus, and Joshua, echo assurances given to Isaac, Jacob, Moses, and Joshua that God would be with them through the crises they faced.

The Gospel of Matthew concluded with the midrashic allusion to these passages to assure the readers that these eschatological hopes would be fulfilled again. The text of 11QT shows only the persistence of these hopes that were based on earlier scripture. It was probably composed independently of Matthew on similar assumptions. Although the temple at Bethel was not the same as the one at Jerusalem, Jewish and Christian composers did not hesitate to apply a text to a context and an identification that was intended for a different purpose.

Malina has astutely shown that Matt 28:16-20 is a literary form similar to the official decree of 2 Chron 36:23, reportedly made by Cyrus of Persia, and Gen 45:9-11, attributed to Joseph from Egypt. He has also shown that these verses were intentionally composed to form an inclusion with the beginning of the gospel, sandwiching in all of the material between, and this done in the form of a chiasm that relates the end (συντέλεια, Matt 28:20) back to the beginning (γένεσις, Matt 1:1).[5] This is beautiful literary artistry! Malina's summary is the following [bracketed transliterations added]:[6]

"Matt i.1 A βίβλος γενέσεως [bíb-los gen-éh-seh-ohs]
2-7 B Genealogy
23 C Μεθ' ἡμῶν ὁ θεός [meth hioo-móhn ho the-ós]
ii.1 D Jesus comes from Bethlehem
11 E Seeing εἶδον [áye-don] Jesus, the Magi adore: προσεκύνησαν [pros-kiu-nay-san]
v.16 Herod rejects
19-23 F Directive from the angel of the Lord--Jesus in Galilee

1. Gospel proper follows: what Jesus commands

xxviii.5-7, 16 F' Directive of the angel of the Lord--Jesus in Galilee

---

[5]B. J. Malina, "The Literary Structure and Form of Matt 28:16-20," NTS 17 (1970/71):87-103. This chiastic structure has also received attention from H. Schieber, "Konzentrik in Matthäusschluss. Ein form-und gattungskritischer Versuch zu Mt 28,16-20," Kairos 19 (1977):286-307, and D. Hill, "The Conclusion of Matthew's Gospel: Some Literary Critical Observations," IrBibStud 8 (1986):54-63.

[6]Malina, "Structure," p. 99.

17 E' Seeing ἰδόντες [ih-dón-tes], Jesus, the disciples adore: προσεκύνησαν [pros-kiú-nay-san]
some doubt

18-20α D' Jesus comes and gives an authoritative decree for all
1. what I commanded
20b C' ἐγὼ μεθ' ὑμῶν εἰμι [eh-gó meth hioo-móhn aye-mee]
B' πάσας τὰς ἡμέρας [páh-sahs tahs hay-méh-rahs]
A' ἕως τῆς συντελείας τοῦ αἰῶνος [héh-ohs tays soon-teh-láy-as too aye-óh-nos]."

COMMENTARY

To the mountain. There are other mountain scenes in the Gospel of Matthew: 1) The mount of temptation (4:8), 2) the mount of the sermon (5:1; 8:1), 3) the mount where Jesus prayed, 4) the wilderness mountain where Jesus multiplied the loaves (15:29), 5) the mount of transfiguration (17:1, 9). These were all occasions where Jesus demonstrated his authority as one like Moses. Just as Moses went up to a mountain top to receive the new contract that bound the people to God, so Jesus would initiate a new contract from a mountain top. Just as God addressed Moses for the last time on a mountain (Deut 34), so here Jesus delivers his final message to his apostles on a mountain top. Matthew did not say which mountain was involved here. Most scholars think it was Mount Tabor, but that was under Roman guard at the time. We probably will never know for certain.

Brooks noticed the literary importance of this final paragraph in Matthew. The two main words were "authority" and "teaching." Both of these are reflected throughout the gospel.[7]

Some doubted. The expression "But some," renders the Greek hoy de (*οἱ δε*) which acts often as a separating term, but it is not perfectly clear who the people are that are separated. Here it distinguishes the "some" from the entire 11 disciples. The "some" could be people other than the disciple or some of the disciples themselves. The context of this pericope pictures only the disciples present, so it can hardly be some non-disciples. Therefore it seems to mean that all of the 11 bowed down before Jesus, but only some of those 11 still had doubts.[8] That

---

[7]O. S. Brooks, Sr., "Matthew xxviii.16-20 and the Design of the First Gospel," JSNT 10 (1981):2-18.

[8]See the debate among K. Grayson, "The Translation of Matthew 28:17," JSNT 21 (1984):105-109; K. L. McKay, "The Use of hoi de in Matthew 28.17: A Response to K. Grayson," JSNT 24 (1985):71-72; and P. W. van der Horst, "Once More: The Translation of *οἱ δέ* in Matthew

seems to be the understanding of the author of the Fourth Gospel. Giblin argued that there should be a period after "worshiped," and the following sentence should be, "But they doubted," meaning all the disciples doubted at that time.[9] Ellis argued that more than one doubted, but those who doubted did not doubt while they were facing Jesus. They first worshiped, while in his presence, but later they doubted.[10] Both translations are possible. There was doubting involved, but we cannot be sure how many apostles were involved.

Matt 28:17 was probably the text that prompted the Johannine author to dramatize this story in detail. According to John the doubting took place within the disciples' camp, but there was only one person who doubted; this was Thomas refusing to believe until he had seen the mark of the nails in his hand and put his hand in the wound in his side. Jesus, then, appeared to the disciples when Thomas was there, and he invited Thomas to put his finger into the holes of his hands and put his hand into the wound of his side. Thomas at once responded, "My Lord, and my God" (John 20:24-29). This is part of the concluding paragraph of the Gospel of John, just as Matt 28 is the concluding chapter of the first gospel. Both gospels conclude with a satisfaction for the doubters. John 21 is apparently a later addition.[11]

<u>All authority has been given me</u>. The passive voice was used to avoid pronouncing the name of God. This means "God has given me all authority." This claim and promise are based on the judgment scene in Dan 7. Dan 7 consists of a mythical judgment scene where God acted as the great judge. The trial was between the horn (Antiochus Epiphanes) and the Son of man (Judas the Maccabee). Antiochus was given a death sentence, and Judas was given the authority to rule over the promised land. Dan 7 was a theological interpretation of the events of history from 168-164 B.I.A. which concluded with the death of Antiochus, the establishment of Hanukkah, and the installation of Judas as the new Jewish political leader.

In Dan 7 it was the one like a Son of man who was given the ruling authority, glory, and kingdom of the house of David. The Danielic son of man was

---

28.17," <u>JSNT</u> 27 (1986):27-30. I. P. Ellis, "'But Some Doubted,'" <u>NTS</u> 14 (1968):574-80, thought the word used for "doubt" here should be rendered "hesitated."

[9]C. H. Giblin, "A Note on Doubt and Reassurance in Mt 28:16-20," <u>CBQ</u> 37 (1975):68-75.

[10]Ellis, "'Some Doubted,'" pp. 574-80.

[11]For similar relationships between the Fourth Gospel and the Gospel according to Matthew notice the following parallels: "<u>After he had seen the crowds, he went up</u> **into the mountain,** <u>and after he had sat down</u>, **his** <u>disciples</u> came to him" (Matt 5:1). "<u>After</u> these things Jesus went away across the sea of Galilee (of Tiberias). A large <u>crowd</u> followed him, because <u>they had seen</u> the signs which he had done for the sick, but Jesus <u>went away</u> **into the mountain and there he sat down** with **his disciples** (John 6:1-3). As in Matt 28, John seems to be secondary here.

Judas the Maccabee, who had won the battle of Beth-horon, the decisive battle of the Maccabean Revolt. This Matthean midrash on Dan 7 placed Jesus as the new Son of man, with extended authority. Judas received the authority to rule the promised land; Jesus was given all authority in heaven and earth. The Danielic author expected all peoples and nations to serve Judas. The Matthean author expected all peoples and nations to become converted followers of Jesus, serving the new Son of man just as the Danielic author expected of the Hasmonean Son of man.

Kingsbury argued that the Christology of this passage is Son of God Christology. He argued that Jesus "is the Son of God in the sense that in his person God dwells with his people," and he was exalted to the position of Son of God by his resurrection. Before that he was the Messiah.[12] It is true that God dwelled with his people through Jesus, but probably not in the way Kingsbury intended. Jesus, as the Messiah, was God's legal agent. Whenever he was anointed as the Messiah, probably by John the Baptist, at that time all authority was given to him. His authority did not begin with the resurrection. Legally, but not ontologically, he was therefore God. Like all agents, he was the vehicle through which the principal acted. He spoke and acted in the name of the principal, in behalf of the principal, and at the responsibility of the principal. When he was present, God was legally present.

In Matt 2, 16, and 27 it is clear that Jesus held the titles Messiah, king, king of the Jews, Son of God, and Son of man with no indication that he advanced in rank from one to the other. As soon as he was Messiah he was also Son of God. The latter title did not originate with the resurrection. Since this text used Dan 7 as an intertext, Matt 28:16-20 is primarily Son of man Christology, but all of these titles have the same significance, so this is a detail of small importance. Son of man is the title implied in the midrash, but all of the rest of the titles are understood. None of these titles has any ontological significance. They are all legal titles that are applied to kings.[13]

<u>In heaven and on earth</u>. This is a <u>merismus</u>. A <u>merismus</u> is an idiom by which ancients mentioned both ends of something to include everything in between. "Heaven and earth" mean all creation. "Sea and dry land" mean all the surface of the earth. "Both great and small" means everything of every size. The terms "heaven" and "earth" are used together in the FT many times. Genesis begins

---

[12]J. D. Kingsbury, "The Composition and Christology of Matt 28:16-20," <u>JBL</u> 93 (1974):573-84, has shown that this passage is coherent with other words and concepts in the Gospel according to Matthew. He presumed that also meant it was "redactional." He thought that because these verses were not in the Gospel according to Mark that therefore Matthew added them when he used Mark. That presumes without showing any evidence that Mark was written before Matthew. There are many problems with this assumption, and his argument would not have been weakened at all had he omitted the redactional claim.

[13]See further the commentary on chapter 3.

with a creation litany in which God created both heaven and earth. When Abraham sent his servant to find a wife for Isaac, he made him take an oath by **the God of heaven and the God of the earth** (Gen 24:2; Deut 4:39; Josh 2:11; 1 Kings 8:23). This may have meant, "This is the God of all creation. He is the creator of heaven and earth" (Gen 14:19; Exod 31:17; 2 Kings 29:15; Isa 37:16; 45:18; 51:12-13, 16; Zech 12:2), and he would create a new heaven and earth (Isa 65:17; 66:21-22). Yahowah makes heaven and earth shake (Joel 4:16; Hag 2:6, 21; Ps 68:8-9). Since Abram lived early in the religious development of the Hebrews, he may not have been monotheistic. He may have made the servant take an oath by all the gods there were--those of heaven and those of earth. The word for "God" in Hebrew may also mean "gods."

Since the word for "earth" can also mean "land," rabbis sometimes interpreted the term one way when it was probably intended the other, but authors of the FT also intentionally put them together so that both meanings were intended. For example in the same narrative where Abram reportedly called the Lord the **God of heaven** (shah-máh-yim, שמים) **and the God of earth** (áh-retz, ארץ) (Gen 24:2-3), he also referred to him as **The God of heaven who took me from the house of my father and the land** (áh-retz, ארץ) **of my birth** (Gen 24:6-7). Yahowah pushed his people to the ends of heaven, but he promised that he would gather them from there and bring them to the land which their fathers inherited (Deut 30:3-5). Since the Messiah was a king, he was God's legal agent, ex officio. Therefore he might claim all divine authority, that is, all authority in heaven and on earth. As king of the promised land, however, the meaning might be that he had all the authority of God only on the promised land. Since, however, the command continued to instruct the apostles to "go therefore and make disciples of all the gentiles," the relevant term here seems to mean "earth."

Make disciples of all the gentiles. There has been a debate among such scholars as Strecker, Lange, and Meier[14] concerning the integrity of Matt 28:16-20. Is it basically a unity composed by the author of Matthew? Is it an earlier source which Matthew edited? None of the above is satisfactory. It is a composition based on earlier sources, to be sure, but those sources are Dan 7 and 2 Chron 36. Matt 28:16-20 is not just an edited source.[15] It is a midrash based on two texts. Except for these two texts, there is only one author involved, and it was probably

---

[14]J. P. Meier, "Two Disputed Questions in Matt 28:16-20," JBL 96 (1977):407-24; G. Strecker, Der Weg der Gerechtigkeit (Göttingen: Vandenhoeck & Ruprecht, 1971), pp. 98-14, 208-217; J. Lange, Das Erscheinen des Auferstandenen im Evangelium nach Mattiäus (Würzburg: Echter Verlag, 1973) pp. 488-506. Meier recognized the importance of 2 Chron 36:23 to this text (p. 419), but he did not notice the midrash. He opposed D. R. A. Hare and D. J. Harrington by questioning their claim that the ethnay in Matt 28:19 were gentiles. See also Meier, "Nations or Gentiles in Matthew 28:19?" CBQ 39 (1977):94-102.

[15]Liturgical or otherwise. See Meier, "Disputed Questions," p. 411.

not the same author as the one who composed Matt 7:6 or 10:5, warning against association with or conversion of the gentiles. This, however, is not absolute.

It is not certain what is meant by the word "gentiles." There are two possibilities: 1) It could have meant to make proselytes of non-Jews. Jews had made converts of gentiles ever since the Babylonian captivity. According to the targum, Naomi did not allow Ruth to follow her into Judah until she offered to become a proselyte (TgJon Ruth 1.16). Without becoming a proselyte Ruth had no right to a portion in the age to come (TgJon Ruth 2.13). Jesus reportedly accused the Pharisees of encompassing land and sea to make a single proselyte (Matt 23:15). 2) Another possibility is that the command was to make disciples of Christ of all the Jews in the diaspora. These were sometimes called "the uncircumcised" circumcised or not.

Rabbis said that there would be no proselytes accepted during the days of the Messiah, because the days of the Messiah would be like the days of David and Solomon (bYeb 24b), meaning that this was the time the land would be acquired and diaspora Jews would be returned. Jews would concentrate on land and not proselytes. There were no proselytes accepted in the days of David and Solomon. This means that the rabbis thought the Son of man would sit on his glorious throne in Jerusalem just as David and Solomon did. The age to come would be the age of peace that followed the Messianic age. That would be the time to make proselytes after all of the diaspora Jews had returned.

There are many prophecies that predict, either before or after the facts that Israelites and Jews would be scattered among the nations (Deut 28:37; Jer 26:4-5; 25:34; 29:18; Ezek 6:9; Hos 9:1). There is also the promise that they would be returned (Deut 30:3; Jer 12:15; 32:37; Mic 2:12).

Following Isa 40:11, Ezekiel promised that God would gather his people from all of the nations, and he would restore them to their own land, and he would feed them upon the mountains of Israel. He would appoint over them a Davidic shepherd who would feed and care for them (Ezek 34:11-25). The author of some of the servant songs held that the servant was called from his mother's womb to be assigned the task of gathering the diaspora Jews together and bringing them back to the Lord (Isa 49:1-5). Rabbi Hanin said that Israelites would not require the teaching of the messianic king in the future, because Isa 11:10 says, **The nations will look for him**. If this is the case, the question arises,

> Why should the messianic king come? What will he have to do [for Israelites]? [The answer is]: He will gather the Jewish exiles (GenR 98).

If the "nations" were going to look for the Messiah, this means the term "nations" was used to mean the Jews of the diaspora, and these were the ones the Messiah should gather. A Jewish nationalistic author of NT times said of the Davidic messiah, "He will gather together a holy people, and he will lead them in righteousness" (PssSol 17.28). The first task of the Jews in the messianic age would be to gather the Jews together from all over the diaspora and restore them to the promised land where they would live in peace and prosperity with the Messiah ruling from Jerusalem, just as it was in the days of David and Solomon. In the days of David and Solomon, before the Israelite and Jewish exiles, the Jews and Israelites all lived on the land. They had not been scattered among the gentiles.

Rabbis said that those outside the land were called uncircumcised and those inside Palestine were called circumcised, circumcised or not (mNed 3.11). It was to the Jews in the diaspora that Paul went, following the promise of Jeremiah that those who had been pushed out of the land of Palestine would be returned after they had paid double for all their sins. The agreement among Paul and the apostles at Jerusalem was that he would go to the gentiles and the apostles would go to the circumcised (Gal 2:7-9), but Paul evidently did not go only to unJudaized gentiles (1 Cor 7:18-19; Gal 5:6; 6:15; Col 3:11). He went to those who attended synagogues and other Jewish meeting places in Asia Minor.

After 11 years, he considered his work in this territory completed, and was prepared to go further. This could not have happened if his work had been among gentiles who had never heard the Bible or Jewish beliefs. Foreign missionaries who have tried to make converts of peoples of other non-Jewish religions sometimes spend ten years before making their first convert. Paul, however, must have worked among people who were already trained in the Torah and prophecies as well as basic Jewish doctrines. They already knew about the expected Messiah. Paul had only to convince them that Jesus was the Messiah for whom they had been waiting. Nevertheless, they were called "gentiles" and "uncircumcised" because they were outside the promised land. There were so many Jews in the Roman empire outside of Palestine in NT times that more than 8,000 appeared in the city of Rome to influence the judgment made when Archelaus was on trial before Caesar (War 2.80). There were so many Jews in Syria and Egypt that there continued to be military rebellions after Jerusalem had been taken and the temple burned (War 7. 43-62; 407-50).[16]

The Pharisees who traveled widely to make proselytes may have made converts from uninitiated gentiles, but that is not the only possibility. They may only have made Pharisaic converts of Jews who belonged to other sects. Fulfilling the belief that all the Jews of the diaspora would have to be returned in the days of the Messiah, the Matthean command may have been designed to convert other Jews to Christianity. Pharisees were making proselytes before the Kingdom of Heaven was established. They may have stopped before the arrival of the days of the Messiah.

At any event Christians, either on the basis of this commandment in Matthew or following the example of Paul had successfully converted many Jews to Christianity by the time of Constantine. Whether the commandment was intended to make proselytes of all non-Jewish gentiles or only Jews of the diaspora, the extensive goal was consistent with the Jewish tradition from which Christianity

---

[16]See further Buchanan, "Samaritan Origin," pp. 173-75.

had its origin. Whatever definition is given to the word "gentiles" here, this commission provides no basis for Cook's claim that all of the Gospel of Matthew is anti-Jewish.[17]

Powell was correct in thinking that the basic plot of Matthew was completed before the great commission, and Cook was mistaken in thinking that the distinctly pro-Jewish passages, like Matt 10:5-6 and 15:24, were only preliminary to Matthew's real message which was pro-gentile and anti-Jewish. It was not Matthew's design to bring the gospel to the gentiles. The theme of the gospel was closely tied to the promised land. Jesus was the new Joshua who was predestined to save the people from their sins and restore the promised land. The Gospel of Matthew was designed to show how Jesus fit into this antitypal pattern.

The passive voice in Daniel and Matthew means that it was God who gave both Judas the Maccabee and Jesus the authority involved, just as it was God who gave authority to Cyrus. Sometimes the use of the passive voice could prevent the speaker from mentioning the name of God. The authority God gave Jesus was that of being God's legal agent. Legally he was identical to God, and all of his actions and speech were to be in God's name, in God's interest, and at God's responsibility. It is because of this legal authority that Jesus was called "God" as well as "Lord."

This commandment may have been made by a different author from the one who spoke of the gentiles as "dogs" and "hogs" with whom they should not share their "pearls" or "that which is holy" (Matt 7:6) and who commanded the disciples not to go into the way of the gentiles or any of the Samaritan cities (Matt 10:5), but that is not certain. The commandments were given for different purposes and at different occasions. The commandment given in Matt 10 was probably given to apostles who were to make hasty announcements on the promised land before the following Passover. No attempt was made to proselytize. The gentiles mentioned there would have been the gentiles who lived in the promised land.

The commandment in Matt 28 was a directive to evangelize. This was a long term project that involved training and baptism. The gentiles there would have been people in the diaspora, either Jewish or gentile. It is true that the gentiles mentioned in these commandments may have been diaspora Jews, and diaspora Jews may have avoided mingling with non-Jews just as carefully as Palestinian Jews had. They might also have called non-Jews "dogs" and "hogs," just as Palestinian Jews did. There are no certain answers to this question.

Father, Son, and Holy Spirit. This is the first use of the Trinity in a formula. The terms, Father, Son, and Holy Spirit were all used singly, but not as a unified formula. Solomon and God were considered a "Father-Son" combination (2 Sam 7:14). The Spirit was used many times in the Dead Sea Hymns. In the Trinity, the legal significance is that God is the principal; Jesus as Son is God's legal

---

[17]M. J. Cook, "Interpreting 'Pro-Jewish' Passages in Matthew," HUCA 54 (1983):135-51.

agent; the Holy Spirit is the legal force that gives authority. Most early Christian baptisms were in the name of Christ, of Jesus, the Lord Jesus, or Jesus Christ (Acts 2:38; 8:16; 10:48; 19:5; Rom 6:3; and Gal 3:27).

I am with you. The author of this section probably intended to form an inclusion with the first chapter where Emanuel is translated as "God is with us" (Matt 1:23). God was with his people during the wilderness wanderings in the Shekinah. He was also present with them through Moses, the judges, and the true prophets, Amos, Hosea, Micah, Isaiah, Jeremiah, and Ezekiel. These were recognized as legal agents who spoke God's word, because God's spirit spoke through them (Matt 10:20). God was present through the agency of his Messiah, Jesus, and by extension, through Jesus' apostles who were authorized to act and speak in his name, in his behalf, and at his responsibility (Matt 10:1). That means God was with them. Through his Messiah, Jesus, God was legally present with Jesus' disciples wherever two or three were gathered in his name (Matt 18:20). This is legal presence the way the president of the United States is with the prime minister of England when the prime minister is in London and the president is in Washington, D.C. The "presence" is certified by a legal agent, usually the secretary of state, who is authorized to act in the name of the president, in the interests of the president, and at the responsibility of the president. When Jesus said he was with the disciples, he meant that they were his legal agents, commissioned as apostles, and his presence was with them legally.

Jesus' legal presence with the apostles made it possible for Jesus' program to continue after his death. He had organized a corporation of legal agents who could continue without his physical presence, but in his name. This was the corpus christi, the legal body of Christ.

Until the end of the age. The age bestowed upon Judas was the Hasmonean age which began with his victory at Beth-horon. The Hasmonean age was the holy age which followed the common or pagan era. The holy age was completely over by the time Herod the Great had Antigonus killed (37 B.C.). The author of Dan 7, however, had expected it to last longer--but not forever. The Matthean author expected the age he mentioned to be short. The age was the Roman age. This was the common, evil age which Jews and Christians all wanted to be over. Jews and Christians looked forward to a new judgment, like the one in Dan 7, which pronounced an end to the Seleucid rule over Palestine. In this new judgment, Jesus would be the new Son of man to set up his kingdom over Palestine, ruling from Jerusalem on the throne of David. They also expected a new Jubilee, like the one announced by Cyrus. Neither of these periods had yet come; the common Roman era continued, so the apostles were given the assurance of Jesus' legal presence with them until the current unsatisfactory political period was over so that the new holy Christian age could begin. The age to come is the one where Jesus would rule from Jerusalem as the Son of man, the son of David, the Son of God, the Messiah, and the king.

CONCLUSIONS

LITERARY STRUCTURE

The Gospel Form. The author of the Gospel according to Matthew probably designed the gospel as a literary form. Based on the Hexateuch type, the author took all of the sources that were available to him and organized them as closely as possible according to the first six books of the Bible, tracing Israel's history from the beginning to its entrance into Canaan. The discovery of a hexateuchal structure in Matthew provides insights that explain old unsolvable problems. For example the two feeding miracles that Jesus performed in the wilderness match the two feedings of the children of Israel under the leadership of Moses in the wilderness. The typology of Joshua suggests why there is a Judaea "beyond the Jordan," as Jesus entered Judah after he left Galilee. Jesus was presented as a new Moses and a new Joshua. It was an ingenious accomplishment, on the part of the Matthean author, tracing the activities of Jesus and his apostles and matching them with the activities of Genesis, Exodus, Leviticus, Numbers, Deuteronomy, and Joshua, not only in order of the books, but mostly in order within the books. He wanted the literary form itself to make the reader think of the new messianic movement as the new Exodus, wilderness experience, and entrance into Canaan. It is impossible to know precisely how much of the gospel the author wrote. The literary form he invented lent itself to further and later additions. There probably were such additions, so critical readers should try to determine where these additions occur. The following summaries show the prevalence of the Hexateuch in the Gospel according to Matthew:

1. Genesis	Matt 1:1-2:15.
2. Exodus	Matt 2:16-7:27 plus the transition sentence.
3. Leviticus	Matt 8:1-10:39 plus the transition sentence.
4. Numbers	Matt 11:2-13:52 plus the transition sentence.
5. Deuteronomy	Matt 13:54-20:16 with transition sentence misplaced at 19:1.

6. Joshua Matt 20:17-27:60 with transition sentence misplaced at 26:1.
Resurrection account in Matt 28.

Not only is this gospel well organized according to a hexateuchal typology, but it is well organized throughout: The genealogy is divided into three units of 14 ancestors; there are three temptations in Matthew 4; there are eight beatitudes in chapter 5, together with midrashic expansions; there are six contrasting legal comparisons in chapter 5--"You have heard . . . but I say." There are ten healing miracles in Matthew 8-9, and six parables dealing with the Kingdom of God are organized in Matthew 13. Seven woes are grouped together in Matthew 23. Like other rhetoricians of antiquity, Matthew liked groups of three, and he grouped 38 of them in his gospel.[1] There are five major discourses in the document, each one concluding with the words, "When Jesus finished . . . they were surprised. . ." This constituted a transition sentence from one hexateuchal antitype to another.[2] Luz argued that "According to Matthew we find no developed consciousness between units of literature (Gattungen) [emphasis his].[3] By this he seems to have meant that Matthew did not label some units as fiction and others as history, but that is not surprising. Matthew did not think all of the literature that Westerners call fiction was fiction. Once he found a unit of literature that was "proved" by two or more FT texts, he thought it was history.

Because there are so many well-organized units in the Gospel of Matthew, most scholars agree that the gospel is a well-structured document, even though they disagree about the structure. Carter has followed Matera, for example, in arguing that there are structured "blocks" in the gospel developed around "kernels," which are turning points in the plot. They do not agree, however, in the identification of the "kernels" or the "blocks."[4] Gooding suggested an outline with seven divisions: 1:1-4:22; 4:23-7:27; 7:28-10:42; 11:1-13:42; 13:53-18:35; 19:1-25:46; 26:1-28:20. This outline was basically organized around Bacon's plan, placing the divisions according to the positions of the connecting sentence, "Now when Jesus finished . . . " appearing at Matt 7:28; 11:1; 19:1; 26:1.[5]

---

[1]A. Plummer, An Exegetical Commentary on the Gospel according to S. Matthew (London: Stock, c1920), p. xx.

[2]On Matthew's structure see F. V. Filson, "Broken Patterns in the Gospel of Matthew," JBL 75 (1956):227-29.

[3]U. Luz, "Fiktivität und Traditionstreue in Mattäusevangelium im lichte griechische Literatur," ZNW 84 (1993):175.

[4]W. Carter, "Kernels and Narrative Blocks: The Structure of Matthew's Gospel," CBQ 54 (1992):463-81; F. J. Matera, "The Plot of Matthew's Gospel," CBQ 49 (1987):233-53.

[5]D. W. Gooding, "Structure Littéraire de Matthieu, XIII, 53 a XVIII, 35," RB 85 (1978):235.

Gooding argued especially that the central unit was not Matt 14-17, as Murphy-O'Conner had suggested, but Matt 13:53-18:35. This unit is preceded and concluded by the familiar connecting sentence. It consists of four units of five paragraphs each. These paragraphs are symmetrically organized.[6] Doyle basically followed Bacon's outline but noted each of the five basic divisions was directed to Jesus' disciples, so he concluded that the book was organized around the authority of the apostles and directed to the later church. Like most scholars, he held that the document was written about 80-90 I.A. to a church in Antioch which was becoming principally gentile.[7] It is true that apostolic authority was an important message of the gospel, but that fact does not require a late date for composition nor a basically gentile reading public.

Davies had never considered the importance or accuracy of the Hexateuch as an antitype for the Gospel of Matthew. He had seen only Bacon's conjecture of a fivefold division, following the pattern of a Pentateuch when he said,

> Thus its fivefold structure cannot certainly be held to have any theological significance, that is, it does not necessarily point to a deliberate interpretation of the Gospel in terms of a new Pentateuch as, in its totality a counterpart to the five books of Moses. At this point, though certainly not in others, it might prove profitable to exorcise the awe-inspiring ghost of Bacon from Matthaean studies. [8]

If Davies meant by this that Matthew never intended to give up the Pentateuch or Hexateuch, he is correct, but if he meant that there was no theological importance to Matthew's design of history, he was mistaken. In any event Bacon should be appreciated. His theory was incomplete, to be sure, but it was the model that provided the inspiration for the typology of the hexateuch. Matthew's typology has important theological significance, not to provide an assumption that it replaced the hexateuch, but to show how carefully the author or editor of this document studied the past in order to understand the present and to predict the future. This same care is reflected in the way he used FT and literary units containing the teachings of Jesus. His theology cannot be separated from his rhetorical and legalistic interpretation of scripture and events of history.

Literary Sources. The author did not compose the entire document de novo. He had at his disposal many previously composed units--chreias, parables, poems,

---

[6]Gooding, "Matthieu," pp. 248-50.

[7]B. R. Doyle, "Matthew's Intention as Discerned by his Structure," RB 95 (1988):34-54.

[8]W. D. Davies, The Setting of the Sermon on the Mount (Cambridge: Cambridge University Press, 1964), p. 107.

the Sermon on the Mount,[9] eschatological passages, woes to the Pharisees, etc. He organized them systematically, putting all of the healing miracles together, all of the kingdom parables together, all of the eschatological units together, and all historical passages together. This organization pattern successfully emphasized points to which the author wanted to call the reader's attention. Eight beatitudes (Matt 5) are more effective than one in persuading the reader of the same teaching. Six parables of the Kingdom make the intended belief more convincing than one (Matt 13). The same is true of other teachings.

Matthew utilized chreias and other small units to fill in places to match their hexateuchal equivalents. He often added another punch line to chreias to provide a second witness as the law required. Sometimes he made small sermons from chreias, according to the techniques taught by the Greek rhetoricians. One example of this is in Matt 15, where he began the chapter with a chreia, added a second punch line, interpreted the chreia on the basis of two intertextual scripture passages. Then he illustrated his point with further chreias and parables, finally promoting a teaching that contradicted the probable meaning the chreia originally intended.

Several scholars have tried to identify units of the gospel as special sources. Parker, for instance, put together a large section of Matthew comprised of that which is uniquely Matthaean (often called M) and that which is parallel to Luke (often called "Q"). Parker called this the K source.[10] Glover accepted "Q" as an unquestionable source, but found units in the church fathers that were very similar to passages in the gospels. He held, however, that they could not have come from "Q." Therefore they constituted a separate source which he called "the terse source."[11] Lambrecht assumed that there was a "Q" source, but he found so many places where Mark and Matthew were in parallel relationship in which the Matthean passage was clearly earlier than Mark that he had to conclude that Mark used "Q." He did not consider the possibility that Mark used Matthew.[12] Argyle found so many places where Matthew and Luke agreed against Mark that he concluded that Luke must have used Matthew; the

---

[9]H. D. Betz, The Sermon on the Mount (Minneapolis: Fortress Press, c1995), p. 86, was correct in concluding that the Sermon on the Mount was addressed to Jewish disciples, and that the Sermon itself is pre-Matthean (p. 145). In fact some of the sermon might have been pre-Christian.

[10]P. Parker, The Gospel before Mark (Chicago: U. of Chicago, c1953).

[11]R. Glover, "Patristic Quotations and Gospel Sources," NTS 31 (1985):234-51.

[12]J. Lambrecht, "John the Baptist and Jesus in Mark 1.1-15: Markan Redaction of Q?" NTS 38 (1992):357-84.

dependency could not be the other way around. Luke could not have been one of Matthew's sources.[13]

Huggins was of the same opinion, arguing that "Q" is an unnecessary conjecture, but his conjecture was based on other hypotheses which he did not challenge. He presumed without question that Mark was the earliest of the three synoptic gospels and that Matthew was secondary to Luke. He did not show that the arguments could be reversed. He did not consider, for example the fact that Luke's beatitudes are not only secondary to Matthew's eight beatitudes, but also to Matthew's midrash on the eight beatitudes in Matt 5:11-12. Neither did he explain Luke's homily (Luke 4:16-24) as a midrash on either Matt 13:54-57 or Mark 6:1-4. Nor did he explain Mark's commentary (Mark 7:3-4) on Matt 15:1-4. There are many instances in the synoptic relationships where it is possible to dogmatize a solution, based on a previously conceived hypothesis, but impossible to show which way the dependency lies. There are only a few places where a common source for two gospels is evident.[14] Our knowledge of the gospels should not be dependent upon conjectured synoptic hypotheses.

Lindsey argued that Luke is the earliest gospel that both Matthew and Mark used.[15] This is thought-provoking, but it overlooks the midrashic relationships. Years ago Plummer found problems with the logic of the popular consensus of synoptic scholars:

1) they assumed that Mark was the earliest source and was written in Greek;
2) they accepted the testimony of Eusebius (HE 3.24, 6; 39, 10; 5.8, 2; 10.3; 6.25, 4) that Matthew was first written in Hebrew;
3) they held that Matthew used Mark as his primary source.

This means, Plummer noted, that someone had to translate Mark into Hebrew for Matthew, and then someone else had to translate it back into Greek, very much like Mark's. Plummer thought this was incredible.[16]

The logic becomes still more incredible when we add to the confusion the geographical hypotheses that accompany the conjectures Plummer found incredible.

---

[13]A. W. Argyle, "Evidence for the View that St. Luke Used St. Matthew's Gospel," JBL 83 (1964):390-96.

[14]R. V. Huggins, "Matthean Posteriority: A Preliminary Proposal," NovT 24 (1992):1-22.

[15]R. L. Lindsey, "A Modified Two-Document Theory of the Synoptic Dependence and Interdependence," NovT 6 (1963):239-63.

[16]Plummer, Matthew, p. viii.

1) Jesus had Palestine as his home base where his activity took place;
2) Mark was composed in Rome;
3) Matthew wrote his gospel in Palestine and saturated his narrative with Palestinian customs, geographical names, and traditions.

This means instead of using primary sources from his home office in Palestine, Matthew would have gone abroad and found Mark in a library somewhere and used it as the primary source for his Palestinian document. Surprisingly enough, scholars 85 years later are still affirming the logic Plummer thought was ridiculous. Scholars who accept the hypothetical "Q" as if it were real have to make further conjectures, such as presuming that Mark and "Q" overlapped and that Matthew and Luke used different versions of "Q."[17]

After observing the careful use that Matthew made of the FT, and the outline that he structured following the Hexateuch, it does not seem likely that Matthew

> walked in the footsteps of Mark, and, if one now asks about his "category" (Gattung), he wants to write a new Gospel of Mark filled out around the teaching of Jesus.[18]

If an attempt were made to follow a Hexateuchal pattern in the Gospel of Mark, he or she might find one there, with units divided by consistent transfer clauses, but the divisions would not always be made in the same places. It was not necessary for either one of the two gospels to have followed in the footsteps of the other.[19] Matthew certainly had a pattern of his own into which he organized his FT passages and whatever other sources he had in his possession.

It seems more reasonable to assume that there were several sources that were composed before any of the gospels was written than to presume that there are several versions of one conjectured source. Some of these sources found their way into one gospel, some two, and some all three. Not all of these can be identified, although some may be conjectured. When the same teachings, narratives, or stories appear in more than one gospel, there are more ways than one by which this phenomenon can be explained. Two or three gospels may have used the same source; one gospel may have used a source and the other two may have copied it from that gospel; two gospels may have used the same source and the

---

[17]D. E. Garland, The Intention of Matthew 23 (Leiden: E. J. Brill, 1979), pp. 14, 16; H. D. Betz, The Sermon on the Mount (Minneapolis: Fortress, c1995), pp. 8-9, 42, et passim.

[18]Luz, "Fiktivität," p. 177.

[19]See further Buchanan, Typology and the Gospel (Lanham: University Press of America, 1987), chapter 2.

third copied from one of the other two. Those who herald only one possible solution to this relationship and group all of the possible sources into one unit and then have to explain that there are several versions of this one hypothetical document are placing more confidence into one conjecture than the data allows. The document called "Q" by nineteenth and twentieth century Western scholars has never been identified or named in antiquity. It is strictly a later Western hypothesis.

The Use of the First Testament. This commentary has attempted to relate the text of Matthew to real, visible, FT intertexts and devote as little time as possible to hypotheses. Fourteen times in the gospel, the author or editor spoke of FT prophecies being fulfilled (Matt 1:22; 2:5, 15, 17, 23; 3:3; 4:14; 8:17; 12:17; 13:14; 13:35; 21:4; 26:56; 27:9). Charette correctly said,

> Even the most superficial reading of the Gospel will not fail to produce the impression that the author has gone to considerable lengths in order to relate the life and teaching of Jesus to the Old Testament, and in particular to demonstrate that much that had been anticipated and expected in the Old Testament scriptures has been brought to fulfillment through the actions and words of Jesus.[20]

Allison was aware of Matthew's heavy dependence upon the FT, but also noticed a fact that most scholars have overlooked: Matthew composed much of chapters 26 and 27, alluding to passages from earlier sections of the Gospel of Matthew itself.

This is consistent with Matthew's intertextual development. He used chreias related to Jesus the same way he used FT texts, treating them as valid documents upon which to comment and clarify. Matthew intended to remind his readers over and over again of certain points that he considered very important.[21] He repeated and reillustrated these points effectively. This was designed precisely the way great rhetoricians, like Aristotle and Quintillian, recommended. One of the best ways to identify sources in the Gospel of Matthew is to observe his method of developing texts.

According to the rhetoricians, the introduction and conclusion of a document should present in summary fashion the basic points of the rest of the argument. Matthew composed the account of Jesus' suffering and death so as to remind the reader of John the Baptist's suffering and death as well as the suffering

---

[20]B. Charette, The Theme of Recompense in Matthew's Gospel (Sheffield: JSOT Press, c1992), p. 21.

[21]D. C. Allison, Jr., "Anticipating the Passion: The Literary Reach of Matthew 26:47-27:56," CBQ 56 (1994):701-14.

servant and the Sermon on the Mount. The passive teachings in the Sermon on the Mount and other teachings that encouraged believers to avoid conflict and lay up treasures in heaven all prepared the reader to realize the importance of Jesus' passive suffering and death. Several special words used at the beginning of the Gospel are reiterated at the end, forming an inclusion of the entire document.

Languages and Libraries. Over the years various scholars have conjectured 37 different emendations to the text of Matthew. Black analyzed these and concluded that none of them had merit, except one: Matt 19:4. Here the text now reads **Male and female he created them**. Sahlin conjectured that this initially read "Male and female he created one." In Greek it originally had instead of "them" an alpha (α.), meaning "one." This Greek alpha, then, was misunderstood by later scribes as an abbreviation for the pronoun "them" (ow-toós, *αὐτούς*).[22]

Downing ridiculed Goulder's suggestion that gospel writers, like Luke, had before them scrolls which were laid out before the author for comparison as each wrote. This seemed rather awkward to Downing, but some of these ancient scholars were very careful in their composition. That is especially true of Matthew, who apparently worked from some library where he had sources before him and spent countless hours organizing them for the composition of his gospel in much the way Goulder pictured.[23] Just as today, ancient authors were free to use their sources according to their own plans and their own judgment.

Eusebius reported that Papias said that "Matthew organized the logia in the Hebrew dialect" (HE 3.39, 16). Scholars have argued whether he meant Hebrew or Aramaic, but that was before the discovery of the Dead Sea Scrolls when most people assumed that Jesus would have spoken only Aramaic. Now most scholars assume that Papias meant Hebrew, just as he said, but Kürzinger thought that he did not mean any Semitic language. Kürzinger took "dialect" to mean not "language," but rather the "Yiddish" way Jews had of speaking Greek. He based his argument on the fact that later church fathers quoted Matthew only from the Greek. When Irenaeus said Matthew wrote "to the Hebrews in their own dialect" (3.1, 1) he also meant that Matthew wrote Greek in a Yiddish style, according to Kürzinger.[24] Of course, this is possible, and the testimony of Papias has to be tested from the text of Matthew itself. There are many Hebraisms in Matthew that make sense only when a Semitic version of Matthew is conjectured.

---

[22]D. A. Black, "Conjectural Emendations in the Gospel of Matthew," NovT 31 (1989):12-14.

[23]F. G. Downing, "A Paradigm Perplex: Luke, Matthew and Mark," NTS 38 (1992):15-36.

[24]J. Kürzinger, "Irenäus und Sein Zeugnis zur Sprache des Matthäusevangeliums," NTS 10 1963/64):108-15.

MATTHEW'S PLACE IN THE SYNOPTIC RELATIONSHIP

This commentary is not primarily concentrated on the relationships of the synoptic gospels. Matthew can be understood as a very useful and important document without so much as a glance at the other gospels. The goal of this commentary has not been to discover which gospel or which hypothetical source each gospel used, but there have been so many obstacles to the two-source or four-source hypothesis and the conjectured "Q" source, observed along the way, that it has been necessary to criticize that hypothesis. The so-called minor agreements between Matthew and Luke against Mark have not been at all minor. This does not prove the Griesbach hypothesis, that argues that the earliest gospel was Matthew which was used by Luke, after which Mark used both. Instead it calls attention to the hypothetical nature of the hypothesis of Markan priority. When the data is as limited as it is, it is necessary for historians to make conjectures and reach hypotheses, but these hypotheses should not be confused for facts nor should they be substituted for real documents. It is better academics to concentrate on real documents and keep hypotheses on the periphery.

Fee attempted to revive the Markan priority argument on the basis of order.[25] Lowe analyzed his arguments, showing that in every case the arguments Fee used pointed instead either to Matthean priority or a proto-Matthean origin--never to a Markan or proto-Markan source. He concluded:

> Consequently, if the Markan priorist seeks to attack the GRIESBACH hypothesis with arguments from order, he cannot advance his cause, but is likely only to cause it unanticipated harm.[26]

Recent efforts to stabilize the "Q" hypothesis have been made by Robinson, Koester, Kloppenborg, Jacobson, and Mack.[27] In response to these Linnemann said,

> Try to imagine flying to a non-existent island on an airplane that has not yet been invented. Even if this impossible trip were to take place during the thirteenth month of the year, it would not be as

---

[25]G. F. Fee, "A Text-Critical Look at the Synoptic Problem," NovT 22 (1980):12-28.

[26]M. Lowe, "The Demise of Arguments from Order for Markan Priority," NovTest 24 (1982):36.

[27]J. M. Robinson, "The Sayings of Jesus: 'Q'," Drew Gateway (Fall, 1983); H. Koester, Ancient Christian Gospels: Their History and Development (Philadelphia: Trinity Press International, 1990); J. Kloppenborg, The Foundation of Q (Philadelphia: Fortress, 1987); A. Jacobson, The First Gospel (Missoula: Polegridge, 1992); B. Mack, Q--the Lost Gospel (San Francisco: Harper--San Francisco, 1993).

> fantastic as the tale, recently christened as scientific certainty by some NT scholars, concerning the 'Lost Gospel' of Q.[28]

After pointing out the problems with this hypothesis and the logic of the professors who uphold it, Linnamann concluded,

> On both historical and theological grounds, there is no reason to give up the canonical Gospels as the original and divinely inspired foundation for our faith.[29]

More than 40 years ago Doeve concluded

> It will be clear that this analysis of the composition is not very favourable to theories assuming the existence of a written source containing words of Jesus, a Logia source, Q.[30]

Howard has aptly studied the gospels to find the instances where lines were composed either in parallel or chiasmically. In the process he found some lines that were structured differently in one gospel from the way they were formed in another. Sometimes the order of the subjects was reversed. This is an interesting observation, but Howard correctly noted that this phenomenon provides no solution to the synoptic problem. The evidence could go either way. There was no pattern which each gospel writer used.[31] This is true of most units in the gospels. Scholars who confidently tell how Matthew "redacted" Mark or "Q," adding or deleting thus and so, would be hard pressed to prove each claim.

A person does not have to be brilliant to be able to show where one gospel tells the same story briefer or more extensively than the other, but it is much more difficult to discern how they got that way. Affirming a hypothesis is not the same as demonstrating a relationship. To do that as well as possible we must begin with facts. It is possible to find all four gospels useful without dealing with any of these hypotheses. In some ways concentration on hypotheses of origin distracts the Bible student from studying the text itself.

Linton found many problems with the general concept of "Q." He said that if there were a "Q" it was unrealistic to think that Mark and "Q" never overlapped or that Matthew and Luke include all of "Q." He correctly thought it

---

[28]E. Linnemann, "Is There a Gospel of Q," tr. R. W. Yarbrough, <u>BR</u> 11, 4 (1995):18-23, 42-43.

[29]Linnemann, "Gospel of Q," p. 43.

[30]J. W. Doeve, <u>Jewish Hermeneutics in the Synoptic Gospels and Acts</u> (Assen:Van Gorcum, 1954), p. 200.

[31]G. Howard, "Stylistic Inversion and the Synoptic Tradition," <u>JBL</u> 97 (1978):375-89.

was strange to think we know the extent of a source that is actually non-existent. He concluded,

> We are entitled to perform a purely analytical examination of the texts independently of any synoptic theory. The analysis, not some more or less current synoptic theory, should be given priority.[32]

Wilkens thought there was a "Q" source, but he was convinced that Luke also had access to Matthew directly.[33] Hagner assumed that Mark was the earliest gospel and that there was a "Q," but he also thought there were other unknown sources behind the gospels.[34] Stein acknowledged that there were many agreements between Matthew and Luke against Mark, but he satisfied himself that there were other ways to explain the data in every case without assuming that one gospel used the other.[35] There are many imaginary solutions possible for these synoptic problems, but since none of us was there, they are all conjectural. Just because someone can conjecture a solution does not mean the conjecture is correct. It is best to acknowledge that we do not know how many sources there are behind the gospels and be satisfied with uncertainties when uncertainties exist.

The first way to study these relationships is with text and commentary. This involves applying the same methodology when studying synoptic relationships as was employed in examining the relationships between FT and NT texts. In the following texts there is not only an intertextual relationship, but also a poetry-prose relationship. The commentary is shown in bold face type.

POETRY AND PROSE IN THE SYNOPTIC GOSPELS

Matthew	Mark
a) 6:14For if you forgive men their trespasses, c) your heavenly Father will also	11:25Forgive, if you have anything against anyone; so that your Father also who is in heaven may forgive

[32]O. Linton, "Coordinated Sayings and Parables in the Synoptic Gospels: Analysis Versus Theories," NTS 26 (1980): pp. 161-62. The quote is from p. 163.

[33]W. Wilkens, "Zur Frage der literarischen Beziehung zwischen Matthäus und Lukas," NT 8 (1966):48-57; "Die Täuferüberlieferung des Matthäus und ihre Verarbeitung durch Lukas," NTS 40 (1994):542-57.

[34]D. A. Hagner, Word Biblical Commentary: Matthew 1-13 (Dallas: Word Books, c1993), pp. 133 and 145.

[35]R. H. Stein, "The Matthew-Luke Agreements against Mark: Insight from John," CBQ 54 (1992):482-502.

forgive you;	you your trespasses.
b) [15]but if you do not forgive men their trespasses,	
d) neither will your heavenly Father forgive your trespasses.	
16:25For whoever would save his life will lose it;	8:35For whoever would save his life will lose it;
but whoever loses his life for my sake will find it.	but whoever loses his life for my sake **(and the gospel's)** will save it.
19:26With men this is impossible	10:27With men this is impossible but **(not with God for)**
But with God all things are possible.	with God all things are possible.
26:11For the poor you have with you always;	14:7For you always have the poor with you **(and whenever you will, you can do good to them)**;
But me you do not have always.	but you will not always have me.

Anyone who presumes that Mark was the earliest source, and that Matthew obtained his material that is parallel to Mark's from Mark has a peculiar notion of the way poetry is composed. In these passages, Mark's account is prose, even though many words in Mark are exactly the same as the poetic passages in Matthew. Does anyone suppose that Matthew copied Mark, omitting only a few words here and there, and thereby arrived at poetry? It is much more reasonable to suspect that Mark composed his material either with Matthew or with Matthew's source before him. He copied down Matthew's very words, but added a few explanatory notes, midrashically, for emphasis and clarification. This, however, does not solve the synoptic problem. It only shows that in this particular pericope Matthew now has the earliest form.

But the plot thickens. Evidence does not all point the same way. Burney, for example, found another poem in Mark that has been abbreviated in Matthew.[36]

Matthew	Mark
20:22**You do not know what you are asking.**	10:38**You do not know what you are asking.**
Are you able to drink the cup I am about to **drink?**	**Are you able to drink the cup I drink**?
	Or the baptism with which I am

[36]C. F. Burney, The Poetry of our Lord (Oxford: Oxford, 1925), p. 63.

	baptized to be baptized?
They said to him, "We are able."	[39]**They said to him, "We are able."**
	Jesus said to them,
He **said to them,** [23]"My **cup you will drink."**	The **cup** which I drink **you will drink.**
	and the baptism which I am baptized, you will be baptized.

The poetry is that which came first, which means that Matthew had access either to Mark or to a Markan poetic source. If they both used the same source, then it was Matthew who abbreviated the source and Mark that preserved the Semitic parallel, which means that in this case Mark has preserved the earliest source. It seems most likely that Mark and Matthew had some of the same sources and that they used them differently. These facts provide more questions about hypotheses than answers.

CHREIAS AND HOMILIES

There is a chreia at Matt 15:1-3 which functions as a text for Mark 7:1-9. There is also another chreia in Matt 13:54-58 which has become a text for a sermon in Luke 4:16-30. The detail of these relationships can be seen in the commentary. In these cases, at least, the text in Matthew is earlier than the expansions in Mark and Luke. It is possible, of course, that all three gospels used the same sources which Matthew preserved without change, and the other gospels expanded. In any case, Matthew now preserves the earliest form. It is no more reasonable to presume that the expansions preceded the texts on which the commentaries were made here than to presume that the gospel commentaries on FT texts preceded the FT texts. In these cases, Mark and Luke used chreias centered around Jesus in the same way they used texts from the FT. More complicated is the following relationship between Matthew and Mark.

COMPARISON OF PARABLES

Matthew	Mark
24:42**Watch, then, because you do not know** on which day **the Lord** of you **comes.** [43]Now, if that master **of the house had known** on which watch the thief **comes,** he would have **watched,** and he would not have permitted his **house** to be broken into. [44]Because of this you also be prepared, because at an hour when you do not suppose, the Son of man **comes.**	13:35"**Watch, then, because you do not know** when **the lord of the house comes--**

45Who, then, is the faithful and wise **servant** whom **the lord** has set over his **household** for the purpose of giving to them the food at the proper time. 46Blessed is that **servant**, whom, after his **lord** has **come**, will find him doing thus. 47I tell you under oath that he will set him over all his possessions. 48But if that wicked **servant** says to himself, "My lord is delayed," 49and he begins to strike his fellow servants, and both eat and drink with drunkards, 50the **lord** of that **servant will come** on a day when he does not expect, and at an hour which he **does not know**, 51and he will cut him in two, and place his portion with the theater actors. There, there will be weeping and gnashing of teeth.

25:1Then the Kingdom of Heaven will be compared to ten virgins, who, having taken their lamps, went out to meet the bridegroom. 2five of them were fools and five, wise. 3For the fools, after they took their lamps, did not take oil with them. 4The wise took oil in the vessels with their lamps. 5Now when the bridegroom was delayed, they all dozed and **fell asleep.** 6**In the middle of the night**, a cry was uttered, "Look! The bridegroom! Go out to meet him." 7Then **all** those virgins arose and prepared their lamps. 8The fools said to the wise, "Give us some of your oil, because our lamps are extinguished." 9but the wise answered, saying, "No! Lest there not be enough for both you and us. Go, rather, to the merchants and buy your own." 10While they were going away to buy, the bridegroom came, and those prepared entered with him into the chamber and closed the door. 11Later the rest of the virgins came, saying, "**Lord, Lord**, open for us." 12Then he will answer and say, "I tell you under oath, 'I do not know you.'" 13**Watch, then, because you do not know** the day nor the hour.

33you **do not know** when the time will be

35dusk, **in the middle of the night**, or cock crow, or at breakfast time. Lest, after he comes, he find you **sleeping**.

I say to **all, "Watch!"**

35**Watch, then, because you do not know** when the lord of the house comes

[14]Just **as a man going**
away on a journey, called

his
servants and gave over to them his possessions,
[15]to one, he gave five talents; to another, two, and
to another, one--each according to his own ability,
and he went away. [16]At once, the one who had
received five talents went, worked with them, and
gained another five. [17]Likewise, the one with two
gained another two, [18]but the one who had received
one, went away, dug the earth and buried his lord's
silver. [19]After a long time, the **lord** of those
servants comes and holds a financial accounting
with them. [20]Then the one who had received five
talents added another five talents, saying, "Lord,
five talents you gave me; look, I have gained
another five talents." [21]His lord said to him, "Very
good, good and trustworthy **servant**. You have been
trustworthy over a little; I will set you over much;
enter into the joy of your **lord**." [22]Then the one
who had received two talents said, "Lord you gave
me two talents; look! I have gained another two
talents." [23]His lord said to him, "Very good, good
and trustworthy **servant**; you have been trustworthy
over a little. I will set you over much; enter into
the joy of your lord." [24]Then also approached the
one who had received one talent. He said, "**Lord**,
I knew you, that you were a hard man, reaping
where you have not sown, and gathering where you
have not scattered. [25]Since I was afraid, I went
away and hid your talent in the ground. Here, you
have that which is yours." [26]His lord answered and
said, "Wicked and cowardly **servant**, you knew that
I gathered where I have not sown, and I collect
where I have not scattered. [27]Then, you should
have invested my silver with the money-changers,
and when I came I would have received my capital
with interest. [28]Take, then, from him the talent and
give it to the one who has ten talents. [29]For to
everyone who has [interest], it will be given and
added to him; but to the one who has not [interest],
even that [capital] which he has will be taken away

[34]**As a man going**
away on a journey,
having left his house

and given to **his**
servants the authority
to each his work.

from him. [30]Throw out the useless **servant** into outer darkness. In that place there will be weeping and
gnashing of teeth."

Here are two passages which contain words that are identical. One is much briefer than the other. A priori this could mean that the longer passage used the shorter one as a text and expanded his text exegetically. That is normally the first suspicion, because many commentators in many centuries have expanded texts in that way. The problem here is that the brief passage does not make sense. Mark's watchman was left for an indefinite length of time and was expected to be on guard 24 hours a day without any sleep. Matthew's virgins were expected to be prepared to watch only one night. Matthew's supervisor was expected to manage the business well during his absence, assuming that he also slept at night.

It is unlikely that anyone would have chosen the Markan pericope for a source. What authority would such a pericope as this have? It would have been much easier to compose something de novo. Furthermore the longer passages, although they contain some of the same words as those that appear in the shorter unit, do not look like exegetical commentaries. The longer passages consist of two parables that seem to be complete and unified in themselves. This means that the more likely relationship is that the author of the shorter unit (Mark) had access to the two parables in the longer passage (Matthew). He summarized the two parables into one, writing a summary that is comprised almost entirely of words that occur in Matthew with the result that his summary is too brief to make any sense. It seems likely in this unit that Mark used either Matthew or the very source that Matthew copied unchanged. If it was a source, it would have had both parables in the same relationship to one another as Matthew now has, because Mark has compressed the two parables together into one.[37]

Although the hypothetical source "Q" may never have existed, it has been necessary in this commentary to refer to its conjecture, because it has been so widely accepted. It exists in the minds of many scholars. Nevertheless, it is only a hypothetical source, and all of its suggested versions are still more hypothetical. No one has ever seen any of them, and no one probably ever will. No matter how carefully and extensively scholars work to conjecture every word, it remains in the area of the unknown. The idea that Matthew shaped his gospel after the pattern in "Q"; that the Gospel of Thomas is "Q-like"; or that there were many hypothetical versions of this hypothetical document has gone far beyond the realm of analysis and has become pure fiction. It would be better academic methodology to refer to the texts that are preserved both in Matthew and Luke but not Mark as the "double tradition."

This commentary is centered on intertextuality. The first step, methodologically, is to notice the FT documents each gospel used. These are not conjectural. Scholars can argue whether or not the presence of certain words in a Mat-

[37]See further B. C. Butler, The Originality of St. Matthew (Cambridge: Cambridge U., 1951).

thean passage are there intertextually or accidentally, but no one can question whether or not the documents of the FT under discussion really exist and can be identified. Other gospels also exist, so that we can note the parallelism that there is among the three synoptic gospels and speak of those passages that are contained in all three synoptic gospels as the "triple tradition" and those units that exist in Matthew and Luke alone, Matthew and Mark alone, or Mark and Luke alone as "double tradition." The first way to study these relationships is with text and commentary. This applies the same methodology when studying synoptic relationships as was employed in examining the relationships between FT and NT texts.

THE BASIC MESSAGE

The basic message of the Gospel according to Matthew is that time had cycled around to the very antitype of the conquest of Canaan by Joshua many years earlier. That point in the cycle also coincided with the return from Babylon foreseen by Second Isaiah, and at the same time the point that was an antitype of the victory over the Greeks and the cleansing of the temple by Judas the Maccabee in 164 B.I.A. All prophecy was destined to be fulfilled during the days of the Messiah. Those days during which Jesus and his disciples lived were the days of the Messiah, and Jesus was himself the new Messiah, heralded, and probably anointed, by John the Baptist. The Kingdom of God, which had been under the rule of the Romans for many years, was destined soon to be restored to the chosen people. It was only the sin of the chosen people that kept the Kingdom from coming. Therefore it was the obligation of the followers of Jesus to forgive one another, repent of their sins, and perform good works that were necessary to pay off the heavy national debt recorded in the treasury of merits and demerits.

Klein examined the materials, apart from the birth and passion narratives, that are peculiar to Matthew. These units are brief, like stories of the workers in the vineyard (Matt 20:1-15), the ten virgins (Matt 25:1-13), interpretations of the law (Matt 5:21-22, 27-28, 33-37), counsel on personal piety (Matt 5:23-24; 6:2-4, 16-18); community rules (Matt 18:15-18), pictures of the judgment (Matt 25:31-46), and the two sons in the vineyard (Matt 21:28-31). These are Jewish Christian teachings that point out the rigidity of the piety required of the community. The treasure in the field (Matt 13:44) and the pearl of great value (Matt 13:45-46) tell of the importance of their goals. The weeds and wheat, the good and bad fish, and the rules for dealing with a sinner teach the demand for perfection. The judgment should not be arbitrary or reckless, but the new kingdom would permit only sinless citizens.[38] Klein thought these reflected more than one position and community. These units may have come originally from collections that different individuals composed, but they do not reflect views sufficiently different in viewpoint to conjecture different communities with different theologies.

---

[38]H. Klein, "Judenchristliche Frömmigkeit im Sondergut des Matthäus," NTS 35 (1989):466-74.

Cook attacked all scholars who thought there was so much as a word in Matthew's gospel that was pro-Jewish. Those passages which scholars have generally accepted as pro-Jewish were only seemingly so, according to Cook. Matthew's plan was to aggrandize the law, "but only as a prelude to its ultimate supersession by the law of Jesus."[39] Matt 10:5-6 and 15:24 were designed to show that Christians were originally Jewish, but that the Jews rejected them, so they were forced to go to the gentiles. Cook imported into Matthew the account in Acts where Paul was reported to have been reviled and opposed by the Jews, so he left them and continued his testimony to the gentiles (Acts 13:46). Cook failed to notice that Paul's travels among the gentiles were really to the Jews in the diaspora and not to gentiles who had never attended synagogue, read the Torah, or learned about a messiah. Furthermore, even if Acts were anti-Jewish, it is not Matthew. When Jesus reportedly attacked the Pharisees, scribes, and chief priests, Cook took another huge jump, and considered this inner Jewish conflict among Palestine leaders to be quarrels between Jews and gentiles. He affirmed this position repeatedly, following an erroneous chain of reasoning, while overlooking well known Jewish traditions reported in the FT and in rabbinic literature.[40]

THE AUTHOR

The author was a very intelligent, skillful, literary genius. He was well informed about FT and Jewish traditions; he was a learned legalist. He argued cases on the bases of that which could be proved legally. A man of integrity, he faithfully represented his sources. Even though he was a legalist, he accurately preserved the teachings of Jesus that were anti-legalistic. If he were not a monk himself, he at least preserved monastic traditions, such as those in Matthew 10, the commissioning of the apostles. After Goulder had analyzed the various features of all three gospels he learned that Matthew's familiarity with all of these far exceeded that of Mark or Luke.

> Matthew's imagination is different. He can use the salient features--the sheep or the way or the house--as themes to develop through his book. But also his mind goes into every corner. When we have given a list of animals, or crimes and punishments, or parts of the body, or religious characters and practices, or marriage and death

[39]M. J. Cook, "Interpreting 'Pro-Jewish' Passages in Matthew," HUCA 54 (1983):145.

[40]Cook, "Interpreting," 135-51. Cook is not alone in his position. He quoted from S. van Tillborg, The Jewish Leaders in Matthew (Leiden: Brill, 1972):, p. 171: "Many attempts have been made to explain the anti-Jewish character of the Mt Gospel. The simplest one, it seems to me, is to start from the assumption that Mt was not a Jew." There is an explanation that is still simpler and more accurate: There is anti-Pharisaic, anti-scribal, and anti-chief priests material, but there is no anti-Jewish character in the Gospel according to Matthew.

> images from Matthew, we feel we have covered the whole field: all that is left to Luke is the gleanings.[41]

Roloff was of the opinion that the author was a member of the later church and, especially in the parables, reflected the situation of the church when he wrote.[42] It is true that Matthew was more interested in the church than other gospel writers, and the teachings of the parables were undoubtedly found useful to the church, but they were not composed by members of the later church. They are coherent with one another and with the chreias. They make the best sense in the time of Jesus and in the geographical area of his activity. There is not one parable that reflects a geographical location outside of Palestine or a date later than the life of Jesus. A person would have to be very credulous to assume that the parables reflected many different authors from many different churches who wrote at many different times, and yet none of them ever indicated his or her own geography or date of their composition. Furthermore they all turned out to be coherent with one another. Matthew composed this document around the Hexateuch more than around the needs of the later church.

DATE AND LOCATION

Date. The events and time reported in the Gospel according to Matthew are centered around Palestine during the time of Jesus' activity (ca. 26-36 I.A.). The materials contained in the chreias are all coherent with one another; when date or location are revealed they all take place in Palestine during the lifetime of Jesus. Their coherence shows that one person could easily teach all of these messages. So coherent are these messages, that it would be difficult to show any way they might have acquired this coherence if their composition had taken place in various other geographical areas at some later time. Furthermore, the parables are also coherent with one another and with all of the chreias. Wherever their geography or time is implied it is also in Palestine during Jesus' time.

The most reasonable way to explain this data is to conclude that these represent the teachings of Jesus which he disclosed to his disciples. As commissioned preachers the disciples had lists of parables and chreias which they used as needed. It was they who wrote down the chreias as summaries of Jesus' teachings, and it was they who wrote down the parables, some of which are literary master pieces. Datable parts of the Sermon on the Mount presume the existence of the temple, where people were still bringing their offerings on the Day of Atonement. The parable of the Pharisee and the tax collector in the temple on the Day of Atonement presumes the existence of the temple. These teachings would

---

[41]M. D. Goulder, Midrash and Lection in Matthew (London: SPCK, 1974), p. 113.

[42]J. Roloff, "Das Kirchenverständnis des Matthäus im Spiegel Seiner Gleichnisse," NTS 38 (1992):337-56.

make no sense after the temple had burned in 70 I.A. Promises made that the Kingdom would come during the lifetimes of Jesus' contemporaries (Matt 24:34) would be unreasonable after the temple had been destroyed. Warning inhabitants of Jerusalem to flee to the mountains if war should come (Matt 24:17) would make no sense after the destruction of Jerusalem. Why would anyone compose the assurance to John the Baptist that he would be rescued after his death had been known? Predicting the good things that would happen immediately after the tribulation would make no sense after 70 I.A. when the tribulation was over and the blessings had not come (Matt 24:29).

The party line for many years has been that reflected by Beare who held that

> Jesus left nothing in writing, and gave no charge to his followers to prepare a written record of his saying or of his deeds. They were commissioned to preach, not to write, and the substance of their recollections was in fact not committed to writing to any degree for a number of years.[43]

Beare thought that the Gospel of Matthew was written many years after the death of Jesus and that the material Matthew used had undergone many changes before Matthew obtained it, and that he made still more. Herbert also argued that Matthew was written for gentiles after the fall of Jerusalem.[44] Bacon presumed that Mark was written after 80 I.A., and that Mark had been Matthew's chief source. Therefore Matthew had to have been written late.[45] According to Beare, Matthew attributed to Jesus sayings which he composed himself. On the validity of the gospels for reporting the teachings of Jesus, Beare concurred with Lightfoot that the gospels "yield us little more than a whisper of his voice."[46]

Beare reached these conclusions without ever learning what a chreia is, how it was composed, how it was preserved, and how it was used. He never studied the coherence of chreias and parables or wondered how they could be as coherent as they are and still be composed by many different people and later edited and changed by others. He apparently never studied the rhetorical and homiletical methods of rabbis and Greek rhetoricians. Therefore his assumptions are understandable, but inaccurate. Abel said there were enough contradictory statements in Matthew to conjecture two different editors: 1) A Jewish Christian who wrote between 64 and 70 I.A., and 2) a gentile author who wrote from

---

[43]F. W. Beare, "Concerning Jesus of Nazareth," JBL 87 (1968):125.

[44]G. Herbert, "The Problem of the Gospel according to Matthew," SJT 14 (1961):403-13.

[45]B. W. Bacon, Studies in Matthew (New York: H. Holt & Co., c1950), p. 67.

[46]Beare, "Jesus of Nazareth," p. 135.

Antioch between 80 to 105 I.A. This is one of the possibilities, but not the only one.[47]

Scholars like Beare thought Matthew was only someone who put together Mark and a hypothetical "Q" and later added some words of his own to expand the document. Since Mark has few teachings, many scholars assume that the teachings in Matthew were later compositions that had little to teach about the historical Jesus. Chreias and parables have been tested in several ways to show that their likelihood of representing the teachings of Jesus is very high. This is not true of the narrative reports in Mark. That which many scholars have dismissed as late and useless can be shown to be some of the earliest datable material. Since many of the parables and chreias occur in Matthew, this is a clue for dating Matthew earlier than has been customary. That which many scholars have claimed to be the earliest material, because it is found in Mark, is not datable and cannot be tested for validity.

There may have been a few post-70 I.A. editorial additions to the Gospel according to Matthew, but internal evidence points to an early date for most of the gospel. What, then, is early? Some parts may have been pre-Christian, such as the beatitudes, and some other parts of the Sermon on the Mount may have been based on earlier Jewish legal code. Parables, chreias, Jesus' response to the disciples of John, prophecies of the end, and references to the temple were all composed before 70 I.A., when the temple was burned. Some small editorial additions have been almost universally believed to have been written after 70 I.A., such as the narrative about Herodias and John the Baptist, the reference to the city being burned (Matt 22:6-7), the reference to wisdom (Matt 11:19c) and the commission to go into all the world (Matt 28:18-20), but closer examination shows problems with these conclusions and other explanations for their composition before 70 I.A. There may still be some additions that have been added after 70 I.A., but they are fewer than most scholars have thought, and they can be supported with less confidence than they have held in the past. There seems little reason to posit a post 70 I.A. date for most of the Gospel according to Matthew. Sibinga compared the parallels between Matthew and the words of Ignatius. He concluded that Ignatius used either Matthew or a uniquely Matthaean source (M). This is one of the earliest witnesses there is to the usage of Matthew by another author.[48]

Via observed that Mark was far enough away from the situation where the parables were used that he failed to see any way in which they were useful.[49] That may be true, but that does not also infer that Matthew was written still later. Parker called attention to many instances where Mark reflected ignorance of

---

[47]E. L. Abel, "Who Wrote Matthew?" NTS 17 (1971):138-52.

[48]J. S. Sibinga, "Ignatius and Matthew," NovT 8 (1966):263-83.

[49]D. O. Via, Jr., "Matthew on the Understandability of the Parables," JBL 84 (1965):430.

Palestinian geography and Jewish customs and practices, whereas Matthew was well informed about these.[50] That is also true of the Fourth Gospel. Both Matthew and John reflect a provincial, sectarian point of view that is not evident either in Mark or parts of Luke.[51]

Noting the things that are Jewish in the document, Plummer mentioned the following: Palestine is the land of Israel (Matt 2:20-21); its people are Israel (Matt 8:10); or the "lost sheep of the house of Israel" (Matt 10:6; 15:24); its towns are the "cities of Israel" (Matt 10:23). God is the God of Israel (Matt 15:31); Jerusalem is the holy city (Matt 4:5; 27:53). There are many references to fulfillment of Jewish prophecies in the book (Matt 1:22; 2:6, 15, 17, 23; 3:3; 4:14; 8:17; 12:17; 13:14, 35; 21:4; 24:15; 26:31, 54, 56; 27:9). The Messiah is the son of David, son of Abraham (Matt 1:1). The Messiah is the messianic king (Matt 2:2; 21:5; 27:11, 29; 37:42).[52]

This commentary has been written, using as comparative sources Jewish traditions and texts, because it is apparent that the Christianity which Matthew represented was Jewish-Christian, and it was composed before there became a severe schism between Judaism and Christianity, and the church was not distinguished from the synagogue. The doctrines, traditions, and assumptions in Matthew are all Jewish. The opponents in the gospel were the gentiles and other sects of Judaism, not Jews per se. At the time this document was composed the only Christians that existed were Jewish Christians. There were no non-Jewish Christians.

Three years after Paul was converted to Christianity he went to Jerusalem to meet with the apostles (Gal 1:18). He left while Aretas was king of Arabia (9 B.I.A.- 40 I.A.) (2 Cor 11:32-33). He went back to Jerusalem for another meeting with the apostles 14 years after his conversion (2 Cor 12:2; Gal 2:1). This leaves 11 years between Paul's first meeting with the apostles and his second (14 - 3 = 11). The latest possible date for the second conference was ca. 51 I.A. (40 + 11 = 51). It was after his collection in Asia Minor (ca. one year) that Paul prepared to go to Rome, but he first had to get the approval of the church at Rome. There was already a church at Rome at that time, and it was a strong Jewish Christian church. Paul had to argue his case to the leaders of the church on the basis of scripture and Jewish tradition. Such a church as this would have been comfortable with the Gospel of Matthew as their primary gospel at that time. This

---

[50]P. Parker, "A Second Look at the Gospel before Mark," JBL 100 (1981):396-98.

[51]That is not true, however, of all of Luke. The two chreias in Luke 13:1-5 were obviously written down when all of the readers knew about the events that occurred in the temple area while Pilate was procurator and also who the 18 men were that were killed at the border of Jerusalem. It was not necessary to explain the details. Without any of the modern means of communication these could not have been composed very far away from Jerusalem or much later than the rule of Pilate.

[52]Plummer, Matthew, p. xxiv.

does not mean that the Gospel of Matthew had been composed by then or that it had reached Rome, but if it had, the community there would have received it gladly.[53]

The earliest report of the Gospel according to Matthew was by Papias, bishop of Hierapolis, writing about 135-40 I.A. By that time the gospel was evidently complete and was called "According to Matthew."

Location. There is no mention in the Gospel according to Matthew of the place of its composition. Therefore scholars can only conjecture possibilities in general terms. Hypothetically it might have been composed anywhere in the Near East by some Jewish Christian who had spent much of his life in Palestine and had access to the necessary Palestinian sources that were used in its composition. Someone in a monastery in Spain or Italy, for example, who knew the land of Palestine well and also had studied carefully all of the data available about Jesus might have composed this literary document based on very early and reliable sources. Although many things might be possible, this is not a very likely conjecture.

Some of the earliest datable gospel material comes from the Gospel according to Matthew. Matthew and John reflect the most reliable familiarity of the geography and topography of Palestine. Matthew was recognized and used in the early church long before any other gospel. The more reliable the data, the more accurate the Palestinian geography and topographical information, and the more faithfully Jewish traditions are reflected, the more reasonable it seems to suspect that it was composed somewhere in Palestine. To narrow down the conjecture still further is to proceed with less confidence.

For years scholars have conjectured some place in Syria, probably Antioch. More recently Viviano has suggested Caesarea for the following reasons:

1) There was already a library there when Origen moved from Alexandria, Egypt, to Caesarea in 215-16 I.A. Archaeologists think they have identified it.

2) Jerome reported that a Hebrew copy of the Gospel of Matthew was kept in the library at Caesarea in his day.

3) In 222 I.A. Caesarea became the metropolitan see for Palestine.

4) Caesarea is only 30 miles from Jaffa and Jamnia and 75 miles from Jerusalem.[54] Scholars have presumed it has to have been composed near some large city where Greek was spoken, because the gospel has been preserved in Greek.[55] The earliest extant report of the Gospel of Matthew, however, is that it was composed in Hebrew. It was only translated into Greek after a Greek

---

[53]See further Buchanan, "Pauline Chronology," H. R. Johnson, Who Then is Paul (Lanham: University Press of America, c1981), pp. 231-33.

[54]B. T. Viviano, "Where Was the Gospel according to St. Matthew Written," CBQ 41 (1979):533-46.

[55]A. J. Saldarini, "Delegitimation of Leaders in Matthew 23," CBQ 54 (1992):661.

reading public was available. That might have been at a different location from the one at which it was originally composed.

That which seems very likely is that the Gospel was used in the library at Caesarea. It may also have been composed there. That is as good a guess as any other. The numerous sources the author would have needed suggests his access to some good library, but there were probably more than one in NT times. In all probability no one will ever know for sure where this document was composed or who the author was. The brilliance of the author and the quality of the document claim only the highest respect, even if we never learn who the author was or where he worked.

The document is pro-Petrine. It probably originated from the Petrine sect of Christianity, which seems to have had its beginning in Galilee and Syria but to have established extension churches quickly in Rome. When Paul went to Jerusalem from Asia Minor to confer with the Judaizing apostles, the council agreed that Paul should go to the "nations" and James, Cephas, and John would minister to the "circumcised" (Gal 2:7-9). Paul's ministry to the nations, however, was not really limited to those who were physically uncircumcised (1 Cor 7:18-19; Gal 5:6; 6:15; Col 3:11). He served instead both the circumcised and the uncircumcised among the "nations"--i.e., Asia Minor--and he planned to move from there west. The contrasting terms "circumcised" and "uncircumcised" were evidently geographical, rather than physical designations. Rabbis said the term "circumcised" applied to the inhabitants of Palestine, circumcised or not, and the term "uncircumcised" referred to those outside of Palestine, circumcised or not (mNed 3.11).

Antioch was somewhere near the northern border of the apostolic division, because it was there that Cephas and Paul had contacts in their ministry. At first Cephas was willing to observe the rules used in Pauline territory, but under the correction of "certain ones from James" (Gal 2:12), he changed to exclusive dietary rules. Eusebius said James was the first bishop of Jerusalem after the ascension of Jesus (HE 2.23, 1; 2.5, 2; see also Acts 21:18 and Hom 11.25). This seems reasonable, because those from James were not always near at hand. They had to come from a distance when they conferred with Cephas at Antioch. Cephas, on the other hand, was nearby. He seemed to be ministering to Christians in the North, perhaps Galilee and Syria.

Most of the geographical locations mentioned in the Gospel of Matthew are concentrated in Galilee and Syria (Recog 1.12). According to Matthew Peter was the rock upon which Christ would build his church (Matt 16:18). Between Jerusalem and Galilee lay Samaria, the territory where the Gospel of John shows the greatest familiarity with the area. Without identifying authors it is possible to put together these loose pieces to make a reasonable conjecture concerning the division of the church from which some of the NT documents originated and the apostles to which they were attached: James was in Jerusalem; Peter/Cephas was around Galilee and Syria; John had Samaria; and Paul went to the "nations" (Gal 2:7-9).[56]

There is an early tradition that Paul and Peter were both at Rome (HE 3.1-2). This does not necessarily mean that Paul and Peter were both there in person. It might mean that they had agents there. If there was a Petrine church there when Paul arrived that would be enough to establish the tradition. Paul's letter to the Romans has been preserved, so Paul probably traveled as far as Rome, but the church there was more Judaizing than Paul's churches in Asia Minor. Marcion seemed to get along well in Asia Minor, but when he moved to Rome he was excommunicated. This church did not accept Marcion's anti-Judaism. Again that kind of church would have liked the Gospel according to Matthew. It is possible that the Petrine church existed in Rome and that it considered Matthew its favorite Gospel. It may have been at Rome that the gospel was translated from Hebrew to Greek, and it may have been at Rome that the final commission of the Gospel was made to "all the nations."

All of this is highly conjectural, and it may be far from the truth, but we do not know the truth by which to judge it. The facts are given here that are relevant to conjecturing dates and location for the composition of the gospel. No one has ever written a commentary and given the suggested date and location of Matthew's composition who has not made a conjecture. Every reader may consider the data given here, and this conjecture, and then make his or her own hypotheses.

THE INITIAL READING PUBLIC

The earliest audiences of Jesus' teachings were sufficiently learned in Jewish tradition and scripture that they understood the codes involved. There were Jews in Palestine who might not have understood, but they would not have been the ones who preserved the materials. Furthermore, it is presumed that the author of this gospel also understood Jesus' messages and wrote them for a reading public that would understand them. These would not have been the masses; they would have been the well-educated Jews who appreciated the message and the literary structure of this document. They would have included early Christian monks. Although there were then, as now, Jews in the diaspora who were as well acquainted with Jewish scripture and tradition as those who were in Palestine, there is nothing in the Gospel that indicates any other origin. Therefore, the most likely supposition is that the author wrote this document somewhere within the borders of the promised land, and that his original readers were there as well.

Kilpatrick noted from the works of Irenaeus, Tertullian, Cyprian, and Augustine that Matthew was the most popular gospel of the NT canon. Wherever possible these fathers quoted from Matthew rather than one of its parallels. For

---

[56]See further Buchanan, "The Samaritan Origin of the Gospel of John," Religions in Antiquity, ed. J. Neusner (Leiden: E. J. Brill, 1968), pp. 173-75.

example they preferred Matthew's version of the Lord's Prayer to that of Luke.[57] Tagawa called attention to conflicting ideas in the gospel; some were pro-gentile and others were anti-gentile. He answered the question to his satisfaction by saying the author and initial reading public were Christians and neither gentiles nor Jews, per se.[58] Where would anyone go to find non-Jewish, non-gentile Christians? Christianity had its origin in Judaism, in Palestine, and later spread to diaspora Judaism. Later there were converts to Christianity that had not first been Jews, but that was after Matthew had been written.

THE PURPOSE OF THE COMPOSITION

Zealous, nationalistic Jews of NT times believed that they were reliving the last 3 1/2 years of the pagan rule of Palestine, just before the beginning of the Hasmonean period. The entire age of gentile rule (586 B.I.A. to 164 B.I.A.) was thought of as an evil age, sometimes called the common era, the profane era, the gentile age, the age of wrath, the age of darkness (קץ החושך, 4Q 462.9), the evil age, and other pejorative names. The last 3 1/2 years of that era was ruled by Antiochus Epiphanes. After the fact this period was known as the "end of days" (buh ah-khah-reét hah yahmeém, באחרית הימים, 4Q 397.13; CDC 4.4; 6.11), the "end of years" (buh ah-khah-reét hah shah-neém, באחרית השנים), or "the end of the time" (buh ah-kah-reét hah áyt, באחרית העת, 4Q 397.33), meaning the end of the evil days, years, or time, meaning a very specific time. It was later also called the "birth pangs of the Messiah," "the messianic age," or "the tribulation." This was to be followed by the holy era, the age of light (káytz hah óhr, קץ האור, 4Q 462.9), the good age, the holy era, the heavenly age, and other complimentary titles applied to the Hasmonean rule (164-38 B.I.A.).

The author of the Gospel according to Matthew believed that the evil age was just about over, and the new age of light was ready to begin. The very time when he was writing was the end of the common era, in his judgment. The age of his lifetime was the messianic age, and Jesus was the Messiah. He wrote this gospel to demonstrate to all readers the way current events had matched up with the ancient exodus from Egypt, the wilderness wandering, and the entrance into the promised land. The messianic age was the contemporary equivalent of the "birth pangs of the Messiah," the "tribulation," or the antitype of the Hasmonean war just before the rededication of the temple (164 B.I.A.). All of this was good news, so the literary form the author designed was called the gospel or the Good News according to Matthew.

---

[57]G. D. Kilpatrick, The Origins of the Gospel according to St. Matthew (Oxford: Oxford U., 1946), p. 77.

[58]K. Tagawa, "People and Community in the Gospel of Matthew," NTS 16 (1969/70):146-62.

Clark proposed that the author was pro-Gentile in his bias.[59] He has been followed by many scholars, all of whom have misinterpreted the data. The four reasons given are as follows: 1) The birth narrative includes a genealogy that begins with Abraham and includes four gentile women; 2) Jesus is to be the light to the gentiles (Matt 4:15-16; 12:18-19); 3) Jesus healed the Roman centurion and praised his faith (Matt 8:5-13); and 4) Jesus traveled to gentile territory, namely Gadara (Matt 8:18-34), Tyre, and Sidon (Matt 15:21-39), and performed miracles there. Sim correctly maintained that this argument is "based on a very shaky foundation which simplifies the evidence by overstating it at some points and by downplaying or even ignoring it at others."[60]

There are real obstacles to the claim that gentiles in Matthew are always treated favorably and Jews, unfavorably. For example, Abraham is called the father of many nations, but he is especially traced genealogically through Isaac and Jacob to the Jews. He is not thought of as an anti-Jewish father. The four gentile women were all presumed to have converted to Judaism. The reference to Jesus being a light to the gentiles is based on the intertext of Isaiah, which is a message of hope. This was spoken when Judah and Samaria were divided. Second Isaiah foresaw a time when Judah would expand its borders to include Galilee. This gentile territory would be included within Jewish borders--hardly an anti-Jewish expectation. It was the gentile, Pilate, who condemned Jesus to death; it was the Roman soldiers who crucified him, according to Matthew. The Gadarene story pictured the gentiles as crazy, demon possessed, and pigs--not really pro-gentilic.

The Roman centurion seemed well-versed in Jewish law. Like many other officers in the Roman army, he was probably Jewish. His being Roman did not keep him from being also Jewish. Jesus traveled into gentile territory, but not exclusively. He only once traveled to the territory of Tyre and Sidon, but these cities and all of Lebanon were once part of the Davidic-Solomonic kingdom. This was not an anti-Jewish act. Although he healed a gentile woman's daughter, he first referred to her as a dog, an anti-gentile, insulting title. Gentiles were given as negative examples, classed alongside tax collectors (Matt 5:46-47). Jews were warned not to be greedy like the gentiles or pray with many words like gentiles (Matt 6:7-8; 31-32). Those excommunicated were to be shunned like gentiles and tax collectors (Matt 18:15-17). Counsel to be isolated from gentiles is hardly a pro-gentile bias. According to Matthew Jesus criticized the Pharisees and scribes from an inner Jewish point of view, but gentiles were treated as outsiders to be avoided and not imitated.[61]

---

[59]K. W. Clark, "The Gentile Bias in Matthew," JBL 66 (1947):165-72.

[60]D. C. Sim, "The Gospel of Matthew and the Gentiles," JSNT 57 (1995):19-48.

[61]For a careful rebuttal of the notion that Matthew has a pro-gentile bias, see Sim, "Gentiles," pp. 19-48.

Matthew was not an indifferent document that was sometimes Jewish and sometimes anti-Jewish. His anti-gentile bias was too strong to be also anti-Jewish. He did not propose that Jews become involved in a war with Rome, but he was nevertheless nationalistic and anti-gentile.

THE HISTORICAL JESUS

There are still those who, like Gager, follow Schweitzer and say,

> There can be no quest for the historical Jesus in any meaningful sense of the phrase.[62]

This amount of skeptism is no longer necessary or wise. Those who are skeptics regardless of the evidence shown are just as credulous as those who believe everything without evidence. There is a certain amount of gullibility to skepticism that is held against all odds. We can know more about Jesus than about most personalities in ancient history, such as Socrates or any of the rabbis, but we must be willing to accept the most logical interpretation of the data possible rather than trying to force twentieth century western concepts on a Near Easterner who lived 2,000 years ago.[63] Scholars like S. Matthews have imagined that Jesus died, paying "for his spiritual democracy with his life."[64] There is not much in the gospels to indicate any democratic tendencies in the life of Jesus. Matthews realized this, so he explained that Jesus was not teaching people how to live for his day; he expected God to introduce a new era that would be democratic. He held that Jesus prepared his followers for this day by his silence.[65] This is pure, unadulterated, Rorschach eisegesis. This is no time to place the historical Jesus off limits for NT research. It is not necessary to argue in terms of silence when there is as much actual data as there is available for research.

A PERSONAL NOTE

I am grateful to anyone who has actually read this entire commentary. I also hope that some of you have become excited, not just about this commentary, but most of all about the Gospel according to Matthew. It is no mistake on the part of Christians that, over the centuries, the Gospel of Matthew has been the most read and best loved of the gospels. The beautiful style, the careful attention

---

[62]J. G. Gager, "The Gospels and Jesus: Some Doubts about Method," JR 54 (1974):272.

[63]See further Buchanan, Jesus: the King and his Kingdom (Macon: Mercer U. Press, c1984).

[64]S. Matthews, Jesus on Social Institutions intro. K. Cauthen (Philadelphia: Fortress, c1971), p. 60.

[65]Matthews, Social Institutions, p. 146.

to Jewish tradition, and the erudition reflected in this gospel deserve careful reading and appreciation. I have tried here to introduce readers to the most important traditions, customs, and data for studying this gospel. I have also added my own interpretations and conjectures. There is no claim to infallibility about either of these. It is more important that every reader study the data critically and make his or her own interpretations and conjectures. Anyone capable of reading this commentary is also able to think critically and make responsible judgments. That is the design and purpose of the commentary.

GENERAL INDICES

WORDS

ANCIENT PERSONALITIES

MODERN SCHOLARS

GEOGRAPHICAL LOCATIONS

BIBLICAL REFERENCES

NON-BIBLBICAL REFERENCES

ABOUT THE AUTHOR

Prof. George Wesley Buchanan, PhD, LittD, D.S.L. has been recognized in academic circles for being the first to achieve the following: (dates of publication)

1. discover how to gain insights from the Dead Sea Scrolls to solve biblical problems (1956).
2. discover midrash (commentary on Scripture) in the First Testament (1965).
3. discover the Samaritan origin of the Gospel of John (1970).
4. discover ways to present intertextual commentaries both in the New Testament (1993), and in the First Testament so that the sources were obvious (1999).
5. discover the northern borders of the Promised Land (1970).
6. discover that Hebrews 1–12 is a sermon based on Ps 110 that was first preached at Zion (1972)
7. discover independently the true location of the temple at Zion as one of two scholars (2003).
8. discover how to separate the teachings of Jesus from the additions of the later church—that which Albert Schweitzer and all succeeding NT scholars thought could never be done (1984).

Buchanan has spent fifty years in research and 31 years teaching, while conducting many archaeological projects in the Near East. He has written 16 books and 63 scholarly articles, in addition to many sermons, church school materials, articles for the clergy, and poems. His latest project has been this intertextual commentary on Hebrews, which has been written so that pastors and church school teachers can understand it, and scholars can learn from it. To help clarify the message, pictures, a map, and a diagram have been included. Buchanan was the first to recognize the importance of Zion to the Book of Hebrews and the importance of Hebrews to Jerusalem archaeology.

www.ingramcontent.com/pod-product-compliance
Lightning Source LLC
LaVergne TN
LVHW010222110826
845148LV00022B/1244

* 9 7 8 1 5 9 7 5 2 8 6 7 2 *